CÉLINE

EUROPEAN SOURCES

SERIES EDITORS

Russell Epprecht and Sylvère Lotringer

CÉLINE
A Biography

Frédéric Vitoux

Translated by
Jesse Browner

PARAGON HOUSE

First American edition, 1992

Published in the United States by

Paragon House
90 Fifth Avenue
New York, N.Y. 10011

Originally published in French as *La Vie de Céline* by
Bernard Grasset in 1988;
Copyright © 1988 by Éditions Grasset and Fasquelle.

Interior designed by Robert Aronds

Library of Congress Cataloging-in-Publishing data

Vitoux, Frédéric.
    [Vie de Céline. English]
    Céline : a biography / Frédéric Vitoux : translation by Jesse
Browner.
        p.   cm.—(European sources)
    Translation of: La vie de Céline.
    Includes bibliographical references and index.
    ISBN 1-55778-255-5 (HC)
    1. Céline, Louis-Ferdinand, 1894–1961—Biography.   2. Authors,
French—20th century—Biography.   I. Title.   II. Series.
PQ2607.E834Z9513   1991
843′.912—dc20
    [B]   90-28174
                                                             CIP

Contents

Acknowledgments

I should like, as is customary, to thank those with whom—sometimes over the course of several years—I have had occasion to talk of Céline, and who were kind enough to answer my queries and offer me their precious testimony, direct or indirect; and those who helped me in my research, bringing to my attention such or such a book, article, or new source of information. I single out in particular Mmes. Arletty, Agnès, the late Jacques Benoist-Méchin, Pierre Bourget, Jacques Brenner, Dr. and Mme. Brami, Mmes. Renée Canavaggia, Simone Carrat, MM. Dominique Charnay, Bernard Clesca, the late Jean Dubuffet, MM. Jean-Claude Fasquelle, Dominique Fernandez, Mme. Édith Follet-Lebon, MM. Jean Guénot, Marc Hanrez, Mmes. Odette Joyeux, Frédérique Laroche, Sergine Le Bannier, M. Massin, Mme. Bernard Ménétrel, MM. François Michel, Pierre Monnier, Jean-Louis Montané, Éric Neuhoff, Serge Perrault, Mme. Pinson, M. Jean Pommery, M. André Willemin . . . and others I may have forgotten and whom I ask to accept my apologies.

Obviously, a biographer relies not only on personal testimony but also on writings or documents compiled by other researchers. I thank all of them. From Céline's earliest letters and the attestations solicited and compiled by Dominique de Roux for *Cahiers de l'Herne* in 1963 and 1965, to the patient and erudite critical editions of Céline in the Pléiade series by Professor Henri Godard, long is the list of those who helped to advance the study of Céline's life. I must thus acknowledge Jacques Boudillet's works on the writer's childhood and genealogy, Pierre Laine's discovery of two of Céline's friends and correspondents, Marcel Lafaye and Joseph Garcin, who played significant roles in the genesis of *Voyage au bout de la nuit* and *Guignol's band*, the correspondence with Albert Paraz edited by Jean-Paul Louis, many testimonies and letters found by Éric Mazet, the information collected and published in Brussels by Marc Laudelout in his *Bulletins céliniens*. . . . It would be impossible to list them all! Over the past few years there has been a great increase in unpublished fragments, letters, and new testimony. Céline's letters to his lawyers, for instance, were published in Paris by Frédéric Monnier under the "Flûte de Pan" imprint, while Gallimard brought out *Maudits Soupirs pour une autre fois*, an early version of *Féerie pour une autre fois* that the writer's widow had rediscovered in her archives. These are but two examples. A synthesis of such discoveries was becoming necessary.

I would like most particularly to mention here the name of Jean-Pierre Dauphin, to whom none of the circumstances of Céline's life can be unknown. His monumental *Bibliographie des écrits de Louis-Ferdinand Céline*, written with Pascal Fouché (published by Bibliothèque de littérature française contemporaine de l'université Paris-VII) is the indispensable tool for all students of Céline. Jean-Pierre Dauphin is above all one of those very rare experts who never hesitate to help their colleagues, answer their questions, and advise them on specific points. For that, I thank him most sincerely.

I should also like to express my profound gratitude to my friend François Gibault. His three volumes—*Céline, le temps des espérances, 1894–1932* (Mercure de France, 1977), *Céline, délires et persécutions, 1932–1944* (Mercure de France, 1985) and *Céline, cavalier de l'Apocalypse, 1944–1961* (Mercure de France, 1981)—contain a wealth of unpublished letters, biographical discoveries, and details. The author was never daunted by many years of patient research, meeting and questioning numerous witnesses, and gaining access to their archives. It will be henceforth impossible for any new biographer or researcher to avoid reference to his remarkable works. I would add that, over the course of our many encounters, François Gibault never hesitated to provide me with such details as I requested on various points concerning Céline's life. I thank him once again.

Finally, I must cite the name of Lucette Destouches, the writer's widow. Without her encouragement, her unceasing help, the many unpublished letters and documents of Céline that she placed at my disposal, without the hours and hours of interviews that she has so affectionately granted me over the years, I would obviously never have written this book.

But neither could I have carried it through without the daily assistance of Nicole Chardaire, the people she helped me to contact, the tape recordings she patiently transcribed, and her rereading of every chapter. She knows what I owe her.

One last word. André Malraux advised the American academic Frederic Grover, with whom he discussed the great writers of his time (Idées/Gallimard, 1978), to meet with Lucette Destouches. "She has an intuitive understanding of Céline," he explained. I had the opportunity to measure the accuracy of that statement. Lucette Destouches helped me to understand the man who shared her life from 1936 to his death, and whom she accompanied with admirable silence, affection, and devotion through the cruelest of his ordeals. I feel it is fitting to make her voice heard here. It is to her, first and last, that I express my deep and eternal gratitude.

F.V.

Translator's Note

With the exception of those passages drawn from Milton Hindus' *The Crippled Giant* (Boar's Head, 1950), all quotations from Céline in this book are my own translations. I should like, however, to acknowledge a debt of gratitude to earlier translators of Céline—in particular to Ralph Manheim, Bernard Frechtman, and Jack T. Nile—whose works were a great source of inspiration to me.

In general I have tried to be as unobtrusive as possible within the text, providing notes only for the most obscure of cultural, historical, or literary references. While some readers may have wished for more, it is my hope that most will be grateful for the chance to enjoy their reading undistracted by superfluous cross-referencing and fact-checking.

Lastly, for their invaluable help and support, I should like to thank Judy Clain, Alain Joly, Richard Miller, Pascalle Monnier, Rosie Sarah Reiss, Fred Sawyer, Frédéric Vitoux, Annette Wagner and Philip Watts. My eternal love and gratitude are reserved for Jacky Baudot.

J.B.

Mystery is the only life of the soul.

—CÉLINE

1

Birth . . . and Before

Courbevoie

First there was Courbevoie.

This is the starting point, the birthplace, at four P.M., on May 27, 1894, at the address of 12, rampe du Pont.

The next day Céline's baptism is celebrated in the superb neoclassical parochial church of Saint-Pierre–Saint-Paul, boasting an elliptical vault and portico somewhat reminiscent of the Roman Pantheon. A few days later his parents send him out to nurse in the Yonne region. His mother believed herself to be tubercular, and the child had to be spared any risk of contagion. He was never to return to Courbevoie, his parents having moved in the meantime. In short, he would never live there.

It would be hasty, however, to see Courbevoie as a merely fortuitous setting, and thus without significance. If we wish to speak of Céline, to evoke his life, to discuss his reference points, we must first refer to Courbevoie for two closely related reasons. We can regard Courbevoie primarily as symbolic, a place that reveals Céline's social, cultural, and geographical position. We will come back to that. But Courbevoie is also the place that inspired a stubborn and powerful loyalty in Céline. He always thought of himself as a child and a native of Courbevoie. Yes, Courbevoie, 1894. He was from Courbevoie and that said it all. That was his calling card.

Let us recall the opening of *D'un château l'autre* [Castle to Castle]: "Frankly speaking, between us, my end is even worse than my beginnings . . . Oh, I didn't start off too well . . . I was born, I repeat, in Courbevoie, Seine . . . I'm repeating it for the thousandth time."

The thousandth time indeed. . . . Let us reread his interviews. To André Parinaud of *La Parisienne*, visiting him in Meudon in January 1953: "It took me 58 years to cross the Seine. Because I was born on the other side, over there, and now, every day, I look at the landscape of my childhood." To André Brissaud, for the newsletter of the "Club du Meilleur Livre," in October 1954: "First of all, I was born in Courbevoie. . . ." To Gérard Jarlot, of *France-Dimanche*, in April 1956, speaking of Courbevoie: "I am indigenous, a suburban 'Fellah.' " And to Galtier-Boissière who, writing for *Le Crapouillot*, had requested a biographical sketch to appear in a dictionary of contemporary writers, Céline, then in exile in Denmark, answers in 1949:

3.

"My dear Galtier, the best thing would be to write me in as 'Louis-Ferdinand Destouches, born May 27, 1849, in Courbevoie (Seine).' That way, my friends and enemies will think I'm a hundred and very near death, and they'll all be very happy."

In the years of imprisonment, exile, and hostile silence which, for Céline, followed the Second World War, Courbevoie would of course be an implicit plea in his defense, a way for the writer to affirm his identity, his love of the soil, his quality as an exemplary Frenchman—whether as the model or average Frenchman it hardly matters, but as someone who could not be suspected of intelligence with the enemy or of anything else. Not a chance—he was born in Courbevoie. . . . And yet, there is more here than artfulness or ingenuousness. There is a definite complicity, a loyalty and harmony that Céline felt between his personality and his birthplace.

For example, the friendship between Céline and Arletty would find its anchorage therein and, in the narrowest sense, its personal common ground. Both were natives of Courbevoie. The same settings, the same *milieu*, the same word to be offered as a password to a shared nostalgia: Courbevoie. And they understood each other.

When Céline and Arletty meet for the first time, at the home of mutual friends in Paris, 1941, of what do they speak? Courebevoie, naturally. Nor should it come as any shock to find, from the pen of Céline exiled in Denmark (in a letter to Albert Paraz dated November 13, 1947), such statements as the following: "Give Arletty a kiss for me. I love her. We said our goodbyes during those pretty awful times, without much hope of seeing each other again. But we share the spirit of the Country, the soul of things, of the *Rampe* . . . I received some news of her . . . It seems things are all right . . . I'm glad of it . . . she is a bit of my song . . . so torn apart . . . Tell her to think of me as she passes along the banks of the Seine . . . I'm still there. . . .

"My heart is on the ramp of the bridge [*rampe du pont*]," Céline had written him once before, on October 25, 1947. Sometime later, Paraz must have sent on some old photos of Courbevoie. On Christmas day of the same year, Céline, moved, answers: "No little yuletide could have so touched my heart like the little snapshots of my quay, of my foggy ramp . . . Dear Courbevoie! old animals return to die where they were born whenever they can. And so would I wish to do, nothing more . . . Best wishes."[1]

But let us leave the final word to Arletty. As Céline, from his Baltic refuge, awaits his trial *in absentia* in Paris, she exclaims: "Céline? He can't be a traitor—he's from Courbevoie." Courbevoie, then, is home ground, the reference point. It can be quite useful to cling to such a point when your life is as elusive as a journey that never ends.

Our image of Louis-Ferdinand Céline is of a man forever on the run, harried, proscribed, exiled, restless, a seeker of fame, of adventures, of clearings at the other end of society or on the other side of appearances, between two wars, from continent to continent . . . Céline, or Velocity. . . .

There is the velocity of language, of course. He is the man who bevels sentences, disarticulates syntax, who warps and straightens words so as to hurl them at great speed toward emotion, the ultimate target. But that is not all. There is also, first and foremost, the velocity of his life (and to retell that life is to throw oneself into frenetic pursuit). Céline involves himself at every instant. Acts of impulse, acts of folly, subterfuges, deliria, in the army, heading for London, in black Africa, in New York, in Leningrad. He is forever dreaming of open spaces. At the drop of a hat, a rejection, a hope, a deal to negotiate, a woman to see again, a ship setting sail, the sea and the wide blue yonder—that's where he wagers his comfort and his everyday life. Indeed, until 1951—the move to Meudon, old age and weariness prematurely born after prison and his Danish ordeal—Céline is on the move.

And the world moves as fast as Céline. Progress, technology, wars, politics, governments, revenge, the victors, the vanquished, morality and culture—is Céline moving to keep up with or to outflank the passage of time? Or, rather, to escape it? To console himself? To intoxicate himself? The reality is irrelevant. The counterpoint is Courbevoie, the starting point of his life, the moment when everything is still perfect, when time has yet to begin and accomplish its slow sapper's work on him, its decomposition, its invitation to death. Courbevoie, or The Blessed Days. The paradise that was, before the accident—or rather, the mistake—that his own birth will forever represent. In other words, this is an imaginary Courbevoie that does not exist, that no longer exists, a moment frozen in 1894. A time imagined rather than recovered. A motionless time.

Is it a town, a village, or has it already become a suburb at the tail end of the nineteenth century? Between the island of La Grande-Jatte to the north, spanned by the Courbevoie bridge and the Neuilly bridge farther to the south, the village (this "curved road," that *voie courbe*, that Gallo-Roman *curva via*) lies on the banks of the Seine to the west of Paris. The pastoral hamlet, the vineyards and the castle have long since disappeared, like so many settings buried in the chronicle of times past—the type of chronicle so adored by Céline, an admirer of Tallemant des Réaux. This is the same Céline who dedicated *Normance* to Pliny the Elder and who invoked the passage of the *Vert-Galant* through Courbevoie in this manner: "Henri IV almost drowned (at the *rampe du pont*) in the old ford on his way to visit some whore or other. More precisely, at the passage de l'Ancre—a little dead end on the other side of the Rampe. Ah, I know a thing or two about the suburbs! My heart is still there."[2]

Courbevoie in 1894 more closely resembles the agglomeration where the sculptor Carpeaux had died twenty years earlier. From that time on, the old village was a gangrenous appendage of the capital. From the Étoile, from the avenue de la Grande-Armée, descending toward Neuilly, and, farther, toward Colombes, Asnières, and Bécon toward the west, came an endless flow of travelers, wagons, handcarts, greengrocers, industrial products. Courbevoie also has a port, just a stone's throw from the rampe du Pont, and even one of the great ports of Paris. From 1839, the town is served by railway. And from 1870, industrialization is setting in. Workshops and factories proliferate, from the perfume to the automobile industries, from tool-making to food products. Activity on the river develops tirelessly, the port is enlarged, while the old laundries go about their flourishing concerns. . . .

Courbevoie in 1894 seemed to be based on a very precarious equilibrium. The city, the big city, was there already, it had reached and eaten away at the old, bucolic village, with its "follies," its gardens, and even its handsome barracks of Swiss regiments. Henceforth, liqueur, Guerlain beauty products, and Dion-Bouton automobiles will be manufactured here. Yes, but behind the suburban homes and newly erected little buildings, the factories and warehouses, one can still discern the same layout of roads and old eighteenth-century houses, the ancient rural paths and the fields still visible a few hundred yards away. In brief, one can still smell a hint of the vanished past.

We have arrived in Courbevoie, a symbolic place for Céline.

Céline the city dweller, the roamer of the suburbs, witness to the misery of the proletariat, the dispensary doctor of Clichy or Bezons, the hygienist struck by the insalubrious living and working conditions of the working class, the writer who would always prefer the most sordid and revelatory byways to the most becoming and illusory of settings—all those Célines found their stomping grounds of choice in Courbevoie.

But the suburbs hover precisely on that edge between town and country, confinement and freedom. And Céline is also the man of escape, the man of water, the man of the West. And through Courbevoie flows the Seine, the river that bears away, that creates distance, that urges one on to dreams and journeys. "In the distance, the tugboat whistled; its call passed the bridge, one more arch, then another, the lock, another bridge, far away, farther still . . . It was summoning every barge on the river, every one of them, and the entire city, and the sky and the countryside, and us, carrying it all away, the Seine too, everything, and that would be the end of it."[3]

Céline may have seen, at the time, one or another of the drawings by Épinal depicting the return of the Emperor's ashes on December 15, 1840, in Courbevoie. The frigate *La Belle Poule* had moored just off the rampe du Pont. With great pomp, the majestic funeral hearse had passed the writer's future birthplace before taking the avenue de la Grande-Armée all the way to the Étoile on its way to the Invalides. And Courbevoie, for once, could shiver in the fine breeze of adventure, of nostalgia for the open spaces.

Courbevoie, finally, is the symbol of the Céline attached to the past and the modern Céline, a window on the hardworking and humble lower-middle classes still close to their rural roots, which the upheavals of heavy industrialization were to sweep away once and for all.

Just about nothing remains today of Courbevoie (or of the "values" defended by Céline's mother). The rampe du Pont disappeared with the widening of the Neuilly bridge and the modernization of roadways in the new neighborhood of La Défense. Courbevoie's town planning has been subsumed. The workshops and decaying factories, the little suburban homes, the two- and three-story buildings have given way to the headquarters of multinationals, underground parking lots, skyscrapers of steel and glass, and the verticality which Céline so admired in New York.

To sum up, Courbevoie in 1894 resembled an accident, a hesitation of history between two slopes. It is the first deal of the cards that illustrates Céline's life and its contradictions.

Branches of the Family Tree

The life of Céline begins on May 27, 1894, at four o'clock in the afternoon. Yet that statement is not strictly true. Louis-Ferdinand Céline was born much later, on October 5, 1932, to be precise, on the day when Éditions Denoël published the first novel of an unknown who had only just chosen the pseudonym Céline to appear at the top of the cover of *Voyage au bout de la nuit* [Journey to the End of Night]. No, on May 27, 1894, in Courbevoie, it was merely Louis-Ferdinand Destouches, the son of Fernand Destouches and his wife Marguerite, *née* Guillou, who was born.

For the life of Céline, we must be patient awhile longer. We must first take a brief look backward—or upward, toward the branches and ramifications of his family tree.

Impassioned Célinians[4] have not hesitated to extend their civil-registry researches on the family as far back as the early eighteenth century, leading us along the way past a great-grandfather, Clément Destouches, born on 11 Brumaire, Year IX, or a great-great-grandfather, Jean-Baptiste Nayl de la Villaubry, deceased in 1801. Such erudition offers little of interest. Without for the moment speaking of the personalities of Céline's uncles and aunts, and of course of his father and mother, of their different backgrounds and culture, we are particularly struck by the grandfather, Auguste Destouches (1835-1874), to whom the writer alludes on several occasions in his writings. But above all, in the eyes of the young Louis-Ferdinand Destouches, there was the hovering shadow of the Destouches "family" in general, with its unknown and imagined ancestors, its distant chimera of glory, mystery, epic, nobility, out beyond, towards Brittany and the Cotentin peninsula. . . .

Céline dreamed of an aristocratic heritage. In 1916 he signed his letters from Africa to his childhood friend Simone Saintu: "Louis des Touches."[5] He may have considered himself a distant descendant of the Chevalier des Touches. His father, in any case, insisted on a definite relation to that more-or-less legendary figure in the Chouans wars, arrested by the troops of the Republic and liberated in Coutances by the famous "Expedition of the Twelve"—a figure who would certainly have been forgotten without the 1864 novel which Barbey d'Aurevilly devoted to him.

And again, to Simone Saintu, in a letter from Africa dated October 30, 1916, Céline alludes more specifically to his distant paternal ancestors and their domains in the Cotentin: "I see that you enjoy Normandy, in that we have similar tastes, just imagine that on the day when, like Tircis, I'll start thinking about retirement, it's precisely to Normandy that I'll make my escape, somewhere around Coutances there's an old family castle that will most likely shelter my peinates [sic] and those of my old friends who have remained loyal. It all leads me to think that we'll have a good old time there, that I'll be a rather merry and bearable old man."6

The family castle of which Céline speaks with such naive complacency was in fact a mere country estate, Lentillière (today in ruins), belonging to the Saint-Aubin-du-Perron parish, a dozen kilometers from Coutances. And Thomas Destouches, Céline's great-great-grandfather, had sold the estate in 1787. He had settled in Le Rocher-Coyer, between Fougères and Dinan— hence, in Brittany.

Could the Destouches family have been noble? The pretention is absurd. It is true that several particulate names occasionally slip, almost fortu- itously, amongst the branches of Céline's family tree, and that his ancestors must have been more or less related to the minor Norman and Breton gentry of the area. The Destouches were neither peasants nor merchants. They held a variety of administrative posts, which do not in the long run constitute definitive proof of true nobility. Nevertheless, in 1916, at the age of twenty-two, Céline still clings to the rather outrageous claim of noble blood. On December 11, 1916, he writes again to Simone Saintu from Africa:

"Anyway, perhaps fate will decree that I end up a harem guard in Con- stantinople, with the particular exigencies (for lack of better) demanded by the job, but faithful to the Des Touches motto: 'More honor than honors!'

"Most sincerely your old friend—Louis"7

This may be a still somewhat adolescent concern with impressing his correspondent. Again on January 11, 1917, in a letter that has remained unpublished to date and is preserved in the archives of Lucette Destouches, he writes to his parents from his cocoa plantation in Cameroon, poorly dissimulating his pride: "I have received an interesting letter from the Normandy Antiquarian Society, congratulating me on being a descendant of the Des Touches, and inviting me to one of its meetings, at my conve- nience."8

We must picture the future writer as visited, even haunted, by the more or less improbable ghosts of the past, the ancestors he has reinvented for himself, the regions he roams in his dreams—those moors of the Cotentin immortalized by Barbey, with their burden of anguish, solitude, romantic magic, or else that Brittany to which he had lost a direct family connection that he longed to perpetuate all the same, like a call to escape, to adventure, to danger, like the unarguable symptom of a dissatisfaction with the present that would never let him slip from its grasp.

In that sense, yes, the Destouches of Lentillière, the elusive silhouette of the Chevalier Des Touches captured by Barbey, a warped and hallucinated specter surviving beyond its exploits, and the tragic eloquence of the

Cotentin, of the château de Fougères and the Breton landscapes—all these boughs on Céline's family tree undoubtedly cast their shadows about him.

Thus, Thomas Destouches had sold Lentillière just before the French Revolution. A strange character, this great-great-grandfather. Thomas already clearly manifested an instability of character, a lack of emotional balance, not to mention a taste for endless geographic peregrinations—in short, all that would later characterize Céline as well.

Having settled down between Fougères and Nantes and married a young lady, Gabrielle Michelle Guerin de Léchallerie, he soon walks out on his wife and conjugal household (just as Céline, later, would leave his first wife, Édith, and their daughter, Colette, in Rennes) to settle in Nantes and then in Vannes where, in 1794, he becomes administrator of the *département* of Morbihan. After his divorce, he will marry a second time. He is widowed. He will marry a third time and the son born of that third union, Clément, will be Céline's great-grandfather. After Vannes, we find Thomas in the Isère, in Vienne, where he will end his days.

We now turn to his grandson, Auguste, the famous teacher of Le Havre, the grandfather whom Céline evokes in his preface to *Guignol's band* in 1944.

He was born in Vannes in 1835 and began his studies in the town of Le Havre. A brilliant student on a state scholarship, he was first a schoolmaster in that same town, then junior master in Rennes, before being named personal secretary to the prefect of Ille-et-Vilaine.

We can easily picture him as one of those provincial scholars who prides himself on his literary facility, never misses a poetry competition, and whom his fellow citizens claim to be gifted with a "lovely turn of phrase." In 1860, with the coauthorship of one Lissilour, he published a serial novel entitled *Une dette de coeur* [A Debt of the Heart] in the *Journal d'Ille-et-Vilaine*. François Gibault cites some of his rather mediocre verses, of the order:

> *C'est l'heure où l'oiseau noir, sur le charnier qui suinte*
> *De tant de cadavres pourris,*
> *Au travers des échos de la funèbre plainte*
> *Va jetant ses douloureux cris.*[9]

To the detriment of his politico-administrative ambitions, Auguste had fallen in love with a young girl from Le Havre, slightly older than himself, Hermance Caroline Delhaye. In order to be with her, he left Rennes, his prefect, and his secretary's position, and sought to reenter public education. He married Hermance on September 20, 1860, and tried, unsuc-

---

* Now is the hour when the dark bird, above the charnel house oozing / With so many rotten corpses, / Through the echoes of the mournful wailing / Hurls its pain-ridden cries.

cessfully at first, for his literature degree in Caen. He eventually passed the examination for his teaching certificate in September 1867. The days of humble salaries and positions in the civil service hierarchy were over. Auguste Destouches was henceforth among the exalted ranks of the titular teachers of the Le Havre high school. He had five children: Georges, René, Charles, Amélie, and Céline's father, Fernand, whose actual given name, according to the civil registry, was Ferdinand Auguste.

But the hardworking Auguste, scholar, notable, literary and family man, would not have long to enjoy his hard-won success. Seven years after his certification, on January 1, 1874, at the age of thirty-eight, he died of typhoid fever.

That same day, *Le Journal du Havre* published the following notice: "With deep sorrow, we have learned this afternoon of the demise of one of our most respected Lycée teachers, one of our young *Havrais* for whom the future also seemed to have held a brilliant career in the arts.

"M. Auguste Destouches, certified special teacher, appointed to teach literature in the trade curriculum at the Le Havre Lycée, succumbed to typhoid fever complicated by bronchitis. . . .

"Following his brilliant examinations, Destouches dedicated himself to the teaching which had provided his earliest successes. The winner of several literary competitions, our fellow citizen was gratified in later seeing his pupils carry off the palms of victory in those same literary tournaments."[10]

Naturally, Auguste Destouches interests us as a somewhat mythical figure on Céline's horizon. The latter, in a letter to Simone Saintu dated October 28, 1916, mentions him for the first time:

"The family is proud to count amongst its members one who held a certificate in French Grammar, and who was often held up to me as an example back when they bothered themselves with such things.

"I hope to be less of a p—— than him; I can hardly think it's a question of spelling.

"For all that, he was a very fine man. . . ."[11]

Above all, these few words reveal Céline's mocking pride and his irreverence toward the "great man" of the family, but they are hardly very meaningful. More interesting, obviously, is the famous preface to *Guignol's band*:

"I've got to admit that my grandfather, Auguste Destouches by name, was something into rhetoric, even taught the stuff in the Le Havre Lycée, and brilliant, around 1855.

"Which is to say, I'm scared witless! In case that tendency is bred into me!

"I've got all grandfather's writings, his files, his notes, whole drawers full! Awe-inspiring! He wrote the prefect's speeches, in a hell of a style, I'm telling you! Couldn't he find just the right adjective! What a way with the flowery crap! Never a blunder! Moss and vine leaves! Son of the Gracchi! Maxims and everything! In verse and prose alike! He ran away with every award from the Académie Française!

"I have preserved them with emotion.

"That's my ancestor! So I know a bit about the language, and not since yesterday like some people! I'm not afraid to come out and say it! in all its subtleties!

"I unloaded all my 'effects,' my 'litotes,' my 'pertinences' into my diapers . . .

"Ah, I'm sick of them! They'd be the death of me! My grandfather Auguste agrees with me. From up there he tells me, he whispers to me from the heavens . . .

" 'My boy, no phrase-mongering!' . . .

"He knows what it takes to make it work! I'm making it work!"[12]

All of Céline's contradictions can be seen in this passage. This preface is one of the rare texts in which the author of *Voyage* explains his novelist's art or undertakes in some way a defense and illustration of Célinian language.

We find above all a nostalgia, Céline's wondrous affection for that lovely era—the era before his birth—when all was in order, when there was a commitment to and even a love for work well done, well tailored, well ordered. Whether in his mother's lace or his grandfather's writing, there was in each instance an admirable professional pride, the same concern for arabesques and embellishments, for the Alençon stitch or the right metaphor. And Céline misses that blessed time.

But he also knows that that era is irretrievable for him, that no one ever again will write like grandfather Auguste or fashion lace like his mother, Marguerite. No one has the time, the patience, the courage, or the humility. So his admiration turns somewhat scornful and desperate. He slams the door on his memories. He's sick of them. They'll be the death of him, he says in essence. And he invents a style that dynamites the lovely turn-of-phrase, pulverizes syntax, shatters the florid rhetoric of yesteryear. Céline shoves his ancestors aside. Farewell, Auguste . . . And yet that is not quite true. Céline approaches his artificing of language with the same meticulousness, the same conscientiousness, the same eternal vigilance that his grandfather had used sixty years earlier to prettify his speeches and fine-tune his disheartening quatrains.

In other words, the legendary Auguste, the pathetic and slightly ridiculous great man, remains a kind of role model for him—not an artistic or literary role model, but a moral one, with his painstaking awareness of a work that is never finished, an effort that must be endlessly repeated in the stubborn silence known only to perfectionists—all that Céline himself will lay claim to through the times of abandon, renunciation, and laxity that he seems to feel go hand-in-hand with the atrocious era he is experiencing and observing.

Fernand's Way and
Marguerite's Way

But let us leave Auguste here, with his receding hairline, his emaciated face, his thin, pinched lips, and the large, anxious, and questioning eyes of an unhappy intellectual.[13] He belongs to Célinian prehistory.

What becomes of his wife, Hermance, in 1874, widowed with five children? A woman of duty, will Hermance, the worthy spouse of the meritorious *lycée* teacher, struggle to complete the education of her four sons and her daughter, Amélie? No, none of that for her. Hermance is a *bourgeoise*, which is not an evil. She is provincial, which is also not an evil. But she is thus a very provincial *bourgeoise*, which is a little more alarming. She intends to continue shining in Havrais society. She is less interested in *belles lettres* than in the salons where they are discussed. All in all, she is a rather scatterbrained muse in a province she deems too limiting. . . .

Her children, on the other hand, take up far too much of her life. One solution jumps to mind: sign her sons up posthaste as boarders at the Le Havre Lycée, and let us hear no more about it, or at least as little as possible. If Fernand, Céline's father, is able to enjoy a communal scholarship (Hermance is still well enough placed to play on her relations and protectors), well, that's just fine! Hermance has other things on her mind.

She is a provincial lady, as we have mentioned. A provincial lady always dreams of leaving her province one day. A provincial lady has thoughts only for Paris. And Hermance evinces, so to speak, an energetic frivolity. She is not the kind of woman to dream long about a goal that does not seem entirely out of reach. Hermance wants Paris? Very well, she shall have Paris! She moves there a year after her husband's death, accompanied by Amélie. Amélie is a young girl who plays the piano nicely, it seems. Amélie will not tarnish her *salon*.

But Paris is not a city that systematically welcomes widows on the rebound engineering the rise of their worldly status. The modest fortune of Hermance Destouches (one is always poorer in Paris than in the provinces) will evaporate as quickly as her social aspirations. She will end her life, a few years later, as a kept woman, or at least a woman kept by proxy. In other words, she will allow herself to be kept by the lovers of her daughter, the beautiful and resolute Amélie, who plays the piano and has no trouble seducing her listeners. In other words, Amélie will be a demimondaine, an expression coined to designate someone who is excessively worldly (*"mondain"*) and who does not make love by halves (*"demi"*).

As for the Destouches sons, cooped up at the Le Havre Lycée all this time, there is no hope of liberation for them in the short term. What with her daughter, the piano, her *salon*, and her relatives, their mama has too much on her hands in Paris to consider taking them with her, even during the summer holidays. And besides, they don't give away train rides between Le Havre and Paris for free, and how can she be sure that those four gawky boys would even be presentable in Paris? It seems they belong, rather, to the vigorous, noisy, and indestructible race of layabouts satisfied with and proud of their place.

Nevertheless, in early 1884, Fernand Destouches enters the Lycée Condorcet as a day pupil. He has grown. One might suppose that he has become a little better behaved, if not more studious. Indeed, he stands out at the Condorcet as neither a good nor a bad student. Prudently, he forgoes competing for the second half of his *baccalauréat.* Why bother when failure is so likely? Which demonstrates at least a kind of clearsightedness or even an intelligence on his part: an understanding of his own limits.

In any case, to evoke Fernand Destouches as a man with his *baccalauréat* or, better yet, his undergraduate degree, is an enormous joke, a great lie of the sort that Céline will love to invent and then lug from one novel to another, from interview to fake confession. It is easy to see, in this specific case, what justified such a fabrication in the writer's eyes. His unlucky father, stuck in a wretched job, embittered, abused by his superiors in the hierarchy, always getting the short end of it, his father crushed by life . . . yes, the inclination was strong to give him an advanced degree as well, so that his fall would be all the harder, so that Céline might better underline the contrast between his hopes and his failures, his virtues and his bad luck. Because that was how the iniquitous weight of the world's misery was manifested.

Céline stated to Pierre Brissaud, for instance, on the television program "Lecture pour tous" in July 1957: "My father, alas, had his bachelor's in literature. He was a . . . he would have been the joy of the high-minded. He wrote well, prettily. He was a correspondence clerk."[14]

To Louis Pauwels and André Brissaud, who, again for French television, interviewed him in spring 1959: "My father was a clerk. He had his degree, my father! And then, my father had literary pretensions. He sure did. Furthermore, he was a literate man and handled the correspondence for the fire department of the Le Pays insurance company on the rue La Fayette."[15]

And to Jean Guénot and Jacques Darribehaude, in February 1960, as they harped on Fernand Destouches' career:

"Mightn't your father have had a better position in education?"

"Certainly, the poor man, but what happened was that he [would have] had to take a teaching degree, and he had a liberal arts degree, and he couldn't study for it because there was no money, his father had died and left his wife with five children."[16]

But, leaving such quotations aside—and there are many more like them—let us return to Fernand without his high school diploma. Collective life (at least at the Le Havre Lycée) must not have left him too many bad memories, since he joins the army, that realm of strong wills if not strong minds, of those who dream of everything—adventure, glory, exotic places

—perhaps because they are good at nothing. . . . And he signs on for five years, with the 27th Artillery Regiment.

A valorous gunner second-class, he is soon named sergeant-at-arms in January 1887. His military ascent will end there, his wild escapades and epic adventures having survived only within the duration of a rather vain hope: the time it took to sign his enlistment papers. He must have imagined that he would fill his lungs with the smell of gunpowder. Instead, he must have gotten only a noseful of the dust and mildew of crowded barracks. . . . Later, Céline, himself a volunteer, will experience the same kind of disillusionment.

In September 1889 he is discharged and drafted into the reserves. Fernand is twenty-four years old, he has no money, no talent, no diploma, and no friends. He is henceforth a civilian. He has nothing better to do in Paris than to watch the Eiffel Tower go up. Throughout his life, he will never stop rehashing his resentments about the social successes that, like the mad hopes of adventure left behind with adolescence, were forever denied him.

Auguste had once had such mad hopes, and Céline will have them: the same old Destouches propensity for traveling and wandering, their allotment of dreams, ghosts, the sea, the distant call like a vague melancholy ringing in their Breton or Norman ears, the chance, for instance, to sail, to build a long-term career in the navy, which, for one brief moment after leaving high school, Fernand had thought a possibility.

Demobilized, Fernand moves into a little place at 12, rue de l'Arc-de-Triomphe in Paris. On July 1, 1890, he wangles a job as a junior clerk in the correspondence department of the fire division of the Le Phénix insurance company. That is when he meets Marguerite Guillou. . . .

The family Guillou, a Breton name, were natives of Finistère. And yet, a change of setting, of scenery, of fortune, of mentality—of everything—is involved in their case. We will not go climbing the Guillou family tree, after that of the Destouches, nor evoke at length the great-grandfather, farmer in the Sarthe, or his canteen-attendant wife under Napoléon III. . . . Let us simply note that the Guillous are of modest means. Céline's grandfather, Julien-Jacques Guillou, was a copper welder; his wife, Céline, *née* Lesjean, a boot stitcher and herself the daughter of a luxury-goods dealer from Verneuil-sur-Avre.

In his grandmother Céline Guillou's maiden name we recognize the pseudonym that the writer will later appropriate in testimony to his fidelity, affection, and nostalgia, homage to the Guillou side of his personality, to the purely Breton patronym and to the woman (the famous grandmother Caroline in *Mort à crédit*) who would die when he was ten, and who certainly represented for him one of the rare *points fixes* of his existence, a model of tenderness, of hardworking probity, of intellectual lucidity. Céline Guillou was a woman allergic to lies, who never let herself be excited by chimera and false promises or dazzled by tinsel. Illusions evaporated before her, as did unnecessary conversation and the frivolous display of emotion. Her affection was silent.

Quite naturally, Céline Guillou, a widow since 1879 and mother of a second child, Julien (who was called Louis), could only oppose her daughter's marriage to Louis Destouches, that worrisome, harum-scarum fellow, his head stuffed with dreams of greatness, haunted by the glorious ghosts of his ancestors, whom he hoarded as his only capital, his military career behind him and his little pen-pusher's job with the dreariest of outlooks.

"I can't say that she was tender or affectionate, but she talked a lot and that's something in itself; and then, she never smacked me! . . . She despised my father. She couldn't bear him, with his education, his scruples, his idiotic tantrums, his loser's hot air. She thought her daughter was a jerk, too, for having married such an ass, with seventy francs a month in Insurance."[17]

Céline Guillou was not rich. At 43, rue de Provence, she had opened an antiques store specializing in old lace. But she was patient, frugal, and shrewd. She had sunk her savings into real estate. Stone, that's something solid, isn't it, you know where you stand with it. She had gone to Asnières, where she had acquired three new villas at 16, 16 bis, and 18, rue Laure-Fiot, to bring in rent money. Later, in 1899, she would buy an eight-room house, also in Asnières.

"When the January quarter came around, Grandmother Caroline went out to Asnières for the rent money. I took advantage of the situation. She had two villas there, brick and clay, on the rue de Plaisance, one little and one midsize, rented out to workers. It was her livelihood, her wealth, her savings."[18]

We cannot help but note in passing Céline's perpetual need to exaggerate when creating his portraits—in this case to make his grandmother appear as less then she really was—to wallow in misery, to highlight the revealing detail, anything to arouse his emotions. And his contrapuntal irony—the "rue de Plaisance" (Pleasure Street), for instance.

The Guillous, then, were of Breton origin. Though obstinate, Céline Guillou wasn't able to oppose her daughter's marriage for long. Marguerite, too, dug in. She married Fernand Destouches on July 8, 1893, in the Asnières town hall. Her dowry was modest: a few thousand francs in a savings account, some cash, some personal belongings, and an inheritance, which had not yet been liquidated, from her father. But as for Fernand Destouches, he had nothing. Worse, he had, as they say, no prospects.

Less than a month after their marriage, the young couple settled in Courbevoie, at 12, rampe du Pont, in a little fashions and accessories boutique with a flat above, from which the previous leaseholders had barely squeezed a profit.

At this late hour of the century, Fernand already seems to bear a precocious plumpness. His face is round, a little chubby, striated by a pointy mustache that in no way lends him a martial air. His features are regular. He would almost be a dashing fellow were it not for the somewhat heavy lower face and incipient double chin. With his little eyes sunken in their sockets and his sagging lids, he seems to be on the lookout for some chimera or other, while the rest of him is draped in a kind of mediocre inertia, wedged as he is into his hard collar and his tight jacket, as if into an absolute banality that squeezes the heart.

Marguerite Guillou has soon become a dignified wife, corseted, delicate rather than pretty, the very picture of the woman of character. She has chestnut hair, a thin-lipped mouth, nose too long, eyes a little frightened. She is a mother rather than a lover, that much is obvious. Lucette Destouches-Almansor would later say that she made her think of a nun. But in 1894 she is still a graceful young woman whom life has already begun to mark with its shadows, that makeup which, little by little, deepens one's lines, tempers the sparkle of one's gaze, slows down one's gestures, and erases the laughing insouciance of youth.

Such, then, are the parents of Louis-Ferdinand, split down the middle between the Destouches side—dreamers, penniless, chimerical, mediocre, clinging half-heartedly to an improbable nobility—and the maternal side—humble, impecunious, frugal, painstaking, never stoking the hopes of excessive ambition, refusing to comfort themselves with fine words, respectful of an established order of which they, the Guillous, would never be anything but the victims, the humble, marginal servants.

François Gibault hit on a happy formula in describing Céline as "raised by *bourgeois* amongst the people, according to aristocratic principles and with proletarian means."[19]

Between Two Crises

Céline the volcanic novelist, Céline the child of an embittered and reactionary petty-bourgeoisie, Céline the hallucinating pamphleteer, the delirious anti-Semite of *Bagatelles pour un massacre* [Trifles for a Massacre] in 1937 or of *L'École des cadavres* [The School for Corpses] in 1938: how tempting it was to connect the year of his birth with the beginnings of the Dreyfus Affair. It was the perfect symbol.

Céline is born in May. A few months later, on Monday, October 15, to be precise, Captain Dreyfus, alumnus of the Polytechnique and the École de Guerre, a Jew of Alsatian origins, is arrested after the notorious dictation session in the War Ministry on the rue Saint-Dominique. Major du Paty de Clam accuses him of high treason. He is immediately brought to the Cherche-Midi prison, locked up, and held secretly. His trial opens December 19. Three days later, the war council unanimously declares Dreyfus guilty. He is condemned to deportation in perpetuity to a high-security penitentiary, and to military degradation.

Looking at it more closely, however, the coincidence is not very revealing. In the little game of life's randomness and ironies, one might also highlight the fact that, a few years earlier, in 1886, in the suburb-town of Courbevoie where Céline was born, a career officer had settled down with the young woman he had married two years previously because her name was Anne de Nettancourt-Vaubécourt and she came with a dowry of 200,000 francs. His name: Esterhazy. Yes, Esterhazy, the culprit, the real traitor in the Dreyfus Affair, the aristocrat of Hungarian origin, swamped with debts, who sold his information to Schwartzkoppen, the military attaché at the German embassy in Paris,[20] thus became the Destouches' neighbor.

But if, in 1894, Dreyfus has been well and truly condemned, if his personal tragedy is just beginning, there still exists no "Dreyfus Affair" in France. After the right-wing Drumont labeled Dreyfus a traitor in *La Libre Parole* of October 30, 1894, Léon Daudet or Maurice Barrès could not, in turn, find enough hateful terms with which to insult Dreyfus. He was of "foreign race," "not fit to live in society."[21] But their statements elicited no public response: after all, Dreyfus' guilt was beyond any shadow of a doubt.

The real Dreyfus Affair that was to tear France apart, pitting the anti-Semites, the defenders of "order," and the army against the "intellectuals" (the word emerges and thrives precisely at that moment), the liberals, and a fringe of the French Left, will not break out until 1897, when the first indications of the innocence of the convict of Devil's Island will be revealed.

No, if one would evoke in one or two words the prevailing climate of France in 1894, it is the word *becalmed* that springs to mind. Like the town of Courbevoie, hovering between its ancient village if not rural traditions and the progress of urbanism and industrialization that were soon to disfigure it beyond redemption, one might also say that France in 1894 is holding its breath, governed by provincial notables, without any jolts or exaltations, undergoing its industrial revolution in a rather somnolent fashion, suffused with a vague liberalism more middle class than socially oriented.

Not too long before, with General Boulanger, it had enjoyed the thrill of the potential military coup d'État and the fall of the Republic. But Boulanger hadn't been able to seize his opportunity, he had fled pitifully to Belgium and, by the World's Fair of 1889, had fallen into the anonymity that preceded his suicide. "He died as he lived, as a sublieutenant," Clemenceau would say of him. At the election, the Republicans won the day over the monarchists and the nationalists of the Right.

After Boulanger, there was the Panama scandal caused by the failure of the *Société* in 1888. But in 1894, that crisis, too, was drawing to an end, after all the virulent polemics and press campaigns, the accusations of corruption, the ministers persecuted and deputies alarmed. The Republic had weathered that "affair." In May, Charles Dupuy succeeded Casimir-Perier in the presidency of the Conseil. The latter became president of the Republic. . . . The new crises, Dreyfus, the quarrel over secularization, would come later, with the turn of the century.

Is the France of 1894 anti-Semitic? To some extent. For several years anti-Semitism seemed to have become the personal monopoly of the antirevolutionary Right, a new phenomenon. It was so reassuring, so tempting to explain by a Jewish plot the successive reversals experienced by the French Catholics. In 1886 Édouard Drumont met with tremendous success in the bookstores with his *France juive* [Jewish France], bloated with a pseudo-scientific racism used to explain the sense of Apocalypse in which he saw his *patrie* foundering. And, in April 1892, he founded his daily *La Libre Parole [Free Speech]*.

But was that anti-Semitism really shared by the majority, had it won over the French middle and lower-middle classes, the Catholic community in general? And had the socialist, secular, racist, anti-Semitic Left ceased to exist? A negative is required in both cases.

Léon Poliakov has shown very clearly that, in that period, French Jews did not feel threatened by the country that had been welcoming them, in some cases, for centuries. Better yet, these Jewish families dreamed of a disappearance, a total assimilation with the French culture and race. "The dominant tendency was toward wholesale gallicization, a fusion that seemed inevitable—and desirable—as much to the 'pro-Jewish' freethinkers, to Renan and Zola, as to an Alfred Naquet or to the brothers Reinach. (For the younger, Théodore, author of a *Histoire des Israélites*, Judaism "could consider its 'mission' as accomplished, and die without regrets, shrouded in its triumph.")[22]

The memoirs of André Maurois or Emmanuel Berl testify to that. And Proust's entire oeuvre, between the intertwined destinies of Swann and Bloch, also illustrates the contradictions and difficulties arising in the willful or chimerical de-Judaization at the heart of French society.

In 1894 Bernard Lazare, a young intellectual who had drawn attention to himself by taking a position in favor of the anarchists and revolutionary thinkers, had published an essay: *L'Antisémitisme, son histoire et ses causes* [Anti-Semitism, Its History and Causes], in which he too envisaged the progressive assimilation of the Jews into the French community. To his way of thinking, the disappearance of the Jewish religious impulse and the Talmudic spirit could only accelerate that evolution. From the moment that the Jews stopped thinking of themselves as Jews, he believed, others would cease to recognize them as such.[23]

To give another example, three years earlier, in 1891, a scientific journalist, future doctor and, most likely, a Freemason, had published, first with Éditions Albert-Savine and then with Chamuel (more or less indifferently, it would appear), an altogether unusual work entitled *L'Agonie d'Israël* [Israel's Death Throes], in which he attempted to demonstrate scientifically, according to biological and statistical determinants, the ineluctable disappearance of the Jewish race. Its physiological deterioration proved that the absorption of the race was inescapable. From which it followed that anti-Semitism was necessarily doomed.[24]

In brief, the year of Céline's birth, the year of Captain Dreyfus' judgment, strangely sees the French anti-Semitic impulse in a lull. *La Libre Parole* experiences financial difficulties and negotiations for its sale are even initiated. That fact is symptomatic.

Once again, everything points to the writer's having been born in one of those indecisive periods of French history, peaceful, without any particular divisiveness—as if better to illustrate the eternal Célinian nostalgia for the good old days, the days before birth, that improbable paradise where everything was static; where hatreds, screams, disorder, revolutions, corruption had yet to unfold, where the world was light, had escaped the seeds of corruption and death; where, finally, traditions were maintained like a form of scaffolding buttressing and consolidating society, creating a sort of check on reality from destroying that chimerical, tranquil construction.

After 1894, and thus after Céline's birth, the dams will collapse. Reality will triumph, with its procession of hatreds, violence and, soon, its wars. The Dreyfus Affair will set France ablaze. Bernard Lazare will take up the condemned officer's cause and struggle against the anti-Semites. The dream of the fusion of the Jews into the national community will have had its day. Racial violence will blossom. The first Zionist Congress, called by Herzl, will be held in Basel in the summer of 1897, and it will be, in part, an indirect response to the Dreyfus Affair, to the fanatical anti-Semitism of a fraction of French opinion, for there were lessons to be learned from it. . . . During that same time the infamous *Protocols of the Elders of Zion* will be formulated in Paris, commissioned by a czarist policeman of high rank, General Ratchkovsky, anxious to please Nicholas II, from a forger of genius whose identity remains unknown. Its title had clearly been inspired by the first Zionist Congress."[25] It was the *Protocols of the Elders of Zion* that, among other things, was to serve as the most frightening and preposterous documentation for Céline in his anti-Semitic writings preceding the Second World War.

But all of this, once again, is what follows his birth, the normal, natural cycle of catastrophes and death waiting to pounce from the moment the first mistake has been made, that is to say, from his own birth. In other words, there is in 1894 a sort of discreet irony of history. That almost peaceful year between two crises gives a semblance of justification to Céline, his obsessions, his deliria. Yes, everything is still held in check. The seeds of violence are there. History awaits. As does death. With Céline's birth, everything will suddenly begin to accelerate.

2

Passage Choiseul, Passage Toward Adolescence

Nurse to Nurse
Shop to Shop
School to School

Nurse to Nurse

Thus, on May 28, 1894, Louis-Ferdinand Destouches is baptized. Holding the newborn babe above the baptismal font of the Courbevoie church are two people: his maternal uncle and grandmother, who will be the godfather and godmother, respectively. The Guillou side has won. As far as education and religion are concerned, there is no question of compromise—such things are too serious to be left to dreamers, to *déclassés* and good-for-nothings. Exit the Destouches. As for the Guillous, they know what things cost, the value of symbols and the potential value of the sacraments, like a mortgage forever waiting to be cashed in on the future.

The child is immediately sent away to his first wet nurse, in a little *commune*, Voisines, eleven kilometers from Sens. The local country doctor watches over his health, takes care of his swollen glands, notes that "the baby is merry, radiant, and with good care he should turn out well, since he has good milk for the asking, which is a great boon."[1] The months pass, the teeth come through, the hair grows, the child wails, the child laughs, he has blue eyes, he's as strong as an ox of the same age, and we may safely speak of an infancy without incident. Or a mother.

The road is long from Courbevoie to Sens. Even when clients are few and far between, the *patronne*—the boss—has to stay. Thus, Marguerite, like Fernand Destouches, has little chance to visit her scion.

That absence probably marked Céline, left some trace on his personality and molded his subconscious. It is for the Freudians, for the traffickers in hidden meaning, the speleologists in depth psychology, to try to answer that one.

In the spring of 1895, about a year after the child's birth, the Destouches decide to change wet nurses. After all, Puteaux is closer to Courbevoie than the *département* of Yonne. And there, at 67, rue des Valettes, a certain Mme. Joualt is ready to welcome Louis-Ferdinand, Little Louis as he is called, to give him her breast and her affection into the bargain. Over the summer, the nurse even takes the child with her to the Mayenne, where she must attend the bedside of a sick father.

One year, two years, three years, the child grows. He is good looking, healthy, jolly. A photo shows him in 1896, sitting in a little carriage. With his large bright eyes, his delicate nose, his wide face cloven by a broad smile, Little Louis already looks a bit like Céline, not the conventional image of the hobolike hermit of Meudon after the war, but the Céline of the thirties, with his piercing eyes, those mocking, anxious eyes, the grown-up Céline wavering between medicine and literature with his air of a nonchalant seducer, aristocratic yet of the people.

But the three-year-old tyke does not have much to say yet, and there's not much to say about him either. If not this, which is crucial: the child is beginning to learn, to retain: "I was raised in Puteaux. On the sentier des Bergères. By a wet nurse—my mother took sick—we looked out over the whole of Paris. Those are my first memories as a kid. Later—thirty years later—I took care of my wet nurse, still on the sentier-Bergères. I was replacing a doctor—Chagnet—a goner himself, since then. After a certain age, old man, you don't die, you're polished off, that's all, you accompany."[2]

In other words, we are now embarking on that narrow path where Céline's life will evermore skirt the territory of his novels, the space of his memory and emotions, those vague landscapes—too vague—with their mirages, their lies, their false perspectives, their shortcuts, their approximations. . . . And how sorely tempting it will be, up to the very end, up to the writer's death, to seek our landmarks in his work, in that borderland of his life, at the risk of losing our way, of coming up against dead ends. To write the life of Céline is to be driven ceaselessly to rely on him—there is no way to avoid it, to ignore the essential part that is always there in what he sees, what he lives, what he writes, what he observes, what he suffers—but it is also to make that reliance into a strength with which to reject his work, distance it, since it is necessarily but a lie, since any work whatsoever, be it the most beautiful and even in proportion to its beauty, is but a work of transposition, of fragile illusions tailored, in Céline, to the convulsive material of his life.

"Memories are stubborn . . . but they break, they're fragile . . . ,"[3] he writes in *Mort à crédit*. We cannot contradict him. Nor can we reproach him for having occasionally shattered his memories or for having in some way reinvented their fragility. Our job, as they say, is to make allowances.

Céline does not have much to say about the Puteaux wet nurse, other than to recall her name as the starting line of his memoirs. In *Féerie pour une autre fois* [Fairytale for Another Time], for example, where he recites yet again the geographical grammar of his origins: "In my schooling and education, I am a brat of the Passage Choiseul; of Puteaux through Madame Jouhaux, my wet nurse (sentier des Bergères); and of Courbevoie, where I was born."[4] Or in *D'un château l'autre* [Castle to Castle]: ". . . my wet nurse, in Puteaux, sentier des Bergères . . . maybe I shouldn't talk about her? . . . forget it!"[5]

Céline is necessarily a little more detailed in *Mort à crédit*, the account of his childhood and adolescence. "When I was even younger, in Puteaux, out to nurse, my parents came up there to see me on Sundays. There was plenty of fresh air. They always paid in advance. Never a penny in debt. Even during the worst setbacks. Only, in Courbevoie, what with worrying and doing without so many things, my mother started to cough. She never stopped. What saved her was a syrup of slugs and later on the Raspail Method."[6]

On the other hand, nothing could save the shop in Courbevoie. While the child was thriving in Puteaux, business was foundering on the rampe du Pont. Who would have had the strange idea of buying lace or house linen in some dark shop in the suburbs? Parisian articles are bought in Paris, and that's all there is to it. And there are neighborhoods for lace or antiques. Grandmother Céline Guillou, with her store on the rue de Provence, had understood that a long time earlier.

Thus, bankruptcy loomed. And to avoid that bankruptcy, which anyone who has ever read *César Birotteau* knows is the ultimate shame of shop-keepers and honest folk, Marguerite and Fernand Destouches resigned themselves to giving up the business, and fast. This was done in 1897, to the profit of one unfortunate squire Voiron, who transformed the boutique into a bazaar which, naturally, itself vanished soon thereafter.

So . . . failure and ignominious retreat to Paris. The hour was ripe for humiliation. How Fernand Destouches must have hung his head, how Marguerite must have blushed for shame and exhaustion under the sad, sarcastic gaze of her mother and brother Louis. . . . On April 10, 1897, the young couple moved into an apartment at 19, rue de Babylone. What was the point of leaving the child to nurse after that? By then, he was weaned, he had grown, and his parents were no longer small-business owners. It was time, at least, that they call in their last and most precious capital, their only son, Little Louis.

Shop to Shop

The 7th *arrondissement*, where, from the summer of 1897, Louis Destouches was to live on the rue de Babylone, is a lovely neighborhood: airy, residential, chic, with its embassies, its ministries, its town houses, its old nobility and its new department store, Le Bon-Marché. A lovely neighborhood, but the family dwelling was tiny. "I slept in the dining room. The missionaries' hymns came over the walls. And there was only one horse left in the whole of the rue de Babylone . . . Bum! Bum! that hackney in tow."[7]

The "Foreign Missions" building is the enduring memory, the indelible image (the bells, the matins, the canticles), the ritualized image, or rather sounds, that infiltrated the child's consciousness, and which he evokes not only in *Mort à crédit* but also in *Nord.* He couldn't see the missionaries "because of the wall that almost blocked up our window" and which "made it a little dark."[8] All that remains, then, yet again, was the sound of bells and the muffled hum of singing, like a distant call, infinitely mysterious and, perhaps, reassuring in its mournful and peaceful repetition, to come and dim the all-too-sharp and wounding noises, tantrums, mediocrities of family life, of life in the foreground.

Fernand Destouches was still employed with Le Phénix insurance company (he would not be named deputy chief clerk until 1923, a year before his retirement). Marguerite, on her side, had had to capitulate unconditionally before her family—or her mother. On the whole, she had played appropriately the role of the returning prodigal daughter. She became once more a shopgirl on the rue de Provence, as if by that act she erased her very marriage, her dreams of independence, the shop in Courbevoie, and her new patronymic Destouches into the bargain.

More often than not the boy remained in the shop with his mother and grandmother. Someone had to take care of him, didn't they? And every morning, after waking up early, the first thing was the great expedition from the rue de Babylone to the rue de Provence, crossing the Carrousel or the Tuileries, past the Opéra. After that, the day dragged on endlessly, hours and hours spent waiting, bored, among the little clocks, the vases, the lace and the old furniture. Was the child naughty? We cannot imagine Louis Destouches as quiet as a porcelain curio. "It was no joke during the day. It was rare that I didn't cry most of the afternoon. I took more smacks than smiles at the shop. I said I was sorry for anything at all, I was sorry for everything."[9]

It is ridiculous to see Céline as an abused child, with his ubiquitous and notorious exaggeration, as if we had to take what he writes as the whole truth. If the Destouches had to count their money over and over again, it's because it must have been as rare as the thrashings administered to their son. It is likely, however, that Céline was a bored child, and that's not much fun either.

Two things, it seems, struck him about his grandmother's shop. He may have reconstituted them after the fact, as if to justify his adult obsessions, or have actually been impressed by them as a child of three or four. There is no way of answering that, but how important is it, really? From the moment that it is in accordance with the facts, the childhood relived or redreamed by Céline is more important to us than the cautious presentation of the few historical certainties we possess.

The shop must have seemed to him, first of all, like a magical world, where the past touched you with its various forms of sediment now up for sale, its hints of bygone eras, its disconcerting evidence of the comforts of yesteryear, as if idealized and at the same time corrupted by the misery and hardships of the present, since, henceforth, silver teapots, china vases, mahogany pedestal tables, or Limoges services became merely objects in a difficult business.

But that is not the essential issue. The world of the shop was riddled with pitfalls. In order to survive, one had constantly to distinguish the false from the real, imposture from sincerity, trash from good merchandise. And Céline was thinking about it again as he wrote *Féerie pour une autre fois II*—

Normance, after World War II: "I can sniff out a fake at twenty-five meters . . . I was raised, myself, among the real stuff . . . in my grandmother's time, the fake had a scent, but it doesn't smell anymore! . . . if it still had its scent you'd have to close all the museums!"[10]

Other than the usual idealization of the past, of the happy days with Grandmother, this passage illustrates the extent to which the shop and life revealed the world of mendacity to the child. To be on guard against illusion, against deceptive appearances and mystifications, to be able to tell the false from the real, such is without any doubt the antiques dealer's overriding obligation, and as a boy of four Céline was in a good school to understand it. Later on, it would also be his duty as a doctor and a novelist: the diagnostic art, the talent for stripping appearances bare.

Once you have learned how not to let yourself be taken, the second point, finally, the second stage that tests the mettle of any good dealer is to learn how to con others, how to bedazzle the customers. "Antiques still make me sick, but that's what fed us. They're sad, these scrapings of time . . . they're vile, sickening. We sold them whether the customer wanted them or not. We wore him down. We'd drown the sucker in torrents of bilge . . . the incredible bargains . . . no pity whatsoever . . . Had to give in . . . to lose any good sense he had . . . He left the place in a daze, with the Louis XIII cup in his pockets, the openwork fan with shepherdess and pussycat in a silk-lined basket. It's amazing how they revolted me, grown-ups taking such crap home with them."[11]

And that, without any doubt, is the origin of Céline's obsession, which sheds light on his work[12] but which, more importantly, reveals his character and defines his outlook: the feeling that language consists of lies, illusion, threats, desperate attempts at survival (the child is well aware that you have to deceive the client to earn your living), and that to be the dupe of such language, on the other hand, is to cherish futile dreams, to ruin oneself, to add to the world's misery and one's own.

During the endless days at the shop, his mother would first dress the windows, then handle the clients while the grandmother watched over the merchandise, assured herself that she wasn't being robbed ("A little chantilly handkerchief flies like a breeze up a well-trained sleeve.")[13] or went off to the auction rooms to replenish her stock, buying "paintings, ciboria, candelabras, parasols, gilt horrors from Japan and god knows what other kind of junk."[14] And in the evenings, Fernand, having left the office after sometimes putting in extra hours that were providential to the household finances, would join them.

"Since the retreat from Courbevoie, Grandma and Papa weren't speaking to each other. Mama babbled on endlessly so that they wouldn't chuck things at each other."[15] Nevertheless, Fernand took charge of deliveries on his mother-in-law's behalf. And again, in *Mort à crédit*, Céline tells of those expeditions from one end of Paris to the other, the father lugging a side table on his shoulders, climbing the stairs, the boy keeping up as best he could, being almost seduced, one day, by the rustling, exhibitionist *bourgeoise* to whom the antique was being delivered, before returning to the rue de Babylone. But how, once again, are we to believe him? It is hard to imagine that such a small child would be made to cross the capital on foot and then allowed to be practically raped in an apartment while his father, unaware, was in the next room. The joke is a little too much to swallow.

For in 1897 (Louis, we may remind ourselves, is under four years old), the shop on the rue de Provence has been left behind. Marguerite Destouches has found work with a hatter, Pestour, on the rue de Rivoli. She had not fought with her mother, to be sure, but she must have been fed up with the humiliations of her position. After that, there was no longer any question of Louis Destouches waiting day after day in the shop on the rue de Provence, even if we can readily imagine his grandmother looking after him quite often.

A year later, in November 1898, his parents moved again, this time to the rue Ganneron in Montmartre. They stayed there ten months. Ever since Courbevoie, his mother had dreamed of getting back on her feet, of opening a new shop of her own. Marguerite was a stubborn woman, humble, self-effacing, hardworking, a woman of silence (lace symbolizes silence, patience, the premonition of infinity), a slightly lame woman with her painful, underdeveloped leg (the consequence of childhood polio?), who limped around at home. But she was above all an obstinate woman, a Breton carved from granite, probably quite lonely and willing to blaze her own trail to her dream of deliverance: a shop where she would be the boss.

This required at least two conditions: to find a shop, and to find the money for the lease and the preliminary stock of merchandise. And no mistakes this time: she would prospect in a good neighborhood and not in the suburban deserts; she would look, for instance, around the Opéra, the Stock Exchange, the Grands Boulevards.

In July 1899 Marguerite and Fernand Destouches finally settled on an "Established Dealer in Curios" located at 67, Passage Choiseul. The rent was modest, but even so they had to spend 1,100 francs to buy out the lease. Yet again—but this was the last time, she promised, swore (and kept her word)—Marguerite called on her family. Her brother lent her the money, her mother gave her a little merchandise, lace, and luxury lingeries. Boutique Destouches, act II, the curtain rises. And the whole family moved in above the shop.

Louis had just turned five.

To sum up: born in Courbevoie, he lived in a little parish in the Yonne, and then with a second wet nurse in Puteaux. He would join his parents in the rue de Babylone and spend his days with his grandmother in the rue de Provence. Then he was moved to Montmartre. And now, finally, to the Passage Choiseul. Enough to make him giddy, in effect. And how should we not believe that all this helped to sow the seeds of instability in him? Céline the nomad, the restless, the man of change and departures—no doubt about it, his earliest childhood gave him the habit if not the need or the taste for such a disequilibrium, which in the long run is but one of the symptoms of the incapacity to live in arrested time.

Céline, or the impossibility of sedentary well-being.

School to School

The Passage Choiseul, which essentially encompasses the author's childhood, became one of the most picturesque settings in *Mort à crédit*, but that is of little account. It remains above all one of the most symbolic. It now figures among the great places of French literary memory, along the lines, say, of 12 Eccles Street in Dublin, where Bloom lives in *Ulysses*, or the gardens of the Champs-Élysées, where the narrator plays in *À la recherche du temps perdu* [Remembrance of Things Past].

Built during the reign of Charles X, the *passage* links the rue des Petits-Champs with the rue Saint-Augustin. A few steps from the Opéra, the Grands Boulevards, the Stock Exchange, the commercial arcade, to this very day, shelters shops that are practically identical: narrow, capped by a tiny dwelling on three levels, the last mansarded and jutting out into the fresh air above the arcade's skylight.

It requires little imagination to picture the Passage Choiseul at the turn of the century, with the bustle of foot traffic, the shoppers, the *flaneurs*, the delivery boys, the assistants, with its small shopkeepers—tailors, jewelers, antiques dealers, haberdashers, milliners—who all knew one another, sympathized and gossiped with one another, spied on or slandered one another. There was the gunsmith Weil, the book dealer–publisher Alphonse Lemerre, and a *patissier*, Charvin, become Dorival in *Mort à crédit.* A little farther up, on the avenue de l'Opéra, the fine carriages rolled by. On the rue des Petits-Champs, it was the hustle and bustle of wagons, handcarts, and deliveries. But there, under the glass that was so stifling in the summer, there were only the shouts, the jostling, the shut-in odor of urine and naphtalene, an echo chamber where footsteps reverberated, the barking of dogs, interjections, conversations, the cries and wailing of children.

"I have to admit that the Passage was an unbelievable cesspool. It was made to kill you, slowly but surely, between the urine of little mutts, the shit, the spit, the leaking gas. It stank worse than the inside of a prison. Down under the glass the sun reached you so dim you could eclipse it with a candle. People began to gasp for breath. The Passage became aware of its own suffocating stench!"[16]

These lines are not merely a piece of literary bravura, and the impression left on Céline by the arcade would survive the publication of *Mort à crédit.* Whenever he would evoke his childhood, he would continue to describe the setting in almost identical terms, as witnessed by this extract from *Féerie pour une autre fois*: "It reminded me of the Passage Choiseul, we were 'gassed' too, in the Passage, thousands of gas jets ... at mid-Lent every asshole from the Boulevards came to toast himself in the Passage, yelling, pierrots, clowns, harlequins, fake aristocrats ... what bedlam! And the grannies, and old farts, and the kids! What a racket! Gas is worse than the moon, it's this pale green that stupefies ... stupefies ... you see some strange ones ... people not quite dead, not alive, not anything ... Those freaks really threw me at the time ... and the Passage was full of 'em!"[17]

Or again, these lines from *D'un château l'autre*: "When you talk about our Passage Choiseul, there's just the neighborhood and the suffocation: the worst of all of them, the most unhealthy: the biggest gas bell in the whole City of Lights! ... three hundred permanent Auer nozzles! ... raising kids by asphyxiation!"[18]

In *Mort à crédit*, Céline calls the Passage Choiseul the Passage des Bérésinas. As we know, his choice of proper names is never innocent. They generally symbolize, with Rabelaisian glibness, the burden of catastrophe attributed by the writer to the places or people he rebaptizes. With "Passage des Bérésinas"* the implications of a murderous bottleneck, a rout, a generalized and Imperial debacle are all there.

Though he caricatured the discomfort, if not the misery, of its inhabitants, Céline did not exaggerate his descriptions of the Passage. For the set is all there, the backstage and offices of the Bouffes-Parisiens theater abutting the Passage (Céline calls it the "Grenier-Mondain"), the glass roof and the shopkeepers' apartments. One might almost be able to revisit the Destouches' lodgings: its three rooms connected by a spiral staircase, the living room/dining room/kitchen on the first floor, the parents' bedroom on the second, and, on the third, above the skylight, the child's room, with a window on the open air but encased in bars "because of thieves and cats," and a tiny dressing room near by.

This home must have seemed pretty pathetic to Fernand Destouches, the bogus country squire plunged by marriage into an authentic, shopkeeping lower-middle class. But from there, for Céline to transform it into a hovel, and the arcade into a Court of Miracles with its inhabitants like broken, docile victims, laborers sleepwalking on a razor's edge, ready to tumble off into irreversible misery, there was but one (long) step, which the writer was later to take with a liberty that made good use of his scrupulous memory for facts.

The arcade discovered by the child Louis Destouches in July 1899 was a symbolic place. He constantly seems to meld the ambiguous, contradictory characteristics of the open and the closed, the fugitive and the sedentary, the invitation to travel and the cozy, nostalgic withdrawal into himself.

Of course, the Passage was open, like life, like adventure, like the imagination. Let us reread the (highly dubious) song of the Swiss Guards that

---

* The Berezina River: Site and symbol of Napoléon's retreat from Russia in 1812— trans.

Céline chose as epigraph to the *Voyage*: "Our life is a journey / Through Winter and Night, / We search for our way / Through a sky without light." And the Passage Choiseul attracted its long procession of middle-class ladies, workers, the curious and the destitute. The traffic was continuous, like a hemorrhage. It offered spectacular possibilities, this Passage. Ah! To be able one day to follow one of these strangers out into the city, into danger, into adulthood! Inside the Passage Choiseul, Louis Destouches was at home. And the hubbub came to him, like a call, a breath of fresh air, or a seduction, all the enigmatic figures, sometimes threatening or cajoling, the strangers who filed past, strolled, bought, loitered, moved off and, perhaps, breathed it in. . . .

But, above all, the Passage Choiseul resembled a belly, a dark, humid, hot, and comforting bell jar. It was a maternal space, where time was suspended. The metaphors Céline chose to describe it are revealing. "I am a child of the Passage Choiseul," he cries in *Féerie pour une autre fois*.

The Passage Choiseul was also a cultural stew, an ideal stomping ground for a child (as later for the writer), where the little race of shopkeepers and artisans swarmed, that humble, laborious, and submissive class that progress, according to Céline, was to sweep away mercilessly. If he is to be believed, businesses tottered on the brink of ruin, tradition was being lost, the competition from the department stores was ruining them. The rich had lost their taste for finery and their understanding of refinement. Beautiful lace had died with respect for manual labor. They were entering the mechanical age. Why fight it? When he left the Passage Choiseul, that was how Céline would sign his farewells to childhood, mothering, a bygone era. By putting the Passage Choiseul behind him, he was essentially pronouncing its death sentence. A mother does not long survive her son's emancipation. He was to enter into active life. Leaving the Passage would be a sort of labor: a second birth into Modern Times.

Already, in 1900, progress loomed in the form of the World Exhibition, the warning sign that so impressed the six-year-old Louis. "Grandma was very suspicious of the upcoming Exhibition. The other one, in '89, had only messed up small business, making idiots spend their money the wrong way."[19] But Fernand Destouches, less perceptive, more of a dreamer, certainly took his son there, and was amazed by it. In short, for Céline, the World Exhibition inaugurated modern life, progress and calamities, along with his entrance into conscious life. On the other side, that formless and euphoric world of childhood, that golden age where his grandmother reigned absolutely, was fading.

We must nonetheless be careful not to caricature Fernand Destouches, that engrossed visitor to the World Exhibition, too harshly. His personality is richer, one might say madder, than the image that is usually drawn. We need only picture him an instant, plump, blond, and baby-faced, with his fat, fairground athlete's whiskers, bitterly unhappy at the Phénix office, where his division manager humiliates him at will and, as soon as working hours are over, donning a sailor's cap to keep his captain's dream alive a little while longer.

Mediocrities do not dream. Or, more precisely, mediocrities have mediocre aspirations. By that account, Fernand Destouches was not a mediocrity. Back at home, he painted endless flotillas of watercolor boats. He would climb up to Louis' room, way up there, as if onto the bridge of a ship, and his brush would spin out naive dreams of another, more beautiful, more distant life, lashed by tempests and the whipping spray of high adventure. Then, "he would stand a long time behind the bars, contemplating the stars, the atmosphere, the moon, the night high above us. It was his poop deck, I knew that. He was commanding the Atlantic."[20]

Of course, to balance that portrait, the man's mediocrities and conformities were glaring. He read *La Patrie* [The Fatherland], a popular reactionary sheet; he must have been nationalistic, anglophobic, anti-Masonic, anti-reactionary-parliamentary, anti-Semitic, anti-Prussian, anti-everything. The Dreyfus Affair was in full swing. Perhaps, in 1898, Fernand Destouches had contributed to the fund opened by Drumont's *La Libre Parole* to allow the widow and orphan of Colonel Henry (who had committed suicide after being convicted of authoring the false evidence that got Dreyfus condemned) to prosecute his accusers and defend the honor of "the French officer killed, assassinated by the Jews." One point is known: Fernand Destouches did read Drumont. But who didn't read Drumont in those circles? And the retrial in Rennes must not have changed his mind: Dreyfus was guilty.

But it is curious to note that in none of his writings did Céline emphasize his father's anti-Semitism, which would later have constituted an excuse, a reason, an alibi with which to justify his own in the end. However, in *Mort à crédit*, in *D'un château l'autre*, and in the series of chronicles, he resolutely avoids any evocation of his father's political opinions, discussions, arguments, or family squabbles that he must have witnessed (even if, for good measure, he was to emphasize the man's violence and closed mind with—excessive?—cruelty).

We will understand nothing about Céline if we gloss too quickly over the dreamer side of his father's character, and the trace, the impression it left on him, his taste for the sea, for travel, for fog; a taste, like a voyeur's restless reverie, to which the writer confesses in *D'un château l'autre*: "I have to tell you that, on top of being a voyeur, I'm a fanatic about port traffic, about any water trade . . . anything that comes floats docks . . . I was on the piers with my father . . . eight days of vacation in Tréport . . . the things we saw . . . the coming and going of the little fishing boats, risking their lives for whiting! . . . widows and their kids praying to the sea! . . . the pathetic scenes on the piers! . . . what suspense! so hold on there! . . . makes the Grand Guignol look like Punch and Judy! and Hollywood's millions! now here, we've reached the Seine . . . I'm enthralled . . . just as in love with water traffic and boats as in my earliest childhood . . . once you're obsessed with boats, their ways, their comings and goings, it's for life! . . . there aren't many fascinations that last a lifetime."[21]

But let us return to the Passage—and thus to the image of the mother with her lace requiring endless repairs, an image that also belongs to the child's memory. François Gibault cites a beautiful letter from Céline to Lucienne Delforge in 1936: "I remember in the Passage when she was younger, the enormous pile of lace to be repaired, the fabulous hillock always overshadowing her table—a mountain of work for a few francs. It was never finished. It was for food. I had nightmares about it, so did she. It always stayed with me. . . . Like her, I've always got an enormous pile of horrors waiting on my table, which I'd like to take care of before I'm done."[22]

As for the meals prepared by Marguerite Destouches, a pitiful cook, it was always bread soup with egg or noodles, those infamous noodles, ad nauseam, because noodles gave off no odor, did not permeate the lace or disturb the clientele in the poorly ventilated Passage Choiseul. The only recipes the tireless Mme. Destouches could master involved boiled foods and meats. Here again, as in the Passage, as in all feminine space, humidity, warmth, and blandness reigned.

But in 1900, it was time to think of removing Louis from this, his only protective environment. He was six years old. In October he began his first year of elementary studies at the public school on the square Louvois.

There is nothing to say about his first years of schooling. He almost never discussed them. He was neither a dunce nor a gifted student, neither a naughty, disruptive class clown as his father had been at his age nor a model pupil. Just an average student who inspired the following appraisal from his principal: "An intelligent child but excessively lazy and encouraged in this by his parents' weakness. Was capable of doing very well under firm guidance. Very lax upbringing."[23]

In short, school was a grayish barracks environment that inspired neither anger nor joy in him. Merely silence, which is worse.

And we are suddenly reminded of the final pages of *Les Beaux draps* in which, caught up in the whirlwind of ruin, soul-searching, ambitions, retreats, and anxieties that followed the defeat of 1941, he settled his frenzied accounts for the last time, summed up (almost) his anti-Semitic deliria, put an end to Freemasonry and the rest of it, and offered up a satirical program for French national recovery, starting with salvation through the schools. What had been the norm up to then, he asks? "Places where perfect innocence and spontaneous joy are tortured, where birds are strangled." And he added: "School must become a place of enchantment or disappear, a petrified prison. Childhood is magical."[24]

In other words, the school on the square Louvois had been a petrified prison for him. And where had he found magic? Very far from school, certainly, and most likely at his grandmother's side.

"Grandma was well aware that I needed to have some fun, that it wasn't healthy to be shut up in the store all the time."[25] He often slept at her place at 52, rue Saint-Georges. She brought him to Asnières when she went to collect the rents on her three villas. That meant fresh air, the countryside, freedom in the company of an elderly woman, once a tireless worker, now suddenly reinvigorated by the lad's cheerful mischief. She certainly left him to his whims and wild gamboling.

Better yet, she had no qualms about taking him to the movies, to the Robert Houdin for the Thursday matinee. "We'd stay for three shows. It was the same price, one franc for any seat, a hundred percent silent, no words, no music, no letters, just the purring of the projector. It'll make a comeback, people get tired of everything except sleep and daydreams. *The Journey to the Moon* will make a comeback... I still know it by heart."[26] Behind the back of his father, who wouldn't hear of such frivolities, she also bought him *Boys' Illustrated Adventures* from the saleswoman sitting at her foot warmer at the end of the Passage. Lastly, Céline Guillou owned a dog, Bobs, a little fox terrier that the boy adored and which he would inherit on his grandmother's death.

And this was enough to open the gates of dream to him, the joys of spectacle, that pure delight that exists out of the mainstream of life, on the fringes of childhood, beyond the Passage Choiseul; that share of enchantment without which existence is a nightmare from which there is no escape. Yes, *Boys' Illustrated Adventures*, *The Journey to the Moon*, or the silent, bouncy presence of Bobs, which he will later exchange for the charms of ballet, love of dance, and the presence of animals, cats, dogs, Bébert and others, always like an act of grace, a magic, a lie that frees you momentarily from the deadly oppressiveness of mankind.

But that oppressiveness, alas, wins out in the end, death waits at the end of the journey, separation on the horizon in the Passage Choiseul. On December 28, 1904, his grandmother Céline Guillou died, she who had enthralled the child and would provide him his pseudonym. A tragic death, a silent death, a modest death. The child's encounter with death, this world's only truth. It was his first desertion, too, his first grief, the first shreds of a dream that was to weaken, vanish into the past, that night of time and memory from which there is no return.

"Grandma looked me right in the eye, but her look was friendly... They told me to kiss her... I was already leaning over the bed. She motioned to me not to... She smiled a little again... She wanted to tell me something... It was scratching at the back of her throat, it wouldn't come... Even so, she finally managed... as softly as she could... 'Work hard, my little Ferdinand!' she whispered... I wasn't afraid of her... We understood each other, deep down... And, in the long run it's been true, I have worked hard... It's nobody's business."[27]

A few months before Céline Guillou's death, the Destouches had moved. From No. 67 they moved to No. 64, on the other side, almost directly opposite, thus obtaining an identical shop, identical lodgings, identical lighting, the identical business, and the same clientele.

They were not on the verge of bankruptcy. In the spring, they bought Louis his first piano lessons—and it was at a recital that he met a little girl, Simone Saintu, with whom he would later correspond, particularly during his stay in Africa in 1916–1917. Clearly, one does not offer one's son piano lessons before one has first managed to set the pot a-boiling and fill it with macaroni. Better yet, with Céline Guillou's death and legacy, the Destouches' modest comfort was to be further consolidated.

Marguerite received the three Asnières villas, which she sold in 1921 and 1923, and a cash sum of 17,750 francs. It was no fortune, but it meant no more scraping and anxiety at the end of the month. Thus, it had nothing in common with the atmosphere of penury emanating from *Mort à crédit*, and which Céline, in his interviews, would help to magnify even further. To give only one example, he asserted to Georges Altman in the December 10, 1932, issue of *Le Monde*, after the publication of *Voyage*: "My mother, a lace worker; my father, the family intellectual. We had a business, we did a lot of cities. It never worked. Failure. Failure. Failure. I was always surrounded by failure as a kid."[28]

In 1904 a certain Louis Montourcy was put in charge of a stock portfolio in Fernand Destouches' account. His testimony was published in the first of the Éditions de l'Herne's *Cahiers Céline*, in 1963. "He came now and then, sometimes alone and sometimes with his little boy, and, having had the chance to send some good things his way, I had managed to gain his trust to the point where, leaving on a month's vacation, he had given me two signed, blank stock orders, so that I might make one or two purchases while he was away if I thought it might be in his best interest."

Another sign of the household's comfort was the child's being abruptly withdrawn, in February 1905, from his primary school on the square Louvois—secular, free, and compulsory—to be enrolled at a religious (and paying) school, Saint-Joseph-des-Tuileries, on the rue du 29-Juillet. Discipline there was strict. There was no trifling with morality and the catechism courses were far from optional. Louis Destouches seemed in general to fit fairly well into the school. Acceptable grades, a docility that was appreciated by his teachers. In short, the child was growing in discretion (perhaps), knowledge (certainly), and piety (provisionally).

On May 18, 1905, at the church of Saint-Roch, he celebrated his first communion. How droll it seems to us today, the photograph of Louis in his Sunday best. He is so well behaved, so stiff in his long trousers rumpling over his patent-leather shoes, with his white armband over his lovely pale shirt with the sailor's collar. Kneeling at a prie-dieu, he holds a prayer book in his left hand. Pretty as a picture, as they say. But that would be a generous interpretation of his pinched lips, the simultaneously scornful and intimidated look of a young bourgeois placidly waiting to grow up, perhaps, before he sends it all packing.

At eleven, of course, the time is not ripe for rebellion. In the summer, the time was ripe for vacations. Sometimes Louis would stay in Ablon with his uncle Louis Guillou (Uncle Édouard in *Mort à crédit*), who ran a raincoat store at 24, rue de La Fayette, under the sign "Imperbel." Or else with his parents, who rented a house there on several occasions. Sometimes, alone or with the family, he went to the seaside, to Dieppe. From there, he would write his parents sober, affectionate, and sensitive letters without notable spelling mistakes. . . . (But nothing of what we know about Céline's life or those of his parents hints at the excursion to England told in *Mort à crédit*, with its apocalyptic account of the crossing.)

The child's education continued. In October 1906 his parents again enrolled him in a public school at 11, rue d'Argenteuil. For the last year before the *certificat* (a primary education exam), the important thing was to cram as much as possible. Morality and religion suddenly took the back bench to pedagogical proficiency. Which didn't prevent him from picking up an award for good conduct. A miracle! That is to say, a miracle that was not often to be repeated in his lifetime.

And, on June 15, 1907, came the great test, the last act, the final rite of passage, the end of childhood and its privileges, the entrance into adolescence, work, worries, travels, exhaustion, and, finally, the farewell to the Passage Choiseul. On June 15, 1907, Louis Destouches passed his certificate of primary studies exam.

We come across that most solemn moment again in *Mort à crédit*, evoked in a cruel and derisory comic scene. The mother closes up shop to escort the child to the primary school near Saint-Germain-l'Auxerrois; she makes him recite his fables and his list of *départements* one last time. The first test is dictation. The oral is taken with a fat, friendly, indulgent teacher who foresees, beyond the examination, the hard life of labor waiting for the young examinees. The teacher is almost tempted to hold them back to protect them one more year, though he doesn't go that far. The narrator is passed; Céline, or Louis Destouches, is passed. The master is going to pass them all. "Now, now, my boy," he tells me, "don't worry! None of this means a thing! I'll pass you! You'll get your start in life, since it's so important to you!"[29]

It probably wasn't all that important to Louis, with his mocking smile, his lovely blue eyes, his cabbage-leaf ears; tough, lanky Louis, boisterous and shy at the same time, solitary the way only sons sometimes are, touchy, without intimate friends or partners in adventure. But his father had plans for him. Starting now, he would have to choose a profession.

Louis was thirteen. A fateful number, a farewell to childhood and to magic.

3

The Schools of Life

Germany, 1907–1908
One Island, Two Schools
Fabric, Jewels, and Freedom

Germany, 1907–1908

The start in life after the *certificat*, getting hired, apprenticeship, the thousand trying little labors of an errand boy or a messenger, those humble intimations of hell evoked in *Mort à crédit*—there was no immediate question of any of these for Louis Destouches. The philosophical examining teacher of the novel need not have worried. In crowning his young examinees, he was not sending them off systematically to the working life, or the slaughterhouse, which came to more or less the same thing in his eyes. For them, the passive or rather the past life, the life of schoolchildren, preserved their rights, like a reprieve, though probably the last. That moment where others are still paying for you, supporting you, making your decisions, holding up that invisible shield, invulnerable and precious above all others, that protects you from the world's misery, from the future, from worries—and thus from death.

"My mother's ambition was to make me a department store buyer. To her mind, there was nothing higher. As for my father, he didn't want me to pursue any studies because he thought that was just misery and he knew all about it since he was in it."[1]

Short of theoretical studies and new diplomas, there remained the acquisition of languages, that supreme trump of commerce, that guarantee of promotion, that weapon of international success. For a salesman who speaks English or German, the sky's the limit. A department store buyer—yes, why not? Or else regional manager, or else, or else . . . The Destouches dreamed. Louis, their only son—that is what we must never forget, their only son, their only hope, their only vengeance—justified sacrifices no less unique. So Louis would speak English, he would speak German, and the more he spoke the higher he would rise on the social ladder. To speak, to persuade, to trick, to triumph, to lie, were perhaps just so many synonyms to them—but were they actually aware of that? In any case, they would be just so many certainties in Céline's work: speak to succeed, to oppress, to buttress one's privileges by founding them on the misery of others.

Therefore, first stop: Germany.

How did Fernand Destouches, the patriot, the nationalist, feel about sending his son to the land of the hereditary enemy, the Prussian, the usurper of Alsace and Lorraine? He may have resented it, but in the end one could not retreat before any concession; or he may have been proud, for there Louis would take the measure of his adversary, conquer his language, and—why not?—do his own form of reconnaissance, informing his father on the morale of the Germans. We won't look too deeply into these opposite and contradictory points of view. And the young man, writing to his family from over there, will for that matter play the accepted game, show himself appropriately patriotic and, on occasion, comment cynically on the news and newspapers from beyond the Rhine.

We do not know how the Destouches were put in touch with a certain Hugo Schmidt, headmaster and teacher at a secondary school in Diepholz, Lower Saxony, who accepted young Louis as a boarding student for 120 marks a month, plus a few marks for pocket money and piano lessons. Let us merely recall the expedition's departure in late August 1907, Louis burdened with his trunk, his bicycle, and an avalanche of advice, but most of all with his father and mother, who wanted to assess with their own eyes the man to whom they were confiding their progeny.

That, then, is the salient image: the only child, let us remind ourselves, accompanied and protected before being abandoned for the first time, which, of course, cripples the entire Célinian mythology promulgated particularly in *Mort à crédit*, which shows us the young Louis (or Bardamu) browbeaten by parents whose sense of duty overwhelms their real solicitude, as endless reproaches do to the least avowal of tenderness. No, as prudence and affection require, Marguerite and Fernand most definitely embark with him at the Gare de l'Est towards Diepholz, with multiple changes at Aix-la-Chapelle, Düsseldorf, and so on, forty-eight hours on the train and, for Céline, the first of his rail crossings of Germany.

A brief parenthesis, or a detour through Céline's work, is called for here. In *Mort à crédit*, Céline jumps straight from the primary studies certificate to the child's hiring by a merchant. "The next day, we started our search for a really solid house where I could get my start in business. A place that was even a little severe, where they wouldn't let me get away with anything."[2] No question of schools, vacations, or linguistic apprenticeships. The reason for that is simple—younger, more helpless and thus more exploited, the hero of *Mort à crédit* is only made more pathetic thereby. Céline is ever concerned with highlighting salient features, darkening already existent shadows, revealing the suffering and thus the truth of this world—meaning Céline's truth—the moment when the nightmare abruptly tears away the smiling veil of appearances, when delirium seizes reality, distorts it, removes it from verisimilitude to restore it, convulsive, at the level of a higher truth that could be called the impressionism of unalloyed emotions.

We later come across a transformed account in *Mort à crédit* of Louis' stay in English schools. But that stay will only arise as a "last chance." A repurchase of the child after his calamitous experiences in business. A final hope that we can already foresee will be in vain. In other words, the stay in

England will be falsely presented as one of the hero's worst afflictions, the moment when he has become as helpless, misunderstood, unhappy, and guilt-ridden as he could be.

Obviously, there is nothing of the sort in Louis Destouches' life as a boarder in Germany and then as a schoolboy in Rochester or in Broadstairs. His stays there seem to have been generally peaceful if not happy. Without incident, without accident, without catastrophe. With the procession of the usual secret joys, exaltations, and sorrows of adolescence and its meta-morphoses, their vague and muddled aspirations to a sexuality comparable to a fog that lifts too slowly—in short, that age that seems essentially so muddy, so opaque, and whose true values, points of reference, and feelings it is impossible to determine afterward. . . . And over all this reigns a deep silence.

Moreover, whatever cannot be dramatized, if I dare put it that way, does not interest Céline. In his books, he hardly exploited his time as a schoolboy in Germany. And that is not all: he never really touched on it in his inter-views when he evoked his childhood, forging his personality with hammer blows of hazy memories, touched-up versions of family portraits, approx-imations, sleight-of-hand, and repentance. Why? Perhaps because the Great War came along with its own share of horrors, blood, absurdity, and hatred, and Céline had some trouble reconciling the carefree months he had spent in Germany, at thirteen and fourteen years of age, with the memories of a front-line fighter. Or else because, after the Second World War, Céline, on the defensive, was not inclined to underline the roots of the complicity which he was wrongly seen as harboring toward Germany and its culture.

Thus, the Destouches left their son in that late summer of 1907 to under-take the endless return journey to Paris, the Gare de l'Est and the Passage Choiseul. But Marguerite had promised that she would return toward All Saints' Day.

Louis' heart must have been heavy. The setting around Diepholz, at the edge of the river Hunte, with its old castle and few thousand inhabitants, was not exactly enchanting or spontaneous. All around were swamps, the Lower Saxon plain stretching out forever, and the great city of Bremen lost to the north, well beyond the horizon. We can understand the disillusioned statements he was still making in the early 1950s as he was writing *D'un château l'autre*: "I was over there with those Krauts, northern Prussia . . . Brandenburg . . . I was just a kid, 9 years old . . . and later, as an internee . . . I don't much like the dump, but anyway . . . it's a plain of poor soil and sand, between two forests! . . . a land for spuds, pigs, and old soldiers . . . and storm plains! hang on! the kind you never see here! . . . and these sequoia forests you never see here either!"[3] Moreover, such assertions were re-doubled a little further on by a no less exaggerated hostility toward the inhabitants themselves: "I know a thing or two about Germany! . . . God help me! . . . more than I'd like to! . . . that violet muslin . . . by God! . . . Diepholz, Hanover! . . . talk about memories! . . . as nasty as they were stubborn, all right! . . . maybe worse than in '44! . . . the thrashings they threw at me in Diepholz, Hanover! 1906! . . . *Sedantag! Kaisertag!* the same savages as in '14! . . ."[4] And we should note in passing the willful mistakes that Céline slips into these few lines, the age of nine, for instance, when he was thirteen, or the year 1906, when it was actually two years later.

In the final analysis, what Louis Destouches was leaving behind him for the first time was not just the gas bell in the Passage Choiseul, it was an entire family world that had nurtured him through thick and thin. And now he was saying goodbye to his father, his mother, his uncle Louis Guillou, the uncle Édouard of *Mort à crédit*—the athlete, dressed in his undershirt like an escapee from a Maupassant short story, with his velocipede, his country house in Ablon, his ingenuous good humor, his raincoat store on the rue La Fayette, his canoeing parties on the Seine and his backfiring automobile. . . .

On the Destouches side, the regrets must been less vivid. Aunt Amélie, Aunt Hélène of the novel, was nothing but a myth of sulfurous seduction at the far end of his horizon. Having traveled around Europe and the block a few times, leaving a wake of gallants, lovers, or clients, as you will, behind her, she had settled in Romania, where she had married a diplomat, Zénon Zawirski. Exit Aunt Amélie . . . Georges Destouches (Uncle Antoine) had entered the civil service. After having occupied the post of assistant chief clerk in the Ministry of Public Education, in March 1906 he had wangled the title of general secretary of the Paris Faculty of Medicine. But he was not on the best of terms with Fernand Destouches, who envied him and accused him of owing his rise to Freemasonry. Later on, Jacques Destouches, Georges' son, would finish his medical studies at the same time as Louis, and relations between the two men would not be any better. In 1932 Jacques would even go so far as to let it be known, through a press release, that he had nothing in common with the author of *Voyage au bout de la nuit*. . . . Charles Destouches, the second brother, was Uncle Arthur in *Mort à crédit*, "a lady's man with a goatee, corduroy trousers, pointy shoes, a long, tapered pipe. He didn't give a damn. He was heavy into womanizing. He often fell seriously ill when the quarterly rent was due. Then he'd spend a week or so in bed with one of his ladyfriends"[5] He had remained a Bohemian, a failure, one day a salesman in a department store, the next sipping absinthe in the back of a café. He was not the best company. . . . René Destouches (Uncle Rodolphe) was hardly any more so, being a little nuts following a fall from a cliff, and dozing away his entire life as an underling at the telephone company. "He chuckled quietly when you talked to him. He answered his own questions. It lasted for hours. He wanted to live only in the open air. He would never have anything to do with stores or offices, not even as a guard, even at night. He preferred staying outside on a bench when he ate. He was suspicious of the indoors. When he got really too hungry he'd come to the house. He'd come by in the evening. That meant things were pretty bad."[6]

In short, it was not the Destouches side that the child missed as he was discovering Germany, taking bicycle rides around Diepholz, doing his scales on the piano, donning his school cap every morning on his way to *Klasse 3* in the austere *Mittelschule* with its typically Nordic, pedimented front landing. "The Passage Choiseul is not indispensable to me," he wrote to his parents at the time. But we are not compelled to believe him. Nevertheless, according to his landlord and teacher, Herr Schmidt, Louis was cheerful, hardworking, athletic. He hiked, skated, did gymnastics. He was handy and inventive. To round out his pocket money, he gave French lessons and did electrical odd jobs for the inhabitants of Diepholz. His dark spot may lie specifically therein: the feeling of guilt he doubtlessly had (and which his parents helped to inculcate in him) in matters of money. The Destouches were not poor, we know that, but they had the sense of being poor, and that may be even worse. To them, every expense was a form of sacrifice. Any happiness was wrongful if it was not productive. Throughout his life, Céline would be marked by the stern demands of duty, of money that must be won by the sweat of one's brow and, above all, that one must save: the under-the-mattress mentality. Céline, or Anti-Wastefulness. . . . On January 1, 1908, for instance, he wrote to his parents: "I thank you with all my heart for the sacrifices you are undertaking for my future but please believe that I will not be an ingrate and that you will later have every reason to be glad of the great sacrifice you are making for me."[7]

And the weeks unfolded, repetitive, lively, or nostalgic. At the beginning of *Voyage*, Céline evokes this *séjour*, transformed, no doubt, by the dramatic requirements of the novel: "I knew the Germans pretty well, I had even been to school over there as a kid, in the Hanover region. I'd spoken their language. They were a bunch of little loudmouthed jerks, with their pale, furtive eyes, like wolves; after school we went together to feel up the girls in the woods around the town, or we'd shoot popguns or pistols you could buy for four marks. We drank sugary beer."[8]

More informative, of course, are the letters he regularly wrote to his parents, which strike us by the imperturbable pains Louis takes to chronicle a little German town at the turn of the century, to describe the death of the station innkeeper's son or the crime committed by the flower merchant of Bremen. . . . And always that reserve, the modesty of a child revealing his emotions, his feelings, as if to the often laconic malaise of that age were already being added a skittish character, perhaps too immoderate in joy, in suffering, but one that was learning at the same time to conceal its various moods.

As previously decided, Louis went home to spend Easter vacation with his parents. And his father took advantage of the visit to put Louis' knowledge to the test. After all, were Hugo Schmidt's favorable reports entirely trustworthy? Fernand Destouches had the somewhat bizarre idea of putting together a little jury (an assize court?) whose president, moreover, was a licensed translator to the Court of Appeals. And the accused was compelled to testify. The jury then deliberated, praised his knowledge and the facility with which he spoke and understood German. However, he was found guilty of weak grammar and composition. The sentence came down: it was desirable that the child should do another stint beyond the Rhine. The court rose. . . .

And, after the summer vacation, also spent with the family, Louis left for Germany for another four months, sometime in early September 1908. This time his destination was Karlsruhe, to a teacher, Herr Rudolf Bittrolff, who offered him a private room, family life, abundant nourishment, and Germanic discipline. As usual, his parents accompanied him.

Everything was in order. From eight o'clock to one, school. Lunch, then a piano session (one hour), German (one hour), free time (two hours) before the studies (another hour) that came before supper. No more goofing off. Louis had to learn to walk straight and to bow to the objectivity of clocks, the *diktat* of schedules, the discipline of the master. We can easily imagine that not even his bicycle outings with the sixteen-year-old son of "Professor" Bittrolff could have taken particularly out-of-the-way or imaginative detours.

Louis, certainly, was not very happy in Karlsruhe. Herr Bittrolff scolded him for his laziness, his faulty pronunciation, his lack of attentiveness, his disorderliness, his negligence, and his superficiality, as shown in the letters that he himself wrote to the father of his student boarder. Louis was simply unable to adjust to a regime so incompatible with his character. But he was a child, that is to say a reed. He bent. He made progress on the piano. He made fewer mistakes in German. He also spent less pocket money (one mark a week) because business was not exactly booming at the store. Financial worries were ever present. And another Christmas spent far from his loved ones, since his stay was paid for up to the New Year. The inescapable hatred of waste.

At the end of December, mercifully, it was over. Louis had been discharged. He returned home to his mother, his father, his dog. In his luggage, the predictable presents: a keg of sauerkraut and a bottle of kirsch. Goodbye, Germany! Louis was fourteen and he was leaving no regrets behind him.

One Island, Two Schools

Louis had barely two months—January and February 1909—to catch his breath, to resume his family life and his Parisian habits, above all to forget Germany, the industrial smogs of Karlsruhe and Rudolf Bittrolff's iron rule, before he had to begin preparing for his next expedition.

For the past two years, his parents had lived not above the store but in a slightly more comfortable and spacious lodging on the rue Marsollier, in a modestly middle-class building whose windows looked out on the Salle Ventadour, which was once near the Opéra, just a stone's throw from the

Passage Choiseul. His mother would live there until her death. Even so, on his return, Louis found the same old shop, lace, clients few and far between, and the arcade's odor of urine—one might say the odor of his childhood.

At the time, France was nursing its wounds from the Dreyfus Affair as best it could. In any case, a new crisis was garnering attention and requisitioning the press: the revolt of the Southern wine growers, who were crusading against the government and the state, protesting the lowering of the price of wine, organizing the sabotage of their province's civil service, and fomenting out-and-out rebellion in the Languedoc. But Clemenceau had sent in the troops. Everywhere, for that matter, in the fight against strikers in the Paris region or the subversion perceived in the intrigues of the unionizing railroaders, the order of the day was repression. The Bloc des Gauches—the consolidated Left—had had its day. Briand, who succeeded Clemenceau in 1909, was to continue the struggle. The bourgeois order had to rule. The railroaders' strike was "illegal." Yes, the climate called for firmness. Fernand Destouches must have rejoiced. His son's education was to be achieved in the same way, through sacrifice and energetic decision-making. So it was England for him, and posthaste!

But business, it was true, was slow—ever the same domestic troubles, the same professional rancor, the same daydreams unfulfilled. No, nothing had changed around Louis. But the child himself had changed. After a year and a half far from home and his friends, whom could he possibly recognize or want to see? His cousin Charlotte, perhaps, "Lolotte," who was his age, Uncle Charles' daughter, to whom he was bound by a solid and affectionate complicity? Perhaps. Or else his piano buddy, Simone Saintu. . . . But he had grown so fast, he had already outgrown his memories and the framework of his life. Childhood companions disperse too quickly after the first betrayals and departures. Louis was thus ready to cross the Channel. Already more autonomous, freer of the bonds of childhood, of his apprehensions, of his family habits and pleasures.

The custom had been established: his father accompanied him. On February 22, 1909, they embarked at Calais for Dover. On to Folkestone and the train for Chatham, which essentially formed one agglomeration with Rochester, that already large city at the mouth of the Medway on the North Sea, on its right bank, barely thirty miles from London. Their destination: the University School, at 5-6 New Road, a pair of semidetached houses on the heights above the town that constituted the school run by a couple, the Toukins.

To Fernand Destouches, everything seemed to be in order. The sloping private garden encircled by a brick wall was perhaps a little damp and dismal. Never mind! At least, right across the street, an enormous public lawn stretched all the way to the top of the hill, an ideal playing ground for the boarders. . . . And then, lower down, there was the port life, the siren calls, the hustle and bustle of the ships, the docks, the fog, the lighthouses and the magic of adventure. Fernand Destouches, the sailor *manqué*, would have been happy to stay on the Rochester heights, watching and dreaming. That hillock certainly beat the upper room in the Passage Choiseul. But his job at the Phénix awaited. He left his son staggering under the weight of his advice, displayed once again that grouchy authoritativeness and laconic tenderness that had the bitter taste of impatience and failure. Perhaps he envied Louis. He needn't have.

For all was not so wonderful at the University School run by the Toukin couple. The food was mediocre and niggardly, if we are to believe Louis' letters to his parents. At lunch, meat pastes or slices of beef as thin as paper, some mashed vegetable of indistinct provenance, and pudding; tea, bread, and jam at five o'clock, and that was about all for the day. When the pupils escaped from the damp basement where meals were taken in the Toukins' presence, it was to the playing fields across the street, where, it seems, afternoons afforded the most complete freedom. But in the morning, during lessons, discipline couldn't have been very strict, either. Which did not prevent Louis' taking a dislike to Mrs. Toukin. . . . "As to the kids they're very nice and the teachers too who look like poor monitors on the take one of them in particular has it in for me. I'm not telling you fibs and you mustn't think it's because I want to leave. Maybe it's the change of life."[9] Even so, Louis did not dare ask for care packages of food. For fear of drawing attention to himself, out of discretion toward his friends and teachers condemned to the boarder's lot.

And the quality of education? "They don't knock themselves out at school if you saw how lazy the English kids are they spend what little time they have in class throwing rubber balls at each other."[10]

The Destouches very soon caught on to the situation. Louis had to be withdrawn from the Rochester boarding school. To justify the hasty departure, Fernand resorted to a pathetic little trick. He wrote the Toukins that his wife had fallen ill, that she had to sell her business and take a rest cure in the South, where the company of her son would be quite invaluable if not to say indispensable. So, barely a month after his arrival in Rochester, Louis was deserting, ostensibly buying a ticket for Paris under Mrs. Toukin's eyes, and goodbye! Once he had arrived in Dover, alone, a change of plan and direction: he took the train to Ramsgate; a few miles from Ramsgate, at the easternmost tip of Kent, was a bathing resort, Broadstairs, where he was awaited in the lovely house of Pierremont Hall, transformed barely two years earlier into a school. There, the Destouches hoped, their son would at least be properly fed (and God knows that a healthy and abundant diet is indispensable to a strapping lad in his last spurt of growth), educated, and disciplined.

This time they got it right. And one could not imagine a more radical change between the two towns, the two hills, the two systems of education. To the populous, industrial, busy Rochester succeeded the pleasant little city of Broadstairs, of which Dickens, who had stayed there on several occasions, had written: "Of all the holiday resorts, it is one of the most charming and least affected." The damp buildings of the University School were replaced by the Victorian majesty of Pierremont Hall, with its corinthian-columned portico, its music pavilion, and its enormous, airy dining hall, all surrounded by a large private park. Louis enjoyed a private room. The food was English—or at least beyond reproach. He participated in almost every sport imaginable; swimming and cricket, tennis and foot-races (he won the 2,000 meters and was awarded a steel watch), lawn hockey and soccer. That's not all. Gilbert Farnfield, the co-owner of the institution and Louis' teacher, took the pupil under his wing. He praised his gracious character, complimented his progress in English. His wife, Elizabeth, gave Louis piano lessons, at least until she fell ill following childbirth. At that time, she temporarily lost the use of speech. A specialist was brought in from London to try to cure her.

Two brief stays in Paris, in May and August 1909, interrupted the rituals of Louis' time in Broadstairs. They are worth mentioning only for the horrendous crossings that befell him from Calais to Dover. Storms, seasickness, the works: Louis was stricken with nausea "and the wind carried it all onto a clergyman's robe." Of course, here is the seed of the family's famous apocalyptic crossing to England related in *Mort à crédit.*

What else is there to say about the nine months—from March to November 1909—that Louis spent at Broadstairs in a flexible discipline that seemed to suit him, between breakfast, lunch, and five o'clock tea, between classes and ball games on the beach, walks, study, and recreation? That everything was going smoothly and that he had escaped the hell of Rochester to land in the paradise of Pierremont Hall? No, that would be cutting corners. I believe we must moderate our evaluation of these two stays. In order to see into it more clearly, a brief detour through *Mort à crédit* is called for.

We note first of all that Céline evokes only one boarding school, that of "Meanwell College" in Rochester, which owes most of its characteristics to the University School. And first, his opinion of the town and the port.

"For fresh air and a view, you couldn't ask for better than 'Meanwell College.' It was a magnificent site . . . From the bottom of the garden, and even from the study windows, you looked out over the whole countryside. In clear weather you could see the whole thing stretched out, the panorama of the river, the three towns, the port, the docks piled up at the water's edge . . . The railway lines . . . all the ships moving off . . . and reappearing a mile farther down . . . behind the hills, beyond the meadows . . . toward the sea, after Chatham . . . It was really impressive."[11]

Or again: "The sounds of the city, the port, rose, filled the echo . . . Especially those from the river down below . . . It sounded like the tugboat was docking right there in the garden . . . You even heard it puffing behind the house . . . It came back . . . It went off again down the valley . . . All the railroad whistles coiled up and away like streamers across the misty sky . . . It was a kingdom of phantoms."[12]

Is this merely the adult, Céline the writer, re-imagining the maritime romance of Rochester twenty-five years later? Or is it, in part, the child already in collusion with that "kingdom of phantoms"?

Let us remember that one is no more serious at fifteen than at seventeen, one is easily soused by beer and outings, the call of the wild, and the heavy and intoxicating temptations of sex, of the unknown, of other places. Thus, at fifteen, Louis Destouches had to fit in with the landscape, the Rochester setting, the revelation that was to become one of his recurrent themes—phantoms, schooners, English fog, the sea—and which found its most perfect expression in *Guignol's band*. . . . All his life, Céline adored England, the English language, the English climate that resonated in his Breton heart. Until World War II, he returned to London over and over again, on a whim, at the drop of a hat, through need or nostalgia. And it all originated with coarse Rochester and not from middle-class Broadstairs. In writing *Rigodon* on the eve of his death, he again returned to his port, the length of a brief parentheses, an evocation, to see once more the ships at dock, the crews on shore leave on a Saturday night, every uniform in the Empire reeling with color and whiskey, the fistfights on the docks, the raw light of acytelene streetlamps, the drumbeat and cornet of the Salvation Army on a streetcorner. Ah, Rochester! A prodigious dream machine for Céline, one of the earliest triggers to his imagination, who knows? . . . "I'm not trying to sell you on these enchantments of days gone by . . . other ports. . . . I'm recapturing them for you! my head's fine, hit with a brick, bleeding through the ears and all the rest of it . . . but I can't give myself free rein . . . respect for the reader, if you please! respect, yes, sure . . . all the same, I take the liberty of letting you know that I miss the scents, the smell of frying food, tobacco and sweat . . . and of all those people, sailors, soldiers, and gangsters . . . the smell of freight, too, lumber, saffron, palm oil . . . absolutely essential if you're going to get a little sense of being there, so it won't be just a dream, those wharfs of Rochester, Chatham, and Stroud . . . anyway, you'll do your best! . . . by the grace of God!"[13]

We have to picture Céline at that age. He has grown fast. Photographed in Diepholz in September 1907, he still has the look of a kid, the mischievous air, the mirthful face, still with his cabbage-leaf ears. Between crises of melancholy, we can imagine him a prankster, bouncy, mischievous, savvy, and carefree. Two years later in England, there has been a change of portrait, of size, of posture, of silhouette, of everything. "I was finishing off my growth double-quick. The violence of the elements stirred a revolution in my lungs, in my height. By dint of hitting the plates and scraping them clean without being asked, I became a kind of tableside plague. The brats eyed my bowl, threw me dirty glances, there was going to be trouble, that was clear . . . I didn't give a damn, I kept my mouth shut."[14]

Louis has become tall and thin. He cuts a fine figure in his tightly laced shoes, his jacket and watch chain, his cap pulled down over his eyes. He is playing the grown-up, that's for sure. Or the young man who retains only the slightly rounded cheeks of childhood. . . .

And what is this young man thinking of? Of sex, naturally, of the unrestrained masturbations in the Rochester dormitory, of first loves—planned or actual?—with the corner prostitutes or the magical initiatresses of his acquaintance. Let us therefore refer yet again to *Mort à crédit* and to the passion he vows to Nora Merrywin, an ethereal, frenzied passion, somewhere between pure poetry and rabid obscenity. Who is Nora Merrywin, she who gives herself to the child, to the narrator of *Mort à crédit*, before disappearing like a tragic mirage and throwing herself into the sea? Did she ever exist? Is she the formidable Mrs. Toukin? Or the sweet Elizabeth Farnfield? Probably neither one nor the other. The former was not seductive, while the other, pregnant, was to fall sick. And probably both. In a word, a pure fantasy, the spark that erupts, illuminating the personality, where reality and imagination rub up against each other.

Moreover, Louis couldn't have been too proud of having deserted the University School, after having "snitched," as children say, to his parents. And in *Mort à crédit*, he works a curious—and telling—reversal. "Meanwell College" goes into decline but he is the last to hold out, faithful to his post, while the boarders give in, one by one. This is due to the construction of a new luxury establishment nearby, the revealingly and promisingly named "Hopeful Academy," which attracts all the business and all the clients. Naturally, this "Hopeful Academy" symbolizes Broadstairs to a certain degree. But the narrator, once again, holds out, does not betray, he does not belong to the too-wealthy, too-protected, too-happy world of Hopeful Academy (or of Pierremont Hall).

In this we touch on something essential, a constant in the Célinian landscape. The universe of Pierremont Hall was not made for Louis Destouches. Happiness, there, was related to wealth, like a sweet amnesia in which one does not fear disenchanting morrows. "We only had one thing in common in our family, in the Passage, and that was worry over grub. We had it bad. I felt it from my very first breath. . . . They planted it in me right away . . . We were all of us possessed by it at home."[15] And by extension, of course, money concerns aroused in him a consciousness of suffering, of misery, of the passage of time that decomposes and unmasks the arabesques and gracious frivolities of life, which leads toward decomposition and death.

But let us return to Broadstairs and Pierremont Hall. How happy could Louis have been there, knowing that his parents were struggling, sacrificing themselves to come up with the £20 of his board? He felt deep down that he did not belong there. His letters to his parents are testimony to that constant, obsessive worry: "I am very grateful to you for having moved me and will do my very best to pay you back when I have 'my position' next year."[16] Or else: "By my conduct and my application I will try to make you as happy as possible, so as to be able to return the enormous sacrifices you have made for me since my birth and especially in the past two years so as to give me an advantage later on."[17]

When Elizabeth Farnfield fell ill, her pupils offered her little gifts. Louis, too, wanted to bring her a bouquet of flowers. But with what money? He had to think twice before asking his parents for a shilling.

We have already asked the question: Who was Nora Merrywin, the tragic phantom of *Mort à crédit*, with her white, tapering hands, her face like a sorcerer's spell, the curve of her lips, and hair that glowed light by the fireside? Yes, she may have been inspired above all by Elizabeth Farnfield, but only to the extent that she was inaccessible, that she was representative of the fairy kingdom. Pierremont Hall was a mirage for rich folk, whereas Louis Destouches was not rich, he was only passing through, it was all a misunderstanding that would soon be cleared up.

Indeed, in mid-November, the call would sound for his return to reality and to France. On the 5th, a farewell concert was held in his honor at Pierremont Hall. Every pupil took a turn with his poem, song, or violin solo. Louis played piano. Then he packed his bags and crossed the Channel, headed for Paris, business, and real life. His beloved dog, Bobs the fox terrier, was dead. In short, sorrow—i.e., reality—awaited him on the opposite shore. He spoke English fluently and his head was still filled with mirages.

Fabric, Jewels, and Freedom

France, work, apprenticeship, here we come! He had barely a month to forget the luxury of Pierremont Hall, the cricket matches and the five o'clock tea, to reaccustom himself to the gloomy lodgings at 11, rue Marsollier, no doubt to lend his mother a hand at the shop in the Passage Choiseul, before the holidays, before Christmas. On January 1, 1910, the official date, he entered the house of Raimon, a fabric store on the corner of the rue de Choiseul and the rue du 4-Septembre. No question, then, of being allowed to cradle too long in the foggy quietude that lingers after waking.

The German painfully learned in Diepholz, and the English easily retained in Rochester and Broadstairs, were not to be of much use to him. What can a fifteen-and-a-half-year-old do without any professional experience other than that of short stints as a salesman or as an assistant of the lowest rank? What can he do, indeed, except obey, observe, and keep quiet?

In January 1910 Parisians woke up with their feet in the water. The Seine was up to its old tricks. The flooding was unprecedented. One needed a boat to reach the steps of the Saint-Lazare station. The boulevard Haussmann looked like the Grand Canal. To start out as an errand boy in Paris in 1910 was a truly Célinian wager. A catastrophe or a big game. . . . But the river soon returned to its bed and Louis to the routine of the store.

Seven months were enough, and he left Raimon with a certificate of good behavior in hand. The shopkeeper could go jump in a lake with his cottons, his brushed wools, and his prints—Louis was going into jewelry. And, more specifically, into the house of Robert, on the corner of the rue Royale and the rue Saint-Honoré, where he remained another seven months, from September 1, 1910, to the end of March 1911.

Once again, his employer well and faithfully declared that he had only praise for the honesty, punctuality, and work habits of this young man, recommendable in every respect. That didn't stop him from getting rid of him (perhaps?), and no more should it compel us to take him at his word.

There was no question, however, of Louis regaining his freedom. Idleness? Never heard of it! The time for dreams, loitering, and English fogs had well and truly passed. Thus, on March 31, he took his leave of Robert, and the next day, April 1, entered the house of Henri Wagner, established at 114, rue du Temple, under the sign JEWELRY, GEMWORK, ENGRAVING, CUSTOM ORDERS.

Why such a dance of employers? Must we suspect awful scandals comparable to those of which the young Bardamu was guilty—or the victim—in *Mort à crédit*, with Gorloge and the others? Having been entrusted with important missions by Wagner—or, more precisely, entrusted with bracelets, brooches, necklaces, and other trinkets of a certain value to be delivered to the authorized person—had Louis been indiscreet or incompetent, had he been conned out of precious gems? There is no compelling evidence to that effect. Céline himself never alluded to it. Perhaps, quite simply, he wanted to vary his commercial experience. Or perhaps he was seeking a more solid house, that is to say a house that offered serious prospects on a more-or-less long-term basis . . . a house that had perhaps been found when the Destouches finally flushed out the rare bird or the choice firm, the jeweler Lacloche of 15, rue de la Paix, where Louis eventually entered as apprentice on October 5, 1911. . . .

What, then, should we retain of his early experiences? We know, at least, what Céline himself recalled in his talks, much later, to critics, friends, or journalists.

For Jean Guénot and Jacques Darribehaude, for example, in 1960, he recalled first the enormous leather sample cases stuffed with lead models of Wagner's jewelry, which he had to carry from house to house, from the rue du Temple to the Opéra. Thus, dragging his sample case, did he visit every jeweler on the boulevard with a salesman. And what he remembered fifty years later was above all his aching feet, his shoes, which were too small, but which he didn't change very often though he was growing so very fast.[18]

For Claude Bonnefoy of the journal *Arts*, just before his death Céline recalled his work in the jewelry trade, the errands that might have been exhausting for the salesman but were more so for him, dragging the notorious sample case stuffed with lead models of tiepins. Ah, those famous tiepins, each one more symbolic, complex, allegorical, and hideous than the next! A nightmare. And in the evening, he found himself on the steps of the

Ambigu (theater) with the other salesmen.... And why should he have walked and walked endlessly in the narrow-toed shoes that were often too small? Well, to save the price of the *métro*, of course! And because he claimed to go just as fast on foot from the rue Royale to the place de l'Étoile.[19]

But in the end, such confidences are of secondary interest, or less significant than his confessions to Robert Poulet, to whom he explained how, while he slaved away for his parents or his bosses, he would save a little pocket money to buy books, cram away in a corner, destroy his eyes and pass his nights away, collapsing from lack of sleep. What was he reading? According to him, textbooks on Latin and Greek, history or math. Of which we find an echo in these lines from a letter to Albert Paraz, dated April 18, 1951: "I studied while I was earning my living before fourteen—it was horrible—I kept getting the boot from everywhere! Twelve jobs thirteen miseries! Shit but I was stubborn! Ah, what a thirst for knowledge I had!"[20]

This may be an *in extremis* explanation of the disconcerting dance of employers. If he didn't actually get the boot, he must at least have discouraged his bosses, reading and reading endlessly in his corner instead of working.

We find it reassuring when a (future) great writer reads. It finally brings us back to the appropriate images, to traditional biographies: the young man seized by literary bulimia, devouring the classics, discovering Shakespeare, Balzac, Dickens, Voltaire, helter-skelter, before finding his own path, his own voice, taking on his own work, defining the unique outlines of his own genius. But the problem is knowing exactly what it was that Louis Destouches read. Good literature or dime-store novels? Everything points to a Céline who, with his confidants or his correspondents, tried to clean up, to forge his image as the typical writer raised in misery and having acquired by himself a prodigious and highly classical education. Why classical? It was quite simply better to suggest the extent to which his own "modernity" was the fruit of resolute labor and not a miracle, an accident, of a naive writer unaware of the past. . . .

All the same, we can get a decent idea of what Louis Destouches was reading by referring to his correspondence. In his writings from Africa, in 1916 and 1917, particularly when he is writing to his old childhood friend Simone Saintu, he openly discusses his education and his reading. He is not yet on his guard, he is not thinking of becoming a writer, he hasn't learned that all unhappiness, perhaps, comes from books, nor that exposing one's reading is to strip oneself bare, to confess. Thus, to Simone Saintu, he speaks just as readily of Pascal and Goethe as of Albert Samain or Émile Faguet, of Talleyrand and Montluc as of Richepin. The least one can say of him is that his curiosity is vast and unoriented. He reads the classics and illustrated editions of the contemporaries. He is moving with the utmost haste, and, in the case of the moderns, toward the most obvious works.

Those, then, were the sixteen-year-old Louis Destouches' likely authors when he sat on the steps of the Ambigu in the evenings after his long errands through Paris and the suburbs, where he observed the shabby, the losers, the bums around him who never stopped exercising their lungs, talking about their connections, chanting their victories, exhausting themselves in speech steeped in lies and illusions, rhetoric designed to mask reality. For his part, the solitary adolescent probably said nothing, shut himself up in the silence of books, a more tightly sealed shelter against the world's howling miseries.

A reader is more likely to be a voyeur than an exhibitionist. And Céline the reader, the voyeur (which will forever be a constant of his character) must have been in his element at Lacloche's, the prestigious jeweler's on the rue de la Paix with shops in Madrid, Saint-Sébastien, Biarritz, Aix-les-Bains and Nice, thank you very much. . . . What was he given to do? To walk the boss's two guard dogs and to clean the silver with "Spanish white" (calcium carbonate) after the customers' constant handling. At least that is what he claims in *Voyage au bout de la nuit*, where Lacloche is palmed off with the name Puta [alluding to *"pute"*—"whore"].[21] But also to watch the clients, remaining hidden in a corner of the store, to check on the little spoons, the costume jewelry, and the pearl necklaces. A voyeur, all right! From there to insinuate that he spent his free moments at a hole in the bathroom door or at a crack in the wall of the boss's wife's room, getting an eyeful of the latter's revels, gymnastics, and natural functions—no, that is strictly within the realm of novelistic imagination, and any resemblance between the hero of *Mort à crédit* and the young Louis Destouches is purely accidental, as the cautious, sanctioned formula goes. The truth, more simply, is that we know precisely nothing about it. Reality or an author's fantasy? Mum. Let us therefore leave Céline to his *fictions* and return to Louis Destouches, a big lad of seventeen and a half, a little pimply, no doubt, as befits his age, and (poorly) paid to eye the great *cocottes* or the *petites-bourgeoises*, the blushing brides or the uncompromising *demi-mondaines* wavering between sapphires and rubies, wedding rings of faceted diamonds or emeralds set as solitaires.

Was this the commercial training that Fernand Destouches had dreamed of for his son? Patience . . . At least it wasn't bad training for a budding voyeur or an embryonic novelist, so long as it wasn't abused, naturally.

He didn't abuse it. In late December he was sent to Nice to work in the branch office. A godsend for him: the Promenade des Anglais and the beautiful foreigners strolling beneath the palms, the luxury of the Riviera, romantic adventures, the casino. For the first time, here was the relative freedom of the boy escaped from the family yoke, from the Prussian *Hochschule* or Kentish boarding schools.

Louis may have been afraid that his father would put a stop to the project and the assignment. He didn't get around to telling him until three days before his departure. A way of backing him into a corner and disarming his suspicions. It showed poor judgment. Fernand Destouches, the pathetic failure, was far too respectful of the established order, far too humble before the "powerful of this world," far too obsequious before his superiors ever to consider displeasing the haughty Monsieur Lacloche. He barely had time to slip into his son's valise one of those comical morality manuals on sex and sexual hygiene that were profuse at that epoque and to overwhelm him with advice on its use (which, for once, would not be wasted!). So, goodnight and all aboard on the Paris-Lyons-Marseilles!

To Louis, a good-looker with bright eyes, mischievous expression, and intrepid curiosity, Nice held promises of paradise. On the financial side, it was the Bérézina. A modest hotel–boarding house, with communal meals, pocket money, incidental and living expenses—there were obstacles to overcome. Lacloche gave him 150 francs a month, the normal salary for an apprentice. Louis spent double that. His father, good egg, made up the difference.

One might object that it was not indispensable for Louis to become a regular at the Eldorado Casino on the rue Pastorelli. That is true. But he had arrived at an age, in the words of Oscar Wilde, where one can resist anything except temptation. And the warm, wintertime temptations of the Riviera are too many to list. Let us add, for local color, that in 1912 the Promenade des Anglais was the ideal site on which to celebrate the Entente Cordiale, and that Raymond Poincaré, president of the Conseil, and the British ambassador worked with appropriate pomp to that end: processions, military maneuvers, infantry, fanfares and orations, especially orations by frock-coated notables of the Third Republic. In the crowd, you would have seen idlers, curious spectators, shopgirls, nurses, nannies, little flower girls dreaming of flirtations—and Louis Destouches, who must have kept his eyes peeled, with his camera in hand, his cajoling smile glued on his face and his reputation as a lady's man that he would soon have to start forging.

The working day at Lacloche must have passed fairly quickly for him: always something to observe, commit to memory, read, or learn, and the constant running about, too, as gofer and delivery boy, from the Negresco to the boulevard Masséna, from one gem to another. "Did I ever run around carrying treasures, diadems to Russian princesses—to the Cimiez, I say! you bet! Ah, didn't I hang out with grand dukes! And the terrific carnivals! Those Vegliones! and Émilienne d'Alençon! And the Tzar's brother!"[22]

In Nice, he not only kept company with marchionesses and old bags, he might even run across real crowned heads. That, at least, is what he wrote to Simone Saintu on November 7, 1916. His letter is worth quoting at length:

"It was in Nice, quite a few years ago already. I was coming back from lunch, taking the Promenade des Anglais to the house of Lacloche, where I worked in those days.

"When my attention was drawn to a discreet circle formed by a few people.

"Upon approaching, I saw that the strollers' attention was focused on a bench, upon which an elderly, bewhiskered gentleman was sitting, alone.

"I immediately recognized this old gentleman as Franz Joseph, having seen his likeness so often in Germany.

"In those days, I was determined to abandon all good taste—with an innate touch for affecting the most relaxed and disingenuous commercial aplomb.

"Like a novice criminal, every opportunity seemed appropriate to strengthen my propensity.

"I approached the old, bewhiskered gentleman and, presenting him my business card, asked with the most gracious and commercial smile if he would have the goodness to sign it.

"The old gentleman looked at the card every which way, then abruptly returned it to me.

" 'Don't you have any others?' he asked me.

"I realized at that moment that I had just committed an enormous gaffe. To redeem myself in my eyes and in his, I babbled a few words of apology in German, but he had already taken a little visiting card from his pocket and handed it to me, saying, 'I too, young man, have a trade name.' "[23]

It would seem that Franz Joseph was never in Nice during the winter of 1911–1912. Never mind. Céline was never too fastidious about his plots. If it wasn't the Austrian Emperor, it was his brother, or a Russian grand-duke, a Prussian highness, a king of Poland or of nowhere. What interests us is Louis Destouches' attitude toward this mysterious and noble personage, his combination of impertinence and timidity, of ingenuousness and discomposure, daring backed by a lack of assurance, as if he were trying, awkwardly as yet, to escape the paternal character. Louis Destouches: a rebel but, deep down, a very nice boy, in Nice, from December 1911 to May 1912.

For make no mistake, he gave satisfaction to his employer. Lacloche was even inclined to take him on permanently, after Louis' military service. Yes, but military service was still to come. And before military service, Louis had to return to Paris, to the family home, under the renewed authority of father and mother.

It was a difficult return. Louis couldn't have been in very good shape physically. Had he eaten his fill, had he even thought of eating regularly in Nice? All those lunches and dinners, those deplorable wastes of time when so many more delicious occasions arose to spend one's few francs? But the pranks had ended for good with the onset of winter on the rue Marsollier. Henceforth, meals at regular hours, peaceful and solitary sleep. And to Lacloche, Fernand Destouches would write a letter of the kind of toadyism of which he was master: "I have spent some time leading my son back to a less independent and more reserved attitude than the one adopted during his training in Nice, and in rectifying the few errors of judgment which that unusual existence had left in him, quite satisfied in the long run but to pay this inevitable tribute to an apprenticeship so important to his future in a house as powerful and as honorable as your own."[24]

There remained another four months of apparent liberty for Louis, spent helping his mother at the shop, idling through Paris, reading Albert Samain or Voltaire, or reuniting—who knows?—with the old salesmen on the Ambigu steps.... And on September 28, most likely after a last family summer at the seashore, he enlisted for three years in the army.

A fit of muleheadedness, a fit of madness, a suicidal haste, a will to escape at all costs the stifling grip of the family circle (he must have been missing the drug "liberty" he had tasted in Nice), a desire to anticipate the draft in order to return on a strong footing to Lacloche, whose own son had also just been called up, Fernand Destouches' will to see his overly boisterous son finally educated with the rod—discipline, discipline, discipline, don't you know!... But now, for Louis Destouches, it was well and truly the end of schooling and innocence. He was eighteen. The curtain was falling on one era, one childhood, on peace, and perhaps on the nineteenth century as well.

"They had closed the door quietly behind us civilians. We were caught like rats."[25]

4

The Good Old Days and the War

Rambouillet

France was waiting for the Great War and didn't know it yet. In 1910 the gunboat *Panther* weighed anchor off Agadir and aimed its guns at the Moroccan coast, but it was France, primarily, that felt itself targeted by Wilhelm II. A year later, Joseph Caillaux, the president of the Conseil, saved the stakes and the peace. Short-circuiting the Quai d'Orsay (The Ministry of Foreign Affairs) and Parliament, he established direct contact with the German secretary of state for foreign affairs. Germany renounced its claims to Morocco and in return France gave her a little piece of the Congo. Unfortunately, it was a step back just to get a running jump—a jump for the bombs, naturally.

For good souls were not lacking in France who wanted to relight the fuse, their ears attuned to Déroulède's trumpet, their eyes so glued to the blue outline of the Vosges as to give them a stiff neck. More active and more French than ever, the Action Française increased its rallies, its marches, its protests at the foot of the Strasbourg statue in the place de la Concorde, rather inappropriately renamed for the occasion. "Jeanne d'Arc, here we come!" the students and dutiful sons repeated. Their idols, masters in thought and writ: Barrès, Péguy, Psichari. . . . But patriotism was not a new idea reserved only for supporters of Maurras. And for every Jaurès, how many Poincarés? And for every pacifist or socialist, how many jingoistic shopkeepers? The papers led the charge: *Le Petit Parisien, Le Figaro, L'Écho de Paris.* In their eyes, Caillaux was a traitor and the accord with Germany—despite being to France's advantage—a disastrous treaty.

So it was that he was succeeded by Poincaré, a *parlementaire*, we should not forget, from Lorraine. He knew that war was unavoidable. He prepared for it. Did he want it? He named Alexandre Millerand as minister of war. He purged the Quai d'Orsay, which was too pacifist for his taste. He attempted to tighten the bonds of the Entente Cordiale and the alliance with St. Petersburg, as if he were tightening a cord around Wilhelm II's neck to strangle him into an apoplectic fit. He increased military appropriations with no thought to a policy of deterrence. Henceforth, the only doctrine of the École de Guerre was a war of movement, a systematic offensive and eastward drive across the Rhine and then look out!

Fernand Destouches could only approve. As to the famous three-year (draft) law, selfishly and in relation to his own family, he couldn't have cared less. It was true that the gap between the Prussian army (850,000 men) and the French army (450,000 men) had to be closed, and thus the length of military service increased. But what did he care for the bitter debates in the Chambre, the polemics, the oratory, the twaddle preceding the shell bursts! On September 28 his son had enlisted under the flag. And he had the three years promised to him in any case. A funny kind of promise.

Rambouillet, October 3, 1912 . . .

"I waited a long time in front of the gate. A gate that made you think, one of those really enormous cast-iron jobs, a hideous trellis of lances sticking straight up into the dark night.

"I had my transit papers in my hand . . . The time was written on them.

"The sentry on duty pushed open the wicket himself with the butt of his rifle. He called inside to alert them:

" 'Sergeant, it's the new recruit!'

" 'Bring the asshole in!' "[1]

And Louis Destouches went in. The gates closed behind him. The 12th Cuirassiers awaited him. He vanished into its depths.

Vanish is the right word. When you enter the army, you enter the barracks as if it were a monastery. Iron discipline and vows of silence. In the army, the Great Mute, cries of rebellion, exhaustion, indignation, or hatred are not heard without. It is an impervious world, inaccessible to civilians. A world with its own rules, its own hierarchy, its own values, aims, persecutions. A world outside of which it is useless to seek help. A world that inhaled and absorbed Louis Destouches, eighteen, strong-minded, impenitent dreamer, professional busybody, eclectic reader, more or less distinguished polyglot, ex-tradesman of dubious experience—Louis Destouches under the flag, in uniform, who must have had all the trouble in the world, in the beginning, staying on a horse.

"Did you enlist out of patriotism, were you pushed into it, or did you have a certain calling . . . ?"

"A certain calling, too, because I have a lyrical bent, maybe a little too much. It was always History. I saw it as something very brilliant, and then, the history of the Reichshoffen Cuirassiers seemed to me something really brilliant, I must say. And then, it was very brilliant because of the spirit of the times."[2]

His lyrical illusions soon evaporated. The "brilliance" of the Cuirassiers was wiped away by the dull brutality of military education. And no more adventures from now on, no more turns about Nice or the Grands Boulevards, the dream erased under the agonizing discipline of exercises, fatigue duty, and reviews. The disappointment must have brought back a lot of memories for the father, for he too had once been taken in by the prestige of uniform, colonies and adventure, he too had been quickly disenchanted by the dusty, severe monotony of barracks.

How can we imagine Louis Destouches in uniform? How can we imagine Céline the recruit? Here we touch on paradoxes perpetuated by the writer throughout his life. It is impossible to picture him on a regimental roll, docile before authority. Céline is above all the grouser, unsatisfied, choleric, imprecating, violent, with many extreme and modest attachments—the man of all solitudes. Admittedly, he occasionally indulges his readers' fancies with reference to sex and the most dubious of instincts. His anti-Semitism of the late thirties would garner him the jubilant support of racists who would never have heard of him without it. But, for all that, he would avoid any ideology codified in little red, black, or brown books; any party memberships; any label devised by yellow journalism. Impossible to enlist Céline under a banner. The socialist or communist intellectuals in 1932, the fascists in '38, and the collaborators in '40 all found that out very quickly. Céline was not one of them. An objective ally on occasion, perhaps, but no more. And this, the Céline compelled to say, "Yessir, Captain!," to sweep the hallways and to march in lockstep, is indeed a Céline impossible to visualize. . . . And yet, Rambouillet, the 12th Cuirassiers regiment, the names, the dates, the places, the flashy colors retain for him a sort of faint odor of nostalgia. There was never anything revolutionary in the ideas of Céline the anarchist. We might even wonder whether he was more conservative than anarchistic, more "Old France" than prophet of times to come. The new order, to his mind, was a joke. He dreamed only of the old orders. And perhaps, in a way, the intractable discipline of the 12th Cuirassiers, the French army that was to bear the brunt in 1914, his sense of duty, his spirit of sacrifice, his heroism, his idealism—these are what he would later cherish and miss, the way he already missed his grandmother, lace, and the port of Rochester in the Victorian era, especially when the debacle of '40 was to shed a cruel light on the uncertain virtues of the present.

But let us now enter the barracks. What do we see? Nothing. One must get used to the dark, or, if you prefer, accustom one's eyes to the nightmare. The barracks of Rambouillet are a bad dream. Céline evoked them in *Casse-Pipe* [Cannon Fodder], the unfinished book he began after *Mort à crédit*, in 1936. It constituted the logical continuation of the latter novel from 1912, when the narrator's uncle vainly tries to dissuade him from enlisting, to the opening of hostilities that begins *Voyage au bout de la nuit.* But Céline soon allowed himself to be distracted from the projected novel, caught up as he was in the political debauch and his feverish composition of political pamphlets. In 1941 he started work on *Guignol's band* and left the book definitively incomplete. Quitting Paris in '44, he left behind fragments and drafts of *Casse-Pipe* that disappeared soon afterward in the upheavals, pillaging, vengeances, and general fireworks of the purge. Thus, only a preface of *Casse-Pipe* was later to be found and published. But what a preface and what a precious picture of Rambouillet as the Célinian memory had transfixed it.

The 12th Cuirassiers does, indeed, have something of the nocturnal vision about it. Let us skirt the "squadron merrymaking" that Louis Destouches discovered and experienced, the life of a squaddie, the absurdity of soldiers who have forgotten the password and desperately sputter out onomatopeia, the insults, the idiocies, the dead-drunk orderlies, the stables with their mountains of steaming manure. For the squadron merrymaking soon transforms itself into squadron nightmare. Until the moment when dawn appears, when the bugle sounds the reveille through the fog, when the visions evaporate and life—what life?—finally begins again.

The Ferdinand of *Casse-Pipe*, like Louis Destouches, had passed through the barracks gate the way Alice passed through the mirror. He found himself plunged into a hallucinatory universe burdened with the heavy, intoxicating, and morbid odors of the guardhouse. "The way it crammed its way deep into your nostrils like a smell made you lose your mind. . . . It was so strong and pungent it made everything smell wrong . . . Meat, piss, chewing tobacco, it hit you like a ton of bricks, and then cold, miserable coffee, on top of that a hint of shit, and then, too, something stale like dead rats in every corner . . . The way it turned your lungs, you couldn't draw a breath."

That smell is one of the leitmotivs of *Casse-Pipe*, like a narcotic. It helps to push the barracks well beyond the mirror into a parallel universe that Ferdinand (like Louis Destouches himself), the civilian, the greenhorn, the novice, can't understand at all. Everything becomes miragelike, menacing, mysterious to him. Even the horses gallop, whinny, loom, as if sprung from some fantastical bestiary. And the stables seem to have escaped from a Gothic stage setting.

The soldiers are Bretons, foreigners with disconcerting names: Keriben, Garec, Le Moël, Kérouëc. On close terms with death and myth, they make sacrifices with ritual invocations that one guesses in this case to be the psalm of military profanity. These soldiers are elves, sorcerers. . . . "Right at the bottom of the gloom, over there in the mist, they were moving about. They poked at the night with their lanterns, they looked like butterflies. They had wings of light. They reappeared from one direction, from another. Their revels were fairylike . . . like passing will-o'-the-wisps, flitting from one shadow to another."

Ferdinand is caught in the spiderweb of his dream. And, in the barracks, there is no longer any waking moment that affords escape with impunity. The military universe becomes the admirable symbol of Célinian society in general, with its injustices, oppression, and pain. The hierarchy there is simply codified, simplified, compared to the more ambiguous and protean civilian world. The sergeant-at-arms insults the lance sergeant who insults the cavalrymen who insult little Ferdinand at the bottom, no longer a civilian but barely a soldier, one might say less than nothing, the ideal victim, helpless, the ideal scapegoat who has no one to turn to, to insult in turn, to console himself.

But beyond the hazings of military life, the raggings, the exhausting exercises of rubbing down the horses, feeding them, riding them, of conquering his fears under the sarcastic remarks and insults of the noncoms, between twice falling and twice getting back into the saddle, Louis did, after all, get a few leaves, a few escapes from Rambouillet, just enough time for a walk around the Renaissance château where François I died, or in the park, idling around the Water Garden as a tiny and derisory substitute for an ocean and longer-term escapes in mind. There may also have been a day or two's escapade into Paris, for the pleasure of impressing and seducing the girls of the Passage Choiseul. Ah! the prestige of a uniform!

We can leaf through the photo albums from 1912–1914. Here is the *Cavalier* Destouches in the stables, black apron tied around his waist, broom on his shoulder, *képi* cocked on his head, cigarette at the corner of his mouth, curled in a superior, disenchanted pout. Louis Destouches has put on a little weight. He is an adult, a man. Nothing left of the arrogant innocence of adolescence in him. In gloves, military boots, and light-colored fatigues, here he is holding his horse by the bridle on the large paving stones of the courtyard. Exhaustion and trials have certainly taken their toll, but he has withstood them, he's drawn up, he's pinching his lips. A grown-up face is often an enigmatic face, one that has learned to hold back its emotions. *Cavalier* Destouches scares us, so entirely does he melt into the other cavalrymen, so crushed does he seem by the barracks' daily grind. One more page of the album and everything changes. Louis poses in the dress uniform of a mounted sergeant-at-arms. It is 1914 and we are in a photographer's studio, with its painted backdrop, potted palms in the background, the whole shebang. Louis Destouches looks as if he were returning to adolescence for the last time. He looks so young, so disarming, armed though he is with his saber hanging to his feet, epaulettes larger than life, well-polished cuirass, shining buttons. He is a military man out of Offenbach and *The Grand Duchess of Gerolstein*. A light down covers his upper lip. Louis Destouches is in disguise. He is still playing, no doubt about it. A fine uniform that he, child of the Passage, is sporting to trouble the hearts of the grisettes, flower girls, and seamstresses around the Opéra. . . . But the illusion is all too brief.

When the regiment left the barracks, not even that could dissipate the nightmare. It changed colors, that's all. Louis participated in the Duchesse d'Uzès' hunts in the Rambouillet forest. "I was a cuirassier, and we held the officers' horses. I remember the Duchesse d'Uzès very well, on horseback, the old bag, and Prince Orloff, with all the officers of the regiment, and my mission was to hold the horses . . . It stopped there. Plain cattle, that's what we were. It was taken for granted, the whole business, taken for granted."[3]

On May 1, on the rue des Pyramides, he found himself facing revolutionary workers who were throwing stones. "There weren't many of them, forty or so. With the 12th Cuirassiers, made up of Breton peasants who barely spoke French, there was no risk of fraternizing. That's why we were called in . . . What was astonishing was the people's acquiescence in living like pigs. Revolutionaries were often treated like louts, even by the people. I myself, at the time, didn't think those guys had anything to offer. We didn't realize. We respected order, discipline. The question didn't come up."[4]

And the nightmare sometimes glowed red, tawdry, striped with the gleam of sabers, pounding to the horses' gallop, as when, in the Cercottes camp, near Orléans, the cuirassiers performed their exercises, bugles blaring, charges, dragoons, light and heavy cavalry, more squadrons and ever more, everywhere, in swirling motion, as if in dress rehearsal for a great spectacle that would soon engulf all Europe with its cast and dead of millions.[5]

So Cavalryman Louis Destouches learned to ride a horse. He was promoted at the same time. On August 5, 1913, he was named lance sergeant. On May 5, 1914, sergeant-at-arms. . . . A brilliant rise through the military ranks? That would be an exaggerated claim. It simply could not have been very difficult for him to distinguish himself from his barrackroom comrades. "They couldn't get it up—pretty much never—and what hayseeds! Specially recruited at the time because of the strikes in Paris—which were hot! A little erection in the direction of the canteen girls—half-formed, barely there. Sad folk—*mystical.* I watched them charging to their deaths— without batting an eyelid—the 800—like one single man and horse—a sort of magnetic force—not just once—ten times! Like a housecleaning. No sensuality—not one out of ten that spoke French—gentle and brutal at the same time—in short, assholes."[6]

Louis Destouches flirted with disaster: desertion and its consequences. This is witnessed by the *Carnet du cuirassier Destouches*, confidences hastily jotted down by the young soldier in an imitation leather notebook, in November and December 1913, a notebook miraculously rediscovered in 1957 by an old cuirassier who came to realize that the Céline everybody was talking about was none other than the young Louis Destouches at whose side he had fought in '14.

The notebook is of immense value—on the biographical and factual level, of course. When Céline evokes his induction, "the noncoms who could crush you with a look," the "horrible reveilles with their falsely merry bugle calls," going down to the stables in the morning fog, when he describes being victimized by a young officer, when he speaks endlessly of sadness, melancholy, and confesses: "How often, coming back from grooming the horses, all alone on my bed and seized by deep despair, have I cried, despite my seventeen years, like a girl at her first communion."[7] And he declares in the notebook: "I began seriously to consider desertion, which was beginning to seem the only way out of this calvary."[8] Luckily for him, he only considered it. But the officers of the 12th Cuirassiers must have been tipped off about the plan, as were his parents.

Marguerite Destouches took it upon herself to go to Rambouillet to meet one of her son's commanding officers, Lieutenant Dugué-MacCarthy, the same way she might have gone to one of his schoolteachers. The lieutenant, it seems, was understanding, and the incident was closed.[9]

If we linger over the *Carnet du cuirassier Destouches*, it is primarily because it is the writer's first text, not a piece of utilitarian writing—a letter or a report—but the confession of a young man of nineteen making a statement about his life that paints an anguished self-portrait, that seeks to describe in order better to understand his exacerbated sensibility, his extreme sensitivity, as well as his pride, which frightens him. He would like to dominate not by the whimsical, factitious power of military rank, but by his education. He dreams of the happy situation wherein all fantasies, all liberties, could be achieved.

What is unusual in that? Many teenagers or young men keep journals or written accounts of their hopes, aspirations, rebellions, or fears. The protective silence of writing is not the monopoly of writers. But the *Carnet du cuirassier Destouches* goes further. Particularly surprising is the penultimate comment, overwhelming in its perspicacity. It seems already to prefigure the great Célinian certainties: "If I get through the great crises that life holds in store for me, perhaps I will be less unhappy than another, for I want to learn and to know."[10]

Did Cuirassier Destouches suspect, in a confused way, that he would never put the great crises behind him and that his only opportunity for reflection, for non-weakness, would consist in confronting pain, poverty, death, and that only at that price could he find his balance, his truth, and maybe even success? Was it already a doctor's opinion? Or a writer's? What, in fact, was he saying in the *Carnet* other than the famous aphorism offered by Bardamu in *Voyage*, and which seems to be the key to Céline's work, life, and philosophy: "Maybe that's what we're looking for all through life, just this, the greatest possible sorrow so we can become ourselves before dying."[11]

Before dying . . . Death, indeed, was lurking in the early summer of 1914. But on the national holiday, Louis Destouches probably didn't give it much thought. He was marching in procession before Raymond Poincaré, President of the Republic, and that alone counted, that ultimate parade, that great shimmering illusion, that last, colorful lie into which he threw himself with the zeal appropriate to the fortunate of this world—to those who have not yet learned to foresee.

"Twenty-seven squadrons at full speed! the whole Parisian cavalry and the Guard and the eleven bands thundering toward the grandstand! 'We who are about to die salute you!' Sixteen regiments on horseback, stop dead, eyes locked on the president! Twelve thousand horses toss their heads whinny send foam high into the air in a white downpour . . . cover everything! in flakes! . . . infantry! Engineer Corps! . . .

"I see umbrellas I see plumes . . . I see boas . . . cascades of feathers . . . blue ones . . . green . . . pink . . . like a waterfall from the grandstand! . . . fashion! high fashion! . . . and the muslins . . . orange tides . . . mauve . . . All the refinements from top to bottom . . . the delicacies. . . .

"From his balcony, all alone, under a red dais, way up high, Monsieur Poincaré salutes us! . . .

"All in all I'm showing you everything, see! . . . everything! . . . so's you won't die without knowing what those high-spirited Reviews were like! France! and July! and families of enthusiasts clinging to the mills, the wings, the ivy, screaming! Some moments are just sublime!"[12]

On June 28 Archduke Franz Ferdinand, Crown Prince of Austria, and his wife had been assassinated in the Bosnian city of Sarajevo, but that was probably about as important to Sergeant-at-Arms Destouches as the first lace place mat in the Passage Choiseul. Was he even aware of it? Did he read the papers? Did he follow the repercussions of the Balkan crisis? What did he think of Austria's ultimatum to Serbia? He probably thought nothing of it, he was out galloping in Longchamp.

And all that time the general staffs in the European capitals were egging their governments on to war, stoking the fire. Russia was hardening its stance. Berlin pressured Vienna without reservation. Despite a Left-leaning and rather pacifist Chambre dominated by Caillaux and Jaurès, Poincaré continued to prepare France for the imminent conflict, while the German army increased its provocations. Henceforth a bagatelle was all it would take to set things off. A bagatelle soon arises. It arose. It was the German ultimatum of July 31, demanding to know whether France would remain neutral in case of war between Germany and Russia. From August 1 onward, the two camps hastened the machinery of general mobilization. On the third, Ambassador von Schoen brought Conseil President Viviani his country's declaration of war. The German armies had already invaded Luxembourg the day before. No more processions at Longchamp, no more reviews or theater, gone was the innocence of happier days. The great initiation was just beginning for Louis Destouches: war, and above all death, that sole truth of this world.

The complete Céline, his despair, his obsessions, his rebellions, his indignations, his deliria, his sufferings, his tendernesses, too, the complete Céline, Céline the doctor and Céline the writer, was to be born out of this first Apocalypse.

"The dead are continually replaced by the living"

And off they went, flowers in their gun barrels, shouting "To Berlin!" in the barracks of France, shouting *"Nach Paris!"* in Berlin, Frankfurt, or Hamburg. Everywhere, the summer was decked out in a festive array. In Paris, the Gare de l'Est became the bawling crowds' prime rendezvous, the family men remembering 1870, excited shopgirls, infantrymen looking for their regiments and regiments looking for their railway carriages. Tiny flags, immense farewells and resounding songs—*allons enfants de la patrie!* . . . The enthusiastic crowds saluted those who were leaving for revenge and adventure, and who would return victorious without delay. No one thought that the flower in the barrel might be a chrysanthemum, or that Europe, the center of the world, was signing its death sentence, the flourish coming a few months later in the mud of the trenches and the bloody absurdity of its millions of dead. The modern era was beginning, with its taste for twilight, for mass murder, its individual rebellions and the slow and ineluctable decay of its ancient social values.

On August 3, 1914, the socialists had put their pacifism in their pockets and their Chassepot rifles to their shoulders. What did Jaurès have to say? He wasn't saying anything anymore. On July 31, he had been assassinated at the Café du Croissant in Paris. At his funeral, on the other hand, Léon Jouhaux, head of the Confédération Générale du Travail, asserted: "I hereby declare that we are entering the battlefield with the will to repulse the aggressor." And to really hammer the nail in (right into the Germans' heads, as was proper), to clear up any misunderstandings, to relegate their past pacifism to the level of capitalism's profit-and-loss, Vailant declared on August 2 at a socialist meeting in Paris: "Faced with aggression, the socialists will fulfill their duty." They would indeed fulfill that duty, as would all the French, all the Germans, all the Russians, all the Austrians, all the Italians, all the Americans, all the Rumanians, Serbs, Bulgarians, Turks and the others (they do call it a world war, don't they?), with profits that remain unclear to this day and losses that are only too clear.

From the ruins of this conflict, from this incalculable earthquake, were later to be born, in the cultural sphere, dadaism and surrealism. But surrealist already, when we come to think of it, was that "Sacred Union" of early August '14 in France, Paul Déroulède's sister in the arms of the secretary of the SFIO (the French branch of the Workers' International) at the Sorbonne, or the Marxist Jules Guesde and the socialist Marcel Sembat in the same cabinet as Viviani. From Left and Right came the same injunction to thrash the enemy, to smash the Prussian, the Kraut, the Hun, Fritz, the *Boche*: there would be no lack of names. And because, without really paying much attention, the French had just occupied Mulhouse, they imagined themselves having already retaken Alsace and Lorraine. They shut their eyes to the early, somewhat alarming dispatches from the front. War was a lovely thing in early August 1914.

From July 31 onward, the 12th Cuirassiers had begun sprucing up its horses and packing its bags. The men had been confined to barracks.

"A little after the evening meal, to the four corners of the neighborhood and until he lost his breath, the bugler of the guard sounded the call to arms. It was war. There were a few minutes of excitement, cries of youthful enthusiasm, and then the regiment prepared to move.

"Colonel Blacque-Belair had received, by official dispatch, the order to ship out; he was to be used as a covering troop.

"The general staff and the first squadron shipped out on an early train, the next morning at daybreak. Three other trains, leaving at two-hour intervals, took the other three squadrons."[13]

Louis Destouches had enough time to send word to his parents from Rambouillet. He told them the regiment's probable destination, the plains of the Woëvre in Lorraine, described the strange calm each man felt before battle, the tranquillity, the silence that followed the stress of the first moments. And he added: "As for me, I will do my duty to the end, and if it's fated that I should not return . . . please believe to diminish your own suffering that I die contented, thanking you from the bottom of my heart. Your son . . ."[14]

This was not at all the affected heroism, the theatrical pose of a young sergeant-at-arms barely twenty years old, very soon to be shattered by the sordid, hellish reality of the first encounters. The cynical, lucid, infinitely disillusioned eye that Céline was to cast on the war would not come until later, say, starting in 1916, when he would write from Africa to his friend Simone Saintu, and twelve years later, when he would write *Voyage au bout de la nuit.* The three months of combat that Louis Destouches would experience until being wounded on October 27 he would go through as in a bad dream, having suddenly been turned into a sleepwalker by the horror, heroic and unconscious, drunk on exhaustion and idealism, and numbed by an overdose of corpses, blood, suffering, screams, sacrifices, mad dashes on horseback, reconnaissance missions in which nothing could be recognized, the bursting of shells and exploding of bombs all around him—enough to make him lose his mind, his reason, his caution, and nearly his life.

There was thus nothing in common between the Bardamu of *Voyage* and the Louis Destouches of the 12th Cuirassiers. Bardamu is clear-sighted, sneering, demystifies the bloody circus in which he is participating in the midst of puppet officers, grotesque in their very bravery, and irresponsible soldiers abused by their orders and their flag-waving delusions. Louis obeyed, indulged himself in the illusion of heroism in lieu of sleep, and believed in victory to the very end of the night. Bardamu unmasks the arrogance of officers and aristocrats. Louis was at times sensitive, in the heat of combat, to the camaraderie of the army where, for a fleeting moment, all consciousness of class and rank was obliterated. Bardamu is prepared to desert, to surrender to the enemy with his inseparable Robinson in order to escape this hornet's nest, this butchery that he denounces with all the solid good sense of the resourceful Frenchman. Louis volunteered for liaison missions under enemy fire. . . . It is worth repeating: those three months of war were revelations for Louis Destouches—about the human condition, the death instinct, social consciousness, the rich, the poor, rebellion, submission, pain, everything. Without Sergeant-at-Arms Destouches, there would never have been a Céline, as he will be the first to admit in 1939.[15] But this revelation will progress in stages. It will require that Louis Destouches, wounded and battered, remove himself from the noise and the furor, reach the hospitals in the rear and then London and

Africa, allow the years to heal his superficial scars and entrench his deep distress, before the great lesson of '14 will finally be understood. And the soldier Bardamu of *Voyage au bout de la nuit* will be Céline's cynical projection of his twenties, certainly not Sergeant-at-Arms Destouches, who in 1914 was only beginning to discover the world, on horseback, for the first time—the revelations of the backstage and wings of the war, with corpses shredded by shrapnel.

One last remark. When Céline wrote *Voyage au bout de la nuit*, he was still only a novice novelist and not the expert in cataclysm we recognize him to be. And we must ask ourselves if it was not a kind of modesty that prevented him from raising the war—that is to say, his own, ever-burning memories of it—to its true, convulsive, howling dimensions. In *Voyage*, he avoids Bardamu's wound and the truth about fighting and mass death with a pirouette, an ellipsis. The hero leaves Robinson with the intention of surrendering. "We each returned to the war. And then some things happened and other things after that that aren't easy to talk about now because people today wouldn't understand them."[16] It is that silence that he will later break, when he finds the right words, in *Guignol's band, Féerie pour une autre fois*, or the final trilogy, *D'un château l'autre, Nord*, and *Rigodon*, to make his peace with dying worlds, landscapes shattered beneath the bombs, and, occasionally, with his memories as an old soldier.

As for the young soldier, it took twenty-four hours on the local train to reach the little station of Sorcy-Saint-Martin in Lorraine, on August 2, 1914, to be precise. The heat was trying but the stops had been many to water the war effort and make the troops' morale bubble. The regiment regrouped, men, horses—650 of them—all present and accounted for. Next came the crossing of the Meuse and the tack to the north, through the forests of the Meuse valley, Apremont, Les Éparges, toward the border and the enemy.

Before becoming a charge to the death, war is often a healthful stroll. Until August 10 nothing happened other than reconnaissance parties, shorter and shorter halts and sleep harder and harder to come by, to the point where there was soon no time to undress or unsaddle one's horse.

"Morale is very high," Louis wrote to his parents, "and after the slight panic of the first days, owing to the new state of affairs, minds are growing calm once more and morale is pretty much like that of a troop on maneuvers.

"It is true that we have not yet been under fire. . . .

"We grab sleep by fragments, here and there, and to the point where one can sleep up to 10 times a day in snatches of 10 minutes to 2 hours, that's the only way in any case since there is no such thing as continuous rest.

"I haven't taken my boots off for 9 days and it will probably be this way until the end of the campaign."[17]

Yes, in the eyes of the (future) combatants, war might still seem like a country outing. But the enemy was approaching, lurking. He was said to be everywhere. On August 11 the regiment was billeted northwest of Les

Éparges, in Mesnil-sous-les-Côtes, about ten miles from Verdun—which was not yet a synonym of Verdun. There, Louis heard the sound of heavy guns for the first time.

But before the onset of the great maneuvers, perhaps a childhood memory came to mind of the first gunfire he had ever heard. A quick return to the past, a flash of memory, as if to hold back the course of time and the approach of death a little longer: "I had seen such things before . . . Fort Chabrol in my childhood . . . the barricaded street across from the church . . . at the end of the rue La Fayette. It brought back memories . . . I stopped listening to their idiocies . . . I was back with my father, after his workday. They were shooting out of the windows, they were under siege . . . anarchists . . . I saw the street again . . . the empty street . . . the barricade . . . we had come from the Opéra, from our Passage really. It was a terrible thing. I think those were the first gunshots I ever heard."[18]

These were not anarchists but Guérin and his band, amongst the most determined anti-Dreyfusards there were. Hostile to the retrial in Rennes that was about to open in 1899, Guérin, along with Déroulède, Habert, and the more important nationalists, had begun a series of demonstrations and conspiracies aimed at bringing down the Republic. On August 10 Waldeck-Rousseau received permission from the Council of Ministers to proceed with their arrests. And in an attempt to escape, Jules Guérin and several of his anti-Semitic friends had barricaded themselves into a building at 59, rue de Chabrol.[19] Ferdinand Destouches' visit with his five-year-old son is very symptomatic of the anti-Semitism of that petty bourgeoisie for whom Dreyfus was simultaneously Jew, traitor, and enemy, no matter what anyone might say or prove. Idlers, they were going to attend the ephemeral resistance of their heroes. How could Céline have escaped such a childhood with impunity?

Another word about Guérin, images of whom were to pursue Céline. The agitator died in January 1910, at the time of the great rising of the Seine, in Ablon, near where the Destouches family was renting a villa. "One winter Sunday in Ablon, 1910, I saw his coffin leaving on a wherry . . . They were taking him from there to the cemetery beyond Athis. The Seine covered the entire plain. I can still see the vast stretch of green water, the waves lapping yellow in the sunshine . . . a bright Sunday in January. It was Guérin who was leaving . . . He had died at La Vigie, his villa over by the sandpit."[20]

Back in Lorraine on the battlefield, on August 21, Louis Destouches and the 12th Cuirassiers were heading toward Audun-le-Roman and a baptism by fire. The retreat was to begin immediately. Hell, too. The German artillery pounded the length of the front. Villages fell like card houses.

As a general rule, the German armies were taking the offensive everywhere. To the north, the largest of the enemy divisions took Liège, occupied Brussels on August 20, seized Dinan, Charleroi, crossed the Meuse. On the allied side, Joffre organized the retreat. The Germans were at the Somme and the Parisians at their wits' end. On September 2 the government fell back on Bordeaux and instructed Gallieni to hold Paris. Then came the "Miracle of the Marne." Drunk on their early victories, the Germans left themselves exposed. In order to pursue the troops of the English General French, who had already fallen back on Melun and was prepared to continue his energetic retreat, General von Kluck took the shortest way to the east of Paris, with no protection on his right flank. "We'll fight on the Marne," Joffre declared. The allied units counterattacked. The English stopped running away. They also stopped the German cavalry. Foch's 9th Army blocked Bülow in the marshes of Saint-Gond. The German army of von Kluck was outflanked to the north. And in one night, Gallieni brought the Parisian army into contact with the enemy. The famous taxis of the Marne! . . . By the end of September the Germans in turn had to withdraw and beat a retreat. The battle of the Marne was won.

On September 4, near Sainte-Menehould, a second lieutenant of the 12th Cuirassiers cut down two German dragoons with his sword. Céline remembered him in *Voyage* and called him Sainte-Engence. The war still seemed like an individual affair. Not for long. On September 12 the Germans prepared to cross the Meuse near Troyon. For three days the combat raged. "The struggle begins something awful, I never have seen nor ever will see such horror, we stroll up and down the length of the spectacle almost unaware of the danger from habit and especially from the crushing exhaustion we have experienced for the past month a sort of veil falls over your consciousness barely three hours a night and walking rather like automatons moved by the instinctive will to win or to die Nothing new on the battlefield almost in the same line of fire for 3 days the dead are continually replaced by the living to the point where they form little hillocks that are burned and at a certain point you can cross the Meuse without getting your feet wet over the bodies of Germans who tried to get through and whom our artillery swallowed up tirelessly."[21]

Then the regiment headed south. On September 22, still on the banks of the Meuse, in Saint-Mihiel, it was nearly encircled. The front was stabilizing. On October 1, coming full circle, the 12th Cuirassiers returned to the little village of Sorcy-Saint-Martin and its station. The battle of the Marne was finished. The regiment took the train northward, to Flanders.

Céline the nostalgic!

He really experienced only the first three months of the Great War, and that in the branch that was fast becoming an anachronism: the cavalry. As if he always had to be slightly out of true, yesterday's man rising up against modern times, charging the guns with saber drawn, confusing Austerlitz and Verdun.

In Céline, there is essentially no remembrance of things past. His work bears witness primarily to an escape—or a critique, which comes to the same thing—of things present. If, by some miracle, Céline had been able to retrace the course of years, these would deflate like a bladder, a useless mirage. Things past are delightful only because they can never return, are only memories, illusions, phantasmal ideals in the far-flung reaches of consciousness or memory. Even the hell of '14 will sometimes be decked out in nostalgic colors when compared to the present—when, for instance, he evokes it in the light of the debacle of 1939. . . .

"We get the order to attack a village we knew to be held by a bunch of German infantrymen. Because, pay attention, in '14, I had been in for two of my three years. A whim. August first, Sergeant-at-Arms Destouches of the 12th Cuirassiers. Not yet the doc and even less Céline. The saddle wadding, the cuirass, the tufted helmet, the saber. A real cuirassier. Three and a half feet long and some grip to it. The lieutenant puts us all in open order. The whole troop. On the trot. At the gallop. He was twirling his saber in the air. And changing stride in midgallop. Perfectly at ease under the machine-gun, the bugger. We were shitting ourselves. We thought he was going to cry 'Charge!' He shouted 'Sergeant-at-Arms!' I catch up with him and he yells at me: 'Take care of that cossack riding Governor for me, the one holding his saber like a candle. Have that fat bastard arrested.' In those days, you occasionally had a change of horse but never of lieutenant. You stayed a lieutenant for fifteen years! We had had the same lieutenant and the same men for two years. Well, believe it or not, our troop leader, under fire, could recognize a horse at thirty meters, but couldn't pin a name on the man who was riding it! Now that was what I call an army! In '14, there was a French army. 'Cause in the clinch, it wasn't the rider who counted, it was the mount. It's the horse that charges. Try to stop a horse that's bolted after others! Or, all the more, to make him turn around when you get the fear in your belly! The only thing a fellow can do is try to stay on and make great sweeps of his saber to the left and right to clear his flanks. It's the nag that makes the cavalryman a hero! Like at Waterloo! At Floing! At Reichshoffen! What hidings, but with glory! What idiocies, but with style! Unfortunately, you always run into infantry or artillery. Half your number has bitten the dust before you reach the enemy! And when you retreat, it's on foot. With your helmet hanging from the handle of your sword and your entire tackle on your head. So long, sweety, the harvests are in! No more horse, no more horseman. In September, when we found ourselves back at the gates of Paris with horses that were fagged, broken down, hopeless, it was the footsloggers that had to follow up the chase. After the Marne. And while we were waiting to be remounted, we stayed there like idiots, with nothing to do. That was the end! A guy without a horse doesn't count for anything.

"At a village water-trough, a bomb goes off, my horse bolts. No way to catch it. We're retreating, of course. I'm on foot behind the squadron. I lose sight of them. Through the woods, on a track, a horse by itself. No rider. Obviously not mine! Attached by the bridle to a birch tree. A magnificent beast. With really plush tackle. I jump up. No luck: I had barely grabbed the reins when an English officer comes out of a bush with his shorts in his hands, running toward me and shouting. I jam the spurs in and split. I could still hear the Brit shouting with rage after I had left the woods. I rejoin the column. The squadron warrant officer says to me, 'Destouches, where did you find that animal?' 'Captured horse, Lieutenant.' If I had pushed it, I would have got a citation. But that was before they invented the *croix de guerre.* I contented myself with calling him 'Uhlan.' But I spent the whole night scratching the [identification] marks from his hoof. I was somebody again.

"Those days are gone. You should have met those men—and not just learned their names. Like a medico his patients: in depth! Nowadays they discuss everything. They're unionized. They have other leaders than their leaders."[22]

A change of setting in Flanders, at Armentières, where the 12th Cuirassiers detrained on October 4, 1914. It's not easy to gallop through a landscape scored with trenches, striped with rivers and canals. The front had not yet been stabilized. The German and allied armies were just about to begin a furious race to the sea in an attempt to outflank each other, Falkenhayn on one side, Joffre on the other. And it was there, in the heat of the Battle of Ypres, when the Germans were unable to force their way between the British and the French armies, that Louis Destouches was wounded on October 27. And it was there too, that the war of movement, old-fashioned war, came to an end. Henceforth, soldiers were to bury themselves in trenches. But without the presence of Cavalryman Destouches. Winter was settling in. A four-year winter.

Advances, retreats, forays and setbacks, furious frays, man-to-man, it is impossible to follow, gallop-for-gallop, the movements of the 12th Cuirassiers along the banks of the Lys, in Warneton, Commines, Deûlemont. As in Lorraine, the massacres went on. Céline recalled them in writing *Guignol's band* during the occupation: "I could tell him a thing or two about the horrors of battle myself! . . . with the blood trickling everywhere! Ah! pardon me, my pretty! . . . Me in the flesh and not by proxy! . . . And then, pardon the machine-gun fire . . . the hell of fighting! the bellies opening! and shutting! the heads bursting open! the guts everywhere! glug-glug! . . . Ah! the massacres, six, four two! . . . Pardon me, sweet thing! . . . Butcheries so red, so thick that it's nothing but a stew on the ground, overflowing the countryside, of meat and ground-up bones, and whole ravines full of corpses, not altogether dead yet and which the guns roll across in the charge, yes indeed, thank you very much! . . . a whirlwind, all right!"[23]

He also recalled the reconnaissance mission of October 8 in the woods of Ploegsteert where the bugler next to him was killed with a bullet to the head and the lieutenant was hit in the right thigh. . . .

"We got ourselves good and peppered by a little infantry post on the way . . . We were coming back from reconnaissance, in single file. We fell on it without seeing it. Des Oncelles got his. The blood was pouring from under his breastplate.

"I execute, jump to the ground, but he doesn't have time to take my box of matches from me, he suddenly flops forward . . . He's collapsed over his boots . . . There was no time to equivocate . . . It was whistling down everywhere. Fritz was boxing us in. We got back on our nags. We lit out every man for himself. We weren't able to rally the regiment until nightfall. We had lost our map and our compass. The lieutenant had been in charge of everything. We guessed our direction, we felt our way, by the wind of the bullets, so to speak."[24]

A vision transformed once again in *Guignol's band*: "How I saved the captain! by dragging him by the hair across the entire battlefield . . . not him blond and curly! no sir! all black! through a mist of bullets, a real cloud! the sky was hidden, the gunfire was so thick overhead . . . above us both."[25]

The nightmare goes on, better and better. Carnage. Hand-to-hand combat in the cemetery of Richebourg-l'Avoué on October 10[26] . . . And sometimes, in Céline's magnifying, phantasmagoric memory, nocturnal visions became baccanals against a backdrop of corpses when mysterious, invisible women came to meet the horsemen, between two clashes, on the banks of the Lys. Mirage or reality? Rather, reality become mirage.

"I don't forget much myself (no boasting), I remember very well that on October 14, the regiment dug in on the right bank of the Lys, waiting for dawn under continuous fire from the batteries opposite, a whole group of girls and ladies, middle-class and working girls, slipped in under cover of night to feel us up, raised their skirts, not a word spoken, not a breath wasted, not one face seen, from one dug-in horseman to the next . . . good manners demand ten months, ten years to drag out an engagement, from one winter sport to the next, one opening to another, surprise parties, broken-down cars, spats big and small, spectacular drunks, belches, the banns, Town Hall, but if need be, circumstances permit whole regiments to copulate willy-nilly with lustful wildwomen, under the arching shells, a thousand ladies at a time! . . . by the minute! . . . no griping! . . . nature shot to hell? . . . dead everywhere? . . . *jiggy! jiggy!* screwing like flies!"[27]

And the soldiers also fell like flies, while as of October 16 the regiment headed back to the north, crossed the Ypres canal, intersected columns of civilians, Belgian refugees, and around October 19 approached Poelkapelle. In the days that followed, it retreated (with the entire front) toward Langemarck. The German infantry was making progress. Shrapnel rained down on an end-of-the-world landscape.

Poelkapelle had to be retaken, a task entrusted to the 125th and 66th infantry regiments, whose left flank was protected by the 12th Cuirassiers. Couriers were indispensable in keeping communications open and to pass orders from one regiment to another. On October 27 Louis volunteered for such a mission. Late in the day, while he was rejoining his unit on horseback and passing through a little wood, he was wounded in the right arm by a ricocheting bullet.

The Célinian version in *Féerie pour une autre fois 2, Normance*: "November 14 . . . *bam!* . . . I was blown away by a shell, blown away! swept off my feet! . . . a big one, mind you! a '107'! In the saddle on Demolition . . . my 'close ranks' filly! Saber drawn! By all the winds! I was blown away! there's your man!"[28]

The next day, Captain Schneider wrote the following note to Louis' father, covering both sides of a little card.

Near Ypres, October 28, 1914

Dear Sir,

Your son was wounded the day after I wrote you that he was doing well. That's the nature of war, where, less than ever before, one can never assume what the next hour will bring. It seems that his wound is not serious, but he has been evacuated, I know not where, under the care of the Infantry. He comported himself admirably, placing himself in the way of danger, with a spirit and a courage that he has exhibited since the very beginning of the Campaign. Please do not worry, I am telling you quite frankly how things stand; it seems his wound is not serious. No doubt your son will write you so himself in the near future, but I wanted to alert you immediately in describing the exemplary conduct that he has never ceased to display. I remain, Sir, most sincerely,

A. Schneider[29]

And on November 5, Fernand writes in turn to his brother Charles:

My dear Charles,

Please find enclosed the letter from your friend, whom I beg you to thank for his kind wishes for Louis' speedy recovery.

He was hit near Ypres, while transmitting the division's orders, under fire, to an Infantry Colonel.

The bullet that hit him by ricochet was twisted and flattened by its first impact; it presented barbs and irregular edges that occasioned a rather large wound; the bone of the right arm was fractured. The bullet was extracted the day before we were able to reach his bedside; he hadn't wanted to be sedated and endured the painful extraction with much courage.

The doctor believes he can state that the arm's freedom of movement will not be compromised but the wound is SERIOUS, it will require many months to return his arm to normal functioning provided there are no complications, which the doctor does not foresee given Louis' robust constitution and the clean state of his blood. We found him quite depressed emotionally under the reaction to the continuous and excessive strains of the past 3 months and especially to what he saw with his own eyes; the deaths of several close friends particularly affected him; he explains that this battlefield camaraderie is deeper than we can imagine and that when death cuts down a comrade there are always painful repercussions amongst those remaining.

The action was so hot, the number of dead and wounded so high, that the first echelon of ambulances couldn't dress his wound, the tents were filled with dead and dying, he had to go 7 kilom. on foot to meet the 2nd echelon, where the fracture was ostensibly reduced and his arm placed in a splint. During the whole journey his fractured arm was held up by his sword belt worn as a shoulder belt, that is, around his neck; he was supposed to go from Ypres to Dunkirk in a convoy but the pain was so severe he wasn't able to finish the journey, he had to get off at Hazebrouck where an English officer drove him to the Red Cross.

He still wonders by what miracle he is still in this world; the presence of extreme danger day and night, which he is only now conscious of having escaped, provoked in him as in others a nervous overstimulation that the almost complete deprivation of sleep could only overstimulate. He refused the morphine injections that the doctor wanted to give him to help him sleep a little because he only sleeps an hour here, an hour there, and startles awake, bathed in sweat. The image of all the horrors he witnessed revolves constantly through his mind. But now all that will subside under the calming influence of the hospital bed and the care he is receiving, even though the guns still roar at the gates of Haze-brouck, but that's a music to which he has grown accustomed. . . .[30]

Dated November 25, 1914, at General Headquarters, signed by Commander-in-Chief General Joffre, order no. 439D stipulated:

"By virtue of Ministerial Decision no. 12285K of August 8, 1914, the Commander-in-Chief has conferred the MILITARY MEDAL, dated November 24, 1914, upon the following servicemen: ... DESTOUCHES, Louis—Sergeant-at-Arms of the 12th Cuirassiers.

"In liaison between an Infantry regiment and his own brigade, volunteered under heavy fire to deliver an order which the Infantry liaison officers were hesitant to transmit. Delivered that order and was grievously wounded in the course of that mission."[31]

So much for the established facts. We will later evoke Cavalryman Destouches' other injury, to the head. It now remained for the Célinian imagination to magnify all this. To transform hell into a still greater hell. For Louis Destouches, there also remained months and years of convalescence. But does one ever recover from war? True recovery is forgetfulness, or a lack of imagination. The imaginative Céline did not have a short memory.

The Hospitals in the Rear

In a field ambulance near Ypres, the medical officer wanted to amputate Sergeant-at-Arms Destouches' wounded arm—might as well go with the fastest, most expeditious solution: an arm, a leg, one more or one less, so what? Let us put ourselves in his shoes: it's easier to remove an arm from a body than a bullet from an arm. That was not the opinion of Louis Destouches, the troublesome cuirassier, opponent of smooth surgical procedure. He refused the operation. He was therefore given a makeshift bandage before being evacuated to auxiliary hospital no. 6 set up in the Collège Saint-Jacques in Hazebrouck. It was only two days later, on October 29, that a local doctor operated and succeeded in extracting the bullet. Louis had refused anesthetic. Was he still afraid of having his arm cut off without his knowledge? He paid for his legitimate suspicions with atrocious pain. The wound, according to official diagnoses, had fractured the right arm and paralyzed extensors of the forearm. There was some fear that the elbow would stiffen at 45 degrees.

But nowhere, neither in the Hazebrouck hospital, later in the Val-de-Grâce or Villejuif, nor in his recovery records, will there be any allusion to a head wound, much less to Céline's famous trepanning suspected by so many of his interlocutors—Évelyne Pollet, Marcel Aymé, Milton Hindus—and which would be made official by Professor Henri Mondor in his preface to the Pléiade first edition of *Voyage au bout de la nuit*. The trepanning may have been just one myth amongst many, but the head wound surely was not: "And at the hospital they thought my leg was so screwed up they were ready to amputate . . . and the arm with it! . . . Was I ever messed up . . . my head as well . . . meningitis . . . a small splinter in my left ear . . . so serious it was and feverish that from one day to the next they wondered."[32]

The only document to confirm that head wound is a photo of Louis Destouches at the Val-de-Grâce, his face wrapped in a heavy bandage. It is quite impressive and it could mean nothing. On the other hand, how can the evidence be ignored, how can one doubt the neuralgias from which he endlessly suffered, the stabbing, screaming pains, enough to drive him mad, of which he complained so often?

From one book to the next, the headaches return, obsessive, unbearable: "I can say that I have slept only in fits since November 14 . . . I've learned to get along with my ear noises . . . I listen to them become trombones, full orchestras, marshaling yards . . . it's a game! . . . if you move your mattress . . . show some little sign of impatience, you're lost, you go crazy . . . you resist, stretched out, stiff, you manage after a few hours to grab a little snatch of sleep, to recharge your feeble batteries, to be able to get back on the job a bit the next day . . . don't ask for more!"[33]

Céline also complains before the majority of his interviewers: "As I speak to you now, I have a train in my left ear, a train in the Bezons station. It pulls in, stops, pulls out. It's not a train anymore—it's an orchestra. This ear has had it. It works only enough now to make me suffer. I can hardly sleep anymore."[34]

Céline occasionally invoked Ménière's syndrome, or vertigo, problems of the inner ear that could give rise to loss of balance. The diagnosis seems a little more specific in *Rigodon*: "I must say I felt some problems, not just from the brick, from the bash between the skull and the neck . . . also from higher up near the left ear . . . no imaginary problems either, very medically verified, with two . . . three expert opinions . . . starting in 1916 and much later at the Copenhagen Ryshospital . . . the skull and the petrous in bad shape . . . God knows I'm used to it! . . . whistles . . . drums . . . blasts of steam."[35]

Lucette Destouches, the writer's widow, brings a valuable insight to the case: "Louis often spoke to me about his 1914 wound. A shell had knocked him to the ground. Once back on his horse, he was hit in the arm. His face had no visible wound. He was simply bleeding from his left ear. Nobody worried about it. Louis was so shaken up by his wound, by the explosion. Louis later thought that he had incurred a fracture of the petrous bone and that perhaps a nerve had been pinched as the bones healed, which explained his constant pains. He could tell when the pain was coming. At such times he wanted to be alone. Alone with the unbearable pain. He drove people away, he didn't want them to observe his suffering, to see him in that state where he exaggerated everything, where the buzzing became unbearable. That wound tended to remove him from the world. You cannot understand Céline, the violence that he is accused of, if you forget the state of his health, his insomnia and all that."[36]

Louis Destouches stayed in Hazebrouck throughout November. His parents made the trip to his bedside immediately. They returned, comforted, to the Passage. His life was not in danger. "My mother was happy to see me again and whimpered like a bitch whose puppy has finally been returned to her. She probably also thought she was doing me a lot of good by kissing me, but even so she was worse than a dog because she believed the words they used to take me away from her. At least a bitch only believes what she smells."[37]

I do not believe this to be yet another one of the typically Célinian exaggerations in *Voyage*. Beyond the obvious cynicism of the comparison, Céline clearly emphasizes the weakest point of his mother's character, her docile resignation. Which, moreover, would later be Lucette Destouches' impression of her (future) mother-in-law: "She was a woman of duty, of sacrifice, she was Louis as a nun. She had a lot of character. Very moral, she couldn't imagine that people were capable of doing bad things or of wanting to enjoy life. She would have given her life for her son, but if her son had died in the war she would have found it quite normal. She would have cried her whole life—but she would have accepted it."

Céline had been the first to define that trait clearly: "My mother whimpered as she took me back to the hospital, she accepted the accident of my death, not only did she consent to it, but she wondered if I was as resigned to it as she was. She believed in fate as much as in the fine standard meter of the Arts and Crafts Conservatory, of which she had always spoken to me with respect, because she had learned at a young age that the one she used in her haberdashery was a scrupulous copy of that superb, official original measure."[38]

On the other hand, what Marguerite and Fernand Destouches found difficult to accept was the sight of their son languishing in the Hazebrouck hospital. They asked Georges Destouches, the General Secretary of the Medical Faculty in Paris, to step in to have him transferred to the Val-de-Grâce in Paris. That was accomplished on December 1. If the care was no better there, the setting, at least, was more prestigious. And it was in the Val-de-Grâce that he was presented with the military medal conferred by Joffre on November 24, in a ceremony described by Fernand Destouches to his brother René: "Louis received a military medal presented to him in a jewel case by the Colonel and officers of the 12th Cuirassiers. It had been sent from the front and the most senior officer in the room pinned the medal to Louis' greatcoat in front of all the patients in anticipation of the official presentation. The play of his arm seems to be improving but they say it will still take a long time."[39]

Another image, a passage from the *Voyage*, comes to mind: "You want physical bravery? Might as well ask a maggot to be brave, it's pink and pale and squishy, just like us.

"As for me, I had no reason to complain. I was even about to lose my innocence, thanks to the military medal I had won and my wound and all. They even brought me the medal in the hospital, while I was convalescing."[40]

The crash of exploding shells henceforth rang like a distant echo in Louis Destouches' battered head. He was putting distance between himself and the horror. He was slowly awakening from the nightmare. He was alive. He was still alive. That was the important thing. He was rediscovering life. He rested, or tried to rest. He began to re-explore Paris, civilian life, to mingle with the slackers, the salon warriors, or the pretty French or American nurses, the latter as sweetly and horizontally consoling as the former were ardently and vertically patriotic. . . . No doubt about it, the transformation had begun that would turn the 1914 Cavalryman Destouches into the Bardamu of the *Voyage*, the hotheaded, blind, patriotic, exhausted, willful, docile cuirassier into the cynical and skeptical observer of a war grown repugnant in his eyes, an ignoble tragedy orchestrated by idiots and pretentious fools.

Louis Destouches' months in the hospital seem like a long and still painful journey to the end of rediscovered lucidity. To the end of solitude. He had lived the first three months of the war in the collective suicidal giddiness of the cavalry. He was now learning the very painful and lucid virtues (painful because lucid) of individualism. And from that individualism he was never to recover.

At the Val-de-Grâce, he developed a friendship with his roommate, Sergeant Albert Milon, wounded in the chest at the outbreak of hostilities. Milon, a Parisian street kid with the rough-and-ready humor of the working-class suburbs, the kind of guy you can't put one over on, was to become Louis' cohort, his buddy. We will find them together again after the war, in Brittany and elsewhere, in the Rockefeller Mission's antituberculosis crusades. Then Milon will become a traveling salesman. Céline evokes him again in *Féerie pour une autre fois*, under the name of Arlon, when his wife, Clémence, comes to visit him in Montmartre, the day after the allied landings in Normandy.

But, first and foremost, Milon is the famous Sergeant Branledore of the *Voyage*, the joker, the crafty hobo of the hospitals in the rear. There is no reason to doubt that it was he, with his hearty good sense, who helped disperse any militaristic delusions still clinging to the bemedaled Louis Destouches. "In the course of his hospital stays, he had learned how to attract and hold the nurses' active sympathy. Branledore puked, pissed, and shat blood rather frequently, he also had some trouble breathing, but that in itself wouldn't have been quite enough to win him the special good graces of the ward nurses, who saw plenty of others like that. And so, if there was a doctor or nurse within hearing, Branledore would cry out, between two choking fits: 'Victory! Victory! Victory will be ours!' Or he would whisper at the bottom or the top of his lungs, as the circumstances required. Thus having harmonized himself with the aggressively fervid literature of the day by a well-timed bit of dramatics, he enjoyed the highest moral standing. He had the knack, all right."[41]

And speaking of debunking myths, this may be an appropriate time to lay bare one of the most beautiful of the Célinian lies, which deceived every one of the writer's biographers and commentators until the early '80s: the famous cover of the *Illustré national* of December 1914, with its inspiring drawing of Cuirassier Destouches, saber drawn, the mane of his helmet in the wind, galloping across the desertlike landscape, ravaged by bombs, streaked with shell bursts, in order to fulfill the mission in which he was wounded. The secret was finally debunked by a researcher/collector, Daniel Bordet.[42] The whole thing had been a fraud, a montage, special effects. To the original drawing had been added the review's cover logo and the inset photo in his sergeant-at-arms' dress uniform. The drawing alone was well and truly published, but in issue no. 52 of Tallandier's *Illustré national*, in November 1915, that is to say a year later, and on page 16. Why so late? Had the Destouches family schemed and pulled strings to encourage such a flattering image? And who was it who later put together the famous collage that Céline willingly displayed, framed and mounted, to all his visitors at Meudon in the fifties? He himself, or, as is more likely, his parents? However it came about, Céline used—mischievously?—this swindle on *Paris-Match* in 1957, on Galtier-Boissière, who reproduced the famous cover in the February 1958 number of *Crapouillot*, and even in 1932, on the publication of *Voyage*, on Lucien Descaves and other journalists who came to his home.

At Val-de-Grâce, Louis Destouches' health gradually improved. On December 27 he was transferred to auxiliary hospital no. 47, at 120, boulevard Raspail. He stayed less than four days. They had wanted to operate on his arm, which he refused, probably out of mistrust of the duty surgeon's medical skills. He was transferred then and there to the Paul-Brousse hospice in Villejuif, run by Gustave Roussy (who would found the Institut de Cancer twelve years later).

There is little available testimony, few letters or documents on Louis' stays in Hazebrouck, at the Val-de-Grâce or in Villejuif. The accounts in *Voyage* shuffle leads, places, and indices at will. In an early version of *Féerie pour une autre fois* published under the title *Maudits soupirs pour une autre fois* [Curses and Sighs For Another Era], Céline describes at greater length his arrival in Villejuif one night, accompanied by Milon (under the name Marcel): "We had ourselves transferred together, they gave us the choice because of our military medals, we chose Brousse, the new *hosto* in Villejuif, we inaugurated it. You can imagine the setting, on the plateau, open to the wind, still all grass in those days, just one or two shacks in the neighborhood, the access road not finished, and muddy as hell, all silt, so that you couldn't even reach the place come first rain."[43]

The journey to Villejuif takes on all the appearances of a burlesque odyssey tinged with blood. Marcel is packed in gauze and compresses, a mummy whose uniform and greatcoat float above his wrappings. Céline is impeccable in his cuirassier's uniform. Having crossed Paris on foot, from one *bistro* to another, toward Bercy, they are soon dead tired or dead drunk, it's hard to say which. They are hoisted into a tram. Night falls. The hospital is even farther, beyond the stop, invisible in the dark. "It was while I was climbing that slope toward the hospital plateau that I first noticed that I was groggy, dead beat ... and what a pain I had there too, climbing that slope! ... I was stiff down to the bones, my dead arm was killing me, my head buzzing so's it hasn't stopped since ... I suddenly felt so weak, down for the count, that I would never be able to bend, to jump like before, to run to leap like the others, that I was nothing but a poor crippled bastard."[44]

The hospital seems abandoned—or not yet in use. They are not expected. Nothing is ready to take in patients. The surgery hasn't been set up yet. One single woman, guard, concierge, and nurse all in one, receives the two patients, leads them to a freshly painted white room. And that night, Marcel has another hemorrhage, his wounds have reopened, the blood spurts, pours, floods. Céline gets up, gropes in the dark, falls, calls for help. "Ah! all that's just memories ... it's a good thirty-three years ago that it happened ... obviously it's pretty weak next to the hideous confusions that haven't stopped since ... the titanic upheavals, the endless hecatombs ... it's just a drop of memory in the great ocean of miseries ... and what cyclones! what whirlwinds! I'm just talking about it."[45]

Memories or fables? Still the same, eternal Célinian enigma, since there is not one conclusive fact to authenticate or give the lie to his delirium. But what, after all, is the Célinian delirium? It is the metamorphosis of a reality under the effect of a fever (the fever of writing, in the final analysis), its transformation into a higher reality, that of the emotions, which never lie since they avoid the order or disorder of discourse. There are scarcely any other constants in Céline's fictional universe.

On January 19, in Villejuif, Louis Destouches finally agreed to undergo the proposed operation on his arm, which consisted of breaking the callosity that had formed at the fracture, on the lower third of the right humerus where the radial nerve passes. It was this nerve, above all, that had to be freed and sutured. It was not Professor Roussy who performed the operation but one of his colleagues, Professor Gosset. Roussy is found only as a guignolesque figure in *Voyage* in the guise of the *agrégé* Professor Bestombes (always that choice of ironic, evocative patronyms), smug, always on his high horse, fuzzyheaded, demented, flag-waving, dreaming of sending the dear patients whose recovery he is hastening back to the slaughterhouse as soon as possible.

Three days after the operation, Louis was awarded a three-month convalescence leave, to be spent in Paris. He moved into the little family apartment on the rue Marsollier. How easy it is to picture him, draped in his uniform and his heroism, boastful, seductive, a little rooster strutting through the Passage or beyond, in the cafés, the salons, the bed-alcoves, from one dubious party to the next, making up for the carnage of the front with the pale debauchery of the capital. The time for debunking had well and truly come.

The first months of 1915 . . . The wounded flowed from the front, the war bogged down in the mud, the trenches, the dawn attacks after the artillery's "softening up" that transformed the battlefield into a lunar landscape. The "trench sweepers" attacked with bayonet or knife. The *poilus*, infested with lice, gorged with warm soup, high on cheap red wine, worn out by the rain, chilled by the cold, had to hold, resist, kill for a gain of fifty or a hundred yards. Meanwhile, the Germans had managed to drag the Turks into the war. The Franco-British alliance had the idea of opening a second front in the Dardanelles, with disastrous results (the peninsula of Gallipoli would soon be evacuated). The Germans were pushing forward on the Russian front and the French lacked arms and ammunition. Imagine: the world had believed the war would be short. But that was far, far away, a hundred or two hundred or five thousand kilometers from Paris, where Louis Destouches, his arm painful and stiff, his brain deafened by too many explosions, was relearning civilian life despite the uniform he continued to wear.

On February 22 he was admitted to the military hospital annex in Vanves. He underwent an electrical treatment that continued until March 27. His convalescence was drawing to a close. He still had the month of April left to rest on the rue Marsollier, to try to forget the war in the fanfare behind the lines and the smiles of women left alone. But he didn't forget it, he would never forget it. He had returned from the war, that's all. In the literal or figurative sense, as you will.

In early May 1915 the authorities assigned him to a desk job at the French consulate in London.

London Fog

And Louis Destouches the adult returned to England, discovered London, plunged into the fog and fauna of Soho. They were strange months for him, enchanting, unsettled, poorly understood—months of intense upheaval, no doubt, and of that pungent, thrilling, incredulous happiness that grabs hold when one allows oneself to get drunk on mirages, that one places a little outside one's life, the thrill of possible adventure, of the unknown lurking, coursing through one's body. Louis observed the docks of the Thames, the ships at anchor or outward bound, he frequented the French *milieu* of the capital of the British Empire, a milieu so poorly named,* since it is in its nature to be precisely on the margins or the periphery of respectable society.

One witness remains of the months Louis Detouches spent working in London at the passport office of the French consulate in Bedford Square: Georges Geoffroy. After having been conscripted into the *deuxième bureau* of the 8th Army in Flanders, in late 1914, Geoffroy had been named to Folkestone and then to London. It was there that he noticed and welcomed Louis Destouches, with "all his gongs," that is, in the slang of those involved, his military medal and the whole bit. Geoffroy suggested that they share his furnished room at 71 Gower Street, whose rent was a bit steep for a single man. The two friends thus spent months together in constant companionship.

Georges Geoffrey had been primarily struck by the curiosity of his friend, who often sought out the company of unusual characters—we might call them outsiders or marginals today—whom he would listen to, study, and observe tirelessly. This character trait of Louis' will be mentioned in innumerable testimonies later on. More passive than active, Céline was a voyeur. But he was also a listener, a stethoscope. He looked down upon the world from the heights of his insatiable and sometimes remote need, eager to understand, to know, to deliver a diagnosis on everything. Certainly, a clinical diagnosis, that of the doctor he would soon be; but a writer's diagnosis, too, hungry for mistaken identities, dramas, violence, the picturesque and the tragic in the human drama.

"Some nights," wrote Georges Geoffroy, "we spent in the *milieu*, that is the 'French *milieu*,' naturally. Or else Louis dragged me to the music hall (his gongs were enough to get us in free), or to ballets. We knew Alice Delysia well, and I personally had met up with an old buddy, Aimé Simon-Gérard, who was playing at the Palace at the time and introduced us to show girls. Louis adored the dancers. He had a passion for dance.

"Our lives were both simple and eventful, with strange encounters, for example, like that with Mata Hari, who invited us to dinner at the Savoy,

---

* *Milieu* means the middle as well as the criminal element.

where she was staying. We had instructions to grant her her visa but, at the same time, to keep her hanging awhile.

"We didn't really know what she was in for in France, but we had a vague idea.

"Some days we had some money, others we were completely broke! Things always worked out in Soho. The French pimps and their girls were nice to us, always ready to stand us a dinner."[46]

Do we have cause to doubt the Mata Hari anecdote? It might be wiser all the same to check the schedule of the beautiful, muddleheaded, and choreographic spy. Her meeting with Céline obviously makes us dream, like the novelistic encounters of characters belonging to different *fictions*, such as a meeting, say, between Sherlock Holmes and Arsène Lupin, between Pardaillan and the Three Musketeers. But how much is actually there?

On November 30, 1915, Mata Hari arrived in England on a boat from Holland, where she had been living. She did stay at the Savoy but for no more than three nights. On December 3 she took the train from London to Folkestone, where she was subjected to a rigorous interrogation. She wanted to reach France, where she was not yet under suspicion. The English didn't trust her. Finally, on December 4, she embarked for Dieppe. But the English had alerted the French military authorities to her presence. In a report by the Folkestone police to Scotland Yard, Mata Hari was described as follows: "Height: 5 feet, 5 inches; carriage: average; hair: brown; face: oval; complexion: olive; brow: low; eyes: grey-brown; eyebrows: dark; nose: straight; mouth: small; age: 39. Speaks French, English, Italian, Dutch, and probably German. A beautiful and brazen woman. Elegantly dressed in brown suit trimmed with raccoon, and various hats."[47]

It is therefore possible that, on December 1 or 2, Mata Hari met Georges Geoffroy and Louis Destouches at the passport office, and that she even invited them to dine at the Savoy. How, of all things, could they have made up such a meeting and Mata Hari's presence in the hotel? It is also likely (according to Céline, who told it to Lucette Almansor) that the three of them slept together. All Louis remembered about it was a fairly insignificant little woman. On the other hand, Geoffroy's version seems dubious, with its second meeting and the mission of delaying her visa application which they were assigned by Paris.

So much for adventure. On the same order of ideas and fables, Louis' first cousin, Charlotte Robic, told François Gibault that Louis had been assigned more ambitious and more dangerous missions at the heart of the French counterespionage effort, that he had even been sent to German Switzerland and then to Germany in 1915.[48] Céline/James Bond—the discovery is tempting. Unfortunately, there is nothing to support it. We must sadly return it to the shelf in the magic store.

Beyond question, however, are Geoffroy's interesting remarks on the music hall; on Céline-Destouches' passion for dance, for the dancers' perfect, streamlined, gravity-free bodies. This is the first testimony to Céline's erotico-aesthetico-philosophical obsession, wherein he repeatedly contrasted the miraculous happiness, the perfect dream, dance's instant of frozen eternity and pure, melancholic grace, with the banal truths of the world: death, inertia, idle chitchat, the body's sad, slow decay.

In 1915 Louis Destouches still had no thought for writing; Geoffroy never saw him take a single note. But he never stopped reading history or philosophy. He sometimes woke at six A.M. to finish a book begun the night before. To his roommate he would recite passages from Hegel, Fichte, Nietzsche, or Schopenhauer. Such philosophical erudition is surprising in a writer who always claimed to be a fortuitous novelist, a cultural autodidact, a man of style and not of ideas, avoiding traffickers in abstraction in order to concentrate on his own quivering, convulsive comments on the world's convulsive events and emotions; on the concrete.

On December 2, 1915, Louis received a provisional discharge, that is, without pension. On December 16 the discharge, ratified by the French consulate in London, became permanent. Louis could doff his uniform. Goodbye, army, *adieu*! He was henceforth free to return to hearth and home, to give new thought to his civilian career and to be rehired by Lacloche the jeweler, as promised and foreseen three years earlier. But those three years represented an eternity, the far side of another world. Louis didn't need to think about it, he was not returning to France. England held him. He was not going to leave for several months. He had tasted London's sinister charms, its nightclubs drowning in smoke, its spectacle of ships at anchor, its pale East End whores, its vulgarly painted dancers in seedy music halls, its pints of beer, everything he had once dreamed of with his father: the spray, the fogs, the rigging of three-masters heaving to, casting off, the smell of the open sea—yes, all that overwhelmed his vagabond, Breton imagination drunk on legends and images of the ocean.

What did Louis Destouches do in London in the three months following his discharge? What expedients allowed him to survive? Faced with the writer's silence and evasiveness, with the absence of documents and eyewitnesses, we must again refer to his work, specifically to *Guignol's band*, which provides his London sojourn with the essence of its setting, its magic, its action. We will later discuss the conditions in which the work was written. Let us note immediately that Céline wrote it in the middle of the war, in the middle of the occupation, as if he had to escape the world's gory reality in the refuge of his London fairyland, exactly as he had done in 1915 and 1916, putting distance, a great distance, between the battlefield and the pure, phantasmagorical, and perhaps happy magic of the city of fog and mystery, that grimacing, expressionistic, aqueous city so far from dull, wounding reality.

What, then, does *Guignol's band* tell us about Céline and Louis Destouches? First, the book evokes the young man's fascination for the nation and the city that he so loved throughout his life, that were in such harmony with his unfathomable melancholy, with the dissatisfaction expressed by an inability to stay in one place, to be happy with what he has already learned, by the almost Baudelairian concern with plunging "to the bottom of the abyss, heaven or hell, it little matters; to the depths of the unknown in search of the new." London allowed him to draw a psychic curtain over the war. It spoke to him of dreams, ships, enchantment, and freedom. "It all depends on what you like! . . . I say that without pretension! . . . The sky . . . the gray water . . . the purplish riverbanks . . . one blending into the other, you can't control 'em . . . gently pulled round, in slow circles and eddies, you're charmed away into new dreams, ever further . . . for all to perish in delicious secrets, toward other worlds preparing themselves in veils and fogs of great pale and fluid outline amongst the whispering mosses. . . . Do you follow me . . . ?"[49]

Of course, the war had not been abolished in London. In *Guignol's band*, we see Louis come across occasionally bizarre echoes of it. The *milieu* of French pimps is seized with patriotic fever! Their only thought is to enlist under the flag, leaving their whores in the lurch. But that is not the main thing. More than that, it is a question of counterpoint. Death, the past, the war, all subside like tides, barely perceptible on the horizon. A source of uneasiness at most. A call to order. Louis, still battered and groggy from battle, is left with the mere foam of visions, regrets, and dreams of the sea that are already Célinian: "Oh, memories all too painful! the grandeur, the misery, the burdens of the deep blue! Dundee Goélettes Cotres in the spray! Dead, les Aliges! Dead, le Charme! Cavalry, foam—evaporated! the muted rumble of high waters! Farewell to Cardiff's grease and misery, coal shovels heavy with scum! Farewell wild jibs and brigantines! Farewell! free and breezy waves."[50]

Céline's images occasionally waver on the edge of delicate and whirling lyricism, of inconsolable sorrows. Dreamy London was also the city of frustration, like a promise of adventure never kept, like the boats at dock, inducing you to believe in impossible ocean crossings. "The most tragic thing is the ropes holding the boat back; as big as it is, enormously pot-bellied, it's light, it would fly away, it's a bird. Despite the tons of cheap goods in its wooden belly, filled to bursting, the wind that sings in its mast-tops would grab it by its branches . . . even like this, in dry dock . . . without sails, it would go, if many didn't slave away restraining it by a hundred thousand ropes shamefully taut, it would leave the docks all naked for the heights, it would go strolling about the clouds, that's what the moment of liberation would be like, it would be the spirit of travel, totally indecent, you'd only have to close your eyes to be borne away on a long journey, you'd have gone into the realms of magic, of freedom from care, a passenger on the world's dreams! . . . Miracles are nothing less! Ah! I'm only happy near boats, it's in my nature, I don't want anything else!"[51]

Not only generalities and abstractions are at issue here. No, it is a question of dreams, which is altogether different. Dreams are the fabric of life. Louis Destouches lived primarily on dreams. To know the man, one must hunt out his phantasms. And his London visions of 1915 and early 1916 are eminently decisive in divining Céline, spying out the course of his life: his emotions, his dreams, his discoveries, and his nostalgias.

In fact, on one side, heavy and sordid reality, on the other an escape from reality—ships, dancers, a moment's grace, it comes to the same thing—constitute the two poles of the seesaw Céline. And London allowed him to fluctuate freely between the two temptations helping to make *Guignol's band* one of his most beautiful books.

We now turn to the reality of London. On that score, the stories in *Guignol's band* are clearly not to be taken literally. It is undeniable that Louis was a regular in the French *milieu*, its whores and their men, and that he lived on precariously legal little odd-jobs. Did he overstep the bounds of legality? "I was pretty casual about my papers! . . . my discharge, my rubbed-out stamps! My, oh, my! Oh, sister! . . . I was in a delicate position with those guys at the consulate."[52] And that is distinctly possible. Was he involved in drug running and smuggling from one boat to another? "It also served for something else, the greasy Anabaptist lot. We buried our tubes of opium in its banks, in the rat holes, in rattan boxes, the river dope, good stuff that the Chinaman sends flying through the porthole, day or night . . . Whoosh! . . . It's off! . . . The ship glides slowly off . . . almost stops . . . turns into the lock . . . the pilot fiddles with his compass . . . 'Ding! Dang! Derang! Dong! . . .' One second! A breath! . . . The box hits the water! Bam! Splash! Dope overboard! . . . Get it!"[53] No, that would seem to be in the purely novelistic realm. In any case, the London fogs have clouded and drowned any of Louis Destouches' escapades. Except for his astonishing marriage on January 19, 1916.

The facts are incontestable, and the marriage certificate known and public. Before the civil magistrate of the district of St. Martin were united on that date Louis-Ferdinand Destouches, lieutenant [*sic*] of the 12th Cuirassiers, bachelor, aged twenty-one, residing at 4 Leicester Street in Soho West, and Suzanne Germaine Nebout, twenty-four, without profession, living at 475 Oxford Street, before witnesses Carolina Ode and Édouard Benedictus. Naturally, the Destouches family had not been informed of this lightning marriage, which was not registered with the consulate. Lacking such registration, it has been generally claimed that the marriage had no legal force in France. That is false. Quite simply, France was unaware of the marriage, which is another thing altogether. But in English law (and in French, if Suzanne Nebout or Louis Destouches had informed the French authorities), he was unequivocally a bigamist.

A few weeks later Louis returned to Paris alone.

Later, Suzanne Nebout turned up on the rue Marsollier and introduced herself to her parents-in-law. Lucette Almansor-Destouches still remembers the accounts of her mother-in-law and Céline himself on that event: "A woman with very beautiful, big, dark eyes came to see her, saying, 'We are married.' The big dark eyes were all that Marguerite Destouches could recall about Suzanne Nebout. For her, Louis had allowed himself to be dragged down by bad women, she had no other explanation to give. . . . Louis often spoke about this marriage. Suzanne Nebout was, more or less, a dancer and hostess. She was French and had a sister. The marriage must have been helpful toward their staying in England, a question of identity papers. Both of them were very nice to Louis. He would have married both of them, he was in love with both sisters! They had taken care of him, he lived in their circle of pimps, etc. They showered him with money. They wanted to pay for his studies, they wanted to keep him. 'Do anything you like, you'll only have to study.' But that went completely against his character."

Suzanne Nebout vanished soon after the marriage.

Back in Paris, then, in March 1916, Louis Destouches was to leave again in May for Africa and new adventures. During that time, the static violence of the war's repeated and useless onslaughts was coming to a head. On February 21, 1916, Falkenhayn launched the great German offensive on Verdun. The fort of Douaumont was taken on the 25th. The rest is well known: Pétain assigned Joffre to face the enemy, the *voie sacrée* was set up to shuttle victuals and munitions between Verdun and Bar-le-Duc, the reciprocal attacks from one shell hole to the next, the mud, the quicksand, regiments swallowed up to the last man—that gigantic, inhuman battle, that foretaste of hell in Verdun that was to last until the end of 1916, for nothing, for 500,000 men lost, a hundred meters more or less of landscape that no longer held any sense or any life.

Louis Destouches was not to experience Verdun. It was no longer his war. He had already given. The unseated horseman was leaving for the colonies, for other apprenticeships, other disillusionments. He was just beginning to cross the night. He had merely finished his preliminary nightmares.

5

Impressions of Africa

On Board the RMS *Accra*
Two Packs of Marylands for an Elephant Tusk
Waves

On Board the RMS Accra

Why go to Africa? Could we imagine Louis Destouches back from England, having hurriedly closed the happy, murky parenthesis of London, settling into a sedentary, middle-class life? Could we for one instant believe that he was done with experiments and travel? No, he had to flee yet again, to experience the great trials to which he had challenged himself in 1913 in writing the *Carnet du cuirassier Destouches* in Rambouillet, the crises necessary, he had said, better to learn and to know. At twenty-one, he thought that physical travel was the surest way to explore himself as well. France was deafening him with its patriotic and bloody clamor. To go as far as possible from the war, from the shells that rang hideously in his head, no longer to cling to the capital's wealthy and its shirkers: Africa suddenly offered him that double privilege. The moment was to be seized. He didn't hesitate.

Knowing its conclusion, a biographer sometimes makes it easy on himself when telling the story. He presents the connecting thread, the logic and coherence of an existence—as if a life were always led like a thread, logical, coherent, ordered, and not the unstable result of a thousand accidents and encounters. The manner in which a character builds itself, inexorably takes shape—that is what he claims to be observing from month to month, year to year, forgetting all the accidents that form a human destiny. Or rather, he disdains to include them as determining elements. And yet, in the case of Louis Destouches in Africa, we find ourselves compelled to play by the rules of this double game. His wanderlust, his thirst for adventure, logically called the future writer to try the African experience, that *accident* that presented itself. And that accident was a determining factor in what was to follow in his life. In Africa, Louis was to discover medicine, as we shall see; it was there, in a very confused way, that he would even begin to envisage an alternative career in literature.

In March 1916 he signed a contract with the lumber company Sangha-Oubangui (headquarters, 5, rue de La Rochefoucauld), holding the exploitation rights to Cameroon. We know the contractual engagement between the two parties.[1] Louis committed himself for a period of two and a half years: six months of training at a monthly salary of 150 francs, then, after appointment, two years at 200 francs a month. However, article 8 specified that he was free to leave the company at the end of a year, with three months' notice, the return voyage in that case being at his own expense. He was to go to Douala on a French boat, leaving Bordeaux on May 2, 1916. The company was merely advancing him the price of the fare, but was committed to assuming his repatriation expenses, even if he had to return early for reasons of health. Louis had to work exclusively for the Company. Article 10 stipulated: "In the case of serious causes or egregious errors and particularly if you undertake business for your own profit, the corporation reserves the absolute right to dismiss you, in which circumstance you are to assume the full expense of your travels to Africa and back, and you will be owed no redundancy compensation."

Habitual intemperance was grounds for immediate dismissal with no compensation.

To understand the reasons for the civil colonization and precipitate commercial exploitation of Cameroon during the war, we must go back to the treaty of November 4, 1911, which allowed Germany to extend its protectorate over the Congo and Cameroon in exchange for official recognition of France's protectorate over Morocco. After the unleashing of hostilities, a Franco-British expedition of naval forces and a landing party undertook to "liberate" that territory. The British troops numbered 3,000 men, the French, out of western Africa, about 2,000. That was more than was required. After a de facto British takeover of Douala in September 1914, an agreement placed Cameroon under joint Franco-British sovereignty a year later. In February 1916 conquest of the country had been completed and it was divided into two zones of influence. The zone near Nigeria was placed under British control. The French part included Douala and extended over nine-tenths of the territory. At first it was placed under General Aymerich's authority, and after September 5, 1916, under that of Governor Lucien Fourneau.[2] We can therefore understand why the French were suddenly so anxious to make up their numbers in order to justify a partition so much to their advantage. The great colonial corporations were assigned the burden of recruitment. Louis Destouches, noncom, discharged, bachelor (or so it was believed) and available, was the perfect stereotype of the colonial robot.

Nevertheless, he did not comply with every contractual stipulation. He neither went to Bordeaux nor embarked on a French vessel as promised. In early May he took a train for Le Havre and crossed the Channel to Southampton. A new adventure, he knew, was beginning, with its uncertainties and its risks. Perhaps he was leaving France forever. That, at least, is what he wrote to Simone Saintu with a touch of erudition and a willfully theatrical humor: "I shall watch without a shiver 'the land of France melt into the horizon' and before that spectacle my eyes will maintain a Saharian dryness. It has long been my habit to exercise calm emotional restraint."[3]

A quick stop in London, and on May 6 he found himself in Liverpool. There, he met an old friend graced with the nickname "Monseigneur Bernadotte" because he had once been the personal secretary of His Eminence in Lyons. This Bernadotte had later tried his hand at just about every profession under every latitude. On May 8, 1916, he was preparing to embark on a steamer for South America. And, Céline concluded, again in a letter to Simone Saintu, "we said not farewell but goodbye—our respective mobility being, to our minds, a guarantee of more or less certain meeting in the short term."[4]

No one knows who this meteoric Bernadotte was: he was never to reappear, it seems, in the writer's life. He would thus be of little importance if his adventurous character, his mobility, the hypothesis advanced by Céline of seeing him again soon under other skies, did not suddenly remind us of another figure, this one fictive—Robinson in *Voyage au bout de la nuit*, Bardamu's alter ego, a vagabond, a messenger of misery whom he is constantly running into in Flanders, Africa, America, the Parisian suburbs, everywhere. Who was the real Robinson? There is probably no one key to the character molded out of the dramatic requirements of the plot, like a guide, a foil, a reference point illustrating the evolution of the hero and his character. This Robinson must have been born and constructed out of several meetings, several attitudes. It is likely that "Bernadotte," the itinerant adventurer, was one of his models.

On May 10, 1916, the RMS *Accra*, regular mailboat of the British and African Steam Navigation Company, raised anchor for Africa. This long, thin, single-funneled ship was carrying only two passengers, Louis Destouches one of them. On three separate occasions in his correspondence,[5] Céline alludes to mysterious difficulties caused by Georges Geoffroy and his friends, striving to hinder his return to England and, consequently, compelling him to embark from Liverpool. What indelicacy had Louis Destouches committed earlier in London? What was the vengeance or warning in question? In his statements on his life with Céline in London, Geoffroy made no allusion to any such settling of accounts.

On May 25 the *Accra* called at Freetown, the capital of Sierra Leone, a British colony at the time. The crossing must have been awful: heat, high fever, boredom. Writing to Simone Saintu, Louis recalled seeing "roving sharks, a few whales, a host of flying fish, Negroes, all on a green background—jumping, bobbing, rolling, waltzing to the sound of an engine piston that I will still be hearing on Judgment Day."[6]

From his parents, he urgently requested 1,000 francs, which he promised to reimburse later, in Paris, by any means available. Sick, prostrated by fever, stuck on the quarantined ship on which two deaths had already been registered, in a heat that qualified as murderous, he waited to reach Douala.

On June 1 a new port of call: Lagos, a city, in his own words, that was evil-smelling, unhealthy, dark, black, and humid—hell's antechamber. And

Louis was still in the grips of "a fever that seems to have taken a liking to me, made slightly short-sighted by the exorbitant doses of quinine ingested, sweating or shivering depending on the hour."[7]

At that point the young colonial saw his future as black as the Africa he was about to take on. In a letter he dissuades his friend Milon from joining him (the latter certainly had no desire to do so). There was potential for business, of course, but there was nothing to be done about remaining healthy or living a healthy life.

On June 16 the *Accra* finally reached Douala. Louis Destouches' crossing had come to an end. One essential difference comes to mind if we try to compare it to Bardamu's in *Voyage au bout de la nuit* on board the *Amiral-Bragueton*. On the *Amiral-Bragueton*, the ghastly climactic conditions— without one atom of moving air, in an "agonizing sweat," a "simmering oven"—are reflected in the murderous slander of the other passengers, of which, in this case, there were many. We find him alone, hell itself: men, others, those who are bored, who backbite, who kill or at least adore the circus games, gladiators, and myrmidons, those who fear their own deaths and who desperately seek out distractions. Louis was certainly never the object of the sailors' hostility aboard the *Accra*. That hostility, the role of scapegoat, he would invent later on. Men's hatred is more terrible and more dramatic than the violence of the elements, of any storm or shipwreck—it was that hatred which the novelist was to discover and exploit.

Two Packs of Marylands for an Elephant Tusk

We know about Louis Destouches' stay in Africa mostly through his miraculously preserved correspondence. Beyond the emotions, indignations, and anecdotes that it reveals, it also allows us to evaluate the future writer's "tone" in a more general way. It marks a stage in the evolution of his style. And he already has a strong taste for stories—for fiction, even.

Céline is beginning to take the measure of himself. He tells stories for the pleasure of telling and, as in his novels, he alternates between story and aphorism, moral judgment and impersonal observation. Above all—and it is here that he reveals a precocious mastery of his art—he is learning both sincerity and mendacity, he dares to indulge himself and is already able to transpose the two. He modulates his effects. With his friend Milon, he claims sincerity in everything, including cynicism; he seeks complicity with him and lies out of sheer high spirits; his sentences become syncopated, allusive. With his parents, he is brief, reassuring for his mother, worrisome for his father; in some measure he embodies the role of the repentant reprobate who is always asking for something. With Simone Saintu, his childhood friend, his wise and distant confidante, his sentences grow more supple;

Céline takes pleasure, now in moralizing and now in shaking her; he considers her above all as the perfect reader, inaccessible, and it is with her that he strives to increase the seductions of high style, that he plays the writer. The game is convincing. The letters are early testimony to his desperate individualism, his hatred of war, of colonialism, and of oppression. Céline is afraid of human beings, he knows their wretchedness and the noisy distractions by which they struggle to forget it; he further reveals his taste for solitude and silence. At moments he betrays his first racist reflexes. But let us return to his work and his days, to Louis Destouches' daily life in Africa. . . .

Disembarked at Douala, he was able finally to recover from his fever, helped by quinine tablets. He discovered a little colonial city, its cosmopolitan population, its voracious mosquitoes and makeshift mosquito nets, its cafés, its coconut palms, its bordellos, its notorious "pagoda" which served "for the entertainment of the colony's exotic erotic tastes," and finally its hospital, one of the largest buildings in town, with an enormous portico running around its circumference.

He was not to remain in Douala (Fort-Gono of *Voyage*) very long. In late June he had to assume the overseer's job assigned to him by the Sangha-Oubangui lumber company on a plantation called Bikobimbo (Bikomimbo in *Voyage*), well to the south of Douala, not far from Spanish Guinea. The closest and largest ports were those of Campo to the northwest and Bata in Spanish Guinea to the southwest, about fifty miles from the southern border of Cameroon (respectively Topo and San Tapeta in *Voyage*).

In Bikobimbo, he claimed, he was eleven days' walk from the nearest European, in a little village of Bantu-speaking Pahouins, hunters and tradesmen, sculptors of masks and statuettes, to whom he of course attributed cannibalistic tendencies. Thus, to the intermittent epidemics of malaria and sleeping sickness could be added the putative treachery of the natives. A Célinian persecution fantasy? "As a result, I go about from morning to night covered in thick veils against the mosquitoes—I do my own cooking for fear of being poisoned—I get drunk on quinine and not a few other drugs as protection against fevers, and I never go out without a helmet and thickly smoked glasses for fear of sunstroke I also have a revolver at the ready night and day to settle my differences with my clients in whose eyes I occasionally surprise a flash of lively covetousness."[8]

As to his commercial activities, he painted them thus, with a desperately playful cynicism: "The business I do is of angelic simplicity consisting of buying elephant tusks for tobacco you cannot imagine how much the negro prefers smoking tobacco to getting cash of which he doesn't know the value it was a rare spectacle for me which I turned to great account to the satisfaction of all by selling to them in kind—2 packs of marylands for 1 elephant tusk[.] No doubt such technical details hold little interest for you, but it's the only incitement for me to remain in this charming country, flooding it with tobacco until the last elephant is dead."[9]

Had he crossed into another circle of Hell, into a country whose hideous colonial human and commercial exploitation he had figured out in just a few days? Surely not. In Africa, in that prodigious isolation, in the heart of darkness, to use Conrad's term, where the white man, having reached the very edges of civilization, can suddenly tumble with impunity into savagery, he suddenly benefited from what he had been clamoring for for years, from what military life had made him temporarily forget, and which he defined as "the utter lack of commentary on my behavior—and grand, total, absolute liberty."[10]

We can already sense and recognize the Africa of *Voyage au bout de la nuit* in every detour, in every letter, in Louis Destouches' agenda, in his encounters, his emotions, his indignations: it is the exploitation of the natives, the solitude, a suffocating yet magical nature, the vicious poverty of insignificant whites brought low by isolation, liquor, fevers, and boredom. We can also see this Africa in the first act of *L'Église*, which, however, lacks the Célinian intoxication, the spaciousness, the sense of freedom perfectly reflecting the terrifying but sumptuous landscapes.

In a little village in Spanish Guinea, where he made a brief stop in July 1916, he stumbled onto the sea and its tireless waves, the dunes covered in pink and white flowers. To Simone Saintu, he confessed that "I take selfish pleasure in the present moment—I believe it is the only form of human happiness, the only one that does not deceive, of which [we] can be really sure, since it depends on no one." And he concluded: "For one moment, I am absolutely, exclusively, perfectly happy—

"The breeze comes off the ocean, fitful, ill-tempered, and sprinkles golden sand over the thousand little pink and white flowers that instantly shake themselves, all together, the way little flowers attentive to their corolla do."[11]

The war seemed suddenly inconceivable to him, so far away in Europe, nowhere. What had become of the 12th Cuirassiers? In a letter unpublished to this day (from the archives of Lucette Destouches) and addressed to his parents on September 29, 1916, he wrote:

Poor regiment, which no longer exists even in name! How many brandished swords lost, how many charges into battle at a thundering gallop, as good as useless!!

Often, on horseback, I think of 'Contact.' I can still see him galloping alone through the Rambouillet forest, cutting down an imaginary enemy with his crop flailing madly.

Poor Lagrange, rotting in a retirement home, half-blind—poor cast-off hung in the great cloakroom of the past, which, when opened, gives off the sweetly antiquated, melancholy odor of old things in old museums.

With great affection.
L. des T.

In contrast, Africa offered him some sublime moments. Unusual moments, to be sure, of great rarity with Céline. Reading "I am perfectly happy" in his handwriting, one wants to rub one's eyes—there must be some mistake, a misprint, it's the effect of a mirage, an hallucination. We must nevertheless accept the evidence: Africa did bring him such moments of calm, which of course he never mentions in his books.

If the equatorial forest, if the lizards, the crocodiles, the monkeys, the edible elephants, if the muddy rivers, the baobabs, the pythons and the like appalled him, they were also in harmony with his sense of excess. In a way, they must have pleased him—a certain Célinian madness responded to Africa's exuberance. Cameroon's morbid, lush, delirious natural state, its tangles of creepers, roots, snake pools, inspired to the point of euphoria his wanderings as an expert in catastrophe, as traveling companion of the Apocalypse, as sarcastic and jubilant witness to worlds dying in grotesque contortions. Ah, the African nights and their low-key charms! Céline remembered them thirty or forty years later when he was writing *Féerie pour une autre fois* and *Nord*, as a delirium, a bizarre concert in the enchanted depths of the forest. And, no, the delirium was not a sad one. It resembled a vast derangement of the senses, merry down to the last grimace and contortion.

"Some sounds I'm stingy with, others I give 'em away . . . the sounds of Cameroon, take 'em, as many as you like! . . . those forest orchestrations! . . . at night, huh! . . . at night! . . . gotta hear the screaming of those great animal loves! . . . it's a thunderstorm of instincts with them! and the village Pahouins feasting themselves on personal viands! . . . Tom-Tom! go to it! hup! . . . and the syncopated beats and the jolting dances . . . don't go to see it! . . . Granny on the grill . . . Is that ever a hollering fest! . . . I give you twenty Pahouins from my village, you make 'em howl! . . . creatures, beasts adoring, snatching, devouring each other . . . I sell you their enormous full moon, that gigantic mirror of the night which the forest kind of hangs in the sky!"

Or else:

"Remember the name . . . the village: Bikomimbo! . . . Rio Cribi! . . . real songsters! At night, that is . . . At night! . . . from the depths of nature! . . . Gotta hear it! . . . Gotta hear them! . . . it's an instinctive understanding accompaniment vocalization: 'Dingua! . . . boueh! . . . saoa! . . . boueh! . . . ding . . . a! . . . boueh! . . . Ding . . . a! . . . boueh!' . . . and all-natural percussion! . . . a hollow tree-trunk with sixteen drumsticks! . . . talk about hoodoo! look out! . . . elementally hollow! . . . you can't get near it! . . . Me, my cabin was a hundred meters away and I never went to see it! . . . the Echo's hollow is sacred! . . . it's something else, a hollow fucking prison! . . . Listen, I can sing Pahouin . . . I still can! . . . "Ding . . . a! boueh! . . . eh sao! . . . a! . . . boueh!' . . . I'm telling you, it carries! . . . I never watched their festivities, it was between them and that was that . . . They liked human meat but other meats too I'm sure of it . . . deer, warthog, buffalo . . . python . . . I had proof of it! . . . Gotta mind your own business! . . . Discreet! . . . discreet! . . . and no lies! . . . I'm not making up a thing . . . the facts that's all! . . . Bikomimbo 1916!"[12]

More prosaically, Louis Destouches continued to run his plantation in Bikobimbo, increasing his outings and excursions, setting out for Port Batanga when the mail arrived by ancient coaster, here and there meeting adventurers, drifters, an American enlisted in the Foreign Legion, a Portuguese missionary.

On July 7 he wrote Simone Saintu that, by the same mail, he was sending a short story to the attention of *Le Journal*, a Parisian daily with a wide circulation. Several months later, Louis hinted to his parents that the story had been accepted by Henri de Régnier, who had just become the paper's literary director. No trace of this text has ever been found. Still, we should make note of the date: Louis' first probable attempt at literature, his first work destined for public consumption, in July 1916. Louis Destouches in Africa was beginning, then, to find himself, slowly to approach Céline.

Here are the poems he sent to Saintu and his parents in late August.[13]

Stamboul est endormie sous la lune blafarde
Le Bosphore miroite de mille feux argentés
Seul dans la grande ville mahométane
Le vieux crieur des heures n'est pas encore couché—

Sa voix que l'écho répéte avec ampleur
Annonce à la ville qu'il est déjà dix heures
Mais par une fenêtre, de son haut minaret
Il plonge dans une chambre son regard indiscret

Il reste un moment, muet, cloué par la surprise
Et caresse nerveux sa grande barbe grise
Mais fidèle au devoir, il assure sa voix

Et l'écho étonné, répéte par trois fois
À la lune rougissante, aux étoiles éblouies
À Stamboul la blanche, qui'il est bientot midi.

["Stambul sleeps beneath the pallid moon / The Bosphorus gleams with a thousand silver flames / Alone in the great Mahometan town / The old crier of the hour remains awake— / His voice, which the echo amplified returns / Announces the hour of ten to the town / But from the heights of his minaret / His indiscreet glance through a window does fall / For a moment he stands mute, rooted by surprise / And nervously strokes his great gray beard / But faithful to duty, he steadies his voice / And the echo, astonished, three times repeats / To the reddening moon, to the bedazzled stars / To Stambul the White, that it will soon be noon.]

And let us not forget the alexandrines of "Le Grand Chêne" [The Great Oak]:

Mais déjà, lentement, le ciel se décolore
Les rayons du couchant, pourchassés par la nuit
Luttent contre les ténèbres et résistent encor
Pour voiler la retraite du soleil qui fuit
En haut du noir rocher qui domine les bois
Le chêne retient encore la lumière qui décroit
Cependant peu à peu l'ombre monte et le prend
Et le plonge à son tour dans le tout inquiétant.

etc.

[But the sky already has begun to pale / Harried by the night, the beams of setting sun / Struggle against the shadows and resist once more / Trying to conceal the fleeing sun's retreat / Atop the darkling rock that overlooks the woods / The oak still holds the last rays of the dying light / And yet is taken by the slowly rising shade / And plunged in turn into the great distress of dark.]

We need not comment at length on the literary merits of these verses. They mostly bear witness to the capricious application of an imaginative young man who is bored, who daydreams, who revels in his literary style, who reads Richepin, Émile Faguet, Albert Samain, as well as Voltaire, Talleyrand, or Montluc, who willingly quotes Musset and Claude Farrère, Pascal and Goethe, Bernardin de Saint-Pierre and Oscar Wilde.

These poetry-pastiches signed Louis des Touches, this game that had perhaps taken him in a little, was also a way for him to reconnect with Europe, to its conventional literary games, to a reassuring manifestation of civilization faced with the strangeness of Africa.

He had just turned twenty-two. He willingly admitted his fear to Simone Saintu, at night, when he pitched camp under the vault of branches, alone with his porters, heating up cans of corned beef while nature, the animals half-perceived in the shadows, seemed to protest his presence. Writing was an escape, an illusion. To escape from the present, from Africa as from the war in France. Anything was better than that conflict which, the further he moved away from it in space and time, the more he was beginning to see in its most brutal light. He had finally discovered that he was attached to life. To die doing one's duty, no, that was no longer the thing. Such a taste for sacrifice can arise from only three causes, he wrote to Simone Saintu: first, the sacred flame, in other words a phobia, a sickness; secondly, a lack of imagination, and how can we avoid immediately recalling the famous aphorism from *Voyage*: "When you have no imagination, dying is no big deal"; third, a derailed sense of self-esteem, the need to pose theatrically as a hero.

In Africa, Louis Destouches discovered the virtues of individualism and mistrust. "Do not think either that I profess any hatred whatsoever for my peers, on the contrary I enjoy seeing them and hearing them, but I do my best to elude their grasp, one hears the sound of a bell better from far away, when too close the noise deafens you"[14] he wrote again to Simone in July.

The African stage is very valuable for our first glimpse of the portrait of the writer as a young man, as an adult. After his return to Europe, the action, the various activities of one kind or another, the encounters, his studies, will lead him into a whirlwind in which he will tend to become hazy, even to disappear. In Cameroon, Louis Destouches has all the time in the world to reveal himself to us, complex, torn by his contradictions.

We have emphasized his individualism. From individualism to anarchy, from anarchy to egoism, the paths are sometimes soon trodden. "I have never voted and will never vote, but if it were to happen I would vote for myself. I claim to be alone in knowing how to lead myself."[15]

Yes, but ... Louis is generous. And more, it is his perspicacity that is generous—or his imagination. In a beautiful letter to Simone Saintu, dated August 20, 1916, he speaks of African women, why he is reluctant to take a mistress among them. These women, accustomed in general to being their husbands' slaves, suddenly find themselves raised to the heights. Once abandoned by the white man, they can no longer readapt and are a thousand times more unhappy than before. "She'll probably carry a millstone around her neck her entire life, unless she commits suicide, which happens often, not because of the loss of the white man, for whom she cares very little, but because of the loss of creature comforts, for which she cares a great deal."[16]

Yes, but ... The cynical Louis Destouches reasserts himself immediately and wipes out the other. The one who warns his friend, in case the latter is thinking of joining him (which, again, he has not in the least attempted to do): "No women they all have the clap."[17]

What are his feelings for the indigenous population? He pities them the way one pities animals, the sick, children, victims, defenseless creatures. Above all, he is in Africa to succeed. To make money.

In mid-September 1916, he left Bikobimbo. The Sangha-Oubangui lumber company had named him overseer of a cocoa plantation, at the Dipikar station, not far from his old post, two kilometers from the Ntem river. The Dipikar region, it was said, had been the personal property of the German Emperor. His new work promised to be more interesting and less tiring. He wrote his father that he had already put 5,000 francs aside. To Milon, he explained how he found himself a month away from his boss, alone with the blacks, managing to set aside 2,000 francs a month (while he was only supposed to be earning 200!). What were company contracts to him! They no longer had any value in his eyes. He was exploiting the region for his own profit.

Yes, but ... He immediately harks back to the distant war, to the nameless butcheries. "I feel a profound disgust for all that is bellicose. I can't help wondering to what extent a victory bought at the expense of a wasted country is a victory— I no longer have any enthusiasm for anything but peace."[18]

He pesters his parents to improve his day-to-day life. In Dipikar, he had only found a camp bed and a camp stove. He asks them for chocolate, sheets, trousers, a pillow.

Yes, but . . . he is also concerned about their lives, their well-being. The letters he writes to them are often affectionate and deferential, as revealed in the following unpublished letter (from the Lucette Destouches archives) of January 11, 1917, which pretty well explains Céline's relationship to money as well as his skeptical individualism:

". . . I am told that life is horribly difficult in France and in Paris in particular.

"Have you had many problems?

"Please don't hesitate to help yourselves to my money, it's only natural. Earned with ease or difficulty, I should like to tell you that I couldn't care less about it. If I make it a point of honor to earn some, it is simply in order to prove to those who take such unwarranted pride in it that it is not worth much. Myself, I firmly refuse, in any circumstances whatsoever, to join the herd. I far prefer the margins. I am as wary of the social organizations of my peers as of the plague and I am skeptical of any changes or comforts brought about in the struggle for life by events of whatever magnitude."

In another unpublished letter to his parents, written the same day (January 11, 1917), a few hours earlier, he speaks of his fears of Cameroon being invaded by German troops, and of being conscripted. Then he refers to some papers that his mother must have found in his room on the rue Marsollier, apparently alluding to some London misadventure. "In one of her letters, Mama speaks of personal papers the tenor of which seems to have raised her brows—I must ask you to be good enough to burn all those that are not specifically addressed to you—I have little taste for reminiscence. The history of men of all stamps proves that one had best consider it as a whole and not dissect it sentence by sentence. . . . Whatever the degree of intimacy binding members of a family as harmonious as ours, there are certain doors, especially among the younger elements, that at certain moments it is vain and regrettable to open and especially to conceal. I am giving up my plantation. I do not know what I shall do I am earning money and sending none—not knowing what tomorrow will be made of—or what it holds in store for me."

And a little further on in the same letter, he writes these lines, displaying a poor sense of premonition: "If, as is possible, we must remain some time without corresponding, do not worry. I am much better behaved than Mama cares to pretend. Only my kind of good behavior is not quite the normal kind. I believe I may end up as a gentle philosopher."

In the meantime, Céline is confronted with the epidemics and illnesses of the native populace. He can not remain indifferent. He again asks his father for a sewing kit for stitches, for absorbent cotton, syringes, alum, colloidal silver, sulfuric ether, citrate of soda, lactic acid, camphorated oil, carbolic acid, antivenom, tincture of iodide, hemostatic clamps, the list of products and instruments he requires is endless. This is his real apprenticeship in medicine, the inclination and need to heal, to ease the sufferings that surround him, the old vocation born, he would later claim, in the Passage Choiseul, when he saw the doctor, that magical and distant being, soothe hurts and cure diseases. That alone was what counted. Dr. Destouches is truly born in Africa. He must have learned the rudiments of medicine on his own, read the books, observed, understood, repeated. "I try to do a little good, I am running a pharmacy, I cure as many negroes as I can, though I am by no means convinced of their usefulness."[19]

And there remains, nevertheless, that racism, the cynicism, and Louis Destouches' taste for experimentation. He does tests on monkeys, he studies vegetable and animal toxins under the microscope, he plays the little Fabre, he says, by examining under the loupe the insects and the thousand little beasties swarming about him.

No, it is not easy to homogenize the portrait of Louis Destouches the trafficker, the impenitently curious, the cynic, the improvisational doctor, obsessed by war, but dreaming of peace, Louis Destouches the sorrowful, the hallucinator, the victim, in late October 1916, of a terrible attack of dysentery, who described himself at the time as a "disillusioned precocious child." And let us not forget the role of dreams. Simone Saintu had him sent the satirical weekly *Le Cri de Paris*; his father also sent him books he requested. And books, his father said, "are still the best thing anyone's ever made."

Céline in Africa. We can judge that by 1916 everything is already in place to make him the writer we know. He has his subjects. His culture is considerable and eclectic, it will hardly evolve any further. And his character is almost formed. We even sense him possessed by the need, the ambition to write. If one prefers, the pieces have been set up and the movement is afoot—which, it should be said in passing, refutes the stubborn myth according to which, at the publication of *Voyage au bout de la nuit* in 1932, Céline was a miraculous novice of thirty-eight. I have spoken of his subjects. His work, we know, unfurls like an immense transposition of autobiographical experience. And in late 1916, not only can he recall his childhood (the theme of *Mort à crédit*), he has also known the experience of war (the theme of *Voyage au bout de la nuit*), has spent long months in London (the theme of *Guignol's band*) and at twenty-two has discovered the reality of colonialism (another theme of *Voyage*). Of course, Céline has not yet become a doctor, but the medical experience that gives his books their singular lighting has already begun.

Nevertheless, this development is not complete. The African experience, and especially the letters and early writings he composes at the time, allow us to gauge the absence of what will later constitute Céline's genius. The sensibility, ambition, bearing, subject, theme, thought, and moral were all in evidence already. But, more simply, he lacked a "little music"—that is, the perfection of a writing as meticulous as lace—and a visionary breath— that is, the perfection of a structure patiently elaborated like all great deliria or all great disorders.

Waves

In January 1917 Louis Destouches went ahead with the liquidation of the Dipikar trading post. Had he given his notice to the Sangha-Oubangui lumber company, as he was permitted at the end of the first year? He was complaining of chronic dysentery. His arm continued to hurt. In early March he returned to Douala by boat.

He was probably not considering an immediate return to Europe. He planned to stay more than another full year in Africa, even to return to the bush to open his own trading business in the Cameroonian territory under British control. The project was just a flash in the pan. A few days after his arrival in Douala, he was initiating the administrative processes for his return to France. On March 10 the French authorities in Cameroon, under the command of Lieutenant Colonel Thomassin, issued him a passport allowing him to embark on the SS *Egori*, leaving Douala for Liverpool on March 17.

But new health problems necessitated his hospitalization in Douala. There, he was issued a medical certificate on April 2 by a Dr. Draneau, certifying motor and sensory problems in his right arm as a consequence of his war wound, and a chronic enteritis affecting his general state of health. In conclusion, he wrote, "these phenomena, which stand no chance of improving if M. Destouches prolongs his stay in the Colony, make it necessary for him to be evacuated to France, where he will be able to return to health and receive the care required."[20]

Louis Destouches eventually found passage aboard the RMS *Tarquah*, of the African Steam Ship Company, which left Douala on April 5. The ship called at Calabar, Lomé, Freetown. It reached Liverpool on May 1.

It was on board, on April 30, that Louis Destouches—*pardon*, Louis des Touches—wrote and signed a short story entitled *Des vagues* [Waves], his first literary foray that we know of.

Had he amused himself by describing the passengers returning from Africa with him? Had he met Major Tomkatrick, who "conscientiously emptied a glass that was continuously refilled with soda alternately mixed with brandy or whisky in respectable proportions," the oily governor of a Portuguese colony, or a Swiss trader of no discernible age, "as peaceful and plump as a Bernese pasture?"[21]

We come back once more to the *Amiral-Bragueton* episode in *Voyage*.

The analogies are self-evident: the same account of a crossing, the same effort to demolish every character (the puppetlike militarist passengers), the same need to exaggerate traits to the point of caricature. Unfortunately, the differences are no less glaring. In *Des vagues*, we sense Céline hobbled by his studied, too polished style, brilliant formulas, and caustic remarks. He is already attacking language, but does not distort it enough to bring the right impression and the sought-for emotion to the page. In short, irony replaces the intended violence.

But there is more. *Des vagues* seems to have been written by a passenger who, in order to allay his boredom, passes the time by setting up a gallery of portrait-victims. On board the *Amiral-Bragueton*, the roles were reversed, and it was the narrator who found himself the butt of the passengers' accusations and threats. He would later avenge himself by writing. Thus developed the dialectic of the persecutor-persecuted that gives that episode of *Voyage*—as to Céline's later work—its ultimate and unique viewpoint. This viewpoint is entirely lacking in the story written on board the *Tarquah*.

In Liverpool, Louis stopped at the Midland Adelphi Hotel. He likely went on to London soon afterward. He plunged, disappeared into London for several months, a summer, who knows, time enough for questionable dissipations. It was as though he wanted to delay his return to Paris and the rue Marsollier as long as possible. That moment when he would again have to grapple with life, more or less accept parental authority, account for himself, plan a career, a training, responsibilities—in short, sacrifice the total liberty he had enjoyed in Cameroon.

In Europe he was also to return to reality. And the reality was an exhausted France of wavering morale. Not a family that wasn't mourning a death in action after the hecatombs of Verdun and the Somme. Penury was settling in. Public opinion was beginning to grow indignant at the senseless massacres, the strategies designed for failure, the fiasco of operations in the East. An end to the fighting was looked for. The war grew worse. In March 1917 General Robert Georges Nivelle promised the government a grand-scale offensive. This time France would show the *Boches!* One hundred thousand deaths were racked up on the allied side in less than five days. The Germans knew the French dispositions. They were waiting for them around every corner. A few socialists suddenly remembered the virtues of peace around that time. Workers' strikes shook Paris in May 1917. Mutinies erupted in the French army. Pétain, rising to the occasion, had about 500 soldiers shot. Germany still didn't want to return Alsace and Lorraine—and what was the good of talking about peace in such conditions?

On April 6, 1917, Louis Destouches was at sea, and the United States, in its turn, declared war on Germany. But the Tsar had been deposed and Russia was giving up the fight; she had too much to do inventing modern revolution. In France, Clemenceau was soon to return to power and galvanize the national energies. In the Chambre, in his most famous speech, he affirmed:

"My foreign policy and my domestic policy are all one. At home, I make war. Abroad, I make war. I make war everywhere."

Louis Destouches wanted to hear only talk of peace. In all truth, he didn't want to hear talk of anything. He could easily have stayed the rest of his life in Africa, on board the RMS *Tarquah*, or in London, anywhere. But how to flee forever?

6

Eureka, Medicine!

Bohemia
The Lecturer in Love
Exams First, Marriage Later
Studies in Rennes
Semmelweis

Bohemia

Paris, autumn 1917.

On October 15, at the Vincennes firing range, Mata Hari, wearing a pearl-gray dress and a coat across her shoulders, was shot "in the name of the French people." It was 6.15 A.M. An unlikely spy, a worldly cosmopolitan with ill-chosen connections, she fell by way of example, to bolster the fighters' vacillating courage, to worry the "shirkers" in the rear, to fight pacifism. She also fell as an illustration of human stupidity, of justice's merciless trial-by-error, and of life's absurdity.

In the France that Clemenceau had taken in hand in November, censoring newspapers suspected of tepid bellicosity, creating the psychosis of espionitis, lashing out against pacifism, attacking Parliament, did Louis look for work? He could have found a desirable position in trade, or perhaps have been rehired by Lacloche the jeweler. Idleness was not the order of the day. But Louis had other ambitions, pretty vague no doubt. At least he knew what he didn't want, and that was to resemble his father, to vegetate as a pen-pusher in a business office or in trade, to allow his early adolescent dreams to shrivel up under the crippling weight, the sobriety, the rancidness, the dust and boredom of one of those humble and laborious existences squeezed into the horizons of office hours or behind the iron screens of shops. Back from Africa, he preferred to continue looking for new jungles, to drift with other outsiders, if not other adventurers, other explorers of those distant continents that were represented for him by the cinema, exoticism, publishing, literature, journalism, anything that came up. He was twenty-three, with a little money left over from his more or less licit dealings in Cameroon. He could play his future by the dice, by the chance encounter, by the whim of his curiosity.

At that time in Paris, he certainly met up with Édouard Benedictus, his friend from London and the witness to his lightning marriage with the enigmatic Suzanne Nebout. A droll sort of fellow, that Benedictus, born in 1878 and a descendant, it seems, of Spinoza. An elusive jack-of-all-trades, he would have deserved the epithet later given to Jean Cocteau—the Paganini of Ingres' violin.* Musician and composer, he was a friend of

* "Le violon d'Ingres"—a hobby that an artist praises more highly than his art itself.

Ravel's. He was a chemist, too, and a physicist, having invented a highly resistant glass called Triplex. During the war he perfected asphyxiating gases and protective measures against enemy gases. He was employed at the Ministry of Inventions at the time. Benedictus was also a decorative artist. He designed bindings, fabrics, rugs, furniture. . . .[1] In a letter to Pierre Monnier on April 1, 1949, Céline briefly mentions him: "I had a friend like that, a veritable triumph of the type, Benedictus. A Jew who worked in the decorative arts. An inventor, too, a blowhard and cabalistic swindler."[2] It is likely that Benedictus was one of the models for the bizarre character from *Guignol's band*, Sosthène de Rodiencourt, a crazy old mystic obsessed with Tibet and the narrator's companion on his long, hallucinatory drift through the British capital in 1916.

In 1917 Benedictus was working for Paul Laffitte, publisher at La Sirène press. We can suppose that he put Louis Destouches in touch with Laffitte about that time. One testimony immediately grabs our attention, that of Blaise Cendrars, an author and the life and soul of the selfsame La Sirène publishing house, when he recalled Laffitte.

"At the time of the foundation of La Sirène, he (Laffitte) was running copper mines in Spain, directing war industries, and giving all his time and care to an invention from which he expected great things in the future, the perfection of Triplex glass. The daily contact he had back then with the inventor of this security glass, the great, absentminded Benedictus, gave him the marvelous idea of opening an agency that would suggest to inventors the things that were in most urgent need of invention, of which the most urgent of all was—a machine to put an end to the war! And if, alas, no inventor ever presented himself in that astonishing research office with plans for such a machine, other devices left it, and more specifically new antiaircraft weapons, funny little appliances for domestic comfort, and even, ten years after it closed, a writer (Fernand, as we called the young man who ran the errands . . . yes, Louis-Ferdinand Céline)."[3]

These recollections were confirmed by Céline himself, fifty years later, as he was writing *Nord*: "In the days when I worked as delivery boy and secretary to Paul Laffitte, I ran around like mad . . . back then, much more economical and agile than the *métro* no. 1, between Gance, Mardrus, Mme. Fraya, Benedictus, and the printshop on the rue du Temple . . . And Vaschid, the 'line drawings,' and Van Dongen, Villa Saïd . . . minds may move very fast, sure, but I'm not scared of them . . . especially on the gallop through the Boulevards, the Champs-Élysées and the Ternes . . . picking up the proofs, never losing them, getting everything together, more, writing commentary in a style so enchanting that the reader can't sleep, can't live, between one 'issue' and the next . . . I must say that the Scheherazade thing, suspense and magic, I had it, right in my pen . . . that was half a century ago . . . as well as deliveries, proofs, engravers, and pagesetting . . . entirely on foot, like an athlete, from sprint to sprint, with no fare for the bus or the *métro*."[4]

It was the review *Eurêka*, of which Laffitte was the director/managing editor, that most likely mobilized the essence of Louis' vague, feverish activities in late 1917 and early 1918. A strange periodical, this "Review of Inventions as They Relate to Industry and Modern Life" was headquartered at 8, rue Favart—a stone's throw from the Opéra-Comique. The idea must have been to extend Benedictus' theoretical research through a journal, or to strive more generally to create a forum, a marketplace of ideas between the public, the engineers, and the researchers. Some revealed their discoveries, others requested technical solutions to works they wanted to undertake. Striving for scientific rigor as its standard, *Eurêka* never hesitated to crush charlatan inventors under that aegis. It noted all the papers presented at the Academy of Sciences. But it is enough to leaf through a few copies, even to consult a few tables of contents. A joyful craziness, an erudite debility, a comforting sense of scientific absurdity, a sort of mathematical dadaism unconsciously reign on many pages. It is the unintentional, inoffensive, and dry-humored triumph of the spirit of Alphonse Allais, the immortal inventor of the left-handed teacup or the bathtub with side entrance for the disabled. *Eurêka* suggested shoes with interchangeable heels, white inks for marking black sheets, or a vacuum cleaner for automobiles to suck up the dust they raise behind them.

Louis Destouches never wrote for the review. We nevertheless find his signature in issue no. 9 of February 1918, as translator of "the most salient passages of a message from the eminent Dr. Nutting of the Associated Societies of Worcester, Mass., USA." The article was entitled "On the Rational Use of Progress." What wonderful irony. The first mention in print of Céline-Destouches appears under a title that is the exact antithesis of his thought, of his artistic sensibility. The Célinian imagination—indeed, even his political obsessions—are in fact dependent on one single constant that could readily be defined as the irrational use of the past.

Eurêka, where Louis came, went, worried, watched, supported, edited, corrected, waited, wasted time and exhausted himself as errand boy, reader, and assistant to the editorial secretariat, was a prodigious crucible in which to melt and feed his excessive imagination. We recognize *Eurêka* under a different title in *Mort à crédit: Genitron*. No mystery in that identification. Céline was the first to point it out. As he specifically identified the famous, lunar, whimsical, pathetic, adventurous, grandiose, and weak Courtial des Pereires with the man who, under the name Henri de Graffigny, was a contributor, and later, from October 1917 to February 1918, the editorial secretary of the review (which was to cease publication in January 1919). ". . . my inventor Courtial des Pereires certainly did exist, his name was Henri de Graffigny—his books (innumerable) are still sold in the little Hachette series—*Genitron* was called *Eurêka*—located on a mezzanine on *Place Favart* across from the Paris Opéra-Comique."[5]

By his real name of Raoul Marquis, Graffigny is indeed one of those extraordinary individuals, an eccentric dreamer, a specialist in zigzagging through every door, every scientific mirage, an explorer of perpetual motion or butter slicers, an indefatigable polygraphic encyclopedist of the risible, a Prometheus never brought to the Garden of Miracles, a tragic Hercules in a trick- and practical-joke store. Born in 1863, Raoul Marquis had begun his "career" in often catastrophic ascents in a free balloon. That was in the 1880s. From his intrepid experiments he drew a "treatise on theoretical and practical aerostatics." Theoretical? Why not? But as to practical, one trembles ... A writer-of-all-trades, he put his name to guides for the motorcyclist, the engineer-motorman, the telegraphist, the telephonist. Artificial diamonds, elevators, tapestry, kites, the miracles of clockmaking or lethal rays were each in turn the inspiration for a precise little manual. For reasons of commercial prudence, he even had his wife put her name to his proper and indispensable advice to young mothers, his secrets of needlework or everything you need to know to run your household. But, above all, Marquis had one sizzling obsession: electricity. It caused him to commit innumerable manuals. Marquis believed in electro-cultivation with all his heart. On several occasions he treated the subject in *Eurêka*, particularly in an article of January 1918: "Intensive cultivation through electricity." And like Courtial des Pereires, though much later, he was the victim of his own perilous certainties. Feeling his age, Marquis retired with his wife to the Seine-et-Oise *département*, on the Septeuil plateau (Blême-le-Petit in *Mort à crédit*). He installed an electrical circuit in his vegetable garden. No doubt, he hoped to harvest peas the size of tomatoes, tomatoes the size of melons, and melons the size of ... *montgolfiers*. A vain hope. Did he even have enough to feed himself on a daily basis? He died in Septeuil in July 1934 at the age of seventy. *Mort à crédit* came out less than two years later. Perhaps the whimsical inventor's widow renewed communications with the writer on that occasion.

According to Lucette Almansor, "Louis liked to get to the end of lives, he wanted to revisit people who had disappeared, find out what had happened to them. In that way he rediscovered almost every witness to his past, except poor Elizabeth Craig.[6] Of course, when we returned from Denmark in 1951, that was over, Louis was worn out, he never moved again, it didn't interest him anymore." And Lucette remembers their visit to Septeuil just before the war. Raoul Marquis' widow was raising Welfare Board children in order to get by herself. Her poverty was atrocious. They saw shacks where the kids lived in total destitution, left to their own devices. "There were fifteen or so, threadbare, we brought them big pots of jam and little cakes, they threw themselves at them. That must have been their only meal that day. Of Raoul Marquis' widow, I retain the picture of a form buried in a bed, under a net canopy, you could make out her head, or rather some hairs and whiskers. It was extraordinary. There she was, buried away, dying, she couldn't get up anymore. Outside, you could still see these sorts of little windmills, or children's toys, all that was left of the installation of telluric potatoes, potatoes grown underground with electricity."

Raoul Marquis, alias Henri de Graffigny—what an encounter for Louis Destouches, what a teacher for the writer! There was something positively Célinian about this character. A sort of merry, desperate madness, a phenomenal curiosity about the world, a sense of the grotesque, an intimacy with the tragic. Is Courtial des Pereires a transformation, a metamorphosis of Raoul Marquis? Barely. "You don't meet a lot of men like Roger-Martin Courtial des Pereires."[7] That's true. But what about Marquis? Everything sticks, everything is fundamentally correct (give or take a thousand chronological details, of course) between the true and the false, the model and the character drawn.[8] In Céline's life, such encounters were rare between individuals and settings truly observed and his own imagination. Marquis was incontestably one such encounter, as, later, was Sigmaringen and the Germany of 1944–1945, the incredible Apocalypse, a Shakespearian circus in harmony with his outlandishness. No, Célinian fiction did not surpass reality. In these two cases, reality had simply found the appropriate form, writing, breath, to become spectacle, literature, an irreplaceable prop to the imagination.

But before such a whirlwind, Louis Destouches himself eludes us somewhat, as if he were the only one to be unfocused in the photo. As he said himself, he was galloping about, hustling, running, observing. That is the essential thing: first and foremost, he observed everything; in other words, he withdrew behind the properties of the spectacle observed.

For him, Bohemia was above all a double form of withdrawal, of retreat. As we have already said, a distancing from the war, from politics, from received notions, from bourgeois complacency, from the right-thinkers' great patriotic fear. A withdrawal, too, from the journalists, the calamitous and polygraphic inventors, the distant writers, the inaccessible publishers, the still marginal painters like Van Dongen, the fake seers, the bazaar orientalists, the whole fauna to which, it seems, he made a deliberate effort not to assimilate himself. In short, he was holding life in reserve. Cautiously. One might say cruelly that he was still the young (petty) bourgeois sowing his oats but not sowing them too deeply—one never knows—to be ready at a moment's notice to dig them back up and return to the security of the well-trodden ruts. In fact, Louis was waiting to choose. To embark on a career. In science or in delirium. Honors or dangers. He didn't know which. The ongoing war, which was escalating with the great German offensive on the Somme in March 1918, allowed him in a certain way to remain literally on vacation, in a state of irresponsibility that he had no intention of disturbing with decisive choices, with a profession to take on with no recourse and no turning back.

Abel Gance, his friend of the thirties, makes his appearance as early as 1917–1918, as evoked by Céline. Was he Gance's messenger, as claimed by Henri Mahé from the writer's probable testimony?[9] Céline also confided to Lucette that he had worked at the time as a courier, messenger, or "go-between" to the director, from mistress to mistress. Gance, the extravagant producer, the visionary handyman, the inspired inventor of films that were intimate with the sublime and flirted with the ridiculous, had the power to fascinate the young man. He was barely five years older, and yet what fertility, what early maturity, what method linked to such madness! By 1918 he had already shot more than a dozen films. He was making *J'accuse!*, in which the dead rise from the battlefield to see if the survivors had been worthy of their sacrifice. Yes, the extravagant Gance, too, had something pre-Célinian about him, but Louis Destouches merely passed through his entourage. Gance, for his part, had no memory of him from those years.

The Lecturer in Love

Bohemia, then . . .

Bohemia implies wandering, a readiness for anything, for adventure, the open spaces, the unknown. Bohemia is the sign of a certain impatience to live, the fear of inertia, the dread of repetition, a flight from boredom. After several months of lugging manuscripts and proofs around Paris, of hanging around Professor Nimbuses,* eccentrics and hack writers long of beard and short of ideas, Louis suddenly experienced the need for a change of air, of setting, of work, of companions, and of ambitions, too. Louis was ready to seize the first opportunity that came along, and happy sailing!

The opportunity came along very soon, if one is to believe Céline's later confidences to Robert Poulet: ". . . having indiscreetly read, in a letter addressed to my director, that the Rockefeller Foundation was looking for qualified propagandists, I bravely offered myself, along with a few friends. An American, impressed by our self-assurance, hired us on the spot."[10] Such confidences become all the more believable if we refer to the interview made by the journalist Charles Chassé for *La Dépêche de Brest et de l'Ouest* in October 1933, in which Céline declares: "I had been discharged; I had to make my living. So I come across this little sheet of paper, no bigger than this, calling for a lecturer for the Rockefeller Foundation to do antituberculosis propaganda. I had never spoken in public; I was a gasbag. . . . But there it was, I had fallen on the paper and I was the first to apply, and then I spoke English, which simplified my negotiations with the American committee. Anyway, I got the job."[11]

Of what, precisely, did it consist? With considerable funds at its disposal and of a philanthropic bent, the Rockefeller Foundation (founded in 1913 by a special charter of the State of New York) had been alarmed by the ravages of tuberculosis in France and by the inadequacy of the prophylactic fight against the disease. Arriving in Paris on July 1917 under the guidance of Dr. Livingstone Farrand, the foundation began by opening two antituberculosis clinics, one in Paris, the other in Eure-et-Loire; it then set about creating

---

* Professor Nimbus: cartoon character; absentminded professor.

propaganda teams whose aim was to inform the public of the risks of the disease, set up the best pedagogical methods for its prevention, and advise on the appropriate elementary measures of hygiene.

Brittany was particularly afflicted. Poverty, alcoholism, ignorance, and cramped housing, where contamination was rife, contributed there more than elsewhere to making tuberculosis a scourge. The urgent requests of Dr. Follet, president of the Ille-et-Villaine Departmental Committee for the Struggle Against Tuberculosis, in Rennes, further contributed to the Rockefeller Mission's choice. The first teams were to travel around Brittany.

In order to land his new job, Louis had had to show himself at his best. Above all, we mustn't picture an unkempt, bantering young man, provocative or insolent, slovenly or casual. Louis had a passion for medicine and he spoke English fluently. We have seen the pride with which he had worn the uniform of a noncommissioned officer in the French Cavalry, and he was now assuming, with a fairly self-satisfied bearing (at least, if we are to believe the photographic evidence), that of an American health mission. It was most certainly this Destouches who had impressed those in charge of the Mission, in particular Professor Selskar Gunn, the man who had hired him as lecturer/interpreter.

He had not hired him alone, moreover. His friend Albert Milon had also been recruited as a lecturer. Not long afterward, the comical Henry de Graffigny was in his turn tempted by the adventure. With a sort of "prophylactic puppet show," he was to teach hygiene to schoolchildren as a buffoon or, more officially, as "mechanic and puppeteer."

So in March 1918, Louis Destouches went to Rennes, from where the first pedagogical teams were to leave. There, he immediately met Dr. Follet, one of the town notables who had been instrumental in bringing in the Mission and who was professor of clinical medicine at the University of Rennes, an *officier* of the Legion of Honor, an official in public education, consulting physician to the State Railroads as well as to the Postal and Telegraphic Service, the colleges and the high schools of Rennes, chief surgeon of the Ambroise-Paré military hospital and at the La Sagesse private clinic, married to a daughter of a great surgeon and member of the Académie de Médecine, Augustin Morvan, deceased in 1897, and the father of a dreamy, graceful, slim, and educated young girl, Édith, age eighteen.

The many-titled Dr. Follet received Louis Destouches and other Mission leaders in his home. In 1985 Édith Follet still remembered it.[12] In early March 1918 her mother had told her that she had seen a charming boy. She was speaking of Louis Destouches. But the first time Édith saw him she was a little disappointed. He had wrinkles, she found him old—he was five years her senior. It was a large dinner at her parents' house. Extensions had been added to the table, with brackets underneath on which she had rested her feet. Actually, she was unwittingly playing footsie with Louis. He didn't move. And she very soon fell in love with him. "He had extraordinary eyes, of a blue that changed according to his feelings. When he was vexed, his

gaze brightened. This overgrown boy, six feet tall, looked like a man to me."
He had "lived," as they say. And yet, compared to the Americans, Édith
Follet still remembers, he had excellent manners.

Was the love at first sight reciprocal? Most probably. But Louis could not
stay long in Rennes, where, on March 11, 1918, the conference marking the
Mission's official send-off was held in the large theatre hall, with the usual
speeches, florid, grandiloquent, lyrical, and grateful to the prefect of Ille-et-
Villaine and to Dr. Follet, before a convinced audience of nuns, military
men, attentive young girls (Édith Follet among them), professors, and magistrates.

Louis, it seems, was at first a shaky lecturer. He confided to Charles
Chassé: "Did I ever stammer the first times! I still see with terror the great
meeting in the Rennes theater, all lit up, and that place is big! I was squeezed
in between General d'Amade and Doctor Follet, who would later become my
father-in-law. It was awful, and then, little by little, I got used to speaking the
way you get used to everything. I spoke and spoke!"[13]

More indulgent, sixty-eight years later Édith could still recall the tall
young man, slightly awkward, buttoned up tight in his impeccable uniform,
who paced up and down the theater's stage, speaking all the while in order
to conceal his timidity.

This timidity was to fade over the following days in Rennes and the
suburbs, during his first pedagogical lectures on the evils of tuberculosis,
before auditoriums of young schoolgirls or coeds, boys from the primaries,
cadres of army instructors, members of Catholic associations, male and
female workers assembled sometimes in cinemas or school playgrounds,
sometimes in markets or youth clubs. The regional press, according to
custom, reported his lectures in terms of glowing admiration, praising the
lyrical clarity of his language, emphasizing the orator's well-deserved ap-
plause.[14]

And always, Louis returned to the Follets, in uniform or in civvies, with a
large white scarf around his neck like a dandy, a fop, a parish Brummell
scented with Guerlain, a dazed and dazzling seducer whose charms Édith
could resist only with difficulty.

He told her right away that he was divorced (his own way of presenting
his lightning marriage in London, unratified by the French consulate), he
more or less recounted his past life so mysteriously and uneasily spent in
Africa, Soho, amongst the blacks, the madams of the Thames or the cannibals of Cameroon, the ivory smugglers or the sidewalk hostesses (but he
would never bring up his months of war, which remained in the realm of
silence or of a men-only complicity). And for the quiet Édith, so frail of
health, whom her father had withdrawn from religious school and was
taught at home by a priest, Abbé Pihan, Louis Destouches' life was beginning to sound like a not-so-proper, even scandalous novel. And the smell of
scandal, naturally, dazzled her as the most desirable of scents.

In her company Louis was so merry, so funny, even if she could sense dark and secret recesses in him. He had immediately known how to make her laugh, he mocking with irresistible ferocity the people he met in the Follet drawing room and serving them up in caricature. In private, he used swear words, strange, exotic words unknown to Édith, words that had the sweet and intoxicating savor of forbidden fruit. How could she have resisted a man like that, who was so mature? Just think! He was almost twenty-four.

On April 1, 1918, the Rockefeller Mission left Rennes. Itinerant propaganda team no. 2, to which Louis belonged, began its tour in Ille-et-Villaine, passing successively through Châteaubourg, Vitré, Argentré-du-Plessis, La Guerche, and then, to name only the principal stops up to June 15, Combourg, Dol, Saint-Malo, Paramé, Dinard, Fougères. . . .

Between 1918 and 1923, the five itinerant propaganda teams created by the Rockefeller Mission visited sixty French *départements*, stopping in every township of over 2,500 inhabitants that asked for them. Every team consisted of a female American director, a French lecturer (Louis' job), a male American lecturer, a French delegate responsible for the mail, for publicizing the mission's tour and organizing its stops with the municipalities concerned, and finally one or two driver/projectionists for the truck (nicknamed the "hygiene trailer") and the movie show. Thus, the team's equipment consisted of a projector and an electric generator (for the townships that were not yet linked to the electrical grid), as well as forty or so educational panels, posters, and a stock of brochures, pamphlets, and postcards which it distributed.

For children, the Rockefeller Mission lecturer began with a basic discussion of hygiene in general and tuberculosis in particular. He then distributed postcards among them, on which were printed lyrics to well-known melodies, which the lecturer would then rehearse in chorus, of the kind: "Microbe, microbe go away" or "Sunshine, sunshine in my room." For the adults, the films constituted the main entertainment.

In none of his novels did Céline exploit the otherwise picturesque experience of lecturing for the Rockefeller Mission. Perhaps this is because it was coeval with the war, close to it, and somehow pushed aside by it, by its procession of horrors, screaming, death. He did, however, describe this traveling job to the critic Claude Bonnefoy, near the end of his life.

"We wandered all through Brittany by truck. There was a Canadian Breton with us who was trailing his wife and five children about with him.

"We gave lectures on tuberculosis in the schools. We gave as many as five or six a day. The peasants we talked to, and who spoke *patois* for the most part, didn't always understand our explanations . . . They listened quietly, without a word . . . They mostly watched the films . . . Very educational, those films . . . You saw flies walking around on milk. . . . The reel broke or jumped the spindle every five minutes. It didn't matter . . . it got fixed."[15]

In these remarks, we sense a sort of ingenuous tenderness in Céline for an activity he deems laughable. But again, there is nothing to make us believe that Céline was not an irreproachable lecturer. Photos of the period show him at times in his American uniform, at others in civvies, a dark suit, tie, and a flat, Buster Keaton–type hat. The bearing of a perfect gentleman, compared to whom his friend Milon, in his light-hued jacket, rumpled trousers, enormous shoes, aggressive whiskers and disheveled hair, looks like a hard-boiled proletarian from the suburbs.

Louis may already have been thinking of giving up Bohemia, of making a career in medicine, of rising to the middle class, but we have no way of knowing. And then, there was sweet Édith Follet, whom he had left behind in Rennes, but whom he had by no means forgotten. He telephoned her from every stop. He wrote her three, four times a day, a torrent. Any pretext was good enough to lure him back to Rennes, between two stops, before returning to his lectures, his little songs, and his chancy screenings. He would go to the Follets', trying to win over the father, that bent, proud, ambitious little man with his delicate mustache and bowler hat, who tried to reconcile the respectability of his bourgeois life, his collection of titles, medals, and honors, with the many sweaty and difficult-to-conceal liberties he took with his mistresses. For Louis, his visits to Dr. Follet were, of course, only a pretext. At each visit he would slip a little change to the chambermaid, who would bring him to Édith or pass messages between them. That lost sense of morality, those myriad lovers' stratagems, have something adorably obsolete about them nowadays. We have to exercise our imaginations a bit to picture Céline as a comic character, a kind of Count Almaviva striving through ancillary complicities to communicate with his beloved.

It is likely that Louis foresaw an immediate marriage. Out of love and probably out of impatience. Édith was one of those provincial, bourgeois young girls, dreamy but strict, whom one marries, who become mothers, not mistresses. She had promised her mother (and her confessor?) to remain pure until she was married. She evidently intended to keep her promise. Louis knew that. So Louis had to marry her. But was that possible? Who was he, after all, this Louis Destouches? He had no diploma, not even his *baccalauréat*, no profession, no money, no genuine title of nobility, nothing. All he had going for him was his charm, his gift of the gab, his fine bearing and veteran's heroic prestige, his street smarts, his curiosity, his insolence perhaps, and his predisposition toward medicine. That may have been enough to amuse the father, who readily received him, but not to convince the latter to give him his daughter in marriage.

Meanwhile, the war went on, desperate, murderous, still indecisive. German troops were returning from Russia in forced marches, while the Americans, barely trained, were moving to the front. In March 1918 the great German offensive on the Somme broke through the English lines and reached the woods of Villers-Cotterêts, where it foundered against the French reinforcements hastily brought forward. At that time, Foch was named commander-in-chief of the allied armies. Time was now against the Germans. "Big Bertha," the giant cannon that could fire over 100 kilometers, was able to reach the capital, destroy the roof of the Saint-Gervais church, give nightmares to the Parisians, and shake the Chambre des Deputés. On the front, the war continued with the same ferocity. It could go either way from moment to moment.

And the war was still the eternal ellipsis, obstructing any future, forcing Louis to live from day to day, far from the nightmare, close to the nightmare, in the daily miracle of merely being alive, of staying alive and nothing more—whence, perhaps, originated his ambivalence. The adventurer, the anarchist, the solitary, the restless and curious survivor of battlefields and agony forever on the outskirts of life—in a word, the man of war—versus the young, well-educated petty bourgeois, the good boy he had been, with his *certificat* and his ambitions, his tie, a fine marriage on the horizon, the prejudices of his milieu, professional conscience, the need to seek a profession (medicine?), to be useful, to live and consequently to make plans, to imagine the future, peace.

Of course, war or peace, Louis will continue all his life to present the double face of rebel and conservative, of foul-mouthed utterer of maledictions and conformist in his social or political ideas, of the man of the past and the man of the future, of a suicidal and a muddler-through, of a cautious reactionary and a hallucinating prophet of decadence. But, for the moment, he was assiduously pursuing Édith. He was also pursuing his educational tours for the Rockefeller Mission.

After Ille-et-Villaine, Finistère: Vitré, Montfort-sur-le-Meu, Saint-Brieuc, Quimper, Rétiers. The weeks passed. The summer was ending. The war, too, perhaps. If the specter of tuberculosis was not exactly beating a retreat before the tireless onslaught of Louis Destouches, soldier of health, the German armies, at least, were finally caving in. The Allies were now reinforced by thousands of Americans and had new assault tanks at their disposal. In late July an attack by Mangin forced the Germans back nearly forty kilometers. Foch was named field marshal. New Franco-British offensives followed in August and in September. Victory was at the tip of the gun, but the guns were still in the combatants' hands.

In Rétiers, the very young Henri Mahé, who was later to become one of Louis' closest friends, saw the Rockefeller Foundation's "Hygiene Trailer" pass by in that final summer of the war. . . .

"I still remember that lanky American soldier running around town with a pile of books in his arms. We kids escorted him, because he made us laugh and gave us *chouine-gomme.* Then you returned to the Hôtel Piton and we crushed our noses against the windowpanes to watch you scratching on your slate with chalk. All alone like that, you were preparing for your *bac.* At night, in the market, the traveling lecturer from the Rockefeller Mission, you bawled out the good people who had come, using a magic lantern to show slides of microbes that really layed it on thick:

" 'The microbe is death! The water's full of it! Milk's full of it! Boil your water! Boil your milk!' "[16]

During the course of that summer, 1918, in Montfort-sur-le-Meu or in

Saint-Brieuc, Louis probably met Dr. Alexis Carrel, winner of the Nobel Prize for Medicine in 1912, who had settled in Canada before the war and then in the United States, where he had been in touch with the Rockefeller Institute, and had then returned to France during the hostilities, still closely linked to the Americans, who used him as a prop against the hostility of the French professorial establishment. They very soon entered into a scientific correspondence that proves the young man's curiosity—at least, his interest in medicine—as well as the scientist's disinterested benevolence. But yet again, there is no perceptible trace or certainty that a meeting took place that summer.[17]

After Finistère and the Côtes-du-Nord in October and November 1918, Louis continued to write to Édith, to call her, to pass through and see her on a whim, like a gust of wind, a bolt from the blue, between two lectures. We hardly need list all of the stops—Loudiac, Caulnes, Évran. . . . On November 11, 1918, Louis arrived in Dinan, where the tour was greeted by explosions of joy. They were not celebrating the defeat of tuberculosis, nor the undisputed merits of the members of the Rockefeller Mission, but Germany's surrender, the armistice of Rethondes and the end of the nightmare.

A photo shows us Louis Destouches that day with members of the Mission's traveling team at the Dinan town hall, swigging victory champagne with the town notables. Strangely, the snapshot exudes no sense of joy. To be sure, there is always a little stiffness in that kind of carefully posed photo. But it's as if the picture's frozen images were emerging abruptly from a bad dream. Louis Destouches, leaning against the wall, his arms crossed behind him, seems barely awake, his eyes still goggling from the horrors he had seen, lived, and would never forget.

Dinan, November 11, 1918. And yet the curtain had well and truly risen that day. Louis would be able to begin living again. That is, dreaming, making plans, building a home or castles in the air (or demolishing them). He was recovering his foothold on life and on the brink. He could think about Édith more than ever. He felt that once again he had the right to picture the future. But he still needed some time to believe it. He may still have been a little skeptical in Dinan. The champagne may have had a funny taste that day.

Exams First, Marriage Later

After the war that had ruined Europe, shattered its certitudes, and decimated its population, there was a postwar world to be built. In June 1919 the impossible Treaty of Versailles was to reveal dramatically the same incapacity among politicians for establishing peace which they had revealed five years earlier for safeguarding it. All the seeds were sown: the imbalances, the bitterness, the eternal spirit of revenge, the economic ruin, the rise of totalitarian ideologies, German militarism, slogans of the "The *Boche* will pay" type (for which France, twenty years later, would pay very dearly), the reparations, the military occupation of the left bank of the Rhine—the seeds were sown that would very soon turn the "madcap years" into the tragically mad years. And it was those years that saw the metamorphosis of Louis Destouches into Louis-Ferdinand Céline, that were the compost from which the writer's dark, rebellious, excessive, untenable, and often unacceptable words were to spring.

In 1932 he called his first book *Voyage au bout de la nuit* [Journey to the End of Night]. It was because he had escaped a first time from the long night of the Great War, because he dreaded and foresaw a second great night into which Europe and the world would plunge, that Céline, man of anguish and sorrows, started to write, to hallucinate. A journey to the end of night, no! He began writing, rather, between two nights, in the pale dawn of the curious sort of peace which other revolutionary intellectuals at that very moment were hoping to subvert, to illuminate with the dark sunlight of unreason, of the unconscious, of libertarian magic. But Céline remained a stranger to the surrealist spirit, which he either didn't know of or disdained. André Breton and his friends instantly avowed a radical scorn for him (even well before the writer's overtly anti-Semitic remarks). They simply had nothing in common. In a way, the surrealists were optimists. They had glimpsed avenues of rejection and flight. They were blazing the provocative trails of individual freedom, of the mind's liberation. They believed in the virtues of revolution, and some among them would later swap, with no apparent difficulty, the surrealist revolution for communist revolution. Céline, however, remained an incurable pessimist, caught in a reality that he was to fashion, transform, and raise to the convulsive and disproportionate levels of an immense hallucination, but from which he would nonetheless be unable to free himself. In other words, Céline remained a realist. The sun would never rise for him. Night would fall once more. He would write only in the half-light.

Great changes often barely affect the daily routines of work and living. Once he had sipped at the warm victory champagne in the Dinan town hall, Louis returned to his antituberculosis propaganda tours, through Erquy, Lamballe, from one village to another, with the same film scarred by a thousand breaks, the same peremptory tracts, the speeches similar to within a decimal point, and the little songs learned more or less by heart by the distracted schoolchildren. One might see something symbolic in that— or at least symptomatically Célinian. Peace, then, hadn't changed anything for him. Death remained on the agenda, on the horizon. The war being fought against it must go on. We might call it the crusade against tuberculosis. The thing was to wear oneself out in vigilant, consoling words—so much useless advice, in essence, as useless as it was indispensable—thus faced with death, the ultimate victor against whom the struggle is never finished before we lay down our arms.

And yet, little by little, peace was changing mentalities. More prosaically, it was also changing the law, creating the necessary measures to reintegrate the troops into civilian life. How, for example, to make up for lost time, studies abandoned by so many young men mobilized for four years under flag and fire? For the *baccalauréat*, a restricted program, a dispensation from the written tests, was granted to veterans by a decree issued January 10, 1919.

Louis began thinking of the *bac* right after the armistice. In early December 1918 he took temporary leave from the Rockefeller Mission. No *bac*, no marriage. And those were the two goals at which he was aiming.

No *bac*, no undergraduate studies either, no medical school. And after his demobilization, his wanderings, his colonial adventures, his poorly paid jobs in Paris, Louis had been able to measure the extent to which his highly developed curiosity about the world, his need to learn, to retain, clashed with the fragility of his basic knowledge; also, the extent to which he was nothing without a diploma, just a sarcastic outsider with no influence. His wound on October 14 in Poelkappelle had perhaps shredded his arm—it had also, dare we say it, put some steel in his spine.

I believe, too, that Louis Destouches was remarkably ambitious—which is not at all incompatible, moreover, with the destructive spirit that moved him. In order better to demolish accepted ideas, to shake up well-oiled certitudes, to mock the proprieties, attack the bigwigs, disturb people's intellectual, mendacious comfort, he had first to take their full measure, to prove himself, as they say, to assert himself, to climb the social ladder four rungs at a time, to attain a rank in the middle class of which his parents would never dare to dream, they who pictured him as the department manager of a great store, even if it meant slamming the door behind him with a great burst of Célinian laughter.

Édith was waiting for him in Rennes. He didn't want to make her wait too long. He joined her, therefore, in December 1918. Dr. Follet apparently did not look too fondly on the union of his daughter with the admittedly fascinating but penniless tightrope walker Louis Destouches, he of the blue eyes, spicy anecdotes, and irresistible impertinence. Follet, an important man stiff with ambition, had vowed Édith an exclusive love. Perhaps he was one of those men spoken of by Jacques Chardonne, "who have known only one love—their love for their daughter—and that's as much love as damnation requires." As the first condition to the marriage, he and his wife stipulated the suitor's obtaining the *baccalauréat*, and then, since he wished it, medical studies if he showed himself capable of such (though they didn't doubt it). In those circumstances, the Follets were disposed to help the young couple.

All the same, Louis was not arriving empty-handed. He could be of some help to Athanase Follet, who was soliciting the post of director of the Rennes Medical School (which was directly annexed to the Paris Faculty of Medicine). Let us recall that Louis' uncle Georges Destouches had been secretary of the Paris Faculty of Medicine for fifteen years; he had a good deal of influence if not very broad ideas or solid connections.

Of course there was no explicit deal made between Louis and Athanase Follet. They both had enough sophistication for that. But with the former's lively, mocking, and lucid wit, and the latter's cunning profligacy, words became unnecessary. The future son- and father-in-law understood each other to a tee. So Dr. Follet went to Paris to meet Louis' parents. Warned by his son, Fernand Destouches immediately found it convenient to avoid considering his quarrel with his brother as a permanent thing. He spoke warmly to the latter of Athanase Follet, and asked him to intervene in his favor. In December 1918 Dr. Follet was named director of the Rennes Medical School (and, on June 8, 1920, elected on the first ballot as a corresponding member of the Académie de Médecine). The Destouches were people you could count on.

Meanwhile Louis was cramming assiduously, boning up on history, geography, and Latin. Édith, pursuing her private studies with Abbé Pihan, had advised him to call on her teacher's services. Thus, the young man developed the habit of dropping in at the Institut Saint-Vincent. His erudition was already enormous. Louis had built up a stock of knowledge in literature, history, and of course in modern languages. Speaking of his student, Abbé Pihan was able to say that "I only had to put some order in it all!"[18] For mathematics, Louis saw another teacher, to whom he went regularly.

On February 5 Athanase Follet officially assumed his duties as director of the medical school. His reception by his colleagues was cool, to put it mildly. The dean of the teaching staff read him a collective letter of protest on the spot. It emphasized the "personal intrigues" and the "unhappy compromises" that had allowed him to solicit and land the job against the formal wishes of his peers. These latter draped themselves in their wounded honor and their respect for the higher interests of teaching; they entreated him, if he had the least sense of dignity, to tender his resignation at once in the face of their outraged consciences. There was nothing doing. Athanase Follet did not have the same concept of dignity as that of his touchy and slighted colleagues. He filed away the letter, he filed away the whole business, and let there be no more heard about it! Indeed, it soon became an unbroachable topic.[19]

In March, Marguerite and Fernand Destouches made the trip to Rennes for the official marriage request, white gloves, necktie, the whole bit. They probably didn't put too much hope in it. Louis continued to frighten them with his independence, his instability, his escapades. They could still see the notorious Germaine Nebout, who had dropped in on them on the rue Marsollier, talking about her sudden marriage to their son. And with their scrupulous sense of honesty, their moral righteousness corseted in respect for order and convention, they wondered whether it was really right to let Édith Follet marry Louis. She belonged to another sphere. She seemed so gentle, so protected. Wouldn't hers be a cruel misalliance with that crackpot? They revealed their scruples to the Follets, they may have tried to dissuade them from the marriage which they were requesting with the same breath, they concealed none of Louis' misadventures. The effort was wasted. For his part, the new director of the Rennes Medical School could see nothing standing in the way of his daughter's marriage. Even so, he later went to the trouble of ascertaining, in London, that his future son-in-law wasn't already married in the eyes of French law.

In the meantime, propaganda team no. 2 of the Rockefeller Mission had left Brittany for the Vendée and the Gironde. Louis met up with it sometime in March. And that is why, in Bordeaux on April 2, he sat the first part of his *baccalauréat* in the Latin-and-modern-languages section. He passed the exam with no problem, picking up a *mention bien*—a laudatory citation—into the bargain. In Latin appreciation: Horace (16/20); French appreciation: Pascal's *Pensées* (18/20); in first and second modern languages, presumably English and German: 18/20 and 14/20; in geography: the Champagne region (11/20); in history: the Revolution's organization of France (14/20); and in mathematics: the volume of the pyramid (12/20).

Thus, a limited curriculum and accelerated process. He was to take the second part on July 2. Meanwhile, and in lieu of last-minute cramming, he resumed his Rockefeller lectures against tuberculosis. If, as he generally pointed out, alcohol was the fearsome ally of disease, he must not have been too popular in Libourne or Saint-Émilion, areas of vineyards and high civilization.

The second part was no harder for him to pass than the first. Again a *mention bien*, a brilliant 18/20 in modern history, the subject: the Republic from 1848 to 1851; a 16/20 in geography on Ireland (a Celtic country, he was in his element); a simple 14/20 in natural sciences, where he was questioned on the kidney; and a modest 13/20 in philosophy, where he had to expound on "pleasure and pain"—a Célinian theme, to be sure, but did Louis Destouches have a philosophical mind? "I am not a man of ideas, I am not a man of messages," he would repeat throughout his life.

It was high time that he return to Rennes for long but still chaste *tête-à-têtes* with his fiancée, the marriage preparations, walks, relaxation, riding. Ever so gradually, Louis was getting used to civilian life again, to the silence of happiness perhaps, to everyday, carefree cheer. The oppressive cloud of fear seemed to be lifting now. He re-encountered the world's fortunate ones, the same class he had glimpsed ten years earlier in the luxurious boarding school of Pierremont Hall in Broadstairs, enlivened by the gentle and melancholy Mrs. Farnfield. But this time it wasn't a mirage, he was well and truly going to belong, if he so desired, to the sheltered bourgeois universe he had only skirted as a child, following what must almost be called a misunderstanding. But that, clearly, was not counting on the granite plinth of misery, the deep restlessness, the impatience that dwelt within him, hindered him from finding rest, made him deem as an imposture, an unforgivable laxity, a deceptive weakness, or an illusion, the simple abandonment of the self to the present moment. The terrible imagination of Louis Destouches, of Céline, endlessly hurled and smashed him against the future while he sniffed out disasters like a hunting dog its prey; he barked, he spotted them, one might have thought he was in a hurry to pounce on them, as if to avoid shirking his duty to see the future.

August 10, 1919. Quintin, Côtes-du-Nord, twenty kilometers or so southwest of Saint-Brieuc: the marriage of Louis-Ferdinand Destouches, profession: medical student (a little ahead of himself), born May 27, 1894, in Courbevoie (Seine), living in Quintin (the simplifying little white lies of official records) and resident of Paris, adult son of Ferdinand Auguste Destouches, chief clerk of Le Phénix insurance company, and of Marguerite Louise Céline Guillou, no profession, both living in Paris, at 11, rue Marsollier; and of Édith Amandine Marie Follet, no profession, born May 12, 1899, in Rennes (Ille-et-Vilaine), living in Rennes, dependent daughter of, etc. At the bottom of the marriage certificate, the future married couple stated that they had established a marriage contract dated July 4, 1919, signed in the presence of M. Joseph Delaporte, Quintin notary. A very boring contract, moreover, establishing a typical joint estate of limited means. But, in order to allow the young couple to live during Louis' medical studies, the Follets settled on their daughter a dowry in the form of a life annuity of 12,000 francs a year.

Why the little town of Quintin for the ceremony? At least two reasons come to mind. After the incident—or rather, scandal—of his assumption of the duties of director of the Medical School, Athanase Follet was inclined to keep a low profile in the good city of Rennes and to avoid offending his fellow citizens with the conspicuous pomp of a large ceremony. For his part, Louis hated social events, big weddings, and all the rest. There lived in Quintin an aunt of Édith's, Mathilde Delaporte, a provincial poetess who had published a few slim volumes at her own expense and for whom Louis felt a lively affection. With her husband, the notary Joseph Delaporte, she lived in a lovely house near the church. There, the preparations for a country wedding could be made—or almost.

The Follets wanted a religious service. Édith had been raised piously. Her father may have proclaimed "progressive" ideas or been suspected of Freemasonry, but he would take no clientele for granted. The high clergy of Rennes already numbered among his patients. Louis acquiesced out of indifference. "He had respect for the Church," Édith Follet says. "He went to see the Quintin *curé* and I think they got along quite well."[20]

There were thirty or so guests. Before the mayor, Louis Guillou served as witness to his nephew. In the church, the groom had forgotten the rings and his (future) mother-in-law had to scurry over to the Delaportes' for them. Dr. Follet kept his boater screwed to his head during the entire ceremony. Incorrigibly absentminded or insolently anticlerical? Louis couldn't have cared less. He was simply eager for it all to end. With his light-hued felt hat, his trousers that were too short, his patent-leather shoes and white gaiters, he watched Édith, all tense and excited, pushing out her chin to get a grip on herself behind her lace veil, the flounces of her dress layered down to her ankles.

A marriage, first and last, is a marriage feast, an endless menu of lobsters, shellfish, York Mortemart ham, ducklings here, truffled pullets there, mushrooms, a *foie gras*, and so on until hunger and thirst have been quenched with great swigs of sherry, Château Yquem, Château Léoville and so on. . . .

Louis the ascetic, the impatient, who all his life was horrified by blowouts, by the nosh-ups and booze-ups which he considered to be the source of decadence and all evil, gave way in the middle of the meal. He made himself scarce and dragged Édith with him. Sixty years later, she would still regret not having tasted the meringues frosted with whipped cream that she had ordered specially. Louis dragged her to Rennes, then to Paris for a speedy honeymoon and toward what was to be their very brief conjugal future.

It is common knowledge that everybody benefits from marriage feasts except the newlyweds.

Studies in Rennes

In November 1919 Louis enrolled at the Rennes Faculty of Sciences in order to prepare for the PCN (the certificate of physical, chemical, and natural sciences studies), indispensable in order to undertake medical studies. On November 16, 1922, still in Rennes, he passed his third medical exam, the final one which that faculty was entitled to administer. A few days later he received the official authorization to enroll at the Paris Faculty in order to complete his studies there.

In the interview given to Claude Bonnefoy in 1961, Céline summed up those three years in a few words: "I had moved into a medical family. In Rennes. I had married a director's daughter . . . Then I did my medical studies under normal conditions, peacefully . . . Nothing to say on that period."[21]

Can we be so certain that there is nothing to say? Are we to picture Céline pampered by his wife, supported by his parents-in-law, a good student, a good husband, soon to be a good family man in the provincial, felt-lined tranquillity of a bourgeois life? Is it because such comfort squared poorly with his character or with the Célinian mythology (perpetuated by the author) of the rebel, the adventurer, the man of the people dedicated to sniffing out misery and humiliation in the lower depths of society, to curing it or bearing witness to it with the choked humor of rebellion, that he drew an opaque curtain across that too-peaceable period? Happy people have no story to tell, popular wisdom informs us. Indeed, Céline never built a "story" around his years of medical apprenticeship. Was he happy, then?

A reading of *Voyage au bout de la nuit* cannot help but be instructive. In that chaotic and haunted metamorphosis of his own experiences, the author slips an abrupt and decisive ellipsis into the center of his book. On the one hand, his hero, Bardamu—his brother, his double—never ceases rebounding from one catastrophe to the next, from war to hospital, from colonial Africa to an America worthy of Chaplin in *Modern Times*. On the other, he finds himself back as a suburban doctor, an exhausted participant in and frightened observer of pain he can barely manage to alleviate. Between the two, nothing. How did he become a doctor? Silence. It was as if Rennes, his marriage, his material ease had suddenly fallen into the pit of oblivion, and that he believed once and for all that he had nothing to say about—or nothing to transpose from—that period. "At the time of my doctoral studies I lived in bourgeois style. Well off, with slippers, a frogged dressing gown, a drawing room buried under slipcovers."[21]

One might think that in order to save face Céline—this time before Robert Poulet—goes too far. We suspect him of lying, or, at the very least, of typical excess. The image of Céline in slippers is comical. One wants to dissipate it or laugh about it with the man in question.

And yet . . . Immediately following his marriage, Louis and Édith had moved into a little two-room apartment on the ground floor of the building at 6, quai Richemont where his in-laws lived. He could also benefit from his father-in-law's library on the second floor. The young couple took their meals with the Follets—one less worry! And what can one say about the quai Richemont, right in the heart of the fashionable neighborhoods of Rennes, not far from the fine arts museum, overlooking the Vilaine River tamely canalized, rectilinear and unspeakably sad? Or about those soulless three- or four-storied houses with their austere and opulent façades of stone? How can one avoid developing an eternal disgust for that repetitive provincial respectability, for that city of Rennes where nothing can ever have happened, where Athanase Follet quite vainly tried to conceal his one-night stands or his lifelong mistress, Marie Le Bannier, whom he would eventually settle in his property in Saint-Malo (where Louis, who felt very warmly toward her, would visit on many occasions), where everyone gossiped about everyone else, where the riverbanks were cemented, where no accident could threaten the course of things? I do not know if we should speak of a bourgeois Céline in Rennes, but it was perhaps in Rennes that for the first time Louis experienced the bourgeoisie from the inside and was from then on seized with horror for it.

"I work like a horse, I was born of the people, and the comforts of the good life in no way breach my decidedly plebeian constitution— In the morning, like the virtuous Achilles, I see Aurora rise, and the Night star accompanies me well into my studious vigils— I see little of my wife, because I am as solitary as I am independent and hate constraint even in its most affectionate guise— It is at the price of the widest independence that marriage is possible for me and, most fortunately, Freedom is understood in its highest potential by the whole family. Here, we do strictly what we like and can spend weeks not seeing one another without taking offense— I often find myself strolling in one direction along the Quai you are familiar with, while Dr. Follet is strolling in the opposite direction— We are free to stroll together if we please, but it's just as fine otherwise . . .— My wife is completing her pilgrimage—enveloped in a comfort that makes me think of so many others whose less happy fate leaves them on their two pain-ridden legs, wandering through the suburban trains or as department store shopgirls!! But poverty is only conceivable to those who have known it—and the bourgeois heart is something unimaginably lifeless and insensitive to the suffering of others— I do not say that about Édith, who is charming though altruism is hardly one of her strong points (where would she have learned it?), but about that pack of hideous egoists whose round, closed mugs I notice at random on the streets— Yes, old chum, I've already climbed and then descended many a rung on the social ladder and I remain confounded by incomprehension of the impenetrable barriers that exist between men— There's a hell of a bigger difference between a French bourgeois and a poor Gaul than between a rich Frenchman [François] and an opulent Teuton."[22]

Céline in slippers—impossible! His inseparable friend from Rennes, Marcel Brochard, husband of Édith's best friend, Denise Ertaud, was also unable to accept such a picture. His testimony is essential, one of the few we have on that period of Céline's life:

"You were already an anarchist, Louis. Crude in your puerile, revolutionary, and egalitarian points of view, sure!

"But you talk such tripe about your father-in-law, Professor Follet, who may have been a bigwig, that's true, but who never asked you to be one too. He knew you well, like Édith and the rest of us knew you, the way you've always been, the enemy of conformism, whether in manners, speech, or clothing. Your entrance into a Rennes drawing room caused a sensation. Your cowboy-style hat over one ear, you gave a general greeting, and once you sat down all we ever saw of you was your big shoes. The man with the big shoes, my little Jacqueline used to say when she was very little! . . .

"No, Louis, the way the others knew you later, even those at the end, that's how you were even at 20! Frighteningly curious, fickle, ironical, vulgar, irritable, a marvelous pathological liar! And paradoxical."[23]

Paradoxical indeed. Like the light and shadows that played across Louis Destouches' life in Rennes during those three years.

On the light side, he worked hard to finish his medical studies as soon as possible, taking advantage of the provisions made for veterans to catch up and, if necessary, to complete the normal cycle of the first four years in two and a half years of strict application. Again on the light side, his father-in-law tendered help, advice, explanations, though he quite rightly never showed the least favoritism during the examinations. And, finally, he lived the serene life so favorable to study, the vacations spent in Brittany, in Roscoff in 1920, in Finistère in 1921 (before a brief outing in the Pyrénées with his friend Francis Vareddes, a young journalist with the *Democrate d'Ille-et-Vilaine*), in Saint-Malo in 1922, where he met up with Édith, was initiated into tennis, rode horses, traveled through the countryside on an Indian-brand motorcycle, a sidecar attached when Édith came along, where the summer skies were luminous as they can be only there, with that miraculous acidity of colors, that sweet respite occasionally granted by the winds and nurtured by the turquoise ocean.

But how many shadows elsewhere!

"There were some terrible things in him," relates Édith Follet. "He liked to mock and destroy everything he came across. His mind was negative in many ways. For a young woman like me, it was a little disorienting. As if the rug were being pulled out from under my feet. What happened with him was that you were never peaceful. The things he said came back to your mind, tortured you. But afterward, when Louis became aware that he had tortured you, he backpedaled, because he was very sweet. You would have thought there were two beings inside of him."[24]

And, like a leitmotiv in his life, in his behavior and his personality, there was that terrible impatience ever gnawing at him—an impatience that might still be classified as an incapacity to enjoy the present, a destructive rejection of what he observed and was already wearying him, without any doubt a great fear, a need to stand back, ever further, to allow nothing to escape, to learn and, above all, to flee.

Having barely arrived at the cinema, which Édith adored, no doubt sensitive to the youthful charms of Richard Barthelmess, the wild energy of Douglas Fairbanks, or the dark, pomaded seductiveness of Rudolph Valentino, Louis already wanted to leave in the middle of the show; he was bored, he wanted to be somewhere else, and she, docile and disappointed, followed him. Having barely sat down in a café, a restaurant, he was paying the bill, heading out. Having barely made himself comfortable in the drawing room of a friend's house, he monopolized the conversation and then vanished without warning. His mind was too quick, lucid, too haughty, probably. He could have claimed as his own the remark of Jules Renard (with whom, incidentally, he has much in common that is rarely mentioned, such as an acerbic acuity of the eye, a total disenchantment, a musical concern for style, the right word, economy of language) who, in 1890, noted in his *Journal* that "supporting the entire burden of the conversation is still the best way to avoid noticing that others are imbeciles."

Of course, Céline was no one-woman man. He loved Édith, he had married her and possessed her at last. He already needed other conquests, other fugitive, pointless affairs that had already begun to exhaust him before they had even been brought to a head. What sort of revenge was he seeking? Did he want to make up for his impecunious youth, where everything had been counted out and measured for him, with a mad and literal debauch, an endless prodigality? Or must we also speak of a ribald, orgiastic Louis

Destouches? On what sort of murky expeditions did he drag his friends Marcel Brochard and Francis Vareddes, those days in Rennes? In December 1920 the latter had introduced him to a young girl of twenty, Germaine Constans, who was able to say of Louis back then that "He was very fond of children. . . . Death already gave him the shivers. . . . He had a craving for cakes. . . . He organized partner-swappings."[25]

Céline was a voyeur, a seducer. He shamelessly courted Édith's best friends and she said nothing, sadly resigned because she knew how useless it would be to say anything. That was what he called his freedom. But his was a sad debauch at heart. None of Don Juan's pride or revolt in him. For him eroticism was an endless flight, a meticulous search for the absolute in a hopelessly mediocre, flesh-bound world doomed to decay—and that search for the absolute was a decoy, a lie, and he knew it too. He wooed a woman the way he might have bought a lottery ticket, in the crazy hope of the grand prize, and immediately pulled up short; he knew that the winning number is never drawn, that one does not escape the physiological fatalities of life, of death. He wouldn't even check his ticket number, he'd walk off alone, before he had the chance to be surprised again, seduced by other images.

He may have been looking for similar consolations in books. He continued to devour book upon book. His father-in-law's library was barely enough. Rabelais enchanted him, as did the *Historiettes* of Tallemant des Réaux. His tastes were classical: Dickens, Ronsard, Du Bellay. "I didn't think in those days that he would be a writer," says Édith Follet, "nor did he. That's an impression I kept, even when I saw him again at the end of his life. But he also read everything that was being printed at the time. He said that Proust, who was beginning to be fashionable, gave him a pain. But he had a great love for Rémy de Gourmont and Anatole France."[26]

Louis lived mostly on the margins of life in Rennes. For him, studies were a kind of retirement. Years of apprenticeship far from the reality with which, from the moment war was declared, he had found himself so painfully faced. The election in November 1919 of the "sky blue" Chambre, Clemenceau's retirement the following year, or the Congress of Tours in December 1920—which saw the historic secession from Léon Blum's old, minority SFIO of the future French Communist Party under Marcel Cachin—were probably matters of as much indifference to him as the reopening of races at Longchamp on the very day of the signing of the Treaty of Versailles. In those frenetic years of the Charleston, short skirts, pageboy haircuts, silk stockings and jazz, Louis worked first and foremost on his medicine. His contemporaries wanted to raise hell. He tried to forget. His arm hurt. His headaches persisted. Édith briefly thought that the humming he complained of was caused by an earwax blockage. Air was blown into his ears in an attempt to dislodge it. The humming was amplified and never stopped.

His medical studies made up the essence of his activities in Rennes. They can be summed up very briefly. Five days after passing the PCN, he entered his name at the medical school for the first time, on April 1, 1920. On April 7, 1921, he passed his first exam, his second on July 22, 1921, and the third on November 16, 1922.[27] Tests that were easily passed by a student who was twenty-six when he entered the faculty and was thus considerably older than his friends, who were struck by his distance, his reserve, his offhand manner and his wide-brimmed felt hat. One of them thought he had the silhouette of Aristide Bruant as immortalized by Toulouse-Lautrec. "His head and one shoulder lowered, he seemed to want to knock down doors instead of opening them."[28] But at the hospital he manifested that astonishing and indispensable ease for communicating with the patient and winning his or her trust. Furthermore, his father-in-law's clinical tutoring, of incontestable quality, was of great benefit to him. In his little laboratory, the latter, aside from his traditional functions, devoted himself to research on the Koch bacillus or glycemia dosage. Louis, indefatigably curious, a seeker in every direction, was part of the entourage that followed him even into that secret garden.

Louis himself, during his 1920 summer vacation in Roscoff, had already performed experiments in a marine zoology laboratory and, in October, written a report on the *Convoluta Roscoffensis* that was presented by Edmond Perrier, the director of the Museum of Natural History, whom he certainly knew through his uncle Georges Destouches, to the Académie des Sciences. Observing his "convoluta" or vermicules fixed within algae, Louis noticed a stronger resistance to the hypertonia or hypotonia of their environment in correlation to temperature. In the words of François Balta, "we should see in this experiment a reflection of the correspondence shared with Alexis Carrel since Louis' participation in the Rockefeller Mission, a correspondence that touched on methods prefiguring artificial hibernation."[29]

In April 1921, again through Edmond Perrier's intermediacy, Louis proposed to the Académie des Sciences a new report on "Extension of life in *Galleria Mellonella*," in which, still as a correlative to temperature, he studied the longevity of or slowing-down of life in caterpillars. André Lwoff, future Nobel Prize–winner for medicine in 1965, who had met Louis Destouches in Roscoff in 1920, was struck by the absence of any bibliographical references in the young student's two reports. "It's easier that way and you avoid unpleasant surprises. Both publications show a certain haste and a no less certain naiveté of thought and expression. The whole corresponds fairly well to the image which the writer would draw, bluntly, in the *Voyage* and which, paradoxically, is his own image."[30]

But before leaving Rennes and medical school, Louis had already gone to Paris, on October 1, 1922, for obstetrics training at the Tarnier maternity hospital under Professor Brindeau, a training course which earned him a *mention bien*.

Finally, on December 5, he was authorized to pursue his studies in Paris.

Semmelweis

In January 1923 Louis went through a surgical training course with Professor Delbet at the Cochin Hospital. On February 15 he took his fourth doctoral exam, which he partially failed with evaluations of "mediocre" in hygiene (which cannot fail to surprise those who are familiar with the hygienic obsessions he would manifest as doctor and writer, and which he had already revealed as a member of the Rockefeller Mission) and "bad" in therapeutics, materia medica and pharmacology with applications in the physical and natural sciences. But on April 10 he remedied the failure by landing a *mention bien* in the same exams.[31] Henceforth, all he had left to do was to complete his clinical tests and write his dissertation.

On May 3 he passed internal clinical medicine with a *mention bien*, on June 27 his external clinical medicine exam, again with a *mention bien*, on June 29 that of obstetrics, in which his examiners seemed more reticent.[32] He was authorized nonetheless to defend his dissertation, and while, back in Rennes, he devoted the second half of 1923 to his internship from June 1 to August 31 with Dr. Porée at 5, quai Lamennais (while at the same time passing his final two clinical exams in Paris), from August 18 to October 31 at the La Sagesse clinic run by his father-in-law and, again, from January 23 to February 23 with Dr. Porée, who felt a friendly fascination for the young intern, so unusual, more anticonformist and brilliant than helpful to a clientele that sometimes suffered from ills too benign for him to bother to be truly interested in.

Louis was thus bouncing back and forth between Rennes and Paris, leaving Édith, rejoining her, an unstable husband and a moderately attentive father. The young couple already felt itself an old couple, if not an ex-couple. Its future was behind it. Its happiness too. Édith could expect nothing more from this most whimsical, elusive man who could live just as well without her, as she must have come to understand pretty quickly. She retained a dazzled memory, moments of uneasy wonder, but, decidedly, she was not up to him. She was too quiescent, too domestic, too protected, no doubt about it. She preferred the tranquillity of her drawing room on the quai Richemont, where she could paint, dream, wait, oversee the education of her daughter, Colette, to Louis' wildly magical and destructive turbulence. Later, after her divorce, she would marry (May 15, 1930) a colonel in the French army and things would work out nicely that way, she hoped. She decided to keep nothing but her best memories of Louis, never recriminating and never forgetting.

But let us return to the years 1923–1924. His medical studies coming to an end, a great time of decision-making was beginning for Louis. What to do? Set up practice as a general practitioner, aspire to succeed his father-in-law in Rennes? The latter, who had sized up his son-in-law perfectly, was not keen on it. Louis was even less so. Take up a medical speciality? He may have considered psychiatry or pediatrics, but those were short-lived plans. Devote himself more exclusively to research? He spent some time at the Institut Pasteur in November 1923 (after having momentarily considered working at the Villejuif Cancer Institute and moving to Paris where Édith could join him).[33] His father-in-law had commended him to Émile Roux of the Institut Pasteur, who introduced him to the researcher Serge Metalnikov. But Louis spent a scant few weeks in the latter's laboratory. He took an immediate dislike to the Institut and to those who worked there. Bearing witness to that dislike are the ferociously comical pages of *Voyage au bout de la nuit* in which the Institut Pasteur becomes the "Bioduret Joseph," Émile Roux and Serge Metalnikov the notorious Jaunisset and Parapine, grotesque, smooth-tongued, impotent and senile scientists among so many losers, pathetic pen-pushers of Research and other "graying schoolboys with umbrellas, stupefied by the meticulous routine, the disgusting experiments, pinned down by starvation wages for the rest of their lives in those little microbe kitchens, endlessly reheating that stew of vegetable scrapings, asphyxiated guinea pigs and other dubious spoilage."[34]

André Lwoff, with his wide experience in that matter, would later fully confirm the barely altered precision of the description: ". . . the figure of the 'high secretary' Jaunisset, the mania of the scientist Parapine, the habits of the old laboratory assistant, the places, the smells . . . it all re-creates that famous place, truer than life itself."[35]

What to choose, then? One final respite remained to him: his dissertation. The subject had been suggested to him by Professor Brindeau, with whom he had completed his obstetrics training, and by his father-in-law. The end of '23 and the early months of '24 saw him working with dedication on *The Life and Work of Philippe-Ignace Semmelweis (1818–1865)*.

It wasn't that he wanted to get the work over with as quickly as possible, nor that he felt himself the victim of the historian's interminable scruples in sniffing out his sources. Above all, the personality of Semmelweis fascinated him, as if, in him, he had suddenly come across a kind of double in the idealized, distorting, and grandiosely tragic mirror of history and of an uncommon destiny. And for Louis, this work (though he may not have been really conscious of it) was also the work of a writer, a stylist, a visionary. Whence the crucial importance of those early months of 1924, when one has the impression of Louis hesitating, as if faced with an accomplishment and a promise, an achievement and an exit, an end and a beginning. What was it he was completing at the time? His last steps as a medical student or his first in a literary career?

His entire dissertation rests on that ambiguity. Who is speaking here? In whose name? A student wanting to display the extent of his knowledge? A (future) doctor examining the life of another doctor? A budding writer already determined to show off his virtuosity? A young, disenchanted moralist striving to tell an awful and thus exemplary story? In those early months of 1924, we sense that Louis Destouches had made an appointment with Céline, that they were already all there, the bantering medical student in a bad marriage, the author-to-be of *Voyage*, the pamphleteering vocifera-tor, and the man obsessed with medical problems linked to hygiene.

We can sum up his dissertation—the life of Semmelweis—in a few lines. A Hungarian doctor, master surgeon, and obstetrician, Semmelweis in 1846 had been named assistant professor of one of the two maternity wards of the central almshouse of Vienna. He was immediately struck by the terrible mortality rate of women in labor and by the ravages of puerperal fever. Following various experiments, Semmelweis attributed the death rate to the dirty fingers of students assisting the doctors during childbirth. In the second maternity ward where he later worked, he required that all students' hands be "deodorized" by washing them in a chloride of lime (bleaching powder) solution, and deaths by puerperal fever fell practically to zero. Semmelweis had invented prophylaxis. He was the inspired father of anti-sepsis. But no one in Vienna—or in Europe—was willing to believe him. He was driven from his position. He was prevented from putting his theories into practice. Madness overtook him, as well as persecution mania. He died in confinement (and of an infected wound) on August 16, 1865.

What a subject! What a character! In his dissertation, Louis emphasized Semmelweis' inner workings over his discoveries. He wanted to explore his conscience, to wax lyrical over a kindred spirit, a victim, a comforter, a creature of misery. In many aspects, *Semmelweis* is the youthful work of Céline, the mirror book, the confession book. *Semmelweis* is a portrait of the artist as a nineteenth-century Hungarian doctor.

Let us listen, for instance, to the writer's confessions: "Those who must create marvelous things could never draw from one or two specific emo-tions the affective forces that enflame their extraordinary destinies. Mysti-cal bonds link them to all that exists, all that throbs with life, all that holds, often chains, them to a sacred enthusiasm. Unlike most of us, they never reach the point of considering the wife or the child whom we love as the most vibrant part of our *raison d'être*."[36]

Preparing to abandon his wife and daughter to flee to Geneva and work at the League of Nations, feeling himself imprisoned, stifling under the yoke of family and bourgeois conformity, wasn't Louis Destouches attempting in these words to justify himself—consciously or not—through Semmelweis?

"To force one's dreams to their very limit is to live in a world of discovery, it is to see in the night,"[37] he would write further about the Hungarian doctor. And Destouches-Céline himself was soon to plunge into the night, to force his dream to the most convulsive plane ever attained in literature. Like Semmelweis, Céline was to be a midwife, a novelistic inventor of forms and characters; he was, in a way, to give his life so as better to examine the brief and atrocious respite, to attend, as a penniless, angry novelist, as the doctor of the derisive, to every rattle and twitch of death.

Historically, also to be noted are traits already indicative of Célinian writing. Certainly, the style is still measured, continuous, occasionally lyrical. But we cannot ignore the gripping intuitiveness of his shortcuts or of his acrobatic metaphors. In evoking the French Revolution and the death of Louis XVI, he notes: "As his head was lopped off, a new feeling gushed forth: Equality." A bit earlier: "Death howled in the bloody froth of his ill-matched legions."[38] As a general rule in the dissertation, feeling overshadows knowledge, emotion overshadows education. Enchantment contrasts with horror, the lightness of the dance with the dead weight of human existence, the unattainable dream with ineluctable agony. Céline was never to escape that duality, to which death, naturally, always puts a victorious end.

"Down through the ages, life has been but an intoxication, the truth is death." In the long run, all of Céline's books will reapply that sentence from *Semmelweis*, modifying it, modulating it, quartering it, turning it over, magnifying it based on the hazards of autobiographical inspiration, so as to lift it to the level of one of the greatest novelistic oeuvres of the century.

We must wonder in passing about the reactions to this dissertation of those who read it at the time, first among whom were the members of the board to whom he dedicated his work: Professor Brindeau, his dissertation adviser; Professor Follet, his father-in-law; Professor Selskar Gunn of the Rockefeller Foundation, who had once hired Louis as lecturer/interpreter; and lastly Henri Maréchal. On May 1, 1924, the board awarded him a *mention très bien* (excellent). But how much importance had it accorded to the role of the stylistic inventiveness of the future Céline, to the occasionally overdone metaphors, to the author's bitter glee in describing the horrible destiny of Dr. Semmelweis, crushed prophet, accursed benefactor? For the dissertation's "medical" qualities, in actual fact, do seem thin. There are few scientific reflections on the works of Semmelweis; it is, rather, a biography put together with some hastily assembled documentation. In a word, was the board benevolent as a general rule, or just an ably selected group of literate men enjoying a study as brilliant as it was nonconformist?

Whatever the case, the work was highly acclaimed by the medical world. Louis had it published at his own expense by Francis Simon in Rennes. He was awarded a bronze medal on January 22, 1925. But as early as June 25, 1924, Louis had prepared a shorter version which he published in *La Presse Médicale* under the title "The Last Days of Semmelweis." On September 10, in the same review, a Hungarian physician, Tiberius de Györi, replied to Louis Destouches, pointing out errors in dates and names, the author's approximations and exaggerations, his tendency to emphasize the tragic. For instance, the death statistics for women in labor at Klin's (actually Klein) were not 96%, but ranged from 16% to 31%. Or anything to do with Semmelweis' death. "The whole scene around the corpse is pure fantasy," he wrote.

Pure fantasy, that's it! Dr. Destouches was already applying to historical facts the lesson that Céline would later exercise within writing itself: to blur the edges or jostle words, vociferate, magnify everything and draw it toward delirium so as to create a sense of emotion or indignation or fear or anxiety or love or revulsion or hatred or tenderness. To force dream through reality.

Let us read the last two paragraphs of the preface to that 1924 dissertation.

"The sad hour always arrives when Happiness, that absurd and superb trust in life, gives way to Truth in the human heart.

"Amongst all our brothers, is it not our role to look that terrible Truth in the face, in the most wise and useful way? And it is perhaps our calm intimacy with their greatest secret which the pride of men forgives the least."[39]

This text—this profession of faith—is marvelously vague. Is it for the physician to face that terrible Truth? Certainly. But wasn't Louis Destouches already thinking of Céline, of the writer whom he would be and who would himself sweep Happiness away, minutely examine his models, his characters, in order to overtake that calm intimacy with their greatest secret—their birth, their agony, their death—and who would provoke such indignation?

On May 1, 1924, it was Louis Destouches who defended his dissertation, but it was a writer who was being born.

The problem of a career still remained for Dr. Destouches. Once again serendipity facilitated his choice. In Paris, Professor Gunn had introduced him to Dr. Ludwig Rajchman, director of the Health Section at the League of Nations in Geneva. An immediate plan was formed for a collaboration between the two men, for Céline to be hired to work with Rajchman. The League of Nations, investigative work, foreign missions, especially to the United States—all of this suddenly enflamed Louis' imagination. It suited his curiosity as well as his taste for travel. The idea of new experiences, his fascination with America, which he had long thought about but had never been able to visit, and above all the fact of escaping Rennes and the quai Richemont, yes, everything about the plan was seductive.

He interrupted a new medical internship in Montmort-sur-le-Meu (Ille-et-Vilaine) to sit for and pass the competitive exam in maritime sanitary medicine. In the meantime he had written and rewritten to Rajchman, had sent him the abridgment of his dissertation published in *La Presse Médicale*, had renewed the deferential and zealous offers of his candidacy.

On June 27, officially employed by the Rockefeller Foundation, he was put no less officially at the disposal of the Health Section of the League of Nations, run by Ludwig Rajchman.

He would never return to Rennes.

7

Final Preparations
Before the "Journey"

From Geneva to New York
Breaking With the League of Nations
The Church
Paris, Progress, Suburbs

From Geneva to New York

In reference to Louis Destouches' doctoral dissertation on Semmelweis, Professor Brindeau said of his student: "You know, he's made for this. . . . He's made to write. . . . That's all there is to it."[1]

And writing was what the young doctor enlisted in the Health Section of the League of Nations would be doing from the word go. Writing and more writing, endlessly, report after report, notes and memorandums *ad nauseam, ad absurdam*. Literature would come later, along with the taste for exaggeration, caricature, metaphor, fables, careful style, and digression. Literature was not on the agenda in Geneva. The agenda was committees, subcommittees, and ever more reports to write and rewrite even flatter, more neutral, more concise, more sycophantic, more stodgy, more embued with confidence and self-importance. Writing and nothing else. Brindeau didn't know how right he had been. Or how wrong.

And yet it had all started out rather well for Louis Destouches. In late June he had moved into the fine modern hotel La Résidence, at 9 route de Florissant in Geneva. He was leaving behind a bourgeois and provincial routine too somnolent for his liking, a wife too well-behaved, a little girl whom he certainly loved but had not really wanted, since his pessimism jibed poorly with the symbol of hope and trust in life that is the desire for children—that bond, that constraint so incompatible with his ever-muddled dreams of freedom. Nor did he have the slightest nostalgia for France, which didn't interest him, for that mediocre and confused political life that he had halfheartedly observed, without paying much attention. The occupation of the Ruhr in January 1923, what was that all about? Poincaré-la-Guerre ("Poincaré the Warlike") clamored against the Communist Party. Electing the Leftist Coalition—what if it were all for nothing? Who cared if Gaston Doumergue became president of the Republic on May 24, or if Édouard Herriot succeeded Poincaré to the presidency of the Conseil? Louis Destouches was royally sick of it all. It all seemed like a barely less futile distraction than the Olympic Games that were to open a few days later in Paris, in an era when one had to reach only 13 feet in the pole vault, jump 24 feet, or run the 110-meter hurdles in 15 seconds to pick up a gold medal under the plaudits of the crowd worn out by the heat wave. Louis was arriving alone in a foreign country, with a monthly salary of 1,000 Swiss francs to start and the sonorous title of Health Section Physician Class B. He found himself face-to-face with the League of Nations, with Power, with International Life, with every possible capital letter. His unquestionable ambition, his will, his hopes, his taste for the unknown were all in their element, no doubt about it. Better yet, his boss, Ludwig Rajchman, had promised him a foreign mission soon, to America, that distant, ancient dream. Yes, Switzerland was beautiful in the summer of '24.

In that great modern palace in Geneva, which even in those days would have been difficult to qualify as Nazi or Stalinist architecture, were grafted onto the Assembly and the Secretariat, the central organs of the League, all the other constellations, some judicial and political, others of a social or economic character, such as an international labor organization, a communications and transport organization, another for intellectual cooperation, not to mention the offices devoted to controlling drug trafficking, abolishing slavery, dealing with the problem of refugees throughout the world, and finally a World Health Organization, to which the famous Health Section was annexed. That is where we'll find Louis Destouches.

And, indeed, there he was. He believed in it. To his friend Milon he writes: "You see—this is where you'll find your old Louis— Here, in the international hive— I am stubborn, you know that— here I am. This time I'm taking on the most far-reaching problems of public health, and my God how I love it."[2]

But not for long. The bureaucracy was going to come down on him, finicky, suffocating, impersonal, absurd. That, at least, is how Louis felt it, experienced it, and later described it. And that is essential. At heart Louis was a man of infrequent enthusiasms and crashing disappointments, as if he wanted to punish with a fit of bitterness the shiver of optimism—that unforgivable sin, that incomprehensible failing of his duty to be lucid—that had earlier cradled it. In any case we have a hard time figuring out what Louis Destouches, indefatigable dreamer, hunter of chimera with the leering phantoms of death at his side, was doing at the League. Taking on problems of public health on a planetary scale? Having done with the France of notables, notaries, subprefects in tailcoats and presidents of the Republic in pajamas, like Deschanel in May 1920, found wandering along the tracks near Montargis, having fallen from the train in the middle of the night? But that was to forget that Geneva was far more provincial than Paris, that the Lake was not an ocean, and that the Health Section had not been set up to cure the world but to grind out endless reports.

His boss's name, then, was Ludwig Rajchman, a little man of forty-three, heart to the Left, mind upright, and body always on the go, of Polish Jewish origins, a graduate of the medical faculty of Cracow who had studied at the Institut Pasteur in Paris and then in London before returning to Poland, where he had run the National School of Public Health and the Central Polish Institute of Epidemiology. A member of the epidemics committee at the League, on November 1, 1921, he was assigned by the secretary-general, Sir Eric Drummond, to direct the international Health Organization.

This methodical man of unquestionable medical and administrative talents was apparently not put off by Louis' character, his Bohemian self-assurance, his obvious lack of rigor, his impertinence. The young postulant must certainly have taken pains to present a well-behaved and reassuring façade. But we can also believe that his charm, his seductiveness, and his intelligence were not lost on Ludwig Rajchman, who would later show him such affectionate and faithful solicitude.

"He (Dr. Rajchman) welcomed Louis with an enthusiasm that contrasted strongly with the strained, British-style courtesy expected at the League. He warmly opened his home to him and introduced him to his wife, who loved to talk about literature and was dazzled by his conversation."[3]

It has often been noted that Ludwig Rajchman was like a father to Louis Destouches–Céline, a Jewish father whom he was to betray cruelly. Céline's "betrayal," the caricature he drew of Rajchman with his racist epithets, can be found on certain pages of *L'Église* [The Church] and *Bagatelles pour un massacre*. He elaborated to the point of burlesque, of caricature, what he had observed in Geneva. But, most importantly, it is solely to Rajchman's allegedly "Jewish" character that he attributes his personality traits, his attitudes, and his faults—Rajchman, who becomes Yudenzweck in the play and Yubelblat in the pamphlet. Céline's special brand of anti-Semitism was already evident. The League of Nations seemed to him like a Jewish affair, an unreal, stateless, and somewhat terrifying ballet. We'll come back to that.

"Gotta give him his due, Yubelblat was a lot less rotten than the others, the way great scientists can be, a lot less petty, less moronic, less pretentious. He had all the tricks down pat. He didn't waste time raving in front of his mirror. But he was erratic, like all true foreskinned folk, he couldn't stay in one place. He had to map things out, lay claims. His favorite kind of trip was to China . . . He went to militate there . . . He'd make a quick hop over to Japan . . . He'd get some little business going . . . And then he'd come home double-quick . . . He'd cross the entire planet for a telegram, a sigh . . . a nothing . . . He was passing through Russia again . . . He wasn't passing through Russia . . . He was coming back via the South. He'd catch up with his telegram . . . his sigh . . . his little nothing. And then wham! He'd just show up! one morning! I'd find him suddenly! behind his desk . . . He'd emerge from the other end of the world . . . just like that . . . He was playing the wandering Jew, the will-o'-the-wisp, the eccentric . . . In order to think, he'd stop, behind his specs, he'd sway forward . . . ever so gently on his shoes . . . regular boats . . . like a pendulum. . . . He was endlessly supple . . . remarkable to look at, but at the tips of his fingers, for instance, he also had claws . . . and poisonous ones like the ornithorhynchus . . . You had to have known him for quite a while before he'd show them to you . . . trust wasn't his weak point . . . Anyway, I can't claim that I was bored under his command . . . That would be lying. . . . In the end he managed to train me, I wrote really clever, amphigorical like a sub-Proust, a quarter-Giraudoux, a para-Claudel . . . I tripped along circumlocuting, I wrote like a Jew, a fashionable and contemporary *bel esprit* . . . dialecticulating . . . elliptical, delicately reticent, dull, schooled, moulded, elegant like all the fine shit, the Francongourt Academies and Anal fistulas."[4]

Céline speaks of training. We begin to understand what he means when we read a little brochure entitled *Quinine in Therapeutics*, signed by Dr. Louis Destouches (of Paris), published by Doin in June 1925, and which was most likely written in Geneva under the inspiration of Dr. Rajchman as a work-to-order, an exercise in style. Supporting that hypothesis is the uncustomary and flat neutrality of style, contrasting so highly with the first pyrotechnic bursts of *Semmelweis*, as well as the determined banality of the little piece, a humble work of historical compilation and classification without a hint of new research or a new idea. The League of Nations, in any case, financed translations of the brochure into Spanish, Italian, and Portuguese during the following years.

Meanwhile there was as yet no talk of divorce between Louis and Édith. But the idea was in the air, a sense that something had been broken, that it was too late, that Louis would emphatically never be a domesticated husband, a vigilant family man, a fireside spouse. Édith, of course, wanted to live with him in Geneva, that was her first thought. On several occasions she made the interminable journey by train to the hotel La Résidence with little Colette. But she was in the way. Louis made little effort to conceal that fact. He was thirty years old, had a good job, an impressive calling card which he shamelessly abused—he was hardly going to spend his evenings, let alone his nights, going through dossiers or writing reports. He could dine in town, pursue the female personnel at the League with his impatient assiduity, fall into debt, have fun, act up and shock the bourgeois or diplomatic world between two migraines and two nasty fits of despair. Édith, during this time, would remain alone at the hotel with her daughter, who bore a striking resemblance to her father. What was there to do in Geneva in the winter? Nothing. Colette was much too young to take to the cinema. Édith waited. And she ended up taking the train home with the girl. A few months later Louis wrote to her again, asking her to come back to him. She returned, docile, for a few days. He loved her in his own way. From afar. He willingly told her about his affairs. "I will not deceive you," he told her. His honesty earned him absolution, he believed. All this was so petty! Hardly convinced, she left once more, wounded and discouraged.

And 1924 came to an end. Kafka died in June. Joseph Conrad in August. In October, Anatole France, whom Louis had read and, at the time, loved so much. In Geneva, meanwhile, lost beneath the paperwork, a writer's birth was being delayed. While waiting, he had thoughts only for the United States.

Let us skip over a brief stay in Paris, between January 19 and 21, 1925, the purpose of which was essentially to initiate negotiations in connection with the mission to Africa in 1926. Louis was assigned there specifically to get in touch with a certain Dr. Abbatucci, assistant director of the Health Service of the Colonial Ministry, in order to stimulate by way of an exchange the growth of health facilities already extant in the English, French, and Portuguese colonies that stretched from Mauritania to Spanish Guinea, and to write a monograph on the organization and functioning of public health services in the French colonies.[5] But the big deal, once again, was the United States.

He was to accompany a group of eight South American doctors first across North America and then across various European countries in order that, with the approval and participation of the local authorities, they might visit the main achievements in matters of public health and industrial medicine of the countries traversed. The mission was to last five and a half months (three of which on the New Continent) and naturally required detailed preparation. Everything was ready when, on February 14, Ludwig Rajchman finally "liberated" his young protégé, who embarked at Cherbourg aboard the *Minnetonka*, bound for New York.

Louis was expecting a shock. The truth was even more dizzying. Here was the New World, with its prodigious vitality, its crowds, its architecture, its poverty, its opulence, its cynicism, its women so beautiful you didn't know where to begin, and its endless factories. . . . The New World and New York first: "Just imagine, their city was standing up, absolutely straight. New York is a city on its feet. We had already seen a town or two, sure, and some beauties too, and even some magnificent ports. But at home, our cities are lying down, aren't they, along the seashore or the riverbanks, they stretch themselves across the land, awaiting the traveler, whereas this American city wasn't swooning at all, no, she was standing there good and stiff, not at all seductive, frighteningly stiff."[6]

These pages from *Voyage au bout de la nuit* are in no way an exaggeration. That, indeed, is how Dr. Destouches, having left the *Minnetonka* and settled into the McAlpine Hotel, lived his first four days in the city, from February 24 to 28, before going to Cuba in early March to meet the colleagues he was to lead on tour—New York all revved up at the time with electioneering excitement (on March 4 President Coolidge would be elected to a second term), New York and Broadway, "like a dismal wound, that endless street," and Manhattan too, "one neighborhood of which is filled with gold, a real miracle, and you can even hear the miracle through the doors with its sound of dollars being crumpled, the dollar itself always too fickle, a real Holy Ghost, more precious than blood . . . ."[7] New York and its women, finally—radiant, athletic, unbound by gravity, like goddesses and who, for him, were like a moment of supernatural aesthetic revelation.

New York, the standing city, the erect city and its women—we touch here on one of the writer's most burning and recurrent sexual fantasies: "These apparitions seemed all the more divine to me in that they appeared totally unaware of my existence on the next bench, all senile and drooling with erotico-mystical admiration, quinine and, I must admit, hunger as well. If it were possible to leave one's skin, I would have left mine at that very moment, once and for all. There was nothing holding me back. They could take me away, sublimate me, these unbelievable shopgirls, all they had to do was make one move, say one word, and in that moment I would have fallen whole into the world of dreams, but I guess they had other things to do."[8]

Céline is yet again speaking in extremes, from the deepest intimacy of his imagination. Ten years later he would write to a friend: "Life here in the United States is out of all proportion. The beauty of the women is as immense as everything else."[9]

Immense. America in his eyes was simply immense. With its paradoxes, its infernos and paradises, its beautiful women and phony dreams. And nothing was better able to sum that up than the Broadway movie theaters into which Bardamu plunges as if into an erotic ecstasy. The choice of metaphors is sufficiently explicit. "It was nice in that theater, cozy and warm. An enormous organ, as gentle as in a basilica, or at least a heated basilica, pipes like thighs. Not a moment lost, you plunge headfirst into warm forgiveness. . . . Dreams rise through the night to catch fire in the mirage of moving light. What's happening on the screen is not quite alive, inside it there's still a great, murky hole for the poor, for dreams, and for the dead. You have to hurry to stuff yourself on dreams to get through the life that's waiting for you outside the cinema, to survive a few more days in that atrocity of things and men. You choose among them the dreams that will keep your soul the warmest."[10]

New York seemed to him as immense as a promise or a lie. The Roaring Twenties roared louder there than elsewhere, the Charleston was more bedeviled, the mechanical fury more thunderous, the Broadway girls more bewitching, the neon billboards more blinding, and the movie screens more enveloping. How could he have avoided getting careless?

Louis Destouches, careless—that's a new one. It had begun sometime before, during his preparations for departure. Louis had left not only some of his luggage in Geneva, but also the addresses of the banks in Havana, New Orleans, New York, and Toronto where the several thousands of dollars necessary to his journey and that of his companions were deposited. Rajchman must have smiled indulgently at this symptomatic carelessness. He answered ironically: "I was not in the least surprised that you had left certain essentials of your wardrobe at La Résidence, but I never would have believed that you could forget the address of the bank where your fortune was to be deposited. . . . Why don't you send us a long cablegram listing all your various oversights, which you have certainly filed in your pocket notebook."[11]

After a brief round trip to Washington to settle the final details with a medical official of the public health service, Louis soon left New York for

Cuba, where he landed on March 1. There he met the nine doctors whom he was to guide, natives respectively of Mexico, Cuba, Venezuela, Paraguay, El Salvador, Brazil, Uruguay, and Peru.

What is there to say of this stay other than that it inaugurated on a sound footing what was to be Louis' and his companions' itinerary throughout their long forthcoming tour: a dizzying dance of visits, receptions, lectures, dinners, inquiries: one moment a tour of a hospital or laboratory for anti-typhoid serums and vaccines, the next that of an antituberculosis center, followed immediately by a speech concerning the water service, a visit to nursing homes, rural dwellings, or to an indispensable center for anti-venereal prophylaxis.

On March 9 the group left Cuba. On the 12th it reached New Orleans for a new excursion through Louisiana, Mississippi, and Alabama. The South American doctors couldn't go on. Dairies to visit or commercial oyster hatcheries, luncheons or dinners offered by the Chamber of Commerce of every town passed through, hospitals for handicapped children, schools for deaf-mutes, sanatoria, de-ratting establishments, salt mines, paper mills to examine, from Morgan City to Jackson, from New Iberia to Shreveport. . . . The group swept along like a tornado, led by the indefatigable Louis Destouches, while a little farther north, in Missouri, Illinois, and Indiana, another tornado, a real one, was ravaging the countryside, destroying towns and killing thousands. But that's another story.

A satirical echo of the story of their too-speedy trip (comparable to the African excursion soon to come), can be found in *Bagatelles pour un massacre*: "Whenever I became inquisitive, my great boss Yubelblat sent me away on a trip, on a study mission . . . That's how I did the continents in search of the truth. If travel molds the ripeness of one's age, I can say that I am well done. Crackling! how I traveled! to learn, to increase my knowledge! I've seen a few hospitals, compared a few laboratories! Ripped apart a few nurseries . . . seen some fine barracks at work! stormed through a few slaughterhouses! Admired many a crematorium! surveyed so many dairies, 'model' ones and some not so clean . . . from the Gold Coast to Chicago! and from Berg-op-Zoom to Cuba! I belong in the Institut, such are the things I've been taught, the techniques and worse yet . . . incredibly boring! . . . I should be almost perfect in ten thousand scientific matters on which I don't know a goddamn thing . . . I'm really one of the rankest jerks on the planet. That's how life is."[12]

After the southern United States, they went on to the Atlantic Coast and the North. New York on April 5, Washington the next day for a brief stay during which—on April 10 to be precise—President Coolidge received the delegation at the White House, paying no attention to the accompanying doctor from the League of Nations.

Back in New York, Louis Destouches and his companions began with a visit to a main sewer, to three slaughterhouses in the company of an inspector of food products, to a quarantine station on Staten Island, and to the immigration facilities on Ellis Island. Little by little, the familiar settings of *Voyage au bout de la nuit* were falling into place. Louis Destouches observed and Céline was to remember.... On Tuesday, April 28, on Pier 8 in Brooklyn, the New Yorkers extended their friendliness to the point of demonstrating to the attentive delegates the fumigation method used to de-rat ships.[13]

Then Bridgeport, New Haven, Waterbury, Hartford, Detroit, Pittsburgh.... But it is only the last two stages of the American excursion that concern us, because they were the object of a double report by Louis Destouches, the first following a visit to the Ford Factories on May 5 and 6, the second to the Westinghouse factory on the 8th.

Céline imposed some strange twists on the conclusions of his "Note on the Organization of the Ford Factories in Detroit"[14] in a lecture given to Parisian doctors in 1928, when he no longer belonged to the League, and then in *Voyage au bout de la nuit*, not to mention in his successive interviews. And a veritable legend has arisen concerning Céline and the Ford factories of Detroit, the writer not hesitating to embroider upon it, writing from Denmark to his Swedish friend Ernst Bendz that he had spent four years as a doctor in the U.S.,[15] managing to convince Robert Poulet and Henry Mondor, the editor responsible for the first Pléiade edition of *Voyage*, that he had even been a Ford house-doctor—a statement repeated in his conversation with Jean Guénot and Jacques Darribehaude.

What should we retain from the first report? Louis Destouches is especially impressed by the simplification and specialization on the automobile assembly line. The workers move in mechanical fashion, one or two gestures repeated around a machine and that's all: Chaplin had exaggerated nothing in *Modern Times*. But that is not the main thing. Such cretinization of labor allows all the flotsam, the old folk, invalids, to find work at the factory. "We attended the entrance exam of several hundred workers who had come to fill jobs vacant for six months. Hirings are held only a few times a year. We watched a clinical museum pass by us, no or almost no healthy ones, some completely down-and-out. Furthermore, the doctor in charge of admissions confided to us that 'what they needed were monkeys, that would be fine for the work they would be doing.' "[16]

Is Louis Destouches exaggerating? Probably. Employing exclusively handicapped workers does not seem to have been a Ford policy. But what is particularly striking is the report's conclusion, which, curiously, is not negative: "This state of things, where everything is accepted from a sanitary and even human point of view, is not at all disastrous for the time being, allowing a great number of people to survive who would not be able to do so outside of Ford's."

On the other hand, at the 1928 lecture, he sees the Ford system as a minor evil, just barely preferable to the system of health benefits then current in France. And in *Voyage au bout de la nuit*, everything topples resolutely into nightmare. Bardamu becomes acquainted with Hell in the Ford plant, in the exhausting roar of machinery. "You give in to the noise like you give in to war." All life is swept away in the deadening repetition of the same gestures. "We only existed in a kind of hesitation between stupor and dream. Nothing mattered except the shattering continuity of the thousands upon thousands of instruments that commanded the men."[17]

It was certainly not a report to the League of Nations that could express this other truth about America. We might well believe that Louis Destouches himself may not have understood it very clearly at the time. He was moving too fast, just skimming the surface, trapped as he was in his official capacity, distant and protected from life. . . . The hallucinatory vision of what daily life must really have been like for a Ford worker wouldn't come until later, when he was writing, *imagining*—from that power of imagination that is always so proximate to death. Whence the comical Célinian myths to justify in actuality, in the eyes of his interlocutors or correspondents, what he had imagined of the misery there.

After Detroit and Pittsburgh, the American tour ended with the inevitable family photo in front of Niagara Falls. There followed a dozen or so days in Canada, from May 9 to 21, for more visits and more receptions: Toronto, Ottawa, Montreal, Quebec. Finally, on May 22, the group embarked on the *Mont-Royal*, bound for Liverpool.

America had overwhelmed Louis Destouches. In 1935 he wrote to Eugène Dabit, who was planning a trip to New York: "I know of nothing more violent in the realm of oblivion. Nothing that buttresses our pride exists over there, and that's exactly what we need, humiliation, i.e., spiritual humility."[18] As if the individual suddenly ceased to exist on that country's scale. As if, in some way, in tribute to its stupendous vitality, the beauty of its women, the vigor of its industry, the fascination of its dream factories and enormous screens, one had to pay with the dissolution of one's personality, a return to anonymity, the man in the crowd. America, for Louis Destouches, symbolized progress. He discovered it, enthralled, in that spring of 1925. Of course, one is always enthralled by the very thing that threatens, and which one rejects. Céline was afraid of America as though it were a mirror reflecting the image of his own future. By the same token he was afraid of the League of Nations and the abstract choreography of delegates reigning over the people's welfare. After America he became a man of the past. Or, as he was to write in *L'Église*, "a fellow without collective importance, just barely an individual." His subsequent rebellion, with all its excesses, were born of that.

Breaking with the League of Nations

On the morning of May 30 Louis Destouches and the South American doctors finally arrived in Liverpool. But their mission of inquiry was far from over. New clinics, new conferences, new antituberculosis centers awaited them in the four corners of Europe. And London first of all.

Édith happened to be right there, and Louis was able to see her. She had certainly not thought of coming to meet him, she understood and was gradually learning to give him up, to stop hoping. She was suffering in jolts, in violent crises, the last feverish twitchings of a great love gone astray. She was simply spending a month with a friend, her dearest and closest friend, who had settled in England and whom she visited every year. This time in London, she fell victim to a violent crisis—she caught the mumps and had to be hospitalized. And it was from her hospital bed that she welcomed her husband, that she listened to him tell of America, talk, soliloquize endlessly, spill over with anecdotes, incidents, and trenchant judgments, profanity, and subtle caricatures, keep talking and not listening, enclose himself in his words so as not to see or hear the world, as if to reject it, which is perhaps as it should be with dyed-in-the-wool storytellers. . . .

Doubtless there was a good deal of haughty misanthropy, of disdain, and, more than disdain, of deep-rooted indifference in Céline toward the people he came across in society and to whom he intimated, in his finely modulated voice, by an irresistible, unpredictable, eruptive, ferocious, grousing, grumbling, and imposing sense of humor, the order to keep silent. Every testimony throughout the writer's life bears witness to it: we must think of Céline first and foremost in terms of the spoken word. From another angle, he was really interested only in people who could hold their tongues: patients, the humble, the suffering, prisoners (not to mention animals, of course, the cats and dogs, those who are "witchcraft itself, the sense of touch in waves," to use his own words). Only these, paradoxically, would he take the time to listen to, to sound out, to understand. This man of language mistrusted the words, messages, and verbal fantasies that he used shamelessly, as if he were shooting off linguistic fireworks for the fun of it, elevating a screen of words and sounds, a smokescreen behind which it was quiet enough to apprehend the world. His was a strange split between reality and words. Perhaps he spoke in a totally irresponsible way. He had trouble understanding that his statements had any impact, any connection with reality. His life and later involvements will provide myriad examples of that. Already with Édith, we will recall, he seemed astonished that his brutal, wounding, and cynical words distressed her. He would then backpedal, erasing with new words the upset he had caused, but he didn't understand. That had nothing to do with it. Words were a game, the opposite of life. With Édith, he would never discuss the essential thing: the affection he sincerely felt for her, and for Colette, too, whom he had not wanted. No, as they say, these are things we don't mention.

From London, Louis went to Geneva for a few days. He had to account to Rajchman for the first months of the tour. His bookkeeping may have been less than precise. What had happened to the funds allocated to a South American doctor who, in the end, had not been part of the group? Little matter, since his traveling companions were pleased with him. One of them had written to Rajchman from Montreal: "Dr. Destouches goes to great pains and all the delegates are grateful to him," while, in a speech, another had exclaimed: "I should also like to express my thanks to Doctor Rajchman and to his colleague Doctor Destouches, who has been tireless, courageous and who, with his astute and critical mind, has on more than one occasion provided the group with excellent ideas."[19] All told, Ludwig Rajchman could be pleased with his protégé. The proof: he raised his salary by 250 francs a month. Louis couldn't ask for anything more. The South Americans were waiting for him in the Netherlands. He packed his bag. He jumped on a train. The exhausting medicohygienic gymkhana was to continue on from Holland to Belgium, from Switzerland to France.

At this stage let us skip the details of the visits to The Hague, Amsterdam, Brussels, Berne, Lille, Dunkirk, and Zuydcoote in late June and early July 1925. Let us catch up with the group in Paris, where they were more likely to have been seduced by the Moulin Rouge or the Casino de Paris than by their visit to the crematory oven at Père-Lachaise, the slaughterhouses of Vaugirard, or the capital's sewer system—Paris still reeling from the impact of the great International Exhibition of Decorative Arts opened on April 29.

That year, while Drieu La Rochelle was publishing *L'Homme couvert de femmes* [The Man Covered with Women], a title which the enterprising Louis Destouches could hardly have rejected, the group reached the south, Lyon and later Turin, near the end of July. Italy awaited them. The South American doctors could take no more. The storm threatened—mutiny. One more quinine factory to inspect and they were ready to chuck it all in, to give up the clinics and sanatoria and take shelter in the fortified castle of Ferrara, to see only the mosaics in Ravenna and only the Borghese Gallery in Rome. Louis therefore deemed it prudent to lighten their agenda considerably. At least he tried to do so. But try convincing the Italian organizers that the Nettuno school of malariology, the Ferrara hydraulic works, the tower to be used to raise sparrows in Terracino, the great Mussolinian effort to drain the Pontine marshes and fight malaria are not of the greatest interest. "Decidedly, the organizers are incorrigible. . . . Alas, we are seeing Italy under the worst conditions—our powers of admiration considerably diminished by six months of 'sightseeing' and Saharan heat."[20] Exhausted, the group broke up on August 8, heaving a sigh of relief.

In Geneva, Louis returned to Ludwig Rajchman, the great palace of the League of Nations, administrative tasks, the La Résidence hotel, the limited distractions afforded by the lakeshore, and to wait for a new departure, for Africa, which explains the brief preparatory trips to Paris, Brussels, and The Hague in late '25 and January '26.

Thus did the months pass, inactivity, inertia, and boredom following upon the exhausting course of the American and European tour. Things always went this way for Louis Destouches, and the same would apply to Céline: a life marked by hesitation, a palpitation between running and stopping, haste and torpor, illusion and dejection, curiosity and boredom, an opening out to the world and the tragic and solitary withdrawal into writing. Louis Destouches had wanted America, he had got it, and was soon tired of it. In Geneva he was back in his old lodgings and habits. Only to begin immediately dreaming about his next mission, to Africa as it happens. But had he been offered an expedition to China, Australia, Jutland, the moon, or Patagonia, he would have accepted without hesitation. Only to begin dreaming immediately afterward about the inaccessible well-being of home, silence, and the lucid privileges of motionlessness.

In late December '25, Louis moved: one takes whatever opportunity for change is available. He left La Résidence for a three-room apartment on the chemin de Miremont, in Champel, a residential suburb of Geneva. A peaceful, drowsy setting, a nice straight street, verdant, lined by three-story houses before which lay sober little gardens hemmed by box-cut hedges. All in all, a prosperous, whispering neighborhood for Swiss contented with their lot, whose incomes were as gracefully rounded as their bellies, and where we have to imagine a French doctor of thirty-one, abrupt, noisy, desperately consuming new books, pursuing new and futile feminine conquests, lampooning the absentminded bureaucrats of the bloated, outsized League of Nations, and who wanted to leave his mark, dig a deep and painful furrow into the epoque he had yet to pass through.

In Champel, Germaine Constans, his friend from the Rennes years and a close friend of Francis Vareddes, came to join him. She was accompanying little Colette, assigned to take care of her for a few weeks. Was she Louis' mistress before she was his friend? It would seem that Constans' tastes inclined her more toward women than men. But the fact is not a determining one. More a voyeur than active participant, Louis readily allowed his women to entertain lesbian relations in front of him. He may even have chosen them by that criterion. Sapphic spectacles, amongst other erotic combinations, excited his curiosity. But once again, there is nothing that allows us to second-guess a relationship between Louis and Germaine Constans. In 1978, with all the vagueness appropriate to distant memories, the latter was to say of that trip: "Dr. Rajchman had a daughter and hoped to marry them ... Louis already had the whole *Voyage* in his head, but he wasn't writing yet ... He was buying a lot of antique things, even a bed of gilt wood!"[21]

Édith, for her part, had renounced going to Geneva. To what purpose? Her husband was eluding her. Her husband had eluded her. She had also renounced her husband, and she now had to give some thought to divorce. Did her father urge her down that path? This has often been claimed, but nothing could be less certain. After all, Athanase Follet had adapted very well himself to a conjugal life ornamented by numerous affairs and faithful mistresses. What did he have to reproach his son-in-law? They understood each other. A divorce, moreover, was a bit of a stain, a disgrace for a family that was bourgeois, Catholic, and provincial into the bargain. One had to think about rumors, gossip, the clients. . . . Neither was Louis much in favor of divorce. What good would it do? He wasn't thinking of remarrying. In his own way, he was as much a man of duty as of dissipation. The current situation brought no opprobrium on him. And since he was a family man, he could continue to accept the role that he had not wanted, remain married, so that Colette would have a father and mother united by law, by civil registry, if not by geographical proximity or a shared roof and life.

No, it was Édith who wanted this divorce (her testimony, which I personally took down, is categorical), egged on by her relations and friends, who urged her to reclaim her freedom. Her father, naturally, bowed to her decision, gave her all the necessary legal help, entrusted her to his own lawyer and his own court solicitor. Louis, a little taken aback by his wife's determined will, did not oppose the proceedings. A mere bagatelle. . . . He accepted the blame for the divorce, no doubt with a slightly bitter sadness, as if, at the moment of regaining his beloved freedom, of breaking the conjugal bonds that he bore so easily, he suddenly came to miss the bygone happiness, that quiet life of the provinces, habits, and comforts that had been so unreal to him. Louis Destouches was a nostalgic: anything about to be lost, to be swept off into the past, took on greater value for him. Louis Destouches was proud, too: he may have found it irksome to be sent packing in this manner by the Follet family, of whom he had taken ample advantage to complete his medical studies. He who slammed doors on his way out may have been less ready to accept being politely but firmly accompanied to the porch—and good night!

On March 9, 1926, Édith's petition for divorce was brought before the Rennes law courts. The reconciliation attempt was set for March 19. But five days earlier, Louis had embarked from La Rochelle on his mission to Africa. Noting his absence, the judge gave the mother custody of the child. The judicial machine was in motion. On June 21, in the Rennes civil tribunal, the divorce was finally granted, with the court ruling against the husband. A letter from Louis to his wife had been added to the proceedings and contributed to the judge's decision: "You have to find something in Paris to make yourself independent, for my part it's impossible for me to live with anyone—I don't want to have you dragging along sniveling and miserable behind me, you bore me, and that's that—don't cling to me. I'd rather kill myself than continue to live with you—be very sure of that and stop bothering me with your devotion and tenderness—it would be much better for you to arrange your life as you see fit. I want to be alone, alone, neither dominated nor protected nor loved but free. I hate marriage, I abhor it, I spit on it; to me it seems like a jail where I'm dying."[22]

Louis may have purposely written this letter as a piece of evidence to hasten the procedure, or it may predate that, evidence simply of the occasionally cruel and irresponsible excessiveness of his words and temperament. In any case the divorce proceedings went ahead in his absence, after his departure for Africa, coming to an end at the time he returned to France.

Louis could not have been presented with a *fait* more *accompli*. There is not much to say, for that matter, about the African mission, the purpose of which was to study the colonial medical organizations of the continent's west coast from Senegal to Nigeria. Louis accompanied sixteen doctors there, Englishmen, Belgians, Spaniards, Frenchmen, Portuguese, a Guatemalan, and a South African. He had left La Rochelle on March 14 aboard the *Belle-Isle*; he reached Dakar on March 20.

Exactly ten years had passed since his first discovery of Africa. Ten years—the passage from war to peace, from youth to adulthood, from the still vague hopes of a boy without a future, without education, called by the Great War, to the inherently more settled and prestigious life of a doctor in charge of a mission, of an officer vested with an authority he sometimes didn't know how to wield. Ten years during which, in his studies, in his marriage, in his many professional experiences, Louis had not only benefited from a kind of blunt confidence and clear-headed philosophy of life, but which had also been for him, like so many, won or lost on the way to death. His wrinkles had formed. His character had hardened. His certainties, his pessimism, his bitterness, his intransigence, and his prejudices had gradually ossified in the stiffening of habits and of impending old age. Louis Destouches was now thirty-two, with the energy of a very young man but the experience of a tired one. He returned to Africa and already his gaze had taken on that brightness in which curiosity masks itself in disenchantment. He now no longer seemed to submit to adventure. On the contrary, he subjected adventure or travel to the whims of his will. That, perhaps, is the goal of education. That instant when accidents, encounters, and upheavals no longer have the power to mold a person; or, contrarily, when accidents, encounters, or upheavals confirm a character's acquired traits, when they have gone from being causes to consequences.

It follows that the second trip to Africa, lasting barely four months, was to be far less decisive than the first. In 1916 Louis had discovered colonialism there, freedom, solitude, his taste for travel, a definitive hatred of war, and the rudiments of medicine. In 1926 nothing awaited him there. Not even the hope of being useful, of acting, of healing, of medically soothing a few miseries. On his return to Africa he would find only exhaustion, disorder, and boredom.

After the relative success of the first mission to America, this one was immediately marked by signs of failure. The blame fell in part on Louis Destouches. He had poorly prepared his end of things. The group was to endure numerous transportation difficulties. Lack of money required them to split into three teams that would initially cover different itineraries.[23] Louis and the few doctors who followed him went from Dakar to Bamako, from Bamako to Kouroussa, eventually reaching Guinea. Train, car, train again: thousands of aimless kilometers, savanna landscapes stretching on to infinity, malaria, dust, and gossip. . . . Finally everyone met up in Konakry, embarked on a run-down steamer for a day in Abidjan, on the Ivory Coast, and then for somewhat longer if no more instructive stays in Accra on the Gold Coast, Lomé in Togo and Lagos in Nigeria. The finale of the mission was played out on May 18 in Freetown, Sierra Leone, where a plenary conference was to decide on the foundation of an epidemiology office on the island of Gorée. But that was without counting on political rivalries, national sensitivities, and egoism of every stamp. English and French bickered. The South African delegate preferred a political position of principle to concrete modes of monitoring epidemics. Each man was dug in to his own position. And the congress participants embarked on the first liner sailing.

On June 9 the steamer *Eubée* landed at La Rochelle.

The League of Nations archives retain no report from Louis Destouches on his African excursion, for the very simple reason that he did not write one. He treated his administrative and editorial obligations with the utmost casualness. On June 19 in Paris, before the 7th session of the Health Section, he made due with an oral presentation to his colleagues on the rather disappointing results of the tour.

Like the previous year with the other exchange doctors, the current one was spent in Europe with visits to Holland from July 21 to 26, to Belgium from July 26 to August 1, to France and Switzerland until August 10. On August 25 in Geneva, at the Palace of Nations, a round table devoted to the relationship between state insurance and public health concluded the mission. . . .

And the summer of 1926 came to an end, having seen the triumph of Adolf Hitler at the first congress of the National Socialist Party in Weimar, and, all over the world, suicides and inconsolable sorrows upon the death of the most handsome pomaded seducer (of uncertain virility) in the entire history of cinema, Rudolph Valentino.

For Louis, it was all simple. Hitler? Never heard of him. Valentino either. And he was fed up to the teeth with the League. He'd had enough of the verbiage, twaddle, and idle natter. Above all, he was sick of what was becoming a routine for him. And that is the main thing. He felt that he had gone the rounds with his work at the Health Section. There were no more surprises and no more hope of any. Too harried by life, he must already have been wondering what he would do after his contract expired at the end of 1927.

But if he was sick of the League, it is only fair to say that the League was probably beginning to be sick of him. The benevolence of Ludwig Rajchman couldn't protect him forever. How could the refractory, disordered Louis Destouches, who hated to write the most basic reports on the missions to which he was assigned, and who must have taken few pains to conceal to his colleagues or superiors the mocking disdain they inspired in him, avoid quickly being labeled persona non grata by the bosses of the Health Section? Moreover, his private life was a bit too conspicuous for the good taste and sense of proportion of the diplomats and appointed bureaucrats. They gossiped about his intemperate life-style, about his debts, about his parties where decency did not always prevail, about his fine new convertible, about his abuse of the credit and name of the League of Nations.

How to get rid of him? By two very simple means. First, by leaving him systematically on the sidelines. And then, by mutual agreement, arranging a long-term sick leave (the malaria attacks from which he suffered furnishing the ideal pretext) until his contract expired. This was essentially accomplished in June 1927, when Céline returned to Paris and his independence for the last six months of his employ.

The Church

It is hard to imagine Louis Destouches in Geneva, idle, cynical, content to pick up his check at the League of Nations, stroll along the lake, and take advantage of the passing time. With him, one activity had to replace another. One ambition expelled the last.

Are the greatest writers, scientists, or creators always aware of their genius? Louis Destouches, for his part, knew himself to be different. It was imperative for him to leave his mark on the world. His sometimes haughty uniqueness could not adapt to the shaded byways. He always had to reveal and assert himself, bear witness or act. We might call that pride. Or, rather, a tragic, obstinate sense of his own solitude. Nothing could satisfy him for long. A "fine" job ceased to be so after he had landed it. He wanted more. He wanted better. He wanted nothing. Or to be known by the world. Or to be appreciated, on the contrary, by a tiny minority. He wanted to understand everything. To collide with things, people, reality, politics. Even if it shattered him. With perhaps just a hint of theatricality. In brief, he wavered between suicide and a taste for dramatics.

If he hated writing reports for the League, it was because he was soon to leave another form of testimony, another more spectacular and more singular account of the experiences he had lived through. Sedentary, suddenly idle, Louis truly discovered in Geneva, in late 1926, what for him would remain throughout his life the privileges of refuge or withdrawal into writing—that moment when the thundering bursts of his memory, his visions, his deliria, his fits, and his impatience calm down and, faced with the white page, reveal themselves in the silence of the study.

Within two years he had explored America and New York, its music halls and dancing girls; he had returned to the African colonies and examined with greater detachment the overwhelming muddle of the medical missions, the egoism of fever-ridden bureaucrats, and the impotence of international missions; above all, he had strolled the hallways of the Palace of Nations, met diplomats, attended congresses, written, read and reread reports. And that was able to furnish him with the principal material for a play of which, at that time (late 1926/early 1927), he very likely wrote the first three acts, and which he called *L'Église* [The Church].

His choice of the dramatic mode, which seems so ill-adapted to Céline's talents, is a strange one. His work touches us most of all through the voice of he who is narrating, writing, commenting, through that unique, subjective point of view, through the narrator's distortion of words and things, his observation and organization of a nightmare, a convulsive truth, a journey to the end of night, of history, of childhood, of memory, of war or the Apocalypse, as you like. How could he have objectively translated his visions, his indignations, his metamorphoses, through the medium of coherent action, of characters who express themselves and share a level of identical reality? The theater also presupposes a craft, an apprenticeship in certain techniques that he was still entirely lacking. Louis was the first to recognize that, or at least to become aware of it later on. And he himself formulated the best criticism of *L'Église* in the July 1, 1933, issue of *L'Intransigeant*: "I'm not a man of the theater, maybe they'll laugh at my dialogue . . . [he laughs]. In any case, there's a special technique, tricks, a certain 'crux' that eludes me . . . Yes, yes! And yet, the theater perturbs me."

And the journalist assigned to review the play would later recall the author's judgment, heard in Dinan over the summer: " 'Don't read this,' he advised me amiably. 'It's lousy.' "24

So why the theater? Louis, who had not yet attempted to write a single novel, who may not even have been considering it, probably thought of the theater as the most spectacular genre, the flashiest, the most eye-catching, above all the most concrete. Also, the one that could bring him the most immediate notoriety and the most hard income. Furthermore, he had written *L'Église* as a catharsis, a revenge. He liked to pay back in cash—and with interest—the slights he received or perceived. His susceptibility was excessive—as was his sensitivity. This Breton-Norman had a Corsican taste for vendetta. He was not a man to flee into the abstract. He was happy to withdraw his words, but the way one withdraws one's dagger from an opponent's belly. Nor was he a man to provoke in the abstract. A play was a way of giving life and breadth to the stooges he was denouncing, to the settings that set him dreaming, to situations he deemed untenable.

In New York, on the other hand, he had discovered dance and dancers. In writing a play, he specifically wanted to recapture them, mold them, to dream concretely of an enchantment finally become tangible. And the dream would never leave him. After some unfortunate attempts at theater, Céline would continue, parallel with his novelistic work, to write ballet synopses. And one of the greatest sorrows of his life, one of the most painful sources of his anger, his bitterness, and even his blind vengeances, would be the impossibility of seeing a single one of them produced on stage, at the Paris Opéra, in Copenhagen, in Moscow, or anywhere. He was never to see a dancer spin in the light, rise up, remain poised, then gracefully leap once more, in accordance with the whims and whimsies of a story that he had written. A voyeur, yes, but, alas, no demiurge! He would never recover from that flaw, that secret and unhealable wound.

In Geneva, late 1926, Louis Destouches took up his pen as a sword for the first time and went off to tilt at windmills, at States, races, international organizations, the mediocrity of the well-to-do, the cold nastiness of the poor, the indifference of the rich, the stupidity of bureaucracies, and the impalpable happiness provided by music-hall girls. He began to write, to indict, to confuse his targets, to reveal violence, tenderness, and hatred for everything that moved around him. Innocent or guilty, who cares! Louis Destouches was settling in, one against all, with the prejudices, class blindness, anti-Semitism, stupefying verbal innovations, generosity, and horribly lucid aphorisms, that left his readers nonplussed.

Thus, the first act, first target of *L'Église*: Africa and colonialism. Dr. Bardamu (Céline's double, his spokesman) has been sent by the League of Nations Committee on Epidemics to Bragamance, a little colony on the west coast. Dr. Gaige, an American epidemiologist sent from his side by the Barell Foundation (read: the Rockefeller Foundation), reclines on his camp bed. In fact, he is dead. Bardamu diagnoses the cause. He has been struck down by an epidemic of pneumonic plague. But neither the administrator nor the inspector general wish to accept such irksome news, which could threaten the colony's economic viability, news so irksome it must be erroneous. Gaige died of smallpox. The official and unquestionable truth. Bardamu, a fatalist, leaves Bragamance with a four-year old African boy whom Gaige had adopted.

Second act, second target: New York, scene from the office of Vera Stern, manager of the Quick Theater, where Elizabeth Gaige is one of the showgirls. Bardamu is there to tell her of her husband's death. But he will not have the opportunity, he will be caught up in a whirlwind of chorus men and girls; of another doctor who, as concerns Gaige's death, will prudently lean toward yellow fever; of Vera Stern, a provocative adventuress in trouble with the police for complicity in smuggling bootleg liquor. A judge has denounced her before the elections. She has to flee. To Paris? She suggests to Bardamu that he marry her. Why not? They leave for Chicago and the French consulate.

Third act, third and final target: the League of Nations, the comings and goings of various committees in which subjects of the utmost gravity are discussed. Should the manufacture of shoelaces be forbidden in time of war? Do nations that manufacture syringes require morphine? Every conceivable accent rings out through the hallways. Hungarian colonels and Dutch merchants want to see Mr. Yudenzweck [Jewish-Goal], director of the Office of Arrangements, to arrange their little currency exchange or compensation deals. Yudenzweck arrives, settles several international disputes, appeases the hurt feelings of the English and the French, who accuse each other of responsibility for the African epidemics. Absolutely not—it's Bardamu's fault! Henceforth he will no longer be assigned to missions. In any case he will be leaving the League. Back in Geneva one last time, Bardamu argues with Yudenzweck, refuses to bow to the bureaucracy's lies and procrastinations. Yudenzweck, who had been very fond of him, gets rid of him and forgets him immediately.

This very schematic synopsis needs no commentary. We recognize in passing a host of autobiographical elements, right down to Louis' lightning marriage with Suzanne Nebout in London, no doubt to help her settle various problems with the bureaucracy, her passport, and others.

But first, why *The Church*? Max Descaves put that very question to Céline for *Paris-Midi* on March 28, 1933. The author's answer: "Because it seemed a pretty good way to sum up the League, a church, you know! with its leaders, its staff. I placed the action in 1922 . . . the grand era of the League, of the international religion of rapprochement between peoples, that is, the Briand era."

And why this "Jewish" vision of the League, Louis Destouches' sudden dread of politics and power, his anger, too, against the impotence, delusions, and disorders of international officers? In February 1960 he was to answer Jean Guénot and Jacques Darribehaude: "And then afterward, I was at the League of Nations, and there, I knew where I stood, I really saw how the world is ruled by The Bull, by Mammon! Ah, no question there! I tell you, inexorable."[25]

Having barely finished writing *L'Église*, limited to the first three acts, Louis hastened to pass his manuscript on to Ludwig Rajchman. The better to turn the knife in the wound, to savor his vengeance and humiliate his protector? Not at all: a sign of friendship, rather, of trust, a kind of complicity; simply a way of showing him what he was made of, literarily speaking. Rajchman would appreciate the satire, he'd be the first to laugh, Louis would bet on it.

In *Bagatelles pour un massacre*, Céline recalls the incident in this way: "I liked him the way he was . . . I even had some affection for him . . . Of course he didn't pass up the chance to rook me every so often . . . to make me swallow some trick or other . . . But I didn't go out of my way either . . . There was a cunning little struggle going on. One day, after he had kept me too long in Geneva, doing idiotic jobs, poring over files, I plotted in my own little way, a little play, it was pretty innocuous, *L'Église*. It was a failure, that's for sure . . . but there was still some substance to it . . . I gave it to Yubelblat to read. He, who had always proven himself the most eclectic of yids, never fazed by anything, that bit got to him even so . . . He made a little face . . . He never forgot . . . He brought it up again several times. I had touched the only nerve that was forbidden, that wasn't to be made a plaything. He had understood completely. He didn't need to be told twice."[26]

There is something stupefying about this anecdote, something that touches the very heart of the Célinian character, and which we have already mentioned earlier: a dissociation between speech and writing on the one hand and real life on the other. No doubt about it: Louis had indeed written *L'Église* in a fit of anger; he wanted to bear witness, denounce, act. But everything points to his anger being exhausted in the very act of writing, as if a peaceful amnesia took hold at that moment, as if all had been said, achieved, concluded, and the rest ceased to matter. Once he had delivered his howl, he could return to the status quo, in the manner of a child who shouts "truce!" and moves on to another game with impunity. Again and again—when he publishes his anti-Semitic works before the war and *Les Beaux draps* in 1941, and when he is persecuted after the liberation—Céline will sincerely fail to understand. As with Rajchman, he would desperately plead not guilty before history. But really, he had only written diversions, trifles, they weren't serious! In Denmark, in a memoir, he would even go so far as to write a "defense," a kind of official document that he would pass on to his lawyer, Thorvald Mikkelsen, in response to the accusations then being made against him in France: "All things considered, honestly examined, without passion, and considering the circumstances, *the Jews should raise me a statue for the harm I didn't do them and which I could have done them.* They persecute me, I never persecuted them."[27]

In *L'Église*, there is a minor character whom we have just mentioned, a New York dancer with morals as light as her figure, who kisses her French secretary, Flora, on the mouth, who dreams of shows and schemes, who generously sleeps with everyone, carefree and pretty, and who answers to the name Elizabeth Gaige. The model for her is obvious, the last name barely changed. The real Elizabeth Craig, but newly appeared in Louis Destouches' life, inspired the dramatic figure.

Louis had recently met her in Geneva, in late 1926 when, after a brief expedition to Cherbourg from October 1 to 3 to accompany a British mission, he was champing at the bit, thinking about *L'Église*, getting bored, constructing castles in the air and lines on the blank page. She was American, slight, graceful, slender of waist, narrow of hip, high and wide in the cheekbones. A beautiful woman? An elf rather, supple, spontaneous, and secretive, free of body and mysterious of spirit.

Henri Mahé, a little later, would describe her thus: "Large cobalt-green eyes . . . A small, delicate nose . . . A sensual rectangular mouth . . . Long, golden russet curls of hair falls across her shoulders . . . Small breasts, firm and arrogant . . . her ass too, nice and high! . . . A dancer's legs . . . You could make a necklace with 'em. . . . She doesn't walk, she glides, very straight. Her proud little head doesn't move. The Earth crumbles! . . . She doesn't speak, she whispers, and her eyes and eyelids flutter. She is often followed and accosted on the street. Phlegmatic, without even a glance, she simply says: 'It's a hundred francs!' Radical! The man moves on, disappointed."[28]

She was born in 1902 in Los Angeles, into a Protestant family of modest means, and that year she was accompanying her parents on a grand tour of Europe—that typically American dream of returning to one's roots at least once in a lifetime. After France, the family had reached Switzerland by

September 1926. In Geneva, Elizabeth (who had taken classical dance classes in California) enrolled with Dalcroze, who ran a dance school of high repute.[29] Perhaps that is where she met Dr. Destouches, became his friend, then his lover—one of the most radiant and decisive encounters of her life. All his life, Louis would love to frequent dance classes, observing the exercises and movements of the dancers, plunging into an erotico-aesthetic meditation that consoled him for the world's stony, clamorous realities. But we possess no oral accounts or documents relative to the exact circumstances of his meeting with Elizabeth.

The impact on Louis must have been considerable. Elizabeth was a sudden embodiment before him of the American dream of feminine beauty, of grace, of dance, that peaceable amorality, in other words the liberation from constraints: ugliness, gravity, prejudices, fear of scandal, bourgeois proprieties, social obligations. She was well and truly a lover such as he would never have dared imagine, the unreal, erotic, foreign, and silent counterpoint to his daily life, to medicine, to misery, and swarming mediocrities.

Obviously, he idealized Elizabeth, whom we should picture above all as a young woman raised in the prudish American provinces. For her, Europe rhymed with freedom. And she gave herself to Europe without the least hint of hesitation. Europe meant sexual emancipation, every possible experience, and perhaps even drugs, why not? Sensual and willful, and docile as well, finally rid of the burden of Anglo-Saxon repressions, she lived with Louis, for whom she certainly felt a very strong attachment and enthralled admiration, six years of a dissolute, adventurous, and Bohemian life in Paris, interrupted by brief visits to the United States. And that, right up to her ultimate departure in June 1933. But Europe was, in the end, but a parenthesis. She had known or sensed it from the very beginning. America awaited her around the corner (of her life), with its respectability, its compromises, the necessity one day or another of bending to the decorum of maturity, the yoke of society, and to refined boredom.

Thus, Elizabeth met Louis Destouches in Geneva and left Louis-Ferdinand Céline in Paris. It was she who was present at, and perhaps in her own way contributed to, the metamorphosis of doctor into writer. Before he met her, he had no thought of writing *Voyage au bout de la nuit*. She left him at the moment when his book—which he dedicated to her—was triumphant. In short, she experienced the years of the novel's composition. And her presence, reflected in characters as diverse as Lola, Musyne, and Molly, brightens the happiest, the most bewitching pages of the book.

The mysterious Elizabeth Craig . . . She left Geneva in May 1927 to move with her parents into a little rented apartment on the boulevard Raspail. There was no longer any question of Louis remaining in Geneva. A final mission for the League brought him to Paris from April 22 to May 6 to attend a series of lectures on rabies. Immediately afterward he applied for the position of physician-consultant in the Paris office of the Health Section. He was denied the nomination—through no particular fault of Ludwig Rajchman's. Little matter! It was to Rajchman that Louis attributed his failure, which meant his separation from Elizabeth Craig. But he wouldn't lie down and take it. He immediately obtained from the League (which asked no better, as we have said) a long-term sick leave calculated to lapse at the end of his contract. He promptly left the shores of Lake Geneva, the Palace of Nations, and the city of Geneva.

He left no regrets behind him. Only debts. Which, for him, was a lot better. "Slates" with the caterer, the decorator (204.80 francs for wallpaper, thank you very much!), and even the mover. He had gotten into the habit of throwing money out the window, a vengeance was taken on his childhood years, his years of hardship, when everything had to be counted, measured, saved. The luxury he indulged in wasn't even a need, it was a provocation, a challenge to good sense, a hatred of pettiness more than folly of grandeur. He threw money out the windows—but the windows were too wide and his wallet, in the end, too narrow. . . . Rajchman, whose benevolence in recent times had been put sorely to the test, agreed to intervene and to appease the tradesmen's hostile impatience. From Paris, Louis very gradually reimbursed his creditors. But God! (he thought), those Geneva merchants were shabby in domestic matters.

Back in Paris, and very soon confronted with socialized medicine, Louis rounded out his play with fourth and fifth acts, on a backdrop of a suburban *bistro*, alcoholic old colonials, and a paupers' doctor. And this play, in all likelihood fairly close to that which would finally be published by Denoël in September 1933, a year after *Voyage* appeared, was rejected by Gallimard in October '27. "Some satiric strength, but lacks consistency." It was a predictable rejection, after all. It would have taken considerable literary perspicacity and a considerable taste for risk to publish the first work (theatrical, what's more) of an unknown, the faults of which were so glaring, in which no action actually evolved or devolved upon the stage, in which the author was pleased merely to tack one rather static episode onto another. As if he had been motivated initially to lay out a certain number of situations, to express a certain number of indignations, and nothing more . . . Bardamu remains somehow passive, inert, at every moment of the play. He is presented to us ready-made, from the opening act, in his fatalistic lucidity, his disenchanted silences, and his generosity disguised as cynicism. He casts a horribly clearsighted and aloof gaze over the world. He speaks in monosyllables or insinuations. What use is interference in human affairs? Dr. Bardamu does not believe in healing. His mission is to be at the side of the moribund, to help them to die. "Getting better doesn't require anyone's help," he exclaims. Whether at the bedside of a convulsive Africa, a delirious America, a psychiatric League of Nations, a poverty-stricken suburb, or a clinic for the dying, he watches, he waits. Forever withdrawn. He resembles the Bardamu of the second part of *Voyage*. He is a character deeply set in his ways, remote and, dramatically speaking, empty. Again, he exists only through the gaze he casts on the world—a world reduced here to its disorder and to the fallacy of its apparent order. A world like a Church, with its rituals, its high priests, its merchants of illusion, its profiteers, and of which he, Bardamu, remains the irreducible scoundrel.

But if *L'Église* touches us today, despite its thinly disguised anti-Semitism, it is because we find in it the first true portrait of the artist by himself, without any doubt, because Bardamu is closely drawn on Louis Destouches. But also because the play presents itself to us as a sketch of *Voyage* and because it is of some interest thus to divine the first tentative gropings of genius.

And yet we instantly recognize a significant difference between the two works. The Great War is missing from *L'Église*, as if the author were still too deafened and shaken by the fighting to consider describing it so soon, as if he did not yet feel himself up to such a subject. Conversely, the League of Nations is missing from *L'Église Voyage*, as if Céline, upon reflection, dared not risk an overly literal criticism of the powers that be, dared not reveal an anti-Semitism that might have done him harm. But as for the rest, Africa, America, the suburbs oozing with filth, and the precarious conditions of socialized medicine, Bardamu's entire itinerary is neatly mapped out. Like his character. And his solitude.

Already, *L'Église* expresses, painfully, with a need, an overwhelming urgency even, that vast Célinian compassion for individuals, for those who suffer and who, through their suffering, occasionally manage to attain the truth. "Anyway, you . . . probably since you've suffered so long, you are more intelligent than the others," Bardamu says for instance to the little hunchback, Janine, in the fourth act. Here already is the Célinian theme *par excellence*. "The truth of the world is death, right? Life is a drunkenness, a lie. It's fragile, and absolutely necessary."

Before such truth one must learn to keep silent. "First of all, writing is disgusting, it's a secretion." This accounts for Louis Destouches–Céline's hatred for gossips, the healthy, the bastards who give free rein to their distractions. "It's like this, I prefer to deal with people who are sick. Those who are healthy are so mean, so stupid; they want to seem so clever the minute they stand up, that any dealings with them are almost immediately wretched. When they're on their backs, suffering, they leave you alone. Understand?"

The essence of *Voyage* is substantially there. In 1927 Louis Destouches is already displaying the disenchanted lucidity, the rage, the emotionality that will inspire the most original pages of the 1932 novel.

Paris, Progress, Suburbs

In early July Louis returned to Paris—and Elizabeth.

A doctor heals, that's his or her vocation. But where, under what conditions? In the hospital, in a clinic, in a private practice? Louis was not very settled. The eighteen months following his return were characterized by a sort of hesitation waltz. He lodged one place, then another. Sought out a private clientele, then gave it up. Wrote a second play, without success. Leaned toward socialized medicine, published a few articles, and joined a pharmaceutical laboratory as a writer.

Louis Destouches may have seemed erratic or weak-willed, but in the long run this was irrelevant. For he was patiently gathering the final documentation for his first novel, though he didn't know it yet. Soon, the final preparations before the *Journey* would at last be complete. Everything would be clear then, and all that would remain would be to write—on the sidelines of medicine. . . .

On July 2 he filed his medical certificate in Paris and declared himself a resident of Croissy-sur-Seine. But did he ever live there? His financial situation was precarious. Rajchman, still inclined to come to his aid, recommended him to Professor Léon Bernard at the Laennec hospital. Louis worked there unofficially from September 1927, learning clinical medicine. At Laennec, he ran into Dr. Guy Morin, whom he had met in Rennes in 1919 at the October reopening of studies for the PCN certificate. Then seventeen years old, Morin had not benefited from the accelerated study cycle granted to veterans.

"The years passed, and I didn't see Destouches again until 1926 or 1927. I was at a Parisian hospital at the time, surrounded by a crowd of students, and we were all listening to Professor X, whose class, in those days, was a prestigious one. All of a sudden, the professor broke off, pushed his way through his audience, and warmly extended a hand to a person who had just come in. That person was Destouches. What had he done since Rennes? I don't know, and it doesn't really matter. But if I mention that the professor was Jewish, one might suppose that Destouches hadn't yet formulated his anti-Semitism. As we left, he threw himself into a speech on medicine in general that would have been flabbergasting if he himself hadn't treated it as a joke."[30]

Léon Bernard was the French representative to the Health Section of the League of Nations. He was also leading the campaign against tuberculosis in France. By virtue of this double involvement, he could not have avoided being in touch with the Rockefeller Mission, so that Louis Destouches, at a humble level of the hierarchy, must have crossed his path frequently. In *Bagatelles pour un massacre*, Céline was again to evoke Léon Bernard on a mission to Geneva. Gratitude was not the writer's strong point. He drew a caustic portrait of the doctor as a comic character in a play. And also, Léon Bernard was Jewish. Alas, that said it all!

"Scientists are ruthless when it comes to vanity . . . Believe me, it's no little thing to reassure a scientist, to really fix it in his noggin, that he is indeed the best in the world, the high *excellentissimus*, that there's no one else like him . . . when it comes to intuition . . . staggering syntheses . . . probity, etc. It takes a lot of gestures and words and constant writing and undetectable ruses, and also an unbelievable nerve, and also an absolutely amazing, faultless, superclear memory for tall stories ... not a moment's rest when it comes to buttering them up, sending them little 'reminders,' a little pocket money, free transportation, a thousand 'expenses,' ten thousand confidences, a hundred thousand compliments and then places on committees, to make them come to Geneva in person, shuffling along ... stretching themselves out, still airing their opinions. Bernard Léon from Paris, that fat medical rabbi, perfectly pretentious and useless, was one of the great courtiers of the Princess of Lake Geneva."[31]

Robert Debré, Léon Bernard's adjunct at the time, remembered Louis joining their team on occasion, wearing a faded raincoat and an unhappy look, his face already carved by suffering and by his life's myriad experiences. "Louis fitted in with the Laennec team immediately. Professor Debré insists nowadays that he worked very hard there, justifying all the good Rajchman had said of him and literally compelling his colleagues' esteem."[32]

What Robert Debré didn't know was that at the same time (September 1927) Louis was writing a new play, *Périclès*, a title he was eventually to change to *Progrès* [Progress] on the cover of the typed manuscript.

Louis never for one moment considered having it published. Gallimard's rejection of *L'Église* in October may have helped to discourage him. But once again, he had no illusions about his talent as a dramatic writer. In the early thirties, Céline admitted, again to Guy Morin: *"L'Église is a flop, old boy, nothing but a flop."*[33]

As for the manuscript of *Progrès*—fifty-five pages sewn and bound—the author was satisfied to present it to his publisher's wife, Mme. Cécile Robert Denoël, and it was through her that it could be published for the first time in 1978, fifty-one years after being written, in a small edition put out by the Mercure de France. The typed facsimile still bore the note: "Louis Destouches, 35 Rue Vernet," the address that was also given on the manuscript of *L'Église* and which was that of the Paris office of the League of Nations. We must not forget that in late 1927 Louis was still under contract to the League, on the loose merely by reason of a long-term sick leave. With no established home, he had his mail forwarded from Geneva.

No question about it, *Progrès* is a mediocre play, its plot murky and disjointed, its characters barely sketched. It is a clash of genres that do not succeed in setting a tone for the whole. The first scene more or less bears upon the bourgeois comedy of manners, with its attendant characters: the feeble, jealous husband, the humble, docile wife, the bossy mother-in-law, the sentimental neighbor in love with the wife. . . . Further along, the action is transplanted to a *maison de rendez-vous*—a brothel—and wavers on the edge of ribald vaudeville. The final tableau is unequivocal fantasy, a musical-comedy paradise with its haloed and bearded God on a tuft of cloud, its choir of little angels singing in a corner, and a sweetly impertinent moral. Certainly, Louis must have had fun writing this insignificant doodle, playing the counterpoint between realism and zaniness.

Nonetheless, we should note that by September 1927 Louis Destouches' taste for speaking from the depth of his experience, his memory, his encounters, his family, is already well developed in *Progrès*. *L'Église* prefigured *Voyage au bout de la nuit*; and we now find *Progrès* giving promise of *Mort à crédit*.

We need not cast around for the model for the gentle Marie, clear-headed, resigned, with a slight limp, so generous, incapable of seeing the evil around her—it's Marguerite Destouches, the author's mother (and Ferdinand's in *Mort à crédit*); Gaston, her husband, irritable, powerless and passionate, an embittered insurance man, is, of course, Ferdinand Destouches. We already find Lempreinte, the assistant office manager who humiliates him in the future novel, and who draws from him complaints of the type: "But I'm being trampled, Marie, trampled—isn't an honest man forever being trampled by the rabble, day in, day out?" Of course, Gaston raves against politicians, Freemasonry rising everywhere, threatening him, isolating him, condemning him to failure. "Everything is in league against the honest man. He's watched by unknown forces, he loves the light, he's not suspicious, and everything is known in the Lodge, no more private life, the honest man has nothing to hide. Luckily he doesn't know how to lie, he suffers in the sunshine! But that's not where they attack him, it's from behind, he's alone from behind, you're always alone when you're honest, you're all alone! Alone! Alone!"

This paranoid, reactionary monologue is one Louis Destouches must have heard in his childhood. But it's one he'll take up again after his father, the Jews and the Freemasons have, naturally, joined forces! Moreover, the scorn is ambiguous here. While laughing at the ridiculous narrow-mindedness of his father, of "Gaston," he does not openly disavow his arguments.

And here, as the action moves along, we find a direct allusion to the Passage Choiseul, where the bilious husband likes to stroll. As to the mother-in-law, Mme. Punais, a widow with a shopkeeper's solid good sense who has managed at the end of her life to get hold of a little antique store and who doesn't hesitate to snub her son-in-law, her model, too, is transparent: we recognize Céline Guillou, Grandma Caroline from *Mort à crédit* already sketched out here, having returned to Louis Destouches' memory for the first time.

But in an even more immediate way *Progrès* reveals the author's concerns and tastes in the year 1927. The debts that continue to burden him are like those contracted by the woman of whom Mme. Punais speaks: "She's one of the artist lot, she is, she doesn't pay her debts and it doesn't upset her." Louis Destouches, the voyeur, confesses his penchant comically in the brothel, where all of the clients want to conceal themselves to watch the ladies' revels but where none want to "consummate," to the understandable desperation of the manageress. Until the American with a capital A makes her appearance, a liberated and mysterious client, beautiful, rich, a dancer, athletic, representing the eternal Célinian profession of faith in beauty, eroticism, choreography, and silence. "The day when women will be dressed only in muscles . . . and music . . . how much less talking there will be." This American emerging thus in *Progrès*, just as she had earlier insinuated herself into *L'Église*, in reality bears the sole, magical name of Elizabeth Craig.

In October 1927 Louis filed his certificate to practice at 5, rue des Saules in the 18th *arrondissement*, but eventually, on November 14, opened an office of "General Practice, Childhood Diseases" at 36, rue d'Alsace, in Clichy, at the corner of the rue du Bois, in an ordinary building with a brick façade, metal shutters on the windows, a building without spirit, without sorrow, without originality, without soul, without anything, a petty-bourgeois building made to lead an ordinary life in. Elizabeth left her parents and the boulevard Raspail to move in with Louis, on the second floor left, in a very humble "three-room/kitchen/bathroom" that was also to serve as the doctor's office, above the butcher's on the first floor.

Louis had returned to the suburbs where he had been born, Courbevoie, Clichy, the same struggle and the same boredom. It was still that sort of undecided territory between town and country, poverty and opulence, progress and the past, a suburban rout of urban planning, houses and buildings all resembling one another, with the Seine winding away a little farther off, trams, bistros, a great, gray desperation beneath the factory smoke and the winter fog: "I had no pretentions, nor any ambitions either, all I wanted was to breathe a little, to eat a little better. Having stuck my sign above my door, I waited."[34]

Those pages from *Voyage* in which Céline describes settling into "La Garenne–Rancy"—one is tempted to quote them all. Which would be exaggerating, of course, but an exaggeration resembling a realist drawing that had been touched up, in which such or such detail had been highlighted with black ink, such or such figure with a tragic shadow, in order to pass effortlessly from Clichy, the model, to "La Garenne–Rancy," the fictive one into which it would be changed by what is sometimes lazily called literary eternity.

"The houses possess you, all pissy as they are with their flat façades, their heart belongs to the landlord. You never see him. He wouldn't dare show his face. He sends his agent, the prick. And yet they say in the neighborhood that the owner's a pretty nice guy in person. It costs him nothing.

"The light in the sky over Rancy is the same as in Detroit, liquid smoke soaking the plain all the way to Levallois. A junkheap of masonry glued to the ground with black slime. From a distance, the chimneys, short ones and tall ones, look like those big posts stuck in the mud at the seaside. Inside, that's us. . . .

"Meanwhile, there weren't a whole lot of patients. You need some time to get going, people said to reassure me. For the moment, the patient was mostly me.

"I found that there's nothing more awful than La Garenne–Rancy when you don't have any clients. You can say that again. You shouldn't think in places like that, and here I had come specifically to think in peace, and from the far side of the planet at that! Was I lucky. Arrogant twerp! It came over me black and heavy . . . It was no joke, and it wouldn't go away either. There's nothing so tyrannical as a brain."[35]

It wasn't enough for him to wait for his few patients in Clichy. Louis wanted to continue being more noticeably, more publically active. After the easy, comfortable student's life in Rennes, after the prestigious cosmopolitan life in Geneva, he was no doubt experiencing the reactive shock of his mediocre position in the suburbs, with a pathetic practice that wasn't enough to make him a living, or worse yet to wipe out his debts. This wasn't the time to be thinking of a rapid and brilliant literary career. Gallimard had ignored L'Église in October 1927 and rejected Semmelweis in July 1928, once again missing the chance of a great writer in his developmental stage. Louis sought compensations in medical circles. It was a last resort.

On April 13 he was elected a member of the Paris Medical Society, having been nominated for candidacy by Dr. Georges Rosenthal.[36] On May 26, before his new fellow members, he delivered a paper on the health service in the Ford plants in Detroit, the kernel of which was drawn from the conclusions of the report sent to the Health Committee of the League of Nations.[37]

In November he published in La Presse Médicale an article entitled "State Insurance Programs and an Economic Policy on Public Health." A very curious and ambiguous text in which one may once again measure the difficulty of classifying the author politically. Is he an out-and-out reactionary? A fantasist? An energetic revolutionary? An irresponsible provocateur? An insignificant utopian? He performs many a conjuring trick in his article. Obsessed with problems of hygiene, concerned with socialized medicine after years of investigation in Geneva and months of solitary experience in Clichy, he is not very sure of where he is going. In this article we can sense the extent of his intellectual disarray. He first takes up the idea inspired by the Ford plants: invalids are just as happy in the factory as they are at home, injected into the active life rather than wasting away in sinister and ruinous homes for the dying. But in that case, he says, we must create a corps of labor doctors. In his practice at 36, rue d'Alsace, he has recently come to the conclusion that his patients are unable to explain the pains they are suffering. "Three months of a public medical clientele are enough to teach us that we have not yet reached that level of popular intelligence. The public does not ask to understand, it asks to believe."[38] It would be better to observe the patient at the factory, in his workplace, to gain an understanding of the medical case in its active milieu, not to ignore the economic realities. "My colleagues know that the sum total of information and knowledge they gain about a patient during a visit of that type is, in practice, far superior to that which they draw from a consultation in their office or at the clinic, where the patient 'appears out of the blue,' with his muddled, insufficient, and disoriented explanations, his almost constantly false data on the hygienic conditions of his life and his work."[39]

That is irrefutable. But Louis condemns collectivism and its dangers while at the same time extolling a socialization of medicine. This would seem to suggest the hint of a medical or employers' police, a concern for employment at any cost, a totalitarianism of medicine. Louis Destouches reminds us that a sick man can make an excellent industrial recruit in the same way that a mildly tubercular man made as good a soldier as anyone else during the war. We must ask ourselves again: a socializing revolutionary who deems bourgeois medicine incompatible with the socialist principle of state insurance, is Louis Destouches a dreamer, an agent of high capital, or a destabilizing anarchist? The article contains all the seeds of the author's inspirations and total confusion of thought, jostling one another into incomprehensibility. Moreover, the journal's editorial board had taken care to precede the article with a cautious disclaimer of Louis Destouches' theses supporting a kind of militarization of medicine.

But if political, economic, and social rigor or the formulation of a coherent structure are not his strong points, daily humanity, at least, is in his realm. A lot has been said about Dr. Destouches, the poor man's physician, about his compassion for the afflictions and infirmities that he must have attempted to soothe, sometimes with more good sense than science. We must re-emphasize that image, and we will return to it.

So Clichy was second-rate, the building on the rue d'Alsace oppressive, the clients too few and far between and too similar to one another in their pains and sickness, their alcoholism and bitterness. On the other hand, Dr. Destouches' home was like no other. Jeanne Carayon, his neighbor who was then studying for her *agrégation* in English, gave us this perceptive and meaty description: "And yet, this apartment somehow reveals the unexpected, the 'waiting room' is not at all like one. Above the windowed bay, against the plinth, a long box trailing clumps of marigolds, somehow artificial without being so, so well do they evoke a garden. Little furniture: ignoring it, the attention is drawn entirely toward the walls, which are hung with masks and objects such as 'colonials' bring back from Africa. A wooden statue—African too, no doubt—set right on the floor, extends a hand. 'It's the gesture of the Gods—they're taking up a collection,' quietly assures the doctor, who has just entered the room."[40]

Dr. Destouches didn't always make his clients pay. The concierge was delighted, the housekeeper enchanted. Louis observed his patients, minutely examining their sufferings and their truth. For the first time he was in daily, repeated contact with human beings, he was working "hands on," observing, learning, realizing his childhood dream from the Passage Choiseul such as he would later claim before his interviewers: "As a little boy, I dreamed of being a doctor, of healing people . . . I wanted to heal people . . . You see. From the age of five, I think . . . as far back as I can remember."[41] His dream, then, was coming true in a way. But it may be less correct to speak of a dream than of a nightmare, something which in any case was not enough to satisfy him, and which he had to supplement with other activities.

"Only the butcheress on the ground floor seems impervious to the man's *fluid*, insensitive to his *aura*. Hostile, she confides to a neighbor buying a steak: 'It seems that there are—things—going on upstairs. I'm sure they dance naked.' Might the butcheress have drilled a hole in the ceiling? Might the doctor, in a hurry one day, have opened the door in his bathrobe? But the suggestion of ancient-style dancing? It is the concierge who, in a burst of pride, enlightens the mystery: 'We have a dancer in the house: the doctor's American.'"[42]

The American's parents had just returned to the United States, no doubt somewhat worried about leaving their daughter in the company of that strange doctor to whom they had nevertheless taken a liking, with whom they had not hesitated on several occasions to go on visits to museums, on walks.

And that strange doctor was short on money. If the clients were not breaking down the door, the Swiss creditors, for their part, made themselves felt much more urgently. Louis had to find alternate sources of income.

At the end of 1928 he took a job with the La Biothérapie pharmaceutical laboratory as a writer cum publicity agent, also in charge of correspondence with the medical profession, for a monthly salary of 1,000 francs. It was a job that he may have deemed humiliating or unworthy of him but which he kept until the 1937 publication of *Bagatelles pour un massacre*. Two chairmen of Jewish origin had succeeded each other to the board of directors of La Biothérapie. Not surprisingly, the presence among them of an anti-Semitic colleague was hardly desirable. La Biothérapie specialized in vaccines and toothpaste. Thus, Louis would be assigned to write (anonymously) the publicity brochure for Sanogyl toothpaste in 1931.

At the time he started work at La Biothérapie, Louis had to resign himself to closing his private practice at 33, rue d'Alsace, keeping only the apartment. The absence of clients was decidedly too costly. He accepted a position at the new clinic that opened in early 1929 at 10, rue Fanny, in Clichy. As director of public health he would earn 2,000 francs a month, which included a daily round of general practice from 5 P.M. to 6:30 P.M. For a time he also worked as consulting physician at the Marthe-Brandès Clinic at 35, avenue de Saint-Ouen.

Louis Destouches was tireless; he really never slowed down. Throughout 1929 he also continued to publish medical articles on the most diverse subjects: "Puerperal Infection and Antiviruses" for *La Médecine* in April, "Notes on the Use of Besredka Antiviruses in Wet Bandaging" for the Paris Medical Society, and many others even more technical. At the same time he obtained Ludwig Rajchman's approval for a Health Section subsidy for a study trip to England, in order to observe the functioning of clinics similar to that of Clichy, their manner of treating venereal diseases and of developing a rational nutritional program for the poor. He received a sum of 500 francs from Geneva, promised a detailed report, and stayed in London from March 26 to April 8. This was right in the middle of the Easter vacations. He didn't see very much, nor many people. He wrote no report. He spent the 500 francs. We dare not write that this came as a surprise to Rajchman.

In August, Louis and Elizabeth moved from their Clichy apartment into 98, rue Lepic in Paris. Their neighbor Jeanne Carayon explains why: "It was those filthy bedbugs that chased him out. The invasion swept from one floor to another, from the fifth to the first. Accusations were exchanged through the concierge: 'It's the people upstairs who spread them, shaking out their bedside rugs.'—'They came from the rafters.'—'They came from the fields . . .' It was action stations in the building, bedsprings overturned, the pleasant smell of Fly-Tox, followed by the more acrid stink of 'Mortis' wafting its sulfurous fumes through every landing, despite the strips of sticky paper. For a while it was hell. The doctor made his escape.

"But the air in the building became insipid once he had stopped breathing it."[43]

Before leaving, Louis had made a whopping confession to Jeanne Carayon: "I'm writing a novel. I've been working on it for four years, mostly at night. If it's published, you'll correct my proofs."[44]

Of course he hadn't been working on it for four years, he had just started writing it. But let us remember those first six months of 1929 and the place, the apartment at 33, rue d'Alsace in Clichy. The Céline years had begun.

8

Finally, on October 15, 1932: Céline . . .

The Doctor Has Fun
The Doctor Practices
The Doctor Writes
The Doctor Publishes

The Doctor Has Fun

Louis Destouches, 1929 . . . Having just moved and settled in Montmartre, he soon made new friendships, fleeting relationships, with painters, artists, entertainers who drew him into picturesque dissipations. The doctor was having fun. . . .

But he continued to perform his daily round at the Clichy clinic. Furthermore, he found work as a researcher in a new pharmaceutical laboratory. He also found numerous pretexts to stay away; Ludwig Rajchman and the League of Nations subsidized a number of study trips for him to the four corners of Europe. The doctor was practicing. . . .

The doctor was writing, too. It was his most secret activity, without any doubt the most important in his eyes. *Voyage au bout de la nuit* was thus developed by fits and starts, bursts of fever, rabid composition, penitently, hours stolen from the night, from his patients, from the clinic. The pages accumulated. . . .

In April 1932 it was all done, written, typed. The doctor was ready to look for a publisher. The doctor was published. It was the final act played out before the official birth of Céline on October 15, 1932, the book's publication date.

1929–1932 . . . Throughout those three years, Louis Destouches continues to appear to us as a man divided. The portraits painted by those close to him are hard to tally. The man is contradictory, or, if you prefer, secretive. A single word, perhaps, allows us to link the various aspects he presents: the word "curiosity"—the curiosity that drives him to explore society's enigmas, its back streets, its disenfranchised, its fringes; the medical curiosity, too, that lures him from one country to another, one patient to another, a hygienist passionately involved with a truly innovative social medicine, and the literary curiosity, finally, that pushes him, perhaps without his being totally conscious of it, to break new ground in the novelistic field.

But there is first of all the doctor and society, the doctor and his private life, the doctor and his distractions. . . .

Thus, in August 1929, chased from Clichy by the building's bedbugs and suburban boredom, Louis and Elizabeth move in at 98, rue Lepic, in Montmartre. A little building, modern but already decrepit, whose streetside façade on the corner of the rue Girardon, on the heights of the Butte, bore a rather sad look, with its cream-colored exterior pierced by only two windows per floor, without the least architectural whimsy, rather like a barn that had been converted into a residential building. Their home was on the fourth floor at the end of the courtyard, in the garret. A setting for *Bohemian life*, already far from the noises of the city and the street, with Paris spread out before their eyes.

The interior disposition was "Bourgeois decor, country doctor style, or perhaps a parson? Rustic table, gleaming polished Breton wardrobes, period armchairs, wide sofa, a high tapestry screen, rugs nicely arranged on the floor, on the wall a little pastel of a dancer signed Degas, two or three decorative knickknacks, and, through the studio bay, the view of Paris! . . . Ah! Paris! . . . Paris and its sky!"[1]

Louis would remain in Montmartre essentially until June 1944, his escape and the end of the war, the end of the world—Montmartre had already ceased to be the village of painters, cabarets, and girls, in the accent of Bruant, under the sign of the Chat Noir and the canvases of Toulouse-Lautrec, but still avoided the bewildering postwar onslaught, cars from the world over, souvenir shops, greasy tourist restaurants and the place du Tertre encrusted with innumerable painters. And henceforth, Céline's friends—Gen Paul, Daragnès, Marcel Aymé, and the others—were his Montmartre friends, his neighbors, his accomplices, somewhat aloof from the city, from the commotion of the Grands Boulevards, from the shady disorder of Pigalle and the bourgeois serenity of the rue Caulaincourt. This was to become the geographical center of Céline's Paris and its observation post. He would contemplate the occupation from Montmartre. And the allied bombings of Paris and its suburbs in 1944. And as a symbol in his apocalyptic and literary delirium of the city's destruction, he would imagine in *Féerie pour une autre fois* the Butte Montmartre crumbling, collapsing on itself, honeycombed with caves and quarries, crushed by bombs, swept away by time. Leaving Montmartre, he would destroy it with a sweep of his pen, as if nothing should remain standing behind him.

But 1929 was a time for discovery, and he lured Elizabeth into it through the bedlam of their stormy affair, intermittent, passionate, detached, amused, fierce, in which voices were more often raised between them than tenderly whispered.

It was a strange affair, in which Elizabeth's remarkable and open vitality contrasted with Louis' cynical despair. She satisfied the part of him that dreamed of the inaccessible insouciance of another world—a world without the weight of sin, without the restraints of morality, as we have said. He loved her and watched her. He demanded no fidelity of her. On the contrary: "She only grants her favors to Louis' old friends and young friends if it amuses Louis . . . It often amuses Louis . . . She wouldn't betray Louis for an empire! In the contests where he presents her, she likes to stand near the '*petits cotres* [little sailboats]' the sweet brunettes whose waists and beauty contrast with her own. But she never loses the dignity of a proud three-master with all sails to the wind, even if it means scuttling on arrival in front of the entire flabbergasted jury, if the latter expresses any doubts on the quality of that race toward happiness."[2]

For her part, she never ceased to be amazed by this strange doctor with the bright eyes and dark thoughts, who dragged her to parties where fantasy easily overcame virtue, amongst painters, *cocottes*, songsters, comedians, down-and-outs, exhausted revelers and petulant filmmakers. Or else, on rue Lepic, while Louis wrote she allowed herself to keep fond company with Louis' friends, Marcel Brochard foremost amongst them.

But occasionally Louis couldn't go on. He stopped having fun. He was tired of watching. His lucidity locked him within himself. He wrote. He suffered from constant headaches, as always. He wanted to be alone. Elizabeth exasperated him. The whole world exasperated him. His auditory hallucinations provoked terrible rages, which writing sometimes attempted to express and to soothe. And a few hours later, the pain would ease like an ebbing tide. Elizabeth would be there, shipwrecked, miserable. He'd return to her. She was indispensable.

But naturally more frivolous, more carefree, with a radiant sensuality that did not restrict her to a specific gender in her sexual choices and roles, Elizabeth began to weary. Every year she returned to America. Each time a little longer. She sought other diversions. Or a port where she could relax for life, sheltered from the storm. Journeys to the end of night were not for her.

In Paris she had taken up dance classes again. She followed Mme. Egorova's course on the rue Rochechouart. There, in the very early '30s, she met a Danish dancer, a tall, slender brunette with light blue eyes, twenty-seven years old, born of a wealthy Copenhagen family, who danced in variety shows throughout the world, in Berlin or New York, Chicago, Copenhagen or Paris, and who answered to the lovely name of Karen Marie Jensen. She immediately fell in love with the young woman, introduced her to Louis in February 1931, and they soon formed an unusual trio of sexual complicity, anticipation, misunderstandings and thinly disguised jealousies. Louis' charm worked on Karen. Did the latter help to oust Elizabeth, did she suggest her abandoning Louis and returning to America forever? The murk of the soul is not easily pierced.

In any case, Louis noticed none of her scheming. "I am entirely French in the sense that the infinite variables surrounding the quite banal and imperious reproductive instinct have always seemed like perfect furies to me—I have lived in Priapus all my life, either as a pimp or a patron, and always for the hell of it! I am unable to perceive the tragedy in ass except for *diseases* and *pregnancy*—but as to the rest of it, like Lenin I accord it the significance of a 'very valuable biological stimulus.' Nothing more—nothing less— Lacking all jealousy, Don Juanism, sadism, etc., I have never had enthusiasm for anything but the beauty of forms, fluidity, youth, gracefulness— . . .

In short, I am a swine! And I consume little, unfortunately, concentrated as I am on my work. So serious—*despite myself*—scrupulous—ferocious at my task— I've always liked women to be beautiful and lesbian— Quite pleasant to look at and never tiring me with their sexual needs! Let them feast on, play with, devour each other—with me watching—that gets me hot! and how! always has! A voyeur, certainly, and a somewhat enthusiastic but perfectly discreet consumer!"[3]

At about the time of his move, Louis Destouches had made the acquaintance of Henri Mahé. Germaine Constans, acting through Aimée Barancy, a journalist at *L'Intransigeant*, had introduced them to each other. This Breton painter cut a fine figure—capricious, boastful, truculent, he preferred the company of *demi-monde* or marginal fauna of all stripes—pimps, whores, artists, madams, singers, and writers—to that of his well-bred clients. With his wife, the daughter of a violin teacher from Rennes who knew Édith Follet well, he lived on a canal boat, the *Malamoa*, at first moored in Croissy-sur-Seine, later on the quai de Bourbon off the Île Saint-Louis, until, moved on by the river police, he ended up off the quai des Tuileries. Mahé had worked as a scenery painter on some of Abel Gance's films, and had been assigned along with many other painters to the appointment of the liner *Normandie*. Louis commissioned a more humble "nautical fresco" from him—for the bathroom on the rue Lepic. Amongst Mahé's more famous extant works are the "Balajo" mural paintings on the rue de Lappe and the interior of the Rex cinema on the boulevard Poissonière (inaugurated the day of Louis' failure to be awarded the Goncourt Prize). But the loud-mouthed Mahé, known as "Riton-la-Barbouille," who would soon begin finding more inspiration at the bottom of a bottle than in paint pots, had made a specialty out of the decoration of brothels and other "parlor houses." The Sphinx, on the rue Montparnasse; the Joubert, on the rue Joubert; Charonne's Hotel, an underworld hangout; or the 31, cité d'Antin were all his. We might say that his minor connections helped him in his major escapades.

According to Germaine Constans, "Henri Mahé had a vocabulary that Dr. Destouches could only find attractive. They had to meet. They thought the same way. They were Vikings, incomprehensible to us little Southerners. Henri began drinking only much later. Their affinities and complicity didn't prevent a certain artist's rivalry from existing between them. As soon as Louis entered a group, he wanted to stir it up. The regulars on the *Malamoa*? Marie Dubas, Eliane Tayar and Nane Germon, Roger Lécuyer, 'expert on poetry and cuisine,' Beby and Antonet, Emmanuel Auricoste . . . Sundays on the *Malamoa* were our wild days. Having sung our hearts out, we would come home hoarse from Bougival on the Saint-Germain bus."[4]

Some very pretty women and some very sinister men sometimes found their way onto the boat. Roger Lécuyer, the poet-grocer, had his own memories of Mahé's other casual friends: Paul Belmondo, Maurice Cloche,

Francis Carco, Mistinguett, Georges Simenon or the Fratellinis. "Henri organized costume balls. Louis Destouches declared himself the vampire of Düsseldorf to an Isabelle of Bavaria, then struck up an American revolutionary song at the top of his lungs. Edmond Heuzé played the accordion. I sang 'Les Beaux Dimanches,' which reminded Louis of life in the provinces. We would leave voiceless at dawn on the tram."[5]

And Mahé recalled the nights on the quai des Tuileries when, under the pale glow of the streetlights, furtive games of hide-and-seek and sleight-of-hand were played out behind the trees, rapid and clumsily executed acts of prostitution well observed by the prowling voyeurs. When the vice squad came around, the frightened ladies took refuge on the nearest barge.[6]

We will soon come across Mahé's infamous barge again in *Voyage au bout de la nuit*, the latest provisional and providential refuge for Bardamu, Robinson and Madelon in the heart of the countryside—a clean, spruced up tub with food on the table, the owner's paintings on the walls, accordion music, festivities and unbridled merriment.[7]

Between Louis Destouches and Henri Mahé, the Norman and the Breton, there was of course that shared ironic and curious joy in coasting the undersides of society, that somewhat loutish, somewhat vulgar, somewhat artistic revelry, but all very cautious, without too much exposure to risk, just to see, to get some cheap thrills. More important was the shared, restless call of the distance, ships, the sea, the oceans. For Mahé, the canal boat was still nothing, a placebo to fool his dream the way one fools one's hunger. Louis loved returning to Brittany at the drop of a hat, any excuse would do. He loved the bustle of the ports, the tugboats, the granite coasts, the iodized smells of seaweed and spray. Over the course of the years, Louis and Henri would go to meet each other in Saint-Malo or elsewhere. At heart that was their true common ground.

In talking about women, their respective merits, their beauty, their promise, maritime metaphors became the usage: "Thus, a promising girl was a 'little sailboat' and as soon as we saw one on the street we moved in head to the wind; even if it meant navigating up close to some fat 'old tub,' the mother, we boarded her! . . . 14, 15 years old? Those were our schooners! There, you had to run before the wind! Declare your freight! A trip to the canal boat. . . . Right! Over 20, long legs, those were our three-masters."[8]

But all this, the meetings with Mahé, nights on the *Malamoa*, the three-master boarding parties and dawn debauches constituted rare interludes in Louis Destouches' life. He wanted to see. He saw. Then he wanted nothing more than to turn the page. Mostly, he worked.

He dragged Elizabeth to the movies on the Grands Boulevards. Unfailingly, he would leave before the end. He understood them too quickly. In other words, he was bored. He was more easily held by musical comedy and the ballet. At least there was dancing, dancers, a sort of enchanted, tangible reality to keep under your eyes, in which to stow your dreams an hour or two. And then there was the theater, to which he had given so much thought in writing *L'Église* and *Progrés*.

In November 1929 he corresponded with Charles Dullin, his neighbor in Montmartre, whose stage productions and settings he was familiar with. Dullin may have considered staging *L'Église*. In any case, at the moment when Louis himself had given up on his career as a dramatic author and on his two overly static works, at the moment when he was launching the extraordinary novelistic enterprise of *Voyage au bout de la nuit*, a letter like the following, sent to Dullin to define his criteria for a good play, seems particularly striking. He writes of the theater, and we think of his novels: ". . . it seems to me that, after all, one has to prefer those that go somewhere. The world, whatever they say, is going somewhere, it only gives the impression of swallowing its own tail. The truly good plays go somewhere. Where? Toward the world's future and that's their role. Almost all of Shakespeare goes somewhere, it's fireworks, it's a release. That's it: a good play must be a release."[9]

The years were passing and his daughter, Colette, was growing. Nine years old, soon to be ten in 1930. Louis saw little of her, thought of her often. She was astonishingly like him, the same clear gaze, the high forehead, the thin lips and the forceful nose. Despite the Follets' comfortable means, he insisted on sending her a maintenance allowance. Ever that same strict sense of duty—in his fashion. If he heard that Colette was ill, he was on the first train to Rennes to comfort her, soothe her, oversee the quality of the care tendered her. Sometimes he took her with him to Paris for a few days, a week or two, whenever he felt like it. Édith did not stand in the way. She even came along to drive her around. She had just enough time to see a slender young redhead, a little nervous, who smiled at her and used the familiar *tu* quite unaffectedly. It was Elizabeth Craig. And a few days later, the vacation over, Colette was back on the road to Rennes, to school, and to respectable society. Elizabeth Craig would occasionally return her to her mother.

"Louis would have been very happy for Colette to become a dancer," admits Édith Follet. "But in those days it wouldn't have done at all, it would have been looked at askance in the provinces. . . . Elizabeth Craig? She was delicate and plump at the same time, she had a monument of red hair on her head, she may not have been a very pretty woman but she had plenty of charm, very nice."[10]

But Louis Destouches' life in Paris, these diversions, Henri Mahé and the others, musical comedy, the theater, Dullin, and the cinema—they were nothing, merely the icing on his days and nights, a sideshow, a cultural soup that Louis Destouches kept on the hob, watched, as if for future literary and human experiments. Whatever he or others might say, he had none of the sensualist about him. He didn't know how. He didn't have the time—or the tranquillity of soul—for it. Above all he had to keep moving. To work. To write. To heal. Hunt down truth from one agony to the next. Observe people's hidden convulsions. Imagine stories, ramblings, and deliria. Howl his rebellion against death from one page to the next. Without illusions and without solace.

The Doctor Practices

Did Dr. Destouches have ambitions to be named head physician of the new clinic in Clichy? It seems likely. In any case he felt a lively hostility toward the man who had very soon taken the position. Grégoire Ichok was a doctor of Lithuanian Jewish origins, born April 22, 1892, in Mariampol. There will naturally be speculation about professional hostility, spiteful jealousy that may have fed the writer's latent anti-Semitism. The fact remains that Ichok was an ambiguous person, disliked by the staff of the rue Fanny clinic, where he never actually practiced. He dismissed another physician, Dr. Waynbaum, a woman pediatrician, for incompatibility of temperament. He was held to be ingratiating with the nurses. Tall (6′ 6″) and of a waxen palor, he was nicknamed *"Pertes blanches"* [vaginal discharge] by Louis Destouches. And because he wished to be called *"Monsieur le Médecin-Chef"* [Mr. Head Physician], Louis inevitably greeted him with a loud and ingenuous "Dear Colleague."

We recognize the enmities that revolve around an obsession, the restrained, obsessive violence born of an unbearable promiscuity prolonged too long. Between Ichok and Céline, the man of the Left and the anarchist of the Right, both suffering delusions of persecution, that was no doubt the case. After the war, the writer further accused his colleague to Robert Poulet of having been a phony doctor, an agent of Moscow. In a letter to Albert Paraz on May 18, 1951, he returned once more to the hated figure of the prewar years, whom he called an impostor foisted on the communist municipality of Clichy by *Pravda*, where his brother was an editor, a man who didn't even speak French, who spied for three or four foreign nations, who had tried to raise the clinic against him, the good Frenchman, the non-Jew, forcing him to quit.[11]

Of course Grégoire Ichok was not a fake doctor. His medical dissertation, defended in Paris in 1927, had been devoted to "suckling rooms." He taught at the Paris Statistical Institute while working as a technical consultant to the Ministry of Public Health. An active member of the Society for the Propagation of Cremation, he was then militating for LICA (The International League to Fight Anti-Semitism). He devoted a book to the cemeteries of Paris. He wrote comfortably in French, English, Spanish, Italian, and German. He counted amongst his close friends Marc Chagall, Julien Cain, who ran the National Library, and Salomon Grumbach, chairman of the Foreign Affairs Committee in the Chambre des Députés. His friends described him as a man passionate about public health, lacking political ambition, and very attached to "his" clinic. Did he have a brother in Russia and another in New York? His sister, it seems, was a Soviet official in Berlin. Was that a basis on which to accuse him of being a spy for the Communist Party, of having infiltrated the Socialist Party, or vice versa? An honors panel convened in the Clichy town hall in 1936 would absolve him of all such accusations for lack of evidence.

The outbreak of war and the Nazi threat naturally affected him to the highest degree. He fell into a deep nervous depression. On January 10, 1940, he took a cyanide capsule from the pharmacy of the Clichy clinic and poisoned himself on the terrace of the Café des Sports in Porte Maillot. Grégoire Ichok's death was instantaneous.

Let us return to 1929. Attacks, insinuations, resentments, and persecution real or imagined were not, after all, the only pastimes of the doctors at the Clichy clinic. Louis Destouches healed there. Come what may, he made his daily rounds.

"This brand-new clinic was the sick heart of a large housing project, half worker and half hobo. The architects had dreamed up a pretty little square to frame the clinic, planting young trees, lovingly varying the species, placing comfortable benches for the mothers and the old people, creating parks of fine sand for the children."[12]

At once attentive, cynical, and philosophical, indulgent and disenchanted, with that perpetually intense gaze that seemed to plumb the sick to the very depths of their bodies, their secrets, their diseases, or their miseries, Louis Destouches saw a procession of drunks and pregnant women file through the rue Fanny in Clichy, tuberculosis victims and cripples, workers after disability certificates, and young men and women panicked by their venereal diseases. He preferred the tried and trusted medicines and the basic rules of hygiene to the more modern, more chemical, more ambitious therapies. He was more a man of common sense than of science. Had he aspired to a middle-class career, he would have been, as they say, the very picture of an excellent family doctor: guide, counselor, confidant, the opposite of a specialist. But the public and proletarian medicine he chose—and suffered through—resulted in less urbanity, fewer smiles and bows. His benevolence must have been tempered by a healthy dose of fatalism.

A tramp, staggering and spitting impressive jets of red wine onto the tiles, lurches into the consultation room.

"You must have a stomachache," diagnoses Dr. Destouches.

The tramp agrees. He stokes the boiler at a nearby factory.

"And you don't drink anymore?"

"No, doctor!"

"Any more than fourteen liters a day?"

"Yes, doctor, not any more than that . . ."

And Louis Destouches, growing suddenly more serious and more tender, grants him two weeks' sick leave. He makes him promise to stop drinking and very gravely announces his prescription: a liter of H_2O per meal.

"The pharmacist knows the formula," he adds to reassure the man. Henri Mahé was present and it was he who retold the anecdote.

There were also the very young girls hovering at the edge of prostitution, to whom Louis gave basic hygiene tips (moral tips, he knew from experience, were absolutely useless), perhaps enjoying himself, like a licentious connaisseur without illusions, before such youth, such timid sensuality and insouciance that too soon would be spoiled by the barbarity of life.

At the Marthe-Brandés clinic in Saint-Ouen, Paris, Louis was especially generous in helping veterans, his ex-companions-at-arms already grown old. He would arrive like a blast of wind. He spoke to no one of his literary projects, as if pretending to attach little importance to them. He maintained a polite reserve before his colleagues, friends, and patients, saying nothing about his private life. "While being tolerant and gentle with people who badgered him untowardly, he had down pat the art of avoiding questions by dissuading the patient from pursuing the conversation, using a paternal but firm tone of voice. His face remained smiling and his eyes betrayed his kindliness. He was liked because he inspired trust."[13]

From 1930 onward, while continuing to work at La Biothérapie, Louis Destouches helped M. Gallier, one of the company's administrators, in a little business he had set up on his own: a pharmaceutical laboratory housed at 38, boulevard du Montparnasse. As early as 1927 he had brought Germaine Constans in as a pharmaceutical salesperson. "Germaine Constans? Blond! Athletic! Raised to the Legion of Honor! Papa! Major Constans died in the middle of a bridge game in the Invalides [veterans' hospital] at the age of 103 . . . She climbs 400 flights a day simpering to the medicos about the benefits of the pharmaceutical products of Dr. Destouches, her good buddy."[14]

With Gallier, Louis Destouches worked as a writer but also as a researcher. There he perfected a medication to treat painful periods, menopause, Basedow's disease, pneumogastric problems, etc.: Basedowine. Offered in the form of pills, this medication, containing ovary powder, thyroid extract, and acetosoluble ovarian hormone, was perfected in 1933 and pulled from the market in 1971. Its commercial success was, however, very modest.[15]

There is no question, then, of imagining for one second a brilliant and remunerative career as a pharmacologist-inventor for Dr. Destouches. For one thing he had neither the time nor the aptitude for it. All this, the Basedowine and the rest of it, was probably no more than a challenge to him, perhaps a game, the proof of his unquenchable thirst to discover—the same desire that made him travel.

In April 1927, as we have mentioned, Céline had gone to London for a brief and disappointing medico-hygienic inquiry funded by the League of Nations. Immediately afterward he planned a new trip to the Nordic countries. On August 20 of that same year, he wrote to Ludwig Rajchman in Geneva: "My dear Director and friend. . . . At Clichy we have attempted an experiment in popular medicine based not on *diagnosis* but on *healing*, verified whenever possible by laboratory tests (Verne, etc.), this for all current and specific ailments, tuberculosis, syphilis, etc. I should like to know and observe what is happening in that regard in the capitals of States more socially advanced, I should also like to learn very specifically about the nutritional, housing, and sanitary conditions of the poorest workers in Sweden, Norway, Denmark, and Hamburg. . . . Here is the itinerary I should like to follow: Paris—(1) Antwerp—(2) Oslo—(3) Stockholm—(4) Copenhagen—(5) Hamburg—Paris. Length of the journey: *one month.* During and at the end of my journey I will send you a report on *Medicine in the public clinics of these respective cities.*"[16]

Rajchman welcomed the request. On September 1 a new letter from Louis, this time requesting that his daily allowance be increased from five to seven dollars because, he claimed, life over there was as expensive as in the USA and England, and that, on top of that, he had to pay his substitute in Clichy out of his own pocket while he was away, seventy francs a day. And he concluded: "I shall send you a very detailed report upon my return, if you should even want me to come to Geneva around December 25 and *at my expense* with Colette, I shall come. Ever yours. Louis Destouches."[17]

This letter proves at least three things: (1) that Louis never tired of making naive promises, of inventing reports which he knew, and Rajchman probably knew, he would never write; (2) that, despite the lampoons of Rajchman and the League in general, and despite the thinly veiled anti-Semitic allusions in *L'Église*, he continued to maintain close and even friendly relations with Rajchman; he even goes so far as to mention a visit to him with his daughter, as if to soften him up; (3) that, more than stinginess or a manifest lack of subtlety (when Louis says, for instance, that he will come to see him at his own expense, underlining this last detail), he still retains an almost maniacal concern for scrounging and hoarding money by any means.

This is one of the most revealing contradictions of the man and the writer. On the one hand, Céline loved to take big risks and was wildly prodigal. On the other, he remained the suspicious petty-bourgeois, the wily peasant who mistrusted everything, preferred gold to scraps of paper, cash buried or kept under a mattress to the fine words of bankers. A penny is a penny and anything he could get his hands on, pile up and salt away, was good for the taking. If he had to complain and whine about poverty, fine, he wouldn't hesitate to do so. But once again his attitude was not petty. Céline was not a man of half-measures, but of enormous, contradictory disproportions. Later on, his scams, the business of his stashing gold in Denmark with Karen Marie Jensen, will prove to be just as magnificently catastrophic as his laments and recriminations raised to the literary rank of fabled wrath.

After several delays, Louis Destouches finally completed this trip to the north from December 22, 1929, to February 13, 1930, stopping successively in Germany, Denmark, Norway, and Sweden. By way of a report, the Health

Section received only a postcard sent from Stockholm, in which Louis set out his list of expenses. But not too much irony! In Louis' eyes, after all, this was not merely a pleasure cruise "financed by the princess" (of Lake Geneva). Socialized medicine held a vivid interest for him. Without doubt he wanted to observe its accomplishments at every latitude, even if it entailed keeping his observations to himself. Destouches the doctor hardly went in for neatly dosed-out writings and prudently self-congratulatory testimonial-reports. He had had more than his share of that in Geneva. Hence, on March 8, 1930, the leftist weekly *Monde*, put out by Barbusse and Altman, published a polemical article on "Public Health in France," in which Louis displayed a healthy virulence.

From journey to journey . . . In the summer of 1930 he left for Central Europe, thanks to new grants from the League. On June 2 he had written to the ever-patient, ever-resigned, ever-faithful Ludwig Rajchman:

My dear Director,

I will be pleased to go to Dresden, Prague, and Vienna from June 28 to July 17 next in order:

1. To visit the hygiene fair in Dresden; gather certain information on mass medicine, antivenereal and antitubercular prophylaxis;

2. To go to Prague for the same reasons and also to visit Dr. Philippe and Dr. Libensky's exhibition at the Polubradi thermal installation, where those practitioners are employing Verne's methods;

3. To learn what has been done in Vienna in the matter of workers' housing *and* socialized medicine, *antitubercular and venereal prophylaxis.*

In Clichy, I am pursuing my work on the perfection of a standard medicine *and I hope to publish a book on the subject in a few months. This journey would be very useful not only that I might collect documentation in Dresden and elsewhere, but also so that I can establish comparative studies and get an idea of the whole in certain areas, which it is almost impossible for me to obtain when I remain in Clichy or simply in France.*[18]

And Ludwig Rajchman allocated him a grant of 140 dollars.

From January 8 to 11, 1931, Louis went to Geneva with Elizabeth Craig. He had asked to see certain documents there. Did the Rajchman family receive her, and what impression did Elizabeth make on them? No one knows. The bridges between Louis and the League had not yet been burned, despite the unkept promises, despite the repeated grants he received and the reports he never wrote. Elizabeth and he stopped in Mégève on the way back.

In late February Louis received a mission of foreign doctors sent to Paris by the League. Amongst them was a certain Dr. Wu of the Quarantine Service in China. Louis wrote shortly thereafter to Dr. Boudreau, one of Ludwig Rajchman's associates in Geneva:

"In Paris, M. Wu visited the medical facilities he had wanted to see: among others—the Pasteur Institute, the Maisons-Alfort veterinary school, the Folies-Bergère, the Institut Verne, the Clichy clinic, the Opéra, a . . . Chinese Restaurant, etc. etc.

"M. Wu was the victim of a minor accident, a slight sprain of the ankle while on his way to the *métro*."[19]

This laconic and derisive sense of humor could hardly have been to the taste of the honorable physician-diplomats of the no less honorable League of Nations.

He was assigned to another brief mission: to serve as interpreter to a hygiene committee convened in Paris from April 22 to 25, 1931, to debate the burning question of ship fumigation. About the same time the following year, he again officiated as guide and interpreter to a new committee convened by the public health section. And that was all. The bonds between him and Geneva would relax after that. He would be subsidized for a final journey to Berlin and Vienna in late '32/ early '33, allowing him to leave Paris in the middle of the Goncourt tempest. After that date, he will maintain no contractual connection to the League of Nations.

Had he exhausted once and for all Ludwig Rajchman's stock of goodwill toward him? More simply, Louis Destouches was becoming a writer. He was allowing himself to be taken over by his new craft and his new role. He no longer took the time to solicit subsidies for medical inquiries. Henceforth he reserved his journeys solely for his own curiosity, the haphazard of encounters, or the fatality of history.

The Doctor Writes

Three years to write *Voyage*, to invent a style and turn French literature upside down—is that a lot or a little? We must judge for ourselves. With his usual taste for exaggeration, if not lying, Céline spoke of a labor of ten years or so. Which might just about be understandable if we include *L'Église* in the process of creating the novel, as one of its early sketches with dialogue, or if we accept Picasso's famous reply to a questioner, astonished that he should have earned so much money for a canvas painted so quickly, to which the painter replied that he may have taken only five minutes to create it but that he had been thinking about it for twenty years.

Céline also spoke to his publisher, Robert Denoël, of about ten successive versions of *Voyage* and of nearly 20,000 manuscript pages. In truth, Céline wrote rabidly, feverishly. A few words per line, a few lines per page, the convulsive trail of his visions, his rhythm, his delirium. He corrected little, preferring to start afresh. Hence, the number of pages is not pertinent in his case. And the novel's early manuscript has disappeared. All that has been preserved is a typed version corrected in the author's hand—which the latter sold to a jeweler, Bignou, during the occupation.

Three years, then, to write *Voyage* . . . A writer's true biography would be precisely that: to observe and describe him as he is writing one book, and then another, and another, his entire oeuvre. The rest is just anecdotes, details, trimmings. "A writer's craft is to learn how to write," said Jules Renard. All his life, Céline sought to learn that craft, to pursue, to deepen, to push to its furthest limits the quest for a style. What an evolution between the relative stylistic moderation of *Voyage* and the sumptuously exploded prose of the later works! From 1929 to his death, Céline would never cease to write or, if you prefer, to learn to write. To tell the story of a life is to tell the story of a craft.

Books are the products of solitude and the children of silence, noted Marcel Proust. How to break that solitude? How to align the sentences, the words, the noise, to discuss that silence? In the end, the Céline that interests us is not the Céline he put on display, the dazzling storyteller, the acerbic witness who wanted to attract the attention of all society, nor is it the intemperate seducer, already wearied at the moment of triumph; it is not the taciturn, disillusioned doctor, the approximating researcher, the man tormented by buzzing in his ears, the vociferator, the tireless voyager to the end of himself and the world; it is first and foremost the Céline who writes, the Céline who recaptures, kneads, grinds, transforms his experiences, his emotions, his hopes, his rebellions, as well as the one who imagines, who remembers, who becomes the demiurge. . . . But there you are, we can only revolve about that silence, detect a few of its signals, pick up some crumbs of a secret that we will never share.

While shooting *Le Mystère Picasso* in 1956, the filmmaker Henri-Georges Clouzot sought to surprise and film the painter in the act of creation. A fascinating endeavor, but an illusory one. A work was indeed being created before us. But what work? Picasso was perfectly well aware of being filmed. As a result, he was playing the role of painter. He was imitating for the filmmaker the activity that was habitually and silently his own. We saw a performance of a creation, not the creation itself. A simulacrum of a life. How much harder is it, then, to picture the filming of a writer composing a novel, to watch a literary work develop hour by hour, day by day, year by year.

Three years to write *Voyage* . . .

"I stuck to it a good deal. An hour here, a half-hour there, at the end of the day. In those days, I was stuck on night duty for the Reds in Clichy. The things I saw, morning to night, you can't imagine! . . . I went home at dawn, I slept my fill. Then came my little writing duty . . . Naturally, what I wrote wasn't stroke for stroke what I had thought beforehand. There was a distancing, owing to what is called the gift, the temperament, whatever you want to call it. An artist is never entirely free."[20]

To the eternal question, "Should we believe Céline?" another question is preferable in this case: Whom should we believe if not him? Of course, one must always make certain allowances. Nevertheless, the idea to keep in mind is that of the fragmentation of the time the author allotted to writing his book. Louis Destouches was a pharmacist in the morning, a doctor at night, a writer whenever he was able, at rest whenever he could find a few hours' sleep, and a casual Don Juan when the whim came upon him. Make of this what you can. What would Céline have recognized here?

"I write as I can, when I can, where I can. All through my working life, which has gone on without interruption since I was 12 (except for four years of war), I have stolen hours from my employers, stolen time from my livelihood, to work on my own little projects. I write on the run, the way I've always lived: on the run. That's how I did my studies, always tearing some hours from the daily drudgery; that's how I wrote my fat books, whence no doubt the hasty, panting tone for which I am taken to task, which people think is made up. And yet that's how I talk, that's all. I'm not 'stylizing.' "[21]

Céline did little editing, as we have said. He preferred to begin his passage, his chapter, his book, entirely from scratch. Like a painter who jumps from one canvas to another so as to pursue, grasp, develop the single dream of a perfect painting. Or a filmmaker who shoots twenty or thirty takes of the same scene so as finally to achieve its perfection.

To surprise Céline in the act of writing—in essence, to tell the story of his life as a writer—is first to picture him as a man of velocity. Seeking to capture as fast as possible the images, rhythms, adventures, and aphorisms that jostled about in his mind. He wrote feverishly, in a single outpouring. His writing was not fastidious; it was flung onto the paper, often barely decipherable. He threw punctuation for a loop, he used hyphens like stepping-stones from one idea to another, an unexpected glissade. . . . Céline was assuredly a stylist. But his style was endlessly corrected, emerging by dint of retakes, repetitions, overhauls, additions, or suppression, and not slowly, silently weighed and thought out before consigning it to paper. Céline's style is based on concreteness, on the very fabric of words, and not on inchoate concepts, internal rhythms, mental images: "The first page, the first sentence . . . That was it, all I had to do was let myself flow along to the end. To the very end of night! . . . The motion had been set. As to the tone, I didn't know, I didn't realize it, despite my analyses and reflexions on other people's books. It just seemed better to me like that. I already had a picture of the whole book in mind; and also bit by bit, the complete architecture. All my works are written that way. Leaving nothing to chance."[22]

Céline is surely not lying here. "I didn't know, I didn't realize." He had probably not accurately weighed his book's incredible explosive charge, its power of combustion. Great inventions and great emotions often arise that way, fortuitously. There sometimes exists a sort of innocence or happy irresponsibility at the source of a literary work. It is a blessed moment, when one is not seeking but one finds nonetheless. And that no doubt was the case of Louis Destouches when he wrote *Voyage au bout de la nuit*. But the rest of his life will not suffice him to understand the breadth of his invention, his style (not only, as he said, the intrusion of spoken language into written literature—which, moreover, is not entirely accurate—but also the shattering of the narrative, the narration, for the sake of the unique presence of a *voice*, a speech, an emotion, a narrator who in some way focuses the book's entire dramatic burden around his own elocution), to deepen it, to carry this literary journey, this adventure, to its conclusion.

More prosaically, what had impelled Dr. Destouches to undertake writing *Voyage* in the final weeks before his move from the Clichy apartment? Céline always gave the same litany in answer to those who questioned him: to earn some money, because Eugène Dabit had had a wild success with *Hôtel du Nord* and he could do just as well.

That is what he confessed from the start to Élisabeth Porquerol, whom he met following her favorable review of *Voyage* in *Crapouillot* in February 1933.[23]

It is what he often reiterated to his friend Robert Poulet.

It is what he expanded upon in his famous interview with Madeleine Chapsal in *L'Express* in June 1957: "I wrote to pay for an apartment . . . It's simple: I was born at a time when we were afraid of rent day! Nobody's afraid of rent day anymore. I told myself: it's the right time for populism, Dabit, all those people were putting out books. And I said: I can do as much! It'll get me an apartment and I won't be bothered with rent day anymore! . . . I wouldn't have gone into it otherwise."[24]

It is what he drummed into Jean Guénot and Jacques Darribehaude in February '60: "I knew Dabit, who was at the Abbesses *métro* station . . . He was a sweet guy . . . You know that he was communist . . . Anyway, he puts out *Hôtel du Nord* with Denoël . . . Me, at the time, I was having a hell of a time paying the rent, as it happens . . . It wasn't so hot, I assure you . . . So, how to get out of it . . . I started to write."[25]

It is that, finally, of which he convinced Claude Bonnefoy, who interviewed him for *Arts* in 1961 shortly before his death. Why had he become a writer? "I should've been a psychiatrist! Why? Not by vocation. I hadn't thought about it before. But I knew Eugène Dabit . . . He had just had a great success with *Hôtel du Nord* . . . I thought, 'I'll do the same. It'll help me pay the rent.' So I really got down to looking for a language, a style charged with emotion, direct . . . I hate flowery stuff . . . nicely spun language . . . facile little tricks . . . It's very hard to concentrate . . . The head is a muscle . . . You have to exercise it every day . . .

"The book caused a fuss. It stopped me from doing medicine . . . I miss it, medicine was my vocation. I never should have written."[26]

Because of Dabit, then, and to earn some money . . . The statement is doubly debatable.

Eugène Dabit's *Hôtel du Nord* was published in November 1929 by the Librairie des Trois Magots, founded in 1928 by Robert Denoël (and which was the predecessor of the publishing house that was to bear his name). By that time, Louis had already begun writing *Voyage*, which we know through Jeanne Carayon, his neighbor from the Clichy apartment that he left in August 1929. That alone is enough to refute his statements. It is likely, however, that the book's success impressed and encouraged him. Especially as *L'Hôtel du Nord* received the Prix Populiste in May 1931. But we must repeat that it had been many years, particularly with his theatrical forays, since Louis had been thinking of writing—and of publishing.

Four years his junior, Dabit resembled him in many ways. An only son raised in humble surroundings, he had been sent into apprenticeship very young. He had enjoyed summer vacations on the shores of the Channel and Sundays in the countryside around Paris. He had fought to acquire an education by himself by dint of clandestine reading and hours stolen from sleep. He had also enlisted in the army. And in his books, *L'Hôtel du Nord*, in 1929, and *P'tit Louis*, in 1930, Dabit gave life to a popular, proletarian world described from memory in the greatest detail, with no stylistic tricks, striving (timidly) for a spoken, popular language without affectation, which in itself was a striking contrast to the literary productions of the time.[27] But Céline was to push that experience much further, above all correcting Dabit's determined optimism with more tragically revealing hues and an entirely different violence of style.

Writing just to earn some money? That, too, is an odd notion. In 1929 Louis was finally enjoying a regular income. He had pretty much wiped out his debts in Geneva—or given them up for good, which comes to the same. His private practice had cost him money, he had closed it. Between the Clichy clinic, his work at La Biothérapie and soon with Gallier, one or two missions subsidized by the League, he was earning a comfortable living. He certainly didn't have anything to worry about. He was no longer at the mercy of a private clientele. His monthly expenses were decreasing regularly. He was entirely at his leisure to think about other things.

He was thinking about them all the more willingly now that his professional life was disappointing him. Socialized medicine? His great humanitarian ideals were being crushed beneath the sullen routine of daily work. With Grégoire Ichok, the atmosphere at the Clichy clinic remained hateful. At La Biothérapie, he was putting in an appearance, some writing, nothing stirring. The same with Gallier. Of course, there were travels. But Louis knew perfectly well that they were only distractions, escapes. Like Elizabeth, like eroticism, like theater, like friends. He thought he was moving ahead while he was turning in circles. From Stockholm to Vienna, from London to Paris. A dramatist? He had thought about that with *L'Église*, *Progrès*, and had then given it up. Wisely. Lucidly. To write a novel, finally to liberate his own *voice*, that, perhaps, was the only issue remaining to him in 1929. The only valve open to this man too full of anger, memory, emotion, rebellion, who felt the contradictory needs for the most intense solitude and the most painful encounters. As if he wanted simultaneously to assert himself, leave a trace—that somewhat pathetic way to exorcise death—and to withdraw from the world, efface himself behind a pseudonym, a new, more secretive craft.

The sources of *Voyage*, the influences that marked Céline, are closer to literary scholarship than to biographical narrative. We should mention, however, Barbusse's *Le Feu*, which Céline doubtless read on his return from Cameroon in 1917, and which he quotes on many occasions in his correspondence. And the translation in June 1929 of Erich-Maria Remarque's novel *All Quiet on the Western Front*, which could not have escaped his curiosity. These are possible starting points, possible examples to be kept in mind for his narrative, which also begins with murderous fighting during the Great War, fighting stripped of its patriotic idealism and grandiloquent prose.

Where did Céline derive his spoken style, the colloquial or slang expressions that he often uses? Surely not from his family environment, where only the proper and strained language of a petty-bourgeoisie hungry for respectability would have been heard. Nor at the Follets', where, as early as Rennes, his plain speaking was found shocking. Colonel Rémy, a close friend of Henri Mahé, said shortly before his death: "Knowing that Henri Mahé was susceptible to alcohol, Céline would get him drunk, work him into a fury, then carefully jot down the words brought on by his anger and born of an entirely personal vocabulary so as to claim their invention in his future manuscripts: indeed, when Henri Mahé couldn't find the right word, he invented it off the cuff, in such a confident manner that one understood what he was trying to say."[28]

It is easy to imagine the extent to which the truculence of Mahé and his friends inspired Louis Destouches. As a rule, Louis enjoyed mingling with people of every condition, workers, the unemployed, tramps, bourgeois, artists, toughs. He was not only a voyeur but a listener. He remembered. Phrases, words, expressions, intonations, distortions, emotions. We should not, therefore, overestimate the influence of one man. It would seem rather naive in any case, not to say spiteful, to attribute to Henri Mahé the exclusive paternity of Céline's lexical or stylistic brainstorms. That would obviously be a misunderstanding of the essential thing: the patient work of transposition, of distorting the spoken into the written, in short, the search for a style. One blushes at having to defend such trivial truths.

Two encounters truly put their mark on Louis Destouches at the time of writing *Voyage*. Those of Marcel Lafaye and Joseph Garcin, with whom he would maintain episodic and sometimes friendly relations and who most certainly contributed in a more conclusive way than Henri Mahé to the genesis of the Célinian oeuvre.

We once knew of only one model for Bardamu, the hero of *Voyage*, and that was Louis Destouches himself, the author, who had undertaken in his first novel to recount, sum up, magnify, and sometimes invent his own life in order to lend his hero consistency. Today, however, our knowledge of Lafaye makes that less certain. "It was the meeting of Destouches with his double, with a Bardamu whose adventures were in a way more consistent than those of the author himself," wrote literature professor Pierre Lainé, to whom we owe the biographical "discovery" of these two friends of Céline.[29]

Louis met Lafaye for the first time in the summer of '28, thanks to some Montmartre friends. He must have been struck by the similarity of their past experience. In August of that same year, Lafaye left for the United States, hired as an aviation mechanic for Pratt and Whitney in Hartford, before joining Ford Motors in Detroit in January '29. After wanderings to New York and Canada, Lafaye ended up in Paris, where he remained from 1930 to 1934 before settling permanently in North Africa.

Louis and Marcel had corresponded between 1928 and 1930, and they sought each other out again in Montmartre. Noëlle Lafaye recalled endless conversations between her father and Céline in the *bistros* on the Butte. Marcel told him about Ford, the factories of Detroit, provided him with information on hiring practices, daily life at the factory, everything that Louis had of course been unable to observe in the course of his barely forty-eight-hour, superficial visit to the automobile plant. Better still, in North America Marcel had had an affair with a certain Dorothy, maternal, gentle, attentive, who, in many ways, greatly resembled Molly, the young Detroit prostitute in love with Bardamu. Noëlle Lafaye also reported the statement of a friend who had told Louis Destouches in 1930, "Marcel's just back from the United States, he might have something interesting for your book."[30]

What a romantic life was that of Marcel Lafaye, and so amazingly parallel indeed to Céline's!

He was born in Paris in 1897. At the age of fifteen, he worked at the National Bank. A foot soldier in 1916, wounded twice in 1917, he later enlisted in the air force. His plane was shot down and he was badly burned. He underwent seventeen skin grafts to his face. A recipient of the *médaille militaire*, the *croix de guerre*, and a class 1 discharge, he took his *baccalauréat* after the armistice. Again a bank employee, in 1923 he signed a contract for a managerial position at a trading post in Cameroon, fell ill, and was repatriated a year later. He then hired on as a telegrapher on board various ships. In Venezuela he was employed by a company importing dye materials and chemical products to Paris. It was then that he met Louis. . . .

According to those close to him, Marcel was a sensitive creature, emotional and patriotic. He was very reticent about the war and his own exploits. Deeply pacifistic, Marcel Lafaye was, like Céline, to become an anti-Semite in the thirties. From 1919 to 1923 he had written a narrative of autobiographical inspiration that had remained in the manuscript stage, *Mon Ami Labiffe, histoire d'un soldat* [My Friend Labiffe, a Soldier's Story], of which Louis was certainly aware. Certain resemblances crop up between that text and *Voyage*. For instance, the episode of the army theater or that of the self-appointed godmother, which, it seems, do not belong to Louis' own experience. Professor Pierre Lainé, who studied Marcel Lafaye's manuscript, was able to detect many similarities between the two texts, indeed, many borrowings by Céline from his friend's story. There is nothing very shocking in that. A novelist is a thief. It's his vocation. His duty. He takes a little from one person, a little from another. He watches, he notes, he hoards, he transforms. The meeting with Marcel Lafaye, the account of his experiences magnifying and complementing his own, served him in the end as an irreplaceable leaven.

Céline met Joseph Garcin in 1929. Marcel Lafaye had introduced them. Like Louis, Garcin had enlisted in the army, was wounded in 1916, and had received the *croix de guerre*, the Legion of Honor, and so on and so forth. In 1917 and 1918 he had lived in London and frequented the underworld. Back in France, his life was shared between Montmartre and the South. Linked to pimping, Garcin was officially a hotelier and restaurateur, a manager of establishments run by his wife in his absence. After 1934 he settled permanently on the Côte d'Azur.

He corresponded with Céline up to 1938. After that date, they seem to have lost contact with one another. Garcin was a faithful friend. And Louis was always on the lookout for new acquaintances, new characters, new experiences to understand if not to share.

Twenty-eight letters written by Céline to Garcin have been catalogued to date.[31] The two men shared the same anxiety, the same memory of the war, of the horror. After that, it was only a question of survival, in a general every-man-for-himself. Decency, morality, legality—what did all that mean? Céline observed the world as if he had somehow taken a step aside. Garcin had taken refuge in pimping and crime, at the fringes of society. They felt strangely close to one another.

On September 1, 1929, Louis wrote to him: "You have understood that we have been living a suspended sentence for 15 years, that we skirted a hell from which there should be no return, and you know better than I, that it is henceforth a question of paying our bill shamelessly. You have grasped the essential, everything else is jumbled words without bearing."[32]

But beyond this intimacy, this sometimes unsettling complicity, the meeting of the two men also illumines the birth of *Voyage*. It demonstrates how Louis thought of integrating logically and chronologically the episodes of his life in London, in 1915 and 1916, to his autobiographically inspired narrative, between the war and the African episodes. And, in that regard, Joseph could be of considerable help to him. "You definitely have a lot to teach me," Céline wrote him in April 1930, "about the London underworld. I spent a little time in it 1915, superficially, I was twenty years old and had too many memories of the front. And then I didn't know how to see the details that count, ah, I sure wasted my time, youth is futility."[33]

More interesting still is the beautiful letter written on a page from a prescription booklet with the Clichy clinic letterhead. It's all there: the nightmare of the war; the obsessive memory; the "truth" discovered by the writer, which is, in the end, that of death; the bitterness; the misanthropy, even contempt for human beings (naturally compatible with his inexhaustible affection for people on an individual basis); and the feeling, too, for standing outside of literature, of the refined game of conventions; Céline's primary concern to exorcise himself of the ghosts of the past.

My dear Garcin,

You are very kind to take an interest in my furtive literary activities. There is no question of an "oeuvre"—no pretensions, and no literature my God no. But I've got a thousand pages of nightmare stored up, that of the war naturally holds the lead. Weeks of '14 spent under the soaking downpours, in that awful mud and the blood and the shit and the stupidity of men, I'll never get over it, that is a truth I pass on to you yet again, one shared by a few of us. It's all there. The tragedy, our misery, it's most of our contemporaries' ability to forget. What a rabble!

I also take my characters through Africa, another significant experience. It's a permanent war going on in Douala, on the quiet, I've really seen people melt, go to seed, swallowed up whole. What swinishness, what horrible poverty. . . .

England, then? She'll have her place, it's too early to say where. But I haven't the faintest idea where all this scribbling will lead. The future hardly belongs to us.

Sorry for the morbid tone, fall's on the way and so are the rains.

Ever yours,
Destouches[34]

At that time, September 1931, we sense that Céline is still hesitating to incorporate the English episodes into the weft of *Voyage*. Nevertheless, he is still pursuing his investigations on London and the underworld. A little later he will plan a short trip there (which he will not undertake on the appointed date). "You'll take me to your killers and to all the whorehouses. I'll confess all your Baron White's little girlfriends," he writes to Joseph Garcin in March 1931. And on April 7: "I'm sorry to impose, but could you send me a *proper* map of London to suit my interests, that is, one that has our gangland neighborhoods on it? Just this one last favor. I'm ashamed to ask."[35]

On July 24, as we know, he gave up once and for all using his London experiences for *Voyage*. For on that very day, he wrote to his correspondent: "I'm giving up the London adventure, a little of the USA and the suburbs I know too well, that's it for the novel, for the short-term nocturnal labors. But the sequel to come will be set in London, it's all bound to end in theatrics, in buffoonery. I'm counting on you, I'm watching over you."[36]

In short, he doesn't want to distract the reader's attention, to hinder his book's dramatic development. London is a chapter that is too important. He is not keen to divulge it, to give it away too fast, especially since the chapter is not always tragic. It has comical, picturesque aspects. It would impede that ineluctably mounting horror, the nightmare contrived by *Voyage au bout de la nuit*. We will thus have to wait for Denoël's publication of *Guignol's band* in March '44 finally to see that masterful "buffoonery" rise to the ranks of a novelistic work. In it, we will recognize Joseph Garcin in the guise of Cascade, the pimp who doesn't know what to do with himself—or his blackjack—since his colleagues enlisted in the army, leaving him with their meal tickets; Angèle, La Joconde, and company.

The friendship/complicity between Joseph Garcin and Louis Destouches is instructive. Is it because he feels his interlocutor to be both close and inapproachable, of another world and involved in other relationships? Louis reveals himself in his letters with an unusual solemnity and sincerity. "You have guessed the root of the problem perfectly," he writes on May 1933. "Distress for the ubiquitous perversity, the obvious observation that everything is already beginning to crumble—that disaster is in the other. The important thing is to enter into intimacy with things."[37]

The Célinian obsession with Doomsday, his certainty of being witness and prophet of an ineluctable decadence, his concern for writing in its most concrete form, in its most intimate connection with things, far from lies, from words, from masks—the writer expresses them all here unreservedly. He is forever haunted by the sense of disaster, possessed by that form of suicidal voluptuousness that allows him to delight only in periods of crisis, of decline, of collapse—as if the world were constantly proving him right.

But can we extrapolate and claim, like certain critics, that the great crisis of 1929 helped to fertilize *Voyage au bout de la nuit*, inspired the author's twilit hues, his determined pessimism, his irreversible condemnation of a satiated, coldly selfish, bourgeois, society which, after war, colonialism, and every form of exploitation, was perhaps watching its values and its well-being disintegrate?

French politics were not disastrous during the years the novel was being written, nor were they particularly thrilling—they were nothing. They dealt with the present. From day to day, between two wars, two parliamentary crises, two elections. The pacifist Briand beaten by Doumer in the presidential election of 1931, the leftist elections of 1932, and the setting up of a Herriot cabinet—who cares? In truth, France remained ruled by the Right. Cautiously . . . What was there for Louis Destouches to pay attention to? In any case, Briand would die in March '32 and Doumer would be assassinated two months later, on May 6. Such was the news, the surface of things, the banner headlines of the daily press forgotten the next day.

On the other hand, what might have impressed Céline more during the years of writing *Voyage* was the acceleration of the world around him. Distances were being shortened. Distant dangers were felt more closely. Crises were taking on speed. The movies began to talk, and the planes to fly ever higher, ever farther, ever faster. In May 1930 Mermoz established the first transatlantic air link between Saint-Louis-du-Sénégal and Brazil. Paul Morand raised a book to the glory of *New York* and jazzed up the French language, as Céline would say. In June French troops withdrew from the Rhineland, but the clamor heard a little later in Germany was more troubling: the elections of September 1930 brought in a National Socialist landslide, the Hitlerite party going from 12 to 107 seats in the Reichstag.

And all the while, France dozed. The government was preparing the great Colonial Exhibition of May 1931 under the leadership of Maréchal Lyautey, an already dusty hymn to a debatable greatness. Dr. Destouches set up his own "colonial exhibition" in the pages of *Voyage* devoted to Bambola Bragamance, and his Africa was tinged with mediocrity, poverty, the bare-faced exploitation of the blacks, the endless torpor of days and nights crushed by fever, humidity, delirium, and a nature dizzily exuberant in its hostility.

The postwar years were truly over. The Roaring Twenties had ceased to roar. People had forgotten to forget, they no longer drowned their sorrows or became intoxicated over the prospect of a glorious future. And that, perhaps, is why Louis Destouches was suddenly able to write *Voyage au bout de la nuit*. Because he had had enough of amnesia and lies, and because, in the great silence of the tired, flaccid France of 1929-1932, as if forgotten by history, he found the serenity, the capacity for indignation, and finally the strength to write, to avoid the general numbness of his fellow citizens.

Defining the end of a postwar era is always difficult. Louis Destouches was surely aware of that. It is an implicit recognition that one has already toppled over to the other side, that one is now in a prewar era, that the Apocalypse is not only behind, but that it is waiting at the end of a new night. . . .

1929, the year that *Voyage* was begun, is exactly halfway between the two world wars. A disturbing coincidence. As if Louis were finally able to de-scribe his war of 1914, in which he had been wounded, and what came after, at the precise moment when his alarum would rattle French literature, and then find a new screen placed before him, a new fear, a new echo to justify his concerns and redouble his fury.

The Doctor Publishes

We do not know precisely when Louis Destouches finished writing *Voyage*. In August 1931 he took several days' vacation in Pau with Elizabeth. A strange vacation—even there he was to work in a state of feverish tension. Months, years of work, and for what? He still had no idea. His plays had been rejected by publishers and producers, but that didn't mean much, they were merely diversions hastily written on the fringes of his professional activity. He proceeded altogether differently with his novel. This time it was his medical activity that seemed to be marginal. The stakes were high—he was essentially betting his life on this book. He was alone with his fabrications, his style, his alarum, without feedback or support. Who, then, would be capable of hearing it? Elizabeth Craig? She wasn't in on the secret, she was a foreigner, she spoke American with him, and she was increasingly intol-erant of his irritability, his pessimism, his restless anxieties.

From then on Louis Destouches seemed to distance himself from her. He abandoned himself to the sole intimacy of his doubles, his shadows, his reconstituted characters such as Bardamu or Robinson. He preferred other women to the mischievous, sensual Elizabeth, other chimeras born of his imagination: Lola, Musyne, Molly, or Madelon. Clearly, their unstable relationship could not long stand the test of *Voyage*.

By the end of 1931 the book was practically finished. Louis offered it to his friend Georges Altman, co-editor with Barbusse of the leftist bimonthly *Monde*.[38] It was a strange idea commensurate with his confusion. Why didn't he go to a book publisher?

But first he had to have the thousands of manuscript pages typed. A secretary of the Clichy clinic, Aimée Paymal, undertook the job. She went at it discreetly, at the request of the author, who wasn't at all anxious to alert Grégoire Ichok and his colleagues—from a sense of discretion, no doubt, and, it is likely, a sense of pride as well. How would he look to them if the text were not subsequently published?

On March 14, 1932, Fernand Destouches died. A laconic letter from Louis to Henri Mahé: "My father is dead. I didn't summon you. I prefer to reduce the sorrow to a minimum. It's not easy. I've reached the age when you don't forget anything."[39]

Germaine Constans attended the funeral, along with the family and Uncle Guillou. Louis cried like a baby, she recalled.[40]

Had he really despised his father? We must once again ignore the overly caricatured picture of the pitiful little insurance man painted in *Mort à crédit*. Édith Follet recalled a distinguished, rather well-educated man. As Lucette Almansor says: "Louis said that his father bugged him, that he was jealous of him, that he didn't want to see him rise any higher than himself. But he got his love of the sea from his father, who was always painting the sea, ships, and also circus girls, the well-muscled riding girls he adored. And, again like Louis, he loved musical comedy. At heart, Louis had more in common with his father than with his mother; he was more Norman than Breton."[41]

Louis had set himself against Fernand, no doubt. He had wanted to emancipate himself from his father's narrow-minded morality, his suffocating concern for economy, his chilly, reactionary prejudices. But he was to come to resemble him more and more. He would have no one left against whom to assert himself. He would be able to reconnect, in his own way, with his petty-bourgeois rejections, his immoderate yearning for the past, his xenophobia.

And Louis cried like a baby. Should that surprise us? On hearing of his mother's death upon his arrival in Copenhagen in 1945, having escaped from Germany, he would sob once more. Without false shame. Without that displaced modesty of men uncertain of their virility, who believe it unworthy to express sorrow. It was simply that, as he didn't like to display his feelings, his pain, his sorrow, Louis preferred to be alone when giving free flow to his grief, or to remain alone in the company of the admirable, faithful, silent Lucette, who understood, who accepted all his excesses and who remembers him still, stretched out on a bed, holding her hand and giving way to a sadness that rocked him like waves. . . . And so we may put to rest the ready-made image of the writer hardened against suffering, sarcastic, stoical, expressing his most secret pains only through that unfathomably churlish sneer. Louis cried, and that's all there was to it.

The death of Fernand Destouches left his wife, if not in need, at least with an income small enough to make it difficult to live comfortably. Louis decided to transfer entirely to her name, until her death, the royalties he was due as inventor of Basedowine. He also found her a place as a pharmaceutical salesperson with Gallier, the same job Germaine Constans had. At the age of sixty, with her lame leg, she thus undertook to trudge through the hospitals every morning. In the afternoon, in her apartment on the rue Marsollier, she pursued her sales and repairs of antique lace. Courageous and proud, Marguerite Destouches would never on any account have wanted her son to give her money directly.

His father—that rampart protecting every son from his own death—having disappeared, Louis was able to write, facing alone his death to come, with the apocalyptic urgency that was to seize him ever more tightly. Now there was no more censure to fear, no screen blocking his memory. In one sense he was free—with the freedom that is also an unspeakable sadness when there remains no solace to shelter you from life. He could make the best possible use of his manuscript. He could make any use of it he wanted. He was soon to write *Mort à crédit*, settling accounts with his family once and for all. With his father? No, that was in appearance only. One does not fight with ghosts. There comes a time when one can strive only against oneself. He was to write it above all in opposition to himself.

Meanwhile Louis sent *Voyage au bout de la nuit* to two small publishers, Éditions Bossard and Eugène Figuière. The choice was preposterous, on a level with his befuddlement. Why not try his luck with a large publisher first? Was he still that unsure of himself?

Éditions Bossard turned him down. The book didn't fit their list, based on an established formula. At Eugène Figuière he was offered a vanity deal: he need only pay 12,000 francs to clinch it. Naturally, the deal didn't come off.

Elizabeth Craig had just left him for her annual trip to the United States, her return to the source. She considered never coming back. On the flyleaf of *Voyage au bout de la nuit*, Louis had written, "To Elizabeth Craig." As a sign of affection, of faithfulness, a way of keeping her near him. No doubt, now that the book was finished, he was becoming aware of the sacrifices she had endured while he was writing it. She generally stayed away for two or three months. This time she remained absent for nearly a year. Louis would not see her again until early 1933. And she would not experience or know the long, dizzy months of uncertainty, joy, incredulity, anticipation, and discouragement that followed the launching of *Voyage*. She had left Louis Destouches. She returned to Céline—before her definitive departure.

On April 14 Louis dropped off his manuscript at Gallimard. A short time afterward he sent it to Éditions Denoël. He probably had several typed copies at his disposal. He also sent a copy to Édith, his first wife, recently remarried to Colonel Lebon, and whom he continued to see every so often when he came to pick up or return their daughter, Colette, or to visit her. "His conversation," Édith Follet-Lebon says today, "resembled his books. He spoke the way he wrote *Voyage au bout de la nuit*. The book, to tell the truth, had shocked me a little. We had received the manuscript. My husband, who was not very well disposed toward him, nevertheless read it in one night and told me, 'This book is going to make some noise. I've never read anything like it.' And, coming from him, that was a compliment."[42]

Jeanne Carayon, his old neighbor from Clichy, remembers having the doctor show up at her door one day . . .

"He puts a fat manuscript on the table. 'It's my rag.' The novel is finished. Has the author so emptied himself of substance to appear this changed, thin, with this brand-new ascetic face? The cardboard cover opens on the title *Voyage au bout de la nuit*.

" 'I sent other copies to Denoël and Gallimard. Take your time reading it.'

"You can't always 'take your time' in the profession. A little later comes the victory notice: Denoël has welcomed the 'rag' and is preparing the contract. Gallimard also accepted, very soon afterward, but a deal is a deal. . . .

" 'So I went to pick up my copy on the rue Sébastien-Bottin. People came out from the woodwork to see what I looked like. You would have thought I was a pretty woman.' "[43]

What had happened, exactly?

At Gallimard, the reading of *Voyage* had initially been entrusted to Benjamin Crémieux. Soon afterward, at the literary committee that included, among others, Jean Paulhan, Ramon Fernandez, André Malraux, Gaston Gallimard, and Emmanuel Berl, Benjamin Crémieux gave a summary of his (incomplete) reading of the work, a few pages of which he wanted to read to his colleagues. The manuscript then passed into the hands of Malraux and Berl. Berl would later confide to Patrick Modiano, speaking of Céline: "He was a real writer. There aren't too many of them. I knew it at the NRF [Nouvelle Revue Française] the moment that Benjamin rejected—or rather delayed taking—*Voyage au bout de la nuit*. So it was passed around and I grabbed it, I read the typed copy with Malraux, and we thought it had a tone to it."[44]

However, despite the support of Berl and Malraux, the manuscript frightened Gallimard's sober literary committee, Crémieux primarily, who suggested changes and cuts that the author would not have accepted. In truth, the question was already a moot one.[45] Louis Destouches had for some time sensed Gallimard's reticence and had dropped off a second copy with Éditions Denoël, which for its part didn't hesitate for a second. For Robert Denoël's enthusiasm and such spontaneous and immediate warmth, the writer was grateful to him all his life. And it was somewhat to embellish the picture, to trump up his legend, that Céline would later claim the two publishers had responded at the same time. As proved, for instance, by this letter sent to Milton Hindus on July 28, 1947: "*Both* of them accepted on the same day but Denoël two *hours* before the NRF. Crémieux was the reader at the NRF., he was raising a few difficulties . . . Anyway, *Denoël* took it—It's the only manuscript of mine he ever had 'in reading.' He printed the others later entirely on trust, never reading them ahead of time— I couldn't care less what a publisher might think of my books— There's no question, even, of seeking his opinion— His taste is necessarily bad—otherwise he wouldn't be doing this half-grocer's, half-pimp's work."[46]

Céline's choice of Denoël was a logical one. He could submit his novel only to the publisher of *L'Hôtel du Nord*, which had so impressed him. For some time Robert Denoël and his associate, Bernard Steele, had made the offices of their very new publishing house in an old, deconsecrated chapel on the rue Amélie.

"Robert was the son of a Belgian university professor. Adventurous, Bohemian, having only a vague idea of the value of money. . . . It was said that his start had been made easier by a woman of delicate health who ran a Modern Art gallery on the Left Bank. It was perhaps through her that Denoël had been put in touch with a rich American, Bernard Steele. These two foreigners from very different backgrounds had their youth in common, both under 30, their boldness, their ambition to establish a publishing house in Paris that would make people talk."[47]

The Renaudot Prize awarded the year before to Philippe Hériat's *L'Innocent* had contributed to the reputation of the house, which also published numerous texts on psychoanalysis and had taken over from Doin the publication of the *Revue Française de Psychanalyse*. It has been claimed that Céline's sporadic interest in psychoanalysis was an extra reason for his choice in publisher. One may reasonably doubt it.[48]

One night, then, Robert Denoël found on his desk a hefty package containing the 900 typed pages of *Voyage*. A little novel was included with the parcel, with a woman's address on the wrapping paper. That night the publisher began reading the fat book in a state of mounting excitement. Max Dorian, who had joined Denoël in 1930 as a general secretary, recalled his boss's telephone call in the middle of the night. " 'My dear friend,' he told me, 'I've read 250 pages of Céline's manuscript in one sitting, and if it sticks to the same tone to the end we have a masterpiece on our hands. . . . I've just called Bernard and I ask you as I did him to get to the office early tomorrow morning. You'll have to give your opinion very fast so we can make a quick decision. We'll have just enough time to put out *Voyage* for the Goncourt. Good night, see you tomorrow, I'm diving back into my ocean.'"[49]

His continued reading confirmed Denoël's enthusiasm. It was a bolt from the blue, one of those very rare bolts that constitute supreme joy, justification, and consecration of the publishing profession, that abrupt certainty of having fallen on a treasure or, better yet, on a unique author and voice, a new vision of the world, a world all his own. Denoël's breath was taken away by the novelistic freedom of *Voyage*, its convulsive lyricism, its tormented daring.[50] The next day, as promised, he had Bernard Steele (who shared his office) and Max Dorian read the manuscript he had just finished. Without his partner's support, Denoël could do nothing. Dorian seems to recall that the house was then experiencing financial difficulties following the unsuccessful launching of a series of children's books. Steele allowed himself to be easily convinced. Being of Jewish origin, it is possible—though highly unlikely—that he already suspected the author's latent anti-Semitism, which was apparent in *L'Église* but was barely perceptible in *Voyage*. As he did not have the funds himself to print the book, he called his mother in the United States. "The conversation, it seems, was long and lively, but to know its outcome one need only have seen Robert Denoël's beaming expression. The question was settled."[51]

Now they had to contact the author of this extraordinary manuscript, who had neither signed the work nor even given his address! The testimony of Robert Poulet, then a young novelist who had published *Handji* and *Le Trottoir* with Denoël the year before, is valuable and enlightening.

"Then we remembered that the enormous manuscript had arrived along with another, one in which the author, less absentminded, had revealed his identity. The Denoël messenger rushed over to the person's home: it was a lady, part painter, part bluestocking. She lived in Montmartre. Based on the acclamation she was given, for a minute the poor thing saw herself as the gods' chosen one, promised the most wonderful literary success and the admiration of the centuries. Up to the moment she was told, between two compliments:

" 'Obviously your book has some racy bits! . . . Let's hope we get it past the censors.'

"The lady jumped: she hadn't written anything daring, on the contrary. The messenger went on:

" 'Our volume will also have to be unusually thick.'

" 'How's that? . . . One hundred and fifty pages, double-spaced with wide margins?'

"It was all cleared up when it was revealed that the object of Denoël's enthusiasm was not the little novel in which the lady had told a sentimental story (her own, I suppose), but the very large novel which her neighbor, the 'mad doctor,' had entrusted to her on the off-chance: 'Since you're sending your book to a paper-pusher, why don't you chuck my rag in with it.'

"The messenger, understanding the mixup, didn't have far to go. On the floor below, he found the mad doctor, who had just woken up, as befits a specialist on night duty. Clichy: knife wounds, delirium tremens attacks . . .

Gallimard's letter, with its mitigated rejection, had just been dropped through the slot.

"And that's how the deal was struck."[52]

Louis Destouches went straight to Robert Denoël's office on the rue Amélie.

"I found myself," wrote the latter, "before a man as extraordinary as his book. He talked to me for nearly two hours as a clinician who had done the rounds in life, a man of extreme clear-sightedness, coldly despairing, and yet passionate; cynical but pitiful. I can still see him, nervous, excited, blue eyes, a hard, penetrating stare, a bit ragged, physically run-down. He had a gesture that particularly struck me. His hand went back and forth as if wiping the slate clean, and all the time, his index finger pointed things out. He spoke to me about the war, death, his book; one minute he would get carried away, the next minute he was blasé, like someone who has seen it all, who has no illusions. He always expressed himself in a strong, imagistic, sometimes hallucinatory way. The idea of death, his own and the world's, kept cropping up in his conversation like a leitmotiv. He described a humanity starved for disaster, in love with slaughter. Sweat poured down his face, his gaze seemed to burn."[53]

Naturally, Robert Denoël expressed his intention of publishing *Voyage au bout de la nuit* without delay. A contract was drawn up and signed by both parties on June 30. There was no question, as has often been implied, of a fabulous offer with fat percentages granted the author by the publisher. There was a boilerplate contract, whose clauses were even somewhat restrictive for Louis Destouches. He received no advance payment on royalties. He would begin receiving 10% of the retail sales of the book only after the 4,000th copy sold, the percentage rising to 12% from 5,000 to 10,000, 15% from 10,000 to 50,000, and 18% beyond that. The book's subsidiary rights were to be split 50/50 between author and publisher. First-refusal rights were set at five prose works (novels or short stories) accepted by Éditions Denoël on the same terms as those set down in the current contract.[54]

Thus the publishing machine had been set in motion that was to lead to the book's appearance in October. It is curious to observe Louis Destouches' behavior at the time, for it sheds new light on his contradictions—his anxieties, his detachment, and his passion.

We have seen his ignorance of the mechanisms of publishing, his curious initial choices of mediocre or obscure small publishers like Figuière and Bossard. Moreover, the manuscript of *Voyage* left with Denoël bore neither name nor address. Strangely casual as he was, he couldn't avoid signing it. That was when he had settled on the pseudonym Louis-Ferdinand Céline, in hommage to his maternal grandmother, Céline Guillou, i.e., in reference to the past, to the happy or idealized days of his childhood. . . .

And now, for him, the die had been cast. The book was finished, accepted; the author's name found. The rest no longer belonged to him. He needed to catch his breath, get his bearings, return to the active life, to pursue new discoveries, new emotions. He especially wanted to get rid of the ghosts, visions, and nightmares that had kept him company throughout the writing of the book. That is why he was unwilling to reread the proofs of *Voyage*. He entrusted the job to Jeanne Carayon, as he had promised.

"The work is now in hand on the rue Amélie, where the author rarely goes. He doesn't want to review the proofs himself: he needs to forget the enormous effort of the past years, the metamorphic spasms that turned him into a writer. And yet we have to explain the delays to him: the typographers, alarmed by this 'weird' text, mangled it with commas. 'They want to make me write like François Mauriac!' The typesetting has to be started over. The proofreader's task requires an adaptation to the vocabulary, style, and syntax of the man who has just moulted into Louis-Ferdinand Céline."[55]

Céline's flight did not reveal a mere need for decompression. It also betrayed a kind of fear. Or, at the very least, an irresponsibility. He had written his book the way one makes waves by deliberately inciting a scandal. But he refused to pay attention to the backwash that came from it, somewhat in the manner of a gambler who places his bet on the roulette table and doesn't dare to watch the bouncing white ball. That attitude will recur with every book to come. Céline will write, then flee. As if all this, the publication, its effect on the press, the public, had nothing to do with him. The tidal waves caused by his writings, no, no, that wasn't him, his book was finished and he returned to medicine, donning another civil status; after all it was only a book, some emotion, some style, so why couldn't they leave him alone and stop talking about it!

The solitude was relative, naturally. After all, he couldn't very well be entirely indifferent to the fate of *Voyage au bout de la nuit*. A few letters available to us, sent by him to Robert Denoël while the book was being printed, clearly reveal his feverish attentiveness. He doesn't give his publisher one minute's rest. He sticks doggedly to his text, refusing to change one iota, no question of suppressing the galley episode that allows the transition between the African episode and the discovery of New York; he even gives his advice on the cover, for which he has drawn up a dummy. For a novelist who refuses to reread his proofs, such vigilance is surprising.

"Old man, I beg you, don't add one syllable to the text without telling me! You'd completely screw up the rhythm— I'm the only one who can relocate it— I may seem like a gasbag but I know exactly what I want— Not one syllable. Be careful with the cover too— No music-hallism— No typographical sentimentalism, no classicism. . . . a fairly somber, discreet cover. That's my advice— Dark brown on black or maybe gray on gray and uniform letters—somewhat thick. That's all— That's enough impressionism."[56]

At heart, it was always fear that dictated such incoherent behavior. The fear of being betrayed by his publisher. Fear of rereading his work, that is, of judging himself. Fear of the future. Fear of everything. Following the long stretches of creative lucidity was a pattern of escape and self-delusion. Céline the writer, i.e., the accuser, abruptly became Céline the anonymous, the doctor, i.e, the persecuted, the paranoid.

Let us sum up. His father died in March 1932. A month later, Denoël accepted *Voyage*. Elizabeth was in America. Dr. Destouches kept up attendance at the Clichy clinic and his writing activities for Gallier and La Biothérapie. He was available. His novel was in the works. He needed a distraction from it. He was ready for new adventures. At least, for sentimental adventures. . .

Enter Erika Irrgang, a young German student come to Paris from Breslau, without money, without friends, just out of curiosity, to try to land some little job "under the table" and attend classes at the university. In the beginning, everything went as planned. And then she fell sick. Her savings melted away. Too proud and too weak to seek assistance, she wasted away without food in a little room on the rue Chevalier-de-la-Barre, where the rent was paid for the next few weeks. Until the day when she fainted on the terrace of a café on the place du Tertre. Louis Destouches was passing at the time. She literally fell into his arms. He got her into a taxi. Dragged her then and there into a restaurant on the Grands Boulevards, where she wolfed down a plate of macaroni with ham. They introduced themselves.

Erika Irrgang was beautiful. Brown hair, perfectly oval face, delicate nose, sensual lips, and enormous dark eyes. He brought her home with him. Offered her the hospitality of a room and a bed, into which she collapsed for a long, restorative slumber. He was there when she awoke. He had just drawn a bath. She moved into rue Lepic for a few weeks. Soon after their first encounter, she became his mistress.

If it were a novel it would be bad melodrama.

Erika Irrgang would later explain:

"The doctor was the most unusual man I had ever met. During the early days I had to strain to understand a little of his fragmented sentences. He spoke unbelievably fast and punctuated his words with bizarre, sweeping gestures. . . .

"The weeks I spent with Monsieur Destouches were somehow unreal, like a dream. That was why his life didn't astonish me, why I gave it practically no thought and passively accepted the extraordinary rhythm of his nights and his days. Apparently his brief explanations were more than enough for me. That he rarely slept he explained with remarks about his head wound, received during the First War. 'They broke my skull,' he said. That was also the source of the buzzing in his ears from which he generally suffered, the awful pains in his head. . . .

"When Monsieur Destouches had finished work on the rue Fanny, we usually ate together. I would wait for him in a *bistro*, often at Pigall's Tabac at 22, boulevard de Clichy. He coddled me when it came to meals; when I wasn't hungry he became almost nasty. Whenever I particularly liked something, they brought me a second helping of the same dish. We never drank wine with our meals. . . . Afterward we would wander through the nocturnal streets of some sinister neighborhood. He spoke to old drunks and pale prostitutes, gave a pass for a municipal shelter to some poor devil with ravaged lungs, shrugged his shoulders violently when the invalid tore up the paper before our very eyes. Then he would give me a lecture on the futility of helping people and describe in hideous detail the 'procession of disease' marching past us. I was very moved by these nighttime excursions. I think he undertook them to set me an example, to show me once and for all how important it was to stay ahead of misery."[57]

In late May or early June, Erika Irrgang returned to Breslau. Louis corresponded with her. He met her again in Germany at the end of the year and then in July 1935 in Berlin. In March 1936 she emigrated to England. She had married. Louis saw her again briefly in Cambridge. Their relationship was over. Erika Irrgang, now Mrs. Erika Landry, published under the name of Nataly Landor a work entitled *Die Kaskaden von St. Cloud* with Piper Verlag in 1963.

Their love affair had thus lasted a short time, at the very beginning of their liaison. For the writer, it was a preliminary. The sexual act was necessary in getting to know a woman, but Louis quickly tired of it. He "consumed" little, as we have said. He very soon adopted a father-daughter relationship to Erika, nevertheless injecting a certain vulgarity into his cynical advice on sexual hygiene. As if he were eager, if not to shock her, then at least to evince a medical lucidity free of all moral preconceptions. Perhaps this attitude also had something in it of the game, a sort of mask, the grimacing reflection of his modesty.

For instance, on June 22, 1932, he wrote her: "Use all your weapons at once, all of them, sex, theater, education, work. But protect your health. No *sex without condoms*, OR ELSE FROM BEHIND. Also, build up your literary and theatrical education if you can use it to get ahead. Keep an eye on the Hitlerites, but be careful about it, read the papers attentively, don't be lazy the way women are when it comes to politics. You are made for politics. The main thing is to make sure to choose the party that will win—and to get a thoroughly good start in that direction. I can't advise you, I don't know Germany."

Or again, on October 3, 1932: "You have charm, you can be depraved whenever you want—Preserve your health—your thighs, your mind— . . . Make love (WITHOUT TAKING RISKS) because it's a stimulant, hold back all your mind for your material success."[58]

The political advice he gives her is also striking for its prudence—or its naiveté. They reveal a Céline as little militant and as little concerned as possible with reality. He risks being seduced by no ideology, enflamed by no certainty; he clings to an individualized, every-man-for-himself attitude. So he ignores the situation in Germany. Hitler? Never heard of him. Choose the party that will win. He has no intention of being intoxicated and carried away by lies, promises, ideals. He has no intention of being like his hero

Bardamu, who enlists in the army on the strength of a fine regiment marching past him with its colonel on horseback, "and this colonel even seemed like a nice fellow, rich and healthy!" All that is over with, he believes. He has just written *Voyage au bout de la nuit* specifically to expunge the follies and illusions of his youth. To have done with imposture, with economic, social, and bellicose exhilaration, with colonialism and the rest of it. He doesn't want to know about anything ever again. He will henceforth refuse to rise to the attack under life's gunfire. Find yourself a chilly, solitary entrenchment, ward off the blows, the shells, accepted opinion, political parties, and human beings—that's what he advocates. On June 29, 1933, he would write to another correspondent, Élisabeth Porquerol: "Do you take me for a woman? with opinions? . . . I have no opinions. There are no opinions. Water has no opinions."[59]

And what about literature, and the "opinions" that emanate from books? How does one judge them in terms of profit and loss? But literature, we must re-emphasize, is something altogether different in Céline's eyes: beyond the pale of life. Furthermore, he doesn't discuss it with Erika. In the spring of 1932 she was barely aware that the strange doctor who had taken her in had just finished a novel. And in September he wrote to her on stationery from Pigall's Tabac, one of his preferred meeting places: "I'm having a lot of trouble here— Everything is very hard. The book is coming out in early October I'll send you a copy right away. But, you know, literature is Death. The only thing that keeps you alive is your affection for people and things. The rest is nothing."[60] We will find such statements often recurring in his correspondence and interviews.

In June '32, with Erika gone, Louis found himself alone in Paris once more. From July 1 to 20 he was in Marseille. Another port, again a retreat into dreams and escape. He spent August in Brittany. And in Paris, on September 4, he met a young Austrian woman of Jewish extraction, Cillie Pam, twenty-seven years old, who ran gymnastics classes in Vienna. That same old Célinian predilection for dance, sports, muscle.

He had met Cillie at the Café de la Paix. He took her for a walk in the Bois de Boulogne, invited her to a restaurant, took her home—the basic, classic seduction scenario. Two days later another meeting at the Café de la Paix. He gave her the keys to 98, rue Lepic. The next day she left her hotel and moved in. A few days later she fell ill, a minor bronchitis, and Louis put her in the room usually occupied by Elizabeth Craig. A strange repetition of the scene played out with Erika. For Louis and Cillie there were outings in Paris, restaurant suppers, brief erotic interludes, one or two orgies in which Louis played the role of voyeur while (on September 15 in his apartment) two women, a working girl named Pauline and the beautiful lesbian mistress of an old Jew (according to Cillie Pam's notebooks), fondled one another on his bed.[61] On September 17 Cillie took the train back to Germany.

Their friendship lasted seven years. From this point we can follow it from letter to letter, or on the occasion of a few quick meetings, up to 1938. But already, in the early months of their brief encounters and their correspondence, Céline behaves much the way he had with Erika Irrgang. Affectionate and fatherly, even paternalistic, hypersensitive and cynical at the same time. Cillie Pam had been struck by the care Céline took in choosing a good restaurant, in carefully ordering a dish that he nevertheless seemed to take no pleasure in eating. No more than he took pleasure in making love. Furthermore, the word "love" disgusted him, that indecent display of emotion. Sex, at the bare limit, could be discussed openly (he called it "popo" with Cillie) as a pure and simple biological given.

He wrote to her on October 3, 1932: "You do love me but I make you angry. I don't talk enough about love. 'Speak to me of love! . . .' I'd like to . . . but I can't. I never speak, I never have spoken about such things. I talk about popo. I understand popo. I'm only good at popo."[62]

He didn't speak to her about literature either. That garden was far too secret to bring strangers into, to let them stroll along its disturbing paths. Céline, a hurried but also a harried man—that was the image of himself he gladly gave to Cillie as well as to Robert Denoël, to Marcel Lafaye as well as to Joseph Garcin or others: "You know how my existence is plagued. I am actually sick myself, chronic. A past of horrible worries, that of a hunted beast, has forever deprived me of a taste for adventure and involvement. I live morally, physically, from day to day. I do what I can—the best I can."[63]

October 1932: *Voyage au bout de la nuit* was finally going to come out. What did Louis Destouches expect from it? Fame? Success? Money? Or was he once again withdrawing into the state of mind of an outlaw, of one who dreams of hiding behind a pseudonym, behind a book, on the margins of life?

Another adventure—the adventure of a writer, of his public life, basically—was about to begin.

9

Story of a Book

The Early Days

Was *Voyage au bout de la nuit* a masterpiece? Robert Denoël was convinced that it was. A best-seller? He hoped so. A literary prize–winner? Possibly.

After the war had ended, the pioneer Bernard Grasset had taught Denoël the publishing profession: the launching of a novel had to be organized; a book was a product that had to be promoted with press conferences and publicity campaigns, with shameless bluffing about the size of the run, with a commercial dynamic adjusted to one's intended market. The 1921 launching of Louis Hémon's *Maria Chapdelaine* and of Raymond Radiguet's *Le Diable au corps* two years later had stuck in everyone's mind.

Unfortunately, Robert Denoël lacked the capital to consider a thundering fanfare for his latest discovery. He nevertheless marshaled his energies and forces of persuasion and inflated his available promotional and publicity budget to the maximum in order to blow the trumpet to the profession, literary chroniclers, and readers.

Already, the blurb for *Voyage* was unequivocal: "A book that is bound to cause a considerable stir. The author makes his debut in full maturity, having led an extremely rich and diverse life."

The book:

"A novel impossible to categorize and difficult to define because of its originality. The author strives to create a faithful image of the city-dweller, with all the complexity, abundance, and contradiction implied in the term.

"He has accomplished the *tour de force* of transplanting vigorous and spicy colloquial speech into the written language. The result is a book that is easy to read and enormously vivid.

"One should not be misled by the tone of *Voyage au bout de la nuit* and take this book, satirical often to the point of ferocity, as a lampoon. The author tells his story in a humble, candid manner: unbiased minds will bow to the fidelity of his testimony."

Its readership:

"Doctors, whom the author attacks with particular virulence, academics, and the well-read."[1]

The press releases and the first advertisements at the time the book reached the shelves also tended to emphasize the provocative novelty of the work. As if in answer to a scandal that did not yet exist. As if they secretly wanted to create one in order to boost sales.

"A work tailored to life. A work enormous in its mass and resonance, delirious and objective, fantastic yet infused with truth. A colorful, cruel work in which the abject and the most gentle mingle, hideous in its bitterness, exquisite in its 'Villonesque' sweetness." Thus began the ad for *Voyage* in the November 1, 1932, issue of the *Nouvelle Revue Française*.

In *Gringoire*, on October 21, the following publicity announcement had appeared: "You will love this book or you will hate it. It will not leave you indifferent."

And in *Les Nouvelles Littéraires* the next day: "A cruel work but one so true, so emphatically painful yet at the same time vibrant, that it will immediately leave its mark, protestations notwithstanding."

Nor had Robert Denoël, who was working so hard, forgotten that a book's career and reputation are established more than anything else by word of mouth, and that in order to initiate such a process, one requires, so to speak, a great number of ears to receive the words of one mouth: his own. So he redoubled his visits and meetings with hacks and columnists. He personally wrote to dozens of journalists. Better yet, in order to alert and flatter the most influential writers, the jury of the Académie Goncourt in particular, he had the idea of publishing a numbered edition, off the market, for their consumption.

And Céline? Denoël may have feared that his rebellious author, hiding behind his pseudonym, would refuse to play the game, preferring to take refuge in an attentive, anxious, or sarcastic solitude. The flattery, the compromises, the worldly, respectful game of the young author plunged for the first time into the literary arena, and who must solicit the attention of colleagues and literary chroniclers without whose help he cannot make his name—was all of this compatible with the personality of the author of *Voyage*? It does seem to have been, and the publisher was pleasantly surprised. Well might Céline proclaim to the heavens his indifference to such fare, that makes no difference. Maintaining an affectation of reluctance and cynicism, the author readily stooped to the public and social constraints of his new role. And he did so with curiosity, docility, and gravity. Never hesitating, even with Robert Denoël, to inject the role with cynicism, as if to save face, to keep up his pose as the irreducible anarchist who is nobody's fool.

Thus, this letter to the publisher, on September 2, 1932: "Tell me how many of the 'Printed for Mr. X' copies which you so kindly told me about I can ask you for. I am very eager to soften up a few patrons with such a tribute.— . . . tional [illegible word]. One can never grovel enough."[2]

Indeed—one never can grovel enough. A few of the author's dedications have come down to us. They bear witness to a deference that is unusual for him, to say the least. Should we see them, against all logic, as a form of superior irony? Thus: "To M. Jean Ajalbert, who lends us courage." Or: "To Gaston Chérau, whose lessons we have tried to understand, a most respectful tribute." The two men were members of the Académie Goncourt. To Henry de Jouvenal, editor-in-chief of *Le Matin*, he wrote: "To the author of the marvelous *Mirabeau*, a sincere tribute." Remains the more casual and nonchalant missive to André Maurois: "It's raining, the wind's up, the weather is awful. A sincere tribute."[3]

Did Céline really believe that he had a chance to snare the Goncourt? He hadn't the slightest idea, of course, but he listened to his publisher and was able to hope. And he was ready to run himself ragged to secure the trumps on his side. In the late summer of 1932 he explained to an anonymous correspondent: "I am running around Paris after my galleys! . . . I hope that you have got our Goncourt business ready, to the extent that such things can be influenced."[4]

But how, exactly, to "influence"? At Denoël's request, on October 31 he wrote to Lucien Descaves, who was potentially his greatest champion on the Goncourt panel. On stationery from the Clichy clinic, he introduced himself modestly, emphasizing his work as a doctor in a suburban clinic and his *médaille militaire*. Following that letter, Descaves met with him on November 2 and pledged his vote. Moreover, the two men would see each other again on several occasions before the awarding of the prize on December 7. Denoël also arranged a meeting with Léon Daudet before that date.

To accompany and assist the book's publication, the publisher suggested the publication of advance proofs of *Voyage* in such reviews as *Cahiers du Sud*, *Europe*, and *Monde*. In October 1932 a full dozen Parisian periodicals carried excerpts of the novel. Henceforth, all that remained was the reaction from the press and public.

In its October 14 issue, the *Bibliographie de la France* announced the book's official publication date as October 20. But many copies were already in circulation. The first mention of the book in the press was on October 17, in *Comoedia* . . .

On the page "By the same author" appeared a note: "*Tout doucement* [Slowly Does It] . . . (In progress)." This furtive, phantom title provokes a smile. For the moment Céline was hardly considering his next book. Or else . . . slowly does it! Was he envisaging the account of his London adventures left out of *Voyage*? Or was he already dreaming of what was to become *Mort à crédit*? Most likely, Céline was waiting to see what would come of his first novel. He was remaining on standby. Anxious, alert, skeptical. For the time being, he was exploring a new world, a new *milieu*. That was enough.

To begin with, Robert Denoël had proceeded with a fairly modest first run of 3,000. He was certainly hoping for popular acclaim for *Voyage*, but he wasn't counting on it. Still less the Prix Goncourt. Three thousand copies was the minimum run. A wait-and-see. And in fact for nearly two months he didn't see much worth waiting for, at least commercially speaking. So much so that, on November 21, 1933, he was able to write to a correspondent: "Last year, before the Prix Goncourt, we made a great publicity push for *Le Voyage au bout de la nuit*, without much success. It was only the scandal surrounding the Prix Goncourt that set off the book's sales. Without that, he might very well have sold no better than 2,000 to 3,000 copies."[5]

On the other hand, the critical response was immediately astounding. Opposing positions cropped up one after another almost instantaneously. *Voyage au bout de la nuit* became, as we say today, a media event. But we must remember that the media did not play a determining role in those years before television, when radio had no cultural influence. The press alone contributed to the animation of the literary microcosm, from one publication to another, and nothing more.

What was initially striking was the confusion of journalists, readers, and writers. How to orient oneself to an unclassifiable text, what point of view to adopt before such provocative novelty, what rules to apply in passing judgment on a novel literally unprecedented?

One man, Robert Poulet, confessed to this confusion with remarkable candor. Denoël had insisted on his reading the proofs of *Voyage*. Poulet was suspicious, he was not terribly inclined to sacrifice an evening following the lucubrations of a beginner. He quickly found himself flabbergasted. He was struck above all by the book's comic qualities.

"I felt as if I were reading the facetious jokes of a plebeian Courteline who, in all four corners of the world in turn, was putting to the test the contradictions and absurdities of the human race. . . .

"I recognized, with great surprise and admiration, the birth of a new species of comedy, quite similar to that of Chaplin. I detected something contrived which was, however, perfectly legitimate and effective. Not only did this opinion disappoint Denoël—it angered him.

"In a dry voice, he told me that I had missed the core of the matter. In the author of *Voyage*, we had the equivalent of Dante and Shakespeare in one, with a good bit of Cervantes thrown in. . . .

"Thus spake Robert Denoël. His tone was a little peremptory for my taste, I stuck to my positions, even dug in. I was wrong."[6]

Lucien Rebatet, a contributor to *L'Action française* at the time, has described the shock of discovering *Voyage*, one autumn afternoon on the boulevard des Italiens: hours of impassioned reading on a bench facing the Flammarion bookstore, where he had just bought the book. But, he adds, "I would be lying were I to assert that, from that day on, and despite my enjoyment, I developed the certainty, later acquired, that Céline was the greatest event in French literature since Proust. Having finished the book, I even allowed myself to detect in it certain tedious passages."[7] He noted that neither Montherlant, nor Bernanos, nor Claudel, nor Giraudoux, nor Jules Romain, nor Mauriac, the leading lights of the day, accorded it any official attention at the time. Rebatet was wrong in the case of Bernanos: following a lengthy and highly critical article by André Rousseaux in *Figaro* on December 10, 1932, the writer was to come to Céline's defense in the same daily three days later (and he would be one of the only ones, along with Ramon Fernandez in *Les Nouvelles Littéraires* of December 10, to emphasize Céline's style, not merely a spoken, colloquial language but, on the contrary, an "extraordinary language, the height of the natural and the artificial").

Charles Maurras, for his part, remained skeptical before the enthusiasm of his partner, Léon Daudet, as seen, *inter alia*, in the famous article in *Candide* on December 22 in which Daudet makes the first reference to Rabelais, the comparison between Bardamu and Panurge. And Maurras remarked to Rebatet: "They already tried that with Rollinat and Jehan Rictus. Believe me, there's nothing more seasonal than that sort of reputation!"[8]

And even a Robert Brasillach, who would later find in Céline an ally in his anti-Semitic crusades, and who we would like to believe was possessed at the time by the intrepid enthusiasm of young people impassioned by literature, striving for the new, seems to have received *Voyage au bout de la nuit* with strong reservations. One must reread *Notre Avant-guerre*. Clearly, the brilliant student nurtured on classical literature had nothing in common with the child of the Passage Choiseul, the literary autodidact, the veteran drunk on the world's misery. In literature, Brasillach sought. Céline found. The former could define *Voyage* only as "a sort of epic of disaster and insult" to be disdainfully filed with the *romans-fleuves*, the epic sagas, of Jacques de Lacretelle.

In analyzing the early reactions of the press, we also come to the speedy conclusion that no definitive rift between the sensibilities of the Right and the Left provides categories for the opinions expressed about *Voyage*. The book finds defenders and adversaries in the bosom of the same publications, to the point where a second or even a third article allows for a correction of the critical stance of such or such an organ of the press. There is no better illustration of the book's ambiguity, of the impossibility of making it the standard-bearer of any party, faction, or class.

Voyage on the Left? Why not? Anarchists, anticolonialists, and antimilitarists were immediately inflamed. "A rebel? Better: a *defaulter*. Defaulting on the criminal laws, on the patriotic, social, and sentimental nonsense and rubbish," wrote Faunique in *Le Cri du Jour* on November 26, 1932.

And Pierre Scize in *Le Canard enchaîné* on December 14: "We read him and love him immediately. We? That is, all those who have kept some fire in their belly, some bitterness in their heart. We accept neither the world as it is going, nor the society in which we live, nor men as they are."

The remarks of the *Libertaire* of December 30 are equally blunt: "How can we anarchists not sympathize with this eternally restless man with . . . his absolute refusal to submit to war and its horrors, to the old, deeply corrupt bourgeois society and its need to dominate the unfortunate."

But is Céline's resolute individualism to the Left? Is the absence of any break in the social cloud cover, of any motivating hope, to the Left? *L'Humanité* remains perplexed. On December 19 Jean Fréville writes: "He

[Céline] irrevocably condemns the corrupt ruling class, but his Apocalypse is lacking in conclusion. . . . He does not see the proletariat as a new force, the revolutionary class that will seize from the enfeebled hands of the bourgeoisie the torch of civilization. . . . Céline remains a stranger to all that causes our hearts to beat. . . . Céline can only come up with a philosophy of abdication, of relentless sorrow."

The socialists are even more severe. In *Le Populaire de Paris*, on December 8, J. B. Séverac comments significantly: "The cynical, jeering confessions of a man without courage or nobility. . . . Nothing escapes his pitiless penchant for showing only the vile side of men (himself included). He excels at diminishing everything—one is tempted to say: at soiling everything. Let us concede that he has managed to do so."[9]

It is harder still to concede the existence of a Céline on the Right. Nothing could be less conservative than this book, which torpedos academic French and the subjunctive mode, middle-class decency, the peace of mind of the well-to-do, and all the values—religion, morality, and so on—that supported them. Whence the great fear of the right-thinkers, to use a term of Bernanos', when faced with *Voyage au bout de la nuit*, the fear and thus the condemnation manifested by André Rousseaux in *Le Figaro* on December 5 ("the basis of anarchy is always the same, and scorn for intelligible speech is an effect of the alienation of the human being pushed to its extremes"), confirmed in those same columns, on January 3, 1933, in the article by Henri de Régnier, and further revealed by the critic André Thérive on November 24, in *Le Temps*, where he in turn vents his indignation before so much vulgarity and obscenity.

Who could love Céline unconditionally? His despair, his mockery, his tenderness concealed beneath rage, and his solitude separated him from all political parties, from all schools, and, even more so, from civilization itself. The words of Alberto Savinio come to mind: "Civilization is a game, an entertainment, the most effective means we possess to remove from our minds the thought of death." Apparently, then, Céline was not playing the game in returning everything to the thought of death, that sole and inconsolable certainty. Céline was therefore not civilized.

Who could love Céline? Loners, perhaps, who were themselves uncivilized, "people without collective importance," anarchists of the Right or the Left, as you will. Or else perspicacious stylizers, the desperate, affectionate beings or dynamiters, aesthetes, the literary fringe, fair-weather accomplices.

Someone like Léon Daudet, for example, so little his father's son, a failed doctor, brilliant pamphleteer, erudite eccentric, pathological anti-Dreyfusard, aberrant anti-Semite, merciless nationalist, the soul of *L'Action française*, the spiritual successor to Léon Bloy, "ardent to the point of brutality, passionate to the point of fury, and anxious to the point of suffering," in the definition of Octave Mirbeau.

Or again, like Bernanos, an expert in suffering, a writer of flamboyant prose on familiar terms with the devil and his works.

Or like the erudite, classical, sensitive Thibaudet who, despite his reservations, understood quite clearly, in *La Dépêche de Toulouse* on January 24, 1933, that Céline "has made literary something which, before he came along, was not so."

Let us get back to the writer, to the man. Shortly after the publication of his book, his pseudonym had ceased to protect him. His identity was discovered. Dr. Destouches had thought himself sheltered, quietly practicing in Clichy, working at Gallier's or at La Biothérapie in the mornings, watching with mocking cynicism the storm gradually rising about his novel. He was wrong. He had to move to the front lines, to confront the journalists' spotlights and pens. Was he really so displeased at having to do so, he who had earlier dreamed of the theater?

On November 10, less than a month after the book's publication, *Paris-Soir* ran the first interview with the author, by Pierre-Jean Launay. A fairly short article in which Céline seems more concerned with projecting a persona than sincere answers. "What does my book matter? It's not literature," he asserts. Well, well! He also claims to be obsessed with human misery, which, on the other hand, is indeed a constant of Célinian sincerity. And in conclusion: "Leave me in the shadows. Even my mother doesn't know I wrote this book. That sort of thing just isn't done in our family."

This pious wish was probably sincere only in small part. On November 13 *Le Matin* revealed his true identity. A few days later was to begin the Goncourt Affair. Soon, in a whirlwind of controversy, invective, and trials, people would be talking of nothing but *Voyage* and its author.

The Goncourt Affair

The autumn of 1932 was a dull one in France. The literary season begun in September-October was no more mediocre than usual. The disputes surrounding the important prizes at year's end—the Femina, the Interallié, the Renaudot, and the Goncourt—involved, among others, the names André Billy (*La Femme maquillée*), Robert Brasillach (*Le Voleur d'étincelles*), Ramon Fernandez (*Le Pari*), Marcel Jouhandeau (*Tite-le-long*), Henri Poulaille (*Le Pain quotidien*), and Maxence Van der Meersch (*La Maison dans la dune*). But these books, we must admit, were not the stuff to create a stir—they went through the motions and slowly sank into merciful oblivion, even if their authors would be remembered for other works. No, the uncontested event remained *Voyage au bout de la nuit*. And since France was seeking distraction, it made of *Voyage* and of the ups and downs of the Prix Goncourt a tragicomic soap opera on which it was to feast for months.

The leading characters of this soap opera were, naturally, the Goncourt academicians.

Presiding was Joseph Henri Boex, better known under the pseudonym "J. H. Rosny the Elder." Born in 1856, an authentic naturalist, he was the coauthor with his brother of works that established their reputation and today molder in the libraries; later he was solely responsible for such astonishing prehistoric novels as *La Guerre du feu* in 1911. At his side sat Séraphin Justin François Boex, known as "J. H. Rosny the Younger," who took a stab at just about every novelistic genre with desperate prodigality, as if wanting to benefit in life from the crumbs of a fame that would elude him in death.

Another founding member of the Académie Goncourt since its first meeting in 1900, where he succeeded his father three years dead, was Léon Daudet. A monarchist and anti-Semitic disciple of Drumont, he was nevertheless the friend of Marcel Schwob, whose *Souvenirs*, written in vitriol, still have the power to charm through the genius of their caricature, and who, several years earlier, had had the enormous merit of placing Marcel Proust on the Goncourt honors list.

The last original Goncourt academician was Lucien Descaves, born in 1861. He had spent his childhood in the clutches of poverty in Montrouge, and those advanced ideas, as they say, had quickly drawn him to naturalism. He sympathized—in retrospect—with the cause of the Commune. Novels such as *La Caserne* and *Sous-Offs* won him a solid and well-deserved reputation as an antimilitarist. He was even condemned for offenses against the army and public decency. Lucien Descaves had a big mouth if not a big writing talent; he was a loner, aloof from the small literary world. He had been openly snubbing his Academy colleagues since the 1917 election of Jean Ajalbert to the Octave Mirbeau chair, when his vote had gone to Georges Courteline. Ever since, he had mailed in his vote or came to dine theatrically alone in the large dining room at Drouant's, sending his ballot upstairs with a waiter.

Other academicians included Roland Dorgelès, whose fame was achieved by one single book, *Les Croix de bois*, in 1919; Jean Ajalbert, who had been a lawyer before becoming a novelist, was the curator at the Beauvais tapestry factory (posterity records only that he voted for Céline in the Goncourt); Gaston Chéreau, whose social, peasant frescoes no one would think of rereading today; Pol Neveux, a notary's son and a librarian, the author of a study on Maupassant and a novelist himself, unjustly ignored by posterity; Léon Hennique, a naturalist grown gray in service, a veteran of the Soirées de Médan; and, lastly, Raoul Ponchon, a small-time Rastignac, an appallingly prolific poet-bureaucrat.

Such, then, were the men who needed to be persuaded of the merits of *Voyage.*

Léon Daudet had promised his vote very early on, as had Lucien Descaves, as we have seen. The nationalist and the anarchist, the militarist and the antimilitarist, the rightist and the leftist had reconciled for the occasion. Bravo! The plump Ajalbert with his patriarch's mustache soon rallied to the Célinian clan. Descaves was instantly ready to forget past differences and shake him by the hand. For Descaves, the movement's bellwether, it remained only to rally the Rosny brothers. With the president of the Academy's casting vote, a majority was thus guaranteed to *Voyage*. And it appeared that the Rosny brothers allowed themselves to be convinced.

It was on November 30, at a preparatory luncheon at Drouant's, that Lucien Descaves, returned from the dead, was welcomed back by his colleagues. An informal vote was taken in which the Rosny brothers, Daudet, Descaves, and Ajalbert thus came out for Céline. Guy Mazeline mustered a few allies for *Les Loups*. Roland Dorgèles hesitated. But in the long run it made no difference—a decision had been reached and Daudet even suggested awarding the prize on the spot, which was hardly likely. A Goncourt prize is not handed out behind the scenes, in the absence of the press. A meeting was thus set for the following week, December 7, for the anticipated consecration of Céline.

In the cab taking him home from Drouant's on November 30, Lucien Descaves tried to bring Léon Hennique around to the cause of *Voyage au bout de la nuit*. He may already have been suspicious of the Rosny brothers, or simply have wished to ensure Céline a triumphant election. " 'May I remind you,' " he told him, " 'that our duty to the Goncourts is to encourage new and bold experiments in thought and form. In that respect, we could find nothing better.' . . . We went our separate ways, agreeing to meet eight days later in order to fulfill our inherited obligations. Our chat had in no way reassured me. Hennique had remained evasive! The rude awakening of our shared recollections seemed to have left him deaf."[10]

As to Louis Destouches, he had allowed himself little by little to be won over by his publisher's enthusiasm. What had initially been but a nebulous hope had become a reality worth serious consideration. We find a reflection of that in his letters to Erika Irrgang and Cillie Pam, brief, evanescent mistresses but faithful correspondents with whom he happily communicated.

"I am rather hoping for the Prix Goncourt on December 10 but it's entirely impossible to predict," he is already writing to Erika by the end of October. And a few days later: "The book is very embattled and highly flattered in the reviews. They mostly talk a lot of rubbish."[11]

To Cillie Pam, on November 12, he writes as if wanting to forestall destiny and not give in to the incurable sin of optimism: "I have a great contempt for literature, Cillie. It makes no more sense to me than the yoyo. I use it just like a yoyo. Because life is awful to me, one has to pass the time somehow and I don't know how to play with a real yoyo. My chances for the Goncourt are extremely slim. They exist but are very weak. It would take a miracle. Not from the value of the yoyo book which is as good as any other (it's a very bad year) but because of my anarchic style which could easily scare them off. The Goncourts used to be anarchic but they've grown old, they're no more than conservative old ladies now."[12]

Nevertheless, on December 6, the eve of the announcement, he cannot quite mask his confidence. Still to Cillie Pam: "I am waiting for the Prix Goncourt, which is being awarded tomorrow. You have probably heard speak of it. It is supposed to be the best book of the year. I am indifferent to the honor but would certainly appreciate the financial consequences, which are quite large and guarantee material independence once and for all, my dream. I am not at all sure of getting it but I have a serious chance."[13]

The chance was so serious that Descaves did not hesitate to consider the prize as won, as he wrote in an article on the eve of the poll. And Daudet, in *L'Action française* on December 6, predicted: "Before the Prix Goncourt is awarded tomorrow at noon, most likely to a colorful, extraordinary work that many will find revolting because it is written in a raw, occasionally slangy style, though of great strength . . ." As for the publisher, Robert Denoël, he had already had the wrappings for *Voyage* printed up: *Prix Goncourt 1932.*

On Wednesday, December 7, the usual crowd of rubberneckers, columnists, journalists, and photographers were gathered outside Drouant's on the place Gaillon, where the Goncourt members dined and voted. On the floor above, the panelists of the Prix Renaudot were also preparing, for the seventh consecutive year, to award their prize—which had been created by literary critics as a kind of foil for the Goncourt, in order to relieve the sometimes long wait on the deliberations and, when necessary, to redress injustices.

Among that mob on the place Gaillon, few would have recognized Dr. Destouches, accompanied by his mother and daughter. His imperfectly dissembled anxiety is easy enough to imagine—that enervating, impotent wait, the sudden feeling that his career, the success of his book, money and reputation were in the making, all depending on ten inaccessible, invisible men somewhere in a dining room of the Drouant restaurant, waiting to gorge themselves on seafood, oysters, *belons*, broiled lobster, goose with chestnut stuffing, and to render their verdict like a trial jury. The unbearable tension, the mad hope, the utter pessimism, the constant ups and downs that may be deemed to have no bearing on the actual proceedings but which, as all successful and unsuccessful candidates have attested, happen thus nonetheless.

The mood must have been rather oppressive at the meeting of the Académie Goncourt. Contrary to custom, Rosny the Elder, the panel's president, proposed that the vote be held before eating. So as not to keep the press waiting, he explained dubiously. *Voyage au bout de la nuit* had unleashed passions, they had to get it out of the way, one way or another the vote should be taken just to have done with it. No one amongst the Goncourts wanted a long meal of mundane conversation and small talk with the question hanging over them: who was for or against Céline, for or against the man who had mobilized Lucien Descaves *and* Léon Daudet?

The vote on Wednesday, December 7, at the 203th meeting of the Académie Goncourt, was eminently straightforward. An absolute majority emerged on the first ballot, and the award winner was declared and acknowledged on the spot. It was Guy Mazeline for *Les Loups* [The Wolves], published by Gallimard.

Mazeline garnered six votes, those of Gaston Chéau, Roland Dorgèles, Léon Hennique, Pol Neveux, Raoul Ponchon, and Rosny the younger. Three votes went to Céline, those of Léon Daudet, Lucien Descaves, and Jean Ajalbert. Rosny the Elder voted for the novel *Les Formiciens* by a certain Monsieur de Rienzi, a personal friend.

The Rosnys had sold out.

Lucien Descaves didn't waste a second. He leaped from his chair, slammed the door behind him, and rushed to the upper floor, where the Prix Renaudot panelists were eating. He described what had just taken place to them. It took Georges Charensol, Pierre Demartres, Pierre Descaves, Marcel Espiau, Georges Martin, Raymond de Nys, Odette Pannetier, Gaston Picard, Noël Sabord, and Marcel Sauvage three ballots for a small majority of six votes finally to emerge in favor of *Voyage.*

Meanwhile, Lucien Descaves was venting his spleen to the journalists waiting in front of Drouant's: "I would have gladly returned to the Académie Goncourt, but I had no idea I would be compelled to go through the kitchen to reach the dining room."[14] And again: "I shall never again set foot in the Academy. It is a marketplace, a fairground, where everything, with very few exceptions, is for sale."[15]

Along with the journalists, curious onlookers, and the neighborhood idlers, Louis thus learned of his failure. Dismayed, he left his mother and daughter and went to the rue Amélie, where the disappointment was no less keen. Jeanne Carayon, his ex-neighbor and proofreader, was there.

"Céline, arriving with Denoël, seemed weary. Having seen the publisher off, he had these unexpected words for the proofreader: 'Don't leave me alone.' If this appeal is worth saving for posterity, it's because it was so unusual for a man of his character. Later on, his pets would be the ones to keep him company.

"He didn't speak of the failure on the rue Lepic. He went to the window and uprooted his geraniums with a fork. He passed around a child's drawings—his daughter's—that he treasured. Then he seemed to be smitten by a sort of torpor and he lay down—his face relaxed, as if pacified."[16]

The Goncourt setback was the first rupture, the first divorce, between the literary world, its institutions, and the writer. Up to that point, Céline's *entrée* into literature had been accompanied by sensation, fame, and the promise of honors. We always become very quickly—too quickly—accustomed to success. Suddenly the door was being slammed in his face.

That, at least, was how it felt. And the writer was mortified as well as humiliated. It inclined him to break from the world of intellectuals. The divorce between him and "them" was brewing. Yet it would be ridiculous to consider Céline as a literary outcast. After all, the list of great works passed over by the Goncourt goes on and on, and the Renaudot, furthermore, was an attractive consolation. But the important thing was that Céline was already beginning to feel snubbed and to believe himself excluded. From then on, he would go to great lengths to justify that impression, so as, in some way and a priori, to justify himself.

The very night of the awards, as tradition dictated, Robert Denoël held a reception in Céline's honor. The writer made a brief appearance. A photo shows him at the side of Philippe Hériat, the previous award winner. Céline's countenance is deeply furrowed, his smile forced. He gives the impression of being on the run, huddled in his herringbone overcoat, a dark scarf neatly tucked beneath his chin. The last thing he wants to talk about is the Renaudot prize. What is on his mind is his failure in the Goncourt, that is what feeds the bitterness that he is already savoring with pessimism and that finally justifies his bilious solitude.

Moreover, symptomatically, he makes no mention of the Renaudot in his letters to Erika and Cillie. He writes only of the Goncourt and the conspiracy surrounding it. He was defeated, he says, "by the wealthiest competitor."[17] He states further: "The Prix Goncourt backfired. It's a matter between publishers. On the other hand, the book is a triumph. Unfortunately, you know how I dread triumphs. Never have I been so miserable. That mob of people pestering and pursuing you with their noisy vulgarity is a nightmare."[18]

And to Cillie, a week later, the same words flow from his pen:

"As to the Goncourt, it was a nightmare, pure and simple. I got no pleasure from it—with or without. It's all the same to me. All I remember of it is the vulgarity, the crassness, the shamelessness of the whole business.

"There are so many people who adore fame or, at least, notoriety. Except for the War, I know of nothing so horribly unpleasant. I'm doing my best to put that disaster behind me."[19]

The writer's words are "nightmare," "disaster." One takes one's Apocalypse where one finds it. History was soon to go much better—and Céline with it—in regard to maledictions, prisons, and death triumphant. For now, the writer could only think of leaving Paris for a new, timely, and final research trip funded by Rajchman and the League of Nations. If the Goncourt Affair was, in reality, only just beginning, it was well and truly over for him, the page turned once and for all, without forgiveness, forgetfulness, or indifference. He left for Switzerland on December 11.

There remains, however, more to be said on the Goncourt Affair. For if it no longer directly concerns the writer's life, the dispute at least still swirls about his name and work. And it required a book as excessive as his, with its terrible lucidity and convulsive style, to denounce the most vulnerable points of the era's sensibility, to inspire so much relentless passion. In the end, *Voyage au bout de la nuit* acted as an extraordinary sort of photographic print. It is up to each of us to accept or reject the image, to accept or reject the human race as described by Céline, in its deadly mediocrity, its hatreds, its peevishness, and its all too rare manifestations of tenderness. Each of us must be prepared or not to recognize himself in that seedy, colonialist France, that America stupefied by King Dollar and the assembly line, those Parisian suburbs foundering in poverty, that endless parade of drunks, the goiterous, soldiers, laborers, madmen, sick children—that panoramic human condition observed by Dr. Destouches and to which the writer Céline suddenly gave a language in harmony with his memory, his despair, and his hallucinations.

What had happened in the bosom of the Académie Goncourt? The Rosnys, first of all, denied having ever promised anything whatsoever at the meeting of November 30. The minutes of that meeting (kept by Roland Dorgèles) do not reveal a firm commitment from each panelist. But all the same, why the vote for Mazeline on the very first ballot? Rosny the Younger offered no explanation. Rosny the Elder explained that he had wished to cast his first vote for his favorite candidate, his friend Monsieur de Rienzi (of whom no mention as a possible candidate had been made at the earlier meeting), even if he were later to rally to another name.[20]

But naturally there were other reasons.

In a letter of December 9 to his childhood friend Simone Saintu, who must have resumed contact with him for the occasion, Louis wrote: "The Goncourt is a joke! Hachette had us in their pocket—it was mine the Wednesday before. I'm leaving for Switzerland right away."[21] Hachette, we should remember, was already the largest book distributor in France and marketed Gallimard, the publisher of Mazeline's *Les Loups*. Hachette lacked neither the power nor the many connections necessary to secure the Goncourt and the large sales it guaranteed.

And that's not all. In *Le Crapouillot*, Galtier-Boissière recalled that the paper *L'Intransigeant* had recently serialized a novel by Rosny the Elder, a considerable promotion for a writer by then somewhat out of fashion. It may have been only a coincidence that Guy Mazeline was a contributing editor on *L'Intransigeant*. And then again, it may not.

Let us recapitulate the polemics as they evolved. The enraged Lucien Descaves vowed never again to set foot in the Académie Goncourt, and to renew his voting by correspondence. Dorgèles justified his vote for Mazeline most ambivalently by declaring that the candidate dearest to his heart was Céline. In the February 1933 issue of *Le Crapouillot*, Galtier-Boissière accused Rosny the Elder of selling his vote and demanded his resignation. The free-lance journalist Maurice-Yvan Sicard went even further. In a new publication he was running, *Le Huron*, reporting remarks ostensibly made by

Lucien Descaves, he wrote in March 1933: "We know how the admirable *Voyage au bout de la nuit*—that 'anarchist book,' according to Sergeant-at-Arms Dorgèles—was gradually pushed aside by M. Guy Mazeline's pomaded rag. . . . Once again, the affair was led this year by Dorgèles and the two Rosnys, one of whom is deaf and the other certainly an idiot. . . . With two or three exceptions, the other Goncourts—Commander Dorgèles at the fore—are authentic cutthroats. . . . Every year the vote of the president of the Académie Goncourt is sold to the highest bidder."

ʻ A lawsuit was inevitable. In April 1933 Roland Dorgèles and Rosny the Elder brought a complaint against Galtier-Boissière and Maurice-Yvan Sicard. The wheels of justice turn slowly. The first trial against Galtier-Boissière was heard on the 15th and 21st of December that year and was settled amicably. Claiming ill health, Lucien Descaves refused to testify or to confirm or deny the remarks that had been attributed to him. In a letter to the presiding magistrate, he denied having wanted to attack anyone; his criticisms were of a general order and that was that. For his part, Rosny the Elder was none too proud of having dragged Galtier-Boissière into court and, through him, his colleague in the Académie Goncourt. He preferred to withdraw his complaint. The manager of *Le Crapouillot* wrote him a letter of apology.

Thus, the affair came to a close. But the court's preamble at the December 21 hearing remains rather spicy, since it presumes to substitute itself for the Goncourt panel in deciding who is worthy of receiving the Prix Goncourt, and condemns *Voyage au bout de la nuit* for offenses against the French language! Ever since *Les Fleurs du mal*, the magistrature had been a laughing stock in its consistently calamitous relations with literature.

Following are excerpts from that preamble: "Whereas Galtier-Boissière's bad faith stems from his desire . . . to create a scandal . . . exploited by *Le Crapouillot*; whereas he failed to notice that the book by Céline which the members of the Académie Goncourt rejected for the 1932 prize contains expressions that are flagrantly coarse, vulgar, intolerable, and capable of disgusting unforewarned readers whom a literary prize must protect against such unpleasant surprises. . . ."[22] And there's more where that came from.

Sicard did not appreciate such evasiveness, which he considered to be cowardly and a false reconciliation. He refused all compromise. On January 4, 1934, he was found guilty on two charges and ordered to pay a 200-franc fine and 30,000 francs in damages and interest.

Meanwhile, what with the controversy and the gossip, the testimony at the public hearings, the ire and insinuation and sensationalized reconciliations, *Voyage au bout de la nuit* was firmly on its way. In the two months following the lost Goncourt, more than 50,000 copies were sold, as well as the foreign rights in a dozen countries. Robert Denoël claimed to have received in that same period more than 5,000 press clippings related to the novel and the news surrounding it.

Escape

Céline's trip to Central Europe—to Berlin, Breslau, and Vienna—fell opportunely. He had at all costs to convince himself that the world and his life did not gravitate around the place Gaillon and the Drouant restaurant. To hell with the Goncourts, literary awards, and shattered self-esteem! He was also a doctor, and he didn't want to forget it.

He took the train for Geneva on December 11.

Of course, Louis had not arranged this medical trip with the sole intention of escaping Paris and the reversals of Goncourt academicians who changed their minds like shirts. It had been during the previous August that he had first thought of it, for at least two reasons. The first was to take advantage of a trip funded by the Health Section of the League of Nations to meet with his two friends, his spring and summer mistresses, Erika Irrgang and Cillie Pam, in Breslau and Vienna. The second was the official, medical reason: to head an inquiry into unemployment and its consequences on the public health of the populations concerned.

Thus it was that he had written to the good Ludwig Rajchman on August 20: "I should like to observe welfare and unemployment medicine, and the antivenereal campaign. There are things going on in the East that I don't know of."[23]

Of course, the things he didn't know of in the East, in Breslau, were primarily concerned with the beautiful Erika Irrgang of the great dark eyes. But Rajchman had no way of guessing that. No more than his partner Dr. Boudreau, who, on September 4, received in turn a letter from Dr. Destouches, as urgent and fussy as ever in his requests for expenses:

"As for Berlin, I should like to take a look at medicine for the poor and the unemployed (general medicine, syphilis, tuberculosis). Same thing in Breslau.

"I should also like to ask you if I can receive 7 dollars a day, since I have to find a replacement for myself in Clichy while I'm away. That is, I give 70 francs a day and am not paid in any of the laboratories where I work."[24]

Social medicine continued to interest Céline even while he was writing and then publishing *Voyage au bout de la nuit.* If we have reason to doubt that, the proof lies in a text written at that time, a memoir, perhaps written at the request of Ludwig Rajchman, the Rockefeller Foundation, or Professor Léon Bernard (it is not known which) on a program of studies related to a course in international hygiene.[25] In it, Céline's thoughts wander and gambol in disorder from one contradiction to another, a confrontation between Céline the optimist and Céline the pessimist. The former, the leftist, invokes the economic crisis, the exploitation of the working classes, the class struggle, the misdeeds of capitalism. To his mind, social medicine is not compatible with capitalism. What, then, is to be done? "This society would have to crumble before we can talk of a truly popularized public medicine, which is only in real accordance with a socialist or communist governmental formula. Popular medicine rests on the simultaneously fraternal and scientific application of physical, moral, and localized comfort to all members of a given community."26

What Marxist could reject such ideas, or Dr. Destouches' lengthy elaboration of the socioeconomic factors of medical destitution in our society? But does he really see revolution as a panacea? He may hope that it is, but without really believing it so. For Céline has no confidence in mankind. Official medicine, confronted by "the monstrous hypocrisy [*tartuferie*] of the great economic interests and thus of the public powers" can respond only with the most innocuous solutions. "We all know perfectly well that the proletariat, unemployed or not, is incomparably more crippled by illness than the rich. The program we would suggest would be not to pretend, through the anodyne measures that alone are permitted to the public health official, to make notable inroads against this morbidity but to render the morbidity itself the least burdensome, the least painful, and the least distressing as possible for the proletariat."27

We do not know what or whose purpose this report could have served. There would be no further mention of the plan for the course on international hygiene or, for that matter, of the role that Dr. Destouches might have played within it.

After the Goncourt, on December 10, Edmond Jaloux had devoted a long critical study to *Voyage* in *Les Nouvelles Littéraires*. In it he spoke of the "great literary discovery of the year," but balanced his compliments with numerous reservations. The same day, on the eve of his departure for Geneva, Louis answered him.

Sir,

I read and reread with much emotion your admirable critique of Voyage *this morning. You are most delicately and deeply right (I am speaking of your grievances). One must be on the lookout for fatigue . . . for babbling, for the paradox that tends, on the Bad Days, to supplant one's weakened animation . . . One's delirium can never be candid enough or simple enough. Never. We want to appear reasonable. We are ashamed, and we are wrong. It wears you down so quickly . . . You must make an enormous effort just to retain a little bit. With the next book (in six years) I should like, if you are willing, to submit the manuscript to you.*28

This letter deserves particular attention. It reveals a Céline who, despite the disappointments, has in no way renounced his new literary career. We must thus compare it to the one sent to his friend Simone Saintu a few days later: "I'll never write again, or at least I won't ever publish anything again— in the current circumstances of my life. All this noisy notoriety adds to the horror of living. Bah."29 But that is pure affectation, genuine resentment on which he plays and which he exaggerates at will. The truth lies more on the side of the remarks addressed to Jaloux. And they reveal a Céline who is not only a writer but a man of letters in the classical sense, respectful and flattering to the tips of his fingers or his pen. Yes, there was a divorce between him and the literary world after the Goncourt failure. But it would be fairer as yet to speak of divorce proceedings. Céline is rushing nothing. An attempt at reconciliation is still possible, and he himself is making the overtures.

One word, finally, deserves to be singled out: that of "delirium." One can never be delirious enough, the writer states, and that says it all. It is one of the most decisive words in the Célinian vocabulary. Delirium is the second state of existence that distances dull, prosaic reality, and an excess of which makes the writer (like his hero) incomparably clear-sighted in the very depths of his misery, enabling him to distinguish the true poetic and convulsive realities contained in life and death.

Marguerite Destouches was supposed to accompany her son to Geneva, but abandoned the trip at the last minute. Louis left alone. By the shores of Lake Geneva, he most certainly met Ludwig Rajchman, to whom he could set out the terms and conditions of his journey. It may have been their last meeting. The writer's life, professional burdens, egoism, political commitments, and especially his rabid anti-Semitism would soon help to put an unbreachable gap between them.

Louis arrived in Berlin on December 18. We do not know his specific itinerary in the German capital. As planned, he must have visited clinics, hospitals, met with doctors and those in charge of social and health services. We know only, from the stationery on which he wrote his letters to Erika and Cillie, that he stayed in the Hessler Hotel, which was not by any stretch of the imagination the most modest in the city.

Once there, Louis found a country riven by political conflicts, the struggles between the socialists, communists, and Nazis, perpetually hovering on the brink of civil war. Since the Reichstag elections of the past July 31, the National Socialist party had been the dominant political force in Germany, having garnered 35% of the votes. The latest poll of November 24 may have registered a slight setback for the Nazis, but it was insignificant. Despite the communists' strong oppositional minority, Hitler remained the virtual master of the game in an exhausted Weimar Republic unable to recover from the postwar economic crisis, when inflation had soared almost surrealistically, millions of marks falling short of the price of a loaf of bread. But in 1932 unemployment was growing even faster than inflation once had. Democracy was in an endless cycle of failure and recovery, as if in perpetual reanimation. Berlin was then experiencing its own version of the Roaring Twenties in a whirlwind of jazz, the Charleston, decadent luxury, white nights, and dazzling flights of artistic fancy. Germany saw its own blossoming of modern art, the abstract explosions of Kandinsky and the stripped-down architectural aesthetic of the Bauhaus, a movement whose achievements continue to be explored today. The faltering President Hindenburg could do nothing amidst all this disorder. He was wearing himself out saving face and counting points, bogged down in futile calculations and laughable political realignments. He was ready to come to terms with the devil—or with Hitler. On January 30, 1933, he was finally to call Hitler to the Chancellory to form a new government. A temporary experiment, he believed. He was wrong. The experiment was to last an eternity. Nightmares, we know, seem to go on forever, and their memory never seems to fade. . . . In short, in December 1932, Germany wavered at the edge of delirium. And Louis Destouches was inquiring into the medical consequences of unemployment.

From the Hessler Hotel, he wrote to Erika: "I won't reach Breslau until Monday and will only stay two days. I'll be working with the doctors and do not MAKE ANY SPECIAL PLANS FOR ME. You know how I hate to cause a fuss. I'll go straight to the hotel and will call you. I'll bring you the newspapers you asked for and we'll talk all this over."[30]

Erika at the time was running a small review that republished current press clippings relating to Germany from foreign periodicals, mostly English and American. Louis, at her request, was bringing her the desired documentation.

He wrote to Cillie the same day, confirming his imminent arrival in Vienna in more or less identical terms: "I'll go straight to the hotel and DO NOT WANT to sleep *at your place.* For several reasons. First of all, it would be compromising you very stupidly in the eyes of your friends and of *your friend.* Also, I DO NOT WANT you to have to go sleep somewhere else, as you have offered. You know, Cillie, how I HATE people to do things specially for me. It embarrasses me terribly."[31]

There is no affectation or coyness on his part here. Apparently, Louis' relationships with Cillie and Erika were not sexual at this point, but simply of warm friendship (even if that friendship is occasionally rather ambiguous). Louis was too attached to his own independence to trample on others'. This violent, suffering, vociferous man, who was able to conjure hallucinatory words of rejection and hatred as if to seal himself off from the world solely by the unbearable hum of his deliria, also possessed rare delicacy, silent and surprising attentiveness. And it would show poor understanding of the writer to neglect one aspect of his personality to the benefit—or the detriment—of another.

On December 25 he arrived in Breslau. He remained there but three days. He left for Vienna on the 28th. Cillie Pam introduced him to a psychoanalytic circle. In particular, Louis met Dr. A. J. Storfer, publisher of Freud and Wilhelm Reich and director of the Internationaler Psychoanalystischer Verlag. Cillie also introduced him to her friend Dr. Anny Angel.

This progressive, Jewish world did nothing to shake Céline's convictions. For his political convictions wavered according to his indignations of the moment. His determined pessimism did not permit him to commit himself too decisively. He was not yet blinded by racial prejudices in the whirlwind of intolerant rejection and violence. His curiosity did the rest. Did he really develop a passion for psychoanalysis at that time? Do we see traces of it in the "excremental" and symbolic convulsions of some of his books? I do not believe so. But beyond any doubt, his interest in psychoanalysis was in harmony with his enormous thirst for knowledge, his curiosity, and his need to violate all taboos. He could only be enchanted by the ambition of becoming a voyeur of the unconscious. In fact, his research was conducted in parallel to scientific analysis, rather like Arthur Schnitzler in Vienna a few years later when he strove to root out the "penumbra of the soul" in his stories, novels, and plays. Dr. Schnitzler himself may have owed little to psychoanalysis; psychoanalysis, on the other hand, owed him a great deal. And Freud did not hesitate to write him: "In plunging into your splendid creatures, I felt as if, beneath the poetic surface, I were looking at my own hypotheses, conclusions, and interests." We might easily say as much for Céline.

Despite her taste for exaggeration and the peremptory good conscience lent by the sense of having known and foretold everything after the fact, Anny Angel nevertheless left a valuable account of the author of *Voyage*: "I met him when he was in Vienna, before he became a Nazi. I remember that, during his stay, he spent an entire night talking about all sorts of childish perversions, sexual practices involving corpses, etc. He had extraordinary gifts, and certainly gave the impression, at that time, of being a pervert and a psychopath. But otherwise he seemed capable of being a good and loyal friend. He was so to Cillie, undoubtedly, and at the time I believed he bore similar feelings toward me. For instance, he offered me his apartment in Paris in case I should have to leave Austria in a hurry with my son, for political reasons, and assured me that not only would I be welcome there, but that I could stay as long as I liked until I found something else—an offer that was certainly not to be taken lightly in those days."[32]

It is from that stay in Vienna, too, that dates the famous letter of December 30 sent to Léon Daudet, and which proves at least that Céline had not forgotten his stature as a writer or the respect and gratitude he owed to those who had supported him. Above all, the letter offers a gripping summary of his poetic and literary art, of his most intimate and most tragic obsessions.

> . . . *You are certainly familiar, Maître, with the enormous festival of madmen by P. Brughel* [sic]. *It is in Vienna. For me, it states the whole problem.* . . .
>
> *I should like to see it otherwise—I do not see it otherwise. I cannot.*
>
> *My entire delirium tends in that direction and I have no other deliria.*
>
> *I rejoice only in the grotesque within Death's compass. All the rest is vanity to me. See you soon,* Maître, *and most sincerely, gratefully yours,*
>
> *Destouches.*"[33]

To rejoice in the grotesque within Death's compass: this sums up Céline, the expert in catastrophe, the dynamiting clown of decomposing civilizations, the patient artisan, fastidiously and sumptuously poetic in a French language that is in an advanced state of decomposition, so as better to retain shards of emotion, memory, and despair within its fragments, its glittering flashes, its many facets.

Louis returned to Paris in early January. A single text bears witness to his research trip: a three-page article that would be published in issue no. 26 (February 1 to March 1, 1933) of *Le Mois* under the leader "Opinions." Its title is desperately mocking: "To Destroy Unemployment Will They Destroy the Unemployed?"

The writer simply concludes that, despite social programs, the unemployed are condemned to die a slow death, one of malnutrition. "Out of four Germans, the first eats far too much, two others satisfy their hunger, and the fourth is slowly dying for lack of food. This is a problem that a ten-year-old child, of average intelligence but not hobbled or stupefied by politics and selfishness, could solve in ten seconds."[34]

He can barely imagine any solution. "German poverty stems first and foremost from chaos." Could a dictator inject some order into the unemployment problem? "Even Hitler, Führer that he is, will have a very hard time getting out of this idiotic alimentary marasmus; nobody is interested in peace, and brotherhood is a pain in the neck to everybody. In truth, he'll find it very difficult to obtain one lump of sugar for organizing peace in Germany, whereas he can get all the blood he can use for war."[35]

Meanwhile, Hitler had seized power. And perhaps, to Céline's way of thinking, it was a lesser evil. But let us not scout the texts too obsessively. He could never have managed to believe in peace in Germany, or in brotherhood—with Hitler or without Hitler.

Return to Paris

Naturally, the journey to Central Europe, that brief interlude, had done nothing to change his literary situation. Céline had not forgotten the events of December, nor had the intellectual world. *Voyage au bout de la nuit* continued to animate conversations, nights on the town, and the newspaper columns, while Dr. Destouches returned to his suburban clinic, the routine of his daily rounds, and the abrasive cohabitation with Dr. Ichok.

In February a journalist from *Je suis partout* amused himself by posing as a patient and catching Céline unawares in Clichy. He wanted to find out if Dr. Destouches resembled Bardamu, if he was familiar or rude with his patients. He was wasting his time. Dr. Destouches addressed him with *Monsieur* and the formal *vous*, sounded him with the most professional attentiveness, prescribed a diet free of coffee, wine, and liquor, and that was all. The doctor had remained a doctor, neither colorful nor scandalous. The journalist, René Miquel, went home disappointed.

Thus, a doctor as before, Louis also remained a *Montmartrois* by adoption in his little garret apartment on the rue Lepic, where he awaited the return of Elizabeth Craig, so long in America. Was he bored? He spent occasional evenings with Henri Mahé and his cronies, enjoyed frequent one-night stands, still loved the dance, music hall, and comic opera, and continued to seek the company of artists and easy [*legères*] young ladies.

The person against whom Céline held the biggest grudge was Robert Denoël. For, with the best intentions, his publisher had promised him the moon—that is, the Goncourt (but what French publisher, with far less assurance, has not promised his young writers the Goncourt?). The writer held him responsible not for his failure but for having almost convinced him. He should not have allowed a friendship to develop between them. Céline's disappointment was in proportion to the trust he had placed in Denoël.

Starting in January, while sales of *Voyage* were growing, the opportunistic Denoël began thinking of his author's next book. But Céline was still wavering between two subjects. Denoël fell back on the manuscript of *L'Église*, which Céline must have mentioned to him. The moment was ripe to publish it, so as to take advantage of the endless controversy over *Voyage*. On that subject, in January or February, Céline wrote him a fairly curt letter in which he put things in their proper perspective, distancing himself once more— the letter of a loner, a skeptic, a cynic who would no longer allow himself to be swayed by the vain promises of life and friendship.

> *Dear friend,*
>
> *I came out of my shell at the time of the Goncourt and have now returned to it. There is nothing left for me to say or to hear. We both came out of it the better— thus everything has been for the best—and I am sure that best will persevere. I despise all that resembles intimacy, friendship, camaraderie, etc.*
>
> *That is one side of life that disgusts me. One cannot change oneself. Think of me as an excellent investment, nothing more, nothing less.*
>
> *That is my wish and my truth.*
>
> *As for* L'Église *(which is not in our contract), I want the final say on all foreign translations (should there be any).*
>
> *As for the rest, let me know your terms. . . ."*[36]

The terms must have suited Denoël since, on September 18, 1933, he brought out a limited edition of *L'Église*, followed by a regular edition. But let us not get ahead of ourselves.

In Paris, without making any particular effort, Céline fell back into the habits acquired some months earlier. He responded to his critics and the colleagues who had encouraged him. He pursued his correspondence with

Eugène Dabit (whom he would finally meet on April 26). He sent a letter to Albert Thibaudet, thanking him for his article in *La Dépêche de Toulouse* on January 24. To François Mauriac, who must have sent him a kindly word concerning *Voyage*, he responded with a quite astonishing note, more Célinian than Céline, in which he bears witness to his obsession with death and rejects any spiritual vision of the world, any light at the end of the night.

Sir,

> *You have come so far to shake me by the hand that I would have to be truly savage indeed not to be moved by your letter. Allow me first of all to express my somewhat bedazzled gratitude to you for such a token of goodwill and intellectual empathy. And yet, we have nothing and can never have anything in common. You belong to another species, you see other people, you hear other voices. For me, a simpleton, God is a trick to help us think more highly of ourselves and to avoid thinking of others; in short, to effect a superb desertion. You see how earthy and coarse I am! I am crushed by life. Before I die I want to broadcast that, and the rest be damned. My only ambition is for a relatively painless but perfectly* lucid *death, and everything else is yoyo-playing. . . ."*[37]

Correspondence was one thing; visits, meetings, professional luncheons and dinners were another. In early 1933 Céline can be seen increasing his acquaintance and contact with writers. He is still the man of the hour, the one his peers want to meet and get to know—like some strange animal. And Céline concedes with good grace. He is glad to make a show of himself, because, more secretively, he too is exploring new fauna. He watches, amused. There is no one better at instantaneously discerning the absurdities, weaknesses, and cowardice of any given individual. His gaze is pitiless, as is his sense of parody. Céline is the stripper of masks. It is impossible to lie or pretend with him. That is something noticed and attested to by all his acquaintances, and is borne out by thousands of examples.

On January 18, for instance, he had lunch with the Descaves, with whom he was already on familiar terms. Also present at the meal were Marguerite Destouches, the writer's mother, the painter Vlaminck, and the Abbé Mugnier, who has left us a delicious account of that get-together in his *Journal*. "Céline speaks fluidly, riotously, you can tell he's of the people, a street kid. He mimes his characters well, makes them speak with all the necessary repetitions and plenty of uhs. He didn't spare my preacher's ears: jerk off, fucker, whore, bitch, tart, cunt; the verbs: screwing, pissing off, going down, sleeping together, one after the other."[38]

The conversation turned to Germany, of which Céline painted the darkest picture, evoking the German people's anarchism and his own fear of communism. To Vlaminck, who asked if he intended to continue to write on the same subject, he answered that he would remain loyal to the *milieu* whose horrors he was describing, since otherwise he would feel like a deserter—the same word, desertion, seen already in his letter to Mauriac and which, to him, is synonymous with untruth. "The truth of this world is death. You have to choose, dying or lying," is what he had written in *Voyage*. As a writer, he could no longer lie. Or desert. He would always continue to speak essentially about death.

At the end of the meal, Mugnier asked him to inscribe a copy of his novel. He did so graciously. "To *M. le chanoine* Mugnier, our companion in infinity, with great friendship and respect."

At about the same time, he became friends with Ramon Fernandez, who had recently received the Prix Femina for *Le Pari*. The two men would remain close until the final days of the occupation.

On February 21 we find Céline dining with Daniel Halévy, who was then running the well-known "Cahiers Verts" series at Bernard Grasset. The journalist Robert de Saint-Jean, another of Daniel Halévy's guests, consigned the evening to his *Journal*. His description of Céline is somewhat unusual.

"Built like a 'journeyman,' big mitts, an enormous head like Bardamu, with a bulging forehead and messy hair, bright blue eyes, small and very thoughtful, the 'serious' eyes of a man who has run a lot of risks, taken on responsibilities, etc., a sailor's eyes (he is a Breton) or a psychiatrist's (he is a doctor). Apparent naiveté. A sporty brown suit. He knows English, he says, admires England, Shakespeare of course."[39]

Once again Céline monopolized the conversation. This time he spoke of Clichy, communists, grass roots militants who understood nothing about Marxist theory, even when it was translated into "the rich man's house is yours, take it." In his eyes, France was nothing but a country of wangling, crumbs thrown out, favors, and privileges. He didn't believe that the Russian revolution could be exported.

Present at the dinner were Robert Vallery-Radot and Georges Bernanos. The two men emphasized the existence of the supernatural, revealed in their deliria, in Céline's heroes. But there was no way the writer could be dragged into a discussion of the spiritual. He preferred to change the subject, speaking of Paul Morand, who had disappointed him, of his own play *L'Église*, which he did not hesitate to characterize as bad and unplayable, or of his work habits.

"I have to enter into delirium, to reach the Shakespearean level, because I am incapable of constructing a story using the intellectual logic of the French. . . . What I can do easily is the romance novel, the ghost story full of kings and phantoms. . . . But I find it impossible to trace a novel's plot . . . I have to feel a resonance, to work in the sinew, to have a strong contact. Then I go on. I never worry about logic."[40]

A few days later, on February 25, Céline paid a visit to Élie Faure at his home at 147 boulevard Saint-Germain. For the next two years, the two men would see a great deal of each other, sometimes for dinner at Lipp's, sometimes at the art critic's home. Above all, they would share a passionate correspondence. At bottom, nothing particularly new. But, from one letter to another, Céline sometimes unleashes his thoughts in gripping aphorisms. Faure compels his friend to surrender himself, as near as possible, to his essential inner truth.

Thus, in one of Céline's earliest letters: "You are so right when it comes to the hideousness of the human heart. One has to enter a nightmare state deliberately in order to approximate its true tone!"[41]

Later, he encapsulates his political thinking: "I am an anarchist to the core. I have always been so and will never be anything else."[42]

Months pass; years pass; 1933, 1934. The fascist threat takes shape. The intellectuals mobilize. Céline does not and will not become involved. A break with Élie Faure, who was more to the Left, is in the cards.

Dear Friend,

I am and have always been an anarchist, I have never voted, I will never vote for anything or anybody. I do not believe in men . . . The Nazis loathe me as much as the socialists and the commies too, not counting Henri de Régnier or Comoedia or Stravinski. They're all in agreement when it comes to despising me. Everything is acceptable except to doubt mankind—*then it's no laughing matter. I've proved it; but they can all go to hell too, as far as I'm concerned.*[43]

Can we already discern in Céline the early symptoms of a form of persecution mania? Doubting mankind is, to be sure, an unpardonable sin, an attitude that forces a person into total isolation. And what we will later have to reproach in Céline is not the manifestation of that universal mistrust but, on the contrary, his rediscovery of a kind of trust, of allegiance to a party or, at least, his designation of enemies such as Jews and Freemasons. As if he had suddenly forgotten his anarchism, his pessimism, in order to make common cause, to fight, and, so to speak, to hope.

For Céline, the world makes no sense, is illuminated by no hope. And yet, by the end of the '30s, in the nightmare that coalesces into war, the writer will suddenly be tortured by the need to believe, to struggle, to become involved. In the words of the philosopher Clément Rosset, he will be gripped by "that madness for meaning that is madness *par excellence*, madness for which there is no other philosophical antidote than a steadfast materialism (that of Lucretius and Epicurus, not of Marx)."[44]

But, of course, Céline manifests no involvement before Élie Faure. He has not yet reached that point. On the contrary, he is developing only his obsession with suffering: his own, that which assails him, his headaches, and that of others, that of accursed humanity. And the more man tries to escape that curse, the more he wishes to distract himself, the more he increases the hideous charms of death. There is no other philosophy than that in all of Céline's work, in that Shakespearian vision of a world full of sound and fury, signifying nothing. And the superb letters to Élie Faure from 1933 to 1935 lay out that vision and further elaborate it:

"You do not know what I want. You do not know what I do. You do not know what awful efforts I have to make every day, and especially every night, just to stay on my feet and to hold my pen—on your deathbed, and only there, will you understand me fully. I speak the language of the intimacy of things—I had to learn it, letter by letter. I have sized it all up. Nothing that I say is gratuitous. . . .

"I speak to you brutally, dear Élie, because you are on the other side, despite yourself—you do not speak our language and you will end up getting nostalgic about wars.

"Élie . . . Man is cursed. He will invent tortures a thousand times more appalling to replace them.

"From the ovum on, he is but death's plaything."[45]

Faure retorts nevertheless, speaking to him of the people, striving to mobilize him. Another wasted effort: Céline doesn't believe in the people either. The proletariat is a farce, an ephemera, an idiotic illusion. He wants nothing to do with abstractions. And to Faure, a critic and art historian whom he otherwise greatly admires, he writes these definitive words: "The escape into abstraction is cowardice itself in an artist—his desertion."[46]

This is Céline's final letter. In July 1935 Élie Faure would write to the author of *Voyage* a letter deeply imbued with benevolence, attentive generosity, and committed optimism: "A society, a form, a statue, music, cannot be based on an absolute that is nothingness, by your definition—and by mine. You are, I repeat, a nihilist in the true sense, metaphysically speaking. But humanly speaking, it is the masses, craving a reason to live, who are right and, take heed, will be vindicated, which is better than being right. . . . Furthermore, man has never built on anything other than illusion, not on reality. Your transcendent realism—and you are well aware of this, which is why you are so ferociously attached to it—culminates exclusively in death, which can be a magnificent tool for development in a powerful individual—as in your case—but can have no impact on the multitudes, whom we need."[47]

Clearly, the two men had nothing left to say to each other. They no longer understood each other.

In late February or early March, Elizabeth Craig returned from America. A discreet return not mentioned anywhere in Céline's writings. That was because Elizabeth belonged to another time, to the years of Bohemia and uncertainty, when Louis was leaving Geneva, settling into Clichy, flirting with suburban destitution and the joyful fantasies of the more or less artistic revelers who gravitated around Henri Mahé. She had left a doctor tortured by the composition of an enigmatic manuscript. She returned to a writer who moved in new circles and had become a celebrity. Elizabeth had no connection to that celebrity. She probably could not understand it any more than she understood the metamorphosis of her lover. At her side, Louis had once been able to laugh, to dazzle with fantasy even in his excesses. More than medicine, writing now compelled him to explore the abysses of his memory and the human condition. Which was far less fun.

The only known photographs of Elizabeth Craig are those taken in Beauvais, when she and Céline paid a visit to Jean Ajalbert in early 1933. They show us a young woman astonishingly thin and as if "gentrified" [*embourgeoisée*] in her little beret-style cap, well wrapped in a light-colored woolen coat. Gentrified is probably the appropriate word. Elizabeth must have realized that she could never be "gentry" with Céline. She may also have been jealous of her friend Karen Marie Jensen, whom Céline had recently seen when she appeared in a show at the Cinema de la place Blanche in March. In any case she must have been wholly indifferent to Céline's literary career, as well as to *Voyage*, which she certainly had not read. She had also grown older. One cannot remain forever so sensual, so winning, so open to men's advances . . . or to women's. She had planned and promised her return to Europe and to Louis, but as if in a last-ditch effort in which she did not really believe. They would not grow old together. She was probably already convinced of that.

It seems unlikely that Louis, for his part, took her to any of his literary dinners, for he went to extremes to isolate the various focuses of interest in his life. She was probably unaware that on January 13 Denoël had given publication rights to Czechoslovakian and Italian publishers, that on January 23 Chatto and Windus had acquired the British rights, that more than 50,000 copies had long since been sold in France, that the Polish translation rights were also being sold, that on March 4 Denoël had sold an eight-day option of the film rights of *Voyage* to Abel Gance, that Little Brown was buying the American translation rights in their turn, or that Denoël was about to take the *Berliner Tagesblatt* to court for having abandoned its serial publication of the German translation of *Voyage*. *Voyage au bout de la nuit* had been dedicated to her, but that was only in token to an already played-out affection and not the promise of a long and faithful partnership to come.

Nor have we any reason to believe that she attended the lunch offered in gratitude by Céline on March 16 to the members of the Renaudot panel, nor that she read, that very morning, the article Céline published in *Candide* at great expenditure of ink. Entitled *Qu'on s'explique* [An Explanation], the text had been presented by its author as a sort of postscript to *Voyage*.

Its origins are most curious. In response to a questionnaire issued by the *Bulletin du Livre* to nonprofessional readers in January 1933, a forester claimed that he tore all the useless passages and pages he considered inappropriate from the books in his library. A journalist from *L'Intransigeant*, Émile Zavie, came across this answer and commented with extreme virulence upon it in his own publication, writing of "dangerous demagogy" and raging about the solicitation of such "writings by illiterates and fools who think themselves educated." Céline was amused by the controversy and used it as a springboard for his own explanation.

The article in *Candide* should be read with the closest attention. In its own way, it constitutes a poetic art in miniature, the first Célinian manifesto that leads its author well beyond even the most frenzied and convulsive realism.

First of all, Céline wants to anchor that reality to the imaginary. He chooses his references amongst the great visionary painters: Goya, El Greco, Brueghel. Next, we clearly see traces of his obsession with time, the agent of decay that washes away and erases. What remains of masterpieces? Oblivion erodes, fashions fade, emotions are attenuated. Later, in a letter to Milton Hindus, Céline will compare the novelist's art to that of the sculptor, cutting his subject from within the clay, stone, and timber of words, cleaning off a sort of concealed medallion. . . . Clearly, the image of the woodsman cutting up his books with a pair of scissors and getting rid of useless words, lightening his load, escaping gravity and the stone that buries dream in reality, was one that could only obsess Céline. Like a representation of passing time. An allegory of death. A lesson for the writer.

It is uncertain that Louis, for his part, was aware of a rift growing between him and Elizabeth. He lived too wrapped up in his dreams, his fears, his memory. Only when Elizabeth left him for good would he realize the extent of his loss and the depth of his grief. But for the moment he felt her presence at his side, and that was enough. He gave her little and demanded even less, neither faithfulness nor declarations of love, those big words he had always abhorred as the most vulgar and hateful shamelessness. He thought of her as free, self-sufficient. He thought of her as strong. There is no question that he was wrong. He didn't look at her closely enough. His gaze was sometimes empty; either too pale or too luminous, as if lit and emanating from deep within, from the realm of his fluctuating nightmares. His gaze was tense, too, febrile, curious and thus unsatisfied, as though he were unable to concentrate on anything—a person or a place—for very long. Strange fatality!

A young journalist, Élisabeth Porquerol, had published a favorable article on *Voyage au bout de la nuit* in the February 1933 issue of *Le Crapouillot.* Céline responded immediately, thanking her, correcting certain details, and suggesting that they meet. Why? Out of curiosity, because she might seduce him, because she might become his mistress, an illusion, an ephemeral attraction in his life, and nothing more.

It did not happen. The young woman—who had written in her article that "Destouches, by himself, has touched off the literary revolution that we had been secretly craving"—and the writer hit it off immediately. They were soon to begin corresponding. But their first meeting, on February 16, 1933, bears strong witness yet again to Céline's haunted instability.

He arrived at her place at ten in the morning, having sent her a pneumatic message the evening before. At her door, dressed in a black oilskin, he introduced himself simply: "Destouches." An Anglo-Saxon profile, she thought. And the conversation, or rather the monologue, began, lasting until 1:30 in the afternoon, without Élisabeth even thinking about asking him to lunch. "I have never met anyone so exhausting, getting up, sitting down, pacing, gesticulating, dancing, for three and a half hours! His raincoat enveloped him in the soft sound of oilcloth: why hadn't he taken it off when he came in? I should have told him to remove it, but was afraid he would use the chance to settle in."[48]

Céline complained to her of the vulgarity of the literati and of their "commercial exhibitionism." He himself was sorry to have become the object of everyone's curiosity. "In the villages of Africa," he told her, "they stick the witch doctor in the middle of the square and then some big crier summons everybody with his tomtom and starts shouting. 'Look at his arms, feel his muscles! He can build you a hut in two hours, he can make love twenty-five times in a row!' . . . Here, publicity does the same thing, so I start feeling like the witch doctor."[49]

Céline occasionally enjoyed being the witch doctor. He gave himself over to it entirely, put on a show, in order to attract. But he would very soon pull himself together, deploring his own excesses, and wrap himself in his solitude and mistrust. Élisabeth Porquerol was able to discern that trait at their first meeting.

Céline told her of his life, of the League of Nations, his family, Courbevoie, his headaches like a freight train constantly clattering past his ear. He spoke mostly about the dance . . .

"What he finds in that exaltation that is dance, in that speech without words, with nothing but gestures, is a straight line, a pointing arrow, a rope to catch on to, *the lightning rod of death*, those are his words. He has the feeling of death, the way others talk about feeling alive. I was quite disturbed. Had we reached the core?"[50]

It is pretty clear that "dance as the lightning rod of death" was not a concept easily grasped by the carefree Elizabeth Craig. Decidedly, the Céline she had returned to was becoming less than ever her lifelong companion. Had an Élisabeth Porquerol become her rival, fine, everything would have been clear. But to have Death as a rival? She couldn't understand. Their separation was becoming inevitable. There was nothing left for Elizabeth Craig but to pack her bags.

Adieu, Elizabeth!

The relationship between Louis and Élisabeth Porquerol, the *Crapouillot* journalist, had remained strictly literary. That was not the fault of the writer, who loved to know everything and, in the course of his first meetings, to try everything with the young women who entered his life, briefly or not. To his mind there was nothing in that which might destroy his understanding with

Elizabeth Craig. As we have seen, sex was a fugitive pleasure for him, a casual cleansing. Faithfulness had no meaning. The concept of sin was foreign to him. Elizabeth Craig could give herself to all his friends, he didn't see any harm in that. On the contrary, it catered to his voyeurism. Which is to say that by his way of thinking, his liaison with a newcomer to his life, Évelyne Pollet, in no way threatened the deep and personal intimacy he had established and shared with the beautiful redheaded American dancer to whom he had dedicated *Voyage au bout de la nuit.*

Évelyne Pollet was twenty-seven, married, the mother of two little boys, and lived in Antwerp. She had recently read *Voyage* and was no doubt bored with provincial life. Can one fall in love with a man simply by reading his book? Évelyne Pollet was by her own admission shaken by the personality of the writer, whom she perceived as a solitary, powerful, fragile man of extraordinary vitality and vulnerability, too, "condemned to roam from town to town, from woman to woman." Perhaps she was also attracted by a kind of erotic aura around him, an immense disorder hinting at affairs and forbidden fruit. Évelyne Pollet appeared so calm, so proper, with her short blond hair, her delicate features, her thin nose, and her plucked eyebrows. But one must beware of still waters. She sent the author a strangely impassioned letter with the coyness of a blushing poetess. "I write, but I am not a literary woman: I detest the very word. Please, do not picture me that way!"[51] Nevertheless, she sent him her first writings by the next post.

Louis, amenable as always to new encounters, had of course responded in the meantime. From January to May 1933 they corresponded in this way, never meeting, as if to prolong the anticipation of their first interview. On the literary side, Céline prudently avoided all compliments and commitments. "I read your story straight away. I dare say nothing. I don't know. We all have a mania for judging according to our own tastes."[52] One could not be more tactful—or more plain. But apparently only those who truly wish to understand do so. And the well-heeled Évelyne must have shivered in understanding only too well at the writer's confession: "It seems that you have guessed that I love physical perfection in women to the point of delirium. That is a truth I present to you. It dominates all others. It is from our refusal to acknowledge it that we slowly die, hideous and futile. But these are the truths of another world."[53]

In short, the epistolary courtship was shaded by an intense and erotic frustration.

Louis promised early on to visit her in Antwerp. Perhaps in April, when he was considering a trip to Sweden, a plan that was soon abandoned. And again in early May. Évelyne must have promised him a ceremonious reception. Céline shied: "Certainly not, awful! Under no circumstances! Tell no one of my coming to Antwerp! Anything remotely resembling a special welcome kills all life around it. Never! One can never be anonymous enough."[54] Finally, the prospects for a journey crystallized for him in late May.

At the time, Céline was watching the rift grow between him and Elizabeth Craig, keeping up his visits to Lucien Descaves on the rue de la Santé, and enjoying his frequent encounters with Henri Barbusse, to whom Georges Altman had introduced him. He was giving no thought to *L'Église*, the publication of which was at hand and beginning to intrigue the literary world. Joseph Delteil, whose novel *Choléra*, was published in 1925 (a novel so free in tone, so disheveled, so excessive, one wonders why Delteil isn't mentioned more often as a precursor of Céline), asked him for a copy of his play. On May 15 Céline wrote to him, sending him the manuscript with somewhat harsh commentary. "Jouvet wanted to produce this flop. Between us, I don't think much of it. You can judge for yourself whether I kept it moving in the right direction. I think the whole thing needs an injection of a certain American delirium that is lacking. Just the same, it stinks of the little French mama's boy. The cautious end of the race. It's Shakespeare via Berlitz."[55]

In the same letter he writes of a trip to London. And for Céline, that trip had become more important than the vagaries of the future publication of *L'Église*, for at least three reasons. In London, he was to meet John Marks, the English translator of *Voyage*. He was to ask Joseph Garcin to guide him through the lower depths of the capital that he had only glimpsed and—more superficially than it has been believed—frequented in 1915 and 1916. And, above all, he was to take advantage of the occasion to return via Antwerp and to meet the mysterious and passionate letter-writer, Évelyne Pollet.

His trip went off without a hitch. By the end of May he was in the British capital. He hit it off with Marks, to whom he had already given copious advice in his letters, stressing the syntactical rhythm of *Voyage*, its liveliness: "It's all dance and music—always at the edge of death, don't fall into it."[56] Joseph Garcin dragged him from brothel to seedy pub, from procurer to prostitute. The idea of a novel inspired by his war years on the banks of the Thames continued to obsess him. . . . And on the morning of May 26 he finally arrived in Antwerp, where he sent a note to Évelyne Pollet, written on the stationery of the Hotel Carlton.

The young woman received him immediately. And for three days, she took him for walks along the Scheldt, where he saw the roadsteads, she brought him to the Steen Museum, they went together to the port, the cathedral, the zoo, the Plantin and the Mayer Van den Bergh museums. To say that Céline dazzled her would be an understatement. His presence knocked her off her feet. Literally.

"He came in, and it was genius entering. Much later, I shared that impression with Paraz, and he told me that many had felt it. Even exhausted, ill, drained by his books, Céline exuded a magnetism; when he was in good form, he expressed an intensity of irresistible power. His eyes fascinated, so changeable, so beautiful, sometimes penetrating, often heavily veiled, lost in the distance like those of a wild animal. I often saw him jump, and I always saw him walk as if heading out for conquest, his hair in the wind, head high, body taut, a lion's gait.

"That first time, he was tense, serious, even harsh at first; he soon became relaxed, eloquent, animated, full of joy, curiosity, and irony, but also of languor, dreams, benevolence. I have never seen him so happy.

"I emerged from a long conversation with Céline feeling wiped out, demolished, in shreds. Then I slowly pulled myself together, and found that I was enriched, even when he had been hard, closed in, barricaded, because Céline attracted people with one hand and pushed them away with another, in his fearful hatred of being possessed."[57]

Wiped out, demolished by his conversation, she says. The images are explicit: Céline's way of talking considered as the ultimate act of love. But his behavior, too, was explicit. There is no doubt that Évelyne Pollet became his mistress then and there.

In a novel entitled *Escaliers* [Stairs], put out in 1956 by a small publisher in Brussels, Évelyne Pollet told the story of her affair with the writer. The transposition is negligible. The writer becomes a painter, Jean-Jacques Charbier, she herself is named Corinne, and that's it. Entire pages seem taken straight from life. The language she puts in Charbier's mouth is word for word that of the author of *Voyage.* One might think she had taken notes after their every meeting. And in that lies the main interest of this little work.

Less than an hour after Charbier and Corinne had met in Antwerp, he was already taking her back to his hotel . . .

" 'Don't you think it's fine, making love?' she said in a caressing voice. 'Don't you think it's very fine?'

" 'Dying, that's what's fine,' " he said wearily.

"For a moment she remained paralyzed, swept by a terrible coldness; then a great lightness of spirit moved her toward him. She took him in her arms.

" 'As for me,' she whispered in his ear, 'for months afterward it will be enough to have been here with you. . . . You've given me memories to last for months.' "[58]

At the end of May, Céline returned to Paris, to the rue Lepic and Elizabeth Craig. A letter from Évelyne Pollet was already waiting for him. The habit was established. He would continue corresponding with her until 1948. He would also see her a dozen times more or so, their final meeting being in 1941. But it would seem that Céline felt less inclined to increase their meetings than his ardent friend.

He remained barely a week in Paris. Time enough to refuse an invitation to participate in the Congress of Anti-Fascist writers and to read an article by Hélène Gosset in the May 28 issue of *L'Oeuvre,* in which the journalist waxes indignant over the treatment accorded to circus animals. Her plea for the beasts, which joined the action already undertaken by Jack London in the United States, could only move the writer. He wrote to Gosset: "You have hit on the sore point of all our foul and sadistic brutality."[59]

For Céline, animals are primarily beings that do not speak and do not lie. They have grace, mystery, an intuitive knowledge of things, a sort of innocence. They recall to men the feeble echoes of a lost paradise. Céline had not shared his life with a pet since the little dog of his childhood. He would not adopt his famous cat, Bébert, until much later, under the occupation. But even so, animals remained for him, in contrast, the glaring and intolerable proof of the ignominy and twofold corruption, moral and physical, of humankind.

On June 6 he left on a new tour of Central Europe, making for Austria and Cillie. This time he must certainly have had to pay for a substitute for himself at the Clichy clinic out of his own pocket (though the first income from *Voyage* would henceforth allow him to do so easily). There was no need for a medical pretext or a mission for the League of Nations.

Céline, ever the man in a hurry, the traveler . . . Nonetheless, he had no intention of abandoning Elizabeth after his interlude with Évelyne Pollet. On the contrary, he asked her to accompany him to Vienna and Prague. He announced his arrival by letter to Erika (whom he would not see on this trip) and to Cillie. And then, at the last minute, Elizabeth would not make the trip. Which Céline explained to Cillie in another letter in early June: "I'm leaving Paris for Basel on Wednesday. I will probably be in Vienna on Friday. I'll go straight to the Graben Hotel. Elizabeth is leaving for America on Friday— probably for a very long time. Things over there are going very badly. I'll stay in Vienna 5 or 6 days and then go on to Prague."[60]

We do not know exactly what problems he was referring to. Perhaps family concerns. Elizabeth's mother had died in April. Or else health problems. In another letter to Cillie in April of '33, Louis mentions Elizabeth's frailty, though in other respects she was very easy to live with, gifted and quiet. Or else, finally, money problems. Elizabeth was no longer receiving any subsidy from America. Whatever the reason, on June 8 the lonely Elizabeth boarded a liner for the United States, alone and for good.

Had Louis actually considered, in boarding the train for Basel forty-eight hours earlier, that they were saying goodbye for the last time, that they were all played out, the split definitive? More likely was a kind of insouciance and lack of awareness on his part. Between two fits of neuralgia and the buzzing in his ears, the nervousness brought on by the *Voyage* and his own sudden fame, his need to travel, his strange erotic frenzy, both passive and indefatigable, and his horribly lucid crises of bitter pessimism, he had not paid consistent attention to Elizabeth's state of mind.

Upon his arrival in Innsbruck, where he had gone after Basel and Zurich, he wrote a two-page preface to *31, Cité d'Antin*, an album that Henri Mahé planned to publish, composed of prints of frescoes he had painted for a brothel located at that address. Mahé wanted to take advantage of his friend's new literary prestige. Céline had to be wheedled into it. Finally, he sent him a fantastical dialogue between two newlyweds hovering outside a *maison close*, the young, rather innocent young woman hesitating to plunge with her husband into the strange house of debauchery so as to consummate their marriage—with whom?—amongst the mysterious erotic figures. With this dialogue, once again we get the impression that the writer is presenting us with a final witness to his carefree years of Bohemia, dissoluteness, fantasies, parties, and amiable provocations preceding the terrible years that Céline—and the world—were soon to experience.

"The preface is done, entirely in dialogue, it'll be 5 large manuscript pages. Your suckers are going to get their 100 francs' worth. Anyway, that's a friend's price. After the next novel it'll be 1,000 francs per word. I haven't worked out the price for commas yet. But I think that for 250 you'll get something pretty decent."[61]

Unfortunately, Céline was disappointed in both his fees and his hopes. The project fell through, but at least we have the preface.

On Monday, June 12, Céline arrived in Vienna. He saw Cillie and her friend Anny Angel. He had asked the former to find him an article by Freud, "*Trauer und Melancholie.*" A few days later he was in Prague, where, thanks once more to Cillie, he met Annie Reich, Wilhelm Reich's first wife and a psychoanalyst in her own right. The writer's—and the doctor's—curiosity about these explorers of the unconscious had remained decidedly strong.

His stay in Prague also had another, more professional goal: to promote the publication of the Czech edition of *Voyage* by Borovy. The German translation had stalled since the double retraction of the *Berliner Tagesblatt* and the Piper publishing house. Still in Prague, Céline met the German-language publisher Julius Kittls, who, in December 1933, was finally to bring out *Reise ans Ende der Nacht.*

He reached Paris on June 25. He was now alone, with Elizabeth on the other side of the Atlantic. And her absence began to weigh on him. Or rather, he was only beginning to gauge its effect. And to suffer from it. In early July he wrote to Cillie: "I'm doing a little work here. I don't have much news of Elizabeth—I don't know when she's coming back. I'm a little bored."[62]

Politics could offer him no distraction. Hitler had seized power in Germany. France was sinking limply into its economic crisis. He expected nothing more from France. Italy had been fascist for more than ten years. He never paid attention to what was happening in Italy. The jeremiads and appeals for vigilance from the writers of the Left exasperated him. For the moment he confined himself to his sullen solitude, his contempt for all involvement. Let every man fend for himself in the slow decay of the social body, and that's all there is to it. His letters to Erika Irrgang, Cillie Pam, and Élisabeth Porquerol are eloquent in their obvious contradictions, repeating the ideas shared with Élie Faure. The writer pleads only for an every-man-for-himself individualism.

He advised Erika on June 27: "Since the Jews have been run out of Germany, there must be some room there for other intellectuals? Heil Hitler! Take advantage of it!"[63]

To Cillie, he had stated in April: "I am sorry to hear that your life is becoming more and more difficult in Vienna, and that lessons are growing rare. What suffering to come if you are invaded by this Hitlerism! Anyway, let's wait and see."[64] He was even concerned, for her sake, that the "Hitler madness" might end up "dominating Europe for centuries to come."

Meanwhile Évelyne Pollet wrote him constantly. She had even entrusted him with the manuscript of a novel, *La Maison carrée*, which the embarrassed Céline passed on to Denoël. The publisher rejected it, predictably. The letters Céline was sending to the young woman in early summer evince an affectionate and distant kindness. He addresses her as "Dear Madame and Friend," asks after her family and her two young sons, tries to offer her some literary advice, without much conviction. "You have a delicate and sweetly sad way of living that is poetic indeed," he tells her.[65] But she failed to grasp his meaning.

The main thing for Céline at the time was finally to begin a new book. His heart wasn't in it. In the same letter to Élisabeth Porquerol, dated June 29, he confesses that he is not starting out in literature but that he's finished with it. He hadn't been able to write a single line since *Voyage*; all the fuss had put him off. And, indeed, if he were rich enough he would never write anything again. In this we recognize the first formulation of a litany taken up again and again after the war, and in which we must gauge the part played by coyness and exaggeration.

The proof is that, in early July, he nevertheless described his plans for a book inspired by his childhood, perhaps in two volumes, with the provisional title *L'Adieu à Molitor* [Farewell to Molitor]. On August 7 he accused Denoël and Steele, the two partners, of cheating him on his accounts. His anger was perhaps a sign of renewed health. In mid-August he left on vacation (until September 7) for Dinard, at the Hôtel Michelet, between Brittany and the Cotentin, in the heart of his double family roots. Before leaving, he had again written to Robert Denoël:

"I finally received my accounts from Steele yesterday: I am still delighting in reading these infamous and elaborate forgeries.

"As far as typhoid is concerned allow me to inform you that the incubation period is longer than the vacation period. In most cases, it is upon one's return to Paris that it shows itself.

"'*Mort à crédit*' [Death on the Installment Plan], but that's what you are, dear friend. What more do you want? A story? I need time, lots of time. Anything that is not somewhat eternal doesn't last—and worse—doesn't sell. I'll need to rove many a day yet before taking pen in hand.

"Begone, greedy parasite!"[66]

Mort à crédit: this is the first explicit mention of the future novel. Henceforth Céline would put *Voyage* behind him, little by little. He was staggering toward new horizons.

And the shadows were gathering over Europe and the world.

The four Destouches brothers in 1905, from left to right and top to bottom, Georges, Fernand, Charles, and René (Collection F. Gibault. Photo J. Lauga).

Louis Destouches ca. 1896 (Collection F. Gibault).

Cavalryman Destouches, far left, 1913.

Louis Destouches in dress uniform, May 1914 (Photo J. Coutas).

Battle news of Sergeant Destouches (L'Illustré National, *December 1915*, photo E. Dézé).

Louis Destouches on sick leave in Paris, early 1915

ernment house, DUALA — Palais du Gouvernement de DUALA, Cameroun

Postcard to his parents (1917) (Document Lucette Destouches).

Louis Destouches, ca. 1918–1920, during his first stay in Rennes (Unpublished document, Sergine Le Bannier).

Edith and Louis Destouches on their wedding day in Quintin, August 10, 1919 (Collection F. Gibault).

Louis-Ferdinand Céline with E. Craig and J. Ajalbert in Beauvais, February–March 1933 (Collection Claude Buffet).

Lucette Almansor in stage costume (*Document Lucette Destouches*).

Gen Paul in his studio (Images de France, Plaisir de France, *March 1941*).

*Céline, Lucette, and Bébert at the Rigshospital in Copenhagen, winter 1947
(Document Lucette Destouches).*

Klarskovgaard, early 1950. Céline and his dog Bessy in front of "Fanehuset" (Document Lucette Destouches).

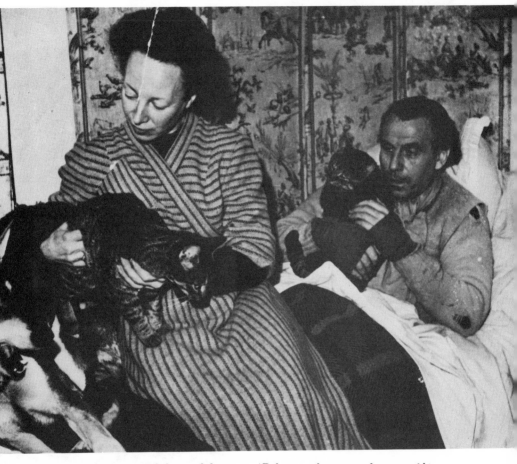

Klarskovgaard. Lucette, Céline and their pets. (Bébert can be seen in the arms of his master.) (Document Lucette Destouches).

Céline, Lucette, and their pets (Document Lucette Destouches) [photo from Vitoux].

Meudon 1959.

10

Chronicle of a "Death" Foretold

Céline Withdraws

From August 1933 to April 1936, Céline devoted himself to the composition of *Mort à crédit*. The publication of *L'Église* might have seemed a palliative to readers and journalists, but in truth it merely offered a new occasion to gossip about the author and his strange personality. The play itself barely counted; it was the novel that was important. In anticipation of which all eyes were trained on Céline. Which would confirm or cripple his reputation. Which had to be a success.

And for nearly three years, in a piecemeal way at the beginning, between frequent journeys, including a long stay in the United States, where he would attempt to reconquer Elizabeth Craig, new encounters, and later, in the final months, with a fervor and application that would leave him almost prostrate, Céline wrote in growing isolation the lengthy account inspired by his childhood, the long-awaited *Mort à crédit*.

What are the important aspects of the writer's life during this period? First of all, his progressive withdrawal from reality. The gossip surrounding *Voyage*—which, moreover, continued to sell (over 700 copies a week in January 1934)—and *L'Église*, grows dim and dissipates. Céline does nothing to revive it. The papers forget him. He forgets the papers. Unlike many intellectuals, he does not come out in public against the rising danger of fascism and Nazism in Europe. He avoids involvement. He lives through these years which, with an anxiety that overwhelms and isolates him, he already recognizes as prewar years. His long stay in the United States, and the ensuing moral and emotional crisis, reinforce his pessimism, his hostility toward the democracies, which he sees as too soft, and the Anglo-Saxon world, cloistered in its prosperity and egoism. And perhaps, too, toward the Jews whom, through what he believes to be their diplomatic stranglehold over the League of Nations, he has already identified as responsible for the evils to come and the current climate of decadence. But there is as yet no public indication of the violence growing within him, which his political writings would reveal in all its hallucinatory dimensions.

All this, we should reiterate, because he is immersed in the long and difficult composition of *Mort à crédit*. In it, he plunges into his past, settles his accounts with his childhood, sketches and caricatures his father, the petty-bourgeois patriot indignant over the Dreyfus Affair, the assiduous reader of Drumont, whose habits, verbal violence, and rancid, anti-Semitic bitterness he portrays with cruelty. How then, could he simultaneously adopt the same obsessions, the same damning intolerant condemnations, the same racist rhetoric?

A last highlight of this period, finally, is his meeting in late 1935 with the young dancer Lucette Almansor, who would soon become irrevocably attached to the writer and would fill the emotional void opened by the disappearance of Elizabeth Craig.

Thus, on September 18, 1933, in the "Loin des Foules" [Far From the Crowd] imprint, Denoël published *L'Église* in a first edition of slightly over 2,000 numbered copies. This time, the "By the same author" page clearly announced "Forthcoming / *Mort à crédit* / Novel."

Over the summer, Robert Denoël had been sorely embarrassed by Céline's harsh commentary on his own play, taken up by certain reporters. An anonymous rumor in the column "Literary Life" appearing in the new daily *Le Rempart* discussed the publication of *L'Église*, which, according to comments attributed to Céline, was "an abortive effort, without interest." Denoël reacted two days later in the same paper, emphasizing one particularly satirical act aimed at the League of Nations, of which no mention is made in *Voyage*, as we have seen.

And now, the book's publicity wrapper bore, on the back, the following blurb: "In this astonishing drama, which no theater dare produce, we see once again the savage spirit and epic inspiration of *Voyage au bout de la nuit*."

For the publisher, the time had come to get the most out of Céline's new work. In an October publicity announcement in *Les Nouvelles Littéraires*, he again made use of this amusing formula: "All who read *Voyage au bout de la nuit* will want to read *L'Église*, the extraordinary drama by L.-F. Céline that no theater dare produce."

In early October, Denoël had gone forward with a new 3,300-copy edition of *L'Église*, which was soon sold out. In a statement appearing in *La Bibliographie de la France* on October 13, the publisher spoke of the "thundering success of Louis-Ferdinand Céline's new book," which "has surpassed all our expectations." When the final figures were in, the thundering success was a modest one. Counting every edition, Denoël had sold just over 12,000 copies by the end of the war. But that is only to be expected with a play.

As a frontispiece, Céline had insisted on the documentary photograph of the death mask of the *Inconnue de la Seine* [The Mystery Woman of the Seine], with the explanation that this was a young woman who had drowned herself in 1930. A strange quirk! The illustration had no bearing on the play, but perhaps for Céline the enigmatic countenance, peaceful in death, with its hint of a smile, betrayed his deepest obsessions: the ubiquity of death and its mystery, as well as his taste for beauty, for the perfection of the feminine form, the miracle of a woman's face, like a secret and a grace that can emerge only outside the bounds of life, in the troubling silence of dream.

The press spoke little of *L'Église* and far more of its author. The few critics who made the effort to read the play and to describe it could not hide their perplexity. One such was Jean Prévost in *Notre Temps* on October 4, carefully noting from act to act every cliché of Céline's foul language. According to him, this was merely an *Ubu roi* without the varied tone or the wit. But Prévost noted above all the writer's latent anti-Semitism. "In Monsieur Céline's League of Nations, every director of arbitration services, every director of migrant affairs or discretionary services—every one of them a *forty-five-year-old Jew*—seems to me to have been born in the popular imagination at the very beginning of the Dreyfus Affair."

In *Marianne* on October 11, Ramon Fernandez, lavishing far more praise on the play, was also struck by its anti-Semitic allusions. "It contains some singular surprises, most notable of which is the concept that the League of Nations is run by Jews, a theory which M. Céline shares with the Action française and M. Hitler."

And though René Lalou, in *L'École libératrice* on October 14, may have deemed the play unperformable, lacking any real dramatic action, he allowed himself to be seduced by its text. While Pierre-Aimé Touchard, in the December 1 issue of *Esprit*, had a most unexpected reaction: having called the character of Bardamu in *Voyage* an abstraction, an "attitude," he now praised the verisimilitude of the *Église* Bardamu, finally brought to life with his faults and weaknesses.

But this time, Céline wasn't lying in wait for the critics; he neither took them to task nor considered responding to them. He was beginning to quietly withdraw from literary life. Thus, just as *L'Église* was being released, it was grudgingly that he received Lucien Descave's request to speak at Médan, where the pilgrims of naturalism gathered every year to pay homage to Zola on the anniversary of his death. But how could he refuse anything to Descaves, who had offered him such support and, soon thereafter, such friendship? He accepted. On September 14 he confided to Évelyne Pollet: "I also have to speak on Zola on October 1, and that just about does me in. To please Descaves and his friends. Lord knows I don't care for Zola at all, so I'll talk about myself, but I don't much care for that either. It's all very boring."[1]

On the other hand, the audience gathered at Médan on October 1, 1933, would be anything but bored. To be sure, the ranting author of *Voyage* was considerably toned down for the event: in a tie and three-piece suit, he spoke for ten minutes or so in an even tone (and even somewhat professorially, several witnesses would claim). It is even much to say that he spoke. He conscientiously read the half-dozen pages he had composed for the occasion. But what pages! With violent turns of phrase, provocative imagery, and a process of thought often more vigorous than clear, Céline skillfully skirted the subject of Zola. For what did he, Céline, have in common with the author of *Germinal*? Had Céline not emphasized delirium and asserted a heritage more Rabelaisian than naturalist? His Médan speech allowed him once again to express his obsession with death. Times had changed between Zola's era and his, he explained. The Great War had taken place. Man had made extraordinary progress in cruelty. He had brought himself a little nearer to the Apocalypse. He had also learned a little better how to pinpoint the death instinct, his universal sadism, and to stop explaining it (as Zola had) by the mere hunger for conquest of the ruling classes.

"In the human game, the death instinct, the silent instinct, is perhaps very aptly situated side-by-side with egoism. Its place is that of the zero in roulette. The house always wins. As does death."

Or: "The Street of Man is one way, death owns all the cafés, and we are attracted and held by the card game played for blood."

How far we have suddenly drifted from Zola and his concerns! Zola would be unable to tell the truth nowadays, Céline further claims, since the truth has become unspeakable. In a tone of almost confessional gravity, as if in defense and illustration of his own philosophy, he goes on to say: "One would need a very strange gift indeed to be able to speak of anything other than death at a time when, on earth, on water, in the air, in the present and the future, that is all there is. I know that one can always go dancing in the cemeteries and speak of love in the slaughterhouses; the comic writer can cling to his opportunities, but it's a last resort."

Céline's speech was published shortly afterward in the *Bulletin de la Société des amis d'Émile Zola*, and Émile Henriot reviewed it in *Le Temps* on December 4. For him, Céline's bizarre obsession with death had soon grown intolerable as a form of despair that could lead only to a dead end. He concluded: "One would hope, however, that he [Céline] is not as hard on his clients as he is on his readers, and that his sincerity does not extend to telling his patients, 'My friend, you are incurable!' as he endlessly does to us in his writings. For my part, I believe that Fontenelle—who saw a great deal and was no more optimistic—was more human than M. Céline. But he was more pitiable and did not seek to drive anyone to despair. Let us recall his gentle and wise saying: 'If I had a fistful of truths, I would open it for no one.' "[2]

Céline was eager to put "that foolishness at Médan" behind him, as he wrote shortly thereafter to Évelyne Pollet. If his despair led to a dead end as Émile Henriot believed, it also led paradoxically to literature, and in no way mitigated the frenzy which the author applied to writing his books. The contradiction is merely superficial. To his cherished Eugène Dabit, Céline confessed:

"You do not constantly seek to surpass yourself, as I unfortunately do, you are not crippled with pride like me.

"I guess I have been so humiliated for so long, so dreadfully and so stupidly by so many men, that I was finally struck by the disease of pride.

"Why play at modesty?

"But I am clear-sighted, that's my saving grace.

"I see myself in a crueler light than anyone else.

"First of all, my dear chap, our literature no longer exists.

"It is an archeological study.

"On Sunday, just to please Descaves, I had to go babble about Zola at Médan. I always hate those events.

"But I was consoled—absolved—by the impression that literature no longer has any meaning in life nowadays."[3]

What, at that time, retained any meaning for him? His new book, *Mort à crédit*, which he had been at such pains to get started? Elizabeth's increasingly painful absence? The medical practice based on his routine at the Clichy clinic with his enemy Grégoire Ichok, the Jewish doctor holding the position that he, Dr. Destouches, should have held? Or, again, the paralyzing obsession with death?

That obsession would lead him on October 19 to attend a dawn execution on the boulevard Arago, where the guillotine had been set up. He found the legmen shivering there, the human-interest hacks come to write their accounts of the final moments of the murderer Roger Dureux. Céline was somewhat out of place among them. Morbid curiosity, a desire for gratification in the "grotesque arms of death"? He told his neighbors before the scaffold: "The guillotine, you see, is the Prix Goncourt of crime."[4] But a paradox or a witticism does not conceal a profound malaise. It was this malaise that haunted him when he insisted on portraying in *L'Église* the death mask of the young suicide in the Seine; that to a lesser extent drove him to write a letter to the journalist Pierre Châtelein-Tailhade of the *Canard enchaîné* (in response to an article on his "Homage to Zola"), in which he evoked his childhood years, his military years, his passive, servile, farcical years: "With ideas, effort, and enthusiasm, I have fed more insatiable cretins, more pathetic paranoiacs, more complex anthropoids than are needed to drive any average monkey to suicide."[5] It was this same morbid malaise, finally, that led him on November 15, 1933, to respond, in the medical and cultural bimonthly *Balzac*, to a questionnaire on the notorious Violette Nozières affair that had enthralled and divided all of France that fall, with the surrealists taking the lead in their dogged defense of the young criminal who had poisoned her father and attempted to murder her mother. . . .

But henceforth and for many months to come, Céline's statements would become less and less frequent. Élie Faure had urged his friend to get involved, as they say. Céline could have joined him in re-enrolling in the Association des écrivains et artistes revolutionnaires (AEAR) [The Association of Revolutionary Writers and Artists], which Malraux had joined early in the year and which united intellectuals from Vaillant-Couturier to André Gide in the struggle against Nazism. The French Communist Party at that time approved of such organizations. It had changed its tune. The times demanded openness (until the next reclusion). For how could one avoid concern over the first months of Hitlerism ascendant in Germany, while that country's last democratic privileges fell away and went up in flames?

The Reichstag burned, most opportunely, on February 27, 1933, and the Nazis found the ideal culprit in Marinus Van der Lubbe. Naturally, the communists were implicated and the roundups increased. In May began the auto-da-fes of subversive, Jewish, progressive, liberal or modern books in towns all over Germany, at those vast, overorganized festivals for a youth that is always driven to fanaticism with astonishing ease. Farewell Thomas Mann, Kafka, Roth, Heine, Döblin, Schnitzler, Zweig, Max Brod. . . . Fritz Lang had caught on early and left Berlin in March to film elsewhere and just as beautifully. Mabuse had found his real name: Hitler. Soon, the unions had been decapitated, political parties outlawed, and the first racial laws imposed. Jewish stores were violently shut down. On March 20, near Dachau, the first deportation camp was opened on the site of a defunct gunpowder factory. Germany, of course, would henceforth have nothing to do with the Conference on Disarmament. On October 14 its representatives stormed out of Geneva, and on the same day made known its decision to withdraw from the League of Nations. . . . Soon, Germany would invade the Ukraine and it would be war, Céline was already predicting in a letter to Dabit. But why should he involve himself? To be useful? How could a writer be useful outside his books? Céline put no stock in these associations of writers and artists—during a period (1933–1936), moreover, when nothing allows us to suspect any sort of indulgence toward Nazi Germany on his part.

In the October 1933 issue of *Commune*, the AEAR review, Louis Aragon asks what he sees as the decisive question: "For whom do you write?" Céline's was one of the earliest answers solicited. It appears in the January 1934 issue.

"If you had asked why men, all men, from their birth to their death, drunkards or not, have the mania to create, to tell stories, I could have understood your question. It would then, as for any legitimate question, require several years to respond. But 'Writer!!!', biologically, has no meaning. It is a romantic obscenity whose explanation can only be a superficial one."

Aragon, who had already manifested certain reservations concerning *L'Église*, deemed this evasive answer to be particularly intolerable. "Why all this confusion?" he wondered in the same issue, before offering his own answer. "Because you find the contradiction between your sympathies and the fate you embrace so unbearable, when all is said and done, that you're afraid to look at it head-on; because you vaguely sense that your way of saying *all men*, emphasizing it solely so as to include the banker with the roofer, draws you disagreeably in cahoots with such vulgarians as Chadourne;[6] and because, deep down, you can't make up your mind to take the side of the exploiters against the exploited.

"And the time has come, Céline, for you to take sides."

But Céline had no desire to take sides. Aragon understood nothing. Céline's despair was beyond all that—like a form of paralysis or extreme lucidity. He withdrew from the arena, a solitary observer "in the Heavens where all is darkness."

Back in the USA

Thus, in late 1933 and early 1934, Céline withdrew into silence. He had no regrets in dropping Aragon, the review *Commune*, and the revolutionary artists. If the writer is someone who takes one step to the side, as André Breton claimed, Céline had already placed himself out of reach. He was an observer. He fretted alone over the rising dangers. But as a novelist, he primarily looked behind him, toward his childhood. In short, he found himself stuck between two nightmares.

He used the problems involved in the English translation of *Voyage* as a pretext for a brief visit to London in December. John Marks, whom he primed with advice and suggestions, and whom he urged to make haste, had also become a sort of friend, accomplice, and guide in his sordid excursions through the London brothels. Once again, he let Marks be his pilot. And back in Paris, he continued in his correspondence to offer him agreeably cynical counsel, suggesting, for instance, that he make a wealthy marriage, learn to dance, cultivate the bourgeois *salons* and the circles of the richest publishing house.

Whatever he would do with the royalties from *Voyage*, he would certainly not throw them away. That would not be in character with his prudence, thrift, and timorousness. The small investor is always comforted by stone and gold, reliable commodities, tangible and concrete. Thus, on December 7, Céline put his first savings into the purchase of an apartment at 1 rue Claude-Debussy, in Saint-Germain-en-Laye, on the top floor of a modern building not far from the Henri IV pavilion. Louis had long loved this town, with its views from the terraces and its walks through the park at the foot of the castle. He would occasionally stroll there on Sundays. He rented out his new apartment immediately; he was never to live there, and would eventually give it up to Joseph Almansor (his future father-in-law) sometime in the 1950s.

These months were hard, in terms of morale, on the writer. "It's cold. Elizabeth is still in America, probably until February. I rarely see my daughter. We really don't have anything to say to each other. Our backgrounds are too different. She's almost hostile toward me. Things remain pretty difficult."[7]

A year earlier it had been the Goncourt, with all its crazy hopes and disappointments. He was still cherishing illusions today, wanting to believe that Elizabeth would return. But was he able to delude himself so completely?

While *Voyage* was being published in Russia, in a translation by Elsa Triolet trimmed by many an excision, he watched the political and social climate further deteriorate in France. The Stavisky affair had just broken. The swindler—with his dubious political connections, his undeniable shadiness, his sumptuous life-style and extravagant politico-financial machinations—cast a dismal pall over the morality of the Third Republic leadership. The deputy mayor of Bayonne, with whom Stavisky had contrived to break the municipal bank, was implicated, and a colonial minister, Dalimier, had covered up the swindle. The oppositions of the extreme Right and the extreme Left grasped the opportunity of this windfall to call for revolutionary solutions ranging from monarchy to fascism. A radical *député* was soon arrested, as were two directors of newspapers. The Chautemps cabinet was toppled by the scandal.... Céline could barely suppress his mirth—a rather dark mirth. Several months earlier, Stavisky had loudly proclaimed his disapproval of *Voyage au bout de la nuit*, which he deemed harmful to the morality of the French; he had then proclaimed his intention of establishing a "decent" literary award.[8] The irony was powerful—the promoter of "decent" literature had turned out to be an expert in swinishness. His timely suicide in January 1934, no doubt aided by the efforts of certain well-wishers, may have allowed the swindler to be buried, but not the scandal.

On February 6 Paris was again engulfed in fire and blood. Members of the Action française, clubs in hand, and of the right wing Solidarité française, the Camelots du Roi, the Croix-de-Feu du général de la Rocque (*les froides queues du général de la Locque*—"the limp dicks of General Wet Rag," as Lucien Rebatet would call them), as well as rampaging veterans and those simply fed up with parliamentary government, marched on the Palais-Bourbon, calling for the return of Préfet Chiappe and the ouster of Daladier. Stavisky's shadow hovered over the riot. The police fired on the crowd during the night. The republican order, as they say, was tottering. The country seemed to be on the brink of civil war. The demonstrators broke through the barricades set up by the security police. In the Chamber, the *députés* were coming to blows. The first wounded policemen poured into the courtyard of the Palais-Bourbon. The *députés* fled and the demonstrators were all for throwing them into the river. Parliament was up for grabs. Most curiously, general de la Rocque did not press his advantage. And Daladier renounced his attempts to form a government.... In the meantime, however, death was no longer working on the installment plan. Its price was paid in cold cash on the pont de la Concorde. Hundreds of wounded, scores of dead among the police and rioters. It was still not enough to maintain the precarious return to calm. In the following days, the parties of the Left called in their turn for demonstrations in defense of democracy and the Republic. The great unrest was just beginning.

On February 17 Louis wrote to Erika Irrgang: "Rather tragic things are going on here at the moment. It will all end, as you know it will, in five or six years—Europe will be united in blood."[9] The calculation $1934 + 6 = 1940$ shows us just how accurate was Céline's vision.

It would have been easy enough for him to find his compensation in some sort of erotic vertigo, as he says, in this case to Cillie: "Thighs, and more thighs. That's my only pleasure. Humanity will be saved only through the love of thighs. The rest is merely hatred and boredom."[10] For if he wished that pleasure on his correspondent, he barely enjoyed it for himself anymore. In the same letter to Cillie, he adds: "Elizabeth should be back soon. She was very sick in America. The nightmare goes on in Clichy—people are nastier than lunatics."

In short, everything still boiled down to Elizabeth, that absence, that suffering which, in his grumpy modesty or his naive pride—it little matters which—he was so loath to admit.

The Nazis did not approve of his first novel, which they found too decadent, antimilitarist, and vitriolic. Harsh criticisms along the orthodox Hitlerite line were made against it in *Die Literarische Welt* [The Literary World]. At the first Congress of Soviet Writers in March 1934, Maxim Gorky violently attacked it. Thus Céline, the expert in martyrology, the misanthrope submissive to none of the totalitarianisms, managed to garner all the honors.

During this time he worked tirelessly on *Mort à crédit*, the book he had taken so long to define, to restrict in its subject matter, before launching himself into its endless composition. He finally managed to establish a silence, to forget the sounds of marching boots, of the vaguely fascistic and undeniably French riots of embittered veterans, of the Soviet people's commissars and the robotic parades of Hitler youth; he strove to clear his mind of Elizabeth Craig and to recapture his childhood.

At the start, at the time of *Voyage*'s publication, he had perhaps considered another subject, medieval or romantic fairy tales written in traditional language to confound his detractors and prove to them that he was as capable as the next man of writing "in good French."[11] Let us recall a statement made one night to Daniel Halévy: "What I'm good at is chivalry, a ghost story with kings and specters." But Robert Denoël must have dissuaded him from taking that path (as shown by the story of "Krogold" in *Mort à crédit*, perhaps a relic of that earliest project). For what he did with difficulty, in the end, was what he did well: torturing his memory and his imagination, attaining emotion on the back of delirium, drawing and quartering the French language according to the rhythmic, musical, panting demands of the dramatic exigencies of his vision. On July 14, 1934, he would write to Eugène Dabit: "By the way, I'm going to bring out a first book within a year, it's decided. CHILDHOOD—THE WAR—LONDON. Otherwise it would take me ten years. Let the chips fall where they may."[12] In other words, his subject matter was still not firmed up at that point, and he was thinking of putting into a single (first) volume that which would provide material for *Mort à crédit*, *Casse-Pipe* and *Guignol's band*.

One thing is certain: during the winter and spring of 1934, he gropingly composed the first pages of *Mort à crédit*. His father had been dead for two years. It was like a liberation of his memory, of the censorship that a novelist more or less imposes on himself or herself with regard to his or her parents. It is also possible that his mother had provided him with his childhood letters, or with a thousand little souvenirs of the past which Fernand Destouches had sentimentally guarded and which might act as catalysts to the slow and dangerous resurrection of his memories.

Céline would soon be forty. He had no time to lose. When the papers still made any effort to contact him, he either gave no response or answered with witticisms. In June, *Le Figaro* launched an inquiry: "Should literary awards be abolished?" Céline got out of it with a pirouette. No, prizes should be increased, like *bistros*, since they worked on behalf of the mind. And he mockingly concluded: "If, well placed as you are, you should hear of any little flower-shows being held in the vicinity of Paris, please be kind enough to let me know. You know my repertoire."[13]

Elizabeth still had not returned. He suddenly decided to go get her. He was ready for anything, to humble himself, to storm, to beg her to return to their life together. In earlier times his travels had been undertaken on the pretext of missions for the League of Nations. With the publication of *Voyage* (and soon, of other books), new opportunities were available: visits to his translators or his foreign publishers, for example. All he need do was to have his travel and accommodation expenses underwritten by his dear publisher, Robert Denoël, who held him in the highest, not to mention the most confounding affection, and who found it difficult to refuse him anything.

On June 12, 1934, Louis Destouches embarked on the *Champlain*. The official explanation was to help launch the American edition of *Voyage*, translated by John Marks, and to prospect Hollywood for opportunities to adapt the book for the cinema. Conveniently, Elizabeth happened to live in Los Angeles. On June 20 the *Champlain* of the Compagnie Générale Transatlantique rounded the Statue of Liberty and docked in New York.

Louis checked in at the Vanderbilt Hotel, paid a visit to his American publisher, Little Brown, and met a few journalists, without showing any particular enthusiasm. He wrote to Denoël:

"I've done the necessary here, seen the journalists, agreed to some pretty ridiculous interviews, including, alas, with photographers.

"Little Brown hopes to hit 20,000 soon.

"Elizabeth has sent me some news about the California Cinema—where they are still hesitating over the adaptation. I have decided to go there in person and to leave New York. . . .

"I'm spending a fortune on eats. I'll need to draw another 4,000 francs on the *Voyage* account. You can give it to me when I'm back. I have some hope for the Cinema—but not too much."[14]

Louis, of course, had only one priority: to take the train to Los Angeles and find Elizabeth. He therefore wasted as little time as possible in New York. He was in California by late June. All we know about this trip is that Elizabeth refused to return to their life together. Céline made but the most passing references to their meetings. In his letters of that period, he described in elliptical terms the nasty violence of their encounters and the hellish times he spent, but without providing any details.

Thus, to Robert Denoël: "Between us, I have had an awful time which can never be described, not even by me, who yet . . . It seems I have only one master, but it has crushed me, and that's my destiny."[15]

Or to Henri Mahé: "Things have come to pass here just as I predicted. . . . An appalling drama, so low, so vile, so degrading that I myself, and yet. . . . I'll be back in Le Havre around August 15. Now I've seen it all."[16]

Or to Cillie: "This trip has been atrocious. I found Elizabeth in a semidemented state that is neither describable nor explainable. An abominable nightmare, I assure you."[17]

He would become more explicit with the passing of the years. He would forge for Elizabeth a tragic and miserable destiny, one to his own scale. From Denmark, on September 10, 1947, he would write to Milton Hindus: "On the off-chance (but the USA is an ocean) you might perhaps run across someone who knows what became of Elisabeth CRAIG—her last address— known to me—1935—(2325 South Ligland Avenue, Los Angeles)—She must be forty-four now if she's still alive! She was living in a miasma of alcohol, tobacco, the police, and the lowlife among gangsters with one Ben Tankle—no doubt well known to the Secret Service—Carolina [sic] Island, etc. Anyway, all this on the off-chance—she's a ghost—but a ghost to whom I owe a great deal— What genius in that woman! I wouldn't have amounted to anything without her—What wit! what finesse . . . What painful and mischievous pantheism. What poetry . . . What mystery . . . She understood everything before you said a word. Rare is the woman who is not essentially a cow or a servant—she's a sorceress and a fairy."[18]

To Lucette, too, he would describe the Elizabeth he had seen in California as already mired in the lowlife, a derelict, an addict, her mind wandering, forever lost to the shadows.

We have any number of reasons to doubt the veracity of such accounts, which harmonize with Céline's need to make reality as nightmarish as his own states of mind. On the one hand he idealized Elizabeth more than ever. To that same Milton Hindus, he had already said a few days later: "She was like a female Molière, with all his wit."[19] On the other, he blackened her fate out of all proportion. "Elizabeth has given herself to gangsters," he wrote to Henri Mahé, who was not about to be fooled and responded: "There wasn't a damn thing in the way of gangsters! Like a goose, the girl just went ahead and married the Jewish judge of her paternal heritage and is playing the pretty milkmaid, like in the good old days of Trianon, in the ranch house of her youth. It's lousy! Unspeakable . . . But none of your tall tales, please."[20]

In truth, Ben Tankle was no judge, but worked in real estate. In sharing his life, Elizabeth undoubtedly wanted to put her past behind her and reconnect with the middle-class, provincial life-style. For Céline, that was indeed unbearable, horrible. And Elizabeth put her past behind her so successfully that she vanished from Céline's life (and that of his students) without a trace.[21]

In Los Angeles, Céline hooked up with Jacques Deval, a best-selling author, a casual and talented humorist who had enchanted thousands upon thousands of theatergoers with the pranks of *Tovarich* in 1930. Céline, whose passion for the theater we know, had undoubtedly gone to enjoy the production himself. They met and struck up a friendship. Deval, who was his exact contemporary (having been born in 1894), introduced him to film circles. It was perhaps through his influence that a six-month option was taken out on the film rights of *Voyage* by Lester Yard, the publisher of *Variety* in Los Angeles. Of Yard, Céline wrote: "Of all the agents, he struck me as the most able, the most roguish. The times may not be propitious for this sort of work, but we can always hope that today's puritanical severity will be forgotten six months from now."[22] Neither his project, nor that of Gance, nor that of hundreds of others would be followed up by production. As if some strange curse haunted Céline and his cinematic adaptations. Perhaps it's for the best that *Voyage* never had the chance to be disfigured on the screen.

With his friend Deval, the opulent exile in the extravagant life of Hollywood, surrounded by the last nabobs and the young first ladies, voracious starlets who would give anything (and gave everything) to be blinded by the sunlights of the great studios whose gates slid open like those of paradise, around pools that were too blue under palm trees that were too green, like celluloid dreams, Céline could have led the most disordered of lives. But he didn't really have the temperament for it. Later, he would tell Milton Hindus: "I was with him (Jacques Deval) in Hollywood—when I was running love-struck after Elizabeth Craig— We lived together for several months, him, me, and HIS women—He lives the life of a nabob à la Alexandre Dumas—He's a good soul and one of the subtlest minds I know. . . . He's the French spirit incarnate—almost hallucinating, he is frightening, monstrous in his witty cruelty."[23]

Actually, he spent very little time in Hollywood, which was still buzzing, that summer of 1934, about the triumph of Claudette Colbert and Clark Gable in Frank Capra's *It Happened One Night*, where Victor McLaglen was shooting *The Lost Patrol* under John Ford's direction, while Jeanette MacDonald played the *Merry Widow* under the carefree and amorous gaze of Maurice Chevalier and the timelessly witty camera of Ernst Lubitsch. For once, Céline had no heart for operetta, comedy, or hectic adventure. He bore no likeness to Douglas Fairbanks. The sumptuous kitsch deployed by Cecil B. De Mille for his *Cleopatra* left him as cold as the swinging banter and wild choreographic embroidery of the blonde, sparkling Ginger Rogers and the marvelous Fred Astaire of Mark Sandrich's *The Gay Divorcee*. Far from being a gay divorcee, he found himself in the role of the inconsolable widower.

He left California in early July. He was in Chicago on the 15th, at the new Lawrence Hotel. In that city of gangsters (as he believed), where the heat was as crushing as his depression, he met up with Karen Marie Jensen, who was dancing at the French Casino. All he wanted was to replace one woman with another, as if one more drink could rid him of his persistent hangover; above all, he wanted to talk about Elizabeth, their mutual friend, she whom Karen—long-legged and temperamental—had certainly helped to alienate from Louis.

"I'm here with Karen and her revue. She happens to live in one of the seediest neighborhoods of Chicago. No more sentiment after midnight. It's on Wilson Avenue. Two rigadoons a week. The cops in shirtsleeves."[24]

Louis had dedicated *L'Église* to Karen. In Chicago, on the spur of the moment, he asked her to marry him. The city must have inclined him toward expeditious solutions—or else toward marriage as holdup. Naturally, she refused. Karen was a free woman, rich, peripatetic, casual, and clear-sighted. She sincerely loved Louis but she knew him too well. And further, she could hardly have liked the idea of becoming his wife by default, like a consolation prize. If Elizabeth Craig was his lost Goncourt, she was not going to play the Renaudot. Instead, she gave him the address of a dancer, Irene McBride, who was making a hit in a musical comedy on Broadway.

In Chicago, Céline was also concerned about the sales of *Voyage* in the United States. According to his American publisher, the book was selling rather poorly. And yet Louis saw it prominently displayed in every bookstore in town.

He continued to work assiduously on his new book in Chicago so as to avoid thinking about Elizabeth, who had left him, and Karen, who stubbornly refused to entertain him.

In Chicago, Louis wrote letter upon letter to Denoël:

Understood for the first volume of Mort à crédit, *in about eight months to a year.*

And I can tell you it's first-rate stuff. But I'm waiting for you-know-which letter from you.

12% from 1 to 20,000.

15% from 20 to 40,000.

18% above 40,000.

All translations, adaptations to me alone.

The letter to Le Havre, please.

Otherwise, you can forget all about Mort à crédit.

See you, lazybones."

L.-F. Céline[25]

Louis arrived in New York in early August. Irene McBride sent him packing. Apparently he had not been the perfect gentleman. In any case there was nothing left for him to do in the States. He took the first available ship, the *Liberté*, a small, economy-class vessel.

On board, he met a young woman who was beautiful, intelligent, and an artist: Louise Nevelson. Out of habit, he asked her to marry him. Out of habit, she refused. They did not sleep together (at least, according to her in her memoir *Dawns and Dusks*, published in New York in 1976). He confided in her. She listened. Louise Nevelson was a quiet woman. She was on her way to celebrity as a sculptor. Louis shocked her by his bitterness, his egoism and, contrarily, by his deep compassion for humanity. Above all, he fascinated her. And she allowed herself to be fascinated, for the duration of an ocean crossing.

Disembarking at Cherbourg, Louis took the long way home. He reached Carteret on August 15, staying just long enough to send a note to Louise, informing her that he would be home on the rue Lepic on the 26th or 27th. Then a stopover in Saint-Malo, one of the towns dear to his heart. Another message (In English) to Louise, in which he waxed ironic on his own behavior on the *Liberté.*

Dear Miss Nevelson,

By now you must have been married over and over again. What passion will be left for me?

I will be in Paris Saturday evening. Have lunch with me anyday you say, but write one day before.[26]

On the 28th, as arranged, he finally reached Paris. He no longer had anything to hope from America—that is, from Elizabeth.

Travels and Encounters

What awaited Céline in Paris? His book, ever his book. The clinic, ever the clinic. The endless jobs for the pharmaceutical laboratories. The garret on the rue Lepic. And, finally, the melancholy moods brought on by his reflections.

The mad, vibrant Raoul Marquis, alias Henri de Graffigny, ex-balloonist and chief editor of the short-lived *Eurêka*, had died in July. Céline probably learned of his death only upon his return. And suddenly he was overcome with memories of years gone by—1917, 1918—during the final atrocities of the Great War, when he was still carefree, running the streets of Paris for the journal, frequenting writers, eccentrics and inventors who behaved like gentle maniacs. His father's death had allowed him to begin *Mort à crédit.* Perhaps Marquis' death allowed him to complete it. For it was after the death of his whimsical old friend that he decided to add to his book, like an endless coda, the episodes relating to the legendary and immortal Courtial des Pereires, the double, and barely concealed reflection of Raoul Marquis. He suddenly passed over the war, the logical, chronological sequel to the adventures of Ferdinand Bardamu (his own), to seamlessly link his childhood life in the Passage Choiseul to his job as boy-Friday to the quixotic, hearty, and crackbrained genius of the journal *Le Génitron.*

Tropic of Cancer had just come out in Paris in its original English edition by Obelisk Press. Its author, the young Henry Miller, had hastened to messenger Céline a copy. Céline found the book on his return from the United States. Miller's admiration for the author of *Voyage* is well known. He had even settled for a while in Clichy, not far from the clinic on the rue Fanny. Céline answered him in a cautious letter, before even considering reading the work: "I take the liberty of a minor suggestion on a topic I am fairly familiar with. *Cultivate your discretion. Ever more discretion!* Learn how to be wrong—the world is full of people who are right—that's why it is so *revolting.*"[27] Clearly, Céline is speaking here for himself, expressing his need to be ever more aloof, far from the loudmouths and pedagogues. This misanthropy could only have been reinforced by his time spent in America trying to reconquer Elizabeth Craig. He had lost everything and could not get over it. Was it also a way of hinting to Miller that he had no intention of developing a dialogue with him? The author of *Tropic* didn't push it. He took Céline's answer as final. They were never to meet (and while Miller would continue to praise the great French writer, the latter, through his interviews and private conversations, would never hesitate to judge harshly the man he considered to be his very pale imitator).

America, which had so bedazzled Céline on his first journey, was now the repository of all evil. America had become that mediocre, spiritless, soulless country that had stolen Elizabeth from him. His letters to Karen after his return are revealing in that respect. In them he does not speak of Elizabeth, but Elizabeth is certainly there in his own suffering and lovelorn spite. How could he forgive someone who had chosen matrimonial bliss and the good life in California over a precarious and radiant existence in Paris at his side? How could he forgive a country whose materialistic mirages had dissuaded Elizabeth from returning to life on the rue Lepic?

"I know of nothing so searing and so dismal as America, that country wholly devoid of serious life from the moment one stops having *fun* and starts to *think*—An outrageous spiritual impotence. A department-store lyricism—elevator enthusiasms. For them, the soul is a shining slide trombone. The more light cast on it, the more they fall in love—a total inversion, perversion, depraving of all that is mystical. A nation of drunken mechanics, loud-mouthed and soon to be Jewish, every last one of them."[28]

To ease his pain, Céline could only increase his travels and encounters. In September he had written to Évelyne Pollet: "I'm going to make every effort to spend a few days in Antwerp in early December. But you know, I too have to come to grips with my little dramas."[29] In late November he did indeed make a two-to-three-day stopover in Brussels and Antwerp. He saw Évelyne once more. But more importantly, he got his second look at the paintings of Brueghel and Hieronymus Bosch in the museums.

On February 10, 1935, he left for a fortnight in Austria, first to Kitzbühel, a ski resort near Innsbruck, and then to Vienna. He had told Cillie: "I have to work on my book on the road. Unfortunately, I also need some air and a rest. I guess I need everything!"[30]

Louis had some vague hope that the Deutsches Volkstheater of Vienna would produce L'Église. He was in touch at the time with a certain Heinrich Schittzler. The project was abandoned. But Cillie, who accompanied him on his journey from Innsbruck to Vienna, at least allowed him a little distraction.

That is exactly what Louis was hoping for: a little distraction, a little comforting, from his old mistresses. And, without pushing his luck, for some mildly perverse and consoling tenderness to interrupt his solitude for a while, to tear him away from his work and perhaps from his despair.

"Even you, Cillie, aren't carefree anymore—or anyway you're not as joyous as you were. Leave children out of it. Humanity doesn't deserve more children—nor do you. I'm still working just as badly. That's my only reason left to live—paper, placebos. Everything else, life itself, gives nothing but pain and sorrow. Except for people who ski. I'd like to be able to build up enough courage to kill myself one day without hesitation."[31]

In late March Céline returned to Antwerp for two days. Évelyne Pollet found him more bitter and laconic than ever. He worked ceaselessly on *Mort à crédit*. He read her a few extracts. And he left just as quickly, chasing after his character, his writing, the dramas he was reliving and reinventing in the urgency of memories from the past and literature of the present.

To Karen Marie Jensen: "*Voyage* is still selling. My other one is giving me a lot of trouble. I'd like it to be more substantial, less declamatory, more musical. I'm trying. I think I've gotten off to a good start, but I have to work nonstop. All this work is making me old before my time. When I'm dead there'll be some money, a fine income for you and my daughter, if only I can live and go on working another ten years. Then it'll be all over and I'll be quite happy to die, Karen, I assure you, but I shouldn't like to die alone. I hope that on that day you won't be in Australia or Shanghai dancing the polka. I'd like to dance the polka too, Karen, don't get me wrong—if only one could die dancing the polka."[32]

He was then acquiring new friends, a new community in Montmartre, close friends who would remain right up to the final days of the occupation.

Among those was Robert Le Vigan, a brilliant actor, unstable and crazed, who posed his characters on the brink of madness, on tragedy's high-wire stretched to the breaking point. He was a paranoid drug addict, and probably a homosexual, though he played seducers. As Pol Vandromme prettily phrased it: "Few film actors bore in their gaze the gleam that warned that they held reason to be of no importance, superficial in men and society."[33]

His thin, sharp profile, his long, chiseled face like a mystical monk by El Greco, was reminiscent of Antonin Artaud. He possessed the sense of the outrageous and the secret. In his small character roles, he was able to embody scoundrels, cowards, the possessed. Le Vigan was a pseudonym. Born on January 7, 1900, his real name was Robert Coquillaud. "I was born in Barbès, Paris 18e, on the rue de la Charbonnière, the street of whorehouses! Like everyone else, a stone's throw from the bidets. And from the rutting."[34]

Toward the end of his life, in a letter to an old friend he described the circumstances of his meeting Céline: "He [Céline] lived in a studio on the rue Lepic, across from the rue Girardon and above a shopfront where an old fogy named Hébert dealt in antiques. It was there that I met C. for the first time. Hébert was a genius at faking drawings and paintings; he had an artistic knack for making the newest piece of paper look a hundred years old; and Céline, like me, enjoyed watching him work and listening to him jabber about his art! . . . laughing out loud, but totally discreet . . . Hébert was an authentic character out of a Montmartre that was already defunct in 1900."[35]

The son of a veterinarian, Le Vigan had been a Greek teacher one year, then he had driven a cab at night before making a brilliant career in the theater, in Gaston Baty's company and later with Louis Jouvet. His screen career began with the talkies. When Céline met him, he had already played the unforgettable cloth merchant/moneylender L'heureux in Jean Renoir's *Madame Bovary*, after a small role in Duvivier's *Maria Chapdeleine*. Renoir was his favorite director. In 1935, when Céline became his friend, Le Vigan brought a disturbing passion to his role as Christ in director Duvivier's *Golgotha*, sharing the screen with Harry Baur (Herod) and Jean Gabin (Pontius Pilate). Duvivier also directed Le Vigan in *La Bandera*, in which he brought an equally sickly conviction to the role of an informer. He would later appear as a has-been actor in Renoir's *Les Bas-Fonds* in 1937 and as a fever-ridden former colonial soldier turned assassin in Jacques Becker's marvelous *Goupi-Mains rouges* in 1943, to name but a few of the most significant roles in his career.

Céline was instantly captivated by Le Vigan, who bore within him the mirages, the deceptive brilliance of the theater and the world of artificial enchantment of which the writer never tired. He also carried within him that vagrant spirit, panic-stricken vividness of dreams; the imagination that rejected prosaic and mediocre existence. Céline would later make of Le Vigan a character in his novels who was certainly very different from the reality. We will see them together in the great postwar debacle, from Baden-Baden to Berlin, from Neuruppin to Sigmaringen. Le Vigan—La Vigue—will become a Célinian hero, a Célinian invention in his own right in *D'un château l'autre, Nord,* and *Rigodon.* The actor, crippled by persecution and denunciation complexes, who would bellow his anti-Semitic hatred on the airwaves of Radio Paris during the occupation, was immediately on friendly terms with the writer, ears open to Céline's powerful voice, and re-echoed Céline's convulsive vision of the world, his sense of the grotesque.

Having mentioned Le Vigan, we must immediately turn to Gen Paul (real name: Eugène Paul), who was about the same age as Céline and like him born in modest circumstances. He was badly wounded in the knee during the war, infection and gangrene followed, and his right leg was amputated. He found himself after the war in the Bohemia of Montmartre, a mocking, cynical, self-taught painter, a friend of Utrillo and others, a hopeless alcoholic (with, in 1936, cirrhosis, delirium tremens, and forced hospitalization), an indefatigable seducer, a first-class reprobate despite his infirmities, an incomparable actor, and the possessor of a rich and phenomenally filthy mouth. Gen Paul liked to shock the bourgeoisie (in itself a very bourgeois obsession). He had made a specialty of it, a trademark. Lucette Almansor remembers seeing him take the hand of a *grande dame* in a nightclub, open her fingers, and urinate on them, on her evening gown, in front of the whole crowd, for fun and as a provocation. When the police passed through Montmartre he insulted them, would have pissed on them too. An obsession. The cops laughed. They didn't dare say a word. Everyone knew Gen Paul on the Butte. A veteran, a war cripple, he was untouchable.[36] His talent did the rest. And, to top it off, he was successful. He entertained Céline. He and the writer were soon inseparable. They told each other everything. They entertained themselves by shocking each other, and Lord knows how difficult a task that was! Sometimes they went on sordid outings, and they disparaged one another. In short, they were the greatest of friends. All that was to disintegrate at the end of the Second World War.

Gen Paul's studio, a wonderful theater with its cast of *cocottes*, pimps, models, intrepid schoolgirls, art dealers, close friends, high-class whores, flamenco dancers, painters, engravers, actors, singers, and middle-class citizens, presented an astonishing human comedy for Céline's delectation. His curiosity and voyeurism were well served by Gen Paul. His studio, at the very top of the avenue Junot, across from the entrance to the Moulin de la Galette, was owned by the city of Paris. "At night," Lucette Almansor recalls, "Gen Paul would climb up to the roof and make holes with a chisel. He would then claim that the roof leaked and that way he never paid rent. He also dedicated Céline's books for people who came up to see him. He was very good at forging his signature."

Sunday morning, people gathered at Gen Paul's. He sometimes got out his cornet. Other musicians would join the fanfare, which soon set out from *bistro* to *bistro,* with more and more pit stops and the music growing more and more short-winded.

A third close friend of Céline's, another inhabitant of Montmartre, and regular in Gen Paul's studio, with its jumbled piles of empty boxes, old encrusted palettes, dishcloths, rotting frames, furniture buried under rags, bottles of oil and jars of brushes, was the writer Marcel Aymé. He was living at 9 *ter* rue Paul-Féval at the time. Younger than Céline (he was born in 1902), he had just published *La Jument verte* in 1933. His success allowed him to turn to writing professionally. It was impossible to tell what the inscrutable Aymé was thinking. He never said a word. His eyes were often concealed behind a pair of dark glasses—eyes which Céline claimed resembled those of a turtle, with their heavy lids. His phlegmatic demeanor only hinted at his fidelity and acid humor. He professed a great admiration and indestructible friendship for Louis. He would never abandon him.

Lucette Almansor soon got to know and appreciate Aymé. "I liked him. He was full of fun. He would come on Sunday mornings. Louis would say very unpleasant things to him. He needed to. He had to have someone to bawl out. Marcel kept silent. He listened to Louis talk. Céline would light into him, like he did with the Jews, like Marcel was his whipping boy. He'd say to him: 'You're a filthy pig' and the like. Overhearing him, I'd ask, 'Why did you call him all those names?' He'd answer, 'Because he doesn't say a word and he knows very well that he has skeletons in his closet!' It was childish. Marcel would stay away for a couple of weeks. Louis would phone him and say, 'Why don't you come over?' Marcel Aymé understood Louis, that's why he put up with it all. He loved him. Céline often abused people. He wasn't going after him specifically. It didn't matter who it was. He was letting off steam and Marcel understood that sort of thing very well."

Among the Montmartre group of which Céline gradually became a part from 1934 to 1936, there are many other names that could be cited: the illustrator and engraver Jean-Gabriel Daragnès, who also lived on the avenue Junot; the cartoonist Ralph Soupault, whose career would take him from *L'Humanité* to the most extreme of the collaborationist newspapers *Je suis partout* and *L'Émancipation nationale*; the playwright René Fauchois; the cabaret singer Max Revol; the painter Dignimont; the film actor and stuntman Pierre Labric, "mayor" of the free Montmartre Commune from 1929 to 1972; as well as such occasional visitors as Vlaminck, Dunoyer de Segonzac, Derain, Dufy, Marie Bell, Florence Gould, Damia, and many others.

On April 4, 1935, Céline attended a recital at the Salle Chopin of a young pianist, Lucienne Delforge, who that night played selections from Mozart, Fauré, Debussy, Liszt, and Chopin. On the romantic level, the writer was available at the moment, still undergoing the long and cruel convalescence following Elizabeth's departure. The young virtuosa, with her melancholy face, thin lips, short blond hair framing eyes of an enigmatic brilliance that were half-shut most of the time, enchanted Louis at first sight. He was a music lover to a certain point, but he preferred vulgar melodies to more sophisticated and serious harmonies, and musical comedy to the opera. But the combination of that romantic music and a woman's countenance was sufficient that night to sweep him off his feet. On May 3 he went to hear her again, this time at the Salle Gaveau. He approached her at the intermission. He told her that he found her playing "moving, profound, simultaneously feminine, gentle, and powerful," and he explained how the manner in which she had played Chopin's so-called "revolutionary" étude the other night had revealed a certain sense of cruelty to him and had helped him to finish the chapter of his work in progress, *Mort à crédit*, in which "the son kills the father."[37] When the concert was over, he invited her for a drink. She soon became his lover.

Their affair proper ended in May 1936, at the time of the publication of *Mort à crédit*. It was not a very possessive affair, since Lucienne Delforge was married and taken up with the many demands of her career and touring. But, as always, sex was soon superseded by friendship and tenderness, as well as fidelity. In a sense Lucienne provided the musical accompaniment to the feverish composition of the last section of the novel. She herself lived in difficult circumstances, what with the ambitions, exhaustions, anxieties, and exhilarations of her work. It was her defense, her safeguard against the overweening presence of the writer and his anxieties. But she was able to perceive in him that searing and tireless search, endlessly confounded and endlessly renewed, for beauty and perfection.

Serving when necessary as her press agent and promoter, Louis wrote of her shortly after their first encounter: "She expresses herself with a natural lyricism. One can count on the fingers of one hand the number of soloists who do not murder Music. Most of them don't know what they're doing: learned and forced, music is not their language . . . they speak it as if it were Latin."[38] Soon afterward he made her gifts of books and a painting by Marie Laurencin.

On May 25 and 26 he took her to London. They returned via Brussels. "I saw the most astonishing things in the London 'underworld.' I made a lot of progress on my new novel. Nothing like a little adventurous travel to rekindle the spark in one's writing . . . The 'wild partys' [*sic*] never stop. They're much more disgusting than in Paris. In Brussels I saw Moussia, who used to dance with Tania. She's the lead dancer at the Brussels Opera."[39]

For Lucienne Delforge and Louis, traveling was the only way for them to spend any time together. In Paris their meetings were necessarily furtive.

On July 4 they left Antwerp for a new journey to Denmark, Germany, and Austria. They stopped in Esbjaerg on the 5th and stayed at the Hôtel d'Angleterre in Copenhagen on the 6th. Karen Marie Jensen, who was dancing at the Tivoli Kursaal, was expecting them. She introduced them to her friends. Louis and Lucienne strolled about the city and the port. He wrote, she practiced on the piano at the hotel. They took their meals at Lucullus or the Bellevue. They visited the castle of Elsinore and the museums. They took a day trip to Malmö, Sweden, on July 13. They eventually left Copenhagen on July 16, taking the ferry to Warnemünde and arriving that night by train in Berlin. They were in Munich the next day. Changing in Salzburg that night, they finally reached the Hotel Grüner Baum in Badgastein, where Emil von Sauer, a professor at the Vienna Conservatory, was waiting to rehearse Lucienne.

Ten days later the couple went to Salzburg and the Park Hotel. Louis had kept Cillie informed of their journey, never hiding anything from her. Secrets were not his strong point. He liked his lovers and ex-lovers to be friends. "I have a lot of work to do during my vacation," he had told her in June, "to finish my book by October and publish in December. I am bringing my friend along to speak French on the road. I lose the music of my phrasing when I am abroad by myself."[40] In the same letter he frets over the health of their mutual friends Annie Angel and Annie Reich, discouraging their dependence on psychoanalysis, "the stupid, sterile subconscious," so far from the concreteness of general medicine, a living science. "A re-acquaintance with meat," that's what they needed.

Cillie joined up with them in Salzburg, accompanying them on strolls through the city, to concerts and museums. That year, Bruno Walter was conducting *Tristan and Isolde* at the Festival. One wonders whether Wagner's long and sublime lyric poem was able to impart its grace to Louis, the lover of operetta, who attended with Lucienne.

On August 2 he abruptly returned to Paris. Alone. Lucienne would not join him for another eight days. What had happened? Had Céline suddenly taken fright at a relationship that threatened not only to curtail his liberty but also to hinder the blossoming of the young pianist? Had they fallen out? Was the life they had been leading too happy, too frivolous, too antithetical to his habits, his penchant for nightmare, and the conditions necessary for good writing? In a long and beautiful letter written to her on August 26, Louis attempted to explain himself:

My little darling,

How happy I am that you have not rejected me once and for all. How I love you! How I need you! You know that I never lie, that I never connive. That I do not sentimentalize. If I left, you see, it was because I was in your way. I am not normal. You need certain things that I cannot give you. The constancy of certain things overwhelms me. In my own way, I am very faithful, I assure you, atrociously faithful, faithful like a Breton, to the death. But I am crushed by life's regularity, life's reality. You know that it's not that I want to play the artist, flighty, hysterical, the special-case-who-needs-to-express-his-whims. God only knows how that kind makes me sick! But you also know, Lucienne, that I cannot, absolutely cannot, be THERE. To be a worthy lover one must be THERE. I am far closer to people after I leave them.[41]

More than anything, what came between them was the writing of *Mort à crédit*. The book could be the writer's only companion. More than ever he needed to confront his memory, his childhood, the bad dream that he was transforming and transposing into a frenetic nightmare. There were words, sentences, and music that he had to find, to mold against the invading silence of mediocrity, in long, endless somersaults. There was the artist's incredible urgency, the need for perfection growing within him, tormenting him, negating everything else: Lucienne Delforge, love, affection, the sweet, fleeting moments of happiness—everything.

"I do love you, Lucienne, you'll never know how much. Times are hard at the moment. I can't claim that it has much effect on me. What does affect me is having to deal with things that are not and cannot be transposed except after many, many years. I should not like to die without having transposed all that I have experienced of people and things. Practically all my hopes are wrapped up in that."[42]

The Final Pages

In early September 1935 Louis temporarily left his apartment on the rue Lepic and moved into the Pavillon-Royal Hotel in Saint-Germain-en-Laye. He needed a change of air, to sequester himself, to escape the distraction of his friends in Montmartre and daily domestic chores. He was finding Paris unbearable. In other words, he wanted to work, to write and go on writing until the very end, the very last word, the very last note, the very last sigh of his novel's score. He would leave his hotel room in the afternoon for the clinic in Clichy. In the mornings and evenings, plunged into a feverish state of excitement, of growing distress and exhaustion, he chained himself to his manuscript. There was no danger of the real world reaching him in the Pavillon-Royal. He was barely aware of Hitler and the racial laws proclaimed in Nuremburg on September 15, of the invasion of Ethiopia by Mussolini's troops in early October, of the demagogic harangues of Léon Degrelle, head of the "Rexist" Party in Belgium, or of Mao Tse-tung's Long March coming to an end near China's northern border. *Mort à crédit* encompassed his entire horizon.

A brief journey to London on November 21 was a mere parenthesis for him, a lungful of oxygen, the chance to revisit the city whose docks, shadows, ghosts, ships, and sinister neighborhoods were the subject of so many of his dreams. He found his excuse for the trip in a concert given by Lucienne Delforge on that evening. He and the young pianist continued to see each other in this manner, sometimes to love or to fear each other— quietly and rarely—in the hazards of their irreconcilable professions. After London, Lucienne left for a tour of Scandinavia. After London and its chimeras and the sordid silhouettes of Soho, Louis returned to Saint-Germain-en-Laye, to *Mort à crédit*, the time for writing and the chance for silence. He had one other distraction, a simple encounter that was to change his life but to which he may not immediately have paid the appropriate attention: that with Lucette Almansor. The longest romantic journeys often start that way, not with the explosive bang of a *coup de foudre*, but with a kind of mutual, subliminal tenderness, a fragile and imperceptible present renewed without a single grand word being spoken, simply the modest affection that extends and perpetuates itself on the sly, until one suddenly realizes that one can no longer live without it.

It was probably in November or December of 1935. Lucette was then taking dance classes with Blanche d'Alessandri on the rue Henri-Monnier. The greatest dancers of the day went to rehearse with the former star, whose career had been cut short by a fractured knee. Her classes were trying, draining. She literally led her students by the stick. One poorly executed leap would bring her cane down across a student's legs. This practice was not uncommon, Lucette recalls, readily comparing sessions with Mme. d'Alessandri to a kind of forced labor. But she admits that it was the best way to really learn how to leap or to execute various figures. The session began in the morning and lasted nearly four hours. "Your calves felt like they were about to explode." Ludmilla Tcherina was there, as was Serge Lifar, whom Lucette met at the time. The four-hour trial demanded by their fearsome teacher was difficult to endure. Later, still at Mme. d'Alessandri's, Lucette commiserated with a young dancer, Serge Perrault, who would soon become one of her closest and most faithful friends and a great admirer of Céline.

But what was the writer doing at d'Alessandri's dance class? He loved the dance, as we know, and loved dancers. His philosophical-aesthetic tastes and voyeurism would certainly have been gratified at such sessions. Spectators were not admitted to the lessons on the rue Henri-Monnier, but Céline's reputation and his manifest respect for Mme. d'Alessandri were enough to soften her. He would sit in a corner of the studio, motionless and invisible. Gen Paul, himself most appreciative of the choreographer's art and its interpreters, had gained him entry there. Louis wanted to learn about the ballerina's training. Mme. d'Alessandri had no doubt been flattered by his curiosity.

"At first," Lucette Almansor recalls, "they came together. Then, little by little, Céline tried to speak with me. I was extraordinarily unsophisticated and shy. I refused to answer him. He would ask me out after class, and I would answer no. It went on like that for months. Eventually he invited me one day to a restaurant in Montmartre. He told me: 'You should eat meat, you need your strength, you work so hard.' I order a steak. Two minutes later he says, 'Come on, sweetheart, let's go!' I hadn't had a chance to touch my meat. He was off. Maybe that's what I liked about him. He wasn't there. . . . I was twenty-two in 1935. I was very shy, educated by nuns. It wasn't normal to go out with a man, even if I was attracted to him, and I was—terribly. He was handsome. There was something of the archangel in him. Those eyes . . . One was drawn to him as to a lover, and I defended myself prodigiously, I was afraid. He was much older than me, and I told myself that it was a fantasy of his to go out with a young dancer. And there had been an incident earlier that had upset me a good deal. I had been having some trouble paying for my classes with Mme. d'Alessandri, so she had let me in for free. One day I see Céline putting some money on the piano. Then she told me: 'My dear, you don't owe me anything anymore.' I wasn't happy with that. There was a big scene. These are the kind of little things that come back to me. I defended myself strongly because I felt too attracted to him. For me, it was too serious. I almost messed it up completely. I was always running away, not answering him. He thought I wasn't interested in him or that I was in love with someone else."

The young woman, born in Paris on July 20, 1912, would soon become the writer's lover and then his wife. She would accompany him on all his travels, wanderings and trials, from castle to castle, from Sigmaringen to Meudon via the exile in Denmark, a silent and devoted presence. Her parents had married in 1910, during the great flood of the Seine, and had moved to the Île Saint-Louis before taking up residence on the rue Monge, not far from the place Maubert. Her father, born in Argenteuil, was an avid sportsman, an all-around athlete, an adept of footracing and cycling, whose fine "belle epoque" presence had turned the head of the coquettish and frivolous girl, chief saleswoman at Lanvin, to whom he soon proposed. He was a chartered accountant, mostly working for dressmakers, cloth and lace stores (such as Lefranc) or haberdashers, for whom he sometimes acted as agent by proxy. Marriages of love rarely resist the wear of time, much less of absence and war. When Lucette was born, her father was doing his military service. Later came the mobilization. In other words, the little girl never really lived with him until she was six years old. Her mother, of course, had had to return to work to provide for the household. Without Lucette, her parents would soon have divorced. But they preferred to wait and to see her education through. Clearly, the child's life was not the happiest or most fulfilling. Her father never got over not having a boy and raised her tough and sportsmanlike. She was put to school with the nuns on the rue des Bernardins.

Unbeknownst to her parents, Lucette studied—alone and without any regular preparation—for the entrance exam to the Conservatory, where she was admitted in 1927 at the age of fifteen, a rare accomplishment. Hearing the news, her father, suffering from ulcers and aspiring to a different career for his only daughter, threatened to lock her up. Lucette held her ground, and her parents grudgingly gave way. She soon won an honorable mention for acting, but she preferred dancing and, after graduating from the Conservatory, was hired for the corps de ballet of the Opéra-Comique. She stayed nearly four years, growing ever more impatient with the rivalries, ambitions, jealousies, and intrigues that held sway there. At the same time, she was appearing at the Comédie-Française in productions of ancient dance or choreographic *divertissements* connected with various plays. Lucette Almansor was also fond of ethnic dances, Spanish dances that she accompanied herself—and very well—on the castanets. She rented a studio at Wacker's on the rue Douai and gave her own dance lessons. Leaving the Opéra-Comique in 1935, she spent some time in the United States. An impresario, Fischer, had hired her as the only Frenchwoman for a variety show of fifteen acts in the spirit of the Ziegfeld Follies. She appeared most notably in a Spanish dance act. Avidly curious, slight of figure, independent, graceful, her brown hair often pulled back, the young Lucette Almansor discovered New York, show business, jazz, the dazzle of costume jewelry and sequins, and above all the exhaustion of highly professional work. On her return to Paris in late 1935, she went back to the ancient dances in period costume to music by Couperin and Lully, and to her Spanish dances to scores by Albéniz or de Falla. But Lucette was basically more of a creator than an interpreter. She was a harsh critic of the vagaries and excesses of classical dance as well as the humiliations of her training. She was already dreaming of a greater liberation of the body, of a stretching-relaxation technique antithetical to dance exercises, at a time when yoga was still unknown in France. Furthermore, her impresario had little trouble finding her engagements for her own pieces, anywhere and everywhere, in France and abroad. She continued at the same time to practice with Mme. d'Alessandri and later with Egorova, a former prima ballerina at the Russian court, the wife of a Trubetskoy prince, exiled in Paris with his family in utter destitution. A dancer absolutely must train for four or five hours a day. . . .

In late 1935 and early 1936, Lucette was a barely detectable presence in the writer's life. He remained holed up in Saint-Germain-en-Laye. He wrote, and wrote constantly. Robert Denoël was impatiently awaiting the novel. He had hoped to publish the work in early 1936, well before Easter. The announcement of the book's publication was repeatedly pushed back to early April, late April, early May.

In mid-February, terribly weakened and having lost over twenty pounds, Céline was forced to return to the rue Lepic and to give up his rounds at the clinic in Clichy. He wrote to Karen at the time: "I've been very sick (my intestines) for the past two months. I'm sluggish and in a lot of pain. I've just returned to Paris. I can barely work. That's life! That's why I haven't written you. I'm very down as well. It's no fun being sick and alone. I don't often complain, but in this case . . . Anyway, I have Gen Paul who comes to see me. I can't go to the clinic anymore. It's better for me to be sick in Montmartre than in St. Germain. I was completely alone there. Gozlan (the little doctor from Médan) is looking after me. That's my news. Even so, I'm working on my book as much as I can. I'd really like to finish it. After all, I've killed myself doing it."[43]

Céline was indeed alone, in that true solitude of the writer who, by definition, can expect no help in reifying his visions, his memory, his nightmares, the whiteness of his page and the blackness of his ideas. Writing is the absolute brought to the world's silence. But he was also alone in his few respites from the composition of the final pages. Lucette had not yet become a part of his life. Elizabeth was still an obsessing and painful ghost. His affair with Lucienne Delforge was coming to an end.

On her return from her tour of Scandinavia and Czechoslovakia, the young piano soloist had found Céline sick in bed, an ice pack on his head, complaining of headaches and fearing cancer. They went out together, to concerts and museums, had lunch at his place or hers. But Lucienne could no longer support the burden of nightmare, of delirious neurasthenia, that the writer always seemed to carry with him. It was as though she were afraid of losing her own balance; as though she were afraid of contagion. After her recital of March 18, 1936, she decided to distance herself from him. The break was finalized in April.

"I've seen little of Lucienne," Louis wrote at the time to Cillie. "She has to work and hang around the reporters and the salons. Anyway, Cillie, you know, I'm so ill-tempered at the moment, I'm so used to being alone, so easily exhausted that I prefer not seeing anybody, when all is said and done. Especially young people—I get fed up with them so quickly—they exhaust me with their little mannerisms. And Lucienne too, in fact, has a bit of the spoiled child in her. Well, she's very sweet."[44]

Louis would but rarely cross her path again, once in Paris and again in Sigmaringen in 1944–1945—brief encounters, friendly, affectionate, and inconsequential.

In the meantime, in order to dot the *i*'s in *Mort à crédit*, Louis left in late March for the Hôtel Frascati in Le Havre, from where he sent this disturbingly solemn message to Henri Mahé: "As you get older, you'll see what's left. Nothing at all. Other than the violent passion for perfection, first cousin to death."[45]

Once again in Le Havre, in the hotel from whose windows he could observe the hustle and bustle of the port, the stately dance of the little tugboats, the smoke of the freighters and the people milling about on the docks, Louis forced himself to reconcile his fantasies with his work, his need for frenzied yet meticulous writing, and his taste for the misty call of distant places.

Jeanne Carayon, having gone to the United States, was no longer there to go over his manuscript. She did, however, recommend one of her old classmates, Marie Canavaggia. It was an excellent choice. Canavaggia was a highly cultured woman who, in particular, was the translator of the great Welsh writer John Cowper Powys (whom Henry Miller claimed to admire as much as he did Céline) and who translated from the Italian such writers as the unjustly ignored Gian Dàuli, who, in his capacity as publisher, was himself the first to make Louis-Ferdinand Céline's name known in Italy.[46] Canavaggia didn't type, but passed on the pages of the manuscript to a typist and oversaw the work. Perhaps she was in love with Céline, but if so with a hidden love, solitary, boundlessly devoted, faithful, and occasionally temperamental and jealous. It was the love of a young woman or an old, unmarried woman, taciturn and lacking in self-awareness. Who could ignore the pull of the writer's fascination?

As Céline's manuscript gradually evolved, it was immediately typed, reread, and proofed by Marie Canavaggia, then abundantly corrected by the author. His new secretary—who would remain faithful to him until 1961, until *Nord*, until the end (she would die in Paris, knocked down by a car, on September 30, 1976)—was thus able to observe the slow evolution of the text, the stages of each "work in progress." Marie Canavaggia never hesitated to badger the writer, to question such or such a turn of phrase, such or such grammatical mistake that shocked her, or some neologism that grated on her lexicological sense of caution. Sometimes Céline was exasperated by this, sometimes he would smile or defend himself patiently.

"Seeing him at work was miraculous," she explained. "He was never at a loss for inspiration. If he decided to change a word, it was never enough to replace it with another. He completely rewrote the sentence, sometimes even the surrounding sentences, according to the demands of his 'cadence.' Sometimes he drummed his fingers as if he were counting the beats of an alexandrine. These corrections almost always entailed some development, some enrichment, like with Proust. Sometimes he'd have another try hours, a night, several days later. He would telephone: 'Reread me that sentence . . .' and go on to make some new transformation. He was prodigious in his invention. A word would change spelling within the same book, whether it was from the Petit Larousse or the Chautard or one he had made up: 'But you spelled it differently a few pages earlier.'—'So what? If you have several women, why would you always sleep with the same one?'

"But what torment was entailed by that need to create form and substance! Watching that face grow more and more haggard, one hesitated to be more complicitous with his fetish for perfection. Rather than point out some trifle, wasn't it better to spare him another attack of his migraine? But that wasn't what Céline expected from Mademoiselle Marie, to whom he wrote one day: 'We have to correct down to the last carat . . . brutally.' "[47]

In this manner the last act of *Mort à crédit* was played out at the Hôtel Frascati before embarking on the great adventure of publishing and the clash with the public. But Céline had yet to submit the manuscript to his publisher and to have it printed.

Was Robert Denoël horrified by Céline's style, far more fragmented, free, and frenetic than that of *Voyage*, multiplying the ellipses, the panting breath of jerky, halting, unfinished sentences, the phantasmagoric urgency of visions spinning between present and past, memory and madness? That at least was how Céline would later describe it to Robert Poulet, painting the portrait of a Denoël perplexed, very dignified and very upset, striving both to warn him against and admonish him for his rejection of tradition and the accepted literary forms. In fact, the problem resided not there but in the novel's obscene passages, for instance in young Ferdinand's revels with his headstrong and alluring *patronnes*.

Céline, again to Robert Poulet: "And then there was something else. Those passages go too far, really too far! . . . Obviously, art has its rights, but really! . . . 'We can't let ourselves be accused of pornography. We've built up a valuable following. Let's not alienate it.' As to the unexpurgated text of the novel, it was very simple: we'd be heading straight for a charge of indecency. We'd missed out on the Prix Goncourt . . . We wouldn't miss out on our day in court."[48]

The negotiations between author and publisher were intense. Denoël refused to print the offending passages. Céline forbade any corrections or expurgations. They finally reached a compromise: with the exception of eleven numbered collector's copies, *Mort à crédit* was printed with blank spaces in the place of the passages, sentences, or paragraphs that Robert Denoël deemed unpublishable! An introductory note explained: "At the publisher's request, L.-F. Céline has suppressed a number of sentences from his book; these sentences have not been replaced. They appear as blanks in the work." This decision respected the author's sensitivity and probity while obviating any threat of censorship. But did it serve the cause of decency? The reader's imagination, running amok through the notorious "blanks," was actually emboldened to overstress the scandalous potential of the scenes. Is that not the very definition of eroticism? On the commercial side, it was also an unintentional stroke of genius.

Even before the book was released, the press had seized on the indecent passages and the notorious forced expurgations. In its issue of March 28, 1936, the satirical paper *Le Nouveau cri* had quoted Céline as saying, "I am not in favor of paraphrase. My name is not Boylesve.[49] I could never bring myself to write that my characters 'embraced passionately while exchanging mad kisses . . .' I've been working on this book every day for four years, losing twenty-five pounds in the process. I won't change a comma."[50]

Indeed, he did not change a comma. But he himself had most certainly changed in writing the book. He had been brought closer to the disturbing and sometimes deceptive ghosts rising from the folds and shadows of his memory; he had grown more aloof from the world and its frivolous pleasures, which he understood less and less; in short, he had been isolated far from society, in an unsettling complicity with pain and the notion of death.

And yet his journey as a writer had only just begun. He would later describe himself as the chronicler of the *Grands Guignols*. And the curtain was but barely risen on the screams, the hatreds, the horrors, and the corpses that would soon be counted by the millions in the forthcoming convulsions of Europe and the world.

11

Cries and Solitude

A Credit Runs Dry
To the Soviet Union and Back
Ballets and Bagatelles

A Credit Runs Dry

On May 12, 1936, *Mort à crédit*, now distributed by Messageries Hachette, reached the bookstores. Robert Denoël wasn't taking any chances. If there was any possibility of Céline's garnering a literary award, it was best not to reduce his chances by having Hachette against them.

Thus, the book, the object, was finally here: an enormous slab of 700 pages with a sober cover. A publicity wrapper encircled the book; on the front: "I took great pains with this work. Whoever puts in as much as me will do just as well—J. S. Bach"; and on the back: "The new novel by L.-F. Céline, author of *Voyage au bout de la nuit*."

The retail price was set at twenty-five francs.

For his second novel, Céline had won his case. Denoël had agreed to modify the publishing contract established between them for *Voyage*. Céline retained the translation rights as well as the film and theatrical adaptation rights. In return he made the commensurate compromise of conceding exclusivity to Éditions Denoël of all his future literary work, with no limit as to number or date. The royalty percentages were not significantly different: 12% of the gross sales up to 20,000 copies, 15% from 20,000 to 50,000, 18% above that.

Denoël was playing hardball with *Mort à crédit*, which had an official first run of 25,000 copies. He followed up the book's release with a heavy campaign, deluging the press with notices and ads usually composed of a short blurb and illustrated with a portrait of Céline by Gen Paul or a photograph. They described Céline as a "satirist of incomparable verve and vigor"; *Mort à crédit* became the "great book of the age" or "the most extraordinary novel of the age."[1] The ads would later evoke the book's *succès de scandale*, the controversy surrounding it, and the 100,000 readers won over to date. A rather inflated claim, since, despite *Mort à crédit*'s undeniable success with the public, sales were far from those vaunted. In late 1938 Éditions Denoël would set the official figure at 35,000 copies sold.

As he had done at the time of *Voyage*'s publication, Louis left Paris just as *Mort à crédit* was about to be released. This time he had no intention whatsoever, either before his departure or after his return, of participating in its marketing: no flattering dedications, no diplomatic visits, no outrageous interviews, nothing. It was not that he had no interest in the critical reception, but he refused to plunge into the literary vanity fair, to play the cheapjack and the buffoon for his own product, as others did, to attract buyers. In his publicity wrapper, he had written of the great pains he had taken; it was now up to the critics, readers, colleagues, and the curious to take their own pains in turn, and that was that.

On May 7 he took the train for Antwerp, where he stayed at the Hotel Century. Naturally, he met with Évelyne Pollet, still as zealous, amorous, and idolizing as ever. Perhaps it wasn't all that unpleasant for him to let himself be loved or idolized this way, for a day or two, on the run. Pollet no doubt took advantage of the occasion to give him a new manuscript that she had just written and hoped to publish. A month later, back in Paris, Louis would write her with polite circumspection and all the allusions that are wasted on those who will not understand. He would explain that he hadn't yet had the time to read her book, that the publishing market was in a slump; and later, that he had read it, that he was a bad judge, that he was incapable of giving an intelligent opinion, that classicism wasn't his field, that people in France didn't read, and so on.

This time he didn't dally in Antwerp. He embarked for England, his country of choice if not of adoption. Was he making the rounds of his old lovers? After Évelyne Pollet, he had plans to see Erika Irrgang, who had married and chosen to leave Hitler's Germany for reasons of conscience, as she explained. Louis had written her: "What hopes you must have, now that you've left Germany—My God, what madness! What a vile, disgusting horror! Married! A baby! A housewife! So many changes! You can tell me all about it soon."[2]

Having passed through Chatham and London, where he made several vain efforts to find a producer for his ballet synopses (evincing the same old taste for fairy tale, graceful illusions, the same old dream of the dance and of liberation from gravity), he reached Cambridge around May 14. A few days earlier he had again written to Erika: "I'll be in Cambridge around May 10. I'll stay with you for a few days—I need a rest—I am exhausted by my three-year, day-and-night task. My book is coming out today. I have, alas, many hopes for it!"[3]

Their re-encounter was disappointing. Louis was indeed exhausted and taciturn, weighed down with worries about his book's release. "I don't know why," Erika explains, "our meeting in Cambridge, which was our last, was somehow depressing; there was something about it that's difficult to describe, something that is born with the instinctive feeling that there is nothing left to say."[4]

The problem, perhaps, was that Céline was unable to forget. He shut himself away in his silence and his piercing headaches. What sort of response was he hoping for to *Mort à crédit*, that message in a bottle launched toward his childhood? He had forbidden his mother to read it and she would obey him. Was he hoping for compliments from everyone else, or some sort of complicity? He didn't know. He couldn't very well expect much from a world for which he had abandoned all hope. Otherwise, he would have found his pessimism contradicted. But who can live without contradictions? One can reject honors and still enjoy being offered them. One can scorn critics and still be hurt when they attack. Céline knew the true value of his book, of its newness, the musical and syncopated quality of its innovative style, the pregnancy of his vision that sometimes burst forth into veritable pantomime. Great writers are always clear-sighted and rarely humble. Céline knew that he had written a terrific book, a *Bildungsroman* that was an apprenticeship to madness. Past and present began to waver until the narrator, the suburban doctor, the author's barely dissembled double, withdrew behind the figure of young Ferdinand and his successive, catastrophic apprenticeships to life. But his book was precisely too new, too scandalous, the way any unique book is scandalous—any book that does not take deferential shelter behind an illustrious precedent.

There was Céline in England, then, stepping back to measure the futility of his efforts. Was the French press ready for *Mort à crédit*? And what about his readers? The press had other things on its mind, his readers had other distractions, and Europe was girding itself helter-skelter for the great bloody spectacle of disasters to come—those one always pictures with indulgence when one believes oneself immune.

In March, in its first warning shot, Nazi Germany had occupied the Rhineland, which had been declared a "demilitarized zone" at Versailles, without meeting any resistance. The French military establishment hadn't uttered a word of protest. In any case, the ultracautious English would not have tolerated a violent reaction. The Germans had actually been bluffing—they did so superbly, and raked in their chips with impunity. They would go on to build their Siegfried Line in answer to France's Maginot Line, where officers snoozed and counted flies instead of their tanks. Belgium declared itself neutral, and thus invulnerable, immune—this wasn't any affair of Belgium's! In any case, the Right in power in France was less afraid of Hitler than of the Front Populaire. Everyone could sleep easily. But there comes inevitably a day of awakening. . . .

On May 3rd 1936, after the second ballot for the legislative house, the Front Populaire was suddenly present in strength with an unprecedented victory: 5,600,000 votes for the Left, 4,200,000 for the Right, and the socialists in the majority with 149 seats. Léon Blum, whose little book on marriage Céline so admired, was quite naturally chosen to form the new government. Yes, France was awakening, but only to plunge into a mad, intoxicating revelry. Ah! bliss was it to be alive in that spring of '36 and the dazzling summer to follow! Maurice Thorez opened the festivities with his open-handed policy: "We communists have reconciled the tricolored flag of our fathers with the red flag of our hopes." In demonstrations, debates, and the press, the "200 families" were pointed to and decried as the source of all past ills. Every fairground needs its Merry-Andrew, someone to throw rag-balls at, someone to provide the belly laughs, to hand out the flags (red ones), and to set you off home on the right foot—the Left one!

Almost everywhere factories were coming to a standstill. Better yet, the workers were staging sitdown strikes. The government had dissolved such groups of the extreme Right as the Croix-de-Feu and the Jeunesses Patriotes, there was nothing left to threaten the Republic, and accordion tunes filled the air everywhere. "La vie est à nous"—Life Belongs to Us—Jean Renoir had proclaimed in his militant film in support of the Communist Party's electoral campaign. And why not? A few weeks earlier, the wonderful film entitled *Le Crime de M. Lange*, again by Renoir, had shown that a business could be run by its own workers. A precursor! In the meantime the workers patiently held their ground, folded their arms, and defied the bosses. People wanted to dance by the waterside, drink a little white table wine in the *guingettes* by the Marne, and be like Jean Gabin in Duvivier's *La Belle Equipe*.

On June 7, after a May paralyzed by merrymaking, the bosses finally ratified the famous "Matignon Agreements." For the workers, it meant a forty-hour week and two weeks of paid vacation. "One must know how to end a strike," Maurice Thorez boasted at the closing ceremonies. But the situation wasn't very dire. Soon enough, come August, the first trains would start out for Le Tréport and Luc-sur-Mer, the workers would discover the ocean, vacations, the sun, sand and pebbles. Fred Addison and his orchestra could be heard on every radio set, rehashing the awful hit tune, "When a Policeman Laughs." In a word, since the workers were less unhappy, they did their best to laugh. As did the policemen.

Céline, however, had no part in all this. He left in May with *Mort à crédit* [Death on the Installment Plan] and its syncopated obsessions with death. France, as we have seen, had other distractions; France was dreaming of its own well-being, or else it was getting drunk and had stopped thinking altogether. It was life that France was buying on the installment plan. . . .

Did the sales of *Mort à crédit* suffer directly from the strikes, the marches, the *guingettes* by the Marne and the union demands? On that note, Céline, frustrated, declared in the satiric paper *Le Nouvel cri*: "The Front Populaire owes me at least 200,000 francs!" A rather rash statement, since his simultaneously intimate and tragic book, too involved with the past and too innovative, out of sync with the era's mass movements, was then experiencing—and it came almost as a surprise—very good sales in the bookstores.

But the critics were not inclined to welcome *Mort à crédit* or to praise it. And while the writer lingered in England, only to return to the rue Lepic in the latter part of May, the barrage fire began, sustained, violent and deafening. It used two basic arguments as ammunition: first, the slang style and vocabulary used by the writer; second, his tendency to debase man, to reduce him to his most ignoble functions and instincts, to a hateful and sterile mediocrity.

"Twenty-five francs' worth of ignominy and abjection," howled *La Liberté* on May 21. "The greatest manufacturer of filth *in the world*, a sort of Ford of sewage," *Combat* commented the next month. "A gutter vocabulary," "a urinal anthology," "an erethism of filth" were among the more subtle comments of *L'Ordre*. Hearts skipped a beat in the provinces, and *Marseille-Matin*, on June 3, spoke of a book that "must not be allowed in the family and should even be banished from the closed stacks of the most private libraries," before equitably concluding that "There are some individuals who must be denied the right to corrupt others." The critic of *Comoedia* came up with a rather novel argument: the characters described by Céline could not be soulless degenerates since they constituted the generation that fought in '14 and had vanquished on the Marne.[5]

Another reproach leveled at him was that his slang style was a false one, artificial if not to say affected. In that vein, Alain Laubreaux, who was to become one of the most extreme journalists of the most extreme collaboration, mused in *La Dépêche de Toulouse* on June 9: "Why . . . does Céline insist on using such a detestable style, which, despite its appearance of rebellion and freedom, is full of the most vulgar literary methods?"

These criticisms echoed to a certain extent those of Paul Nizan in *L'Humanité* on July 15—after an earlier review of the book on May 18 based on the advance proofs, in which he had spoken of a "singular work" and "one of the most original and powerful books of recent years." For Nizan took care to emphasize that evidence: "It is not true to say that Céline's slang is simple transposition of authentic slang: it is a slang reinvented on rhythms not found in colloquial, spoken French." But this was only in order better to denounce Céline's total lack of style, which obviously should not be confused with the banal invention of a language. He went on to accuse Céline of achieving only stereotyped effects where Aragon, in *Les Cloches de Bâle*, had excelled. That wasn't all. There was Céline's contempt for humanity. "*Le Voyage au bout de la nuit* gave promise of a writer with some potential. He has already taken to self-parody. Ferdinand is merely the moribund reflection of Bardamu. *Mort à crédit* is merely an enormous pastiche of *Voyage*. People will not care to waste much time on this rendezvous of ghosts. . . . There was a memorable denunciation of war and colonialism in *Voyage*. Today, Céline is merely denouncing the poor and the disenfranchised."

But Nizan saved his greatest indignation for the character of the prostitute marching on Père-Lachaise on Federation Day, brandishing a portrait of Lenin on a pole. Here, Céline was throwing off his mask, revealing "his thoughts on things political." It was no coincidence that he had made "a prostitute the only communist character to which he refers," he concluded earnestly.

To the Left as to the Right, then, the rift between the writer's admirers and detractors was not a political one. Further evidence of that was the reaction of Robert Brasillach in *L'Action française* on June 11, his collegiate sensibilities and well-bred monarcho-fascistic audacity offended by the writer's "exasperating techniques." But Brasillach had one comfort *in extremis*: "Such books, which will be incomprehensible in twenty years, . . . seem to me to be the very antithesis of art." It was a close call, but France would soon be back amongst its own, amongst persons of good breeding and repute, amongst artists worthy of the name.

There were, of course, more subtle analyses, as well as favorable ones. Gabriel Brunot, in *Je suis partout* on June 6, could not help but hail, despite everything, "700 pages of reality, seized at the very gates of nightmare, that leave you reeling and nauseated." The book had "a kind of awkward and barbaric genius."

In *Les Cahiers du sud* in July 1936, Yanette Delétang-Tardif spoke of a "terrific book" that had to be taken as a whole. In *Marianne* on May 27, Ramon Fernandez dwelt primarily on the "incantantion of a style," and Noël Sabord, journalist and member of the Renaudot panel, had also taken up the author's cause.

In *Le Merle blanc*, somewhat later on September 19, Pierre Scize responded in turn to Céline's critics, evoking the author's "negating genius" and the frenetic violence of his "satanic work." Certainly, the author was a negator. He might one day prove useful to the enemies of the Left. Pierre Scize was quite correct. And his article, written from Moscow on September 10, 1936, ended with these prophetic lines (which, moreover, recall the endless disputes between Céline and Élie Faure): "Céline, from now on you can say and do anything you like. You have given a voice to human despair. A voice that can never be silenced. As for those of us who will continue to hope despite having heard your howl, we shall go to work—without you? Too bad. Too bad for you!—to give the human community a less dismal face and a less sordid appearance. Even if you condemn our task, I tell you: You will have helped our undertaking."

Writers dropped Céline as fast as the critics. From Malraux, Aragon, Sartre, Beauvoir, Mauriac and the others, there was either no reaction or else gestures of disgust, disappointment, indifference. Céline was not of their number. What he wrote was argot, not literature, or else it was precious and contrived—and still not literature. There was no way around it.

But Céline wasn't looking for a way around it. His ever more desperate solitude, the glee he seemed to feel in inspiring these attacks—his hypertrophied sense of pride, the clownish and paranoid cackle that seized him— found their cause and justification in every article, every attack. That was all he heard and remembered. The rare compliment was soon forgotten.

He had written to Marie Canavaggia: "The die is cast! What you tell me is quite comforting. The commercial aspect is all I really care about. The rest was done as well as it could be. Nothing those gasbags might drivel can add or detract from that. It's just free publicity."[6] And to Henri Mahé, later in the month, after the first articles had sunk in: "Forty-two-years old two days ago, thirty-two years of anguish, enough said. The criticism has been filthy, from the Left and the Right. I've made myself the sole receptacle of all blind, jealous hatred from every boorish bastard! . . . Daudet and Descaves have really been shown up as cowards this time."[7]

And yet he had counted on their support. Hadn't they been really responsible for launching *Voyage au bout de la nuit?* But now, even Lucien Descaves, to whom *Mort à crédit* had been dedicated, remained silent. His silence was a public disavowal and that is how Céline took it. Actually, Descaves was more perplexed than hostile, defeated by his inability to come to grips with the enormous book. An outline for an article, kept in his files and never published, bears witness to his diffidence. In it, Descaves vindicates the bleakness of Céline's vision and the vulgarity of his language, but condemns the abundance of ellipses.[8] Léon Daudet, for his part, expressed no opinion on the book, with which he seems not even to have been familiar.

And yet, Céline had written to him, asking for his help in the face of the rising tide of insults. He spoke in his letter of the enormous work he had undertaken and his meticulous stylistic efforts. He appealed to a kind of Nordic solidarity: "I am not a Southerner. I'm a Parisian, of Breton and Flemish descent. I write what I feel. I am accused of being a filth-monger, of writing smut. In that case, Rabelais, Villon, Brueghel, and many others should be so accused . . . Not everything stems from the Renaissance. I am accused of systematic cruelty. When the world changes its soul, I'll change my form." And he concludes: "I write in the *waking dream* mode. It's a northern mode. I'd be very pleased if you would earmark an article for me, not to praise me (such a request would be worthy neither of you nor of me), but so as to define clearly, as only you with your great authority can do, what is and what isn't in my book."[9]

But Daudet, yet again, failed to earmark such an article.

In the meantime, Céline had returned to France, had resumed his rounds at the Clichy clinic, was lingering ever longer at Mme. d'Alessandri's dance classes, beguiling and being beguiled by Lucette Almansor and her timid silences. He did perhaps accept a few "literary" luncheons, with Antonin Artaud, Charles Braibant, Robert Desnos, and Carlo Rim at the home of Bernard Steele, or on June 21 at Louis Laloy's with Ramon Fernandez (with whom he often met on friendly terms) and Francis Poulenc. But he remained a distant spectator of the literary life.

He spoke up but once, not to talk specifically of his book or to offer glimpses into his private life, but to respond to a *Figaro* critic, André Rousseaux, who, on May 23, had described in an article a conversation with Francis Carco and had emphasized, with reference to Céline, the ephemeral character of slang. Selections of Celine's letter appeared in *Le Figaro* eight days later.

"I cannot read a novel in classical language. Such books are novels in progress. They are never novels. All the work remains to be done . . . Their language is impossible. It is *dead*. . . .

"A language is like anything else, it is continually dying. It must die. We have to accept that. The language of most novels is dead, their syntax dead, everything—dead. Mine too will die, no doubt soon enough. But they will have had that little superiority over so many others, that for a year, a month, a day, they had *lived*.

"That is the all-in-all. Everything else is just vulgar, stupid, and senile boastfulness. In all this search for an absolute French language, there is an unbearably idiotic pretention to an eternal quality in any form of writing."

And then, faced with Céline's almost unbroken silence and the polemics that *Mort à crédit* continued to inspire, an astonishing thing took place in July: the publisher himself went into the breach and gave open battle to defend his author against calumny and insult. Under his own name, Robert Denoël published a thirty-two-page pamphlet in a run of 3,000 copies, entitled *Apologia for Mort à crédit*. In it he spoke of Céline, his discretion, his rebelliousness in interviews and inquiries, his contempt for cliques, parties, salons, and editorial bureaus. He attacked Céline's most unrelenting critics head-on. He particularly strove to draw a parallel between the insults inspired by *Mort à crédit* and those aroused in their time by Zola's *La Terre* and *L'Assomoir*, characterized at best as "putrid." The analogy, indeed, was almost perfect.

And Céline remained silent. The civil war was beginning in Spain. In July, General Franco offered his *pronunciamento* against the Republic, supported by Moroccan soldiers and the Spanish Legion. Another warning shot across the bows of European peace and stability, the beginning of an endless conflict that was to bathe the Iberian peninsula in blood; a procession of horrors that would serve as a dress rehearsal for the exhibition of German military matériel, Italian pugnacity, Nazi determination, the ineffectuality of a distant Soviet Union, the courage of the international brigades, and the indifference of the Western democracies. But in July, public opinion was barely ruffled. Paid vacations were no longer just promises in France. And the more athletic workers merely speculated on the outcome of the Olympic Games to be held in August in Berlin, and whether the black American athlete Jesse Owens was really the athlete he was said to be, the fastest and highest hurdler; so much for the Aryan superiority so dear to the Nazis.

Céline, then, remained on the sidelines. He absorbed the blows, saving up his responses for a later date. Noël Sabord had met with him, and described him thus in *Paris-Midi* on July 27, 1936: "The baseness and ignominy of the attacks against him are enough to raise his spirits, and he distances himself, retreats, secretive, silent, alone with his disgust, swallowing his bitter, explosive bile. 'No soap boxes!' he told me. 'I'm not interested in histrionics. They won't force me to reveal myself, to get up on stage. From now on

they'll never see my face, not even the color of my ink. They haven't dared to publish the few letters I've already written them.' "
They would see the color of his ink soon enough.

To the Soviet Union and Back

The best thing to help Céline forget about *Mort à crédit* was to go on a journey, as was his habit. He had been considering the Soviet Union for several years. It piqued his sense of curiosity, as well as appealing to his sense of thrift, for reasons we will soon see. Sometime in mid-August he set off for Leningrad.

Immediately after its publication, *Voyage au bout de la nuit* had been translated into Russian by Elsa Triolet, a translation that was edited, corrected, and expurgated in Moscow by an obscure and zealous bureaucrat in the Ministry of Culture and then published there in 1934. The book had enjoyed heavy distribution, in successive runs of 6,000, 15,000 and 40,000 copies. The press had given him a good deal of coverage, and the inevitably Stalinist intellectuals (the rest were in exile, in the gulags, or dead) had been struck by the inspired, refreshing ferocity of Céline, a true writer of the people. Only Gorky had later expressed his reservations, severely criticizing its "decadence." But that was in the past. Céline had since been informed of the butchery to which his first book had been subjected. He held Aragon and Triolet responsible, and it was the deciding factor in their quarrel. Then came *Mort à crédit*. There was no question this time of a Russian translation. The critic of the *International Literary Review* deemed the work mediocre, anarchistic, cynical, nihilist, the perfect example of literary degeneration. That did not change the fact that Céline had earned some hefty royalties in the Soviet Union and that he had no choice but to spend them within its borders.

Those famous trips to Russia! Over the course of the 1920s and 1930s, they had become virtually *de rigueur* for any intellectual worthy of the name. One had to go at least once to see that still enigmatic giant, that hope or terror arisen in the East, to size up that new world, if not to say new humanity, to view the achievements of the regime and bear witness to what one had seen. The same phenomenon would be repeated in Mao's China in the late sixties, and on the basis of one or two weeks on a highly organized tour, writers and politicians would air with utmost equanimity their judgments and opinions, as blind as they were peremptory.

Romain Rolland and Henri Béraud, Georges Duhamel, and Henri Barbusse had been among the first to accept the Soviet government's invitation. Then it was the turn of Malraux and Marc Chadourne, Roland Dorgèles and André Chamson. For the Russians, of course, the risk was in disappointing their guests, but one had to seize the opportunity offered in the wonderful new field of public relations aimed at the intelligentsia. Accompanied by

Louis Guilloux and Eugène Dabit, André Gide was the next to go, on June 17, 1936. At seventy, Gide had the enthusiasm of a neophyte. This bourgeois writer, having gradually been drawn toward a more defined political involvement, had for several years been bouncing from congress to meeting, from conference to petition. He announced at the time, with fine bombast: "If I had to lay down my life to ensure the success of the Soviet Union, I'd lay it down on the spot." No wonder the Soviets welcomed him with every honor, finding a private railway car for him and his companions, organizing receptions and official tours. But they had forgotten that Gide the writer, though leaning to the Left in his liberal commitments, was an intellectual first and a party man second, a loner who valued nothing above the independence of spirit necessary to the writer, that is, someone who held the search for truth above all tenets and could only bear witness to what he had seen. After his return from Russia on August 22, Gide published his notorious and courageous *Retour de l'U.R.S.S.*, angering the writers of the Left. Gide, tormented and bitter, could not keep silent, despite all the safeguards and stylistic precautions with which he surrounded himself. Romain Rolland and the others accused him of playing a double game.

As for Céline, no one was waiting with honors for him, no bouquets of flowers or private trains. No one was waiting at all. He traveled alone, and that was how he wanted it. Lucette Almansor, who was not yet living with him on the rue Lepic but whose presence was becoming daily more necessary, considered going with him. Louis had suggested it, and she was very excited at the thought of seeing Leningrad, the Winter Palace, and especially the ballets of the great Russian dance academy. Unfortunately they were not married, and it proved impossible for them to share a room at the hotel. Morality and its appearances were no joke to the Soviets. Faced with the growing administrative obstacles, visas and so on, Lucette had to abandon her travel plans. Louis embarked alone on the S.S. *Polaris* bound for Helsinki and Leningrad.

Later, upon his return from the USSR, when he published *Mea culpa*, a rash journalist would call him a turncoat. The offense enraged Céline and inspired some ferocious pages in *Bagatelles pour un massacre*. It was his chance to recall his utter lack of ideological commitment, stressing the fact that he paid all the expenses of his trip. "You didn't see me going to Russia 'on the house' . . . In other words, minister, envoy, pilgrim, lapdog, art critic, I paid it all out of pocket . . . with my own duly earned dough, everything: hotel, taxis, travel, interpreter, soup, grub . . . Everything! . . . I spent a fortune in rubles . . . to see everything at my leisure . . . I never balked at any expense . . . And the Soviets still owe me some dough . . . Let it be known! . . . If people care to. I don't owe them a nickel! . . . not one favor! not the price of one coffee!"[10]

Aboard the *Polaris*, Céline wrote a letter to Cillie, now married and pregnant. He gave her news of Lucienne Delforge, whom he had not seen again and who was said to be in love with a journalist. "By the way, I've had a lot of trouble with *Mort à crédit*. Just about every critic against me, and with what virulence! They haven't even read it. I couldn't care less what they think of me, but it's had a terrible effect on sales. I'll be lucky to sell 40,000— and I had such an awful time with it! Much worse than with *Voyage*! But all this is pointless. I'm not feeling too well. I was really exhausted by that damn book. I'm going to Moscow to get some money, if possible."[11]

It is unlikely that he went. The few testimonies and documents available to us concerning his trip to Russia, particularly the pages in *Bagatelles* devoted to it, mention only his stay in Leningrad. In all probability, he never left the city and its environs.

"From noon to midnight, I was accompanied everywhere by a (police) interpreter. I paid full rate for her . . . For that matter, she was very nice, her name was Natalya, a very pretty blond indeed, eager, all aglow with communism, enough of a believer to knock you off if necessary . . . Absolutely serious, for that matter . . . don't go getting any ideas in your head! . . . and under surveillance! Good God! . . .

"I was bunking at the Evropeiskaya Hotel, second class, cockroaches and waterbugs on every floor . . . I'm not trying to make a big deal out of it . . . of course I've seen worse . . . But still, it was hardly spic and span . . . and just for the room, it cost the equivalent of 250 francs a day! I went to the Soviets, sent by no newspaper, no company, no party, no publisher, no police, entirely at my own expense, just out of curiosity."[12]

What did he see in Leningrad, where he must have arrived shortly after the death of his friend Eugène Dabit in Sebastopol on August 21, during his "official" tour with André Gide? Misery, ruins, poverty, the resigned docility of the people, the small-time prosperity of the *apparatchiki*, propaganda, hypocrisy, oppression. . . . He would later discuss it at length.

Leningrad itself enchanted him. "In its own way, it's the most beautiful city in the world." And it inspired some wonderfully lyrical lines from him: "Just try to imagine . . . the Champs-Élysées . . . but now, four times as wide and flooded with pale water . . . the Neva . . . It stretches past . . . keeps on going . . . toward the pallid expanse . . . the sky . . . the sea . . . ever further . . . the estuary at the very end . . . goes on forever . . . the sea rising toward us . . . toward the city . . . the sea holds the whole city in its hand! . . . diaphanous, fantastical, extended . . . at arm's length . . . along all the banks . . . the whole city, a strong arm . . . palaces . . . more palaces . . . Hard rectangles . . . domed . . . marble . . . enormous hard gemstones . . . at the pale water's edge . . . To the left, a little canal, quite black . . . throwing itself there . . . against the colossus of the Admiralty, every slab a golden one . . . bearing a shimmering figurehead all in gold . . . What a trumpet! right in the wall . . . what majesty! . . . what fantastical giant? What theater for cyclopes? . . . a hundred staggered ornaments, each more grandiose . . . toward the sea."[13]

He must have visited hospitals. A public health specialist, he had developed the habit, if not to say the taste. To his eyes, a country revealed itself first through its health facilities. *Bagatelles* also describes a comical visit to the central hospital for venereal diseases where, in a dismal, grotesque atmosphere, a jovial colleague gives him a tour of wards fallen into utter decay.

One afternoon his young guide-interpreter, Natalya, brought him to an island to watch a tennis match between Cochet and the Soviet champion Kudriakh. And speaking of Natalya, he would later lead Karen Marie Jensen and Lucette Almansor to believe that he had managed to seduce her. According to him, Natalya even wanted to marry him to leave the Soviet Union legally, if only to divorce as soon as they arrived in France.

As could be expected, Louis also visited the Hermitage Museum, the esplanade of the Winter Palace, and the home of Nicholas II and his family. In *Bagatelles* again, he describes his shock, on the way back from Tsarskoy, the tsar's last palace, over the impertinence with which the guides harped on the absurdities of the ruling family. He mentioned this to Natalya. "This visit . . . to the victims' home . . . this exhibition of ghosts . . . embroidered with commentary, a thousand facetious remarks . . . The casual, snarling enumeration . . . pouncing on every little fault . . . poor taste . . . and obsession with 'Romanoff' absurdities . . . concerning their amulets, their rosaries, their chamber pots . . . She wouldn't admit . . . She thought it perfectly right, Natalya. I was insistent. Despite everything, it was from there, from those few rooms, that the Romanoffs all left together to their common fate . . . to be butchered in the cellar . . . One might consider . . . being mindful . . . No! As for me, I found it in bad taste! Even much worse than bad taste, a hundred times worse than all the Romanoffs together . . ." An argument arose. "I was beside myself! with brutishness! I became quite Russian! . . ."[14]

But most of all for Céline, Leningrad was dance and the Marinsky Theater (now the Kirov) for his delight. "The most beautiful theater in the world? The 'Marinsky,' of course! no contest! . . . It has no rival! . . . It alone is worth the whole trip! . . . It must seat at least 2,000 . . . It's in the Grand-Gaumont class . . . the Roxy . . . in capacity . . . But what style! . . . What a marvelous, unique achievement! . . . how dazzling! . . . Like a mammoth . . . perfection . . . nimble . . . unparalleled . . . a nimble mammoth . . . airy in its grace . . . done all up in sky blue, pastel streaked with silver."[15]

He attended a production of Tchaikovsky's *Queen of Spades* there (for we must attribute to Célinian exaggeration his claim to have attended six consecutive performances). "Among the dancers: two marvelous subjects . . . Lyricism, high technique, tragedy, real poets . . . The women? excellent artisans, very talented . . . no more . . . one ballerina excepted: Ulianova . . . But their ensembles? Divine! . . . Pipe organs of human movement. Swarms of ballerinas to fill the sky . . . Their pas de quatre? shimmering comets . . . the glimmering wellsprings of Dream . . . the edges of Illusion! . . . Every evening at the Marinsky!"[16]

He attempted to meet with the director of the theater to offer him his ballet *La Naissance d'une fée* [Birth of a Fairy], or at least so he claims in *Bagatelles pour un massacre* (where the ballet's scenario is published). The director apparently told him that his theme, unfortunately, was not "sozial" enough but that of course, another time, another subject, the following season, the Russians knew of his marvelous gifts, etc. A tall story? Not necessarily.

His journey came to an end on September 21, when the *Meknès* of the Compagnie Générale Transatlantique left Leningrad for London and Le Havre, where Céline disembarked four days later, on the 25th. He took a room at the Hôtel Frascati, where he was known, before returning to Paris shortly thereafter. He assessed his trip without mincing his words: "I'm just back from Russia, what a nightmare! what a disgraceful sham! what a nasty, stupid business! It is all so grotesque, theoretical and criminal!" he wrote immediately to Cillie.[17] He used the same tone in a letter to Karen Marie Jensen on October 15: "I was in Leningrad for a month. It is all so *mean*, appalling, unbelievably *foul*. You have to see it to believe it. A horror. *Dirty, poor—hideous*. A prison full of worms. All police, bureaucracy, and filthy chaos. All sham and tyranny. Anyway, I'll tell you all about it. I passed through Copenhagen on the boat and stayed for three hours! What a paradise after Russia!"[18]

Louis returned to a France that was slowly awakening from the euphoria of the spring and summer, mourning the loss of Major Charcot aboard the *Pourquoi pas?*, accepting with resignation the devaluation of the franc (the bill must be paid after the feast), and fretted over the ever more bloody civil war in Spain. Léon Blum was tormented by the question of whether or not to commit himself to the Spanish Republicans at the risk of triggering a European war. The tone was hardening in the papers, in Parliament, everywhere. The Right was decidedly not coming to terms with the Front Populaire; the extreme Right was just coming into full stride and fulminating against Blum in openly racist terms. Léon Daudet and Charles Maurras indulged joyfully and openly in anti-Semitism. *L'Action française* spoke of the "Cretin-Talmud cabinet" and raged against "the Jews in power." In this chaotic climate, the Salengro affair erupted. Over the summer, *L'Action française* and particularly *Gringoire* had relentlessly slandered the Minister of the Interior, accusing him of treason during the war. He committed suicide by gas on November 18, leaving a note by his side: "The strain and the calumny are too much. They, and sorrow, have defeated me."

In Paris, the backlash, controversy, and broadsides of insults surrounding *Mort à crédit* were finally tapering off. It was in that context that the incident with the magazine *Le Merle blanc* took place. Though it was essentially unimportant, Céline was nonetheless particularly vulnerable to it, exhausted and depressed as he was upon his return from the USSR. Following Pierre Scize's laudatory article on *Mort à crédit*, a reader from Biarritz named Etcheverry had written to the satirical weekly a letter so savage that he challenged the editors to dare publish it—the letter, of course, appeared in its entirety in the September 26 issue. According to Etcheverry, workers found Céline disgusting, a charlatan of smut. "Céline is darkness, hatred, fury, disgraceful, loathsome cowardice before life, mud, shit. . . . When one writes what Céline has written, one does not broadcast it: one commits suicide. I am waiting for Céline's suicide. . . . Céline: to be eliminated—and the first—on the day when, having been stabbed in the back by idealism, we'll do the same to bastards like him who, not content with disgusting us, live off us, vultures starved for any pleasure."[19]

The writer's riposte, also published in full, appeared in the next issue on October 3, backed up by a eulogistic editorial under the by-line of Chatelain-Tailhade, who emphasized the "vast, dissembled tenderness of Bardamu" and again spoke of the writer's solitude, his rejection of the star system. Céline himself emphasized his solitude, far from cliques or parties, and he took the call to murder him very seriously indeed. We can detect what might be called the earliest evidence of his persecution complex, aggravated by the criticism of *Mort à crédit*, which had shaken him badly. Céline in turn evinced a savagery to which his writings would soon give free rein: "Anyone who wants to kill me is free to! perfectly free! I'm not in hiding. I have no police protection. . . . What struck me in that letter, Etcheverry, was its demonstrative value. It finally represents the full attitude of the criticism directed at me, the cowardly propaganda of partisans. If they were all lucky enough to be anonymous like Etcheverry, they would all write pretty much just like Etcheverry. They're more visible, so they have to be more crafty, but it comes to the same thing in the end! As soon as a man thinks he's safe, hidden, he shows himself for what he really is in the depths of his soul. An ass and a murderer."[20]

And 1936 was coming to end. On October 10 Louis recorded with SACEM (Société d'auteurs, compositeurs et musiciens) a song entitled À noeud coulant [Slipknot]. Just as he wrote ballets, he also amused himself writing two or three popular songs about gangsters or sailors, the illusory exoticism of ports and the underworld, a pastime that sheds some light on one facet of his personality. Not having the least rudiments of music, he had made up the melody as he went along. As he could not register under his name with SACEM (not being a professional musician, known and licensed), his friend from Montmartre, Jean Noceti, claimed its official paternity.

On December 2 Charles Gervais directed a single performance of *L'Église* at the Théâtre des Célestins in Lyons. Its success (a euphemism) was not such as to encourage the company to extend the run. Céline hadn't even bothered to attend, which was probably just as well.[21]

On his return from the USSR, while his British friend John Marks translated the ballet *La Naissance d'une fée* in a vain attempt to get it performed in London, Louis resumed his medical and pharmaceutical activities, with a brief distraction in Antwerp on December 6 and 7. Mostly he plunged into the feverish writing of his short anti-communist pamphlet, *Mea culpa*. His work was barely interrupted by Gallimard's publication on December 7 of an anthology of Renaudot prize-winners, entitled *Neuf plus un* [Nine Plus One] to commemorate the prize's tenth anniversary, and in which Céline's *Secrets dans l'île* [Secrets in the Island] appeared. This curious text should be noted in passing: a sketchy film treatment which the producer Pierre Billon briefly considered bringing to the screen in 1943, it is set in that imaginary Brittany of wind, moors, boulders, and passion, through which floats a beautiful foreigner, rich in grace, nimbleness, and love, leaving jealousy, vengeance, and horror in her wake.

In those days, recalls André Pulicani, a friend of Gen Paul's who had met Céline in the painter's studio, the pamphlets of the journalist Henri Béraud were all the rage. One day, Céline turned to Pulicani and asked him: "Do you think I measure up to Béraud?" Céline went on to regale his friends with the story of his stay in Leningrad. His scornful, ferocious truculence turned the epic voyage into a journey to the end of grotesque horror.

There came to Montmartre one day a certain M. Braun, the Soviet consul general in Paris, seeking to gather the writer's impressions upon his return from Russia. Céline received him with great courtesy and a no lesser caution.

At that point, as Pulicani recalls it, the "Consul—who had nothing Slavic about him—felt encouraged enough to reveal to Ferdinand the extent to which Moscow appreciated everything he wrote. The proof was in the publication and wide distribution of the Russian version of *Voyage*. Monsieur Braun was equally eager to read the fine pages which Céline could not fail to write on Soviet Russia. The diplomat did not forget to drop a subtle hint about the number of readers represented by vast Russia. The great writer's next work, he stated, would be translated as soon as published, and would guarantee the writer substantial royalties.

"I had a fine time of it, knowing that Céline, a pure and upright man without needs, without vice, without a car, without a maid, drinking only water and not a smoker, was one of the very rare beings on whom no one had a hold, a man who could not be bought."[22]

In order to write *Mea culpa*, Céline abandoned the new books he was already thinking of undertaking, *Casse-Pipe* and *Honny soit*, which are described as "forthcoming" on the flyleaf of *Mea culpa*, released by Denoël on December 28 and supplemented by *Semmelweis*, the first commercial publication of his medical thesis.

Casse-Pipe was the description of his years as a cuirassier in Rambouillet from 1912 to 1914, *Honny soit* (which would eventually appear under the title *Guignol's band*), of his years in London in 1915 and 1916; in a word, everything that had long been on his mind, that he had hoped to be able to include in his first two novels and which, in a way, filled the narrative gaps in the novelistic sequence of his life as he had undertaken it. As we saw earlier, he had already compiled ample documentation for *Honny soit* from Joseph Garcin and others. He must have written the first pages of *Casse-Pipe* in the summer or fall of '36. But his heart wasn't in it. The critical reception of *Mort à crédit* had not only given him ulcers, it had also temporarily discouraged him. So much work, so much effort put into the style, and for what? For all those misreadings? His trip to Leningrad had managed to distract him—or to distance him from a new and imminent novelistic project. For the first time, he—the silent, solitary one who avoided any political and public stance—felt the urgent need to speak out. He had been attacked once too often. The hypocrisy of the Left, which he saw as self-congratulation with an incorrigibly clear conscience, had become unbearable. He had seen Russia, he had just returned. The bankruptcy of the Soviet system justified all his fears, all his ideas. For the first time he did not spend months and years over a carefully crafted and cadenced text, with its rhythms and transports. It took him a mere two or three weeks to complete his work. He felt himself to be the bearer of a message. He wanted to deliver it, and himself from it.

In his anger, Céline seems to suffocate, to lose his footing, his breath, and occasionally his train of thought. His images clash and bounce off one another. Ellipses proliferate between sentences and words, like so many vast silences, hostile, hissing, panting. What, in essence, was Céline trying to tell us? First, there is no question here of anti-Semitism, personal attacks, dance, or ballet, nor of any of the excrescences found in *Bagatelles* and thereafter. Only one subject is dealt with—communism—and not even a precise description of his journey (as Gide had provided), and little information; it was simply an attack on the principles of communism alone. It gave Céline the opportunity to return to one of his obsessions: the cruelty or egoism dwelling in the heart of every individual.

His attack on the communists is no rallying cry to the bourgeois order, however. He is equitably intent on chucking the conservatives along with the people's commissars into the wastebasket of history—and his own literature.

Why is Céline not a leftist? Because he does not believe in progress, in the "inherent" goodness of humanity, the masses. Because he believes only in the individual, a ghostly individual, miserable and violent, who needs to rely on a misery more awful than his own in order to convince himself that he is not completely wretched, in order to rejoice. Céline condenses in more abstract form the entire thrust of *Voyage* and *Mort à crédit*. From the moment that society promises man a perfectly egalitarian system with equally distributed well-being; from the moment when humanity, one's neighbor, one's rival, cease to act as a counterbalance to all one's own miseries; in a word, from the moment that "others" vanish, each man is condemned to his own hell (to use Sartre's famous image). And at that moment, without a doubt, communism becomes a nightmare. It is too antithetical to every basic impulse. Consequently, it is a failure, an appalling failure, since it goes without saying that fundamental individualism cannot be suppressed in the Soviet Union. "A rabid, bitter, muttering, undefeatable egoism saturates, penetrates and further corrupts that atrocious misery, oozing every which way and making it fouler than ever."

But one has to lie, one has to defend the system, which Céline sums up in the formula "Cleansing by Idea"—a cleansing in the name of progress, of bright tomorrows, of determined optimism. "Massacres by the millions—every war since the Flood has had Optimism as its musical accompaniment. Every assassin sees a rosy future, that's part of the job. So be it."[23]

Who today would dare contradict Céline, in our great débâcle of illusions and ideologies? But in late 1936, ideologies were on the rise, to the Left and to the Right. People went to battle armed with "isms"—fascism, communism, socialism—they were polishing their weapons for the great exegesis of war, each man raised Optimism as his banner, and Céline was not understood. *Mea culpa*'s publication barely caused a ripple. The book should be read and reread today.

Ballets and Bagatelles

In early 1937 Bernard Steele sold his share to his partner, Robert Denoël, now the sole master of the ship. As of January 25, then, the official name of the company was Éditions Denoël, and no longer Denoël and Steele.

The house had as yet no reason to complain of its star writer, Céline. *Mea culpa* had admittedly not provoked any significant critical reaction; one favorable article by Jean-Pierre Maxence in *Gringoire* on January 19 and that was about it. The book would nonetheless sell nearly 20,000 copies (the announced run: 25,000; copies sold by the end of the war: 28,435). But the two important novels continued in particular to attract readers, and the sales of foreign rights were growing. After the translation of *Mort à crédit* in Germany and Czechoslovakia, and a new edition of *Voyage* in America, translations of *Mea culpa* into German, English, and Spanish were announced, as well as a Polish translation of *Mort à crédit*. In February Céline left for New York for about three weeks. Not much is known about this trip. It may have been during the crossing aboard the *Champlain* or on some other journey that he became friendly with Jean Gabin and ran into Danielle Darrieux. And it may have been on the return trip that he met Jane Bowles, the wife of the American writer Paul Bowles, author of *The Sheltering Sky*, who influenced such writers as Gore Vidal and Truman Capote. "She traveled a good deal," her husband recalls. "One day, on a ship, she had a little adventure with Céline. I have never read Céline myself. I'm too lazy, and his language is too difficult. I tried *Guignol's band*, but no. As for Jane, she was sitting one day reading *Voyage* in a deck chair on the bridge of an ocean liner sailing from New York to Le Havre. A man came along, approached her and said, 'Oh, you're reading Céline?' 'Yes, as you see.' And the guy answered, 'Well, I'm Céline.' They spent the rest of the trip talking. She found him very nice."[24]

In New York for the third time, Céline no longer knew many people. Elizabeth Craig had vanished somewhere in California. He probably visited with Louise Nevelson, whom he had met returning from his last trip. Of course he was still fascinated by chorus girls, a gold-spangled mirage syncopated by the great jazz bands. He spent many an evening at Radio City Music Hall and frequented the American School of Ballet, as he told Karen Marie Jensen. He went on: "Otherwise, I found New York greatly changed. Not nearly as arrogant as it used to be. Americanism has disappeared. They're following the same revolting path as Europe. They're completely in tow to Europe and the Jews, from strike to strike and the demagogy of revolution, which can't be far at this rate. The great American era is definitely over."[25]

While he was in New York, Lucette moved into rue Lepic. It was the first time since Elizabeth's departure that a woman was prepared to share his life. For it was a kind of emotional upheaval and, in a way, a guarantee of stability. Lucette's parents had by then begun divorce proceedings and the young dancer, upset by the oppressive atmosphere of the family home, had accepted Céline's offer to move in while he was away. He had left her a blank check and smothered her with affectionate advice. On his return, of course, she remained with him. She recalls: "I had a tiny room overlooking the rue d'Orchampt. The kitchen couldn't have been more than five feet long, and also served as the bathroom. A cleaning lady came every so often. Louis didn't want anyone to touch his papers. We didn't have a very bourgeois lifestyle nor a particularly comfortable one. We never went to the restaurant. No dinners with friends. I've never seen someone so possessed by his work, what with his practice and his books. Sometimes, on Sundays, we'd go to Saint-Germain-en-Laye. We'd take a walk, get back on the train, and he was back at work."

Much has been said of the writer's supposed sexual impotence at an early age. Supporting this theory is an enigmatic letter by Céline to his friend Marcel Brochard, written at the time he was working on *Voyage*, in which he blurts: "How's your health, pal, still keeping it up? This is the 'dangerous' age."[26] Brochard interprets this letter as a reference to the writer's ("dangerous") impotence. The truth is that Céline—whom his parents had had circumcised as a child, whether for health or medical reasons is unknown— was more of a voyeur than a participant, as we have seen and as he himself said quite openly. He was easily bored by lovemaking, at least with the same partner. Some critics have also sought to see Céline's impotence in the panting style of his pamphlets, as if the writer, seized by a febrile and frustrated rage, wanted in some way to recapture in writing, in spasms and volleys of words and insults, some grotesque and vain power to take the world and rape it in breathless and aggressive rancor. But facts are stubborn. Céline was not impotent. He was growing indifferent—which is not at all the same thing—a decadent spectator of sex between others, of female homosexuality in particular, a lover himself from time to time, briefly. There is also another explanation. Céline, as he confided to certain close friends, didn't want to waste his energy on sex. This attitude has a rather Oriental tinge to it. He wanted to focus himself on one goal: writing. We must therefore see his writing not as a confession of frustrated impotence but, on the contrary, as the eruption of a highly focused energy.

Sex, spectacle, dream . . . There is no doubt that his taste for dance was connected to such fantasies. Céline also wanted to see himself as a fairy tale writer, light-handed and graceful, a teller of tales. He had churned up reality in *Voyage* and *Mort à crédit*, nurtured his fears, grasped the world in its saddest and truest palpitations. But there was another side to Céline, the one that was dazzled by the intoxicating lights, glitter, and fantasy of spectacle, the one that enjoyed theater, musical comedy, vaudeville, just for a moment, no more, a distraction, a sense of well-being, a lie. And it was that Céline who had written two plays before attempting any other literary venture, as if to reconcile the magic of the stage and the horror of his universe; who stubbornly wrote outlines to ballets, as if he desperately wished to get a hold on the chimerical world of dance, enter the looking glass, give life and substance to his imagination, compel his dream into reality. A whim? No, far more than that. The search for an easing of his suffering, a respite from his viselike obsession with death, a little music and a little silence away from the droning world. In a word, a desperate attempt at being happy.

After the jolts of *Mort à crédit*, and faced with the political and warlike storms gathering all over Europe, Céline needed a little respite, some magic. He had already written several ballets and the enchanting and tragic screenplay *Secrets dans l'île*. On his return from America, in the new connubial life he had undertaken with the young and graceful Lucette Almansor, he conceived and wrote a new ballet, *Voyou Paul. Brave Virginie* [Hoodlum Paul. Gentle Virginia] and, close behind, a song, "Règlement," which he brought into SACEM on March 21 under the same conditions as the last, with Jean Noceti to sign his name to the music.

He was hoping to see the ballet eventually performed at the great International Fair of Arts and Technology that was to display its pomp in Paris from May to November. He therefore offered it to the appropriate committees, but without success. Another hard knock, another source of bitterness, another grudge against the Front Populaire, which the Right endlessly attacked and harangued and which the writer was beginning in turn to blame for all his troubles. The Front Populaire was too jingoistic and powerless against Hitler's threats, too complacent toward the communism infiltrating it, too obtuse regarding economic realities, too progressive as far as Céline, who didn't care for progress and didn't believe in it, was concerned. The Front Populaire, with its Léon Blum was, finally, too Jewish—"Jewish," the key word (along with communism) that crystallized all the writer's fears, hatreds, and rejections.

The letters written to Karen Marie Jensen in early 1937 testify to his new, dismayed state of mind and to the way in which the Jews somehow explained the apocalyptic times for which he was preparing himself. Thus, on

April 5: "In Russia it's awful! that verminous shit heap! a hundred times worse than the Poles! The Jews will finally win out everywhere—the Asiatic avant-garde, their triumph will be brief! Whites will vanish! overcome by avarice, egoism, alcoholism, and serve them right! What a mess! I'm not speaking of the USA—everything's already in utter decay over there—and at what speed! Prodigious!

"Here in Clichy I'm surrounded by assassins, as you can imagine. I don't go out anymore. I only see Gen Paul. But the Jews and communists are becoming more and more arrogant—the time may not be far off when I'll have to flee or die. Unfortunately I have very little money. I can't sell my house—no buyers."[27]

The ballets, as we have seen, were to be a compensation, a promise of happiness. To Karen, on April 30: "I still love dancers. That's all I love, really. Everything else I find horrible."[28] He who refuses you happiness logically inspires you with undying hatred. The Russians, the French, the English, and the Americans had one by one rejected Céline's ballets. He would therefore despise the Russians, the French, the English, and the Americans—or to simplify matters with the lowest common denominator, he would despise the Jews.

On May 4, then, President of the Republic Albert Lebrun opened the Paris World Exhibition. The plaster had barely dried on the new Palais de Chaillot, designed in the taste of the day with its Stalino-Nazi architectural aesthetic. As for the French contributions, nothing was ready. It would take another month. Blum could galvanize the workers all he wanted with his speeches on the rightful pride France would take in their labors and efforts; they themselves clung tenaciously to their forty-hour week, they struck at a moment's notice—and who dared blame them (other than the Right)? It was *Je suis partout* and *L'Action française*, it was Maurras and Rebatet, it was Brasillach and the rest who laughed up their sleeves and spotlighted the carelessness and confusion of the new leaders. "The Eiffel Tower is ready, so is the Seine," they jeered on the opening day. The Japanese, Italian, and German pavilions had been at the ready since March. A sinister alliance. Across from the Nazis, the Soviet Union had raised its pavilion in a conquering architecture suggestive of bright tomorrows. As a challenge? Or to prefigure a certain August 23, 1939, the date when Comrades Molotov and Ribbentrop signed the sinister Nazi-Soviet nonaggression pact on the backs of Poland and the Western democracies? The Spanish pavilion was preparing to display Picasso's *Guernica*, the sublime response to the bombing by Heinkels and Stukas of the little Basque-Spanish capital on April 26 in which more than 1,500 civilians had perished.

The French could be carried away by the vaporous, seductive, and hardly picturesque flights of fancy of Dufy's *La Fée Électricité*, spread out over 600 square meters. But they were not to see Céline's ballets. Nor Céline himself, who left in early May for Saint-Malo and Jersey, where Lucette was supposed to meet him. He left the Exhibition to the "dreaming bourgeoisie," whose ineluctable decadence had recently been the subject of an elegant novel by Drieu la Rochelle, or to the people of Paris of whom, after all, he was one, and of whom Maurice Chevalier sang in *La P'tite Femme de l'Expo*. The only World's Fair that Céline cared to remember was that of 1900, the one he had glimpsed while trotting behind his grandmother, the one that had inaugurated modern times and nightmare, that had marked the end of any pleasure in being alive.

The trip to Jersey was to take a tragicomic turn: after the abdication of Edward VIII—who, now just a common Duke of Windsor, was free to marry the divorcée of his heart, Mrs. Wallis Warfield-Simpson, in France on June 3—the English were preparing to crown their new king, George VI, on May 12. The police were watching over the four corners of the United Kingdom, hunting down suspects and expelling undesirables out of fear of assassination and embarrassing incidents. In Jersey, where Céline had gotten it into his head to check out the territory and seek a refuge in the event of a European or world war—of whose imminence he was now convinced—the Bobbies were also on a state of alert. What was he up to, this dubious Frenchman with his large, bright, slightly crazy eyes, his tousled mop of hair, his weird and disjointed appearance, this solitary, taciturn, and suspicious Frenchman snooping all over the place? The agents of Scotland Yard didn't waste a moment and brought him in on the spot. Better safe than sorry. It required the intervention of the French consul, M. Delalande, to put things back in order. A few days later Céline wrote to Robert Denoël:

"You almost lost an author! I was deemed so suspicious on my arrival here that Scotland Yard put me in quarantine, practically under arrest, took my passport, etc. Luckily, the Consul was warned and identified me straight away. He recognized me from Rennes and Brittany! Even so, the cops didn't want their prey to get away . . . We had to fight and struggle for my freedom! and I had come looking for possible refuge!

"My papers were scrutinized and, worst of all, deciphered, interpreted . . . and how! They suspected me of having accomplices on the island . . . a plot to kill the King! My face, my hair, everything worked against me!"[29]

Louis therefore met Lucette in Saint-Malo. They returned to Paris but did not stay long on rue Lepic. For Céline, any excuse was good to travel, to get away from the Clichy clinic where, since *Mea culpa*, relations had been more strained than ever with the head doctor, Grégoire Ichok, whose strong leftist sympathies were known to everyone. In July he moved into the Hôtel Frascati, into a garret room overlooking the port. Lucette, of course, was with him.

And it was there that, in less than a month, he wrote the greater part of *Bagatelles pour un massacre*, feverishly, rabidly, anxiously, a disordered writing at top speed, without regrets, without caution, without moderation, without order—like a whim, a fit of anger, a warning, a declaration of hatred, a delirium out of control, a deep chuckle that racked him like a sob, a hint of farce, irresponsible comments, gratuitous, smutty, occasionally

fantastical, the great unpacking of his grudges, past humiliations, bitter-
nesses, his petty bourgeois fantasies, the unbearable aftereffects of the
auditory hallucinations and headaches that isolated him from the world and
from a clear perspective of things. This confession book, this awful book,
would long haunt him like a curse, but at the time he wrote it as a maledic-
tion on others, all others, the Jews, the communists, the Freemasons, the
Russians and—why not?—the entire world: in a word, *Bagatelles pour un
massacre!*

Lucette remembers. He sometimes gave her pages to read, by the armful.
This time he wasn't going to spend three years weighing each comma,
ellipsis, and the *mot juste*. In one outpouring and have done with it! The war,
with its processions of dead, was drawing closer. He had already done his
bit. He had become a die-hard pacifist. And if he had to shout "Long live
Hitler," well, he was ready to shout it. Or to scream "Down with the Jews,"
OK, he could be counted on. Better yet, he'd set the example. He was in tune
with the times. France, in the main, was anti-Semitic, with that widespread,
mediocre anti-Semitism, almost visceral like the fear of the future and the
rejection of "the other," that anti-Semitism fed with nauseating demagogery
for nearly a century by a propagandist press that often tossed it out casually
like a mere rhetorical device. But he was louder and even more irresponsible. His shout became so excessive that he ended up treating it like a game;
a shout that became almost an affectation; a shout that came to resemble
bagatelles. And bravo for bagatelles if they could prevent a massacre! This
was one of his great certainties, his disturbing aberration, one is tempted to
say his *grande illusion*, to borrow the title of Jean Renoir's film that was
playing that very year of 1937, adopting the same pacifist point of view.

Thus, Lucette read, telling him: "But you don't realize, you're hanging a
millstone around your neck." He answered: "Idiot! They're all going to kill
each other, it's going to be an awful mess." And Lucette: "But you're the first
they're going to knock off, the first to be assassinated." He looked at her,
incredulous. He imagined that the whole world, yes, the whole world would
thank him for such a book. "At least," he told her after a pause, "I'll have
done something."

After Le Havre came Saint-Malo, where Céline continued to work on
Bagatelles through August. He felt more or less at ease in that town which he
loved, being closest to his double ancestry in the Cotentin and Brittany.
There, he was the guest of Marie Le Bannier, the old lover of his former
father-in-law, Athenase Follet, and a woman with whom he was still on very
friendly terms. He was very attached to her adopted daughter, little Sergine,
who was not yet ten at the time and still recalls the mysterious and affectionate Dr. Destouches, that strange grown-up who used string to hold up
his trousers and anchor his pocketwatch, who would take her on his knee
and compete in games of spitting in each other's faces. Marie Le Bannier had
a fine, terraced apartment in the old Franklin mansion, a stone's throw from
the ramparts, beyond the walls on the Paramé road.

While Céline wrote with increasing febrility, in a little storeroom he used for an office, overlooking the sea (a panorama that was becoming indispensable, like a drug, leavening his visions and deliria), Lucette persevered with her stretching and dance exercises for hours on end. A dancer's training can brook no interruption. In Montmartre, at Sigmaringen, in Denmark, everywhere, Lucette would continue her exercises. Better yet, she had just landed an engagement at the Dinard casino that summer. She had gone to the manager with a proposal for a show, and he had given her carte blanche. She performed seven or eight numbers of her choice, about one every half-hour, as entertainment over the course of an evening. Henri Mahé's first wife, a native of Brittany who happened to know the Follets and was a talented musician, accompanied her on the accordion. The two women occasionally took a little boat as a shortcut between Saint-Malo and Dinard. If a gale arose late in the evening, the pilot would refuse to set out for Saint-Malo, and the two women would spend the night where they were. And Céline—who hated casinos, who hated gambling as he did liquor, tobacco, and overeating—was furious.

He was both jealous and possessive, but would admit to neither. He had made no promises to Lucette, nor had he demanded any from her. The concept of conjugal or marital fidelity was alien to him. His life with Lucette would not stop him from meeting—though ever less frequently, to be sure—with Évelyne Pollet, as one example. He had asked the young dancer only to curtail her regular visits to her family. His attachment was to a certain extent exclusive. Lucette had entered his world but he had locked the doors behind her. He was not prepared to welcome in anyone else. Similarly, there was no question of their having a child. To what purpose, since any future was precluded and the worst was sure to come? But nothing could have persuaded him to perform an abortion. If Lucette had found herself pregnant—by him or anyone else—he would have asked her to keep the child, more out of respect for life, because of his personal morality, than out of medical conscience.

In September he returned to his regular work schedule in Paris. He finished the last pages of *Bagatelles* at this time. A new ballet, *Van Bagaden*, to round off the work, a final melancholy fairy tale set at one of those nineteenth-century Flemish feasts, a mournful farandole in Antwerp, with its drunks, its painted banners, gay lotharios and inconsolable lovers, and that was it, it was over.

He submitted the work to his publisher. Together, they came up with the publicity wrapper: "For a good laugh in the trenches," and with the short blurb published in *La Bibliographie de la France* on December 3, 1937: "The most atrocious, the most savage, the most hateful, but the most unbelievable lampoon the world has ever seen." Ever the superlatives, but for once they were appropriate.

Céline was well aware that his situation at the Clichy clinic would become untenable, what with a leftist municipality and the administration of a head doctor of Jewish descent, after the publication of *Bagatelles pour un massacre*. For this time he had cast his mask aside, loudly proclaiming his anti-Semitism and dislike of communism. He therefore took the initiative and, on December 11, wrote to the mayor of Clichy to tender his resignation as attending physician of the municipal clinic, a post he had held for almost nine years. Shortly thereafter he quit his job at the La Biothérapie laboratory for the same reasons.

And on December 28, the 379 pages of the outrageous lampoon were put on sale, at twenty-seven francs. At this point there is no evading the question that always haunts readers of Céline: what logic or lack of it had impelled the author of *Voyage* to throw himself into the prewar political and racist fray? The question immediately raises others: Was the climate of the day favorable to such excess? How was *Bagatelles pour un massacre* received?

12

Phony Peace, Phony War

Racism, Ordinary and Extraordinary
The School for Anti-Semitism
War Forever Renewed
The Rout

Racism, Ordinary and Extraordinary

France was largely anti-Semitic before the war. Lucien Rebatet, an expert, stated it, and Robert Brasillach sanctimoniously elaborated upon it in *Notre Avant-guerre* in 1941: "Blum's accession to ministerial power even revived a movement almost unseen in France since the Dreyfus Affair—I am speaking of anti-Semitism."[1] Was this their way of justifying, and banalizing racism? Perhaps. But the facts remain, and sociologists and historians of the Third Republic or of anti-Semitism in France will confirm it: the lower-middle and working classes, the Camelots du Roi, and even certain communists or ex-communists of Doriot's Parti Populaire Français were often anti-Semitic, instinctively, out of habit. There was no ideology in their attitude. Nazi theories were and continued to be foreign and incomprehensible to them. Their anti-Semitism was primarily a question of a reflex, a mood; of ill-humor, of immediate advantage and smug chauvinism.

Blum's accession to power, then, rekindled in many their xenophobic tendencies, a latent hatred of Jews all the more readily expressed since it involved no commitment, since France had not seen pogroms or mass persecution for centuries. It was therefore easy to rant, requiring little thought. One could proclaim one's fear of war, disgust with politics, rejection of disorder, indignation against politicians, resentment of poverty, all thanks to the most visible and eternal scapegoat: the Jew. Blum in power was a godsend. It explained everything. There was no need to seek any further, beyond the Rhine, or to worry about Adolf Hitler's bellicose provocations, no need to pity the persecuted Jews seeking refuge in France, no need to be political. Anti-Semitism was the easiest and foulest reaction, and thus the one most often used.

Of course, the politicians and intellectuals set the example. We can always count on them. Xavier Vallat in the Chambre des Députés ironically hailed the day that "an ancient Gallo-Roman country" first acquired a Jewish leader. Town Counselor Darquier de Pellepoix ran a viciously anti-Semitic journal, *La France enchaînée*, and demanded, to even things with the Front Populaire, that a street be named after the rightist Édouard Drumont. *Gringoire*, which had exposed itself by driving Salengro to suicide, repeated the offense by compiling a list of Jewish ministers, cabinet aides, and departmental heads in Blum's government. The weekly *Je suis partout*, founded in 1930 by Arthème Fayard and originally run by Pierre Gaxotte, prepared a special issue in April 1938 on the Jews of the world. It would do a similar issue in 1939 on Jews in France, striving for precise guidelines for a legal definition of the Jews. In a word, *Je suis partout* laid the groundwork. Soon Hitler would only have to come in and complete the work already begun.

Anti-Semitism had experienced a lull during the Great War. Hatred of Germany leveled differences. There was a natural integration of the Jews into the national community. But very soon, the Soviet's rise to power awakened one form of anti-Semitism. France had to protect itself against the "Jewish" Bolshevism, against Trotsky and his ilk, that threatened Europe. It was a short step from there to claiming as Caillaux did in his *Mémoires* that "the Jew, in whatever sphere of work, carries within him a taste for destruction and a hunger for domination,"[2] and that set the ball rolling again.

From the 1920s on, the press—*L'Action française, La Liberté, Le Petit Parisien*—set the tone. Albert Londres, in *L'Excelsior*, wrote ironically of the new masters of the Kremlin, the Jews, who were preparing the massacres that would drown the world in blood. The theme of England Judaized, an egoistic England wrapped up in its own interests, its colonial empire, favoring Germany over France, would also become a leitmotiv of the political discourse of the Right. *Le Régime d'Israël chez les Anglo-Saxons* [Israel's Rule over the Anglo-Saxons], the title of a 1921 work by Roger Lambelin, a follower of Maurras and the French translator of the *Protocols of the Elders of Zion*, needs no commentary. The Jewish bankers of the City, with Lloyd George wrapped around their finger, were behind an international plot that obviously included the United States. Seeing Hitler's threat take shape, they would soon be clamoring for war against Germany, naturally dragging in France, that ready-made supply of cannon fodder. Such were their theories and litanies. Blum would soon become their ideal target as he wavered between his peaceable desire to oppose Hitler's maneuverings and the policy of rearmament, which he never fully carried through. The nationalization of industry and aircraft factories had thrown France's military potential into disarray. To sum up: by late 1937, anti-Semitism was taken for granted throughout France.

And on the intellectual side, Barrès, Valéry, Léon Daudet, Maurras and several others had already more than revealed themselves as Drumont's followers during the Dreyfus Affair. Jouhandeau and Gide had been firmly anti-Semitic, as had Claudel and Léautaud; Giraudoux would follow suit. Before the 1930s, Bernanos had declared himself essentially a Drumont disciple. More insidiously—and Léon Poliakov pointed this out very clearly in his *Histoire de l'antisémitisme*—there existed an image of the Jew in the French novel of the period, a vehicle for every commonplace of the more or less acknowledged and more or less conscious anti-Semitism of French ideology. It represented the Jew as either ugly, Levantine, or as a profaner of the Christian religion; either his nose was hooked, his ears flapping, or his lips thick; he might also possess the unnerving Oriental mildness of his race. In a word, he was striking for his *otherness*. One need only reread, among others, Jouhandeau, Mauriac, Martin du Gard, Pierre Benoît, Georges Duhamel, or Jacques de Lacretelle.

In his earlier books, Céline had not succumbed to such commonplaces. There was nothing in *Voyage* and nothing in *Mort à crédit* to feed this crude, trite, even unconscious racism. Not one Jewish character appears in these novels. Moreover, in *Mort à crédit*, the author makes fun of Ferdinand's father, that grotesque and vociferous anti-Semitic loser, a reader of Drumont, winded by his own pathetic grudges. The Jews in *L'Église*? They were not personalized, they were merely stick-figures, symbolic characters, abstractions, ideas—one way for Céline to write about the Jews (in a style already polemical) as the secret masters of high-level politics, of the League of Nations, of the world; basically a disturbing little tirade and nothing worse.

And then came *Bagatelles pour un massacre*.

How does one become a racist, how does one come to commit such absolute crimes against the spirit as racial discrimination and defamation, and more specifically, anti-Semitism? Each individual, of course, lives with his or her own contradictions, his or her own zones of shadow and light. It would be singularly naive to claim to be able to explain every facet of a personality, to reveal every reason behind a person's behavior. History, sociology, psychology, and psychoanalysis are helpless before it. There exists within each of us a solid core of unyielding opacity. We can only orbit around it and try to shed light on merely fragmentary aspects of that mysterious (and dubious) unity known as man. In the case of Céline and his anti-Semitism, several answers allow only a part of the enigma to be dispelled.

1. Céline's anti-Semitism goes back to his earliest childhood. The world before Dreyfus, before the 1900 World's Fair, represented to him an imaginary and thus perfect paradise. His father insisted that the Jews were the cause of every evil and every decline. If the lace market was no longer viable, for example, it was the fault of the Jews. How could such ideas fail to leave marks on the consciousness of the teenager, the adult? From his childhood, anti-Semitism had been banalized, a thing coeval with his entry into life, into awareness, i.e., into the feeling of death. From there to associating the Jews with the very concept of decadence . . .

2. At the heart of all forms of anti-Semitism we must seek out the personal hatreds, bitterness, and humiliations that the individual then raises to the level of generalized assumptions, as if to justify his or her own failures, to find the pettiest, easiest, most across-the-board revenge. Why should Céline have been immune to this petty-bourgeois attitude? He had felt himself barred, rejected, at the League of Nations, where his mentor, Ludwig Rajchman, ran the Health Section. At the Clichy clinic, Grégoire Ichok had

usurped what he considered to be his rightful place. Elizabeth Craig, whom he adored, had left him for an American whom he suspected of being of Jewish descent. The Soviets, all Jews in his eyes (though Stalin had already begun to liquidate his rivals), had rejected his ballets. The Left rallying around Léon Blum had blasted *Mort à crédit*. And there was no question of producing his ballet at the 1937 World Exhibition. It was too much. It was intolerable. It was a conspiracy. It was the group against the man alone, the Jews against Céline. Something had to be done!

3. The writer's anti-Semitism was connected to the pacifist trend of the times. Anything rather than war! As Léon Poliakov wrote in his dissertation of this widely shared idea, "was it conceivable that, threatened as he was by Hitler, the international Jew should not seek to encourage a general mobilization? Consequently, death to the Jew."[3] Thus, the frantic Céline, wounded in '14 and having retained an hallucinatory image of the war, was inclined toward any excess if it could prevent further massacres. The most striking pages of *Bagatelles*, and especially of *L'École des cadavres*, develop that obsession:

"Above all, war must be avoided. War, for us as we are, means the end of the show, the final tilt into the Jewish charnel house.

"The same stubbornness in resisting war as the Jews display in dragging us into it. The Jews are motivated by a fearful, talmudic, unanimous tenacity, an infernal perseverance, and we oppose them only with a few groans.

"We will go to the Jewish war. We are only fit to die."

And Poliakov notes: "Here, the demented style expresses terrors that were no less real for being demented, and which one need not have been anti-Semitic to share."[4]

In short, Céline could have dedicated *Bagatelles* to his friends with the same inscription penned by Bernanos to Jacques Vallery-Radot on his copy of *Grands Cimetières sous la lune*: "I'd like to throw this book into the starving faces of idiots to prevent them from devouring the world."

4. To be astonished by Céline's racist theories is to forget the public health specialist he had always been. The author of *Voyage au bout de la nuit* remained obsessed with the idea of decadence. A "bastardized" France, alcoholic Frenchmen with otiose digestions—these were scourges he had long denounced. The distance is not that great between certain developments in his novels and the arguments in his political writings. Everywhere we find the same obsession with race, the Chinese in France, the death of civilization, etc. Hitler's concepts of the chosen people, the Aryan people, pure blood, discipline, and public health found fertile ground in him, ready-tilled.

5. Analyzing communist ideology in *Mea culpa*, Céline had demonstrated the danger of any system that draws up plans for a rosy future, forcing men to be happy according to its personal vision of progress. The supreme imposture, he believed, is hope. For it is hope that seeks out hostages and

condemns them, that inspires acts of revenge, that fills the gulags. Steeped in misery, Céline had up to then bound himself to the narrow attitude that consisted foremost in denouncing the imposture of all rebellion, that is, of all hope. Man was cursed. Progress was a mirage. And it was this not easily tenable position that he abruptly renounced when war threatened, when an existential misery was faced with the imminence of historical, if not to say planetary catastrophe. In his pamphlets everything seems to indicate that Céline had succumbed to hope, had finally found an explanation of the evils he had been denouncing. Jews, communists, and Freemasons could now be shown up for what they were, the problem with everything. "Aryan idiocy" did the rest. The passengers aboard the *Admiral-Bragueton* in *Voyage*, all those indigent, sickly, worn-out, humiliated people doing their best to slander the narrator, to create someone even more miserable than themselves, simply for entertainment, comfort, and a momentary escape from their own nightmare—Céline had shown them up in his first two novels. And now he had gone over to their side. He sought and found his scapegoats, as if he were unable to escape his fear, to bear his skeptical solitude any longer, as if he needed answers at any price.

6. One last point. We must always keep in mind the image of a Céline wounded, solitary, isolated by the humming in his ears, his headaches, his auditory hallucinations. When an attack came upon him, when he was in pain, he didn't want to see anyone, he brutally evicted his visitors, slammed the door, retreated to his office, lay down for a rest, and then wrote. Writing protected him, carried him to life's other dimension, that of dream, fairy tale or wrath—it little mattered which, so long as he achieved the state in which he no longer felt responsible. "I'm still a few hatreds short, and I'm sure they exist," he had written in the afterword to *Mea culpa*. These hatreds, which he nurtured and developed with such intolerable energy, were, I repeat, *fictitious* hatreds to him, solitary and rhetorical hatreds, neither real nor personalized. To the extent that, with all the conviction of sincerity, he was able to tell Pierre Dumayet, for example, on the television show "Lecture pour tous" aired on July 17, 1959: "I don't see myself at all as violent. Not in the least. I have never been violent. I have always cared with great gentleness, if I may say so, for all those who have come to me. I have saved a great many people, animals . . ."

He was barely aware of the effects of his writing. Why was Ludwig Rajchman upset by *L'Église*? Why were the Jews after him when the war ended? He seemed astonished because he really was astonished. All he had done was write, develop a voluminous rhetoric—trifles, nothing more. Céline the man was bitter, close, finicky, suspicious, bad-tempered, thrifty, resourceful, and anything else you could think of. But he did not harbor aggressive, racist vindictiveness toward any particular individual. He saved up and magnified his hatreds and ill-conceived banalities for the convulsive solitude of writing—that other universe. He also took them lightly, wanting to get a laugh out of them. History had yet to catch up with him. Hitler's nightmares—very real nightmares this time—had not yet provided their disastrous mirror image of his own.

There remain in any case two arguments that must be explored in order to explain Céline's anti-Semitism—arguments often advanced and, moreover, conflicting. There is first the idea that Céline was not anti-Semitic but that he had used this generic, abstract term to define all his fears and targets, such as alcoholism, war, and warmongers. That is false. From the very beginning, Céline possessed the basic anti-Semitism of the embittered and insecure lower-middle class whose characteristics he adopted. But he accelerates the tempo of that anti-Semitism, elevating it to the level of delirium and a universal condemnation of humanity's evils. There is the further idea that Céline, moved by suicidal rage, wrote his political books to set himself up as a victim, to cultivate the art of being in the wrong. In other words, to play the persecutor so as to be better able to claim the role of persecuted later on. The theory is seductive. Céline often falls into paranoid delusions, believing himself the target of endless conspiracies and ill-will. But now, in 1937 and 1938, his writings were aimed at the greatest number of readers, humoring them, amusing them, provoking them. It was not until later, after the liberation, that he would discuss, with a sometimes morbid pleasure, all the misinterpretations and misunderstandings that had made him hated, as though he drew his strength only from the bitterness and hostility he aroused.

Which finally brings us back to the contents of *Bagatelles pour un massacre*. A hold-all book, certainly, as we have said, an open floodgate of excess and belly laughs, too, a book of racist slurs of the worst sort distorted and transformed into a world of delirium.

The cultured, academic, and literary worlds—which had slammed the door in his face after *Mort à crédit*—are the first to be hauled over the coals. And Jewish Russia, oppressed Russia, Soviet Russia, steeped in frightful misery. Jews clamoring for war against Hitler are a leitmotiv. "A Jew in every turret, right from the start of mobilization. As if by magic, you'd feel a breeze—what am I saying?—an irresistible, blasting gale, veritable cyclones of pacifist protestation! across every border! it would rain turtledoves!"[5]

And the English? They would leave the French to be massacred. "Let us never forget that the Jews are kings of the City . . . one of their supreme citadels, along with Wall Street and Moscow . . . Not much will be destroyed . . . you can be sure of that . . . Patience! a lot of patience, a remarkable 'wait and see' . . . The Jews, the Jewish House of Lords, the magnates of England, won't rush into anything . . . They'll send a few planes . . . a few generals for luncheon with Maurois . . . and to discuss the Channel tunnel a little at the Ministry."[6]

Hitler? Céline does not much care for him, but throws off his own mask nonetheless: "I don't want to go to war for Hitler, I'll admit it, but I don't want to go against him, for the Jews . . . You can bawl me out all you want, but it's the Jews and they alone who are dragging us to the firing line . . . Hitler doesn't like the Jews, nor do I! There's no point getting all upset over so little . . . It's no crime that they make you sick." And further on: "Taking it to the extreme, I'm not one for beating about the bush, I tell it as I think it, I'd prefer a dozen Hitlers to one all-powerful Blum. Hitler, at least, I could understand, while with Blum it's pointless, he'll always be the worst enemy, absolute hatred, to the death."[7]

He also settles his grudge against the 1937 Fair that rejected his ballets, "a magnificent, crushing example of the Jewish colonizing fury, less and less worried about resentment and native reaction."[8] Which naturally leads into Céline's denunciation of French decadence, the lack of culture, the alcoholism, and the educational system that are killing its ordinary citizens, turning them into robots, stifling their emotions, teaching them a dead, stilted, academic language. From one ideal to the next, the output of the publishing industry is catastrophic, literature is washed up, culture has become a meaningless word. "The poor little market for French literature, already so stunted, on the run, its back against the wall, has quickly found itself crushed under the novels and serializations of Mr. and Mrs. Lehmann Rosamonde, Virginia Woolf . . . Wicki Baum . . . Mr. Ludwig . . . Mr. Cohen . . . Mr. Davis . . . Miss 'Chat qui pêche' . . . all Jews and Jewesses . . . each one of them more tendentious, more talentless, more plagiaristic, more fake, more of a 'genius,' more thieving, corrupting, cunning, depraved, contemptuous, sniveling, humoristic and sententious than the next."[9] And the great French classics? "Racine? What a sweet-talking, weak-kneed exhibitionist! What an obscene, groping, swooning mongrel! Part Jewish, as it happens!"[10] There's more: the Bourbons who ruled over France—just look at their noses! And let's not even get started on the cinema.

Scatological, sneering, vulgar, incoherent, and comical, Céline strews his book with phony numbers, insane statistics culled from the anti-Semitic den of Darquier de Pellepoix, quotations from the *Protocols of the Elders of Zion*, that notorious invention of anti-Semitic propaganda, which he uses without batting an eyelid. He also slips in his ballets between chapters—chapters of one or sometimes two pages, like quick belches, sneezes, bouts of nausea, of hatred, of revenge. The Jews, whose intelligence and solidarity he cannot help but admire, are constantly used as the most convenient shibboleth (along with communists and Freemasons) on which to focus his rejections and to base his anger. Logic and fact are thrown out the window.

Published in late 1937, *Bagatelles* was a great success with the public, as we have said. The first run of over 20,000 copies was soon sold out. Denoël ran a second edition of the work. By the end of the war, total sales would be around 75,000.

No surprise, the critical reception was neither fierce nor hot-headed, and once again provoked no radical differences between Left and Right, due to the fact that no one knew whether or not to take Céline seriously. Of course, for militant anti-Semites, the author of *Voyage* had suddenly become a choice, unhoped-for recruit, and they weren't about to split hairs. "The surprise was extraordinary," Lucien Rebatet would later explain. "I got into a race with Brasillach over who would be the first in with his article, him in *L'Action française* or me in *Je suis partout*. I think it was Robert who won, by a nose."[11]

But it was precisely in his *Action française* article on January 13, 1938, that Brasillach hinted at his reservations concerning Céline's rationality. Brasillach would have preferred a more coherent, well-argued, persuasive anti-Semitism. He was concerned lest that "vast, monotone obsession," Céline's excesses, tirades, and blatant lies should work against the anti-Semites themselves, such moderate rational folk as they were. But he soon redeemed himself. "What can you do? If you want to be in a lion's company, you don't feed him spinach. And my word, while I was reading his book, I enjoyed every minute of M. Céline's company." Even so, there was no better way of saying that, in normal circumstances, Céline was not his social equal. And Brasillach concluded his article on this sympathetic note: "Think what you will of the Jews and M. Céline. We do not agree with him on every point, far from it. But we said it first: this vast book, this magnificent book, is the opening shot of the 'native rebellion.' You may find this rebellion excessive, more instinctive than rational, even dangerous: but after all, *we* are the natives."[12]

The most memorable article is undeniably that of André Gide in the *N.R.F.* of April 1938. Gide had been harshly taken to task by Céline but did not seem to hold it against him. He set the tone from his opening line. "It seems to me that there has been an awful lot of nonsense written about *Bagatelles pour un massacre* by its critics. What surprises me is that they could all have been so mistaken. For, after all, Céline was playing for high stakes, even the very highest, as he always does. He has always come straight to the point. He has done his best to warn that all of this is no more serious than Don Quixote's tilting at windmills." The entire book, he basically went on to say, was one big joke. Céline was never better than when he abandoned all moderation. He possessed a gratuitous excess of lyrical ire. "It is not reality that Céline paints; it is the hallucination brought on by reality, and that is where he is interesting." It could not have been better put. And Gide concludes: "Certain other readers might not be comfortable with a literary game that, with the help of stupidity, runs the risk of tragic consequences. If one were forced to see in *Bagatelles pour un massacre* anything other than a game, then Céline, despite all his genius, would have no excuse for stirring up our commonplace passions with such cynicism and casual levity."[13]

Among the other critical reactions to *Bagatelles* we should note Georges Zérapha's quite appropriately harsh analysis in *La Conscience des juifs* in February-March 1938. He perceptively noticed that "all [Céline's] statements on the so-called Jewish domination are contradicted in his latest work by the simple presentation of a real Jew, Gutmann, who is his friend, has none of the defects attributed to Jews, and in whom we detect no particular capacity for corruption or domination." He adds: "Here we touch on proof of the metaphysical nature of anti-Semitism in general, and Céline's in particular. The corrupter, the dominator, is not the concrete Jew, who, based on personal affinities, is always given a special dispensation by anti-Semites; it is the symbolic Jew, the Jew as abstraction, who is cursed; it is, as we shall see, the devil."

After pointing to Céline's cowardice, his fear of love, his incapacity for life, his doctrinal impulses akin to Hitler's theories, Zérapha specifies: "What, finally, does a call to massacre mean to Céline? Céline has not for one moment considered that an Aryan reader would take him seriously and respond to his call by murdering one or several Jews." There always lingered the suspicion of a huge joke, which Zérapha denounces all the more vehemently for its reliance on a pseudoscientific documentation. "A writer worthy of the name can write an anti-Semitic book, grotesque though it may be, but he disgraces himself by reproducing propaganda leaflets and passing them off as the fruit of his own research."[14]

René Vincent, in *Combat* in March 1938, found Céline's tone so artificial, so surreal, so embued with Freudian concepts, that he detected a Jewish influence upon it. Someone had to think of it. "Furthermore, since Louis XIV is Jewish, since Racine is Jewish, since the Pope is Jewish, why shouldn't M. Céline himself be a Jew?"[15] In support of his thesis, he quotes a line from *Bagatelles*: "Thanks to my incantatory manner, my smutty, vociferous, anathematic lyricism—in a very personal manner that has certain Judaic aspects to it—I excel over the Jews, I can teach them a thing or two."

In *La Revue Hebdomadaire* of July 1938, Gonzague Truc pointed out Céline's enthusiasm for filth, turpitude, and his relentless wallowing in the dregs of human ignominy. Not in order to attack him but on the contrary, to defend, to emphasize the necessity of Céline's protest in the face of the terrifying imbecility into which the world, civilization, was stumbling. He concluded: "We must therefore admire his courage. We must better learn how to find the wisdom and beauty hidden within such demented books, and in that same, almost sacred delirium, the divinatory panoramas unseen by good sense; we must sense through these moldering garbage heaps the healthful breezes of the seas."[16]

We are shocked today by the moderation of such reviews, a moderation barely disturbed by H. E. Kaminsky's widely ignored pamphlet, *Céline en chemise brune* [Celine in a Brown Shirt], published by the Nouvelles Éditions Excelsior in late February 1938, a pamphlet that was less aggressive than its title would lead one to believe. But to be shocked would, again, be to forget how banal xenophobia and racist sentiment were at the time. One could write against the Jews with impunity. One could joke, bluster, rant, play dirty. One could lie, invent, discredit oneself. It was of little consequence—or so it was believed.

The School for Anti-Semitism

What expectations could Céline have after *Bagatelles*? "I'm not too sure what the future (if there is one!) will bring. We'll see. I have no more expectations. For that matter, I have never had any expectations. I shouldn't like to suffer so much that I'd have to flee. That's my only wish. It's a modest one. But I know from experience that I don't have much luck."[17]

Even so, not leaving it to chance, in early 1938 he deposited some gold coins—184 ten-florin coins to be precise—in the Nederlandsche Bank of Amsterdam. He took advantage of his travels to see Évelyne Pollet in Antwerp. As soon as he had left, she offered the Belgian weekly *Cassandre* (where, in May '37, she had already published an encomium on "Céline and the Scheldt") a paper in defense of *Bagatelles pour un massacre*. The editors rejected it. Céline learned of her effort and showed extreme irritation over it. Be it from generosity or pride, as an individualist he rejected as a general rule any offer of assistance. He hated to be beholden. As things stood, he did not wish to compromise her or her family in the event that this political affair "should finish tragically." He wrote her violent letters: "I loathe, truly loathe, friendships that end up being helpful. *I do not want* anyone to help me, assist me, defend me. *Once and for all.* Neither you nor anyone else. I know what I'm doing. I know the risks. That's how I like it and that's all that matters."[18]

Céline had written his book feverishly. History was moving no less so and was about to catch up with him. The government of the Front Populaire—under which Céline was proud to have written *Bagatelles*, not waiting for the Jews to be persecuted to abuse them, as he later said—had had its day. Hitler pursued his expansionist policies. On March 12 his troops occupied Austria. It was the Anschluss, a flouting of international law. The unfortunate Chancellor Schussnigg was forced to resign. A European country had been annexed just like that, on a roll of the dice, an easy bluff, and a roll of the drums. The Austrian Nazis, led by Seyss-Inquart, had worked things out pretty neatly. Courageous but not foolhardy, England for its part let it happen, would not intervene in Austrian affairs, and made that very clear to France, which asked for nothing better. Chautemps' new government came out of it looking pathetic. Blum then tried to form a new "National Unity" government. In vain. The French couldn't see the need for it. Communists and rightists refused to cohabitate. Susceptibilities were easily wounded. War was still someone else's problem. After six weeks of Blum's interim leadership, the Daladier government took power.

Céline took to the road. It was an old habit. When things were going bad, when he wanted to escape harsh realities and the pressures that followed the publication of a book, he ran away, to forget and be forgotten. The launching of the American edition of *Mort à crédit* was the perfect excuse to cross the ocean. He decided to begin his tour with Canada, and said *adieu* to France, to Europe, to the Anschluss, and to the coming war.

In Bordeaux, he boarded the freighter *Le Celte*, which was on its way from Zeebrugge and weighed anchor for Saint-Pierre-et-Miquelon on April 15, after having first taken on 240 tons of cargo and four passengers, amongst whom were Céline, a young woman, and her ten-year-old daughter, Jeanne Allain. "I'll always remember Louis-Ferdinand Céline, that big nice man, who was equally liked by the crew of *Le Celte*, with whom he talked about Saint-Pierre. He gave me a little note and his autograph. I've lost it all, unfortunately. At that age, I didn't really understand why he told me to remember him when I got older."[19]

On April 26 the ship docked in Saint-Pierre, that island of heavy winds, ocean, fog, and oblivion at the end of the world. A romantic landscape, a savage and desolate Célinian landscape, Saint-Pierre certainly enabled him to indulge his nautical fantasies. In Sigmaringen, he would write in *D'un château l'autre*, and he would ask Laval to appoint him governor of the Saint-Pierre-et-Miquelon islands. A fairy tale? Perhaps. And Laval had answered him:

" 'Whatever put that into your head, Doctor?'

" 'It just came to me, Mr. President! The attractions of Saint-Pierre-et-Miquelon! . . .'

"I start to tell him . . . I'm not speaking on hearsay . . . I was there . . . in those days it took 25 days from Bordeaux to Saint-Pierre . . . on the very fragile *Celtique* . . . they still fished on Saint-Pierre . . . I know Langlade and Miquelon well . . . I know the road well . . . the only road, from one end of the island to the other . . . the wheel and the marker of the 'Souvenir,' the road dug through solid rock by the sailors of the *Iphigénie* . . . I'm not making any of it up . . . these are real memories, a real road! . . . and not only the sailors of the *Iphigénie* . . . convicts too . . . there was a prison camp on Saint-Pierre . . . it left its own marker! . . .

" 'That's what you'd see, Mr. President! In the middle of the Atlantic!'

"The main thing is, I was named Governor . . . I still am! . . ."[20]

What was he doing on Saint-Pierre-et-Miquelon in 1938, and afterward in Canada? He was not a tourist, nor was he on the lecture circuit or promoting his books. He was pursuing his obsession, continuing to explore future and potential places of exile, after London and Jersey. This later caused Henri Mahé, an invaluable witness to Céline's ramblings, to say: "That year, a kind of foul whiff of Apocalypse hovered over Europe. . . . It was high time to unearth some island that no one wanted or would fight over, where lovely peace was assured and you could get yourself some. Saint-Pierre-et-Miquelon would stand a chance."[21]

This intention was confirmed by the testimony of René Héron de Villefosse, who had met Céline in 1936 aboard Mahé's little boat, the *Enez Glaz*, then docked in Paris, on the quai Conti, across from the Institute, and who recalls his prophecies:

" 'Only one country in the world will be left in a century, the one where parish priests are kings, and that's Canada, the most damned boring country there is . . . but I'll go, say the Mass. I'll teach the catechism. There won't be much choice if you want to save your ——— and I'm rather fond of mine.' "

"In verbal gales, a bit like in *Mea culpa*, he described the coming upheavals, Europe in flames, the last chance one had to get safe by leaving *pronto*, without delay, without a second thought, with a bundle of clothing."[22]

And then came Montreal.

As soon as he learned of Céline's arrival in town, a Canadian academic, Victor Barbeau, then president of his country's writers' association, wanted to meet him. He finally found him at a meeting of the extreme Right, where Céline was attending as a simple anonymous spectator. He introduced himself and greeted him as *"cher maître."* Céline burst out laughing. They became friends. Barbeau would have liked to persuade Céline to give lectures. Nothing doing, neither in a tuxedo nor in a lounge suit nor for any fee proposed. Play the clown to entertain society folk? Not a chance.

"A supper for writers? Yes, on the condition that there be no more than ten of them and that it all be set up without ceremony, like a party for cabbies and truck drivers.

"There were more than twenty of us. Despite the good food and fine wines, Céline never unclenched his teeth. Showered with questions, bewildered by the chatter of a woman of letters who knew all the Paris phonies, he hardly touched his meal. I was expecting the worst, but the ogre didn't devour a soul."[23]

Later in the evening, Barbeau brought Céline to a friend's house. And suddenly the writer revived. He had been taciturn. He became irrepressible. The intimate atmosphere aroused his spirits. He soliloquized on the Apocalypse. No dialogue, just the long retailing of anecdotes, predictions, fits of anger, Céline's great scope that people found so dazzling and frightening. This was Céline in his entirety: the man who spoke too much, the man who remained despairingly mute, the man who could never hold a real conversation. Who could flatter oneself by claiming ever to have had a proper discussion with Céline?

In its Anglo-American translation by John Marks, *Mort à crédit* was published in America by the Boston firm of Little Brown, which also published *Voyage*. Céline's presence in the United States does not appear to have contributed significantly to the book's launching. The writer was drawn to New York for other reasons, the usual ones: the music hall, the chorus girls, his friends, the comforting oblivion one always feels in plunging into a large, foreign city.

He headed for home on the *Normandie* on May 18.

On the 23rd, Lucette met him in Le Havre, where they remained for about a week. Louis soon fell back into his Montmartre habits. Now he need no longer be distracted by his medical and pharmaceutical work; he could shut himself away, write, remember things past and weave them into nightmares present. Technically, *Casse-Pipe* was still the work in progress, the chronological sequel to *Mort à crédit*, young Ferdinand's conscription into the army before 1914. And from one war to the next. But it was precisely that next war to come that he wished to forget momentarily by wandering through his past, writing, seeking his music and doing a little daydreaming.

He put it very prettily to Évelyne Pollet in a letter on May 31: "I am just a workman in a certain kind of music and that's all and everything else is immaterial, incomprehensible, desperately boring to me. This world seems extraordinarily wearying to me with its characters dependent upon, stubbornly wallowing in, and bound to their desires, their passions, their vices, their virtues, their explanations."[24]

Lucette left him occasionally for brief engagements or tours of France and abroad. That summer she was dancing in Poland and Lithuania. Louis let her go but was soon anxious and impatient with her absence. His letters became ever more urgent. "Come home! Come home!" Had Lucette's manager made her sign a one-month contract? "Screw your manager! Come home!" was his answer.

He left for Saint-Malo in mid-July, again staying with Marie Le Bannier. When he came to write *Féerie pour une autre fois*, in the torment of exile and prison in Denmark, he would recall these summers in Saint-Malo, of which we get a fleeting glimpse in a photograph taken on the beach, at the foot of the ramparts, with a smiling Céline in his bathing suit, his friends Henri Mahé and the doctor/colonel Camus at his side, while Lucette squats in the foreground performing her stretching exercises, and a very young Sergine Le Bannier plays and crawls in the sand. And in *Féerie*, the images, the sounds, the music of those summers in Brittany will return to charm him.

"Three rooms under the rafters, a sublet from my old pal Mlle. Marie . . . You can imagine, I heard a thing or two! bangings and passions! and sea gulls crying in the storm . . .

"Fantastic romantic summers! What equinoxes!"

After having been Marie Le Bannier's *de facto* guest, he would rent a little apartment from her on the second floor of the Franklin Building. Only one summer, during the war, would he take an apartment on the Saint-Malo ramparts, lent to him by his old friend, the museum curator André Dezarrois, who was proud of belonging to the school of Breton bards.

"I'm in my memories, please forgive me . . . All in all, those were happy times . . .

"Tonight, speaking to you from my pit, I can hear, I hear again . . . say! . . . the sobs of vioooolins! miaowing to me! and the foghorns' 'pwah pwah' from the docks! . . . the 'huff-huff,' their asthma! . . . the Cancale race! . . . the hurrahs! the crowds . . . now that's your authentic cinema of the time!"[25]

Saint-Malo and the sea—poignant . . .

"I don't know if you can see it? . . . it's a charming bay . . .

"The old *Terranueva* rotting there at the dock, its yardarms falling on the bridge, snapping, worn out . . . its holds empty, bowsprit crushed . . . you couldn't tell, it's full of people. . . .

"I love the whole bay and the clock towers and the ruins and the vanished belfry and the Corsairs' Palace."[26]

During the summer of '38, he probably strolled idly along the ramparts or the strand, mused before Châteaubriand's tomb, rambled as far as Cancale, spent hour after hour with his friends—Henri Mahé, a sailor as makeshift as he was stubborn; the Breton poet Théophile Briant, who edited an astonishing little sheet, Le Goéland; the Le Coz sisters, authentic locals who ran the Breiz Izel restaurant where he enjoyed eating. He would recall all these characters in the melancholy pages of the aptly named Féerie pour une autre fois. He may also have argued with such hotheaded and ferocious separatists as Olier Mordrel who, in the heat of the Munich crisis, had no qualms about posting a bill: "Not one drop of Breton blood for the Czechs!"[27] Céline enjoyed their occasional company, he felt a certain indulgence for and empathy with them, for his curiosity was always aroused by impassioned, excessive dreamers. But he spent most of that summer locked away in his little office in the Franklin Building, writing the more-feverish-than-ever pages of his second great political book, L'École des cadavres.

Daladier had by then taken power, stabilized the franc, and abolished the forty-hour week by decree. He wanted to revive the economy, and committed France to a policy of rearmament. They weren't striking in the German or Italian factories, he told the strikers and communists who claimed to be anti-fascist, with some justification. Hitler was pursuing his adventurous schemes and his Greater Reich policy. After Austria, Czechoslovakia soon became the next target, with its three million Sudeten Germans led by a party that took its orders from Hitler. In short, war remained on the daily agenda.

After Bagatelles, there was nothing left for Céline to say or argue. But he could repeat himself with greater force, greater provocativeness, greater delirious intensity, without being sidetracked this time by considerations connected to his trip to Russia, his ballets, or literature. He still felt the need to howl out his abiding thirst for peace, his hatred of Jews, and thus his desire for an alliance with Hitler at any price.

Each time Céline sat down to write, he fell into an altered state, a state of trance, a strange arousal that might be called erotic. He fantasized: about dance, dancers, anything! It was a curious "erection" that writing alone could soothe, could cap. Or else he had to reach a sufficient degree of rage, like a drug, to unleash his incantatory writing, to achieve, as Gide rightly put it, a state of hallucination.

This phenomenon appears clearly from the very opening of L'École des cadavres. The narrator meets an old mermaid, her body covered in scales, an erotic, sarcastic muse dripping with oil and tar, basking in the Seine somewhere between La Jatte and Courbevoie. They soon begin to argue, to insult one another. Céline defends himself, attacks, vituperates. And his story grows precisely out of this quarrel. Without this summons, this contrivance, he could not have expressed himself. Further, in the following pages, he invents—most probably—a contradictor, a correspondent who sends him a poison-pen letter signed "Salvador, Jew." Which allows Céline to retort, to fuss over his anger, to achieve the ecstasy of hatred.

His book then descends into a vortex of madness. Words pile upon words, sucked into a revelry, an alliterative delirium, an abusive music, shimmering insults, a euphonic ebb and flow of his fears.

Novelists and reporters who boast of having abolished war are incompetents: "They've never fucked, bucked, hustled, muscled a damn thing! those be-peacocked parakeets, not the least butt or babe, the least complicament, never unfinagled, discombobbled the weakest mitigated litigation! Not a thing! Never! short-sighted sleazes! Pencil-necked shitslingers!

"The fuming, destructing Furies of War scoff at your woggish emotings to the ends of hell! your silent, anathematic farting.

"You cowardly, shit-scared gropers! I'm enfulminating I admit! I'm moiling! I'm boiling! I'm humbugging my wig! I'm fuguing! I'm shrieking! I'm breathless! I'm belching roiling vapors! I don't give a fitting fuck anymore!"[28]

What a confession! What a wonderful concentration of Céline's stylistic genius and rambling! In this extract we see perfectly how the writer frees himself with his valise words, his speed, his hallucinations, his rhymes—as if the music within him moved continually faster than meaning, emotion preceded reason, with his acknowledged anger, his immense fear, his racial hatred of the "Kikish carrion corps" and other nauseating niceties.

What would be the point of accusing Céline of racism? It would not be an insult. It's patently obvious. He says it, admits it, shouts it: "Racism! Of course! And how! The more of it the merrier! Racism! Enough of our soft religions! We've been stuffed enough as it is by all the apostles, all the Evangelists. All Jewish, by the way, from Peter the founder to the present Pope via Marx!"[29]

And always, to underlie the book, to give it its only possible illumination, there remains that overweening fear of war and massacre.

"The Aryan States: wilderness parks for Jewish bloodfests. Ritual battles for knackers, lowings, wholesale meat of every kind, various social phenomena, a milking of the cows between the intermissions."[30]

The solution? There is only one, which Céline repeats until he's hoarse: "Franco-German union. Franco-German alliance. Franco-German army."

"It's the army that makes alliances, solid ones. Without a Franco-German army, treaties will remain platonic, academic, fickle, erratic . . . Enough slaughterhouses! A Franco-German army first! The rest will follow of itself. Italy, Spain into the bargain, will quite naturally join the Confederation.

"Confederation of the Aryan States of Europe.

"Executive power: the Franco-German army.

"A Franco-German alliance, for life, to the death."[31]

And at the same time that he was writing these final pages of L'École des cadavres, he was also dabbling with the same peace of mind—or rather the same tortured and delusional anxiety—in writing the outline, the ballet, the fairy tale that he called *Scandale aux abysses* and which he would publish for the first time in 1950, thanks to Pierre Monnier, under the aegis of Chambriad Éditeur. In it, Neptune, Venus, the island of Terranova, long-haul sailors with short-lived destinies combine their charms, their melancholy loves, and their whispered poetry.

Elusive Céline! During the summer he had stopped over in London with Mahé to withdraw some gold he had deposited at Lloyds Bank, before renting a safe deposit box at the Privat Banken of Copenhagen. Céline's early assaults on the world had brought him large amounts of hard cash, and he was keeping his feet firmly on the ground. That much is true, but a novel, a book other than *Bagatelles*, could have brought him just as much. And it is obvious that he had not written this one to indulge his readership's baser instincts and to get rich. He explored the furthest boundaries of his delirium with total conviction, one might say integrity. It was simply that Céline, haughty, sly, and suspicious, more from the gold-coins-under-the-mattress school than from that of paper money, was also willfully sensitive and proud. He wanted to be in no one's debt, ever! The idea of one day being dependent or at the mercy of others made him tremble. Dignified, silent, like his mother and grandmother, he had not forgotten the lessons of a poverty dissembled and borne without complaint. If he was earning far less money since the loss of his medical jobs, that was all the more reason to save. In that way he hoped to ensure himself a shelter far from Paris, far from France and the battlefields, a nestegg, a hidden treasure that would perhaps allow him to exist, to survive the Apocalypse without having to beg. And the future would prove him right—to a point.

In September the political crisis took its most dramatic turn to date. War seemed imminent. In Nuremberg on September 12, Hitler called for the outright annexation of the contested Sudetenland. Daladier pressured the Czech government to yield. The English leader Chamberlain, anxious to stall for time—England had to be rearmed, equipped with an air force, without which it would be crushed in the event of hostilities—hesitated to react. Hitler immediately formulated new and unacceptable demands that the Czechs evacuate those territories without repatriating their property. Czechoslovakia began mobilizing on the spot, France and England called up several reserve divisions, and Hitler massed his troops. At the last minute, Mussolini's initiative brought together the "big four" of Western Europe—France, England, Italy, and Germany—at the Munich Conference on September 29-30. Chamberlain and Daladier yielded to the main points and signed a nonaggression pact with Hitler (who agreed to a gradual occupation of the Sudetenland from October 1 to 10).

It was, as Blum said, speaking for the Left, "a cowardly appeasement." Peace had been saved *in extremis*. Daladier was welcomed in Le Bourget with hurrahs and sprays of roses. Peace, yes, but for how long? Daladier was not too proud of himself. They still had to prepare for war. The English, who for so many years had diplomatically played Germany against France, were finally beginning to understand that. The French too, but a little late. Lucette and Louis had rushed back to Paris on September 20 to figure out how best to save their furniture in case of hostilities. There were no hostilities. Not this time. A drawn hand. Céline finished the last pages of *L'École des cadavres* and submitted it to Denoël. An urgent book, it had to be published urgently. And while the first critical reviews appeared of the Italian translation, *Bagatelle per un massacro*, published in Milan in April, and the advance proofs came out for the future German edition of the same book, to be entitled *Die Judenverschwörung in Frankreich* [The Jewish Conspiracy in France] (Dresden, 1939), Denoël got to work on the second book, which ran to 25,000 copies and went on sale on November 24, at 30 francs.

It was less successful than the earlier one. It came at the worst possible moment. Who could possibly follow and support Céline in his madman's lucubrations? *Bagatelles* had won over the fascistic extreme Right which until then had ignored him, like Brasillach. *L'École des cadavres* would isolate him once more. Did this unduly upset him?

Lucien Rebatet has explained it very well:

"I must say too, to be truthful, that if we fascists had done the war dance around *Bagatelles* in 1938, *L'École des cadavres*, a year later, broke our backs. Hitler had just entered Prague. And that was the moment that Céline chose to call for a total, military, political, and economic alliance with Germany. Even for us, it was impossible to print a single word on such commerce. It was decided rather hypocritically that, in any case, he was repeating himself, spinning it out, and I agreed, despite the cries of joy which that whirlwind had often elicited from me.

"Céline, as always, had gone too far."[32]

L'École des cadavres, like *Bagatelles*, would be pulled from the shelves in 1939. Its commercial exploitation was thus of short duration. But even taking the 1942 reprint into account, its sales would remain far lower than that of the earlier work.

"God is under repair" was Céline's epigraph to the book, a marvelous, mocking aphorism that chills one to the bone. Like the entire book, for that matter, with its stupefying, grotesquely poetic developments and its descents into hatred or unequivocal dementia. If a little perspective might help someone to speak about it, who, in that case, could boast of such objectivity in those final months before the war? A Henri Guillemin, perhaps? In the Cairo newspaper *La Bourse égyptienne*, he wrote with surprising serenity on February 19, 1939: "We have to know what it is we want from Céline. Ideas, a doctrine? If so, then we are obviously misguided. But a certain literary pleasure that only he can bring us? That, yes, and that alone; and that, to my mind, is no mean feat."

And he concluded his article thus:

"Once again, one needs to don armor—or better yet, steel plating—to approach Céline. He must be taken as he is or not at all. If I had opened his book intending to argue with him, I would have seen red myself, I would have had a stroke. To trample down the Jews, when they're enduring what they're enduring on the sacrificial pyre at this very moment, is a disgrace. But Ferdinand is well aware of that; and, as regards abominations, he has always enjoyed 'laying it on thick' on his adopted characters. A law of the genre.

"As long as one understands that this is a juggling act, one can go, free of reservations, and applaud this extraordinary juggler."[33]

War Forever Renewed

The countdown had begun. Céline had howled out what he had to say with the madness, violence, and fear that moved him in the wounded solitude of his deliria. From now on he had only to keep his silence and catch his breath. He had only to keep his distance. He would stop militating. He would stop publishing. In any case, he would never join any kind of party. His philosophy could be summed up in the maxim of the pre-Socratic philosopher Bias of Priene: "Most men are wicked." If one accepts this, there is nothing left to be said, and everything can fall by the wayside: confidence in progress, Christianity, Marxism, hope, political involvement, democracy, and so on. After the howling, silence. The countdown to war had begun. He could only watch it, alone and despairing.

A witness reports Céline's attendance at a public meeting organized by Darquier de Pellepoix on December 2, 1938, at 8, rue Laugier, in a gymnasium not far from the offices of the Anti-Jewish Assemblies of France. "He sat, anonymous, among the crowd. His shyness or modesty shied from public acclaim. As he had asked us to do, we respected his anonymity."[34]

After the meeting, Céline accompanied some of its organizers to a neighboring café. To the exalted dynamism of Darquier de Pellepoix, future General Commissioner for Jewish Affairs in the Vichy government, the writer responded with hopeless disillusionment. The *patrie* was done for, he kept repeating in his monologue. No, he had nothing left to say, nothing left to hope for, like some connoisseur of decay. Too bad if Darquier was scandalized by such defeatism.

In early 1939 Céline learned of the death of Cillie's husband in Dachau. On February 21 he wrote her this astonishing letter.

> *Dear Cillie,*
>
> *What awful news! At least you're far away, on the other side of the world. Were you able to take a little money with you? Obviously, you're going to start a new life over there. How will you work? Where will Europe be by the time you receive this letter? We're living over a volcano.*
>
> *On my side, my little dramas are nothing compared to yours (for the moment), but tragedy looms nonetheless . . .*

"Because of my anti-Semitic stance I've lost all my jobs (Clichy, etc.) and I'm going to court on March 8. You see, Jews can persecute too.[35]

It will be said that Céline was irresponsible and paranoid. But he wasn't joking, he wasn't displaying a macabre sense of humor—he was dead serious. He believed that the Jews were persecuting him. He felt like a hunted man. And it was in part for that reason, because he was convinced that a still more-or-less latent hostility would one day rise up against him in the early days of war, that he left the rue Lepic and that he and Lucette moved in with his mother, in the little, comfortless apartment without toilet at 11, rue Marsollier, a stone's throw from the Passage Choiseul, on June 10, 1939.

After his letter of February 11, Cillie never saw him again and stopped writing, not surprisingly. The trial of March 8, to which Céline refers in his last letter to account for the "persecution" he too was suffering, followed a complaint lodged against him by Dr. Rouquès after the publication of *L'École des cadavres*. Already, in early January, the leftist journalist Léon Treich had felt attacked by Céline, who had wrongly called him a Jew; he had responded through the bailiff, and Céline wrote the required retraction, which vacated the legal proceedings. No such luck with Rouquès, who felt he had been libeled by the same token. On page 302 of *L'École des cadavres*, Céline, citing an article published in *L'Humanité* on November 5, 1938, that described the opening of a clinic owned by the Paris local of the metal-workers' union in the presence of Drs. Kalmanovitch, Oppman, Rouquès, Lecain, Bli, etc., had slipped in the parenthetical remark "all Jews," which was not true in Rouquès' case. Céline's lawyer, André Saudemont—who would be brought before the courts after the liberation, declared guilty of offenses against the nation and struck from the Paris bar for his radio transmissions during the occupation—noted that to call an Aryan a Jew was a mistake, not an insult, unless the victim were himself a racist. The argument was a rather clumsy one, since Céline invariably associated Jews with Evil, with a thousand offensive and insulting epithets, at which point the characterization became indubitably libelous. The 12th Chamber of the Court of Summary Jurisdiction handed down its verdict on June 21. Céline and Denoël were each fined 200 francs. Rouquès had asked for 50,000 in damages and interest. The court awarded him 2,000 and ordered the deletion of the offending passage, under penalty of 200 francs for every day of delay.

Céline had finally taken on his role as persecuted. In the prewar days, so steeped in tragedy, he had begun to live tragically; he saw the world foundering in horror, he saw himself, and he saw nothing between the two. In short, the line had been blurred between the general situation and his personal predicament. Céline was living, sleep-walking, at the center of a nightmare.

On April 21, 1939, Garde des Sceaux [Attorney General] Marchandeau issued the so-called "Resident's Law," which applied to the press and was aimed at protecting racial minorities. It was a question of reining in the anti-Semitic frenzy then current in the papers of the extreme Right. On May 10 Céline and Robert Denoël decided to pull *Bagatelles* and *L'École des cadavres* from the shelves, though the Marchandeau decree did not target them directly.

Their retreat was not to the liking of *Je suis partout*. Under the precautionary pseudonym Midas, on May 26 the paper published a paragraph summed up in one sentence: "Céline—you're chickening out!" Céline attributed this to Robert Brasillach and answered him fiercely on June 2. This time it was Brasillach who chickened out and did not publish the letter, in which the author of *Voyage* denounced his "cowardly little trick." Of a new letter from Céline written later in the month, *Je suis partout* published only four telegraphic lines. Céline had written: "You're splitting hairs, Brasillach, if I wanted to call you a pansy or a bastard, I wouldn't need an excuse. I'd say it like a man, to your face. . . . I told you that we've already been to court twice. Do we have to go thirty-six times to make you happy, little girl?"[36]

But all of this was a sideshow. History was on the move. And the last happy months, days, hours were slipping by, running out, vanishing with every warning shot heard in the news. Peace hung by a thread. And it was losing its grip.

The Jews were leaving Germany in haste, having lost every right but that to be persecuted, deported, with worse to come. On January 26, 1939, Barcelona fell to the nationalists. Madrid fell a few days later, and London and Paris scurried to recognize General Franco's government. France's first ambassador to Spain was Pétain—there could be some understanding between military men. They understood each other. On March 15 the Nazis were in Prague. This time Czechoslovakia found itself well and truly dismembered. England and France pretended not to have seen a thing. On April 7 Italy in turn invaded Albania, and hastened to reassure Greece that it had no designs on its territory, at least for the moment. On May 22 Mussolini and Hitler signed a pact of mutual assistance in Berlin; they were beginning to get along very nicely.

As for Daladier's France, it was getting along on its own. On April 27 Paris acclaimed the premiere of *Ondine* at the Théâtre de l'Athénée. Giraudoux's shimmering phantasmagoria was enough to keep it happy. Well might Renoir, in his masterpiece *La Règle du jeu* that same year, denounce a frivolous and worn-out middle class, isolated within its privileges, selfish, stupid, and satiated, unconcerned by and unaware of the Apocalypse—Renoir was a voice in the desert, no one cared to hear him. "Must we die for Danzig?" mused Marcel Déat in a famous article for *L'Oeuvre* on May 4. The French had no desire to die for the Poles or for anyone. The French were afraid. They amused themselves, or they waited, passively.

As in earlier years, Lucette and Louis left for Saint-Malo in July. Évelyne

Pollet, who had undergone surgery in December of '38, had been recuperating for several months in the south of France. Céline suggested that she come to see him in Brittany, and reserved her a hotel room in Dinard. The offer was as generous as it was rash. Possessive and passionate, Évelyne could only be jealous of Lucette's presence at his side. Already the previous year, Céline had had Lucette accompany him on a brief visit to Antwerp, and they had gone to see her together. Évelyne suddenly refused to leave her room. And while Lucette and Évelyne's husband stayed in the living room exchanging small talk, Louis had gone up alone to see Évelyne, who had wanted to express to him the strength of her nonplatonic feelings. But now, in early July in Saint-Malo, she was forced to face facts: Lucette shared the writer's room. A scene ensued, shouting, despair. That very night, Évelyne Pollet tried to poison herself with an overdose of digitalin, a cardiopathic medicine. A real or a staged suicide attempt? Louis would not stand for the theatrics of this grotesque situation. He calmed her down and put her on a train for Paris the next morning.

The summer in Saint-Malo was getting off to a bad start. Céline had no heart for continuing work on *Casse-Pipe*. On July 5 *Le Canard enchaîné* wrote of the expulsion of German ambassador Otto Abetz and the espionage incidents that had justified the measure. There was no mention of Céline in the article, but he felt himself targeted nonetheless and wrote a letter to the weekly on July 12. Lucien Sampaix, on the other hand, virtually accused Céline, in *L'Humanité* on July 10 and 11, of collusion with Darquier de Pellepoix's anti-Jewish leagues. Céline wrote a response that the paper declined to publish. A few days later, inspired by an antipornography and pro–higher birthrate bill tabled by a certain Senator Pernot and a company president named Boverat, the weekly *Le Merle* (formerly *Le Merle blanc*) published a derisive article that characterized Céline in passing as a "monster of genius." The writer wrote to the weekly on July 14, once again offering a diagnosis of his country's decadence: "In truth, France can barely get it up, we're as stingy and cautious with sperm as with everything else, but we're frighteningly heavy drinkers. Will Péguchet attack the bistros, our innumerable kings? Not so brave, the sneak! Down with the writer! What risk is there in that? None!"[37]

On July 21 and 22, *Je suis partout* published part of Céline's letter to *L'Humanité*, a response that also appeared in *Le Droit de vivre*, the journal of LICA (the International League against Anti-Semitism), then headed by Bernard Lecache.

In this way did Céline pass his days, by Lucette's side, reading, writing letters, waiting, loafing, fearing the worst in that city of pirates, through what he knew would be the last summer of peace.

The French government would have been happy to negotiate with Stalin and establish a military alliance with him against Hitler. French and British experts had even gone to Moscow in August to discuss its guidelines. But then, on August 23, came the thunderbolt of the German-Soviet pact. Hitler and Stalin understood each other. France didn't understand a thing. Poland understood only too well. It would bear the costs of implementation. In every movie newsreel on every screen in France, from Douai to Villefranche-de-Rouergue, from Menton to La Rochelle, one saw the bright and jerky image of Stalin, the very picture of bewhiskered mirth, offering a toast to the health of the German chancellor. This was a difficult pill to swallow for the French Communist Party, which Daladier outlawed posthaste. But communists can sometimes give proof of a sound digestion. The communist representatives might well lose their seats if they accepted the pact; many militants approved of it because they had no choice. Even Maurice Thorez, a future minister of the Republic, would be seen on October 4 to desert his 3rd Engineer's Regiment, which had been mobilized on September 3, 1939. The ways of dialectic are often inscrutable.

On September 1 the German army invaded Poland. On schedule. The Poles had clearly foreseen that any negotiation would have been useless. France and England had just mobilized their troops. On September 3 the two allies made the first move and declared war on Germany.

Céline returned to Paris. A young conscript, Pierre Ordoni, ran into the writer on the boulevard Saint-Germain. They had been introduced by a mutual friend. They talked on the street for a while, and then in a bistro.

War was here. It was all starting over—another nightmare, new absurdities, and it was as though Céline's past came back to him, grabbing him by the throat—the Great War, Sergeant-at-Arms Destouches, the galloping squadrons. What was left today? The soldiers were union men, no one was prepared to obey, let alone to resist and withstand the first quarter-hour's assault, that decisive quarter-hour; the Gare de Lyon (where trains leave Paris for the South) was a lot more crowded than the Gare de l'Est (where they leave for the East). Those were Céline's observations.

"I looked at him askance," Pierre Ordoni would write. "Exhaustion had etched his face, where there flitted something melancholy and bitter. I could only see him as the target of persecution by mediocrities and imbeciles. . . .

" 'Will you be mounted?' he finally asked me.

" 'Yes. Battalion adjuncts 'earn' a horse. I happen to be a fairly good rider, too. A colonel's son.'

"He smiled imperceptibly.

" 'In that case, one last piece of advice: above all . . . no boots! Gaiters! Good old-fashioned regular-issue gaiters, bought in a store before you leave. With a flap over the shoe. Hmm? Watch out for your feet. Your butt will tan soon enough, but with boots, ten kilometers and your feet will be bleeding. There's no need to put on airs. War? It always ends with the infantry. Remember: gaiters!"[38]

It was as if Céline could already see the rout, the great footrace between France and its army as far as Biarritz or Carcassonne.

The Rout

France settled in to the phony war.

"We're going to hang out our washing on the Siegfried line." This refrain was unconscionably repeated on the radio, with the digestive bravura that comes at the end of a banquet. The fact is, the French army had no desire for a change of linen. It preferred to adopt a defensive stance. A hasty attack on the Saar in early October had ended in a pitiful retreat and the loss of Forbach. The order of the day was not yet "Courage, run for it!" but was already "Courage, wait and see!" The Nazis weren't fooling around with their *Panzerdivisionen*, and Poland could attest to that. Might as well spend the winter in the warmth of the Maginot Line bunkers. And what if the phony war were followed by a euphoric peace? People were still ready to believe in miracles, between verses.

Céline was not fit to fight. On November 9, 1939, the draft board confirmed his degree of disablement at 70%. Not eager to write, and preoccupied with returning to work, in early September he had the half-baked idea of opening a medical practice in Saint-Germain-en-Laye. With the exception of temporarily replacing one colleague or another, he had not had a private clientele since Clichy and 1928. The new initiative was no more successful. He moved into a charming little rented house at 15, rue de Bellevue, one of those provincial dead-end streets far from the shops, from the bustle of downtown, where nothing filters in, nothing moves, where life seems to doze, lethargically, in the peaceful quietude of boredom. Who the devil would want to go to the rue de Bellevue to be sounded by an unknown forty-five-year-old doctor of rather Bohemian aspect, to say the least, who had hastily printed up calling cards replete with the seasonal patriotic references: "Dr. Louis F. Destouches/ Graduate of the Paris Faculty of Medicine/ War Invalid, *Médaille Militaire*/ General Practice/ Consultations every day from 1 P.M. to 3 P.M."?

"His mother," recalls Lucette Destouches, "had come to help me hand out the calling cards. We were not always welcomed with open arms. I had hung some little curtains on the windows. We had put a table and some chairs into the room that was to be used for consultations. You would have thought you were in a theater. We had also had a telephone installed. As for us, we lived in the kitchen, because of the cold, with two mattresses on the floor. Looking at the house from the outside, you might have thought it was uninhabited. It didn't look professional. In three weeks, there was maybe one phone call. We didn't see a single client. Louis loved Saint-Germain and its terrasses. He would have liked me to give lessons at the local Conservatory. Why not? But first we had to get a foothold in the town. Louis was very impatient. If he had waited a year his practice might have gone somewhere, but after a month of fruitless waiting he wanted to leave. Louis was always like that. He had dreams and when the dream was over he dropped it and moved on to something else. The day before he died he was still saying: 'We drop everything and head for the sea. You love the sea.' He was like that, and I was ready to follow him."

The couple returned to the rue Marsollier in October.

The war went on, endlessly dragging out its prelude. The winter of 1939-1940 was harsh. Louis was bored. Having shouted himself hoarse a year earlier in *L'École des cadavres* with "Long live Hitler! Long live peace and the Franco-German alliance!" he was again caught up in the patriotic fever that had never really left him. There remained something of the veteran in him. There was nothing to do about it, Germany was still the hereditary enemy, he had known it since childhood, all his life. Phony war or no, the die had been cast, the *patrie* was in danger. He wanted to serve, one way or another, unable though he was to enlist for active duty.

On December 11 he found a job as ship's doctor with the Paquet navigation line. And on the 15th, in Marseille, he boarded a liner requisitioned for the transportation of troops, the *Chella*, which was detailed to the Marseille-Casablanca route. He made two round trips before the accident on January 5.

Lucette continued to live on the rue Marsollier during his absence. She had just wangled an engagement at the Ledoyen restaurant on the Champs-Élysées, a dance number that she performed during supper. Around 2 A.M., Mme. Destouches would pick her up in her dressing room. Louis may have jealously asked her to watch Lucette's every move. Rich clients mistook her for Lucette's own mother and presented her with flowers to butter her up. The very dignified old lady, more "nunlike" than ever, understood none of the implications.

Louis had only a temporary contract with the Paquet company, at a very modest salary. On the night of January 5-6, off the Gibraltar coast, around 10 P.M., the *Chella* rammed a British torpedo gunboat, the *Kingston Cornelian*, which was on submarine detail and sailing blacked out. The British warship, full of explosives, caught fire and sank within a few minutes. Having sustained damage to its prow, the *Chella* was able to reach Gibraltar, where it was hastily caulked. It then made its way back to Marseille on its own steam on January 23, hugging the coast at reduced speed.

Without the twenty or so deaths aboard the British gunboat, the accident would have had its grotesque, comically Célinian, and frankly absurd aspects. Picture a military ship sunk by a civilian ship, and the English going down just a few furlongs from Gibraltar, sunk by their allies the French. It is surprising that Céline never thought to use the episode in his writing, except for a fleeting reference in *Les Entretiens familiers avec le professeur Y* [Conversations with Professor Y]. Which did not prevent him from writing on January 9 to his old friend Dr. Camus:

"Valor and discipline, and always the first. Thus was I sailing the other night on the treacherous seas, a highly respected man, when my ship, moving at full speed, rammed an English torpedo boat, which exploded with one of those bangs that is decisive in the life and death of a ship, and sank with all hands in less than a minute.

"We were in pretty bad shape ourselves and in distress all that night. It goes without saying that, throughout that tragic night, with its dead, drowned, and wounded, your friend brought honor to those who taught him the profession of arms and drill and valor and discipline. I wonder at this point if my talents won't be honored in high places. We finally limped into port by the skin of our teeth. We later returned to Marseille after a hasty patchup . . . and then we disarmed. Where will I go? Ah! how savage is destiny these days. I'm hoping that, what with my valor and discipline, I'll be found some other cushy number where I'll hit the jackpot, the good life full of thrills. Between ourselves, I've never had so much fun."[39]

We should not be shocked by the word "fun." We must take it in its most extended sense. A doctor aboard a ship which, for its last voyage, had finally been equipped with cannon, Céline must have felt that an old dream had come true—one might say an old family dream, since his father had shared it too. He was no longer a mere passenger! A ship's doctor, almost a military doctor, he was sailing, braving dangers, storms, and the submarines of the Kriegsmarine. . . . The German battleship *Graf Spee* had recently been scuttled in Montevideo Bay, having been relentlessly pursued by British and New Zealand cruisers. The papers carried the news in banner headlines. Of course, the *Chella* incident was not quite the same thing. It had ended in farce. But a bloody farce all the same. It had skirted grand adventure. Céline the Breton, the pirate, the adopted son of Saint-Malo, was in his element.

In Marseille, the *Chella* was first disarmed and then dry-docked for repairs in March. But the Paquet company did not wait that long to cancel Céline's contract. It had let him go in late January. There were no other positions available. Louis had nonetheless hoped for a new appointment.

"A nice stay in Gibraltar then back into the storm on that patched-up old tub—creeping past the rocks on the Spanish coast! And then upon arrival, the eternal question: *Am I fired?* No! It seems . . . the reason—'that I performed above and beyond the call of duty' says the captain's report—but if repairs take too long . . . heroism is forgotten—the bell-pulls remain . . . they never get tired."[40]

In February Louis returned to Paris, Lucette, and the rue Marsollier. In March he accepted a daily round in general medicine at the Sartrouville clinic, replacing the head doctor, who had been drafted.

Sartrouville, past Clichy and before Bezons, was decidedly no escape from the northwestern suburbs of Paris. A gloomy municipality in a wide curve of the Seine, it sat between Houilles and Argenteuil, just across the river from aristocratic and residential Maisons-Laffitte.

The war was continuing on every front. Daladier resigned on March 22. Paul Reynaud, who succeeded him in the Republic's leadership, decided to speed up military operations. British and French troops occupied the port of Narvik in northern Norway in April. The "iron road" had been cut between

Sweden and Nazi Germany, which in the meantime had occupied Denmark and a part of Norway. But all of this was nothing, the mere preliminaries to the great offensive unleashed by the Germans to the west on May 10, with their 105 divisions backed up by Panzers hastily recalled from Poland. This, in the words of Benoist-Méchin, a historian of the war, was the beginning of the "sixty days that shook the West." Everything happened too fast. Everything crumbled. France was in an advanced state of decay and didn't know it. The communists didn't have their hearts in it, to say the least. In any case, the anti-communist struggle prevented any mobilization of the "Sacred Union" type. The extreme Right believed the war to be pointless. It was the Front Populaire with which it had failed to come to terms. What was the use in fighting Hitler? The Right rejoiced only in disasters, it awaited—hoped for—defeat as its vindication. The Right is never so inveterate and arrogant as in disasters, in the decline it greedily prophesies, or in the *décombres*—the ruins—to quote the word that would make the fortune (and the title) of Lucien Rebatet's 1942 book. Most Frenchmen, furthermore, could not see the need to double their stakes in the great roulette of uniformed massacres—they had had their share of dust and ashes twenty years earlier in the Great War. Stalin wasn't stupid, he had arranged things with Hitler, or so he thought. War was for others, on the Western Front. We should have done as he did. Too late!

Fifteen hundred tanks led by Guderian took the narrow, winding route through the Ardennes. They weren't expected there, but over by Belgium and Holland. The front collapsed. The Germans crossed the Meuse. Their infantry followed the tanks. The Luftwaffe harassed the allied columns, the Stukas stung, strafed, and bombed through an empty sky, since the Spitfires and Hurricanes were holding back for the main event—the Battle of Britain.

Gamelin was dismissed and Weygand named Commander-in-Chief on May 19. In Dunkirk, the pincers closed on the allied troops. The English first embarked what remained of their own army, 270,000 men, and then the French soldiers who, under a hail of fire, the pounding of German artillery, aerial attacks, pleaded to be taken next. Meanwhile the Panzers marched onward toward the south. On June 8 they reached the Seine. On June 10 the French government withdrew to Tours en route to Bordeaux. With admirable fearlessness, the Duce declared war on France that very day in the name of Italy. He may have been thinking of the witticism attributed to Charles Maurras: "They say you should not kick an enemy when he's down; fine, but in that case, when should you?"

It was exodus, rout, soldiers in flight, NCOs in confusion, officers nowhere to be seen, populations seized with panic, toward the south, ever southward, Biarritz, Béziers, the roads overflowing, German planes attacking, the whistle of dive-bombing Stukas, cars, wagons, piled mattresses, tears. Anything sufficed—hearses, garbage trucks, vans, and carrier tricycles—for loading up gear, the wardrobe and the grandfather clock, and trying to get across the Loire. Soldiers threw their weapons into ditches, the bourgeoisie conscientiously put their dogs to sleep before heading off with their art works. There was no gas. All the gas flowed into the black market. Tanks and armored trucks stood motionless by the roadside or in the shelter of the undergrowth. People slept by the road, in barns. They didn't really sleep— they were living a bad dream.

"Bicycles were fastened between the fenders. Twelve-year-old children had left clinging to the doors of little jalopies, whose floors were a tangle of arms and legs. Some cars had bedframes secured to their trunks. The most expensive ones carried on their roofs, wrapped in dirty sheets, two or three of the famous June '40 mattresses, and vanished beneath parcels of God-knows-what tied up in newspapers and old dishcloths, hanging all along the fenders. Women factory workers and shopgirls had set out on foot, bare-headed, in slippers or Louis XV heels, pushing two little ones ahead of them in a pram, a third clinging to their skirts. Cyclists had somehow managed to get this far, bearing a pack camel's load on their bikes and their backs. People had carried away bathrobes, vacuum cleaners, pots of geraniums, fire tongs, barometers, umbrella stands, in the panic of waking from a nightmare, a desperate jumble, the chaotic pillaging of a home by its own residents."[41]

And Céline? On June 10 the mayor of Sartrouville decided to evacuate part of the population. The fire truck, the archives, the provisions were all to join up in Pressigny-les-Pins, south of Montargis, on the Gien Road. Céline found himself in charge of the municipal ambulance. He slipped on a white smock with a Red Cross armband. Lucette did likewise. A driver took over at the wheel. They escorted an old lady and two newborns out of Sartrouville.

"I did the retreat myself, like many another, I chased the French army all the way from Bezons to La Rochelle, but I could never catch up. It was one of those neck-and-neck races that are rarely seen. I just made it out of Cour-bevoie on the morning of the 13th. I wanted to see everything! The Fifth Column! You get me? Caught in the crossfire! Between the firing line and the butt, to be more precise! I don't know what the law says in such cases. I left with two little girls—I'll tell all this another time, at my leisure—two newborn infants and their grandmother, in a tiny little ambulance. I cer-tainly protected them in their helplessness from the most dreadful of perils. (They'll put all this on my tombstone.) Believe it or not, we couldn't go any faster, we did our level best to catch up with the French army, road after road, zigzagging, stretches at breakneck speed, the French army kept throwing us off the track, never let us catch up. Its wheels were giddy. Oh! that motorized retreat! Oh! that prioritized prudence! Oh! that police force retransformed into men! every trembling man for himself! I saw forty-ton tanks shove our orphans aside, force us into the beanfields in their dash for cover, a juggernaut free-for-all, a thundering panic of scrap iron. Charge of the lightweight brigade! The thrashing of '71 followed by 40 years of shame was a munificent feat of arms compared with this latest stunt. You can't make this sort of thing up. This is no ugly treachery. There were 15 million of us who saw it."[42]

The exodus of Céline, Lucette, the two bawling newborns, the grandmother straining at her bottle of cheap red wine, and the panicked driver, should first be reduced to a few dates and events. On June 15, the day after Hitler's troops reached Paris, they were in Gien and stayed in a cinema, the Artistic, which was already full of patients evacuated from a Paris psychiatric hospital. The town was bombed in the middle of the night with incendiary bombs that leveled entire neighborhoods. It was impossible to cross the Loire. They made their way upriver to Cosne-sur-Loire and crossed the river on the 16th, at around 10 A.M. That afternoon, the Cosne bridge was destroyed in turn by a bombing raid. They took advantage of a few hours' rest in a military field hospital to change and feed the infants. Then they were off again toward the south, to Sancerre, on the banks of the Allier. Then a westward turn to Issoudun on June 18, where Céline hoped to remain after settling the children in a nursery. But on the 19th a squadron bombed the town. Fires, the dead and wounded all around. Céline again found himself responsible for the two children and their grandmother, and trundled off with the ambulance towards La Rochelle, where they arrived that night.

We also have Lucette Destouches' account of the exodus. Though somewhat muddled as to events and chronology, she gives a pretty good picture of the terrible confusion of the days and the feverish chaos of the nights.

"The nurse had disappeared in Sartrouville where, in normal times, I would go to meet Louis at 5 or 6 P.M. There was just an orderly who worked as a driver. I put on a nurse's uniform, we got the little ambulance, and took the old lady, who was a patient at the clinic, a one-month-old baby girl and another one whom we found on the roadside—her mother had forgotten her, left her behind in the general panic. We loaded them all aboard and left. All Sartrouville was leaving, we headed out with the fire trucks and the moving vans. We took what we could, there was such confusion! Gas soon grew scarce, the firemen left their vehicle on the road, all the vans came to a halt. We still had some gas in the ambulance. On we went. We slept by the side of the road. In Issoudun with the bombing—I can still see the children in the courtyard of the nursery where Louis had wanted to place them, they were left there while the buildings burned and the dead lay all around. We got back just in time. They looked like little monkeys. I had never looked after children myself, I gave them some powdered milk in a tin can, we had no water or talcum powder, the poor things were beet red, we took them back with us. Earlier, we had been with some loonies in a movie theater. We also spent the night at some woman's. The walls of her house were lined with cakes of soap! Everyone had stockpiled something—with some it was sugar, with others soap. It wasn't much fun sleeping out in the open. It was early summer. With the grandmother and her bottle, the two kids, the orderly, and the two of us, the ambulance wasn't big enough to fit us all. The orderly tried to paw me. At one moment, we had reached a little woods, the

Italians were bombing us, and the orderly panicked and couldn't go on. I took the ambulance, the road was mostly gone, I didn't know how to drive, but I still managed to get the ambulance back on the road and we made it to a military hospital. Then we went on to La Rochelle."

Most probably, Louis considered trying to reach England. On the 20th he offered his services to the La Rochelle naval superintendent's office. A doctor, the public health inspector of the Charente-Inférieur *département*, recommended him to the inspector of the port of La Pallice: "This doctor [Céline], a naval medical doctor offering his services, would be pleased to accept any available position, either aboard ship or in any other capacity."[43]

Lucette states: "Boats were leaving for England. I said to Louis, 'Let's go!' Louis loved England, he thought about it. He would have found some medical work there, I would have been a dance teacher in London—why not? And everything that followed would have been different. But no, he said to himself: 'The kids, the old lady, I have to take them home.' After the exodus, the panic, people were returning to their homes. Louis also said: 'You don't leave your country because things are going bad.' And then, he was curious, he wanted to see what was going on. And how could he forget his mother, who was still in Paris? She hadn't left because of her furniture, her chandelier, she was attached to her furnishings, she was afraid it would all be stolen. We found her surrounded by her furniture."

So they did not board ship in La Rochelle, and continued on their way as far as Saint-Jean-d'Angély, where Louis was assigned to the air force. With Lucette, he moved into a barracks for refugee workers from an aircraft factory. His assignment ended on June 30. And by July 14 he was in Sartrouville with the ambulance and the survivors. He did not resume his medical functions, which were paid only by the visit. As he would later mention in a letter to a commission looking into the circumstances in which some doctors had left their posts, the whole odyssey ordered by the mayor of Sartrouville had cost him a small fortune. Traveling expenses, the cost of gas, of repairing the vehicle, the upkeep for driver and patients, food, had all come out of his pocket. And he ended: "Curious by nature and, if I may say, by calling, I was very glad to participate in an adventure that I imagine takes place only once in three or four centuries."[44]

He was wrong. The dark years had only just begun. And as to adventures, the most dramatic and peripatetic ones awaited him at the twilight of the war, during the death throes (still unimaginable in 1940) of Hitler's Third Reich.

13

The Occupation

A Fine Mess

Very few Frenchmen heard de Gaulle's famous call to resistance broadcast on the BBC on June 18. They were on the road, fleeing. They believed that their country had lost not only a battle but the war. All they were waiting for was peace and the demobilization. On June 22 the armistice was signed at Rethondes in Foch's railway wagon, the one from 1918. Hitler prized that symbol. A ceremony in the form of revenge and humiliation. The tone was set. The collaboration would be a suckers' market.

Wagon or no wagon, France was well and truly derailed. What to do? "The time has come to stop fighting." Pétain said, and was heard. And the French delegation had to sign every clause imposed. Woe unto the vanquished. France was divided into free zone and occupied zone. It had to pay an enormous occupation indemnity. Pétain the savior and father, Pétain the bewhiskered old debonair, the defender of Verdun, had given himself for France, he was there to comfort his fellow citizens, to speak to them about Work, the Family, *La Patrie*, and national recovery. On July 10 the Third Republic scuttled itself to a man—or almost. Only eighty-four *députés* voted to deny Pétain full powers to define the new regime to be set up, a vague absolute monarchy ruled, the French believed, by an indulgent daddy who, as they would later discover, turned out to be a senile daddy.

If the war and the defeat had been a bad dream, it was time to wake up. But for many the awakening would be more nightmarish still. A four-year nightmare, which Céline would experience in its every paradox, its every malaise, its every hatred, fear, suspicion, blindness, brutality, and skepticism. Four years of occupation, four long, endless, awful years in which the contradictory Céline, the man of excess, silence, and clamor, would be more than ever contradictory, excessive, silent, disgusted, rebellious, devoted, visionary, and totally short-sighted. It was as though, in the very depths of that foggy night hanging over Europe, the compass needle had suddenly gone haywire. The horror, the absolute horror, preconceived and meticulously organized by the Nazis, the deportations, the camps, the final solutions, the millions of dead—yes, unalloyed horror would be a constant presence in the background, sensed and occasionally glimpsed, blinding and invisible to those who would not see or dared not imagine the unimaginable.

345.

It is thus difficult to understand anything about Céline, shut away in the neuralgia, the buzzing in his head, and in the armorlike deliria that protected him, wounded him, and cut him off from the world. He is silent—and then suddenly he won't shut up. He wants to see everything—out of curiosity—and he sees nothing. He abhors the Jews but joins no party, rejects all official, regular, remunerative journalistic collaboration. He provokes the Germans in public and predicts their defeat, but does he really believe in it? He does not hesitate to help fugitives from the STO, the *Service de travail obligatoire*—forced labor in Germany. Resisters are all around him in Bezons and Montmartre. He closes his eyes—or opens them. He lends a hand in healing a wounded man who bears a striking resemblance to a paratrooper or a liaison agent from England. Which does not prevent him from writing impassioned letters to ultra-collaborationist newspapers, from regretting and forgetting nothing, from loudly proclaiming his racism and then falling silent, tormented by the thought of death, incredibly lucid and visionary, before writing *Guignol's band*, pursuing his fairy tales. He takes the sly petty-bourgeois precautions of stockpiling sausages and jam, afraid of going without, and then he rails against the Freemasons, the communists, the Allies, the Jews. He encourages the anti-Bolshevik crusade, but despises all forms of war. It would be simple to tell the life stories of Brasillach, Cousteau, Laubreaux, Jean Luchaire, and their ilk. They throw themselves into the struggle, they hold convictions occasionally adulterated with opportunism, they nourish themselves on hatreds, strategy, rejections. They denounce, they settle grudges, they hold out hope for a New Order, they believe in a French-style fascism and nonetheless in the Franco-German alliance and the struggle against Bolshevism. Nothing like that with Céline. He is not a party man. He has only prejudices, which, moreover, he can take or leave as he pleases. He is a writer, an inventor of a language. His "little music," his own revolution—that is what he believes in and makes him great in our eyes. But he nevertheless wants to be of his time. He committed himself on the eve of the war. He committed himself a little deeper after the French defeat. One step forward, one step backward, one step to the side, and many a false step. This is Céline in his entirety—torn, ranting, taciturn, generous, imposing, sad. Clever indeed is the person who would claim to understand him, to draw his identikit in a few sentences.

Vichy France established itself at a record pace. On August 13, 1940, Freemasonry, "guilty of being a canker in the body of France," was abolished and its adherents hunted down. It began with the publication of their names in the *Journal officiel.* On October 3, 1940, though the Germans had as yet made no requests or exerted any pressure, the stupefyingly zealous Vichy government passed a Jewish law, an exclusionary program aimed at expelling Jews from positions of authority and responsibility in the army, the magistracy, and public office. They were banned from any cultural activity in the cinema and the theater. Jewish foreigners were subject to internment.

France had been defeated, had she not? The guilty had to be ferreted out, while Pétain strove to mobilize youth "body and soul" with his Compagnons de France, his Youth Camps, and other scouts and torchbearers for the national revolution. The evildoers, then, were the Jews, Freemasons, the Front Populaire, and earlier governments. It was all very well to point them out, but the main thing still was to pass judgment on them. October 20 saw the first session of the Riom court, where, among others, Léon Blum, Georges Mandel, and Paul Reynaud would be tried.

But intellectuals, too, were eager to participate in the great examination of conscience (the examination of others' consciences, to be sure) to determine the causes of defeat. The task had been thrust upon them. The press was to be skewed by creating or nurturing collaborationist periodicals, which they intended to dominate under various slants, from the ultra-fascism of *Je suis partout*, in which Rebatet and Brasillach lost no time in accusing the Vichy government of being too soft, to Marcel Bucard's "Francism"; from the politico-cultural weekly *La Gerbe*, run by Alphonse de Châteaubriant, a fervent defender of the Franco-German alliance, to the newspaper *L'Oeuvre* run by Marcel Déat, leader of the pacifist Left until September 1940, then a Vichy opponent, and then the unfortunate partisan of a "single-party national revolution." Books, too, were to be skewed. Pierre Drieu La Rochelle drew up an entire agenda in his *Ne plus attendre* [No More Waiting]. Lucien Rebatet began writing *Les décombres*, which would become a runaway bestseller on its publication in 1942. Benoist-Méchin put his name to *La Moisson de Quarante* [The Harvest of '40], which gained him immediate recognition. Céline, for his part, having returned to the narrow little apartment on the rue Marsollier that he shared with his mother and Lucette, undertook the drafting of *Les Beaux draps*—A Fine Mess—during the late summer. His way of participating in the great washday.

Meanwhile, publisher Robert Denoël had not lost his sense of direction, i.e., his business sense. The collaboration could also be a remunerative market. Barely a month after the Montoire meeting and "handshake" that solemnized the policy of collaboration between Pétain and Hitler, Denoël founded, on November 20 to be precise, les Nouvelles Éditions Françaises, a publishing subsidiary headquartered at 21, rue Amélie (Éditions Denoël had fine offices at no. 19), and immediately launched an edifying series characterized by him as being in the "national interest" and entitled "The Jews in France." The first title to appear was Dr. Montandon's *Comment reconnaître le Juif?*—How to Recognize a Jew. Soon to follow was Lucien Rebatet's *Les Tribus du cinéma et du théâtre*—The Tribes of Filmmaking and the Theater. It was for Denoël's subsidiary that Céline wrote his third and last great political diatribe.

This was hardly enough to fill his days. As a doctor, he felt unemployed, or demobbed. He soon began looking for a new posting in public medicine, disgusted as he was by private practice. The head doctor and founder of the

Bezons clinic, Dr. Hogarth, of Haitian nationality, had been barred from practice because his country had joined the Allies. Céline learned of this and moved heaven and earth to take his place. He wrote to the president of the Bezons Special Delegation, who had replaced the ousted communist mayor. He explained how, to his mind, there were a few too many Jewish doctors in Bezons and that a native of Courbevoie would fit in perfectly there. He called on the director of the departmental health service in Versailles. In short, he had no trouble getting nominated by the Bezons Council on November 21, rewarded with a yearly salary of 36,000 francs and the rank of municipal officer. Then, by decree on December 21, he was further named the accredited physician to the administration of the Seine-et-Oise *département.* Naturally, he swore an oath that he was neither a Jew nor a Freemason. He did not require much persuasion.

The job, which he began on December 1, 1940, and would keep until leaving for Germany in June 1944, consisted mainly of three long shifts a week at the clinic, in the unspeakably bleak suburb between Sartrouville and Colombes, a gray, impoverished urban sprawl, a kind of foretaste of purgatory. As an accredited physician—i.e., a forensic pathologist—he had also to make house calls, notify the administration of deaths, sign burial certificates, etc.

The war was now raging in the skies over England. London was bombed, Coventry razed, but the British air force held its own. Hitler was beginning to realize that his troops would not be disembarking at the foot of the cliffs of Dover anytime soon. In France, Pierre Laval stoked the fires of the collaborationist policy, believing as he did in Germany's inevitable victory. Field Marshal Pétain dragged his feet. Laval had no qualms about negotiating behind his back. On December 13, as if in a vague burst of authoritarian energy, Pétain had his minister arrested and replaced by Admiral Darlan as the government's leader. The Germans frowned, their ambassador in Paris, Otto Abetz, made his disapproval clear, and Laval was released forthwith. The collaboration still had some fine days ahead.

Between Bezons and the rue Marsollier, Céline completed *Les Beaux draps* in a few months, with the same anxious haste betrayed by the large, sprawling handwriting, indefatigable and almost sickly looking, leapfrogging from one page to the next, and which is explained by the partial paralysis of his arm resulting from his 1914 wound. The bundles of paper were held together with clothes pins, thrown into the wastebasket, or hung from string. He wrote with a kind of mad empiricism, an unruly meticulousness, pages by the hundreds, by the thousands, a few lines, a few ideas, a spinning music, dissonant shouts combined with the gracefulness of a Couperin melody.

What did he have to say in *Les Beaux draps,* dedicated to the victimless noose, as if the hangman had failed in his office, as if those responsible for the mess of '40 still awaited punishment—or else, a disturbing ambiguity, as if the noose were being made a good-luck charm in the hope of better tomorrows without any further deaths? It has been claimed that there is no anti-Semitism in the work, his only political piece written under the occupation. That is untrue. Céline begins by deploring "More Jews than ever in the streets, more Jews than ever in the press, more Jews than ever at the bar, more Jews than ever at the Sorbonne, more Jews than ever in the theater, in the Opéra, the Comédie Française, in industry, in the banks. Paris and France more than ever under the sway of Masons and Jews more arrogant than ever."[1] And he adds a little further on: "I say it's not enough to beat on the Jews, it's running in circles, it's a game, a song-and-dance, unless we grab them by their pursestrings and strangle them with them."[2]

Nonetheless, anti-Semitism is not the book's dominant theme, not by a long shot. For a very simple reason: his anti-Semitism had once been a form of hope, and he had voiced it with a specific goal—to avoid war, save the peace, peace at any price. But war had come and nothing had changed. The same swarms of mediocrity, selfishness, and misery. What was the point of being anti-Semitic? He now portrays anti-Semitism as a kind of permanent presence, a symptom of the French illness. As a result, that anti-Semitism becomes an excuse. When he states that Jews are everywhere, that is all he means. The dream of the French bourgeois is to be Jewish, i.e., according to Céline, to worship the Golden Calf, to be devoid of wit, spirituality, subtlety.

"France is Jewish and Masonic, once and for all. That's what you have to get into your noggins, dear diplomats! Their teams are innumerable . . . Hardly is one exhausted . . . than another steps in . . . ever more 'conciliatory,' naturally . . .

"It's the Hydra with 120,000 heads!

"Siegfried can't get over it!"[3]

The Catholic religion, of course, is implicated by Céline in the same condemnation.

"Crime of crimes, throughout our history the Catholic religion has been the great pimp, the great crossbreeder of the noble races, the great procuress for the corrupt (with all its holy sacraments), for the rabid contaminator.

"The Catholic religion, founded by twelve Jews, will have proudly fulfilled its role when we have all disappeared under the great boggy waves of that gigantic asiatic whorehouse brewing on the horizon."[4]

Not a word in *Les Beaux draps* about Vichy, which of course is incapable of pulling France from the mediocrity in which it is sinking. Jewish, not Jewish—for Céline it has become no more than an arbitrary criterion, an aberrant typology for distinguishing, for example, the writers he enjoys, the musical, light-footed writers, from those he condemns, the abstract, heavy, or gossipy writers.

"What the hell do I care for preacherman Mr. Ben Montaigne, the sly old rabbi? . . . He's hardly the joy I'm seeking, fresh, roguish, mischievous, passionate . . . I'd like to die laughing, but gently . . . Bellay is more dear to me than Racine for two or three verses . . . I'm happy to weep a little, but while I'm dancing . . . I'm of the 'flighty gang' . . . Iphigenia's sobs bore me . . . Hermione is obscene and self-involved . . . Gloomy tales about sex.

"Mr. Montaigne lacks all lyricism and that's a great crime in my eyes, he constructs his cunning Talmuds, his fat manuals on the 'Perfect Jew,' stifling in their tepidity, in their captious yellowness, with their 100,000 explanations where one would do . . . Unspeakable!"[5]

There's certainly nothing optimistic about *Les Beaux draps*. France will forever remain just as dirty, washday or no. Nothing new or lasting will be built on such ruins. The ideal future that he sarcastically suggests to the French, with that wounded laughter drawn from the depths not of his disappointment but of his affirmations, is a petty-bourgeois communism with an hereditary suburban bungalow and a national salary of 100 francs per day for everyone, "dictator included."

The most vivid and most melancholy pages are the final ones, in which in his itemization of mediocrities he evokes education, a debraining machine that, with its closely reasoned, repetitive, and anemic idiocies, kills the inate poetry in children. Céline summons harrowing tones to condemn the entire French educational system, that "disaster of the imagination." "We're dying for lack of legends, mystery, grandeur," he exclaims. "The heavens abhor us. We're dying a stockroom death. . . .[6]

"It requires a long, strenuous effort on the part of the masters, armed with programs, to kill the artist in the child. It doesn't happen by itself. That is the purpose of schools, to be places of torture for innocence, spontaneous joy, the strangulation of birds, the manufacture of a sorrow that already oozes from every wall, the original social ill, the muck that seeps into every corner, suffocating and smothering forever any pleasure in living."[7]

No, there is no anti-Semitism left here. In any case, anti-Semitism for whom, to what purpose? We must remember, any effort is pointless. The laundry will remain dirty. What's the point in purifying, damning, cleaning? Céline has returned to his old certainties; Céline's wash comes out blacker still. Who could guess that *Les Beaux draps* would suddenly become a mobilizing force for the collaborationist powers then establishing themselves? On December 4, 1941, the Vichy government would even ban the work in the unoccupied zone. Céline's sarcasms were too vitriolic for the believers in Work, Family, and *Patrie*. Pétain needed the support of the Catholic and Protestant churches, so the irredeemable Céline's furious anticlerical diatribes were even more unwelcome.

In early 1941, the book was sewn up. Céline signed his contract with Denoël (on behalf of the Nouvelles Éditions Françaises) on February 3. The contract was favorable to the author, with royalties set at 18% from the outset and payable in advance for each new edition, the first being set at 10,000 copies (to be sold at 24 francs). Freed from this work, Céline then began thinking about a move, for at least three reasons.

Living with his mother was becoming more and more difficult, especially in the cramped and comfortless apartment on the rue Marsollier. Céline and

Lucette's very bohemian life-style was hardly suited to the chilly quietude of a housebound and rather possessive old woman.

Moreover, he no longer had to fear any imagined persecution, as he had in the tense prewar climate when he had felt strangely hunted. The worst was now a certainty, the worst had come to pass, the worst was settling in with a war that threatened to drag on and a German occupation to which no end could be foreseen. He could now return to a lodging with his own name on the lease.

Finally, with his new position as head physician of the Bezons clinic, and his royalties from *Les Beaux draps* (along with those from his earlier works, which Denoël put back on the market without altering the text in September 1940, so as to liquidate his stock), he could afford to pay rent. He wanted to return to Montmartre, his neighborhood of choice, to his inseparable friend Gen Paul, to the taciturn Marcel Aymé, and to Le Vigan, consumed by the madness of his roles.

Gen Paul found him an empty apartment for rent at 4, rue Girardon, just a stone's throw from his old garret on the rue Lepic: a three-room apartment this time, on the fourth floor of a rather ugly and very petty-bourgeois brick building on the corner of the rue Norvins, across from the entrance to the Moulin de la Galette. Had its old tenants been Jews or foreigners forced to flee Paris?

"Three cozy little rooms, well-lit, perhaps a little narrower,"[8] decorated with the same curios brought back from Africa, books everywhere, a Dutch brass chandelier, "the kind of rustic Breton furniture that an office worker come into an inheritance might have chosen,"[9] and Louis' office in the wildest disorder, books scattered everywhere, strings strung from one wall to another, bundles of manuscripts hanging from those famous clothespins. This, then, would be the setting for their life in Paris as of February 1941, the probable date of his and Lucette's move.

To sum up: a municipal doctor's job in Bezons, a new apartment in Montmartre, his book of reckoning finally finished, Céline had now put the most urgent things behind him. The setting was now in place. He could settle into his new life. Look around. Live, survive, protect and give himself thoughtlessly over to the four long years of occupation.

To Write or Not to Write?

In the earliest days of the occupation, Lucien Rebatet paid a visit to Céline the way one might consult an oracle, the unheard prophesier of national disaster. Rebatet was animated by the rash zeal of those intellectuals who dreamed of rebuilding France and the world, of finally shaping them to their own exalted ideology. But his meeting with Céline, from whom he hoped for advice and encouragement, was a terrible letdown. The author of *Bagatelles pour un massacre* began by telling him:

" 'Vichy is a mirage, smoke and shadow. What is true is that Fritz lost the war.'

"I looked at him, stupefied. What had happened to him? This was around October 12 or 15. The most unbridled Gaullists of the Hôtel du Parc would have been staggered by such a statement. Churchill himself . . .

" 'No kidding, Louis? What makes you think that?'

" 'They blew it, and us with them. In wars like this, an army that doesn't bring a revolution with it is all washed up. The Jerries have had it.'

" 'Come on, what can the English do to them, on their island?'

"He shook his head, scowling:

" 'The Krauts have had it, even if it takes awhile. And it'll be ugly.' "[10]

This conversation is most revealing. It immediately sets Céline apart from the collaborationist circles. French intellectual fascists like Rebatet or Brasillach took Germany's victory as guaranteed, and saw only one hope of recovery for France: a close alliance with her ancient foe. Céline doesn't believe in France's recovery and no more believes in progress in 1940 than he did in 1932 or 1936. He will never be a man of the future. He is a man of the past, i.e., despairing, like all nostalgics. The future inspires only cynicism in him. *Les Beaux draps* bears that out. What is more, the victory of the Third Reich does not seem to him at all guaranteed. In short, he apparently shares no common ground with *Je suis partout, Au pilori,* and their writers.

Is he, however, really that sure of Germany's defeat? Other testimony or fragments of correspondence sometimes allow us to question that certainty, particularly at the very beginning of the Nazis' successful lightning offensive against Russia, after June 22, 1941.[11] But that may be merely a matter of circumstantial optimism masking many a doubt. When he goes around saying and repeating that the Jews are everywhere, that nothing has changed, that France is immutable, he is only revealing in his own way his profound pessimism.

Céline doesn't know where he or the world is headed. The worst seems certain to him. He has no strength to fight against worst-scenario politics. He protests, whispers, then falls silent. He'd prefer to take refuge in literature. Too late. His discourse was defeatist from the outset, wildly provocative. He remains alone. He asserts his solitude, fiercely, rashly, painfully.

There is no question of regretting what he has written or of pulling his prewar anti-Semitic books from circulation, at a time when the Germans occupy (for starters) two-thirds of France and the deportation of Jews is getting underway. Is he even aware of what is going on around him, of the great "Vel'D'Hiv" raid on the night of July 16, 1942* and what was to follow? His short-sightedness and sincerity seem as inordinate as they are indisputable. In life, as in his books, he twists and distorts reality to suit it to his desires and fears. What he can't adapt to his own logic he sweeps under the carpet. Visionaries see nothing that might disturb them. Céline sees the

---

* The Vélodrome d'Hiver: Site of a roundup of Jews prior to deportation.

triumph of Jewish plutocrats. Who could change his mind? By dint of frenzy and delirium, he has ended up emptying the word "Jewish" of all meaning, making it the shibboleth of his anxieties and rejections. He remains isolated in Montmartre, surrounded by friends who live on the edge. From day to day he heals the miseries of Bezons. He writes. He flares up. He understands nothing. On March 9, 1951, in the last days of his Danish exile, he would again confide to his friend Albert Paraz: "Mme. Rothschild was marvelously respected at the Ritz throughout the occupation. The Kraut is venal, servile, he idolizes the Yid."[12] It seems that history has no lessons to teach anyone.

But he neither cares to commit himself more deeply, nor to write, despite everything, for the collaborationist periodicals. Never to write an article for money is a principle to which he had doggedly adhered since the publication of *Voyage*. Never to be in anyone's pay or at anyone's mercy.

His thinking can be summed up in one formula: What he had to say he has already said, in 1936 or 1937, under the Front Populaire and afterward; he has no intention now of repeating himself and running with the wolves. An undated letter to Jean Lestandi, editor-in-chief of the weekly *Au pilori*, summarizes his attitude: "You ask me why I no longer write? It's kind of you to ask. My answer is a simple one. What is written is written, nothing more, at the right moment. The moment past, the danger past, make way for the tradesmen! For the dogs and the sheep! For the retailers in everything! For the bleaters in everything . . . We need slanderers, duffers, fiends. For my part, I always have a good pack of them on my tail. Whether it's Blum, Daladier, Monseigneur Zazou or Laval, their number pretty much stays the same. If I had to kick all their asses, I'd have been going barefoot long since."[13]

Not writing, as he claims to Jean Lestandi, is a slight exaggeration. In fact, more than thirty manifestations of Céline would appear in the occupation press. More specifically, twenty-five letters, three interviews, two responses to questionnaires, a signature on a manifesto, and three extracts from reviews of public speeches. Seven times in *Au pilori*, six times in *Je suis partout*, four times in *La Gerbe* and *L'Appel*, three times in *L'Émancipation nationale*.[14] He would occasionally complain of expurgations, falsifications, betrayals of trust. His writings would always retain a private format. Indeed, in the strict sense of the word, there were no articles.

Céline's signature appeared in Alphonse de Châteaubriant's *La Gerbe* for the first time on February 13, 1941, under the title "Act of Faith." This was a fiercely anti-Semitic statement condemning with bitter irony the cautiousness and second thoughts of the new leaders in Vichy:

"A hundred thousand shouts of 'Long live Pétain' aren't worth one little 'out with the yids!' in practice. A little courage, in God's n . . . !"

He added: "That's your Revolution? For the birds! Wake me up when the trusts are abolished. Not before! Spare me!"

And he ended by upbraiding the politic and hypercautious intellectuals:

"All who hold pen in France, stage, film, scribblers, should—like members of one Lodge!—fulfill their duty on the spot. May it be so recorded! Let us commit ourselves! Freely, of course, spontaneously, backs to the wall. Without any pressure. And then we'd know who was who, finally. Baptism isn't enough! An act of faith, outright, in writing.

"Are the Jews responsible for the war or not? Come on and answer us black on white, dear acrobat writers."

Does this letter, solicited by the editors of *La Gerbe*, reveal Céline's true thinking? Had he gone too far? Had he already begun to regret his rash whimsy? So it would seem. He immediately complained to Lucien Combelle—a rather anarchistic populist with whom he was on closer, more intimate terms than with the aristocratic Châteaubriant—of the modifications made to his text.

Dear Friend,

I would like you to know that my letter published in La Gerbe *was totally tampered with, prettified, truncated, falsified, that I* no way acknowledge it—that it has nothing to do with me—*These goings-on only hurt their perpetrators—Much good it'll do them! As dumb as they are inept!*[15]

A young German diplomat assigned to the Ministry of Foreign Affairs, Eitel Moellhausen, was acting editor-in-chief at *La Gerbe*. His relationship with Alphonse de Châteaubriant was not always of the smoothest. It was perhaps against the advice of the latter—who, furthermore, had just temporarily quit the paper in protest over its adopted political tack—that Moellhausen published (and altered?) Céline's text. He explained the matter some years later, in an account published in *Rivarol* on January 17, 1953: "From the beginning, Céline told me he wanted nothing to do with the collaboration and that he was determined not to write again, since having had the courage to favor the Germans while they were far away, he couldn't bring himself to do so in current circumstances. . . . I then asked him simply to write a letter to Châteaubriant explaining his position and, to my great satisfaction, he agreed to do so. A few days later his letter arrived at *La Gerbe* and, as I had hoped, it was an excellent piece. . . . The issue had only just reached the stands when Céline sent me a resounding protest in which, after accusing me of betraying his trust, he threatened me with a lawsuit."

A few days later, on February 22 to be precise, Lucien Combelle published another letter by Céline in *Le Fait.* An ambiguous, contradictory letter in which he hedged. The writer began by demanding a certain discretion: "That our profession is all hysteria and narcissism I accept, but still, a little decency is our only redemption, a little transposition the only atonement we can use as our only little excuse. Without that, what abjectness!" He goes on to express his shock at his colleagues' cowardice: "What are they up to? Where are they? What's their price for betrayal? How much an hour? That splendid elite. America? England? Marseille? The time has come to know, to know everything . . . Over to you."

Les Beaux draps went on sale on the 28th. There was no significant critical reaction. The book had come at a bad time and fell flat. In whose interest could it have been to recruit Céline? Vichy's? The Gaullists'? The early resisters'? The fascists'? The pro-Germans'? This time, no doubt about it, Céline had done everything to put himself in the wrong. But since he had lent much credibility to the nascent anti-Semitic hysteria before the war, he was occasionally praised out of pure gratitude.

Undoubtedly, the most penetrating and significant critique was that of Drieu La Rochelle in *La Nouvelle Revue Française* on May 1, 1941: "There is something religious about Céline. He is a man who feels things deeply and who, being seized by the spirit, is compelled to cry from the rooftops and howl at streetcorners the infinite horror of existence. In the Middle Ages he would have been a Dominican, God's watchdog; in the XVIth century, a *moine ligueur* [a member of the anti-Protestant 'Sainte Ligue']. There is something religious about Céline in the larger sense of the word: he is bound to the totality of the human entity, though he may see only with the immediacy of his time. And is there perhaps, in a narrower sense, something Christian about him? That abhorrence of the flesh. But, in the final analysis, no: his abhorrence is only for corrupt flesh. Beyond it, Céline espies a flesh cleansed, glossy, redeemed, sparkling with cheer and bursting with joy. This shines forth, among other places, in the final pages of his book *Les Beaux draps*."

And that, indeed, is Drieu's only reference to the book, which finally he used as a mere pretext.

Why would that same Céline who had refused to grant an interview to Lucien Combelle agree to one, in March '41, with Henri Poulain, the subeditor of *Je suis partout*? A momentary whim? Publicity acumen? Brasillach's weekly enjoyed a much wider circulation, a detail that is perhaps not insignificant.

Poulain, whom Céline had known before the war, dropped in on him at his clinic in Bezons. The author of *Les Beaux draps* warned him right away: "We can talk about the book . . . if that's what you want! no talking about me! I'm not Madame Darrieux! The literary question is a feminine thing, foolishly feminine! Also, no talking about the fellow himself, never! What a lousy thing is man!"

Poulain expressed his regret to Céline that the Jew is not enough of a central theme in *Les Beaux draps*. One can never be anti-Semitic enough for other anti-Semites. Céline hastened to reassure him: "I did all I could on the Jew in the other two books . . . For now, anyway, they're less arrogant, less swaggering . . . Still, we shouldn't kid ourselves. The secretary of physicians of Seine-et-Oise is named Menckietzwictz. For that matter, I also happened to overhear a woman on line who said: 'We ate better in the time of the Jews!'"[16]

We see here how Céline, too cautious, too distant, too skeptical to commit himself, to write articles for money, could allow himself to be "trapped" by a journalist. His words are terrifying. Céline, irascible and intemperate, who played on his anger and rhetorical excesses, who roared out the false to whisper the true, who wouldn't hesitate to provoke the entire world, could thus be caught in his own evasions. His words linger, crushing at times, petrified, distorted, stripped naked, without the vocal inflections and comedic play that occasionally parodize and save them.

Céline's responses to the press attacks on *Les Beaux draps*; his letter to the editors of *Aujourd'hui* insulting Robert Desnos, accusing him of gibberish and *philosémitisme*; or that to *Le Pays libre*, which, under the by-line of Maryse Desneiges, had reproached him for ridiculing the French army— all these are noteworthy only for their muddled wrath, an anti-Semitism that is made all the more feverish and attenuated by Céline's contempt for the whole stupid business. "In the end, we all deserve to croak, and that is my abiding hope."[17]

Far more interesting are his letters to the press after the Axis powers opened hostilities against Russia on June 22, 1941, as if Germany's early victories over the Bolsheviks had somewhat revitalized his passions, if not his faith.

In *Au pilori* on October 2, he writes to Jean Lestandi, again concerning the General Commission for Jewish Affairs created by Vichy on March 2 with Xavier Vallat as its chief officer: "In these conditions, what dare the Jewish Commission attempt? Making faces. Might it be nice if it were to act? It wouldn't last twenty-four hours! French public opinion is completely philosemitic, and ever more so! . . . In order to re-create France, it would have to be entirely rebuilt on racist-communal foundations. With every passing day we move further from that ideal, that fantastical goal. The lark has remained valiant and joyful, still wheeling in the sky, but the Gauls no longer hear her . . . Bound and chained to the ass of the Jew, steeped to their very hearts in his droppings, they're sitting pretty."

More cautiously, he avoided a clear response to an inquiry published in *La Gerbe* on October 23, whose very question is nauseating: "Should the Jews be exterminated?" He got away with a few generalities and references to his earlier books.

It should be noted that there was nothing exceptional about such an issue. On December 20, 1940, the editors of *Au pilori*, whose circulation ran at about 60,000, launched an important competition for its readers on the subject: "The Jews: Where to dump them?" One reads these lines, which need no commentary:

"The only required measure is that of total purification through expulsion.

"But it seems that Palestine is too cramped to hold them, and that Australia is not overeager to receive such a gift.

"What are we going to do with them? . . .

"Our Management has allotted sensational prizes for the best answers to this unique question:

" *'Where to dump them?'*

"(Any measure of radical destruction is acceptable.)"

Céline hoped for a German victory over Soviet Russia. He had therefore warmly welcomed the creation of the LVF, the League of French Volunteers against Bolshevism, on July 6. The Soviet barbarity that he associated with a Jewish triumph seemed a thousand times more disturbing than the triumph of National Socialist ideology. No doubt about that. It was the West that had to be defended above all else. "At least the Legion exists, that's something, there are some people who are bothered by that. And what are they doing? I'm telling you myself, the Legion is great, it's everything that's good. That's what I think about all this."[18]

Was Céline trigger-happy, a saber-rattler? That, once again, would be to misunderstand him. Writing to Alphonse de Châteaubriant, he suggested a campaign, not to send his fellow citizens to the slaughterhouse on the Eastern front, but to finance, in one instance, a French medical service. "Enough arms striking out! a few hands repairing . . . a little charity, some goodness, some active help in this vast charnel house, and let the initiative be a *French one*—less anti-communist, pro-Nazi politics, bla bla bla . . . still following Germany's lead, but with a little of our own stuff . . . with the appropriate publicity, of course—a corps of physicians . . . of transfusion medics . . . a corps of surgeons—of nurses . . . I know Russia well—come the winter, we'll certainly need as much medical and epidemiological help over there as we will artillery reinforcements! If the idea took root I'd be happy to join—but frankly, killing, and I've done a lot of it, doesn't do much for me anymore."[19]

While Denoël brought out a new edition of *Bagatelles* in November '41, Vichy declared a ban on *Les Beaux draps* in the unoccupied zone on the 4th of that month. That same day, coincidentally, Pierre Constantini's *L'Appel* (a paper that survived only on German subsidies) published a letter from the writer, who had suddenly taken a dislike to Charles Péguy, "that moron for life," and concluded: "In the end, only Chancellor Hitler can say anything about the Jews. . . . That's the side of him that people like the least, the only side of Chancellor Hitler, apparently, that they're really afraid of, deep down. It's the one I like the most. I was already saying so in 1937, under Blum."

Shortly after the Vichy ban, the police seized copies of *Les Beaux draps* at bookstores in Marseille and Toulouse. It was another opportunity for Céline to react. To affirm to Pierre Lhoste of *Paris-Midi*, on December 29, 1941, his indignation over the measure: "On principle, a writer must be on the outs with authority. So this way . . . it's perfect. Banned by Daladier, banned by Pucheu . . . It used to be, only the Jews were persecuted. Nowadays, they have to have an official victim."

And on January 8, 1942, he wrote another letter to Jean Lestandi at *Au pilori*: "The Toulouse police department took the trouble to go to a bookstore and seize seventeen copies of *Les Beaux draps*. Why? I haven't the slightest idea. A year after publication? Perhaps I'll find out one day. Virtue is on the rise beyond Moulins! The rifles of the retreat, certainly dry by now, are going off by themselves in the South! There must be other, far more upsetting tragedies in the world at the moment. But the police department has no greater concern than to go seize my poems while the earth comes tumbling down, while the flood is at its height!"

Céline was not alone in taking a stance against the measure by Vichy—"that den of Jewish muck"[20]—which had been officially undertaken for "offenses against the army." Marcel Brucard's *Le Franciste*, Alphonse de Châteaubriant's *La Gerbe*, and Brasillach's *Je suis partout* joined his protest.

His disgust with Vichy after the ban on *Les Beaux draps* certainly contributed to pushing Céline toward deeper political involvement. Thus, the December 11, 1941, issue of *Au pilori* quoted Céline's words in favor of a single party. "Anti-Jewish from the very beginning, I sometimes have the impression that certain newcomers, if not having actually superseded me, at least have very different ideas from mine on the Jewish problem. That's why I have to meet with them, I have to explain myself to them." Once again he took his colleagues to task for their silence, their caution, urging them to declare themselves racists, to define their positions.

A meeting was organized in the paper's offices on December 20, with the participation of Céline, Pierre Constanti, Pierre-Antoine Cousteau, Marcel Déat, Georges Montandon, Henri Poulain, Georges Suarez, and other French anti-Jewish personalities. Xavier Vallat, the High Commissioner for Jewish Affairs, had been invited to the meeting. He did not attend. Jean Luchaire (*"louche Herr"*—"shifty Herr"—as he was called by the London Radio), Drieu La Rochelle, Châteaubriant, Rebatet, and Ramon Fernandez made their excuses. The December 20 issue of *Au pilori* reported Céline's statements at the meeting, in which he entreated the Church to take a position on the Jewish problem, called for a minimum wage for the working classes, and ended with these general thoughts: "It is necessary to re-instill a sense of beauty and hard work in the French people, and to replace the sordid materialism in which they have been living with a little idealism. Only then will France be able to rise from the degradation in which three-quarters of a century of Jewish domination have steeped it."

Of course, this involvement did not involve making common cause with a specific political party. Céline went only so far as to offer, with infinite disillusionment, generalized ideas.

Doriot would have been well pleased to welcome him into the ranks of his Parti Populaire Français. Céline met him on three or four occasions at the home of his friend Dr. Bécart. Their relationship grew no closer. At Sigmaringen, they would not even see each other. Céline would later write of him: "The man was interesting but I hated the clique of little political pimps surrounding him, and the PPF returned the favor. Fossati—Sicard—that girl

Moreau, Raymondi, etc. Doriot, a good friend? For eight months, we lived sixty kilometers from each other in Germany— He never came to see me."[21]

The fact remains that on February 1, 1942, Céline attended the rally held by Doriot in the Vélodrome d'Hiver before nearly 15,000 people, and that *Les Cahiers de l'émancipation nationale*, the official organ of the PPF, published a long letter from Céline to Jacques Doriot in March 1942. Maurice-Yvan Sicard (who thenceforward wrote under the name Ivan-M. Sicard) later recounted: "The letters sent to us by Louis-Ferdinand Céline were delirious and difficult to publish. Sometimes they took the form of morbid prophecies."[22]

Céline's text came out just after Doriot had left for the Eastern front. It is more striking for its tone than for its contents. Did he sense the Nazi armies' growing exhaustion in Russia? Did he know that by now all was lost, that Bolshevism would not be defeated, that the end of the war would witness new massacres and new infamies? More than ever, the word "Jewish" was becoming a shibboleth for him, a stubbornly empty word used to designate evil, the venoms of the past, the symptoms of decadence. His letter to Doriot in March 1942 has the knell of a death march.

"To hell with anti-Semitism! To hell with all the Aryan assholes! Such is the watchword of the day! That, in the end, is the summary, the simple, gloomy result of Aryan rage in action, the demented disparagement, the delirious passion for the 'Self.' The cause is lost.

"It ends up taking your all, and even disgusting you a little, this impossible Aryan cause.

"Since we're so corrupt, so hopeless, so stupid, all us bastards should just disappear!

"The story of Vercingetorix is starting all over again, identical, in a new format. All has been written.

"Who's gloating? cheering? jeering? The Jew, of course! What a windfall! Try putting yourself in his place!"

Let us recall René Vincent, the *Le Combat* critic who in 1938 had accused Céline of being Jewish. Was this provocation so very absurd? Deep down, Céline was very jealous of what he called Jewish solidarity. He hardly denounces it in his writing. Mostly, he scolds others, Aryans, Bretons, writers, Montmartre or Saint-Malo natives, for their terrible lack of it. Céline occasionally dreams of an ideal community, bonded, based on support, mutual help and devotion. In that sense he should have liked to be Jewish, as he admitted on several occasions, without irony or violence, to Lucette. And his admiration for what he saw as the Semitic communal spirit turned to clownish, tragic rage when he felt deprived of a happiness to which he aspired and which others possessed instead of him.

His article-letter to Jacques Doriot develops that regret with a desperate and blinding clarity:

"One day, chatting a little about such things, Lucien Descaves told me: 'You see, Céline, the Aryan has no Family.'. . . .

"That's the essential horror of it, and our condemnation.

"Our defeat is moral, not one of intelligence.

"We are 'antisolidarity' out of principle, religion, damnable habit, and the Jew has nothing but that: 'Solidarity.'

"A single family, he is 'Mr. One-Family,' Mr. 'All-in-the-orgy.'

"We must lose."

And his letter ends with the usual visions of Apocalypse, the tide of blacks, Asiatics, and cutthroats sweeping across Europe—

"Aryans, I'm very much afraid our fate is sealed; we haven't managed to unite ourselves, we don't like one another at all.

"Never mind! Let it rip!

"It's the sharks' turn now!

"Let death rejoice!

"It's all we've got left!

"Congratulations, we innocent and aggrieved!

"We just came a little too early to be niggers, that's all!

"Be hip when it all crumbles around you!

"We'll die refusing! That, friend, is my final word!

"May your victory in the East upset the course of things!

"How I'd like to be proved wrong in the end! To die mistaken!"

On March 17 Céline complained to Combelle of having been "tampered with by *Les Cahiers de l'émancipation nationale* . . . I absolutely refuse to have my texts expurgated—I'm free of charge but absolute."[23] A sentence naming the Church a "great crossbreeder," and "the archcriminal procuress, the ultimate antiracist" had been censored by those in charge of Doriot's paper.

But for Céline, the time of his most ferocious invective was now past. Weariness, discouragement, and caution were his basic motivators.

On February 19, in Riom, the trial brought against those responsible for the defeat—General Gamelin, Blum, Daladier—finally began. The trial was characterized by total confusion and Vichy hastily cut it short. Céline read the testimony of the officers at the bar and thought of the ban imposed on *Les Beaux draps* by Vichy. On April 5 *Révolution nationale* published his letter to Lucien Combelle in which he remarked that "the generals of the defeated French army express themselves with a candor and ferocity about the soldiers of '41 that reduce me with my *Beaux draps* to the rank of gossipy commentator, a little harum-scarum."

On April 2 Pétain was forced to recall Laval. On May 6 Darquier de Pellepoix succeeded Xavier Vallat as General Commissioner for Jewish Affairs. On May 29 a German statute imposed the obligatory wearing of the yellow star by Jews. On July 17 came the Vel'd'Hiv raid. The nightmare loomed ever more tragically, and fatally, over the Jews, over France, over the world. The Germans marked time outside Stalingrad. On November 8 the Anglo-American forces landed in North Africa. On November 11 the Germans occupied the free zone.

It would be an exaggeration to claim that Céline was silent during this period. Denoël—who in March had brought out a new edition of *Voyage*, illustrated with drawings by Gen Paul that were marvelously in sync with the novel's whirlwind, anarchistic violence—doubled his stake in September with a *Mort à crédit* also illustrated by Gen Paul. Most importantly, in October '42, he undertook an illustrated re-edition of *L'École des cadavres* and a new edition of *Bagatelles*. In the political atmosphere of the time, this decision was disastrous.

Might Céline have been able to oppose it? He later claimed that Denoël, always short of money, had forced his hand. Moreover, in a statement written in his Danish exile and sent to the public prosecutor in response to the accusation brought against him, he explained that Denoël had probably tried to compromise him on purpose, as if to win points with the Resistance, with which he had secretly joined cause: "I knew that Denoël was more or less hiding Aragon at his place . . . I had good reason to be suspicious. In any case, Denoël represented the re-edition of *L'École des cadavres* to me as vital to the state of his finances—an always precarious state. On top of that, given the 'Publication Regulations' of the time, I had to furnish Denoël with a preface to justify the book's price increase. That's how I came to write the offending preface."[24]

The defense is not entirely convincing, no more than Denoël's supposed Resistance activities. It is easy to believe that he pushed Céline to reprint his works. But it is equally hard to doubt that Céline let himself be pushed. Every book sold was another penny in his pocket, a provision against hard times. The thrifty Céline, ever hoarding against the Apocalypse, could not ignore that. On the other hand, he was always ready to ignore the rest, or not to see it, so much so that he had no qualms about writing directly to Karl Epting, director of the German Institute in Paris throughout the occupation, to ask him for paper. The letter, written on April 15, 1942, on stationery from the Bezons municipal clinic, bears witness. "Dear Epting, You were once kind enough to inform me that in the event of *my publisher* lacking paper to print my books—you might be able to come to my assistance. I have not forgotten those tempting words—up to now we have struggled against growing penury but we have *reached the end of our rope*— To reprint my principal works we would need *fifteen tons of paper*. That is the naked truth—Do you think you can help me? [In English] *That is the question—Be or not.* Most cordially yours. Destouches."[25]

After this, Céline's letters and public speeches would become increasingly rare and less meaningful. That the war was lost for the Germans was no longer possible to doubt. On February 3, 1943, the German Sixth Army capitulated at Stalingrad and Field Marshal Paulus surrendered to the Soviets. It was the slow beginning of the retreat. And Laval, who on June 22, 1942, during a radio discussion, had declared: "I wish for a German victory because without it Bolshevism would take over everywhere," would long have cause to regret the sentence that aroused indignation and wrath in many French hearts.

Caution or no caution, from then on Céline was associated with the most extreme journalists, writers, and pamphleteers of the collaboration. On August 2, 1942, his name had already appeared on a blacklist published by *Life*, and the BBC had named him as a "collaborating writer" in its program "The French Speak to the French" on October 15. For his part, he now wished to speak to no one. He isolated himself further. He wrote a new novel. In other words, he abandoned one war to return to the last, he deserted the present to take refuge in the past. In short, he wrote *Guignol's band*, as if he were joining the French in London, in his own way. Not the Gaullist resisters on the BBC, but the patriotic pimps of Soho, 1916.

Another letter on May 4, 1943, written this time from the rue Girardon: "Dear Dr. Epting, I have the honor to bring to your attention one naked fact. Neither *Bagatelles*, nor *L'École*, nor *Les Beaux draps* have been on sale or *in print* for nearly *a year* for lack of paper—without a miracle I will run out of paper. Denoël has barely 5 tons a year in all! And if he prints so many things . . . It is thus a question of *3 or 4 tons* of *good-quality paper*. I wonder my dear Director what are your thoughts on this?"[26]

During this time, Parisian journalists subjected to German censorship were having a very hard time transforming the successive setbacks of the Nazi armies into soothing communiqués. Their dailies had to publish the OKW (Oberkommando der Wehrmacht) official communiqué every day. How could a journalist, writer, or mere observer obtain any real news?

In January 1943 Darnand established the Militia. The collaboration was to stiffen against the Resistance, the "terrorists," with bloody relentlessness. Rommel's Afrika Korps was defeated in Tunisia, and the Allies landed in Sicily in July. As for Céline, he continued to tune up his guignol's band in Montmartre. And what had originally been intended as the final section of *Voyage* gradually became, in the eerie fogs of London, a great novel in its own right. For the moment, Céline took virtually no time out to write letters to newspapers, only an insignificant note to Lucien Combelle, which *Révolution nationale* presented as an article on February 20, 1943. It was simply an opportunity for Céline to say, "Once and for all I NEVER write articles. I have not written you an article, but a *letter* and *for free*. I'm sticking by that."[27]

He wrote another letter to *Je suis partout* on July 9, 1943, to condemn the French bourgeoisie, denounce its cowardice, greed, and parasitism. The word "Jewish" appears here only as an epithet not serving to distinguish the chosen and accursed race from "good" Frenchmen, but to disqualify precisely those Frenchmen—all Frenchmen and the officers foremost—who had recently carried off their mirrored wardrobes in the retreat. The word "Jewish" is again emptied of its strictly racial meaning. We are all Jews because we are all decadent, selfish, cautious. And Céline more than most. That was his statement.

Céline was certainly on the defensive, weighing ever more concretely the dangers he would run come the end of the war and the liberation. Another letter to *Je suis partout* on October 29, 1943 bears witness to that: "What about the full roll-call of all those who benefited from the Germans? Now, those were the *real* collaborators, not the idealists and intellectual dilettantes."

Céline was equally embittered, violent, and resentful, in his reaction to the death of Jean Giraudoux on January 31, 1944, with a sarcastic letter: "The Jews must be having a good laugh with Giraudoux's obituaries! A roundabout way of kissing their asses! Suppose I snuff it or am snuffed, I'd like to see *Izvestia* throw obituaries my way! My God! Every day makes you sorry to be an Aryan."[28]

Is this paranoia? Mad Céline, the fierce, grotesque moralizer, the anti-Semite whom the war and occupation had taught nothing, since he had managed to see nothing and to remember nothing, was also setting himself up as a target. For several years, however, his paranoia had been belied by unspeakable persecutions against his perceived enemies.

To Claude Jamet, who interviewed him a few weeks before the Normandy landings, Céline could not help dropping these despairing remarks, in which anti-Semitism no longer plays any part: "Hitting on the Jew, or the Mason, isn't much of anything. It's negative really. Laughable, if you like. It raises no enthusiasm. It's only anti, abstract—bagatelles! It doesn't grab the masses. You can turn your record over all you like, slow it down, speed it up, or make it play backwards. What we need is a change of record. With calculation. Race? Family? Country? Sacrifice? All that's idealism. It soars, it floats, it hovers—too high. You have to get at the people where they are, at their basest level. Communism will be overthrown only by being superseded, only if we can do better."[29]

The Céline of the occupation years cannot be summed up in thirty-odd statements to the press of the period. There is also and primarily the Céline of Montmartre and that of Bezons, the novelist and the doctor, the harried man, the wounded man, the curious man, the private man, the silent man, the arrogant man, the man who sees Paris and its suburbs under the bombs. We'll come to that.

To write or not to write? A few letters, some interviews and commentaries—is it a lot or is it little, at a time when polemicists, political journalists, professional anti-Semites, ideologues, and assorted carpetbaggers were raging by the columnful, the weekful, the microphoneful?

One thing is certain: through the ferocity of his voice and the respect in which it was held, Céline had made himself the most popular and resounding spokesman of prewar anti-Semitism. No one had forgotten that. In other words, after '40 he was watched like an oracle. People tried to surround him. They sought his endorsement. And he strove to disengage himself. To endorse as little as possible. He wrote parsimoniously. And, objectively, he was little heard from in the dissonant uproar of occupied France. He did not, like Professor Georges Claude, do the lecture circuits to justify Vichy policy. He did not become directly involved in politics like Abel Bonnard. Did not thunder on the airwaves like Jean-Hérold Paquis, every day forecasting the destruction of England. Did not call for the systematic deportation of Jews, including children, by the Germans, like Robert Brasillach. Did not launch into dithyrambic praise of Hitler's visions for Europe, like Georges Suarez. Is that enough to characterize him, given his own earlier commitments, as a man of no consequence, a crank, conceited, chicken, yellow—in a word, irresponsible? Certain people, such as Robert Brasillach's brother-in-law Maurice Bardèche, tried to do so, essentially reproaching him for having betrayed his camp.[30] But whose camp? Theirs? His own? That is absurd. It is once again the error of seeing Céline as a party man: a man of plans, a man for the future, when he was a man only for the past. Anti-Semitism, for him, had coincided just before the war with a moment of hope, a moment when he had believed himself capable of influencing the course of events, of preventing another conflict. It no longer made any sense on the morrow of the German victory, which Céline did not believe in anyway. For him, I repeat, any future could only be disenchanting. Drieu, who, like so many other intellectuals, had believed that France's salvation depended on the Reich's triumph, thus bitterly defined after the war the policy of collaboration he had felt correct in following: "Germans who did not believe in Hitler enough, assigned to indoctrinate Frenchmen who believed in him too much."[31]

Céline believed in neither the Germans nor the French. And so he spoke, against all reason and evidence, to declare the Jews triumphant at a time when they were being marched by the millions into the camps and the death chambers, and to repeat that decadence, egoism, mediocrity, fear, and cowardice no longer knew any bounds. He hazarded every so often to speak, to vomit up a few hatreds, a few belching spasms, bitter, inaudible, and clinically morbid. It was too much. It was pointless, unexploitable by the Germans and incomprehensible to the collaborators—as to everyone else.

Bezons and Montmartre

In order to meet Céline under the occupation, there was no point in seeking him out at home in Montmartre, because he didn't receive visitors; nor in hoping to catch him in the editorial offices of the ultra-collaborationist newspapers, since he never set foot there. There was no chance of finding him at the soirées held by Otto Abetz at the German embassy—he only went once or twice, out of contemptuous curiosity. More often than not, he was bored at the theater or the movies. It would have been pointless looking for him in the worldly social circle of cocktails and the chic and frivolous *Tout-Paris* undaunted by the sight of Wehrmacht officers. For the Céline of the years '40 to '44, one had to cross Paris, the Seine, Courbevoie and Asnières, finally to catch a glimpse of him, every day of the week or very nearly, at the municipal clinic in Bezons.

More than ever he gave the impression of a doctor little interested in conformity, unrecognizable as the young propagandist of the Rockefeller Mission he had once been and whom Édith Follet had met in 1918, elegant if not quite a dandy, with a long white scarf around his neck and smelling of Guerlain eau-de-cologne. Now Céline dressed with bohemian casualness, in ragged clothes, suits that must once have been fashionable in a very English sort of way but were now seedy and misshapen. Strings took the place of belts and served to hang his gloves around his neck. He wore a khaki raincoat lined with sheepskin or a putty-colored, oil-stained mackintosh. He occasionally used public transportation but more often went to Bezons on an asthmatic moped, the make of which Lucette can no longer seem to remember.

Healing the sick, the contagious, the maimed, the rheumatics, and the heart patients was obviously his primary task, which he sometimes dispatched with a distracted offhandedness. Not that he was uninterested in their fate, but their ills had to harmonize with his preconceived ideas. Céline became convinced, for example, that the inhabitants of Bezons practiced lax hygiene. He treated them for scabies at the drop of a hat, and too bad for those who didn't have it, they should have! Schoolchildren found themselves prescribed withering doses of cod liver oil, and adults had to swallow liters of phosphated iodotanic syrup.[32]

The destitute, the dispossessed, and the poor interested him more than the sick. He would open the clinic doors during the winter and the homeless would come to find a little comfort in the well-heated waiting room. When there were few clients, Céline wrote at his desk, expediting his private correspondence but also writing his books, *Guignol's band* in particular. He was unable to sit and do nothing. He handed out milk vouchers and ration coupons to mothers and the needy, and had to pull strings, see officials, exploit his connections to obtain further privileges for his people.

"It's true there were a lot of them . . . a whole crowd to be examined . . . a really faithful clientele·. . . one, two, three, four prescriptions . . . and then a voucher . . . that's the rhythm . . . one . . . two . . . three vouchers . . . a prescription! . . . That's been the cadence since winter . . . fewer and fewer prescriptions . . . more and more vouchers . . . each time a quarter . . . a half-liter . . . I get an enormous number of requests . . . I panic on the telephone . . . that it'll ring, that there's no more . . . that I've given out all the milk in town . . . as the purse strings tighten, fewer and fewer prescriptions . . . more and more vouchers . . . 25 sugar cubes . . . a little bucket of coal . . . that the misery will never end . . . that it keeps increasing . . . that it'll soon cover everything . . . and finally medicine itself . . . that it won't leave anything untouched."

These pages, among the last of *Les Beaux draps*, are no exaggeration. To Céline, no emergency was as serious as that of these undernourished children, whose fathers were prisoners in Germany and whose deficiencies he tried to palliate with sugar, milk, fats, meat, vitamins, not to mention the allocations of coal that had to be distributed to old people during those endless wartime winters.

In Bezons, Céline was on good terms with his predecessor, Dr. Hogarth, who was prevented from practicing but whose wife, a Frenchwoman and physician, continued to ensure the examination of women and children at the clinic. She held watch during Dr. Destouches' frequent absences.

Another Bezons personality was Dr. Joannin Vanni, with whom Céline—a forensic pathologist, we must remember—was to establish professional ties, and to whom he was soon linked by an abiding friendship. But Dr. Destouches remained highly secretive about his private life. Despite their friendship, it took the commissary a year to learn that the doctor was also a writer. He found him occasionally "a little too favorable to the Jerries" but had no trouble agreeing with him on anti-communism. They argued for hours. Joannin Vanni was not strictly speaking a resister, but he nonetheless did not hesitate to use every available channel to warn the men whom the STO had selected to leave for Germany. Of course Céline's colleagues kept him carefully isolated from the still inchoate networks and organizations of the Resistance. All the same, the commissary and many people in Bezons knew that Dr. Destouches readily signed medical certificates, out of pure generosity, for STO evaders and some Jews. Like this certificate of May 7, 1943: "I certify that M. Marcel Plazannet has been under my care for some time, and that, over the course of the winter, I have observed in him symptoms of apical inflammation by means of radioscopy of the affected apices, generally poor health, short bouts of fever, coughing fits—we feel that M. Plazannet should be seen by a medical board before being sent to Germany."[33]

Céline had also long felt an abiding friendship for Albert Sérouille, a retired teacher and, according to some, a former dance instructor at the Opéra-Comique.[34] He had been named municipal librarian of Bezons under the occupation. Céline urged him to write a *History of Bezons* and the old man jumped at the chance. Céline helped him to get his book published by Denoël in January '44, writing for the occasion a sumptuous preface that resonated with the great melancholy lyricism of a Courbevoie native, a kind of tragic fidelity to his modest origins.

"A poor Parisian suburb, a doormat before the city where each man wipes his feet, spits lustily, and passes on—who thinks of her? No one. Benumbed with factories, overflowing with muck, tattered and torn, she is now but a soulless land, an accursed work camp, where a smile is vain, effort lost, suffering drab, Paris 'the heart of France,' what a joke! What an advertisement! While the suburbs all around it die away! A Calvary permanently flattened by hunger, labor, and bombs—who cares about her?

"Therefore, long live death in Bezons! I know a little bit about it. M. Sérouille adorns it for us. Long live Montjoye and Saint-Denis! Not far at all! Long live Courbevoie! my birthplace. All the homeland I ever had is buried there. I can't help my interest in it. A last glimpse. . . .

"Bezons in the dictionary? Two depressing lines. What meanness! What filth! But all of French history passes through Bezons! Right through! Across the bridge of Bezons, more exactly. Are France's years full of abundance, prosperity, happiness? The Bezons market is in full swing! They're hunting in Maisons-Laffitte, the troops are parading around Carrières, there are processions, joy and feasting, all is well on both banks!

"Are the years dire? Do misfortunes rain down on France? The advance guard of the calamity camps in Bezons . . . The bridge blows up! . . . That's the great sign! . . . Go see it . . . They're only just starting to repair it."[35]

History was catching up with Bezons, a victim of Royal Air Force bombardments in 1943 and 1944. The bridges were targeted, as was the nearby industrial zone in Argenteuil. Céline was called to the scene with the rescue teams. Having grown gradually attached to the town, having helped to develop its school fund and municipal library, having relentlessly solicited his friends, like Marie Bell, to contribute gifts to those two entities, he could not help but be moved by the systematic destruction. It further justified his Anglophobia.

If he was afraid of falling victim to the bombs himself, from 1941 onward he mostly feared assassination. He again saw himself as a marked man. He was a little ahead of history, however. For the moment, others were being marked, hunted down—Jews, foreigners, resisters. But Céline wasn't interested in details. Thus, from 1941 on, he began limiting his visits to Bezons to two or three a week, not counting his travels, vacations, and expeditions to the country to stock up on the black market. But once he was there, his solicitude never slackened.

The case of D. is exemplary. This girl of eighteen, holding a Red Cross diploma, offered her services to the clinic, as a volunteer if need be. She was desperate to escape her family environment at all costs. Her father, a police sergeant, was the perfect specimen of a brute. Her mother beat and mistreated her relentlessly. Céline took her under his wing. He got her into a nursing school. He oversaw her studies. He was like her mentor, an adept in clear-thinking, bitterness, and cynicism, he strove to arm her against all of life's dirty tricks and traps. It is unlikely that he was also a distracted, shortlived lover to her, as he had been to Erika Irrgang and Cillie Pam, whom he had once taken in and plied with advice as valuable as it was crude. He did try to lure her to Gen Paul's and make her pose as a model in his studio, but he did not press her when she balked. His lighthearted voyeurism no doubt found more minimal, more subtle satisfactions with her. Which in no way detracts from his generosity. For her, Dr. Destouches remained the only person who had helped her to "overcome misery" with his "unflagging kindness."[36]

To the professional Céline of Bezons we must of course contrast the private and secretive Céline of Montmartre, not the doctor but Céline the patient, racked by the never-ending humming in his ears and his neuralgia; the Céline whom any noise sent running and who for that reason never allowed a typewriter in his home. In the days before the war he would go to Marie Canavaggia on the square du Port-Royal. Marie's two sisters would discreetly withdraw when Céline was expected. He spoke little, ever anxious and tirelessly perfectionist. He would leave his manuscript with the young woman. The text brought up to snuff, after many comings and goings between Marie Canavaggia, the typist and himself, he would bring it back to her a last time, without looking at it again, leaving her to oversee it to the final printing. He trusted her implicitly. But for some time he had stopped taking the road to the little apartment on the square du Port-Royal inhabited by the three Canavaggia sisters, who seemed somewhat Chekovian to him. Instead, Marie came to Montmartre, to the rue Girardon, entered his office to find an arrangement of things that would look like clutter to the uninitiated, his folders piled up, chapter upon chapter, held together by the famous clothespins. And yet everything was meticulously ordered, Lucette Almansor affirms. An order perceptible to him alone.

Like Flaubert subjecting his manuscripts to the test of speech, Céline needed to read his. Lucette was his audience. She assumed this entirely passive role at the beginning of the occupation.

"I didn't make any comments. I laughed or I cried. I didn't allow myself anything else. I would only tell him whether it gave me the feeling he was looking for. In any case, he could see it on my face. He read out loud for himself. The whole time he was writing, or in the evening, he would tell me: 'Sit down, don't move!' I had a really hard time sitting still. He would say: 'Enough with the dancing, come sit, don't move!'

"He did this as soon as he had finished a chapter. So I didn't say a word. I listened. I was his witness. He could have done it with anybody else. He had to be listened to, to read out loud to make sure that it worked, that the music was there. It could last an hour. I didn't make a peep. And if someone was stupid enough to speak or call on him, he didn't answer. It was like he was in a trance. He worked in trances. I think musicians must work like that. He was somewhere else. . . .

"He wrote at 6 A.M., or in the evening, or at night toward the end of his life, to be sure there would be no noise. There couldn't be any noise. That's another reason we came here to Meudon. He wrote as long as his energy lasted. Sometimes he had attacks, pains that lasted two or three hours. At those times, it was as if he were dead. You couldn't talk to him. As soon as his strength returned he was back at work. As early as Montmartre he was having these moments of exhaustion. I'd see him turn green, he'd lie down, he couldn't talk, and later, without a word, he'd get back to work."

Lucien Rebatet, visiting the rue Girardon, was surprised to find no bookshelves, no evidence of a library at his home. "Not a trace of an artistic or intellectual life, the books were hidden like with those old peasants who read but think it would be dangerous if their reading became known."[37] There is no point in looking for scholarly or psychological explanations. Céline had moved to the rue Girardon in difficult circumstances. He had left book crates at the warehouse. Others were stacked in Lucette's room. But it is true that Céline did not treat his books as treasures. Once read, they had served their function. He neglected them as he neglected his comfort, or rather his interior decor. In the past he had been something of a collector. He prized his African objects, his masks brought from Cameroon, the valuable furniture he had bought in Geneva, his rugs. Lucette remembers a very fine Boulle chest of drawers he had from his mother, which vanished during the liberation. But in any case, he never really settled in on the rue Girardon, he merely camped there. A three-year bivouac that few people had the chance to observe, other than his Montmartre intimates—Gen Paul, Le Vigan, Marcel Aymé—or the occasional visitor, amongst whom was Marie Bell, sometimes accompanied by Florence Gould, French by birth and married to an American millionaire.

"... she forced her way into our humble abode, with Marie Bell (of the Comédie-Française). They brought their own dinner! I, who never received anybody, found myself compelled to receive her! She was determined to buy my manuscripts from me. I refused, not wanting to owe anything to the American millionaire. But she was neither unpleasant nor silly—in her rushing around, one night, and drunk, she broke her leg at the bottom of my stairs on the rue Girardon—I refused to go see her in her bed, to take care of her as she invited me to do! *By telegram.*"[38]

From the windows of his apartment, the view swept across Paris. He, the visionary voyeur, was in his element. He was mildly interested in the daily lives of the French under the occupation. But it was universal life, the general perspective, that fascinated him. The allied bombing in the north and west of the capital, the antiaircraft searchlights streaking and sweeping the sky, the conflagrations of the bombs, the tawny glow of fires over the Renault factories in Billancourt on March 3, 1942 ... there he was in his element, "chronicler of the grands guignols" in his first-tier box seats on the top of the Butte Montmartre, where reality met fiction and history mingled with his deliria. A trifle could have set Paris ablaze, Montmartre collapsing into its own cellars and quarries like a house of cards, the RAF bombers in the sky like the Horsemen of the Apocalypse.... A trifle indeed; a little deflection of the imagination, of madness, the bringing into play of a distorted writing and stupefying speed, as, for example, with *Normance*, that phenomenon of a book written shortly after the war, that long nightmarish rambling over the course of a single nighttime bombing of Paris.

Lucette was not always by his side, having sometimes to go on tour for a few days, to Brussels with Serge Lifar or elsewhere. She was also pursuing her classes with Mme. Egorova. She rented a room at the Wacker studios, where she taught the Oriental dances or the Spanish castanet dances of which she was so fond. Her pupils paid her when they could, or they didn't pay at all, it depended. In the evenings Lucette sometimes performed short cabaret numbers. Louis would come to pick her up.

Karen Marie Jensen remained one of the couple's closest friends. Céline corresponded with her constantly. Denmark loomed still as a refuge in his mind: Karen's presence there was not irrelevant. He hoped that the young woman would come to Paris. In vain. From her native land to Spain, the unsettling, worldly Karen avoided occupied France. Céline wrote her on April 20, 1942: "I'm going to find out why you're not allowed to come to Paris, probably because of the food—already hard enough to come by— I'm going to spend all of June in Brittany—precisely to stock up before winter—which I'm afraid will not be easy—Lucette is starting to get students— I'd like her to open a little studio—like Mme. d'Alessandri! I want to end my life in dance classes—With yours in Copenhagen— I'd also have a good excuse to travel— You're going to be very busy this summer! with your troupe! but what a charming occupation! You are the happiest of women and the kindest and most devoted of friends—and the most beautiful—we must see you again soon, we are all bored without you and me especially. You know how faithful I am to you without seeming so! well, in my own way . . . You'd have made a pretty Duchess of Brittany indeed if I had been Duke— . . . Montmartre is turning green and flowering—we have 100 sparrows on our balcony who unfortunately claim an enormous amount of bread! Thus life goes on, not very merry but happy all the same for having seen you!"[39]

The difficulties in obtaining provisions to which Céline refers were the common lot of all Frenchmen. They filled the writer with a panic of going without (i.e., of being in anyone's debt), his need to stockpile, preserve, and hoard gold coins or sausages. Céline's known letters to Henri-Albert Mahé, his friend Henri Mahé's father, who lived in retirement in Rétiers, in the *département* of Ille-et-Vilaine, are not without pungency. Henri-Albert Mahé died on December 16, 1941, at the age of sixty-one. That year, the author of *Voyage* sent him more than thirty letters requesting parcels of provisions, thanking him, making new, ever more pressing and plaintive requests.

"I'm going to send you Fr 100 tomorrow by way of credit . . . on a running tab! I should like to place my next order for butter, *rillette* and a roast, like this one, really marvelous, but no pâté, which I enjoy less than *rillette*, certainly excellent but we lack the country air and the sharp appetite needed to appreciate such substantial delicacies! Butter, *rillettes* and roast are perfect for our current penury, some bacon if there is any" (letter of March 1, 1941).

"I take the liberty of sending you a carton containing three zinc boxes— for butter. Would you be so kind as to fill them." (letter of August 6, 1941).

"Must I again bother you for some butter and cheese and ham? The cheese, if you have any, might be shipped in the zinc boxes. Anyway, at your leisure." (letter of October 20, 1941).

"You are very kind indeed to have sent us these wonderful cheeses— which we shall savor very slowly—since they have to last. Please let me know how much these beauties cost. Think of us for some *butter*. It is in cruelly short supply here—and is apparently sought after rabidly everywhere. I must also remind you about the ham." (letter of late October 1941).[40]

Céline was no sensualist, no Lucullus, no glutton, as we know. He was a man of anxieties. If the past rhymed with nostalgia, then the future was in tune with every sort of danger. *Rillettes*, ham and butter in the cupboard could no doubt go a little way toward dispelling the fear of tomorrow, like an exorcism—which was not after all so laughable in those years of hardship, ration coupons, lines at the food stores, and a lively black market, when one crossed Paris on foot in the more or less chimerical hope of a ham.

Three important events mark Céline's private life under the occupation. First was the marriage of his daughter, Colette, on June 10, 1942. Of course, he had not directly supervised her education, she had lived with her mother (and stepfather), but Louis had continued to see her regularly, fretting over her health, her studies, her happiness, and certainly more possessive of her in his own way than he had been of any of his wives or mistresses. He had pictured a glorious future for her, a medical career, as if to seal their affinity. She never had any such plans. When she told him that she was pregnant and intended to marry the child's father, a certain Yves Turpin, Louis blew up. He tried to dissuade her. He could not accept his daughter being taken from him. He did not attend the ceremony, and broke off relations with her. He apparently took not the least interest in the birth of his grandson, Jean-Marie, on August 3, 1942. He saw Colette again only much later, upon his return from Denmark in 1951.

Another marriage, his with Lucette, was celebrated on February 23, 1943. Why such a delay? Probably again out of fear of the future—to guarantee Lucette a minimum of legal protection at a time when he felt Germany's defeat to be inevitable, when the Wehrmacht had surrendered at Stalingrad, when he himself would probably have to flee one day—and in what circumstances?—to escape retribution.

Lucette: "I didn't want to marry. When Louis felt constrained by something he started to hate it. A little like an animal. Affection could be a trap, and he ran away. What was the point of getting hitched? And yet he had often talked to me about marriage. And then it would fall through. And then one day he made some arrangements. He told me: We're getting married on such-and-such a day. His witness was a boy who worked at the town hall, people called him the Poet of the Butte, Victor Carni, in charge of provisioning. We went off to the XVIIIth *arrondissement* town hall and Louis went straight back to his clinic afterward. There was nothing, no celebration lunch, nothing. Even his mother only found out about that marriage fifteen days later. Our witnesses, Gen Paul, and that town-hall worker, that was it. I hadn't told my parents either.

"His mother wanted us to marry. She kept asking me: But why don't you get married, my dear? Louis, too, talked to me about it all the time, starting in 1936. But I had the feeling that marriage would ruin our understanding. In fact, it didn't change anything between us. He had also given me the excuse:

• It'll be better, you see, it's more practical if we want to travel. He was thinking of the trip to Russia when I hadn't gone with him.

"Denoël was very worldly, brilliant, intelligent, and somewhat scornful. We weren't on very good terms, the two of us. He was very much in love with Louis, he was his creature. The day we got married (I sensed he would have done anything to stop us) he sent a magnificent bouquet of flowers anyway. It was the only one, since we got married without telling anyone. We came home. Louis went back to work. A day like any other."

On February 10, in the offices of Robert Thomas, notary of Bougival, Céline and Lucette signed a marriage contract. They had opted for a separate administration of property settlement, which was more advisable for Lucette in the case of Céline's being prosecuted or having his property seized. On the other hand, he drew up a will benefiting his wife.

Lucette: "Louis had his motorcycle. I came by bike. He had told me to go to the notary's. The weather was quite nice that day. So Louis arrives first and the notary tells him: you can sign here and here, but where's your wife? And he says, she's coming, she's coming! In fact, I got there a half-hour later. And then we left, him on the motorcycle and me on my bike. And it's funny, that gave the old notary a real kick! He'd never seen anything like it. He mentioned it every time I saw him after that."

The third important event in Céline's private life, after Colette's marriage and his own with Lucette, was his meeting with Bébert, the famous, immortal Bébert, his companion through the débâcle, Bébert the faithful in Neuruppin and Sigmaringen, who would be there at every odyssey and in every exile, in Copenhagen and on the Baltic shore, Bébert, who would return with him to France, who would end his days in Meudon, Bébert the hero of *D'un château l'autre*, *Nord*, and *Rigodon*, Bébert of the gentle gaze and the sharp claws—Bébert the cat, Céline's illuminator and key character of his novels, about whom enough books can never be written.[41]

Bébert was a fine, fat European tabby whom Le Vigan had bought at the La Samaritaine department store in 1935 to celebrate and symbolize his meeting—and cohabitation—with a young woman, Tinou, whom he had met in Algeria while shooting Duvivier's *Golgotha*, in which he played the role of Christ. From then on, Bébert lived in Montmartre and Le Vigan's house, the home base for his raids and expeditions along the gutters of the rue Norvins or the avenue Junot. Depending on whether he was plump or lanky, his master's friends could tell whether the couple was getting along or on the outs, whether Le Vigan or Tinou had thought to feed him. In a word, Bébert's stomach was like a barometer of their love life. The couple broke up in late '42, and Bébert was eventually taken in by Lucette. Louis protested at first. What would he do with a cat? He had never lived around them. And with the war heating up, the future was as grim as could be. In the end he let himself be persuaded, grudgingly. Bébert immediately became "his" cat, his companion, his accomplice, his silent witness, "magic itself, tact by wavelength."

Bébert, "the merry sprite," sometimes accompanied Louis and Lucette on their evening walk around the place Blanche or La Trinité. A terror of motorbikes would send him leaping on his master, claws out, as if jumping for safety in a tree.

Céline has spoken so well about Bébert—soberly, with impish tenderness and overwhelming intimacy, as if in his cat he found every compensation for the wretched dealings of mankind. Bébert the clear-sighted, "aware of tragedy . . ."; Bébert, "faithful like a wild thing"; Bébert the disobedient, yet always at heel; Bébert the voracious, the seer; Bébert, who knew that words were suspect, lies.

Yes, Bébert was one of Céline's decisive encounters under the occupation. And no irony or paradox should be read into that claim. Bébert, adopted in late '42, became one of the most significant characters in his life, one of the most powerful triggers of his sensibility and perhaps of his imagination.

In a way, his meeting with Bébert eclipsed many another—perhaps even that with Arletty, whom he met during the same period. The writer and the actress were introduced to each other at the home of the legal counsel to the German embassy, William von Bohse, in the presence of Josée Laval. "A woman friend offered me a coffee and a surprise. Standing in a corner of the drawing room, a very handsome man with gray eyes. Introductions:—Céline.—Arletty. Together: 'Courbevoie.' A long embrace. The beginning of a friendship that nothing could disturb."[42]

Yes, he loved Arletty, his countrywoman from Courbevoie. He met her again on his return from exile. A close and affectionate complicity linked them. But Bébert was more, he was a reflection, a projection of himself, his first discovery of a perceptible and forever mysterious universe.

Robert Le Vigan, the other Bébert, his former master, the son of a veterinarian, sometimes climbed the four flights of stairs to drop in on the cat . . . or Lucette.

Lucette: "Le Vigan watched for Louis as he left for his clinic. Everybody knew everything that happened on the Butte. Then he'd come knocking on the door: 'Yoo-hoo, it's Bébert!' he'd say. The first time, I open—I thought he had something to tell me. But he wanted to jump me—we ran all around the furniture. I threw stuff at him. I chucked him out. Later on, he could say 'It's Bébert' all he liked, there was nothing doing. He didn't get upset. He'd start in again. 'It's Bébert!' He knew very well I didn't dare say anything to Louis. Even in Germany he continued. He wasn't good-looking but he was intelligent. . . .

"He spoke to Bébert (the cat), it was fantastic, he spoke cat, really, the two of them argued together. All of a sudden, Bébert would disagree. They began clouting each other. Le Vigan was a very engaging person. He told you stories, he had a gift for that, he was a storyteller, he was never himself. For once, with Céline, I think it was Le Vigan who talked more. Louis enjoyed hearing him. He listened. He was very funny, Le Vigan, and a stoolie. He ratted on all of Paris, the whole Comédie-Française, all of [the theater] Marigny. Everyone went through him. He denounced his pals. He sent long letters to the Gestapo. Everybody knew it but they forgave him. He was like that. He was living at the time on the avenue Junot, near Daragnès. He had transformed his apartment into a blockhouse, with sandbags, like he was digging in."

Bébert the cat was the lodestar, the magical reference point of Céline's domestic intimacy in Montmartre, with whom it seems opportune to close this section, as if with a magical fade to black. . . .

Through Occupied France

Bezons and Montmartre, then, were two stationary worlds, two worlds of daily life in which current events, the unforeseen, and the haphazard played minimal roles during the early years of the occupation. Basically, all that mattered was the routine of work, withdrawal, secrets, silence, emotions, writing, and the passing days.

But between Bezons and Montmartre, Céline had to cross Paris, occasionally run into people, and show himself one way or another. Moreover, he managed to get away, too, beyond Montmartre and Paris. To Brittany every summer, or for a short visit to Holland or Germany. In a word, the Céline of the occupation must also be described chronologically, as a witness to History, a modest participant, a watchful and listless observer, an obstinate hermit and an indifferent provocateur.

The occupation years did not begin for him under the most auspicious star. On March 14, 1941, his deposit box at the Paris branch of Lloyds Bank was opened by order of the German authorities. The measure was not aimed at him specifically. It was the bank—foreign and enemy—that was concerned, but what difference did that make? The thrifty Céline hated any interference in his affairs. Any tampering with his hoard was out of bounds. And this was just a warning of things to come.

Céline, the thundering prewar anti-Semite, had been asked right after the armistice to support the policy of collaboration. We have already seen him in action as a journalist and writer. But it is likely that Vichy had sounded him out for the establishment, on March 29, 1941, of the General Commission for Jewish Affairs. The writer naturally got himself off the hook. Xavier Vallat became the first Commissioner, and then Darquier de Pellepoix on May 6, 1942.

The Institute for the Study of Jewish Affairs was founded shortly thereafter at the instigation of the Germans, who already controlled the General Commission. Its headquarters were established on the rue de la Boétie in a building symbolically confiscated from a Jewish owner. The Germans were going all-out to discipline the French, to embue them once and for all with ideological anti-Jewish feeling. The difficulty of the task is borne out in this letter of February '41 by SS Colonel Knochen, immediate superior to Lischka: "It has become apparent that it is virtually impossible to cultivate in the French an anti-Jewish feeling based on ideology, whereas the potential for economic benefit would more readily awaken sympathies for the anti-Jewish campaign. The internment of nearly 100,000 foreign Jews living in Paris would give many Frenchmen the opportunity to raise themselves from the lower to the middle class."[43]

For the Germans and their ambassador in Paris, Otto Abetz, Céline figured prominently among those Frenchmen of intellectual stature whose anti-Semitism was irreproachable. His name accordingly appeared on several lists: one which an anonymous informant had written to the Germans advising them on people they might contact to participate in the consultative committee of the Central Jewish Office; another, from Otto Abetz to his expert on Jewish affairs at the embassy, in which Céline's name again appears (with those of Jean de la Hire and the Comte de Puységur) as a sympathizer or potential collaborator with the Central Jewish Office. But Céline became a member of no committee and no administration. He balked unambiguously. He never provided any assistance, either by report, advice, or information, to the German ambassador, let alone the Gestapo or the Central Jewish Office.

Let us return to the Institute for the Study of Jewish Affairs, which was inaugurated on May 15, 1941. Céline attended the ceremony, as did Lucien Rebatet . . .

"I was invited. I noticed and immediately greeted Céline, incognito, lounging at the back, in the corner, buried in his sheepskin and faded scarf, his gaze barely filtering through his dozy eyelids. There was no empty seat near him. I sat down nearer the front.

"On the podium, the presiding chairman droned on, sweating under the load of a thick wad of typewritten paper. He pronounced 'Léon Blum' as if it were 'plume.' Among the committee members was an old captain, retired from the colonies, flopped down next to him. The captain was drunk as a lord and had obviously been juicing it up at the party.

"While the chairman hemmed and hawed, from Ferdinand's corner I heard grumblings, the tones of which could not be mistaken. As the lecture droned on endlessly, Céline's bass-baritone grew ever more distinct.

" '. . . Judeo . . . judeo-marxist . . . tyra . . . tyranny . . .'

" 'Hey, why don't you talk about Aryan stupidity?'

"Fifty pairs of amateur detectives' eyes, darting every which way, tried to identify the source of the sacrilege.

". . . I made for the door through a hopeless uproar. Céline hadn't moved. In the lobby, the fattest of the Krauts was moaning: 'Ve vill neffer be able to built anytink vit dees French!'

"That's how I watched the author of *Bagatelles* sabotage anti-Semitic meetings, which would have gone off fine without him, and come within an inch of being lynched for patent Judaism."[44]

Céline the impossible—how can we not be astonished by such enormous contradictions? He goes to the inaugural ceremony of this institute. Who asked him? And why does he compromise himself? He is and remains an anti-Semite, as we know. His boundless curiosity does the rest. And his jeering impertinence caps it off. Céline was a saboteur, no doubt about it. Abetz and the others would catch on quickly. There was nothing to hope for from him.

And what, indeed, could they have hoped for from such a foul-mouthed ranter who occasionally showed up at colloquia or receptions in rumpled pants held up by string, wearing a three-day beard, spewing forth streams of invective and gibes at his hosts. Abetz would have personal experience of this at the embassy in 1944. But as early as 1941, Céline caused a fine ruckus during a reception given at the Café de la Paix by Kuni Matsuo, correspondent of a large Tokyo newspaper, who had just been named private secretary to the Prime Minister and was celebrating his departure. A headwaiter first asked the writer to clear off, having taken him for a bum or a scrounger. Later, Céline sarcastically asked a colonel of the Wehrmacht how many months he thought it would be until Germany's defeat. Châteaubriant made certain comments about Céline's choice of attire; Céline called him a scumbag collaborator.[45]

In May 1941 Cocteau's *La Machine à écrire*, showing at the Théâtre Hébertot with Jean Marais and Gabrielle Dorziat, was subjected to a particularly despicable attack by Alain Laubreaux in *Je suis partout*. So much so that, one night, Jean Marais took the journalist to task in a restaurant on the boulevard des Batignolles, insulted him, and gave him a spectacular smack. This resounding slap to the cheek of Laubreaux, a Nazi and Germanophile by nature, a hateful and exulting insulter of his persecuted enemies, reverberated like an echo from street to street, through every *salon* and editorial room in Paris, to the gleeful, vindicated, or horrified commentary of all. After the incident Céline generously sided with Cocteau (and Jean Marais): creator against critic. He had not forgotten the lacerating of *Mort à crédit*; for him it was as much a reflex of *ésprit de corps* as a moral one. He offered to mediate, to encourage if not a reconciliation then at least a civil discussion with Laubreaux. But a few months later, in a second move, Céline made peace with the slanderer. He wrote Laubreaux a letter published in *Je suis partout* on November 22, 1941. "Reasons of race must supersede reasons of State. No explanation necessary. It's very simple. Fanatical, unequivocal racism or death! And what a death! They're waiting for us. May the spirit of the mongoose move and fire us! So what if Cocteau is decadent!"

Meanwhile, Céline had spent two weeks in Brittany, in northern Finistère and Camaret, in early June. He was back in Paris on the 21st, the eve of the Axis powers' declaration of war against Russia, when Stalin, surprised (whatever some may say) by his former ally's about-face, was at first powerless against the march of the Reich's armies across his territory. But with the new front, the tables had definitively turned. War against Russia would prove to be Hitler's great mistake, his last gamble, his final mad wager. With the war against Russia the balance of forces would change, the balance of numbers and ideology.

In July '41 Céline had other concerns. Certainly, he was pleased by the Wehrmacht's lightning victories. But he was beginning to curse the Germans with no less ferocious surliness. The occupation authorities in Holland were blocking the bank accounts of foreigners and commandeering their deposit boxes. Céline had deposited 185 gold coins at a bank in The Hague in 1938. From July 15 to 20, he took a trip to Amsterdam, in vain. He was not allowed access to his deposit box, much less to withdraw his property. On the way home he stopped in on Évelyne Pollet in Antwerp. It was a brief meeting, after the tragicomedy of the young woman's fake suicide attempt in Dinan on the eve of the war. Happily for Évelyne, Céline was alone this time. That's all she wanted. She was able to throw herself on him. But there was no question of being able to keep him. She had no idea that she would never see him again.

And the story of the gold in Holland goes on. In August, the Amsterdamsche Bank of The Hague wrote to Céline officially requesting the return of his keys by reason of Nazi enactments. Céline immediately applied to his connections and friends, to the Germans and the French. He complained, he threatened, now flattering, now insulting. My box, my box! So this is how the Germans treat their friends! A letter to Alphonse de Châteaubriant on August 30, 1941, sums up his indignation: "I consider the violation of my deposit box to be a *personal insult* and a *cowardly and disgusting act of banditry.* . . . That they should behave this way with Gaullists or Jews—fine—But with their few friends, those who were censured, hunted down, persecuted, slandered for their cause and *not today*, but from '36 to '39—under Blum—Daladier—Mandel—it *takes the cake*—a monstrous piece of dirty work—*What a lesson for their faltering collaborators!* . . . It's probably a question of gangsterized military gorillas pouncing on their plunder . . . I have no choice but to yield to force, but violence will have been done to me and they may have an opportunity to regret it someday —You know, my dear Châteaubriant, that I have never taken a penny from Germany and ask nothing from it. I merely request the German authorities to be so kind as to leave me the hell alone, to *consider me as some sort of neutral party*, from Guatemala or San Marino— Is that too much to ask? I already feel put upon enough for being deprived of the use of my property—may they have the *goodness to leave my box alone and wait till the end of the war*—when everything can be settled. This acme of shoddiness, this unspeakable monstrosity, comes at a time when I was planning to launch a campaign supporting the anti-Bolshevik crusade."[46]

Neither Châteaubriant (or Otto Abetz, with whom he interceded), nor Fernand de Brinon, likewise informed, nor Karl Epting, the director of the German Institute, to whom Céline had also applied, were able to do anything. The gold had been well and truly confiscated. A pure and simple theft.

The gold coins were never returned. And for Céline, shut in on himself with his hallucinations and neuralgia, this took on the dimensions of a perceptible, concrete, and intolerable persecution, an unbearable torture, while the other, real horrors seemed remote to him, not worth the effort of imagining.

To the words "impossible" and "contradictory," we must add the word "paranoid" to the writer's pedigree—Céline, or persecution mania.

He spent the summer of '41 in Brittany. On September 5, at the Berlitz palace in Paris, there opened a great anti-Semitic exhibition, "The Jew and France," which would have been comical with its maps, statistics, profiles of Jewish stereotypes and the myriad ways of recognizing them, had it not been so loathsome. The Parisians flocked to it without any apparent disgust. Céline lost no time in going, similarly without disgust. His books were not exhibited there. And he, who rejected any public display, who blasted the Institute of Jewish Studies with his jeers—he took the thing badly. Persecution, yet again. He wrote to Captain Sezille, in charge of the exhibition, to complain, to condemn the frightful deficiency of intelligence and Aryan solidarity.

On December 7, 1941, at the German Institute, Céline was introduced to the novelist Ernst Jünger, who noted in his *Diary*:

"He has the gaze of a maniac, inward-turning, that shines as if from the depths of a pit. For such a gaze, too, nothing exists either to the right or to the left; one gets the impression of a man hurtling toward an unknown goal. 'I have death constantly at my side'—and so saying, he seems to point to a little dog that could be lying by his chair.

"He says how surprised and stupefied he is that we soldiers do not shoot, hang, exterminate the Jews—he is stupefied that someone availed of a bayonet should not make unrestricted use of it. 'If the Bolsheviks were in Paris, they'd show you how to go about it; they'd show you how one purifies a population, neighborhood by neighborhood, house by house. If I carried a bayonet, I'd know what I had to do.' "[47]

Naturally, the German writer was horrified by such talk. And he added the following comments on their meeting:

"Listening to him talk like that for two hours, I learned something, for he was clearly expressing the monstrous power of nihilism. Such men hear only one melody, but that is singularly insistent. They're like those machines of steel that go about their business until somebody smashes them.

"It is curious to hear such minds speak of science—of biology, for instance. They use it the way a Stone Age man would; for them, it is exclusively a means of killing others."[48]

Céline was a brutish nihilist, delirious and bloodthirsty, according to Jünger. But we should remember that Jünger probably represented all that Céline hated: aristocratic militarism, refined aestheticism, detached morality. Jünger was the kind of man who was interested in mineralogy and botany, who could speak enraptured of the roses in the Bagatelle Gardens and at the same time deplore the fate of the Jews who were being deported en masse. Jünger was self-controlled, reserved, and haughty, never allowing his feelings to show through—"It is unworthy of great souls to broadcast their distress." Jünger, dispassionate and enigmatic, had very eighteenth-century sensibilities. Céline, an anti-Jünger, knew how to see through appearances to the underlying reality. One look and he knew a person inside out, stripped him bare, broke through his masks and postures. Céline wanted to provoke the repressed Jünger, push him to the limit. Cocteau spoke of "those intellectuals who have clean hands but don't have any hands." As he did many a time with journalists after the war, Céline amused himself in Jünger's presence by blackening and artificially besmearing his own hands. As if he were essentially telling him: You expected to see a monster, a bloodthirsty collaborator, very well, I'll give you your money's worth! And he hit the mark. It was an indirect way of mocking the self-conscious courtesy and sensitive soul of the meditative Jünger, whose courage remained secret (he would participate in the failed plot against Hitler) in the face of the bloody nightmare of war. Jünger was horrified; Céline was delighted that he was.

It is worth noting that the two men had further occasion to meet. The first time was on April 22, 1943, at the home of Paul Morand, in the company of Countess Palffy and Benoist Méchin. The German writer felt the same incomprehension and fear when faced with Céline.

"Doctor X. then spoke of his practice, which seems to be characterized by an abundance of sinister cases. Furthermore, he is Breton—which confirms my first impression that he is a Stone Age man. He constantly visits Katyn, which is being exploited for propaganda purposes these days. It's clear that he is attracted to such places."[49]

Céline never went to Katyn. Some Germans had indeed come to solicit his participation, with a delegation of French writers led by Fernand de Brinon and escorted by Robert Brasillach, in a field trip to visit an LVF unit on the Russian front and then to the Katyn gravesite, where the Nazis had recently discovered the corpses of 4,000 Polish officers executed by the Red Army, a revelation that came at just the right time to justify their crusade against Bolshevik barbarity. But Céline unequivocally declined the offer.

Their third and last encounter took place on November 16, 1943, again at the German Institute, when Jünger no longer cared even to identify Céline or use his name. In his *Diary*, he deliberately and scornfully associates him with the anonymous mass of "hired scribblers, fellows one wouldn't touch with tweezers. That whole crowd simmers in a stew of self-interest, hatred, and fear, and some already carry the stigmata of horrible deaths on their foreheads. I am at present entering a phase where I find the sight of nihilists unbearable."[50]

There were no significant meetings or moves in early '42, other than Céline's attendance, on February 1, at Jacques Doriot's rally at the Vel'd'Hiv, of which we have already spoken. A few days later, he gave a lecture at the

École Libre des Sciences Médicales on "standard medicine." Nothing political in his statements, but a return to his old public-health preoccupations, with off-the-rack aphorisms: "At medical school, one learns a medicine of the Right; in life, one practices a medicine of the Left . . . A basic but true medicine is worth more than a scholarly but false one . . . What distinguishes a state of health from a state of sickness in a proletarian is his ability to work and to go to the movies."[51]

Céline's thesis was a simple one. According to him, out of 2,200 cases in a clinic's clientele of outpatients, 300 required a specialist and specialized treatment, while the other 1,900 fell into five or six categories to which the same number of standardized remedies could be perfectly adapted. One might as well encourage medical students to forget nine-tenths of their learning to concentrate on the remaining tenth. It is doubtful that such summary views on the "Taylorization" of medicine could have convinced Céline's audience. Was he really convinced himself?

What continued to preoccupy the writer, during the long war that was to finish so badly for him, were his possessions held abroad, like life rafts and survival rations for the great shipwreck that was to carry him off. He had not forgotten the confiscation of his gold in Holland. He wanted to withdraw that which he held in Copenhagen, but the Germans refused to issue him the traveling papers to get to Denmark. He then came up with the idea of meeting Karen Marie Jensen in Berlin and giving her the key and combination to his box, so that she might put the money in a safe place, bury it in her garden.

But what excuse could he use to go to Berlin? Louis applied to Karl Epting, informing him of his desire to visit the medical facilities of a factory and a suburban clinic in Germany, and to meet a few physicians working in public health. Gen Paul, he added, wanted to accompany him to see a few fellow artists in Berlin. The director of the German Institute happily acceded to his request, officially invited him to participate in a scientific and medical journey to Berlin, and requested the French authorities to grant him the necessary papers.

Having specified his time of arrival to Karen, Céline took the train to Berlin on March 8, 1942. Gen Paul and Drs. Bécart and Rudler accompanied him. He found a young doctor from Argenteuil to substitute for him in Bezons while he was away.

Berlin was an uneventful trip over the course of which Céline, hirsute and unshaven, sought out the company of dancers more than that of public-health specialists, and strove in vain to wangle a visa for Denmark out of the Ministry of Foreign Affairs instead of visiting suburban clinics. At the hotel or in restaurants, he grumbled: "Their ministries are full of Jews and they don't even know how to spot them!"

One evening they were the guests of Dr. Conti, Minister of Public Health. Several officers back from the Eastern front told them of the astonishing morale of the Russian prisoners and of their faith in communism. Was Nazi ideology as mobilizing as Marxist ideology they wondered. On their way home on the U-Bahn, Céline drew Dr. Rudler aside: "These people are washed up, the others are going to win."[52]

Of course Céline saw Karen on several occasions, the cosmopolitan Karen who could pirouette and turn men's heads, who had alienated Elizabeth Craig from Louis and was one of those women who could put him in a trance—precisely the state he sought for writing.

Lucette explains: "Louis always told me, 'Women are there to drain your sap,' and he hated the ones who forced him to make love, because he said 'If I make love to them, I've got nothing left.' He used women only to get himself excited. Anyway, he'd become more and more fussy, 'and since perfection is becoming more and more rare, there's no danger of my getting carried away,' he'd also say. He was so critical that he never managed to find the object that would fulfill his desires. Yes, he was looking for the ideal. He used to say, 'I've gotten closer and closer to the ideal, that is, the dancer, the woman whose feet don't touch the ground, who is of perfect grace, perfect everything. The rest of the broads don't exist, so I've got no reason to run around anymore.' He used to give women points. When he saw a dancer, 8 ... 6 ... 5 ... On a café terrace, too, he gave points to the women passing by ... 2 ... 3 ... 0 ... He looked for an absence of defects. It was his game. But it was also for his work; people don't seem to realize that. He got high on this so he could pass into another world, like a junkie. He got high on fantasies."

It would be exaggerating to portray Karen as an ideal. In her own way, she must have embodied a fragment of the ideal, a persistent fragment of dream, a burst of fantasy. Louis had some affection for her. He trusted her. He therefore gave her the key and combination to his bank box so she could withdraw the gold. For her part, she officially authorized him by letter to occupy her apartment at 20 Ved Stranden in Copenhagen in her absence, whenever he liked. Two months later she would indeed withdraw the gold from the bank in Copenhagen and bury it in her garden.

During his stay in Berlin, the German authorities asked Céline to speak for propaganda reasons before French workers in the STO. The writer would later describe the meeting: "I was so displeased with the Germans, so infuriated by their hangman's courtesy, their policeman's solicitude, that when they asked me to say a few words to the French Workers' Club of Berlin—asked with some insistence that I justify my coming to Berlin—I said these words to the workers, which I can still remember perfectly: 'French workers. I'm going to tell you something really good. I know you well. I'm one of you, a worker like you. These guys (the Germans) are *lousy*. They say they're going to win the war. Maybe so. I don't know. The others, the Russians, on the other side, are no better. They may even be worse. It's a question of choosing between cholera and the plague. Not much fun. So long!' The Club's dismay was great. There was again serious talk of incarcerating me (Laval, too, could think of nothing but incarcerating me ...)."[53]

These are more or less the same words—the plague or cholera—that

Céline used in his speech at the closing banquet at the Hotel Adlon, in front of dignitaries, before the delegation's return to France, apparently without causing any significant trouble for himself or his colleagues. On March 13, 1942, they were back in Paris.

Céline was persona non grata for the Germans, and he did his utmost to provoke them. But that did not prevent him from meeting and admiring Karl Epting, who, at the German Institute, had forged friendships with Giraudoux, Montherlant, Jacques Chardonne, Ramon Fernandez, Jean Giono, Paul Morand, Jacques Audiberti, and Paul Valéry among others; nor from admiring the sculptor Arno Brecker, whom he had met before the war and continued to see under the occupation; or from occasionally frequenting certain German functionaries, such as Dr. Knapp, head of health services in Paris, or Miss von Steeg, Epting's secretary; or from visiting on two or three occasions with Hermann Bickler, head of political intelligence for Western Europe, at his office on the avenue Foch, on the way to Bezons. He did so purely out of curiosity, out of that intense and devious curiosity, that bizarre voyeurism hinting of the forbidden, that continually drove him. Céline, for his part, amused Bickler. The German received him offhandedly. Céline poured out his bile to him, spoke about the foolishness of Hitlerite politics, called Laval a "typical yid." It didn't matter. Bickler enjoyed listening to him, taking short walks with him along the bois de Boulogne road, allowing his intellect to be intoxicated by the wild deliria of this man whom the German guards, a few minutes earlier, had not wanted to admit into his office, because he looked like a terrorist.

But the high-placed Nazi ideologues in Berlin were leery of Céline, considered him intolerable. Who could blame them? They believed that Epting was too close to him. The German writer Bernard Payr, head of the "Amt Schrifftum," the literary department of Alfred Rosenberg's propaganda service, also emphasized, in a report written in January '42, the extent to which Céline's personality seemed suspect to him. This, after all, was the man who had celebrated conscientious objection in *Voyage au bout de la nuit*: "He has questioned and dragged through the mud almost everything of positive value in human existence. For several years now he has been writing books against the Jews and Freemasons, whom he hysterically thrashes in a smutty, colloquial French. Is this really the kind of person who should have the decisive word in the great struggle against the supranational powers, a person who deserves Germany's attentions and support?"[54]

On May 29, 1942, a Nazi statute decreed the mandatory wearing of the yellow star by all Jews. The next day, in his *Parisian Diary*, Jünger noted a stroll he took in the Bagatelle to admire its "collection of various species of clematis, whose blue and silver-gray stars adorned the drab wall. The roses, too, were already in bloom."[55] One wonders whether Céline—who thought he saw Jews everywhere—in Vichy, in Berlin, at the Opéra, in Montmartre, and in the Gestapo—saw the blooming of yellow stars on the streets of Paris. He may indeed not have noticed them, with his sadly banal aptitude for distinguishing nothing that did not square with his own visions.

On June 10, 1942, at the Cercle Européen, he attended a lecture by Dr. Hauboldt on "the medical service in repatriation and emigration." Hauboldt was one of the bigwigs of the Reich health services, and he would particularly attend to Céline during the writer's stay in Germany. A few days later, Céline left for Brittany with Lucette.

Saint-Malo was forbidden to them by the Germans as a defense zone off-limits to nonresidents. The couple went to Finistère. They spent a few days in Beg-Meil, in a caretaker's cottage on the property of one of their friends— "a little house," says Lucette, "with a fireplace and a marvelous kitchen garden where green peas were growing. On the beach, no one, I was by myself all day, half naked on the beach. Louis was working. . . ."

They spent the rest of the summer in Quimper with Dr. Mondain, the director of the psychiatric hospital. Lucette continues: "Athanase Follet was the founder of that hospital. We lived in the asylum director's apartment. His bathroom was filled with canvases, since he would go off to paint in the dead of night, and come back with black canvases! We were really among loonies. It was tough. It frightened me. Another supervisor played the violin all night long. Almost all of them had been attacked or injured by the loonies. But for them, the danger was natural. . . . They'd bring a loony from his cell and tell him: 'Here, sing us a song over dessert.' I found it morbid. One day, the loony smacked the director's face for him. He was right, I don't think he was so crazy.

"I had found a little cat that followed us around. I wanted to keep it. . . . There was a nut who would chop wood into little matchsticks; he chopped vegetables for the soup the same way. Later, the director's wife threw herself out the window. It all ended very badly. . . .

"Louis liked to go back to Rennes, to the past. He always liked to go to Brittany. There were crows in Brittany, I remember, it was creepy. I exercised under an open lean-to every day. The loonies watched me. A little like ghosts—they appear, you don't know how, they vanish, they're lost souls, they're everywhere."

A strange vacation, as if reality were continually pursuing and mingling with Céline's most macabre fantasies—a vacation that put some distance between him and the realities of Paris, of the Vel'd'Hiv raid and the thumping commercial success of Rebatet's *Les Décombres*. He himself was working on *Guignol's band*, whose unfinished manuscript still bore the title *English' bar*. He most likely met with friends such as Dr. Tuset, health director of the Finistère prefecture, who had introduced him to Max Jacob before the war, or Dr. Georges Desse, who did not conceal his participation in Resistance activities from Céline.

Céline was back in Paris in September. There he was soon overseeing the illustrated re-edition of *L'École des cadavres* and the new edition of *Bagatelles*. There, on November 8, he learned of the Anglo-American landing in North Africa and, three days later, of the German occupation of the free zone. The Germans began their retreat from Russia. The countdown had begun for Céline. When would he have to flee Montmartre? It was a matter of days, of months.

Anxious Days in Montmartre

1943 . . .

The war continued to set the world ablaze from the Balkans to the Pacific. Germany was yielding on every front, in Africa, in Sicily, and later in Italy. The Russians were regaining the offensive. Allied bombers were destroying the industrial cities of the Reich. Hamburg was leveled in late July and civilian casualities numbered in the tens of thousands. And yet this was only a dress rehearsal. The Anglo-Americans would go much better in the course of a single night in February '45, with 250,000 citizens of Dresden dead under their phosphorous bombs. A good German is a dead German. The old American school of behavior that had won the West from the Indians was experiencing a revival.

Meanwhile the Nazis were methodically perfecting their rhythms and output as they set up their Final Solution. Jews and Gypsies were vanishing by the millions into the death camps. Were people aware of it? Who in France could dare to think the unthinkable, the hideous specificity of the Holocaust? Who could accept even a hint of that ultimate horror, that calm, premeditated, rationalized crime of crimes? A few amongst them would sometimes whisper the truth, catch a glimpse of it, denounce it in the midst of so many other, more comprehensible horrors, corpses, crimes, and destruction. But even those who talked of it often refused to believe it. As Léon Poliakov put it, "a complete and widespread certainty concerning the fate of the deported Jews was not acquired until after the liberation of France."[56]

The Militia founded by Darnand on January 30 was multiplying its exactions and parodies of justice in France, with its court-martials followed by the immediate execution of "traitors," i.e., Resistance fighters or anyone suspected of being a terrorist. The nightmare loomed larger with the specter of defeat, the burgeoning underground movement, and the STO's requisitioning of French workers for Germany. The anxious Wehrmacht feverishly constructed the "Atlantic Wall," to the profit of a few French entrepreneurs, authentic collaborators if ever there were.

That year, the Resistance paper *Le Père Duchesne* published a special issue devoted to the press and to literature, in which was described "a haggard fanatic, a half-mad Céline congratulating Hitler for having brought a Negro-Jewish France to its senses" and "shameful little hysterics like

Rebatet and Cousteau, swooning over the beauty of the Wehrmacht."[57] On the other end of the spectrum, Jean-Hérold Paquis published violent articles in May '43 in the form of calls to murder: "If a modicum of power were given to the revolutionary that I am, to the revolutionaries whom I know—we with our empty bellies and our furious visions—I know only too well that our first act would be to open a legalized Katyn ditch on the place de la Concorde . . . and in order to fill it, to shoot several hundred hostages."[58]

Actually, Céline the haggard fanatic, the half-madman according to the underground press, had thoughts only for his novel. In August '42, his name had appeared among the members of the honors committee of the Cercle Européen. On May 15, 1943, he officially requested it to be removed. He explained that he had never intended to be a part of it. This we can readily believe. He spent over three months in Brittany, from June 15 to September 25, in order to work on *Guignol's band* at his leisure. And this time he managed to return to Saint-Malo. The police commissioner of that town had granted him a certificate of residence, as a result of which a Gestapo superior at the Rennes Kommandatur, a certain Hans Grimm, issued him a residence permit. This gave *L'Humanité* the opportunity in January 1950 to affirm without batting an eyelash that Céline was a Gestapo agent, that he undertook surveillance missions in Brittany for the Germans and that, had he not done so, he could never have obtained a pass to a forbidden coastal zone. The accusation, of course, was spurious, but happened to fall just a few days before the writer's trial in absentia. The only concrete fact: Céline had seen Grimm on several occasions, had contacted him and, to curry his favor, had sent him a deluxe edition of one of his works. And yet, his stay in Saint-Malo hung by a thread. He was tolerated because he was supposed officially to practice medicine there. In other words, it was in his interest to keep a low profile. And in fact, he remained most inconspicuous, in that genuine, febrile silence of the writer who, in the little apartment in the Franklin Building that he rented above Marie Le Bannier's place, wrote and rejoined his friends of yore—ghosts distorted by a wayward memory and too much imagination: prostitutes running wild on the docks of London, the foggy rounds of drug traffickers, pimps, policemen, and fantastical inventors on the banks of the Thames. . . .

Céline had no lack of friends and connections in Saint-Malo, which he had been visiting for so many years. Journalists, Breton autonomists more or less in with the Germans, artists, restaurateurs or carpenters, he saw them from time to time. But not too often. He valued his solitude. In 1943 he also met once more with the old poet Théophile Briant, who noted in his *Diary*: "A visit from Louis-Ferdinand Céline. A little aged, eyes more hollow, altogether pretty grimy. Still makes elegant gestures with his hands and has kept his torrential vocabulary. Jokes or cackles all the time." Or again: "Saw Céline at the Franklin. Pretty slovenly, feet in old sandals, wearing sailor's pants. His hair still covered with 'grease,' eyes hollow and fiery, lips moistened with spittle. From his window we can see the Saint-Malo clock tower and a corner of the Fort National Beach. The swell at high tide sends us its distant murmur and spray. . . . Céline foresees the triumph of Bolshevism and his own potential hanging, which, he adds, will get a good laugh, since deep down he's an aristocrat, has only aesthetic convictions, and has done all this (like Byron, Hugo, or Lamartine) merely for the thrill of danger and the need to challenge death."[59]

In September '43, Céline returned to Paris. Marcel Aymé had recently described the group of friends on the Butte in his short story *Avenue Junot* and in another fantastic-burlesque story, *La Carte*, published in the collection *"Le Passe-Muraille."* The theme of the latter story has a certain spice: to stave off famine, it was arranged to distribute time cards to the populace that would allow each man to live a certain number of days a month, depending on his level of social utility. Aymé goes on to describe daily life in Montmartre and the lines at the 18th *arrondissement* town hall to collect one's time card. "On the waiting lines, I recognized, not without emotion and, I must confess, with a secret satisfaction, some Montmartre buddies, writers and artists: Céline, Gen Paul, Daragnès, Fauchois, Soupault, Tintin, d'Esparbes, and others. Céline was in a foul temper. He said that this was another Jewish scheme, but I believe that, on that particular point, his ill humor led him astray. Indeed, by the terms of the decree, each Jew, without distinction of age, sex, or function, was allotted a half-day of existence per month."

The mockery was gentle, even affectionate, like a wink. Who could be unaware of Céline's anti-Semitic feelings? But he was only partially amused, for by now he was suspicious of everything, afraid of everything. Was he being denounced, pointed out to future purgers? Was Marcel Aymé trying to clear himself, even if his short story had first been published in *Je suis partout*? His suspicions were unfounded, Marcel was still family, one of his closest friends. Céline knew it perfectly well, in his heart. And the future was to prove him right: Marcel Aymé would always remain one of his most ardent defenders and friends. No matter. His laughter was forced; then he wasn't laughing at all. "He played me a few nasty turns there . . . in his nutty stories, so-called slapstick, some little stories that come across all harmless . . . where he sets me up very nicely . . . 'Death to the Jews!' he has me saying, just like that, to get a laugh . . . No better way to get me killed . . . the world understands a joke . . . it's as facetious as can be . . . It hurt me at first, and anyway I've seen it so often . . . I was really mad at Marc [Marcel Aymé] . . . anyway, two or three days . . . That's about as long as my grudges last."[60]

Céline was also not in the mood to joke on the evening he attended a dinner given by Abetz at the embassy on the rue de Lille, to which Drieu La Rochelle, Benoist-Méchin, and Gen Paul had also been invited. After Drieu and Abetz had talked at length about Germany, the setback at Stalingrad, and the Axis powers' chances of pulling off a victory, Céline exploded. A German defeat was inevitable, he proclaimed, and added in substance that

Hitler was dead, that he had been replaced in power by a double, a false Israelite Hitler who was setting the stage for a Jewish triumph. Gen Paul then got up and, at Céline's insistence, began playing the fool by imitating the old Hitler, the real one, his Nuremberg speeches, while Céline followed up his inflammatory commentary with worse still. No one could make him shut up. Abetz was horrified: the servants would report to the Gestapo the statements made at the ambassador's own table. There might be talk of a plot. What to do? Finally, Abetz chose to act as though Céline had lost his mind. He had been seriously wounded in '14, hadn't he? He had Céline escorted back to the rue Girardon, ostensibly as a sick man. Appearances had been saved.[61] Once again Céline had spoken sincerely, to the point of obliviousness and dangerous provocation.

Occupied Paris was trying to forget the war and hardship. Rarely had the screen seen cinematic works of such quality or the blossoming of such new talents. Robert Bresson completed his first feature, *Les Anges du péché.* Theatrical productions flourished as well. Montherlant's *La Reine morte* was performed at the Comédie-Française, Claudel's *Le Soulier de satin* was hailed with enthusiasm by Robert Brasillach, and Sartre's *Les Mouches* was occasionally criticized but fervently defended by the German columnist of the French-language Nazi magazine *Signal.* Before the same audiences of Parisian intellectuals, enchanted bourgeois, and attentive Wehrmacht officers, Sacha Guitry's comedies packed the halls, as did Cocteau's *Renaud et Armide.* Marie Bell had the lead in the latter play. Céline went to cheer her on, probably on opening night on April 14, 1943. Immediately afterward he wrote to her:

Dear Friend,

Magnificent evening thanks to you—a thousand thanks and affectionate thoughts! Superb play, marvelous actors, you the most beautiful, perfect. . . .

It could use more music— Like all great plays, this one verges on opera— more atmospheric noise, the last act is very successful because [sic, in English], but the music a little too muted. Everything should come together— voices and music. Never forget that Man sang before he spoke. Song is natural, speech is learned. The sources of poetry are in song—not in chatter. Had Cocteau introduced a little comedy—he would rival Shakespeare. Even as is it's quite enjoyable—and you set the standard for all that is magnificent. There's no praise for a single Jew, unless a little for Ben-Jesus. I can breathe.[62]

Occupied Paris . . . The shopgirls wore wooden-soled shoes and drew fake nylons on their legs. The German levies and the "upkeep costs" of their armies were ruining the French economy and lengthening the desperate lines in front of the food shops. As early as 1940, many shopkeepers, good, shrewd apostles, began plastering their windows with stickers such as

"Catholic business" or "The management of this house is Catholic and French, as are its employees." Drancy became "Drancy-la-Juive" [Drancy-the-Jewish], since that was where arrested Jewish men, women, and children were held in deplorable housing, lacking sanitation and food, before being sent to Germany and the death camps. Militant Doriot followers or militiamen sometimes paraded down the Champs-Élysées. Every so often bombs would go off in front of hotels barracking German soldiers, the *Pariser Zeitung [Paris News]* building, or an STO recruitment office. The curfew emptied the streets of the capital every night, deserted and tragic like a surrealist bad dream. The Gestapo increased its arrests, tortures, condemnations, and executions of hostages or any suspected culprit in the hellish cycle of assassination attempts and repression, while Philippe Henriot, head of Vichy propaganda, continued his radio speeches in favor of the policy of collaboration with such lyrical fervor and burning eloquence that it became urgent for London and the Resistance to silence him with a bullet—which would be done on the morning of June 28, 1944. A curious France indeed, so contradictory, where Charles Trenet was breaking hearts with his ever-so-melancholy song, *Que reste-t-il de nos amours?*—What's left of our love? And what was there left for France, other than to fight or to sing, to wait, to fear or to hope?

Céline had still not finished *Guignol's band*, which was taking on the dimensions of an enormous book. And yet time was of the essence. The end of a world, the ebb tide of the war. Already, in late 1943 and 1944, the Resistance was openly organizing against the Militia in the countryside, occasionally in pitched battles as in a civil war. And it was indeed a civil war, lost in a conflict of planetary scale. In Paris, silences became more pregnant, inferences more weighted, looks more charged with hidden meaning, and anonymous letters more numerous. The author of *Bagatelles pour un massacre* was beginning to receive his share of bereavement letters from the AAA (Anti-Axis Association) or little coffins, and Céline expected more and much worse. In January 1944 he wrote to Alphonse de Châteaubriant: "I no longer dare look to the future, all the complicities, subterfuges, ambiguities . . . And that abyss I see at the very end . . . you must see it too."

And yet, to the extent his means and connections allowed, he had done what he could to help those around him. The young Pierre Duverger, whom he had met in Saint-Malo, was supplied by him with false papers and certificates to escape the STO. "At the rendezvous he had set up with me in Paris in the winter of '43-'44, he arrived on his belly, having missed the last turn before the sidewalk, his motorcycle on one side and him on the other . . . it was nothing, and we were able to ride back to the Butte, with me on the back. Céline was a man who often asked favors, but never for himself. In a few days, I had the papers, all in order, that allowed me to stay in Montmartre until the Allies arrived. I owe him a great debt of gratitude, but I'm not the only one."[63]

In a similar way he helped Serge Perrault, a young dancer friend of Lucette's who instantly fell under the spell of the writer's aura, his magnetism, and incredible physical presence. Paris was still the best place to hide to avoid the STO, Céline had told him. Perrault, on his advice, took refuge in Gen Paul's studio, where Céline saw him every day on his way to or from Bezons. Perrault had a young woman friend, Mireille, like him a dancer, who sometimes came to the rue Girardon for tea and was also invited to Gen Paul's studio. One day when she had quarreled with Perrault, she went to sulk at the far end of the studio, stretched out on a sofa. Coming upon her, Louis saw that she was sad and sullen. "Hang on," he told her, "we'll get you out of your funk, we're going to show you something that no one has ever seen nor ever will again!" Gen Paul then took up his flute and Céline began to dance a jig. Mireille laughed herself silly.

Simone Mitre, Fernand de Brinon's co-worker at the office of the French delegation to the occupied territories, described Céline's arrival at the delegation's office. "He'd arrive at the place Beauvau, always quick, unaffected, pleasant, a touch of irony at the corners of his mouth. He hardly had to say anything; his penetrating gaze, so pale blue, had asked it all already. Then, in that staccato voice of his, he would describe some sad case, relay some request for mercy or freedom, or try to obtain passes for people he had taken an interest in and wanted to see across the demarcation line. He'd quickly lay his request down on my desk, and that seemed to relieve him: 'Thank you, thank you, I'm counting on you,' he'd say and just as quickly he'd be gone, having nonetheless taken the time to repeat, with a mischievous glint in his eye, at almost every one of his visits: 'You know, the Germans are going to lose the war.' "[64]

And Karl Epting, too, at the German Institute, having met Céline in Paris in the thirties and being one of the only Germans under Hitler to praise him, in an essay published in late '42, often received his visits and his solicitations for help on behalf of others. And all of this, his awestruck friendship for Céline, he described in a lovely melancholy text with the eloquent title *Il ne nous aimait pas*—He Didn't Like Us. "It is as a physician that Céline appears before my eyes when I think back to our many encounters from 1940 to 1944, in Paris, Berlin, or Sigmaringen; perhaps a rather strange physician, when one thinks of his deliberately shabby appearance, but a physician who was always on the move, with or without Bébert, and one, too, who always had a request to make for someone else. He never sought anything for himself except some paper so as to be able to print his books. . . . Céline was closely linked to Dr. Knapp, a liberal old Swabian whose own peripatetic existence had led him to the foreign department of the Reich's Office of Public Health, in which capacity he was in charge of liaison between German and French doctors during the occupation. Knapp received Céline's innumerable applications in the medical field and tried to respond to them positively, to the extent allowed by the great material difficulties of the time. Céline's applications were for medical assistance to the French populace, such as he was able to observe the need for in his daily work at the municipal clinic in Bezons or elsewhere."[65]

Naturally, Céline did not for an instant consider joining the Resistance. On the other hand, his neighbors downstairs on the fourth floor on the rue Girardon, Robert Champfleury and his mistress, Simone Mabille, played an important role in the underground. Many a messenger, parachuting in from London, found shelter with them before leaving for other missions. Roger Vailland, who belonged to the same network, often went to the Champfleurys'. In an article in *La Tribune des nations* on January 13, 1950, entitled "We will no longer spare Louis-Ferdinand Céline," he describes how he and his friends had once considered assassinating the writer, who was being visited by Ralph Soupault, the caricaturist and PPF member, and Alain Laubreaux. Should they chuck a grenade in the street when they passed by or should they down them with machine guns from the little square on avenue Junot? After all, the concierge at 4, rue Girardon was one of their mail drops, and Simone and Robert Champfleury's hideout was worth saving. Finally, Vailland explains in the article, they decided not to kill the writer: "I think that our clemency was a sucker's game and a bad deed into the bargain."

Céline was indignant at this braggardly article. He answered it belatedly in *Le Petit Crapouillot* in February '58, under the title "Illuminations."

"How could Vailland, imbecile that he is, imagine that I was unaware of what was going on in my building in the rue Girardon? The sap. The little babe in the woods. My concierge was a mail drop? Of course! the whole neighborhood knew it! The Champfleury couple on the 4th, under my bedroom, kept a safe house for STO deserters? The whole Butte was in on it! This Vailland discovers the moon! it staggers him! he's flabbergasted! . . .

"I'd like to ask him, even with his miserable imagination, if he couldn't conceive the possibility that if I had wanted to, knowing perfectly well from Champfleury, the horse's mouth, what was going on downstairs, with a word, a whisper, with some vague hint, since according to that halfwit I was in cahoots with the highest authorities of the moment, I could have put a swift end to all those goings-on and buffooneries? What generosity! Sure, those people changed later on, when the danger was past, into ferocious champions of justice . . . implacable avengers of bellyaches.

"As to those hypocritical, sneaking lies, I can make ready hash of them! I never received a single editor of *Je suis partout*, not by day or by night . . . nor anyone in the high collaboration . . . I never had to accompany them . . . especially while shooting my mouth off . . . (just my style . . . dumb jerk!!).

"The truth is, almost every morning one of those young STO men would knock on our door on the fifth, having mistaken the floor . . . my wife or I would take them to the Champfleurys', one floor down . . .

"Champfleury always gave me the latest news from the Beebeecee, he even turned up his set so I could hear it . . . our radio didn't work right.

"Truly charming neighbors.

"Now that idiot with his rotten gossip comes and spoils a nice memory for me! I don't have many nice memories. Naturally I'm fond of them."

Champfleury endorsed the writer's response. He wrote him soon afterward:

"I fully agree, my dear friend, when you state that you were perfectly well aware of our underground activities during the German occupation, which consisted of distribution of ration cards (counterfeited in London) and travel expenses, allocation of lodgings to escaped prisoners and parachutists, directions to pipelines across borders and demarcation lines, forwarding of mail, radio transmission to and reception from London, meeting place for the National Resistance Council, etc.

"All of this involved comings and goings at my apartment, located directly beneath yours, that could not have gone entirely unnoticed either by you or by the other neighbors.

"I well remember one night your telling me very candidly: 'Don't worry, Champfleury, I know just about everything that you and your woman are doing, but you have nothing to fear from me . . . I give you my word on that . . . and even if there's any way I can help you!'

"There was such a tone of sincerity in your statement that I felt completely reassured. . . .

"Moreover, I came knocking at your door one day, accompanied by a Resistance fighter who had been tortured by the Gestapo. You let me in, you examined my friend's bruised hand and, without asking a single question, you bandaged it in the appropriate way, having rightly guessed the cause of the wound."[66]

Champfleury guessed the dangers that would befall the writer after the liberation. According to Céline, he offered to find him shelter with the Resistance in Brittany. True or false, it made no difference from the moment Céline refused. In any case, there wasn't much his neighbor could do for him.

In *Maudits soupirs pour une autre fois*, the earlier version of *Féerie pour une autre fois*, written in Denmark from 1946 to 1947, Céline gave a precise description of the final anxious days in Montmartre, on the eve of the landings. "I have received three little coffins, ten letters announcing my death, at least twenty threatening letters, two switchblades, a little English grenade and fifty grams of cyanide . . . they're thinking of me already in the shadows . . . Everything about this falling night speaks to me of my death, the starry blue up there above Sacré-Coeur, turning purple and then dark, dark. . . . All this is over for me, for the two of us, Lucette . . . All that's left for us is that chasm out there, across the hall past the window, that enormous valley, all Paris millions and millions of who-knows-what vengeances, roofs stretching on forever, pointed, sharp, cutting, hideous, filled with people who hate us . . . The vast chasm yawns for the two of us . . . the whole world is carrying us there . . . the whole world has stopped breathing, lives only for our death, our torture, there under those roofs turning blue, dim, dark, the thousands upon thousands of cunning, wicked houses, still discreet as yet, whispering . . . millions of people awaiting their joy . . . the promised day . . . Every word on Radio London is a threat, Brazzaville's hints more specific, they read out 'lists,' all the silted-up souls are boiling over with all their nastiness, envy, covetousness, the shit springs from millions of hearts, all modesty cast aside, every dam broken, millions upon millions of murderers, cannibals, howl out their vocation night after night, want to drink our blood, they have to, *La Patrie* demands it."[67]

In this melodramatic, Shakespearian, end-of-the-world climate, with its crimes to come, its revenges and universal fear, Céline decided to speed things up. Not to leave a final testament—the word is perhaps too strong— but at least to leave a trace, a sign, the musical and anguished echo of his visions and dreams. He hadn't yet finished *Guignol's band*. Too bad. He decided to publish at least one volume of it. It might be his last work, Denoël's last book, who could say? And after the war, peace, and for whom? For a new set of prisoners to be reduced to silence, shot? Céline, who had long since appropriated the role of the damned, was beginning to be proven right: damnation was approaching with the allied armies hurtling against the Nazi divisions, with the ardor of the communist FTP's already planning their people's courts on the morrow of the liberation.

On January 13, 1944, Céline signed the contract for *Guignol's band* with his publisher—the work was initially intended for three volumes—with the clauses that had been established for his earlier books and his royalties set at 20%. The final printing of *Guignol's band* was completed on March 15: a first run of 5,000 copies; sale price: 65 francs; the frontispiece, a photograph of the prow of a sailing ship in front of a wharf and docks.

In a short preface, Céline took the trouble to explain: "Readers friendly and less friendly, enemies, critics! Here I am giving myself more headaches with Book I of *Guignol*! Don't judge me too soon! Wait a bit for what comes next! Book II! it all becomes clear! develops, gets straightened out! As is, you're missing ¾ of it! Is this any way to do things? It had to be printed fast because with things so serious you don't know who's going to be alive and who dead! Denoël? you? me? . . . I was shooting for 1,200 pages! Just think!"

And in the same preface he goes on to elaborate an elliptical poetic art, a defense and illustration of his style; in short, a last manifesto in which to explain himself before the end of the war, before his envisaged death.

He anticipates attacks on the notorious vulgarities for which he had already been reproached. "Oh yes—I see it coming! It's so easy to talk! Got to know where to put them! Just try! Not everyone can shit to order! That would be too easy!"

And his punctuation, his commas, his famous ellipses . . . "Yes, I'm stubborn, untamed! If I fell back on 'complete sentences!' . . . Three dots! . . . ten! twelve dots! help! Nothing at all if that's what's needed! That's how I am. Jazz replaced the waltz, Impressionism killed 'faux jour,' and you'll write in 'telegraphic' or you won't write at all!"

All this to a single end: emotion. That is the key word in Célinian poetics: not ideas, messages, sweeping declarations of intent, but emotion, that unpolished fragment broken from Céline's prose, from the myriad repercussions of his anger, his unblinking stare, his exaggeration, and his enchanted breathlessness.

"Emotion is everything in Life!
"Got to know how to use it!
"Emotion is everything in Life!
"When you're dead it's all over!
"Up to you to understand! Get emotional!"

Guignol's band I had little impact and little success. That is hardly surprising. The anti-Semitic intellectuals and the champions of the policy of collaboration had other things to worry about. They were succumbing either to despair or to fanaticism. Céline and his London ramblings from 1916, his poetry of Northern mists, his wanderings in the fog, the wild bedlam of the pimps JoJo, L'Allumeur, or La Poigne, the appalling London Freeborn Hospital where Clodowitz works, the grenade thrown by Borokrom into the seedy pub, the elephantine figure of Titus Van Claben the pawnbroker, and that mystical old madman, Sosthène de Rodiencourt; all the grimacing, grandiose, and absurd faces surging from the depths of his memory and imagination, all the settings attesting to a prodigious remembrance of things past, of things illusory, of things impossible, were solely part of the Célinian universe and had nothing to do with current events. Alas, the day belonged not to literature, however pure, serious, or necessary. The day belonged to vengeance and civil war.

Typical in that regard was Jacques de Lesdain's article in *Aspects* on June 2, 1944: "I was expecting to find in Céline's new work a clear and unequivocal stance on the political and social questions of our time. I was compelled, however, to accept the truth. *Guignol's band* is nothing more than a kaleidoscope of painful, often smutty images. It is, if you will, a fresco covered from end to end with drawings of thugs, pimps, whores, procuresses, madmen, and thieves. Whether you start the book at the beginning or the end, it makes no sense, serves no useful purpose."[68]

The same tone is found in the criticisms leveled by François-Charles Bauer in *Je suis partout*, April 14, 1944, or by Georges Blond in *L'Echo de Paris*, April 15-16, 1944. Rebatet would admit much later that at the time he had seen the book as a mere epileptic caricature of Céline's earlier style, and that he had been wrong, that with hindsight *Guignol's band* struck him as a comic masterpiece. And it's true. In it, Céline's writing has become further perforated, further shattered, with the meticulous and poetic frenzy of an apocalyptic fretwork. Only Lucien Combelle's paper, *Révolution nationale*, offered unmitigated support to the newly released book.

No, the day did not belong to literature. The air raids over Paris had been increasing since January 1944. The most spectacular of them, on April 21, had thrown Paris and Saint-Denis into panic. Allied planes had blitzed the La

Chapelle train station, first lighting it up with tracer rockets. German anti-aircraft units had responded with a barrage of flak. Hundreds of planes had wheeled through the night sky, rendering the station useless to the Wehrmacht but also causing hundreds of civilian casualties buried beneath the rubble. In the provinces, Le Mans, Chartres, Tours, and Rouen suffered similar strategic raids. Pétain felt obliged to undertake a tour of the stricken cities soon afterward. He was in Paris on April 26, cheered by school-children and thousands of adults.

Spring '44. There were rumors of an imminent allied landing on the shores of France, while Rome was about to be liberated. Céline, feeling ever more haunted, now went about in the streets with a pistol, for which he had obtained a permit from the German authorities. He would have to flee. Where? He would most likely be unwelcome in Switzerland. He considered Spain. His friend Antonio Zuloaga, press attaché to the Spanish embassy in Paris, had offered him his apartment in Madrid for as long as he wanted or was necessary. Furthermore, Karen was spending most of her free time there, with a Spanish diplomat whom she was seeing. Céline described all this in the pages of *Maudits soupirs*, in which he melancholically evokes his last strolls through Montmartre, the familiar streets, his close friends, the painter Jules (Gen Paul), Marcel Aymé, the cabaret singer Max Revol, Ralph Soupault, Noceti, Pierre Labric, the "mayor" of the Free Commune of Mont-martre, Dignimont, and others. We see him going from street to street with a bundle of manuscripts under his arm, seeking a safe hiding place for them. He regrets never having had his ballets and fairy tales performed. A little earlier he had been hustling to find some gasoline for his moped, a Cyclo-zephyr one HP, he says, which he used to go to Bezons. Two packs of Gitanes got him five liters of gas.

"I'm clumsy, I'm grotesque, I'm too distracted, that's what . . . it's that *Guignol's band* that put me into such a funk . . . I paid no mind to the threats . . . and yet they were growing . . . Lucette saw it coming a lot better than I did . . . 'Come on, let's head for Spain!' She always wanted to see Spain, it would've been the right time, as it happens . . . it was exactly what we needed . . . I didn't owe Fritz a thing, after all . . . I'd have hit the road and that was that, neither hide nor hair . . ."[69]

On June 6 "Operation Overlord" began on the beaches of Normandy, between Ouistreham and Saint-Vaast. Utah Beach, Omaha Beach, the names would become part of the legend of the "longest day." The allied armies got their foothold in France. A new front opened for the Germans. Fierce and bloody fighting was unleashed on the first beachheads, where the Anglo-Americans were dug in to stay. Caen crumbled under the bombs. Throughout France, the Resistance fighters, FFI or FTP,* stepped up their attacks and acts of sabotage. On June 10, in Oradour-sur-Glane, a detach-ment of the SS division "Das Reich" massacred the village populace in

---

* Forces Françaises de l'Intérieur and Francs-Tireurs Partisans.

retaliation and burned the church in which the women and children had been locked up.

Céline decided to hasten his departure from Paris. "Strangely," says Lucette, "he, who was usually so nervous, didn't see a thing. I was the one who said: we're leaving. He was convinced that if he left he would be back in three months."

Leave for where? There was always Denmark, Céline's obsession: Denmark, the North, where Karen had buried his gold, where he believed no one would look for him. In order to cover his tracks, moreover, he had had false identification made for himself and Lucette, with the help of a brother of Serge Perrault who worked at police headquarters. His name was henceforth Louis-François Deletang, born in Montréal, sales rep, residing at 161, rue de la Convention. She was Lucile Alcante, born in Pondicherry, gym teacher, residing at 12, rue de Navarin. The documents had been drawn up on February 8, 1944.

It does not appear that Louis and Lucette used these falsified papers. There was only one way to reach Denmark: through Germany. Two days after the invasion, the occupation authorities issued their visas for Germany. Bébert the cat had also been given a sort of *Fremdenpass*. Céline took special care to specify this in *Nord*: "Bébert is neither of breeding stock nor a pedigree . . . and yet I have a passport for him . . . I took him for a checkup at the Hôtel Crillon . . . by a colonel-veterinarian in the German army . . . 'The cat named Bébert, owner Dr. Destouches, 4, rue Girardon, does not appear to carry any infectious disease (photograph of Bébert) . . .' the colonel-veterinarian had not specified the cat's race."[70]

And yet, they had planned to leave him in Paris, Lucette explains. "We had a kind of cleaning lady who came from time to time. We wanted to leave Bébert with her, Louis agreed . . . And I can still see us going to this woman's house, opening the door, handing her Bébert, and then, no, at the last minute we put him back in his sack and went home with him. We couldn't leave him. The same in Germany: we were never able to part company with him. And yet we knew that he would have been happier that way. We always took him along. When we look back at Bébert's travels, at that cat who followed us everywhere, in the worst conditions, under the bombs and all, it seems so improbable. But it was his fate."

Before leaving, Louis entrusted his manuscripts-in-progress, particularly the sequel to *Guignol's band*, to Marie Canavaggia. But he left many others at his place—large sections of *Casse-Pipe*, *La Légende du roi Krogold*, and various versions of *Guignol's band*—as if he had every hope of a speedy return to France, safe and sound, to his apartment with its furniture and personal effects inviolate. What was to follow—the confiscation and disappearance of his property—was quite different.

Before taking the train at the Gare de l'Est for Baden-Baden, the first stopover, Céline liquidated all his holdings, including his checking account and some gold coins from a deposit box at the Crédit Lyonnais that he slipped into a jacket which Lucette had sewn especially for that use. François Gibault has calculated that when leaving Paris, Céline had approximately 1 million francs in hand.[71] Marguerite Destouches had been informed of her son's departure, as had Karen, to whom Céline had written. Their other intimates were kept in ignorance. Suspicion . . . Even Lucette's mother was unaware of her daughter's hasty flight.

In their luggage, along with her castanets and stage costumes, Lucette had insisted on taking a saucepan, a teapot, and a supply of tea. Across ruined Germany, through one air raid and derailing after the next, this teapot played a precious role for them, an illusion of domestic comfort between two nightmares. Céline had brought along two vials of cyanide. A way of keeping death in mind, the certainty that the worst was always sure to occur.

Lucette recalls: "A friend piled our luggage on a trailer hitched to his bike. At the Gare de l'Est, we took the second-to-last train. The one after that was bombed. Louis always burdened himself with useless things. A basket was immediately left behind in Baden-Baden. In any case, we lost everything. All our luggage was scattered that way. Later on, we reached Copenhagen without a thing—except Bébert."

14

One Summer, '44

Baden-Baden
Kränzlin

Baden-Baden

Baden-Baden, everybody off!

Actually, in June '44 there were as yet few to disembark in that city of old-fashioned charms and straight-cut gardens, soon to become a revolving door to French castaways of the shipwrecked collaboration: compromised artists, panicked politicians, routed journalists, and cynical intellectuals.

Baden-Baden, a few short kilometers from the Rhine and the French border, less than sixty from Strasbourg, still retained all its grace and luxury from the days when Napoleon III came to take the waters, when Queen Victoria sauntered beneath the elms and chestnuts, when Bismarck found himself surrounded like an oracle by diplomats, and when everywhere, along the Lichtentaler Allee lined with tulips, magnolias, and rhododendrons, before the Trinkhalle, or around the Casino steps, all was but a play of parasols and crinoline, the sharp cracking of whips, the trundling of tilburies, the sparkling laughter of young girls, the black shadows of top hats, and, in the background, the dull bouncing of the white roulette ball in the Casino halls hung with red velvet as with the heady luxury of fate. Céline hoped to stay a few hours, a few days. In transit, urgently called to other destinies to the North and in the Denmark that obsessed him. He would remain for over two months.

Tucked at the foot of the Black Forest mountains, displaying its luxury hotels, family boardinghouses, neoclassical bathing establishments, and residential villas along the Oos Valley, Baden-Baden had just been transformed into a butterfly net, a refined trap, an enchanted, unreal city often rocked by the distant thunder, way up in the sky, of dense formations of allied bombers. Of course, a spa didn't count, a little stain of color that hardly merited the attention of those far-off squadrons of Boeing B-17 flying fortresses, Lancasters, and Liberators on their way to rain bombs and death over the industrial cities and great urban centers of the Reich. A spa, it was an improbable prison for its guests, an illusion of luxury, of well-being, of opulence, of exquisite courtesies and sentimental graciousness, abandoned there in the middle of the war, while men died by the millions, barbarism triumphed, and Nazi ideals peaked then crumpled beneath the ruins of their own savagery in the setting sun of fanaticism. Baden-Baden, in short, was a fantasy, a diversion of time and space.

Céline, Lucette, and Bébert were immediately housed in the Brenner's Park Hotel, the most sumptuous in town, with swimming pool, private garden on the Oos, and immense drawing rooms decorated in eighteenth-century style with stucco work ceilings, thick rugs, and endless hallways. The hotel had recently been commandeered by the Reich Ministry of Foreign Affairs.

The master of ceremonies was one Josef Schleman, assigned to watch over Baden-Baden's political refugees. Once a vice-consul in Marseille, he now found his duties and responsibilities multiplying as the successive setbacks of the armies of the Reich drew diplomats and refugees of every stamp in their wake. His primary task was to collect the passports of the foreign guests at Brenner's. Céline and Lucette had to comply. Bébert, too, perhaps with a show of claws. Without passports it was pointless to think about moving on. Denmark remained out of reach. There was a fine line between fairy tales and witchcraft. The Destouches family were prisoners of a mirage.

In his last trilogy, *D'un château l'autre*, *Nord*, and *Rigodon*, Céline would memorialize and bear witness to the years 1944–1945 and his wanderings through the death throes of Germany. There was no need this time to reinvent the Apocalypse or to imagine it—he watched it from a front-row seat, more sumptuous and tragic in reality than in his wildest imaginings. At the beginning of *Nord*, he reveals his approach:

"So you call yourself a chronicler?

"Neither more nor less! . . ."[1]

It required a hallucinating writer and a language shattered into a thousand shards, reduced to the formidably dissonant harmonies of a great lyrical music, to recall and translate the death of the Third Reich, the laughable and pathetic epic of the narrator, his female companion, and his cat through the rubble and illusions of a dying world. But in Baden-Baden, in June and July of 1944, it was still a matter of pleasant and colorful illusions—illusions as fablelike as the horrors so close at hand: ". . . the banks of the Oos, that little stream sparkling with such distinction, lined with all sorts of rare trees . . . the seat of perfect refinement . . . weeping willows with silver hair hanging down to the water, along twenty . . . thirty meters . . . gardens fussed over for three centuries . . . the 'Brenner' accepted only the best-bred guests, former reigning princes or Rhine magnates . . . those old ironmasters with a hundred . . . two hundred thousand workers . . . at the time I'm describing, July '44, they were still very well and very punctually provisioned . . . they and their people . . . butter, eggs, caviar, marmalade, salmon, cognac, Grand Mumm."[2]

That incredible dream of abundant, succulent food, in Brenner's unheard-of luxury, for the survivors of four years of hardships and sordid black-market dealings in Montmartre! . . . "The end of meals, flushed with

leg of lamb, heavy secrets, and Burgundy . . . menus not to be resisted! . . .
delicious end to end, hors d'oeuvres with strawberries and whipped cream
. . . melba . . . syrup? . . . more? . . . less? . . . lemon peel? . . . and all those
waiters, so attentive, standing by with pen in hand, hesitations, *ja*, and
sighs."[3]

At the Baden-Baden Casino, once the meeting place of Europe, red-faced
colonels, wan refugees, and declining matrons with diseased hearts, according to Céline, played their last chips when they had already lost everything,
when the roulette of war had just raked in their last counters, their last
trumps, and when all they had left was to await the worst while pitifully
deluding themselves that for them the chips were not yet down.

The food, at least, kept going down. The Casino's pastries bloated the
German war widows, consoling themselves by gorging on cream puffs, rum
babas, blueberry tarts, and chocolate éclairs—widows whom the waiter
would then escort gently outdoors, a little drowzy. And they could be seen
beached in the park, on a bench, belching, pensive, still.

That was Céline's vision, perhaps a little exaggerated. And that Mlle. de
Chamarande, "a very nice, even sympathetic person," who, at Brenner's
poolside, drove the masseurs, croupiers, towel boys, and convalescing
officers to distraction with her daily more provocative bathing suits. Did she
come within a hair's breadth of being raped one fine morning? Is she an
illusion, an invention of the writer's? Hardly. Maud de Belleroche, who had
been Jean Luchaire's mistress, recognized herself in the gently caricatured
character.[4] As to old Mme. von Seckt, with her vast knowledge, her smiling
generosity, her humble confidence, her tragic lucidity, who didn't care for
Hitler and said so in a passionate whisper—Céline had only to alter her
name minimally. Her name was Mme. von Seeckt, the widow of a World War
I general, and she had taken a strong liking to Lucette.

The days passed, and the weeks. They could do nothing without papers.
Lucette took Bébert for walks, sometimes on a leash, through the gardens of
Baden-Baden. Louis champed at the bit. Josef Schleman had summoned the
writer and essentially told him, according to Lucette:

" 'People who are in Germany must serve the country. You must do some
propaganda, talk on the radio, for instance. One cannot live without a job!'

"Céline answered him:

" 'You must be mad. Forget it!' "

Schleman must have insisted, threatened, repeated to Céline that, in any
case, he would not be allowed to leave. A wasted effort. The writer retorted
once again that he would do nothing, write nothing, not a word, that they
could kill him and it was all the same to him. Schleman conceded defeat.

The situation could not go on forever. Since Céline could get no results in
Baden-Baden, he decided to try his luck in Berlin to finally obtain the
necessary passes for Denmark. In early July he managed to reach the capital
of the Reich. "They sent a lady doctor to escort us. Louis met with Dr. Knapp
in Berlin. It came to nothing," Lucette recalls.

Louis knew Knapp well and had often seen him in Paris when he had been in the foreign section of the Reich Public Health Office. But what could he do for him in Berlin other than soothe him with fine words and promise that his inquiry would be taken under advisement? The same answer at the Ministry of Foreign Affairs, where Louis had also knocked on a few doors. All they could tell him was to return to Baden-Baden, where he would be notified of the official response.

Thus, life went on at Brenner's, with its ever more numerous refugees, its ever more noisy squadrons in the skies, its ever more blossoming magnolias and hydrangea—and its ever less secret anxieties.

Lucette recalls: "These very worldly people continued to live their normal lives, which had lost all meaning since they no longer had lives, personalities, identities, papers, anything. They continued to form social circles, to gossip at table, invite each other to tea. I watched them from time to time. I could have joined their groups if I hadn't been a dancer, if I hadn't devoted so much time to my exercises. Céline gossiped every which way, out of curiosity. Did he work on any manuscripts? I seem to remember him saying, 'I want to go on with my work but I can't, I'm not in the right frame of mind—we'll see about it later.' It was all very distressing. Louis saw himself being thrown in a prison camp for refusing to work for the Germans. He helped out on the spot, treating people. He had his first-aid kit, his syringes, emergency materials. But medicine was already growing scarce. Especially morphine. I remember the German officers who were there, convalescing or on leave. There were a lot of hospitals in Baden-Baden. You came across seriously wounded people, amputees. I can still see these German officers with enormous bandages, each one escorted by a nurse, going for walks. And one of them—I can suddenly picture him—rips off his dressing and starts screaming, his skull exposed. Scenes like that . . . The Germans had organized soccer games for one-legged amputees. It was awful. They played, they managed to play, they kept on playing. You also saw German youths, little kids drafted at fourteen, who paraded down the streets of Baden-Baden in their short pants and cried out, Heil Hitler! Every shop you went into, it was Heil Hitler! just for a bit of bread. It was an obsession. People were scared sick, terrified by the idea of not being loyal enough to the government."

On July 20, while the Red Army pursued its relentless counterattack in the East and the Allies finally broke out of Normandy to begin liberating French territory, came the botched assassination attempt on Hitler, at Rastenburg in East Prussia. Lucette and Louis caught a hint of its repercussions in Baden-Baden, in the jubilant climate that suddenly swept through the German guests at Brenner's at the hope—unfortunately soon to be disappointed—that the attempt had succeeded, that the bomb placed by Stauffenberg had managed to kill the Chancellor. Banquets, champagne, and laughter. The Germans saw the conclusion of peace, at least on the Western front. *Nord* barely exaggerates the fleeting joy: orgies and drinking bouts. "From the minute anything is being celebrated, good or bad, the human being swells up, stuffs himself to the max."[5]

And again the days passed, and the weeks. Céline was bored. In early August he wrote to Karl Epting, asking him to send books, Châteaubriand, Ronsard, and the chroniclers of the Middle Ages, as if he were already confusedly thinking of following their example. Meanwhile France was being liberated at the speed of General Patton's tanks. Around mid-August the first battles began for the liberation of Paris.

At Brenner's, the squeeze was on. The Destouches were ousted from their fine room on the second floor and installed in the garret. This signaled the arrival of the stars of the collaboration. Food, too, grew scarcer. Gone were the legs of lamb and cream puffs: now it was Jerusalem artichokes, rutabaga, and ersatz sausage.

Despite everything, the new refugees still lived in a dream world, in the comforting illusion of the triumph of their ideas and interests. They became restless. They created this committee, that committee. A pathetic restlessness.

Lucette: "I had said, 'I don't mind taking care of the animals.' So they named me Commissioner for Animals. The Germans didn't want to let dogs into the restaurant, and poor old Alphonse de Châteaubriant, whom Louis didn't much care for, had a cocker. The Germans thought that the animals should be gotten rid of—they were superfluous mouths. I insisted, playing my role, that Châteaubriant's cocker be fed. All this was a farce, a circus. Louis took no part in all the committees. He looked at these people the way you look at fleas fighting. It was really stupid. They fought over everything, over food, over rooms. They were living in the illusion that they were going to survive. They all left after two or three weeks."

Among the new arrivals were Marcel Déat, Pierre Costantini, Jean-Hérold Paquis, Fernand de Brinon and Mme. Mitre, the Englishman John Amery, a minister's son who had aligned himself with the Nazis. There was also Jean Luchaire, who in 1941 had been elected president of the Paris Press Association, with his family.

His daughter Corinne had had a meteoric career in French cinema: eight films, a beautiful, childlike and aggressive face, hard, burning from within. An awkward but strangely haunting actress, she harbored a certain desperation. Life had turned her head, success, liquor, and other, even harder drugs—like that of celebrity. She was a strange, fascinating, and tragic character, a romantic figure through the nights of the occupation.

"I went out quite often at night with young German officers I had met by chance, who were very eager and took me to Scheherazade, the fashionable club. It was full of Germans. There was no dancing. It was forbidden. But we drank a lot as we listened to the music. . . . On the one side, luxury, lights, money and champagne flowing like water; on the other, the mysteriousness and darkness of Paris, asleep or conspiring. My young Germans behaved very pleasantly. They asked for nothing more than to be there, for an evening. They never talked politics, which would have bored me, or of their assignments."[6] And now Corinne was there with the rest in Baden-Baden, not quite understanding how, awaiting the worst. She too had had to relinquish her passport, as she would later write, "to a hateful German, Mr. Schleman, and his secretary Miss Fischer, who claimed to have been whipped by French Legionnaires in Morocco. Good for them! It avenged us for that disagreeable reception."[6] We will shortly see Corinne Luchaire again in Sigmaringen, fleeing to Italy with her family, emprisoned in Nice (her father would be shot), condemned for "national disgrace," before writing her memoirs, *Ma drôle de vie*, and dying of tuberculosis in 1950, at the age of thirty.

To paraphrase Oscar Wilde's witticism, it was a wonderful case of nature imitating art, as reality became *de plus en plus célinien*. The pianist Lucienne Delforge, too, vaguely compromised by some illicit liaison or other, had recently arrived in Baden-Baden. Her affair with Céline, in 1935–1936, was so long ago. . . . And Le Vigan arrived in turn on August 16, half-mad, penniless, without luggage, nothing. In Nice he had begun shooting the role of the clothes merchant in *Les Enfants du paradis* when the announcement came of the allied landing in Normandy. Seized with panic, he disappeared. According to Marcel Carné, his acting in the film had been extraordinary. As he had shot only one scene, he was easily replaced: Pierre Renoir took the part. Le Vigan wandered, hither and yon, his persecution more or less illusory, before hopping on a train and rejoining his old friend Céline and his old cat, Bébert.

Lucette: "We did nothing in Baden-Baden. I kept on with my practicing. I spent my whole life practicing, there and elsewhere. I did my exercises in our room. Little Lucienne Delforge asked me to give her lessons. I had her work out in a parlor. My practicing was everything. Louis would tell me: 'If you get out of this, you'll have to be able to work. That's what a dancer is. It's not like a writer, who can sit around doing nothing. A dancer who stops practicing, it's like she never danced.' Le Vigan arrived in a train that had been bombed. He was all scorched. No more luggage, no more clothing. Louis had to give him his lumber jacket, which he kept. He didn't have a stitch of clothing. As for our cat, Bébert, he behaved himself very nicely. He had taken a shine to a Swiss couple staying in the next room. And Bébert, the pig, slept with them at night, leaving via the roof to fool us! During the day, I used to take him for walks in the garden. He never tried to get away, except at night when he slept elsewhere."

August came and went. Although he had been promised an answer, Céline still had no news from the Ministry of Foreign Affairs. As a result, there was no visa for Denmark in sight. He appealed once again for help to Karl Epting, who had in the meantime been called back to Berlin. Epting spoke to the Ministry, which assigned Dr. Hauboldt to take care of the writer/doctor, to find him some sort of "post." In early September, summoned to Berlin, Céline left Baden-Baden, this time for good, with Bébert, Lucette, and Le Vigan.

On August 24 General Leclerc's 2nd Armored Division had entered Paris, cheered on with the wild joy of nightmare's end. People laughed, sang, showered the tanks with flowers and the soldiers with kisses. Teenagers brandished pistols and played war games—now that the Germans were gone. Temporary prisons were set up everywhere, the first at Villa Saïd, Pierre Laval's mansion. The heads of women guilty or merely suspected of "horizontal" collaboration were shaved, which is still better than lopping them off on the guillotine. Sham FFIs and real FTPs alike hunted down militiamen. Denunciations rained down with the laughter and the joy. The definition of a *collabo* was someone on the outs with his concierge, would say Sacha Guitry, arrested on Liberation Day. The firecrackers carried the smell of gunpowder. Gunfire rang out, laconic and lugubrious. How many summary executions in liberated France? Ten thousand, twenty, more? Historians do not agree. One dare not hazard an answer.

And who would have dared to answer for Céline's life in those wild times of celebration, coeval with terror for some? The Resistance fighter Pierre Petrovitch, who had been a companion of Jean Dasté in the underground since '41 and a member of the first committee of the National Liberation Movement organized by Paul Reynaud, Bloch-Lainé and d'Astier de la Vigerie, had often run into the writer in Montmartre, before the war and under the occupation, "much more concerned with obtaining coupons of every sort than with playing a political role as a lecturer or journalist." And Petrovitch was the first to admit it: "L.-F. Céline did well to flee Paris at the liberation, not because he had anything to fear from *résistants* who knew him, but because certain hotheads were capable of anything. Some obscure commando would have unthinkingly shot him down and nobody would have been able to prevent it. Paris was in revolution."[7]

Kränzlin

Bébert, in his famous game pouch punctured with little holes, Lucette, Le Vigan, and Céline arrived in Berlin in early September. Their last visit had been back at the beginning of July. In two months the city had suffered numerous air raids. They barely recognized it. Buildings destroyed, rubble and debris. "It remained a city only as a stage setting . . . entire streets were mere façades, all the interiors gone, collapsed into pits."[8]

They stayed about eight days.

Louis first went to the Hotel Adlon, no doubt the best in Berlin. Though thrifty, he had gotten into the habit when abroad of staying only in luxury hotels. He had had the chance to enjoy the Adlon during his brief visit to Berlin in March 1942, when he had given Karen the keys to his deposit box in Copenhagen.

" 'You would like a room?'

" 'Two rooms! . . . one for me and my wife! . . . and one for our friend here!'

"This clerk is out of the old days, his frock coat more than ample, very delicate frogging, grand-admiral's hat . . . but he notices Bébert! . . . his head! . . . Bébert stares back . . .

   " 'You have a cat?'

"Shit! he's seen him! . . . whap! . . . he slams his register shut! . . . any excuse to get rid of us!

   " 'No animals allowed! . . .' "[9]

The group had to resort to more modest lodgings, which Céline calls "Zenith Hotel" in *Nord*, run by a bearded *muzhik* in boots and baggy tunic, a native of Siberia and possibly a deserter from Vlassof's army.

Thanks to Epting, Céline met with Dr. Hauboldt, to whom he had been briefly introduced in June 1942 at the lecture given by his German colleague at the Cercle Européen on the health and prophylactic problems posed by the repatriation and emigration of ethnic Germans during the winter of 1939–1940. Hauboldt's exact title is uncertain. In *Nord*, Céline promoted him to the rank of SS Reichoberarzt. At the trial that followed the publication of *Nord*, in a lawsuit for slander brought by the Scherz family, the plaintiff described his duties as more humble: he was only in charge of the office dealing with ethnic German émigrés, and had been inducted into the Waffen SS. In any case, he held the high rank of Standartenführer and was actively involved in foreign relations at the Reich Chamber of Physicians. In that capacity, Dr. Knapp was one of his subordinates. In Berlin, Hauboldt worked and lived at 62 Königsallee in the residential neighborhood of Grunewald. He occupied a fine, vast house in the classical style, the basement of which had been transformed into a bunker that served as offices for his agencies. According to Céline in *Nord*, Hauboldt (who would become Harras in the new edition of the work that followed the trial) received them in a "lemon and sky-blue" bathrobe just as he was preparing to take a dip in his private pool. Extravagant luxury, abundant food, muted lighting, a hive of gorgeous typists, with teleprinters humming in the background, while in the distance, far above on the surface, the city was crumbling building by building, haunted by more ghosts than living beings.

Hauboldt authorized Céline to practice medicine in Germany. The reciprocity of degrees between France and Germany made this significantly easier. It would further seem that he offered Céline a well-paid, permanent medical position, which the author refused. He then offered him a refuge outside Berlin at an enormous house owned by friends, the Scherzes, which already housed several health agencies under his authority. It was difficult for Céline to refuse. The house in question, Kränzlin, was near the village of Neuruppin, about sixty kilometers northwest of Berlin. This already brought Céline and his companions a little closer to Rostock and Warnemünde, where they might be able to board ship for Denmark.

In Berlin, Céline still found time to dine with Karl Epting on September 10, at a basement tavern on the Wilhelmstrasse. Alain Laubreaux, the zealot from *Je suis partout*, joined the group. It was probably a melancholy meal that Epting and Céline shared, a conversation between two men of culture too clear-sighted for their own good, recalling the prewar days in a landscape of ruins.

Around September 15, the quartet of Bébert, Lucette, Le Vigan, and Céline arrived at Kränzlin, perhaps driven by Hauboldt himself in full Waffen SS uniform. "So be it! life goes on! . . . a very large car . . . not gas powered . . . gasoline-powered! . . . he takes the wheel . . . this is September . . . the weather's lovely . . . their countryside in September is going to red, the leaves . . . it's already more than brisk . . . he drives slowly . . . we pass through all of Grunewald, avenues of houses in ruins . . . and then stretches of gray land . . . where surely nothing grows . . . kind of ashy . . . not a pleasant landscape! . . . two . . . three trees . . . a farm in the distance . . . a little closer, a peasant hoeing, I think."[10]

And then they came upon the Scherz's vast agricultural estate, Kränzlin, where they would stay for nearly six weeks.

First the manor, a large and beautiful rectangular building, most likely built in the nineteenth century, with two corner half-towers on either side of the main façade, one rising a full story above the building's roof. The first floor was above ground level, with a single story above it. The windows that opened at ground level belonged to rooms sunk below it: kitchens, storage rooms, offices. Virginia creepers partially covered the walls. The manor was surrounded by an enormous lawn dotted with trees that dated back a hundred years or more.[11] A little farther off stretched the estate with its farmhouses, barns, and recently built barracks. Lastly, not far from the main house stood a residential lodge in the style of a rather plush gardener's cottage, surrounded by a wooden porch.

In the manor lived Erich Scherz senior, eighty years old and a former captain in the cavalry, the very picture of the Prussian soldier. Céline made him a notorious old goat who strove to sleep with the Polish girls on his estate or to urinate on them. There is no evidence to authenticate the assertion, which the Scherzes had every reason in the world to deem slanderous. On the second floor there also lived his late wife's sister, Fräulein Käthe Lake, who played the piano with more vigor than talent. Employees of Hauboldt's health service (*Dienststelle*) were also housed in the building, to which Céline and Lucette were welcomed with undisguised scorn as undesirables to be avoided as much as possible. They were put in a little closet on the first floor without running water or heat, while Le Vigan was allotted a basement room without ventilation, hard by the kitchens, which were off-limits and tormenting.

Erich Scherz junior was de facto manager of the estate since his father's retirement. Forty-five years old, he lived in the lodge with his wife, Asta, and their two children, Ugo and Anne-Marie. Paralyzed for the past ten years by polio, Erich junior never left his chair. A Russian prisoner of monumental girth and strength escorted him, carried him, and set him down to order.

Lastly, various communities lived side-by-side on the estate: a few French

prisoners, German conscientious objectors (*Bibelforscher*) who were building barracks, Ukrainian and Polish refugees, former Berlin prostitutes recy-
cled in forced labor, and even a group of Gypsies housed in the barracks or
in caravans.

"In the manor house," Lucette describes, "I particularly recall the stair-
way, under which was a swinging door that gave onto a broom closet. But
instead of brooms, we were the ones inside. There was a dormer window
and just enough room for an iron bed. To one side, a tiny sink. It was cold in
there. Through the window I could see a very thick bough and a sort of
courtyard overrun with pigs and geese. Birds perched on the thick bough. It
was an entire world, a show. Louis went for walks. I went with him. Other
than that, we didn't move. We ate in a big gloomy dining room along with
the health-service employees, who all had nice rooms. We went there to eat
a bowl of hot water with little bits of rutabaga and potato floating on top. I
put the little bits of potato aside for Bébert. Nothing else to set the rhythm of
the day. There was also a road that went past there, it was built to go very far
and nowhere, it cut through the property and vanished over the horizon. It
was nothing but gravel on a sandy base. There was no telling where it was
supposed to go on that totally bare plain. It gave an extraordinary impression of infinity."

The famine rations reserved for the Destouches and Le Vigan were all the
more objectionable for the smells of fine cooking that escaped from the
doors of the *Dienststelle* employees, who copiously supplemented their
fare, naturally with the Scherzes' complicity. "Old Scherz had an enormous
personal kitchen where lots of good things were prepared, and in the
kitchen next door, ours, they cooked up that pathetic soup. Le Vigan would
hang around there trying to seduce a girl he hoped would give him something to eat. You'd find him by the door, on the verge of fainting. The smells
made him weak. We bought bread, from the Gypsy prisoners I think. We
paid a lot for it. And that bread was like cement, it stayed in your stomach
for eight days. It was crazy, all the dealing that went on there. The best off
were the Finnish doctors, in striped uniforms like a chain gang. They got by.
It was every man for himself. The Gypsies had spotted my ring straight
away, they wanted to buy it. They had a superb white horse they were
hiding. I can still see them in their caravan. The summer was over and it was
getting cold. It was always cold in our broom closet."

And Bébert? Lucette still remembers a little German maid who worked in
the Grunewald bunker and who had fallen in love with the cat. Every
weekend she took advantage of a departmental shuttle between Berlin and
Kränzlin to bring him some awful little fish she must have caught in some
lake or stream. Lucette was touched.

One day the Scherzes asked the Destouches to give them the cat to hunt
mice in the basement. "So we lent them Bébert one night, we took him down
into the basement. They were very embarrassed. It was like Ali Baba's cave,
that basement, crammed with victuals. Bébert couldn't have cared less

about mice. He didn't nab a thing. We had to bring him back. This caused more arguments with the Scherzes. They had borrowed Bébert like you borrow a tool. We had seen hams, sausages, everything. Bébert hadn't eaten a thing. He wasn't such a big eater."

Another local character was the Landrat, the chief administrator of the Neuruppin district, of whom Lucette was not overly fond ever since he had threatened to do away with Bébert. "He had taken him by the paws and wanted to kill him by dashing him against the wall. I didn't really understand. He was saying that Bébert was not a breeder. Castrated domestic animals had to be killed. I never saw any cats in Germany, for that matter. Were they eaten? I pounced on the mayor, and Bébert left with us. The mayor kept saying, 'That useless beast must be killed!' He would have done it."

Louis, Lucette, and Le Vigan were virtual prisoners on the enormous estate, which they could not leave without authorization. Twice at the very most did they go to the neighboring village of Neuruppin, where the populace met them with hostility. There was little to break the monotony.

"Louis had hoped I would be able to work on my dancing on the first floor, in the parlor used by the old owner's sister-in-law. I went there a bit to start, but I didn't care for it. I didn't like these people, who never showed us the least kindness. Old Scherz, the cripple's father, looked like a Kaiser, a very great lord. He owned a twenty-five-year-old mare that he still rode. There were two little Lithuanian girls who served barefoot, in pretty costumes. They were ten or twelve years old. They laughed all the time. They closed the doors with their rumps. They always seemed to be cleaning."

On two occasions Lucette, Le Vigan, and Céline were invited to lunch at the lodge by Asta and Erich Scherz, the paralytic. Strained courtesies and, for the three French, more than usually decent food.

"Suddenly, in the middle of the meal, a terrible explosion, a plane had just crashed a hundred yards from the house. A little German plane, whose pilot was killed instantly. Everyone looked. And then the Scherzes returned to the table as if nothing had happened. The very day that we had been invited! We couldn't go on with our meal. But we brought something back for Bébert."

And Lucette can still see the Russian who carried Erich Scherz on his back. "A big Russian, who Louis said had once chucked Scherz into the pond, and no surprise since his master treated him so badly, like a horse, he beat him, and that poor miserable Russian was doing everything he could. There were also some Russians among the prisoners, badly underfed. They were the worst off. They did the hardest work, you'd see them drop from starvation, they didn't defend themselves."

Céline was offered a distraction one day in the form of an unexpected visit from Karl Epting, and then an excursion around the estate on the occasion of a visit to Kränzlin by Asta Scherz's mother. A picnic had been organized. Louis advised Lucette not to eat any of the sandwiches. He was afraid they had been poisoned. His paranoia was proportionate to his idleness and despair. He also had occasional discussions with Hauboldt, who would come to inspect his offices and to present his most eager and humble compliments to his hostess, Asta Scherz, at forty-three proud and still beautiful. Furthermore, Lucette goes on, "Hauboldt was writing some kind of book on the Apocalypse and he wanted Louis' opinion. To him, the Apocalypse was Germany and all that was going on there at the time. I don't think that Louis was very enthusiastic about his book, and he told him so. He wasn't one to make concessions. People would immediately take offense and that was it. They didn't want to see him after that."

How, generally speaking, could Céline ever have been favorably welcomed at Kränzlin? He spoke German too well and received too many official figures (Epting, Hauboldt) not to be suspect in the eyes of the French prisoners and of the other opponents to Hitler's regime who broke their backs morning to night digging up rutabaga. He spoke too openly about his possible flight to Denmark not to be judged an enemy by the local Nazis. He did not conceal his scorn for Prussia or his certainty of the Reich's imminent defeat in order to avoid antagonizing his hosts. Finally, he criticized Hauboldt's literary works with a candor too excessive to remain in the latter's good graces.

At least he was better off there than in France, where the purge was finally underway after the inevitable disorders of the liberation. On September 4 the National Committee of Writers had published its first blacklist of twelve names, his among them. Tribunals were being set up at a record pace. Among the first to be condemned to death was the journalist Georges Suarez, publisher of the collaborationist daily *Aujourd'hui*. Unaware of any of the conditions under the liberation, Céline only had thoughts for reaching the North. Neuruppin is 130 kilometers as the crow flies from Rostock and the Baltic and, perhaps, from the crazy dream of setting sail for Denmark. He explained his plans very clearly in a letter to his lawyer Tixier-Vignancour on June 23, 1949. "Still planning my escape to Denmark, I cooked up a story about establishing myself as a doctor in Rostock so as to be able to study, on site in *Warnemünde*, the means of *illicitly getting to Denmark*. Le Vigan stayed 5 days in *Kräntzlin* [sic] while my wife and I were in *Rostock* talking nonsense to the Rostock Chamber of Physicians and requesting their permission to travel by rail to Warnemünde (a nearby port) on a day trip. We spent twenty-four hours in Warnemünde studying the possibilities of stowing away. We were noticed almost immediately. I have never seen so many policemen on a beach or so many machine guns on breakwaters. We were challenged 20 times in a few hours!"[12]

According to François Gibault, it was Hauboldt who first offered the writer a position as doctor in an arms factory. Louis had pretended to accept in order to be able to visit the site. Whatever the case, it proved impossible to find passage on any ship.

Louis and Lucette had had to entrust Bébert to Le Vigan before leaving for Rostock and Warnemünde. "There were little fishing boats," she relates.

"We tried hard to bribe a sailor with a view to a future departure. Nothing doing. On that strand at Warnemünde, with its black and white pebbles, that terribly poor and deprived setting, all you saw was soldiers and machine guns. On the train that took us there from Neuruppin, we met a Greek doctor who had been a prisoner in Russia for ten years. He was the one who told us: 'I learned to stop thinking because my thoughts can be seen. Over there, in jail, if you were thinking they knew that you were thinking. So I learned to stop thinking.' And sure enough, you had the feeling of being in the presence of someone who was empty. He was looking for work and he was looking for his wife, who had been in a camp. She was Greek, and a doctor too. All around us there were prisoners, displaced people, it was horrible."

Back in Kränzlin, Louis and Lucette found Bébert skeletally thin. Le Vigan had devoured all the provisions, the potatoes and ersatz sausage that had been set aside for the cat. I was hungry, he explained. Fortunately, Bébert was from the school of hard knocks, a real Montmartre tom. But his masters were desperate. With the Danish border definitively closed, their only choice seemed to be to stay at Kränzlin in that relentlessly hostile atmosphere, while autumn was already setting in, the air raids over Berlin shaking the horizon and reddening the midnight sky, while the privations grew ever more cruel, the isolation ever more unbearable, the waiting and the feeling of uselessness ever more urgent.

It was soon after the woeful return from Rostock that Céline first learned that in the little castle town of Sigmaringen on the Danube, the Nazis had created an enclave to regroup the French government in exile together with the last militiamen, the survivors of the Charlemagne Division, fleeing intellectuals, and all other collaborators threatened with high treason by the new French government. As long as he was stuck in Germany, Céline thought, it might as well be with other Frenchmen, speaking his own language, treating his compatriots and—who knew?—if all else failed, crossing the Swiss border. So he wrote to Fernand de Brinon, an eminent member of the phantom cabinet responsible for guaranteeing the problematical legitimacy of the "New Order" that awaited on the enemy's coattails and depended upon the reconquest of the land by the counterattacking armies of the Reich. Brinon answered him immediately. Céline would be welcome. A doctor would be welcome.

According to Lucette, it was Le Vigan who first pressured them to leave for the South. "Louis was in anguish. For him, every second was a contemplation of horror. That's what people don't understand. He was incapable of being like that Greek we ran into on the train, who had managed to empty his head completely and had stopped feeling. With Louis it was just the opposite, a tireless agitation. And since he wasn't writing, he concentrated that enormous strength, that intelligence, on thoughts of escape. Every second brought him a new idea for escape, by train, by boat. He couldn't help himself. I told him to sit still and wait—a kind of fatality—that we should let ourselves be carried along, wherever. Louis wasn't willing. That's why we left for Sigmaringen after putting all our efforts into fleeing in the other direction. I wasn't keen on Sigmaringen. It was partly Le Vigan's fault. He thought there'd be something to eat there. Boy was he wrong! Louis wavered, he sensed that it was a sanctuary for apes, and since he had nothing in common with them, nothing to do with them, he had no reason to join up with them. No nostalgia, nothing in common. He simply said that at least he would be serving Frenchmen, without deluding himself any further. He saw things very clearly. Arriving at Sigmaringen, I felt like I had fallen in with lunatics or semilunatics. One guy told me: 'I killed fifty of them,' another, 'a hundred.' They were boasting about having killed Frenchmen. Each one hung on to his shred of power. We didn't have a radio in Kränzlin. Maybe we heard about the existence of Sigmaringen through Hauboldt."

Thus, in late October, with the permission of the German authorities and, of course, of Dr. Hauboldt, Céline and his companions left the Kränzlin estate and the home of the Scherz family, who watched them go with no regrets. How could they know that later, with his visionary delusions, his distorted chronicle raised to the level of a grinding, clownish tragicomedy somewhere between laughter and the death rattle, Céline would turn Kränzlin (Zornhof in the new edition), at the heart of the dreary Brandenburg plains, into a setting that was based on reality, yet one of the most incandescent and flamboyant in modern literature?

15

Castle and Prison

Sigmaringen

When, in the years 1955–1957, Céline was writing the new novel that was to open the "chronicle" of his tribulations through Hitler's Germany, he immediately thought of the title *D'un château l'autre* [Castle to Castle]. It seemed logical to link in one dramatic movement the castle of Sigmaringen, at the foot of which he lived from November '44 to March '45, and the Vestre Faengsel in Copenhagen where he would be incarcerated for eighteen months, from December '45 to June '47. In the end, the setting of Sigmaringen alone would encompass the bulk of the narrative, making the title both obsolete and incomprehensible. Céline had fled France and now found himself in close proximity to Pétain, Laval, and the elders of Vichy in Sigmaringen's microcommunity—yet he had no access to the castle that housed only the privileged members of the former French government and their families. His war would end in the bowels of another castle, this one damp, frigid, hostile, where he would be the guest of honor, the *ne plus ultra* of prisoners.

But first things first—Sigmaringen.

Lucette, Le Vigan, Bébert in his sack, and Céline thus left Neuruppin in early November 1944 for a fairly uneventful journey, in trains that were not yet derailing and stopping in stations that had not yet been entirely reduced to ashes by allied air raids. Their route across Germany took them from north to south—Berlin, Leipzig, Fürth, Augsburg, and Ulm—from Prussia through Bavaria to Baden-Württemberg.

In Ulm, a few days earlier on October 18, the spectacular national funeral of Rommel had unfolded in the presence of Field Marshal von Rundstedt. This gave Céline the chance to disrupt his chronology and to describe in *Rigodon*, as if he had been there, the solemn pomp of the burial and the immortal and imaginary meeting of Field Marshal von Rundstedt with Tomcat von Bébert.

There was nothing imaginary about the Sigmaringen station. It was a long, one-story building of grayish stone nestled in a curve of the Danube, which was still a wide, muddy river and would require a respectable number of tributaries and miles yet before earning its overgenerous epithet "the beautiful blue Danube." French refugees, directed by the German authorities, crowded into the waiting room after being met by militiamen under the command of the police and the arrivals authority. In this way, prostitutes on the run, Gestapo informers, former mistresses of SS officers, and other losers of the civil war, all more or less liable before the courts, were sorted out and occasionally turned back by the overburdened city administration. One had to a greater or lesser extent to prove employment to stay in Sigmaringen, this new French enclave in the heart of German territory.

Céline and his companions, of course, had nothing to prove, arriving as they did with papers in order and after the great rush in September and October, when the earliest refugees, mostly coming from Baden-Baden, had settled in. Despite himself, Céline was still one of the VIPs of anti-Semitism, if not of the collaboration. Céline was also a doctor. He was awaited almost impatiently.

Lucien Rebatet described his arrival: "One morning in early November 1944, the rumor spread through Sigmaringen: 'Céline has just arrived.' The guy was coming straight from his Kränzlin. A memorable stage entrance. Still shaken by his trip through devastated Germany, he wore a bluish canvas cap, like a locomotive engineer's circa 1905, two or three of his lumber jackets overlapping, filthy and ragged, a pair of moth-eaten mittens hanging from his neck, and under the mittens, in a haversack on his belly, Bébert the cat, presenting the phlegmatic face of a native Parisian who's seen it all before. You should have seen the faces of the hard-core militants and the rank-and-file militiamen at the sight of this hobo: 'That's the great fascist writer, the brilliant prophet?' I was speechless myself."[1]

To speak in theatrical terms as Rebatet does of Céline's "stage entrance" into Sigmaringen is not a gratuitous metaphor, for Céline himself described the castle and the town as an illusion, a showman's dream setting: "you'd have thought yourself in an operetta . . . the set was perfect . . . you were expecting sopranos and light tenors . . . the whole forest for echoes! . . . ten, twenty mountainsides of trees! . . . the Black Forest, waves of fir trees, waterfalls . . . your platform, the stage, the city, so prettily done up in pink, green, a little sickly sweet kind of pistachio, cabarets, hotels, boutiques, all rickety for the "director" . . . All 'boche baroque' and 'white stallion' style . . . You can already hear the orchestra! . . . the biggest trick of all: the Castle! . . . the sort of centerpiece of the city . . . plaster and papier-mâché! . . . I'll say more about this picturesque vacation! not just a spa and tourist trap . . . amazingly historic! . . . An important place! . . . take the Castle! . . . stucco, brickwork, incongruities in every style, turrets, chimneys, gargoyles . . . unbelievable! . . . super-Hollywood! . . . every era, from the melting of the snows, the narrowing of the Danube, the death of the dragon, the victory of Saint-Fidelis, right up to William II and Goering."[2]

Why was Sigmaringen selected? By late August Hitler had had to concede that the battle for France was lost. The retreat was directed toward the Rhine. He reserved space on his coattails for Pétain and his followers. Not so much to save their lives as to provide for the future, to maintain the fiction of a French government in exile, to weaken and divide his enemies in anticipation of a possible reconquest of French territory. And it was the little town of Sigmaringen, less than fifty kilometers north of Lake Constance, that he chose as shelter for the refugees of the "open collaboration." The princely Hohenzollern-Sigmaringen family, directly descended from the old Imperial family, received the order for an emergency evacuation of its castle, and was confined to lodgings not far from there by order of the Reich. The town populace, often anti-Nazi and Hohenzollern partisans, thus met with sullen hostility the first Frenchmen who began settling into the town and castle on September 7.

Moreover, not all had come willingly. Pétain had been forcibly brought there by the Germans, along with his wife and a small company of the faithful, first among whom was Dr. Ménétrel. Laval, who had planned to contact the Americans as soon as Paris was liberated, also found himself a virtual prisoner of the Germans, along with other ministers of his old government, brought to Belfort and then to Sigmaringen.

What were conditions like in the little Baden-Württemberg village when Céline arrived in November, six weeks into the French presence, to discover its charming half-timbered houses, the fine town hall with its flower-bedecked balconies, the chapels with their domed steeples, and the exuberant baroque decor of the little church of Saint John? First, there was the castle and its occupants. The building, which still draws crowds in the tourist season, was a labyrinthine amalgamation, a confusion of every style and every century, gothic and neo-gothic, renaissance, and the eighteenth and nineteenth centuries to boot. How do you say Viollet-le-Duc in German? Built on a promontory, its north face plunging down to the Danube, and encircled by a chestnut- and willow-shaded promenade, the castle of Sigmaringen retains romantic aspects overhauled and corrected by a Metro-Goldwyn-Mayer set designer for a chivalric film by Richard Thorpe or Henry King. Past the Blue Room, with its Napoleonic memorabilia and its portrait of Caroline Murat, come the Green Room, the Black Room, the Red Room— one for every color—until one reaches the ancestral hall with the full-length portraits that so impressed Céline—every Hohenzollern from Charles I, invested with the fiefdom of Sigmaringen in 1535, up to the very last in line—not to mention the Saint Hubert gallery with its hunting trophies, or the immense armory still piled high with halberds, armor, culverins, and crossbows.

Otto Abetz, as a protocol expert and former "ambassador" of Germany to France, was in charge of overseeing the refugees' accommodations. Thus, at the top, on the seventh floor, Pétain dozed away his impotence, accompanied by his retinue. On the sixth, in the luxurious apartments reserved for guests of honor, were Laval, bitter and despairing, and his wife. Nearby had also been gathered the "passive" ministers, those who knew the score and acknowledged themselves beaten, who refused to lend themselves to the

little game of governmental legitimacy and did not participate in the cha-
rades of Fernand de Brinon and his followers. Chief amongst them was Jean
Bichelonne, a graduate of the Polytechnique, who had a prodigious memory
and was a workaholic, a prototype technocrat and the youngest minister in
Laval's government, having only three months earlier been responsible for
industrial production. The victim of an automobile accident in 1943 in
which he suffered a triple fracture of the knee that never knit, he continuously and painfully dragged his leg. He barely had a chance to socialize with
Céline. A few days after the writer's arrival, he checked into a clinic in East
Prussia, in Hohenlychen, and was operated on by Dr. Gebhardt, a surgeon of
repute and general of a Panzer division on the Russian front. He would not
survive the operation.

Other "passives" included Maurice Gabolde, former Minister of Justice,
Pierre Mathé, Charles Rochat, and Paul Marion, one of the few with whom
Céline got along and who had been Secretary of State for Propaganda under
Vichy after having been on the central committee of the Communist Party
and later in Doriot's PPF until 1938. At Sigmaringen, there was nothing
official or formal about Marion. "His jacket down to his knees, in baggy
trousers of coarse cloth, hobnailed shoes and wide-brimmed hat, he's
followed everywhere by a zoot-suiter named Travaca. He tromps through all
the hallways prohibited by Brinon, calls the latter a 'usurper,' makes fun of
the committee members."[3]

Another wing was used to house the "active" ministers, those who took
part in and hence constituted the Government Committee by shaking their
last rattles of power. At their head was Fernand de Brinon, fifty-seven,
former general representative of the French government to the occupied
territories, whom Céline knew well, as well as his faithful secretary and
paramour, Simone Mitre, whom the writer had often canvassed during the
occupation and who found him now in Sigmaringen, wonderfully devoted,
caring for the sick, walking through the snow, bankrupting himself on
medicine to ease the worst of the suffering. Assisting Brinon was Joseph
Darnand, head of the Militia, come into Germany with 10,000 men and their
families. He was given the "Interior" portfolio but was barely seen in Sigmaringen, as he was supervising the settling-in of his troops in Ulm. Marcel
Déat, head of the Rassemblement National Populaire (RNP), still kept close
to General Bridoux, former Secretary of State for Defense, while Jean Luchaire, running the newspaper *La France* and the local radio station, was
named Commissioner for Information.

As his daughter, actress Corinne Luchaire, explained, "accommodation
for my father and my mother was arranged at the castle. My sisters and I had
to stay at a hotel, the Lion Hotel, which was really frightful. Protest as I
might, there was nothing to be done about it this time. We were treated very
badly. The food was less than scant. Things were definitely beginning to
go bad."[4]

Finally, there was the aloof minister Abel Bonnard, whom his friends,

enemies, and even Pétain nicknamed La Gestapette ("Queen of the Gestapo"). A sexagenerian who strove to be gallant, his white hair thrown back
and lightly powdered, he was one of the rare "passives" not to be housed in
the castle. The former minister of public education and member of the
France-Germany Commission lived in town with his ninety-year-old mother
and his brother. He aired the elegant ennui of an Academy member, throwing out his *bons mots* like tidbits at the end of meals. Rebatet? "A man
crushed under his own ruins." Darnand? "Chief of Distaff for the State of
Molasses." De Gaulle? "A dwarf who has been considerably stretched,
except for the top floor."[5]

These, then, were the privileged, the castle-dwellers. There remained the
plebeians, the 1,200 or 1,500 French refugees scattered throughout the
town, living in tents, in schools, squeezed into the few local inns—
the Bären, on Burgstrasse, not far from the Danube, with its pointed roof
and lovely half-timbers, the Altem Fritz, or the Löwen on Karlsrasse, less
than 100 meters from the castle and the station, a cubic and spiritless place
with its hunting trophies on the wall and its inevitable crockery beer steins
in the dining room. We shouldn't even discuss the food, or if so only to
mention the *Stammgericht*, Sigmaringen's nauseating local specialty, a
gruel of red cabbage, turnips, and rutabaga fed to the proletariat of the
collaboration, the survivors of Bucard's Francist Party, Déat's National
Popular Youth, or Darnand's Militia, in perpetual conflict with one another.

Céline's daily life in Sigmaringen was of the simplest. Officially named
physician to the French colony by the Government Committee, he undertook the medical care of the French refugees throughout his stay, without
ever extending it to the castle, much less to Pétain, as has sometimes been
suggested. He shared this task with one of his colleagues, Dr. André Jacquot,
a former colonial army physician and a member of Marcel Déat's National
Revolutionary Front during the occupation.

Like Corinne Luchaire and her sisters, Céline, Lucette, and Bébert had
been housed at the Löwen (second floor, room 11), while Le Vigan found
himself at the Bären, along with Lucienne Delforge, and Véronique and
Lucien Rebatet. Le Vigan was unable to wangle the post of nurse. However,
in order to have room and food vouchers, one had somehow to prove
employment in Sigmaringen. In order to avoid any threat of expulsion, Le
Vigan was therefore compelled shortly afterward to accept, most
grudgingly, the job of newscaster at the radio station run by Jean Luchaire.

Moreover, Dr. Ménétrel, who was treating Pétain, noted in his private
diary (unpublished to this day) on November 21, 1944: "Yesterday met Le
Vigan, a film actor whom I don't know but who played in *Goupi-Mains
rouges*. Friendly, graying hair, seems honest, polite, and respectable. He's
depressed, he seems sad, woebegone, he wonders what he's doing here . . .
he's been forced to speak on the radio, and it disgusts him . . . I feel sorry for
him. He says he'll come see me, so I can 'buck' him up too."

In Sigmaringen, Le Vigan's friendship with Céline began to cool. He begrudged Céline for having forsaken him. Which did not prevent Céline, when Le Vigan fell sick in early '45 of the flu and a carbuncle in his ear, from taking care of him with all possible dispatch and devotion.

For Céline and Lucette, of course, there were no comforts in room 11 at the Löwen, a closet with two single beds hard by the only toilets on the floor, usually overflowing, while just down the hall were living Dr. Müller, responsible for overseeing the French colony, and especially the sinister SS officer Boemelburg, ex-chief of the Paris Gestapo and the top man in charge of law and order in Sigmaringen.

There was no lack of work for Céline and Jacquot in Sigmaringen, what with the winter's chill, the precarious lodgings, the insufficient food (the notorious *Stammgericht* was a powerful laxative), the promiscuity of the young paramilitaries, and the dubious hygiene. Influenza, consumption, and otitis followed one after the other, not to mention lice and fleas, scabies, and every possible variety of venereal disease. Céline would go to the old Fidelis convent, now transformed into a maternity ward that was never empty. He held his consultations in the afternoon, in an office by the Danube that had belonged to a German dentist who had been mobilized. He obligingly handed out certificates by the armful so as not to send the young recruits of the Charlemagne Legion back to the front, where they faced almost certain death and a defeat that was in any case inevitable. At night, he received more people in his hotel room, transformed into a ward.

"The French 'Government,'" recalls Lucien Rebatet, "had made him Colony Physician. That's all the title he wanted anyway. He did many good things there. Abel Bonnard, whose mother was dying at ninety in a room in town, never forgot the gentleness with which he soothed her long agony. He could also be an excellent children's doctor. During the last days, in his room at the Löwen Hotel, which had been turned into a stifling slum (and to think he was a public health specialist!), he cured a series of Célinesque illnesses, an epidemic of scabies, another of militiaman clap. He painted startling pictures of it."[6]

And Lucette bears witness as well: "We had a room with two bedsteads, not even a table, just a stool. That's where Louis saw his patients, especially the ones with scabies. I acted as his nurse for the injections and bandages. But there wasn't much we could do without medicine. Céline, with his own money, tried his damnedest to obtain some in the town pharmacies. He also bought black-market morphine that came from Switzerland. He never took a penny for his troubles. In the morning he treated the pregnant women. We used to get up early. I went to practice in the castle. I had ended up finding a frigid room with a marble floor, decorated with mythological statues, not far from the music room where Lucienne Delforge practiced."

We have mentioned the food and the infamous *Stammgericht* at the Hotel Löwen, built to house thirty guests but holding five times as many. It was difficult to improve one's fare through the black market. The Germans didn't want money. They would accept exchanges in a pinch. The barter economy had returned. Laval traded his cartons of cigarettes for ham and butter. But generally speaking, the hardship extended to the German populace as well.

According to Rebatet, Céline, though he ate little, was haunted by the provisioning dilemma.

"Through the black market, he collected hams, sausages, smoked goose breast. To prevent any suspicion of hoarding, one of his naive tricks was to come to our inns from time to time, to the 'Altem Fritz' or the 'Bären,' as if he had no other option, and share the official rations, the 'Stammgericht,' a hideous gruel of red cabbage and rutabaga. While he was conscientiously swallowing this pittance, Bébert the 'pussy' would pull himself half out of his bag, flare his nostrils suspiciously at the plate for a moment, then return to his shelter with offended dignity.

" 'Picky, is Bébert,' Ferdinand would say. 'He'd rather die than touch this bilge . . . Amazing how much more refined and aristocratic they are than us vulgar shitbags. We just stuff ourselves. We'll stuff ourselves on even more sickening filth before its all over. We'll have to.'

"Then, satisfied that he'd made us laugh, he'd launch into an outrageous monologue: death, weapons, peoples, continents, tyrants, Negroes, 'Yellows,' intestines, the vagina, the brain, the Albigensians, Pliny the Elder, Jesus Christ. The pervading tragedy pressed his genius like a harvest of grapes. The Célinian wine gushed forth everywhere. We were at the source of his art."[7]

Lucette does not have quite the same memories. She can still see the hideous *Stammgericht* that she and Louis brought up to their room, picking out the little bits of potato, which she gave to Bébert, and the miserable portions of ersatz sausage allotted them by their ration cards. Luckily there was a grocer in town who had taken a liking to the cat. "He'd put some trimmings and bits of sausage aside for him. When we left Sigmaringen, he wanted to keep him. Sometimes we took our meals with the Bonnards. They ate better there. There was a cook who fried with goose fat. And we kept the drippings for our soup or to give to Bébert. Marion, who ate at the castle and sometimes came to see us at night, stole rolls from the table for us. The ministers would get upset: 'What happened to our rolls?' We were all frighteningly thin, bags of bones. I must have weighed 90 pounds. I called Le Vigan the scarecrow. His limbs looked like sticks. But were we that obsessed with food? I don't think so. We were weak, but even so we weren't fixated on food or our physical appearance. I was dressed like a workman, in velvet pants and combat boots."

Céline was never employed in any kind of propaganda capacity. He watched with grieved irony the court intrigues, the underhanded plots of Bridoux and Brinon (who was kind to Céline despite the writer's defeatist sneering) to compel Pétain to return to active duty; the rivalry between Doriot (who was playing the hail-fellow-well-met on the shores of Lake

Constance) and the Government Committee in Sigmaringen; and the gossip sessions at the Schön pastry shop, where Guy Crouzet, Alphonse de Châteaubriant, and Jacques Ménard held forth on the latest news, events of the war, and their own dashed hopes. Rivalry, gossip, and drunkenness held sway throughout the town. At the Deutsches Haus, Lucienne Delforge played Bach or Frescobaldi. At the Löwen Hotel, Corinne Luchaire, who had made fruitless attempts to slip into Switzerland with her daughter and was now socializing with a young starlet, Monique Joyce (suspected of belonging to the secret service of the French Resistance) was feeling ever more feverish. Her friend, the German officer Gerlach, had been compelled to leave her. The militiaman and former swimming champion Jacques Cartonnet came to see her. Otto Abetz insisted on bringing her to a sanatarium, and eventually sent her to Saint-Blasien in the heart of the Black Forest.[8]

Laval and the other "passives" invited Céline and Lucette to dinner at the castle on three occasions, giving the writer his chance to talk about the end of the world and perhaps, one evening, to hear himself jokingly appointed governor of Saint-Pierre-et-Miquelon. For Céline, as for Rebatet and other intellectuals, the Castle meant above all a chance to visit its 80,000-volume library. "Céline had selected an old collection of *Le Revue des deux mondes*, 1875–1880. He kept going on and on about the quality of work he found in it: 'Now that was serious stuff . . . deep investigation, educational . . . Good style, hand-crafted . . . No blablabla.' It was the only reading he ever talked about in front of me."[9]

Bébert, who sometimes accompanied his mistress in the morning and spent a moment observing her dance exercises, soon learned to prefer exploring the hallways and hidden stairwells, running around beneath the graphite-covered coffered ceilings, looking at his reflection in the Venetian mirrors, and scampering behind the Genoa curtains. He was perhaps alone in not being intimidated by the ghosts of the Hohenzollerns or the arguments over seniority between Bridoux and Gabolde. At night, he had endless fun jumping from one bed to the other in the tiny room at the Löwen, or allowing a scarf to be draped around his neck because, when he winked his eyes and pointed his whiskers, he looked just like Lucien Descaves, to the great mirth of Céline and Marion, his audience of choice.

So much for daily life. There were also notable events, or accidents. Just a few days after Céline's arrival, on November 6, 1944, Karl Epting held a "Day of Study for French Intellectuals in Germany" at the Deutsches Haus. Brinon and Déat spoke. Céline had been invited as guest of honor. "Within half an hour, he had turned it into a bedlam that yielded absolutely nothing."[10]

Rebatet's statement is confirmed by a letter from Céline to his lawyer Tixier-Vignancour, dated June 23, 1949, in which he defends himself against the accusations brought against him by the Commissioner of the Republic. "I told the conference of intellectuals held at the Sigmaringen town hall, in the presence of *Déat, Sieburg, Lucienne Delforge, Jamet, Epting* (Rive Gauche Lecture Series), etc., etc., a lecture held to bolster the *intellectuals' morale* (*terribly depressed*), a conference held under the nonstop droning of enormous squadrons on their way to destroy Dresden, etc., amid the echoes of the French army's artillery already reaching the Black Forest. I said, I *shouted* at that conference: '*I think that all this propagandist nonsense is disgusting!* I think that Sigmaringen is a suburb of *Katyn!* And soon you'll all be paying the price for this *disgraceful idiocy!*'

"And it was infinitely more dangerous to talk that way in Sigmaringen, in front of *Baumelburg*, than into the microphones of Oxford Street! Yes indeed!"[11]

Eight days later it got even worse. Léon Degrelle, the head of the Belgian Rexists, newly arrived from the Eastern front in his dashing Walloon Legion SS uniform bearing a sparkling Iron Cross, came to speak of the New Europe and the recovery of France. "Don't be afraid of being real Frenchmen and Europeans at the same time. . . . Europe will perish or it will survive!" he exclaimed. Who today could contradict him? Except for the fact that De-grelle's Europe was a Nazi Europe, an anti-Semitic Europe, a Europe that condemned the "Anglo-American plutocracy." Degrelle had no doubts: "This is a soldier speaking to you. We'll return to our countries, to Brussels and Paris. We'll be the first in Brussels, you be the first in Paris . . . *Vive la France!*"

Céline couldn't take such idiotic bravado while the armies of the Reich were on the run on every front. He got up in the middle of the lecture and made for the door, grumbling for all to hear: "Who is this king of the jerks? With his ugly mug he won't even look good at the end of a rope."[12]

On November 22 a new crisis arose in Sigmaringen with Dr. Ménétrel's arrest by the Germans, the perfect illustration of those pathetic struggles, arguments over seniority, and Florentine political intrigue in the miserable atmosphere of abandonment and defeat. Ménétrel was Pétain's confidant and intimate and the man whom Fernand de Brinon suspected, if not of treason, then at least of hostility toward the Government Committee. If Pétain refused to collaborate, to lend his name and authority to the actions of the Committee, it was Ménétrel's fault. Whence the idea of denouncing him, of removing him in order to weaken the field marshal's moral resistance and resolve. Brinon and Bridoux chose to replace him with a young lieutenant physician, Dr. Schillemans, a prisoner at a nearby *Offizerlager* who was not involved with the gloomy and buffoonish atmosphere of the dying collaboration. Schillemans suddenly found himself at the Castle in the forced intimacy of these ex-notables, ministers without portfolios, secretaries of state without states, and chief envoys with no other authority than that which they wielded over their own imaginations.

Schillemans naturally had many opportunities to meet with Céline. His testimony is particularly valuable to us. "He [Céline] was tall and thin. His eyes, bright, shining, sunk deep in their sockets, overhung by enormous bristling eyebrows, had a disturbing gleam in them. When he looked at you, his pupils had a strange steadiness, and his eyes seemed to be constantly questioning you. He wore a faded lumber jacket that must once have been brown, and dark blue trousers that bagged over his thin legs. Two enormous fur-lined leather mittens were hung around his neck with string, and in his left hand he held the handle of a sizable travel bag into which he had poked some ventilation holes. I learned shortly afterward that he carried an enormous cat in that bag. That was how this curious character was dressed; as to the cat, it was a magnificent beast of which I caught only a glimpse. It was almost as big as a lamb and it seemed perfectly happy to travel about in that bag; a curious creature."[13]

Quite naturally, Schillemans was wary of the evil reputation of the author of *Bagatelles pour un massacre*. He was surprised to hear Céline openly declaiming against the Germans. "In front of the German consul, he had told me he was in charge of medical care for the French colony and the Militia; now, talking so fast that he didn't even stop to hear my answers, he questioned me on the circumstances that had brought me to Sigmaringen. He seemed to think it was a strange idea to come poking about in such a hornet's nest. With vivid imagery, and using altogether unexpected expressions with irresistible clownishness, he painted me a picture of the military situation as he saw it: 'I get the feeling that they're stratified this time, crystallized,' he told me concerning the Germans. 'The elastic bounce-backs are over, the rubber has hardened.' And then, still in the same mocking tone, his cocky Parisian accent contrasting strangely with the feverish gleam of his pale eyes, whose enormous pupils stared tragically at you: 'I wonder what's going to come from this mess? What do you think, being from the other side?' In asking this question, he seemed truly to want the war to end as quickly as possible and, rather curiously for a Sigmaringen resident, with the total collapse of the Reich. 'They should know by now that enough is enough,' he said a moment later. 'It's no laughing matter; they shouldn't prolong the party any further; the kids they're mobilizing now could almost be my grandsons. If you could only cure it like the pox!' "[13]

Sometime later, while he was still talking with Schillemans, Céline noticed SS officer Baumelburg with his dog.

"Céline said to me, but now almost in a whisper: 'Do you see that man talking to Müller, the owner of that bear lurking near them?' I had indeed noticed the strapping fellow who was sizing up Doctor Müller from head to toe, and his superb boxer, which was running around like a wild beast. Céline went on in an even lower voice, comically rolling his eyes: 'I couldn't tell you which of them, man or beast, is the more ferocious: they both eat human flesh. I'm not kidding,' he assured me. 'That guy is the head of the Gestapo and he feeds his animal on scraps of flesh that he strips from his victims.' He gave me an intense stare before continuing: 'Watch out for him, he's really dangerous; you're not used to it, so watch out!'

"What a curious fellow, this Céline. It was my turn to wonder why he had taken part in the exodus that had brought him here and, since we were alone, I asked him. It's true that there were a lot of things I didn't know about him, and still don't. People usually have some justification prepared for such questions, but instead of answering, he merely raised his eyes to the heavens and shook his head wearily. . . .

"Céline seemed to have a lot of regrets at the time. I couldn't forget the sight of his great, hungry eyes looking at me; those eyes seemed to call out for help, in strange contrast to the man's mocking voice, his sense of humor, and the slapstick, nightclub-singer-from-Montmartre side of him. Even now I feel a weird sense of pity for that man, whom I barely knew."[14]

A few weeks later, Schillemans decided to leave Sigmaringen, where he really had nothing to do and could only compromise himself. He imprudently stated his intention. To Fernand de Brinon, this was treason, desertion. He was placed under close arrest, with a guard at his door. Céline then intervened to spare him any "damned problems." He applied to Brinon. Schillemans was allowed to return to a stalag far from Sigmaringen.

The war was inexorably approaching the little town on the upper Danube. Allied bombers were destroying Ulm and Stuttgart. On November 23, at the head of his 2nd Armored Division, General Leclerc liberated Strasbourg to the wildly ecstatic acclamations of the crowds. It was not taken half so well in Sigmaringen. Luchaire let blow with rancorous commentary on the castle radio station. That night at dinner, Brinon told him (and the fact is again reported by Schillemans): " 'Luchaire, I was not at all amused by your piece on General de Hautecloque. He is an exemplary officer and an excellent Frenchman, even if he has involved himself in an indecent venture. I cannot allow you to cast aspersions on his honor.' And then, to finish him off, he scornfully added, 'Especially *you*, Luchaire.' Naturally, this unexpected sally cast a pall, and in the gloom I saw an amused smile blossom on Darnand's face: he couldn't stand Luchaire."[15]

On the night of December 15–16, 1944, von Rundstedt launched the famous Ardennes counterattack—the Battle of the Bulge—supported by 250,000 men, 2,000 artillery pieces, and 1,000 tanks. A last outburst, a last hope. The Germans penetrated deep into the American lines, benefiting from the element of surprise, but they were eventually stopped at Bastogne. Sigmaringen immediately went into ecstasy. The talk centered on the Wehrmacht's and Luftwaffe's new weapons, the Rheinbote long-range missile and the Messerschmitt 262 jet. One writer was heard to proclaim: "My bags are packed. In eight days I'll be sleeping in Paris." And Luchaire wrote in *La France*: "The German offensive will astound the entire world."[16]

The only one not to be astounded, not to indulge in high-flown language or illusions, was Céline. Bichelonne had gone to Hohenlychen to have his knee operation—on December 21, his death was officially announced. He had succumbed, it was explained, to a pulmonary embolism during the course of surgery, which had itself been a success—naturally. Gabolde, Marion, Guérard, and Darnand took a special train to Stettin, in East Prussia, to attend his funeral, a grandiose ceremony that reflected the Nazi taste for theater and pomp. In the afternoon, they were even shown the film taken during the operation, with commentary by the surgeon. Céline had not gone along, but Marion must have described everything to him on his return. And, in *D'un château l'autre*, he made Bichelonne's funeral more truthful and more grotesquely grandiose than it had been in mere reality. He reinvented the place, the emotions, the rituals, and the journey by train. His vision was faulty; his vision was true; his vision was better.

He didn't need to hear that his political books had been officially withdrawn from circulation, by order of the War Ministry on January 5, 1945, to know that his life was no longer worth much in France. On February 6 Brasillach was executed. The pleas for mercy formulated by Mauriac, Cocteau, and many intellectuals who were not indentured to the Communist Party were ineffectual with General de Gaulle. Céline hadn't waited for this news to consider decamping. For him, Sigmaringen could be only a stopover, an ever more uneasy shelter as the vise gradually tightened, the allied armies crossed the Rhine, and the Americans and French reached the Black Forest.

On January 22, 1945, he officially applied to the Swiss consul-general in Stuttgart:

"I have the honor to request an entry visa into Switzerland for myself and my wife. Currently a *refugee in Sigmaringen*, I am a medical doctor from the Paris Faculty and a war invalid at 75%—writer under the name L.-F. Céline.

"My name may be familiar to you and explains why I had to leave France, where at the moment I would almost certainly be sentenced to death.

"I do not intend to remain in Switzerland beyond the usual period for politics to cool down, a year, perhaps.

"I am carrying with me gold coins and jewels worth approximately 12,000 Swiss francs. Moreover, upon my arrival in Switzerland, it would be easy for me to obtain three times that amount from Spain, through friends to whom I have entrusted large sums of gold."[17]

His letter went unanswered. The Swiss federal authorities did not particularly distinguish themselves during the war years by their generosity, their sense of hospitality, or their willingness to grant political asylum. How many German Jews and opponents of the Nazi regime, having entered that country surreptitiously, were escorted back to the border and consequently to certain death? Céline, at the other end of the spectrum, didn't have a chance. He made the effort nonetheless. Lucette remembers training with Louis and Bébert by walking through the snow, so as to be able one day—who knew?—to cross the border on foot. The Löwen Hotel was 100 meters from the station. They occasionally lingered on the platforms and watched for trains leaving for Switzerland, for the moment to be seized. Flight remained Céline's obsession. Once they almost succeeded. The train had just begun to move off when they jumped into it. But German guards noticed them at the last minute and threatened them. They had to get off.

The atmosphere in the town was growing ever more stifling and Ubu-

esque. On January 20 Epting organized another meeting of French intellectuals. A dinner followed, attended by many German military and administrative authorities. On the menu, a single fish course and a significant number
of bottles of red wine. "Céline, who hadn't touched a drop of wine, drew a
parallel between the fate of the 'Jerries' who had managed to get themselves
beaten but would soon be going home, good citizens and good soldiers,
their consciences clean, not having to answer to anyone and having fulfilled
their patriotic duty, and that of the French *collabos* who were losing everything in this idiot's game: their property, their honor, their lives. So he,
Céline, couldn't see why he shouldn't proclaim that he had always hated the
sight of the German uniform, and that he had never been slow-witted
enough to imagine that the collaboration wouldn't turn out to be a horrible
curse in similar garb. The military big shots chose to find the joke excellent,
they laughed heartily, and Ferdinand was sorely missed when he went off to
bed."[18]

On February 22 came the news that Jacques Doriot was dead, machine-
gunned on the road a few kilometers from Lake Constance, shot down by
allied infantrymen, which seemed dubious to some,[19] or perhaps by the
Germans themselves, who were beginning to find him an embarrassment.
The mystery has never been solved. For the past week, Dresden had been
nothing but a smoldering ruin. The Red Army was advancing. The American
army was advancing, as were Leclerc and his divisions. And Céline was still
driven by the same obsession: how to escape? Failing Switzerland, to reach
Italy, the Merano aerodrome, and from there to fly to Spain—why not? But
how? Denmark required a visa. Céline applied to Epting, but the latter could
do nothing for him. Lieutenant Heller, the former chief of German censorship in Paris, had paid Céline a visit on February 15. Already suspected of
defeatism, he was in no position to help him either. The writer then thought
of Hermann Bickler, the old head of German intelligence for Western Europe, whom he had occasionally met at his offices on the avenue Foch in
Paris, and whose department was then relocated in the Black Forest. Bickler
came to see him in Sigmaringen in late February.

"Leave as soon as you can," he told Céline, according to Lucette. "Germany is falling apart. Get to Denmark if that's what you want. I don't know if
your papers will do you any good, there are almost no more trains, the
borders are closed, but at least give it a try."

Bickler then did everything he could to facilitate their getting visas,
identity cards, authorizations, etc. He wrote to the German diplomatic
envoy to Denmark (still occupied) requesting that Céline, Lucette (and
Bébert) be admitted. He used his influence with Baumelburg to renew their
foreigners' passports, which were to expire in December, and to procure
them the administrative documents necessary to travel through Germany. A
certificate was also issued to Germinal Chamoin, an LVF vet who had been
called back from the front for health reasons, posted to Sigmaringen, and

had assisted Céline there as an orderly. Chamoin, it seems, was remarkably resourceful. He had no equal for finding medicine and foodstuffs, or for picking up the latest town gossip in that "community of cacklers," as Alain Laubreaux described it.

On March 6 Marguerite Destouches died in Paris. In Sigmaringen, Céline knew nothing about his mother's death. No news was getting out of Paris.

Drieu la Rochelle committed suicide on March 16. He had been wrong. He had lost. He withdrew silently from the game, with the dignity of the intellectual confronted with the shipwreck of his illusions. Nothing like that in Sigmaringen, where the rats were furiously scampering about, clawing at each other, wondering how to save their skins, jump ship, forget everything, deny everything, and goodnight! . . . On the banks of the Danube, where some were preparing their flight to Switzerland, others to Spain, Austria or South America, no one had heard about Drieu's suicide. Every man was preparing to change his identity and memories the way one changes a jacket.

Céline, at the fringes of this panic, had nothing to deny or to forget. Amnesia was not his forte. On March 18 he officially obtained his visa for Denmark. On the 24th, at 7:30 P.M., he took the train for the North. The day before, he had entrusted Bébert to the grocer who was fond of him. But the cat couldn't endure his gilded, well-provisioned cage in Baden-Württemberg. On the morning of their departure, he smashed a grocery window, boldly crossed town, and rejoined his masters at the Löwen. Immortal Bébert! Hup! Into the bag and on his way to Denmark, other Célinian adventures or, if you will, disasters.

Lucien Rebatet watched them leave. "As the night fell, we met on the station platform. There was my wife, Abel Bonnard, Paul Marion, Jacquot, 'La Vigue,' reconciled with Ferdine after their umpteenth quarrel that winter, and two or three other close friends. The Destouches household, Lucette immaculate, serene, and sensible as always, carried by hand some 200 kilos of luggage, no doubt the remainder of those famous trunks, sewn up in sailor's bags and hanging from poles, a veritable kit for a safari in Bambola-Bramagance. A lad, some sort of orderly, would accompany them to the border to help with the transfers. It promised to be a rough epic, crossing that crumbling and burning Germany. Céline, with Bébert on his stomach, was beaming. No more bombings, no more resigned waiting like a rat in a trap. We would not weigh heavily on his memory. The train pulled up to the platform, one of those pathetic trains of dying Germany with its wood-burning locomotive. We embraced at length, the gear was laboriously stowed. Ferdinand unfolded and waved his unbelievable passport one last time. The train moved off like a miniature toy. The rest of us stayed, our hearts heavy, in that infernal cauldron. But there was no envy. If we had to die there, at least the best and greatest of all of us would escape."[20]

Last Train for Copenhagen

The little narrow-gauge Dubout, with its wood-burning locomotive, left Sigmaringen on the evening of March 22, reaching the suburbs of Ulm, seventy kilometers away, in the middle of the night. All that was left of the station were some makeshift shacks. The city was in ruins, a ghost town which they had to cross at dawn only to find more shacks on the east side and another narrow-gauge bound for Augsburg. For Céline and his companions, the mad odyssey to the North, Denmark and the promised land was beginning, between one air raid and the next, one derailing and the next, like damned souls, dazed by exhaustion in a twilight landscape, cities adrift, a troglodytic populace awaiting the worst—death or the Cossacks— dreaming with incredulous horror of the already outdated Hitlerian dream of the Greater Reich that was to have lasted a thousand years.

Odysseys are endless. Lucette says it seemed to last a month. In a letter to his friend Dr. Camus, Céline speaks of an expedition of nearly three weeks. "Lucette had put [Bébert] in a game bag. She carried him around like that, without food or drink or without pissing and the rest, for eighteen days and eighteen nights. He didn't stir or make a single meow. He was aware of the tragedy. We changed trains 27 times. Everything lost and burned along the way except the cat. We did 37 kilometers on foot, from one army to the next, under worse fire than in '17."[21]

Actually, their journey lasted less than five days. But five days can seem like an eternity. Five days suffice to supply a novel (*Rigodon*) with its subject matter, its burden of adventure and drama, its never-ending developments. Five days can nourish the nightmares of a lifetime.

From Augsburg to the Danish border, they blindly made their way north. Nuremberg, Fürth, Bamberg, Göttingen, Hanover.[21] There were no more stations, ticket booths, conductors—nothing. Police barricades and identity checkpoints and that was it, as if to provide a semblance of order, legality, authority to the bewildering chaos of a routed country. The routine of their journey became stops in open country or in tunnels to escape the allied planes, Nuremberg in flames, long wanderings through suburbs or towns, between marshaling yards that had nothing left to marshal, luggage piled on wheelbarrows and gradually lost along the way. By what miracle did they come through? Outside of Hanover, an air raid hurled them onto the banks of the tracks. "Only Lucette was hurt, in the knee. She rolled under the train, blasted by a bomb, with Bébert."[22]

All along the course of their journey, they ran into other ghosts, half-crazed witnesses to Hitler's debacle, refugees, foreigners, people from nowhere on their way toward fates that were as opaque as the smoke rising from the flames of Hanover, three-fourths destroyed. A crippled Englishman was their traveling companion for two or three stages. An Italian too.

Here, in the terrible confusion of those tragic days, Lucette Destouches' testimony is particularly valuable for the way it recaptures the madness.

"We took train after train, in which we would sometimes remain for only ten minutes. We would hardly have emerged from a tunnel when the first English or American plane to come along would use us for target practice. Everything was blown up. The Germans rebuilt the tracks right in front of the train. Immediately upon pulling into a station we'd find another train, any train, so long as it was heading north.

"It was during one of these pit stops that we met an Italian who was desperately looking for his factory. He had promised his boss he'd be back. People came and went, turned in circles, never finding a way out. Everything was blowing up, everything was in flames. There was nothing left but ruins, there were no more factories, the Italian was probably pursuing a mirage. We stopped everywhere. There was nothing left of the port of Hamburg. The ships had been sunk. All you saw was wreckage, bits of floating wood. Every city looked the same. You could make out their flickering glow at night, like will-o'-the wisps. We didn't sleep, we didn't eat. My little teapot never left my side. With our Italian, Pipo, we sometimes waited for hours. As long as I have a little bread and some sunshine, he told us, I'm happy. A remarkable man, and wonderfully clever. He'd go find little pieces of wood, he'd cut them into sticks, and put some water on to boil in a tin can for our tea.

"In Nuremberg, we were joined by an Englishman who was paralyzed. We perched him on a baggage cart, right at the top, and wheeled him all the way across town to another station and another train. For us travelers without tickets, there was no day or night, we moved on as if we were drugged. And when we reached Flensburg, on the border, we suddenly collapsed in a heap, we fell asleep, we were stunned. And then we suddenly had to wake up again. Pipo came to tell us the train bound for Denmark was pulling in. He urged us to take it. We ran. And that's how I tripped, with Bébert on my back. I fell, Louis ran up, and we were incredibly lucky to be taken aboard. They pulled us up. The Italian stayed on the platform. He was still looking for his factory. He had promised to go back to work.

"Throughout the voyage, Bébert rarely left his bag. Sometimes he'd scamper into the ruins. One day I tried to follow him and I almost got stuck in a hole. That scared him. Afterward, he stuck close by us.

"The most extraordinary image I've retained is that of a city in the middle of the night, under the full moon. I saw a wall and, in front of it, some soldiers lined up, standing, leaning on their rifles. In that half-light, they looked like they were waiting. We came closer. They were dead. They'd been knocked off. And when we touched them, they toppled over. Of course, those weren't the first corpses we'd come across, but that image remains especially vivid and bizarre."

Their boarding in Flensburg for Copenhagen was almost miraculous. They had arrived at midnight on March 26 at the station of that border town, where they spent the rest of the night. They had put some distance between themselves and the front. The threat of air raids had dwindled. There was no question of Germinal Chamoin crossing the border. His duties stopped there. He was returning to Sigmaringen. Céline wrote letters for Fernand de Brinon and Dr. Jacquot, which he entrusted to him. He also gave him the rest of their German money and restaurant vouchers.

"Poor Chamoin, I'd do anything to help him, anything to ease his calvary. He was sublime with us—we'd never have gotten through the four battling armies without him, my wife and he literally carried me. I couldn't go on. And then, alas, we had to plunge back into the fray. The Furies don't let you go that easily! Lucette has been divine through this hell, which unfortunately is still far from over!"[24]

The train that appeared at dawn on March 27 was a special convoy of the Swedish Red Cross assigned to the emergency repatriation of that country's nationals. Céline approached the physician-colonel in charge of moving the wounded and, papers and passports at the ready, asked him for permission to travel as far as Copenhagen. The answer must have been no. But at that very moment, as the train was already moving off, Lucette collapsed from exhaustion. She was in danger of slipping beneath the wheels and being crushed. Someone on the train grabbed her by the armpits and managed to lift her into the car. Céline followed. Germany was behind them. Forever. One nightmare was over. "Copenhagen is still at least 300 kilometers away . . . I think so . . . I think so . . . the two arms of the sea to get past . . . the Little Baelt . . . at the Little Baelt, a bridge . . . the Big Baelt, a ferry . . . anyway, the train's moving, no cuts or bumps, I tell you, like before '39 . . . when we get to the Little Baelt I'll look around . . . we'll be out of danger . . . I think."[25]

As soon as they arrived at the Copenhagen station, Céline and Lucette had themselves driven to the Hôtel d'Angleterre. The doorman didn't want to let them in, Lucette remembers. They looked so disheveled, worse than tramps, menacing, he with his stubbly face, she haggard in her trousers and workman's boots. And yet, Céline was an old guest. He had always stayed there before the war. But how could they recognize him now? He must have negotiated, explained himself in English, shown his papers, mentioned his Danish connections, in order to allay the suspicions of the hotel staff. In the end, they managed to get a room.

They slept like logs, hours and hours, a dreamless sleep; they rose the next day and took their first walk through the streets. Denmark was still under German occupation, but life seemed to be peaceful there. The stores of Copenhagen were well stocked. "It was suddenly like a dream, opulence," Lucette explains. "We went into a store and I see cheeses everywhere, eggs, butter. I began laughing hysterically, I was thinking 'It's not possible!' We had gone through so much privation for so long. And I suddenly felt as if I could order three kilos of butter, a hundred eggs, anything I wanted. 'But it's not possible, no one can have all this, it's not possible!' I laughed out of exhaustion, out of sheer nervousness."

Denmark, Year 0

Through a handwritten letter given to Céline in March 1942 in Berlin, at the same time that he had given her the key and combination to the deposit box at the Copenhagen bank where his gold was stored, Karen had authorized the writer to stay at her apartment in her absence. But he did not have the key. From the Hôtel d'Angleterre, he got in touch with a friend of Karen's, Mrs. Lindequist, a professional photographer who had taken numerous portraits of the royal family, Lucette recalls, and whom Louis had met ten years earlier. She referred him to a cousin of Karen's, Hella Johansen, who supposedly had the key and first put the couple up for a few days at her country house, some fifty kilometers from the capital. After these temporary lodgings, Louis, Lucette, and Bébert finally moved into Karen's apartment (Karen herself was still living in Madrid with her diplomat lover), on the fourth floor of a building that had once been home to Hans Christian Andersen, at 20 Ved Stranden.

According to Lucette, "it was a pretty building overlooking the canal, near the fish market. Opposite, you could see the big square in front of Parliament. The apartment, on the top floor, was paneled, with mansard windows in the rooms, but also lit by fanlights."

They lived hidden this way for months, one cannot say happily. Louis feared denunciation, arrest, a settling of accounts, death. He adopted the name Courtial, in certain deference to the fantastical inventor of *Mort à crédit*, and he allowed his beard to grow in a pathetic attempt to cover his tracks. Lucette went by the name of Lucie Jensen. They very soon wrote to France to give news of themselves, pass on their address, and indicate the names to which they were now answering. Only a few intimates were brought into the secret: the Pirazzolis, that is, Lucette's mother and stepfather, Marie Canavaggia and, of course, Karen. No friends in Montmartre were informed. Louis only partially trusted their discretion, let alone their goodwill.

The first letter that Céline received in Copenhagen was from his uncle, Louis Guillou, informing him of Marguerite Destouches' death on March 6. Exhausted, nerves frayed, the news hit the writer hard, and he collapsed in tears. He spent hour after hour prostrate on his bed, holding Lucette's hand. He may have been revisiting in his thoughts his last meetings with his mother, during the occupation, when she came to see them on Thursdays, getting off at the Abbesses *Métro* station and climbing the stairs of their building on the rue Girardon. He would barely greet her: "Hi, Mom, how are you feeling, Mom?" before closing his office door behind him. Marguerite remained alone with Lucette, she made conversation for hours, telling her about Louis' childhood, giving her her own untransposed version of *Mort à crédit*. In her own way, Marguerite Destouches was modestly happy; she chatted, gave her son a last farewell, and then climbed back down the stairs and got back on her train at the Abbesses station. And now all that was over for Louis. His father long dead, his mother gone, there was nothing left to protect him against his own death. A new curtain was drawn across his past, that is, across one of the rare possible forms of happiness. The people he had loved were being transformed into ghosts, memories, regrets, sorrows. And he, so far away in Copenhagen, in the awful uncertainties of the ending war, so vulnerable, had only to give himself over, orphan that he was, to his childhood fears. He wasn't ashamed to do so.

He wrote to Marie Canavaggia at that time:

Dear Friend,

You can imagine how overwhelmed I was by the two letters I received from you today! My poor mother! She haunts me I can hardly think of anything else she was the weakest the most innocent she paid for the whole world. She was a veritable martyr. I feel horribly guilty for my hardness to her. Life has been atrocious to me too but even so I can only think about the Père Lachaise [cemetery] and being beside her soon. I have said so since the very beginning of this awful, improbable journey. I can still see her taking leave of us at the corner of the avenue Junot like some poor abandoned dog. But what else could I do at the time.[26]

In France, the courts of justice were proceeding with their work with commendable zeal. On April 19 Examining Magistrate Zousman issued an arrest warrant for Céline on a charge of treason (articles 75 and 76 of the Penal Code). The hunt could now officially begin. Everything was straightforward, the dangers clearly defined: Céline was liable to be sentenced to death.

The war was coming to an end in Europe. On April 21 French troops entered Sigmaringen, while the Russian army camped on the outskirts of Berlin. Roosevelt had recently died of a cerebral hemorrhage. On the 28th, Mussolini was executed by the Italian Resistance. On the 30th, Hitler took his own life in his bunker. Pétain survived, imprisoned since the 26th in the Montrouge fortress. On May 4 the German occupation troops in Denmark surrendered and the English army liberated the country. Finally, on May 8, in Berlin, Field Marshal Keitel signed the act of Germany's final surrender.

Was it all over? The truth was only just beginning to come to light. The world was discovering the extent of the Holocaust. No more lies, whisperings, fears, rumors, partial truths, or half-voiced outrage. Instead, raw, total, and absolute horror on a scale without precedent in human history: the martyrdom of the Jewish people, the image of millions of men, women, and children whom Hitler's ideology had hunted down and put to death, meticulously, scientifically, not only in the name of its hatred but, far worse yet, in the name of its rationale. The unbearable images of charnel houses revealed to Europe and the world the sight of those few, dazed survivors of Dachau,

Ravensbrück, those skeleton-men liberated by American or Soviet troops, men who had been to the other side, who had seen death, who had been stripped of everything, right down to their hope, their future, forever haunted by fear, dread, the indelible memory of that which cannot be told and must never be forgotten.

What relationship does this bear to Céline? None except that which an intellectual marginal to parties and political life bears to the course of events. Did Céline's writings have the least influence on Hitlerite politics? Of course they didn't. But can the question be asked in those terms? Céline's writings had permanently marked French ideology, supported and furthered its anti-Semitism and consequently its complacency toward the Germans. That cannot be denied.

The writer and Resistance fighter Vercors deemed the writer's responsibility to be far more serious than that of industrialists who had collaborated. That opinion is a good reflection of the climate of the times.

"What the writer offers the enemy is not himself: it is his thought. And with his thought, that of others. That of all those whom this thought will persuade, seduce, or disturb. Comparing the industrialist and the writer is like comparing Cain with the Devil. Cain's crime stops at Abel. The Devil's threat is infinite.

"We fought passionately, stubbornly, fought—and many of us died in the fight—so that everyone, and the writer especially, might freely express his thoughts.

"In the name of that freedom, we are today allowing those to be punished who did not think as we did.

"Are we not betraying ourselves?

"The contradiction is merely superficial.

"A human society is homogeneous only if each of its members is responsible for his actions. . . .

"Published writing is an act of thought. The writer is responsible for the consequences of that act."[27]

Céline in Denmark, within the day-to-day preoccupations besieging him, seems fundamentally divorced from the upheavals of the immediate postwar period, from the shock that was the graphic revelation of the Nazi abominations. He would later refer to the Jewish martyrdom. But allusively, without wanting to truly size it up, as if, in any case, he had had absolutely nothing to do with it. Is this the consequence of an appalling egoism or of a lack of imagination? Or of a barely conscious effort to avoid any sense of guilt? It is obviously difficult to make a clear distinction. His anti-Semitism had nothing to do with logic, with reality. That was clear from the outset of the occupation. Watching German soldiers parading down the street, he had no qualms in turning to his friend Ramon Fernandez and commenting on their shortness and swarthy complexions: "Dagos and Jews, the lot of them!" Later, Malraux would say: "Neurosis is characterized by the development of phantasms. Anti-Semitism is one of those phantasms. It spreads continuously, like a cancer. Céline's anti-Semitism has no rational basis—it is a sickness."[28]

Céline apparently never experienced a sense of guilt. His letters to his lawyers, his memoirs and defense pleas, would soon prove that unambiguously. A lack of imagination, perhaps. But Céline held himself aloof from life. A prophet of dying worlds, an imposing vociferator, he still strikes us today as a creator of the close-up. There is nothing contradictory in that. His genius is never that of the wide, clear field of vision. It is that of meticulous observation of minutiae. Céline is simultaneously intimist and cosmic, an intuitive writer of pure *dilatation*, whose blind spots are as significant as his lucidity. He does not paint frescoes. He does not write by metaphor. He paints miniatures. He writes by synecdoche. In short, he takes the part for the whole, he sees only the part—and that part becomes immense, becomes a universe. Céline is interested only in himself, in what he feels and observes. But then he transfigures his sufferings, his observations, his misadventures to the plane of a fantastic delirium. Whence the miracle of his later books, when his intimate experiences and individual adventures, his crossing of a Germany in flames, harmonize with the tragic finale of the Hitlerian grand opera. We dare not ask more of him. A man who lives with his nightmares and terrors cannot be asked to assume the nightmares and terrors of all humanity: he is simply unable to see them. While the world was discovering the scope of Hitler's genocide, Céline in Denmark, cut off from all news, strove to survive from one day to the next—the unique victim, he believed, of a world pursuing but one aim: to imprison and kill him.

In the meantime he still had to live, find money, work, feed himself, wait, clarify his situation with the authorities.

His resources? There was above all the gold that Karen had withdrawn from the bank in 1942 and, after various hiding places, had buried in the garden on Hella Johansen's estate, the very place where Lucette and Louis had stayed after leaving the Hôtel d'Angleterre. Moreover, the writer had arrived in Copenhagen with the gold coins sewn into the belt that never left his sight. But possession of and particularly trading in gold were prohibited in Denmark. So the gold coins, placed in a cookie box, were unearthed by Hella Johansen in his presence, kept by her, and gradually and surreptitiously exchanged at jewelers' or by friends traveling abroad. Louis and Lucette were thus supplied from time to time with Danish money to take care of their most basic needs. But there could naturally be no official reference to such transactions.

As to Céline's civil status, under the German occupation there was no problem; he had been authorized to stay in the country. Things changed after the liberation. They now had to square themselves with the new national authorities. Since September 1944, no official Danish organ of government had collaborated with the occupation troops. Parliament, the police, and the government put a halt to the endless negotiating, trying to confine the damage, and allowing the heads of ministerial cabinets free rein in managing day-to-day business: a kind of protest strike. From May 1945 onward, all was quickly re-established in a climate of purges prepared by the Resistance and officially ratified on June 1 by King Christian X. The trials and indictments for treason began. More than 12,000 people would be given prison sentences. Céline had nothing to reproach himself for in Denmark, obviously. Nonetheless, in that atmosphere of witch-hunts, it was better to be safe than sorry.

The writer got in touch with a lawyer to help him with the government and to obtain official residency status. This was Thorvald Mikkelsen. "Louis didn't know him at the time," Lucette explains. "We had met him through Mrs. Lindequist and through a photographer and pharmacist, Mr. Ottoström, who was one of Karen's friends and whom Louis must have run into in the old days. Mikkelsen spoke French well. He had been married to a Frenchwoman who had recently died. Mikkelsen had also been very close to the Danish Resistance, he knew the Minister of Justice and many other members of the government. So he volunteered to put our papers in order and get us the right to stay there."

On May 16 Mikkelsen met with Céline for the first time at Karen's place, less than two minutes from his own apartment. He may have chosen to help him out of feeling for France, out of loyalty to his late wife, his companion of the past twenty-five years. But also because the sixty-year-old jurist had a passion for art history and literature, preferring to discuss Cicero, Horace, or Homer to questions of legal process. He was an individualist and a liberal. A large man, his eyes protected behind thick glasses, his graying hair swept back and parted on the side, he had the look of a businessman, the gravity of a jurist, and the mischievous spark of a man devoted to culture. From their first meeting, Céline opened up to him without reserve, explaining his writings and the circumstances of his flight. But he naturally made no reference to the arrest warrant issued against him, of which he was most likely unaware. Mikkelsen, for his part, was beginning to be shocked by the excesses being committed in the name of the purge, in Denmark as abroad, and did not hesitate to denounce them with the authority accrued from his past as a member of the Resistance. He was thus fully disposed to help Céline in Denmark. Furthermore, the writer represented for him a symbolic and enjoyable case: that of the intellectual pursued by the political powers, the political writer subjected to official persecution, the solitary man hunted down by the powerful and cast out by his fellow citizens.

Mikkelsen immediately vouched for the two foreigners, morally and materially, before the police in charge of foreign nationals. On June 1 he wrote a personal letter to the director of the Danish national police in Copenhagen, as well as an official request for a residency permit.

Dear Sir:

In my capacity as lawyer to Dr. Louis Destouches and his wife, Lucie Georgette Destouches, née Almansor, I have the honor to appeal to your deep goodwill that a permit for residency in Danish territory be issued on a temporary basis to the two above-named persons.

Under the pseudonym of Céline, Dr. Destouches is a well-known writer not only in France but throughout the French-speaking world, while his wife is a famous dancing star of the Paris Opéra.

Céline's best-known book is Voyage au bout de la nuit, *which brought worldwide fame to its author; some of his more recent works, of an anti-Semitic and pacifistic bent, are banned in France and Germany. . . .*

It is imperative that Dr. Destouches obtain a residency permit in our country because on the one hand the current state of his nerves threatens to lead to a complete collapse in the event that he be compelled to face the dangers and stress of further travel, and because, on the other, he is not at all anxious to return to France given that country's prevailing climate.

In these circumstances, I hereby request that, by virtue of the liberal traditions on which our country has always prided itself, the right of sanctuary on Danish soil be temporarily accorded to this so variously distinguished writer.

Taking into account the exceptional circumstances currently prevailing in Denmark, I can attest that Dr. Destouches is not under indictment as a war criminal, that he has never involved himself in politics, and that he has never been a "collaborator," but that his unpopularity in France as in Germany is due solely to his anti-Semitic and pacifistic works.[29]

On June 20 Céline and Lucette were summoned before the national police in charge of aliens, with Mikkelsen in attendance. The writer accounted at length for his life, his antecedents, his family, his marriage, and his service record during the two wars. He had never been a member of a political party, he had never been a war criminal or a collaborator, but it was true that his books were no longer especially "popular" and it was possible, he further explained, that certain people would take advantage of circumstances to bring action against him. Hence his wish to wait a little longer before returning to France. He had been to Denmark several times before the war and had entrusted a sum of about 30,000 crowns to some friends there. Those were the official—if not tangible—resources that he could count on. The Danish police noted his explanations. Residency permits were eventually issued to both of them.

Once their situation had been regularized, Céline should have been able to lay some of his anxiety to rest, to give himself over to the charm of the port of Copenhagen, with its canals crisscrossing the city, its boats and three-masters at almost every street corner, its little brick or pastel-colored rough-cast houses with their pointed roofs, to idle through the old royal city, as in the old days, to dream about the sea, about voyaging, to rediscover his nebulous Viking's soul. But no, for him it was still a time for fear, for solitude, for cold and painful withdrawal into himself.

"The atmosphere was dreadful after the surrender of the German troops, whom we saw march past a final time from our windows, in perfect order, as if on parade, with their wolfhounds on leashes, without a single shot, on May 4, 1945," Lucette recalls. "For the Danes in the shops, I was identified as French, that is, a spy. They tried to figure out what I was doing there. Louis rarely went shopping. He didn't leave the apartment. He barely slept. It was awful."

Life was expensive in Copenhagen. Lucette's mother sent her care packages and clothing. Out of caution, she sent them—always addressed to "Lucie Jensen," Lucette's assumed name—care of the ballet instructor of the Copenhagen Opera, Birger Bartholin, with whom Lucette had become friendly. With his help, she was also able to give dance lessons, unofficially of course, since she did not have a work permit. "Bartholin had asked me to come to his class to give lessons in Spanish and ethnic dance. His lessons were given in the foyer of the Copenhagen Opera. Harald Lander, the great ballet teacher, the opera's choreographer, threatened to dismiss his male and female dancers if they took lessons from me. Even so, a few stuck by me. And I also gave lessons farther away, in the warehouses where they sold fish. I rented a room, moved the crates, and was soon teaching Spanish dances, zapateados! I brought in five crowns a lesson. The Danes loved those Spanish dances, dances from the South. Even Lander's wife came to learn castanets and flamenco. Of course, if the authorities had learned that I was giving lessons, I ran the risk of being shown to the border. I was often followed by a policeman. He must have turned a blind eye. It turned out that he was a pretty nice guy."

Céline was secretly hoping that Karen wouldn't return, which would have forced him to give up her apartment, to find a new place. He wrote her long letters in Spain. He described Lucette's dance lessons with Bartholin. He complained about the cost of living. He urged her to be cautious, not to speak of him to Gen Paul, whom he didn't trust. He asked her to send his regards to Abel Bonnard, who had sought refuge in Berlin. He asked for news of his old friend Antonio Zuloaga, the former press attaché to the Spanish embassy in Paris.

Above all, he had begun to write again. That was all he had to do, other than watch Bébert, who had resettled into sedentary life and indulged in the guilty pastime of sharpening his claws on Karen's Louis XV armchairs. (Later, on his release from prison, Céline would tell his Danish friend, who had found her apartment in a pitiful state upon her return, "Don't worry, I'll replace all the armchairs!")

Before leaving Paris, he had entrusted Marie Canavaggia with a copy of *Guignol's band II*, which would be posthumously published under the title *Le Pont de Londres* [London Bridge]. Another version of the manuscript had accompanied him through Germany and then to Copenhagen, miraculously preserved through all their adventures, the wanderings, and the air raids. He may already have considered writing about more recent events, describing his life under the occupation, his *Féeries pour une autre fois*, but those events were still too close, too painful. The time had not yet come to put them into words, into music. He lacked that frontier of silence; the veil, the screen, the distance in whose shelter he could freely transpose his memories.

On the other hand, he could write as compensation for the violence and pain of the moment, indulge his dreams of new ballet synopses. As a friend of Birger Bartholin of the Copenhagen Opera, why shouldn't he try offering him an original work? That dream eternally pursued, that ever thwarted ambition to contribute to the intoxication of the stage, of spectacle, to participate in making the dancers and ballerinas spin, to free them, howsoever briefly, from gravity! During that summer of '45, he wrote a version of the ballet *Foudres et Flèches* [Thunder and Lightning] in which, in a fantastical Olympus and highly stylized Greece, a lascivious Juno, a prankster Jupiter, a mischievous Cupid, a bantering Vulcan, and a few mythological heroes whirled about in horror, festivities, and total confusion. He never finished this ballet. Even so, it is difficult to see how it could have entered the Copenhagen Opera's repertory. Céline the writer multiplied his stylistic effects and character confrontations. He was incapable of creating the simplicity, the schematic amplification of character, the clear outlines, purged of conflict, which alone make choreographic drama intelligible.

Days are endless in Copenhagen in the summer. Still, Céline did occasionally go out on errands, to buy the paper or provisions. He probably visited Mrs. Johansen on several occasions at her country house, where his gold had been buried and exhumed. Mikkelsen also invited him to his estate of Klarskovgaard, for a day, in the company of the Copenhagen police chief and his family, the Seidenfadens.[30] This friendly encounter would have decisive consequences. Aage Seidenfaden and Céline got along well. And several months later, the former's intervention would be crucial in preventing Céline's extradition after his arrest.

Far from there, Pétain's trial before the High Court in Paris had been passionately followed by all of France, from July 23 to August 15. Vichy politics had been laid bare. France was examining her past. She didn't have much to be proud of. At eighty-nine, in a state of prostration, Pétain seemed unaware of the proceedings or the crimes with which he was charged. Mauriac wrote in *Le Figaro*: "We must not flinch from the thought that, at certain times, a part of us all was complicitous with this devastated old man." And Camus answered him in *Combat*: "If he gave himself, it was as a prostitute—but not to France. Let us hope that the French people will not allow themselves to be seduced or made to feel pity once again by the stratagems of age and vanity."[31]

The eternal debate between justice and charity. But what sort of justice, what sort of charity? France wanted to cleanse its conscience by forgetting that it had been overwhelmingly Pétainist and had endorsed the politics of Montoire. Except during the final days of the occupation, its majority involvement in the Resistance was pure, self-congratulatory fantasy. Pétain was condemned to death. De Gaulle commuted his sentence to life imprisonment. The old man would end his days in the citadel of Île d'Yeu.

"For the liberation government to be legitimate, Pétain and his followers had to be guilty. Guilty they certainly were, but proof of their guilt was very difficult to come by at the time. Whence the paradox: even if the Field Marshal's guilt was obvious in the eyes of liberated France, the trial itself (like many of the important purge trials, for that matter) raised many juridical problems that were not resolved."[32]

At the other end of the world that summer, clouds blossomed into the shape of a mushroom above the cities of Hiroshima and Nagasaki on August 6 and 9. At ground level, two cities had been razed, swept away by nuclear radiation, shock, and heat waves. A few hundred thousand dead—civilians, Orientals—was America's price to Japan for a speedy conclusion of an unconditional peace after a merciless war.

But was any of this discernible from Copenhagen?

The quick trial of Pierre Laval, from October 4 to 9, surely did not escape Céline's attention. It is generous to call it a trial. The game was lost from the beginning. A hasty investigation, jurors who insulted the accused, lawyers—Albert Naud and Jacques Baraduc—who refused to plead under such conditions, every legal rule flouted—it hardly mattered, speed was of the essence, it had to be shown that the purge was being carried out energetically. On October 10 Joseph Darnand, head of the Militia, was executed by firing squad. Laval's death would follow with no more formality. On the morning of his execution, the former prime minister tried to poison himself with a vial of cyanide. A doctor pumped his stomach. The condemned man, half-conscious, was dragged to the execution post under the insults of his guards. No one had any reason to be particularly proud of this task, which capped off the sabotage of his trial, as the communist August Gillot, president of the Justice Commission of the National Resistance Council, was the first to acknowledge.

Autumn was now falling on Copenhagen. The vise was tightening on Céline. The French legation in Denmark received an anonymous letter indicating the writer's presence in the city. On October 1 Guy de Girard de Charbonnière informed Georges Bidault, his Minister of Foreign Affairs, of this by telegram. His zeal in pursuing a "notorious collaborator" was only just beginning to manifest itself. He asked for instructions. Should he officially request extradition? Bidault answered that an arrest warrant had been issued for Céline on April 19, and suggested that he so inform the Danish government. The French legation's file was rounded off with copies of the documents supporting Céline's indictment: a statement in *Le Cri du peuple* on March 31, 1943, concerning Doriot, a letter appearing in *Germinal* on April 28, 1944, the publication of *Guignol's band* and the preface of

Bezons à travers les ages (considering the latter two pieces as evidence for the prosecution was frankly grotesque). He was also accused of having been an honorary member of the Cercle Européen and of having fled to Germany in the summer of '44.

On November 23 Bidault finally ordered Charbonnière to seek the writer's extradition.

The Céline affair was a sideshow, given the opening on November 20 of the Nuremberg trials, which the whole world was now watching as if to exorcise a dream, finger the guilty, perhaps to reassure itself, to justify Dresden, Hiroshima and the war crimes that the Allies must have committed but which they did not need to justify (the victors always write the law) in the face of the terrible fact of the Holocaust, the unspeakable madness of Hitlerism, its crimes against humanity.

On December 1 Sartre published his "Portrait of an Anti-Semite" in *Les Temps modernes.* He wrote of the author of *Bagatelles pour un massacre*: "If Céline supported the social theories of the Nazis, it was because he was being paid." The accusation was ridiculous and untrue, but it clearly sums up the confusion of intellectuals determined to find motives for racism. The accusation also clearly demonstrates how Céline symbolized that anti-Semitism, which it was necessary to understand, dissect, prevent, and punish.

Robert Denoël's death on December 2 may have been directly connected to the atmosphere of denunciation and revenge that pervaded the purge. Was the publisher of the writer of anti-Semitic works—who had also published Lucien Rebatet and so many others under the occupation at the Nouvelles Éditions Françaises—a victim of purgers, hoodlums, or more simply some criminal, male or female, with a private grudge? No one will ever know.

For nearly two years pending his divorce, Denoël had been living with Jeanne Loviton, who was known in literature under the pseudonym Jean Voilier and had once been Paul Valéry's mistress. Was he about to break it off with his mistress and return to his wife? So the latter claimed, though she provided no evidence in support. For her part, Jeanne Loviton had provided financial support for the publisher at the end of the war, requiring as equity the assignment of convertible stock—stock which reverted to her at Denoël's death and allowed her to take immediate and effective control of the publishing house. On December 2 Denoël and Jeanne Loviton took their car to go to the theater. Denoël had been lying low for months. Céline had advised him by letter to leave France. He was mostly involved in preparing for the trial brought against his company for collaborating with the enemy. He could argue that he had also published Elsa Triolet and Louis Aragon under the occupation, but would it be enough? That night, shortly after nine P.M., their car, a Peugeot 202, stopped on the boulevard des Invalides, at the corner of the rue de Grenelle. They had a flat. As Denoël prepared to change the tire, Jeanne Loviton went to the nearest police station to call a cab. A few minutes later, while she was there, the station received a telephone call: Robert Denoël had just been found dead in the street, a bullet in his back. The victim still had 12,000 francs in his pocket; it was hard to assume robbery. And how could members of the Resistance have known that Denoël's car would come to rest precisely at that spot? Was he being followed in another car? It seems improbable. A series of legal investigations were never able to reach any conclusion. The case was closed.

Denoël's death was a painful blow to Céline. Despite their occasionally strained professional relationship, Denoël had been his friend and companion throughout his literary career, the first to have shown confidence in him, to back him, support him, launch him. He belonged to Céline's past, to his memory, and that was the only loyalty which the writer had stubbornly maintained. Denoël had also been the screen, the mediator, between him and his public. Céline would later come to suspect Voilier of having set up the murder. But his first reaction was to believe that the attack on Denoël was in some way an attack on himself, and that he would be next. The two letters that he wrote at the time to Marie Canavaggia allow us to measure the full extent of his confusion:

"And now that tomb is sealed. Yet another . . . Many things are buried with that unfortunate man . . . so many things that life itself has come to a halt . . . that it has ceased to beat . . . that the heart beats to a new rhythm. Poor Denoël, his Renaudot! the two of us already so miserable at the time . . . and then that fixed Goncourt, filched. . . . There it is! A very bitter, very demoralizing weight has been added to our bag of sorrows. Still we must travel on. . . .

"I have just received your letter after the burial. This calvary of memories is awful and irresistible. Right at the time of the Goncourt. Fifteen years later . . . what a curve . . . what a mortal journey! That poor man, fate has caught him as if in a net . . . You must have attracted a lot of curious attention at the funeral . . . How did people seem? He was very well known on the scene. I can't get my mind off that horrible moment. I feel as if I've left a double in France who's being wantonly flayed . . . first one thing then another . . . a slow and vicious curse wantonly mauling me. And so powerless. No one."[33]

Céline was then living his last days of freedom in Denmark.

"Protective Custody" in the Vestre Faengsel

Lucette Destouches: "Christmas was at hand. In the Nordic countries it's a big holiday that people prepare for long in advance. Louis was very depressed. He had premonitions. He would hear the furniture creaking while I was out giving my dance lessons at the fish warehouses. And yet he wasn't like Victor Hugo, consulting spirits and making tables spin. But there was a weird noise from a large cupboard that seemed to move and moan when we were near. For him, no doubt about it, it was a sign, a warning. And then, on December 16, I get a phone call: 'Lucette, both of you should get out of here—you're going to be arrested.' It was the wife of the Copenhagen police chief's son, whom we had met through Mikkelsen. But how could we leave? We didn't have passports, money, anything. We stayed. We knew that something was going to happen but we couldn't do anything about it."

On December 15 the newspaper *Samedi-Soir* had revealed Céline's presence in Denmark—news that was reprinted the next day in the Danish daily *Politiken* with this front-page headline: A FRENCH NAZI IS HIDING IN COPENHAGEN—THE WRITER CÉLINE, WHO ESCAPED WITH THE VICHY GOVERNMENT. From then on, things were to move very quickly. That very day, the 16th, at 7 P.M., a newspaper vendor called Copenhagen police headquarters, having recognized Céline as one of his clients. The next day, the 17th, after office hours, the head of the French legation in Denmark, Guy de Girard de Charbonnière, called the office of the Danish Minister of Foreign Affairs to inform him of Céline's address and appeal for the writer's immediate arrest. The official extradition request would be sent him the next day, but they had to move fast, he added, to prevent the traitor Céline from escaping.

With remarkable zeal, and without even waiting for that extradition request, the minister of foreign affairs, Mr. Gustav Rasmussen, ordered Copenhagen police headquarters at 7:30 that very night to arrest Céline and his wife and to lock them up for breaking the law pertaining to the status of foreigners. Three officers of the judicial police immediately went to 20 Ved Stranden.

Lucette Destouches: "We thought that they were assassins come from Paris to execute us. We refused to let them in. I looked through the keyhole. They were dressed as civilians, we didn't believe that they were Danes. They knocked harder. In a panic, we considered slipping out across the roof, as Bébert had already done. But a dormer isn't easy; Louis couldn't follow me. I telephoned Birger Bartholin, he lived nearby. Finally, the policemen came in. They found the revolver that we had on hand. Of course, we wouldn't have used it on them, but we might have tried to kill ourselves, you know, out of panic. In short, they packed us off in a Black Maria. Louis was locked up in one cell, me in another, in the women's wing. Bébert was also caught and confined to a pound at a veterinary clinic, in a cage."

The next day, December 18, as foreseen, the official extradition request from the legation of the French Republic in Denmark arrived at the Ministry of Foreign Affairs:

Dear Sir:

> *It has come to my attention that M. Destouches, Ferdinand, alias Céline, a French national indicted for treason and the object of an arrest warrant issued on April 19, 1945, by the Examining Magistrate of the Seine Court of Justice,*

has taken refuge in Denmark and was last known to be living in Copenhagen, Ved Stranden 20, top floor, #10.

By order of my government, I have the honor to request you, by virtue of reciprocity, to order the immediate arrest and extradition of the party concerned.

Your Excellency will please find enclosed a copy of the arrest warrant as well as the writs (Penal Code articles 75–76) on which M. Céline's indictment is based.

> *Sincerely,*
> *G. de Girard de Charbonnière*[34]

As long as no charge had yet been brought against Céline, he could not be defended by a lawyer in Denmark. Furthermore, in a stroke of particularly bad luck, Thorvald Mikkelsen had left two weeks earlier for a long business trip to the United States, and his partners did not seem very familiar with Céline's file. But was it really bad luck? It is possible that, in the end, Mikkelsen's absence (he would not return until March 10, 1946) caused the Danish authorities to equivocate. How could Céline be extradited before his lawyer—whose past as a member of the Resistance was known and valued—could be heard? Time could only work in the writer's favor.

While waiting to make a decision on his extradition or to investigate his foreign-resident status, mightn't some other grounds be found to prosecute and indict Céline immediately? The Danish police tried, though without much success, as Lucette Destouches further explains:

"We spent our first night as prisoners in a cage, a sort of telephone booth with a grating on top. We didn't have time to say a word to each other before they separated us. The next day I was stripped and searched. It took hours to get my ring off. I had some castanets with me that I was determined to keep. Nothing doing. They were the only things I had brought with me. Days passed. I wasn't eating. I was alone. And then I got a cellmate, an old woman who had lost all her teeth, had murdered somebody or other, and who tried to get me to eat. In vain. I couldn't. I was dying of anxiety. I didn't know what had happened to Louis, whether he had been sent to Paris, whether he had been killed. I couldn't stop thinking: that's it, he's been shot! I was taken for interrogation. I told my life story, what I had been doing for years, our life in Denmark. I got the dates a little mixed up, I was never very precise, I had trouble expressing myself in my stilted English. They compared my different statements, they weren't right, they didn't jibe, the basis was the same but they were completely different. They kept interrogating me and I had nothing to hide except one thing: my dance lessons, which were illegal.

"One day they brought out a blanket that contained enema bottles, cannulas, rubber tubes that they had taken from the apartment, and they said: 'Your husband performed abortions.' That's all they had come up with!

Actually, Louis had amoebas, he had been taking enemas constantly since his days in Africa. But they were satisfied with their explanation. They didn't want to give it up. On top of that, young dancers had been seen entering our place, whom I had been teaching the castanets. Girls from the building, gossip from the neighbors, the concierge, it was all there. They figured the girls had come for abortions. As if that was Louis' thing! He had always told me that if I got pregnant he would never perform an abortion.

"And the interrogations continued. I still had no news about him. On Christmas day, we were taken from our cells, gathered in the hallway to sing, and each given two pounds of sugar as a gift. I can still see myself that day, with a Bible in my hands. I collapsed. I don't remember a thing. They took me to the infirmary to calm me down. I still couldn't eat or drink, on the verge of hysteria. I was sick, I had fainting spells. And that's where I met a young nurse who spoke French and told me: 'I've seen your husband.' It was amazing. He was alive.

"The Danish authorities were afraid I'd die. But there was nothing they could do, I still couldn't swallow a thing. In the end I was set free. Hella Johansen took me in, in Copenhagen. She had been married for twenty years, and for twenty years she and her husband hadn't said a word to each other, not even to ask to pass the salt! A nightmare. I couldn't stay with them too long. After I picked Bébert up, I went back to Karen's place, to the apartment we had lived in before the arrest."

Lucette spent over ten days in prison, until December 28, 1945, before eventually returning to the apartment at 20 Ved Stranden in early January. What of Bébert? He had been taken the very night of the arrest to a veterinary clinic, against a fifty-crown deposit. The sum was deducted from the money found in the apartment, precisely 3,675 crowns, after the police search carried out on Tuesday, December 18. On December 20 Bébert was officially released and boarded with a friend of the couple's.

There had been no justification for Lucette's detention. Furthermore, the Danes were soon to realize that the Destouches were perfectly within the law as foreigners in Denmark, with a duly issued residency permit.

Like Lucette, Céline was imprisoned at the Vestre Faengsel, in the southern part of the city, an imposing red-brick edifice in the shape of a cross, built in the late nineteenth century next to a cemetery—a holistic program. On the 19th, he had been subjected to his first police interrogation. The accusation of illegal residency no longer held water. Céline, like Lucette, was crushed, a nervous wreck in constant tears. He was watched carefully. They feared an irreversible act.

In a very rounded handwriting to make it easier for her to read, Céline had immediately written a pathetic letter to Bende Johansen, Hella Johansen's seventeen-year-old daughter, who had taken dance lessons with Lucette. This cry for help—hitherto unpublished (Archives Lucette Destouches)— is worth quoting in its entirety:

Dear Bende,

I've had a change of prisons, I don't know where they're holding Lucette. I don't know why we were suddenly so brutalized separated treated so cruelly. I don't understand anything. I'm going crazy with pain thinking of Lucette so devoted, so gentle, so innocent in all this. Something at least should be done for her. She must be suffering agonies of anxiety and sorrow. Nobody's told me anything explained anything. I don't know what they want from me. I can't ask anything nobody understands me. I should have the right to a lawyer so that he can at least explain my crime to me and what they intend to do with me and especially to find Lucette. I shall die of sorrow thinking of her. I never stop crying. I don't count but I can't bear that innocents should be made to suffer. And our poor little Bébert our last keepsake of our poor life. For pity's sake Bende find a lawyer to defend me a little and especially Lucette and who can finally explain what they want from me—what they expect from me. For nine months the police gave me my ration vouchers every month I wasn't in hiding. I went to the Danish police with Mikkelsen on the very first days of my arrival. Try to find poor Lucette. It's really inhuman to treat us so cruelly. What crime have we committed? And especially after nine months of perfect forbearance—if we're not wanted in Denmark anymore it's easy enough to say so and I would understand without torturing us like this. I am often hard on you Bende you must forgive me. I have had too much pain and sorrow—I only ask for a little compassion—I am happy to die if they absolutely insist that I die but I would have liked Lucette to stay with Bébert. Who could take any pleasure in making Lucette suffer? You see, all of this seems too cruel to me to be true—and yet it is happening. Try to find someone to come explain what's wanted of me. This complete isolation is appallingly cruel— Just think, I don't speak a word of Danish. It is hard to be more miserable than I am— And above all think of Lucette (and Bébert).

With great fondness, dear Bende, and all my regards to your mother—I think that we can receive letters and visits—

Louis Destouches

On December 20 he was informed, in English, of France's request for extradition. He disputed the accusations that it contained. On the 25th he wrote an SOS letter to Thorvald Mikkelsen, pointing out that he had never worked for anybody, newspapers, radio, or parties, that he was just a writer and claimed political refugee status. There was nothing against him but hatred and the spirit of revenge. To extradite him to France would be to torture, to murder him. Lastly, he asked him to intercede on Lucette's behalf. "I am so worried about my poor wife, who is perfectly innocent in all this. Please, I beg you to go see her and comfort her a little. Tell her that I'm constantly thinking of her and live only in the hope of seeing her again. She is incapable of hurting anyone, she is generous and honest. We are deeply unhappy at being separated. . . . Please try to dispel this horrible nightmare for us. I am going mad with grief. I feel that I am completely innocent. But first take care of my poor wife, *try to send me news of her.* I am so worried."[35]

He was doubtless unaware that Mikkelsen was then in the United States. The same day, he wrote in almost identical terms to the Copenhagen Director of Police to convince him to dissuade the Danish authorities from proceeding with his extradition. On the 28th, the director (whom we know to have been sympathetic to the writer and his wife) forwarded Céline's file to the Ministry of Justice with a note in which he made two essential points: that first, the extradition request carried no specification of concrete facts imputable to the writer; and that further and above all, infractions of articles 75 and 76 of the French Penal Code were not included in the extradition treaty ratified between the two countries on March 28, 1877. In brief, he recommended that Céline not be extradited until an intelligence report became available.[36]

Aage Seidenfaden's letter was decisive. It prompted the Ministry of Justice to re-examine the case. Without it, the writer might very well have been extradited posthaste. Mikkelsen had only just been informed. He would begin to follow the case—by correspondence. One of his partners in Copenhagen requested the Ministry of Justice to grant Céline political asylum, pointing out that from an economic point of view Dr. Destouches would not be financially dependent on the Danish State.

The Céline affair had begun. It was a case that would be marked by vagueness, equivocation, lack of evidence, and the relentlessness of the French authorities in general and Guy de Girard de Charbonnière in particular, who was to become the writer's *bête noire.* The legation chief would increasingly intervene to the point of antagonizing the Danes. He was the first to acknowledge it, as in this memo of January 7, 1947, to Léon Blum, then head of the government and Minister for Foreign Affairs: "Over the course of the many steps I have taken toward that goal [the extradition], I have pressured the authorities far more than the incriminating evidence at my disposal would allow."[37] The case was also marked by untenable shilly-shallying from the Danish authorities, the Ministry of Justice soon taking Céline's part while Foreign Affairs was rather inclined toward extradition. In the meantime, the writer remained in jail, "in a state of availability" to use the official terminology, shuttling between death row and the infirmary with some frequency while his health deteriorated, his morale faltered, and no charge had yet been brought against him.

Did Denmark save Céline? The jurist Helga Pedersen, who was her country's Minister of Justice from 1950 to 1953, used that question as the title of a work that she devoted specifically to the Céline case. Yes, there is no doubt that Denmark did save Céline, but at what a cost! Eighteen months of detention for what? For nothing. For whom? To please France, for public opinion, for no one. Or else to mark time, to give itself the opportunity to rehash a thousand legal scruples, to note that while they were under no obligation to extradite Céline they remained free to do so, to proliferate meetings and interministerial briefings, and to come to the conclusion that it was essential not to come to hasty conclusions—while a man waited for his fate and his life to be determined, and moldered in a cell, suffering from dysentery, pellagra, and headaches (they considered trepanation), lost his teeth, and would soon be down to under 130 pounds on a six-foot frame.

More specifically, on January 31, 1946, Danish Foreign Affairs finally brought itself to ask the French authorities for the full particulars of the charges against the writer. To which the French legation replied with a simple memorandum calling for an acceleration of the extradition process and repeating the same general accusations: Céline, an honorary member of the Cercle Européen, author of *Guignol's band* and *Bezons à travers les ages*—which is again confounding, showing as it does the incompetence of those in charge of examining Céline's file, since other statements the writer had made in collaboration publications would obviously have been more persuasive than those two completely apolitical works.

On February 15 Mikkelsen's right-hand man implored the public powers to await the lawyer's return, set for March 10, while revealing a letter recently received from him: "I ask you to do everything possible and, at any event, to arrange that the extradition be postponed until my return. Dedichen and I possess very important information regarding this case. I have also obtained certain details here in New York. By extraditing Céline on the data currently available, Denmark will be setting a precedent before the world that it will later have great cause to regret. This is a matter of the highest principle and one whose consequences we are not now in a position to measure. The ill-will of the head of the legation is nothing compared to the painful consequences that would result from an extradition undertaken on dubious and unverified evidence. The Minister of Justice and the Minister of Special Affairs must be fully aware of that. In all events, it would be improper to extradite Céline while Dedichen and myself possess information that we will be in a position to supply in a month at the very latest."[38]

Having fallen ill, Céline had been transferred on December 28 to the prison infirmary, where he occupied a private cell and remained until February 5, 1946. After that, he returned to the western wing, cell 84, and then to K section on the ground level—death row—cell 603.

Beginning in January, Lucette was allowed to see him every Monday. She brought him reading material, newspapers, and food—ham, cookies, lemons and oranges that she herself received in care packages from her mother—to counterbalance the awful fare provided in the prison.

How can one describe the writer's distress, or the indefatigable loyalty and solicitude of Lucette, herself alone in a foreign and hostile city where she did not speak the language? Céline sent her over 400 letters from the Vestre Faengsel. In them, his feelings, his moods, his rebelliousness, his despondency, his encouragement, his bursts of hope, and his grief rise to the surface. He occasionally makes efforts to avoid demoralizing Lucette, and then falls back into endless complaints. He writes to her of Bébert, offers her myriad affectionate pieces of advice. He describes his life as a prisoner for her in detail. And he finally gives in to his melancholy or to imprecations against all those who are seeking his head out of literary jealousy.

This unpublished letter (p. 450-451) of Wednesday, February 6, written the day after his return to his cell from the infirmary, is typical of the state of mind that drove him: "My darling Lucette. I went back to prison yesterday as I thought I would but now all alone in a cell and I like it very much this way. The guards are very friendly to me. I wasn't happy in the hospital. I feel much better alone. My head hurts less this way. I take two walks a day for instance I have so little strength that it's quite hard. But they let me go by myself at my own pace which at the moment, alas, is like that of my poor mother. I'm very well fed. They spoil me. Don't be sad that causes me more pain than anything else. I'd rather die than to think of you unhappy. And then for one thing all of this won't last long a decision will be taken one way or another but we'll be rid of this awful uncertainty which I think no constitution could long resist and mine wasn't worth much to begin with. I received the French books it's unfortunate that I can't receive French newspapers not even *The Times*—or *Le Figaro*. I wish Mikkelsen would get back—but I'm as comfortable as one can be in prison. All alone like this my nerves are gradually recovering only this time it's the heart that seems to have given a little. I've even been given some paper so that I can start getting back to work. If you were here I'd never ask for anything else again. But on the other hand it would also be stupid. Éliane's arrival is really something miraculous! The whole past flooding back in a whirlwind. I see myself as a young doctor in Clichy, she was five years old! And now she sees us again under such conditions! I hope this letter reaches you fairly soon. And then I'll see you Monday. You see time passes pretty quickly all the same. I talk to myself and to you and to Bébert. I can rebuild myself a bearable existence quite quickly if I'm left alone. It's the abrupt changes that completely undo me, my heart and my head are too sick at the moment for me to regain my balance as I should. I'm with you all the time my little darling and you know that for me a Breton the absent counts more than the present. Love to all. Destouches."[39]

In this letter Céline refers to Éliane Bonabel, the niece of a Clichy record dealer who had been a friend of his. Éliane met Lucette in Copenhagen but was not permitted to visit Céline. In 1959 she would illustrate with gracefully childish drawings the edition of *Ballets sans musique, sans personne, sans rien* [Ballets Without Music, Without Anyone, Without Anything], published by Gallimard.

Certain letters show that faced with imprisonment and possible death, Céline was stoical, even religious on occasion: "One must achieve mysticism in the manner of the desert hermits—a sweet, strong obsession—infinity for two and Bébert. Much joy can be had that way—nothing can bother you anymore—it hurts to cling to the world, personally I'm dead myself." And further on in the same letter to Lucette: "Don't grieve for us

Unpublished letter from Céline to Lucette, dated March 28, 1946, on Copenhagen prison stationery and officially addressed to his lawyer, Mr. Mikkelsen. It contains the writer's first reference to Féerie pour une autre fois, *which he was considering entitling* Du côté des maudits *at the time.*

KØBENHAVNS FÆNGSLER

Den 28 Mars 194 6

Vestre Fængsel

VARETÆGTSFANGE: Destouches

(Lukket Brev i Medfør af Retsplejelovens § 784, Stk. 3).

Mon cher maître, Je viens de changer de cellule et même je crois de "quartier" de Prison. Enfin je suis toujours seul c'est le principal. Dans cette nouvelle cellule j'ai deux chaises mais par contre je n'ai plus de table. Je m'arrange tout de même très bien pour écrire et lire. J'espère que la solution de mon terriblement délicat problème diplo--matico-judiciaire ne sera plus trop longue a intervenir a présent! Je commence a me sentir vraiment a bout de forces — Un petit repos au grand air me ferait bien du bien! Mais je sais que vous êtes a la fois Minerve et mer... Je me contente simplement d'adresser un petit rappel a mes deux protecteurs — Ma Lucette chère lorsque j'ai appris hier que l'on nous déménageait encore j'ai été pris par une épouvantable une frayeur irraisonnée que je me serai tué le chagrin. Dans cet état je redoute n'importe quelle annonce et moindre changement vous fait redouter aussitôt le pire. En réalité on nous a transféré tous la Récréation vers les femmes dans un petit quartier de la prison moins triste peut être tout compte fait. Je suis toujours seul les gardiens sont bien convenables, le lit est meilleur. Encore une station du Calvaire! afin j'ai des journaux je m'engage. J'ai perdu mon infirmier par exemple. Je ne connais pas encore la nouvelle! Toujours cette abominable question des lavements. Je n'en demande qu'un par semaine. J'ai avancé notre récit des maudits par le bombardement de la B…… Comme c'est drôle a remémorer. Je place feu Paul en chef d'orchestre du bombardement — et dirige tout or la haute plate forme du monde avec sa cerne. L'esprit ni mal. J'ai lu le paysage s'envole

enfle gonfle les maisons perdent leurs formes – Tout chahute. c'est
si c'est fait de ses tableaux que se realise – c'est le sabbath o Bosch–
et puis d'abord la vie de ce brave milieu et de tous les gens qui ont
absolument peur je leur de race deux livres avant que l'on me
fusille. "Ça aura du prix" nous en avons vu de choses nous
J'aurai un grand choeur et éprouvé surtout et si pas belle ! S'il me
reste quelques années à vivre mon Dieu aller se perdre fuir replier jamais encore
risquer de pareils supplices ! Il faut tout de même que je sauve mes manuscrits.
Je les vendrai à Mignon. Rien que le papier nous fera de quoi nous racheter
le lit et les trois meubles dont nous aurions besoin. Tout le reste parti
aux vents du cyclone ! au pillage des Furies ! Et pourtant qu'il mal
je m'étais donné ! Tout cela ne compte pour rien. La méchanceté et
la haine seules comptent. Je vois qu'à Paris les Triomphateurs se déco-
rent déjà matériellement mais pas encore assez pour notre compte. Il
faudrait que de Gaulle revienne dictateur. Alors sûrement il fera
une amnistie générale de joyeux avènement mais ce n'est pas
près tout cela. Et pourtant je voudrais tant rentrer. Toi aussi bien
sûr. on en a tellement assez d'être méprisé, jaugé, jugé, déchirer
humilié de mille et cent façons. Par la Photo maison en plus c'est le
comble ! Il faut avoir été méprisé par de telles épouvantables ines-
–fables âneries pour être bien de goûter. Jamais de s'occuper
des êtres humains ! mon Dieu quelle immonde race ! Il faut les
prendre par leurs charmes physiques (s'ils en ont) mais le moral
mon Dieu dans 999 cas sur 1000 quel cloaque ! quelle gluante
empestante infectieuse haineuse sottise ! On ne laisse aller
à toucher à ces têtes et l'on est perdu ! On se damne facilement
Ce sont toutes des viandes d'abattoirs – Il faut leur laisser
leur destin. Je suis bien inquiet pour toi toi. Je n'ose pas parler
de Bébert lui même le pauvre petit fragile animal ne fait de
la peine dans tout ce cyclone. Pourrons nous jamais ma pauvre âme
reprendre tous les trois avant la mort un petit instant de repos ensemble
nous laisser t'en respirer quelques mois au milieu de ce cauchemar
que semble ne plus finir. Enfin tu vois que je suis chaque seconde
avec toi. Je ne te quitte jamais. Le temps passe vola. La bonne
aussi peut être... plus tôt. De tout coeur à toi nous de...

nothing can get any worse! It's all over we are nice, affectionate little corpses— You'll come see me at the Père Lachaise. I will always be with you. I have already suffered so much in exile that death will be very sweet to me there." And he finishes: "You must never be sad again but on the contrary laugh heartily—like the monks of yore—all that's needed is a faith. And you have all that—martyrdom is a pleasure once you learn to truly scorn the executioner."[40]

As a writer imprisoned and persecuted, Céline does not hesitate to blame his fellow writers first and foremost for his condition. It is a way for him to remove all political import, to comfort himself and fortify his self-esteem: "The relentless hatred directed toward me is of a literary order, the jealousy of writers currently in power Mauriac Malraux who'd like to see me dead. Everyone knows it."[41]

That Céline is mistaken is of little importance in the long run. What moves us above all in his letters from prison is the mixture of complaints, illusions, hope, lyricism, and his affection for Lucette; it is above all his need to write as if clinging to a life raft, remolding the past, emphasizing his suffering and, as he himself admits, detaching himself from life for a moment. "I am with you and Bébert at all times. I'm always talking to you. . . . You know it is easy for me to remove myself from life. My arm has also started to hurt very badly. They were massaging it. They've stopped. Take care of yourself my sweet little lovely I beg you don't wear a sad face. I wish we were locked up together but I can also spend years alone here in prison. Anything as you know so long as they don't send me back. I am asking for two or three years' asylum. You know the situation as well as I do. I am a writer nothing but a writer. All French writers have had to leave the country on one pretext or another. Any excuse is good for persecuting writers in France. The list is endless. I only name the main ones who have had to flee through the ages— Villon, Agrippa d'Aubigné, Ronsard, du Bellay, Châteaubriand, Jules Vallès, Victor Hugo (at 20), Lamartine, Rimbaud, Proudhon, Verlaine, Léon Daudet and lastly at this very moment Bonnard, Laubreaux in Spain, Paul Morand in Switzerland— Nobody's handed them over to the hangman—it's a matter of waiting two or three years. My offending books are already nearly 10 years old—when I'm better they'll have to let me write the dreadful story of all this."[42]

At times, Céline has no qualms about putting a somewhat happier slant on reality in order to calm Lucette's fears. Coming from him, the paragon of complainers, the suffering man with his violent ranting, the rebellions and deliria, that would seem to indicate a surprising effort, an effort revealing the delicate affection he bears for Lucette, which his ordeal in Denmark would cement forever. "My little darling don't bring me any more cheese or ham we have an abundance of all that and plenty of butter as for me I'm on a special and very privileged diet! Rest easy the food is very well prepared I eat three times as much than at home. Only bring crackers I prefer them to cake which is a bit too heavy, I eat them with milk and oranges and lemons and that's all. I'm not gaining weight because my head still hurts a lot and because I'm depressed but the care is perfect and I am now well used to this kind of unhappy passivity, all the more so since I'm still dependent on the hospital for my care and I take medicine for my head 4 times a day. I keep thinking of that awful accusation and my little darling I can't swallow it and I'm not ready to swallow it and they are well aware of that. By God! They'd be very pleased in Paris to hear me rail against the wretches in Sigmaringen and elsewhere. The scalp dance. How do they go about it? Some joke! A warrant for treason! That's always the way with our poor homeland, gall and bad faith and disloyalty. I'll say it again there were other ways for them to get my testimony. Once I'm in their claws they'll have no choice but to cling to their imposture to save face, so then the farce becomes really contemptible, the whole press jumps into the fray, like with the Sampaix campaign, and what was make-believe becomes true and who was innocent guilty. It's the tune of slander—but I've no intention of playing the 'poor scoundrel.' I am seeking political asylum in Denmark just as the Jews sought it in Hitler's day nothing more nor less. I'll have to wait at least two or three years before returning to France until they're all so caught up in their own nastiness and fanatical dissensions that they don't know where they are."[43]

It is not in this correspondence that we should look for a portrayal of prison as hell, but in his literary work, *Féerie pour une autre fois* in particular. There, the amplification of Céline's vision is given free rein, the nightmare unfurls, the truth may or may not be apocalyptic.

When night is falling, for instance, when the shouts and howls of the tortured and condemned reverberate in echoes and suffering, horror reaches its peak. "A prison is hollow!" Spy holes are closed, doors locked. "Three Monts Saint-Michels! A Creusot of locks! . . ." And he remains glued to his stool or his pallet, in the blackness of his thoughts in K Wing, on death row. "They're not all killed! Allow me to tell you for your edification that at the bottom of the pit the body is overtaken by mold, I mean the limbs, the trunk, the skin and even the eyes!"[44]

And what can be said of his chronic constipation, the enemas he had to take with boiled water, his misery? No, the writer is not making it up. He merely highlights. He reveals. Life in prison is excessive enough in and of itself. In his writings and hallucinations, he is no more so than reality forces him to be.

Céline was able to return to *Guignol's band 2* in the Vestre Faengsel. But he had trouble working on it. He also made an effort to read. Lucette brought him whatever books she could get in Copenhagen and, later, those she would borrow from Mikkelsen's library, such as Châteaubriand's *Les Mémoires d'outre-tombe*, novels by Pierre Loti, short stories by Marcel Aymé, and copies of *La Revue des deux mondes*, the old collections of which he had already devoured with pleasure in the Sigmaringen castle.

On her Monday visits, Lucette sometimes brought Bébert, to whom he so often refers in his letters, into the visiting room. Animals were prohibited.

Lucette somehow managed to keep him hidden . . . "She comes to see me with Bébert . . . seven minutes . . . Bébert in a sack . . . He can't move a muscle! . . . total immobility . . . the guard's watching . . . and then we're not supposed to speak French Arlette and me! . . . only English! . . . French is forbidden! . . . English, us? . . . She was born French, French, French on the rue Saint-Louis-en-l'Île! . . . me at 11, rampe du Pont, Courbevoie! . . . Bébert in the Samaritaine department store! . . . force us to speak English! . . . with my abhorrence of foreign languages! . . . cockeyed circumlocutory babblings! . . . It's capital humiliation! And us natives of the Seine like no one else!"[45]

It is likely that the guards spotted the cat and turned a blind eye. One of them, Henning Jensen, was a painter who felt a sincere affection for Céline. His job was really only a stop-gap measure to get by while waiting for better days and buyers for his paintings. By a stroke of luck, he even spoke French quite well.

Back in Copenhagen in early March, Mikkelsen met with the Minister of Justice and several high-ranking bureaucrats on the 18th. The decision to extradite Céline was far from final. Nonetheless, there was talk of expelling him subject to his being guaranteed an entry visa to another country. The possibility was broached of transferring him to a hospital (which would be tantamount to freeing him) if he gave his word not to try to escape. But none of these suggestions were followed up.

Céline's confidence was bolstered by his lawyer's return, as his letter to Lucette on March 20, 1946, testifies. For once, the Danes found favor in his eyes. "My little darling, I hope this letter reaches you fairly soon—but now that our friend is back all my hope and courage is returning! So that's the whole accusation? A trifle in itself and an absolute lie to boot! These people must really have the demon of hatred in them to come up with such ridiculous schemes! So they will have made us so atrociously miserable purely for the pleasure of it! and without even a respectable motive! Really there's no way out of this nightmare. Just think of such bad faith! such iniquity! Luckily our friend knows France and its political ways and its crazy fanaticism. Such utterly mad behavior is incomprehensible to people who don't know French history—*Malraux* the writer, cocaine addict, thief (condemned for theft!), a homosexual pathological liar and jealous to the point of delirium is capable of anything, as is Cassou. Unfortunately they're all-powerful at the moment. Aragon is no better. Just think that his wife *Elsa Triolet* who's reached such a high point in French letters (Russian born) translated *Voyage* into Russian! All just to keep me down and wipe me out. I know too much I'm too familiar with the puppet show— That's why they killed Denoël—he was the one who launched—in what shabby conditions!—all those giants of contemporary literature— Anyway, let's take heart a little, now that the truth is out—that is, the abominable imposture of my enemies. They certainly counted on hustling the Danish government. They were dealing with masters at law! They have a tradition here in that sort of thing that's at least a thousand years old! I'm still suffering all over of course but a bit like poor Scarron in fairly merry spirits —The days without sunshine are awful and sleepless. I dream of the countryside of real coffee and of an armchair—and of being able to sleep but my head still hurts a lot— I'm waiting for Dr. Levison to come talk to me about that operation. At my age having your head opened again carries a lot of risks but I'd risk quite a lot to end the pain— The newspapers get to me fine they convey the tone of things and of France and thus allow me to come to grips with the attacks against me. Without French papers I'd be struggling in a fog."[46]

On April 1 Céline was again interrogated in English by the Danish police, with an interpreter present, about the accusations made against him by France. He again refuted them. No, he had never been a member of the Cercle Européen, *Guignol's band* was a totally apolitical book, and the innocuous preface to *Bezons à travers les ages* was written to ensure the author better sales.

On April 8 he left K Wing to return to the prison infirmary, where the detention conditions were less harsh. A letter from Céline to Lucette allows us a clearer understanding of his daily life at the time. "I'm woken up at around 4 or 5 A.M. I can hear the guards come in. The prison begins to stir— I get up at 5. I'm a little groggy at that point. I make my bed and clean up very slowly no one hurries me—all the time I need— I wash the floor twice a week but without tiring myself. The guards are very nice to me. Then I walk to my enclosure where I'm alone and spend 25 minutes in the open air, which is a kindness, I look at the birds and the sky and the treetops the whole enchanted spectacle of the world of the living. I don't move about much because I'm still weak and prone to dizzy spells but I'm left to go peacefully along at my own pace. After the walk over, back to my cell where I wait for lunch. I rest my head in my hands I'm more comfortable that way I think about my little concerns and also about plays that I write and rewrite. You know it's pretty easy for me to dwell inside myself in a state of semi-trance not at all painful and quite pleasant in my current state. They take good care of me in the mornings I'm given a painkiller of paraffin and linseed—comes lunch nicely prepared and very hearty—around 1 P.M. (at a guess I don't have the exact time) after lunch if I'm feeling up to it and my head doesn't hurt too much I work on the account of our sufferings (*du côté des maudits*) that I'm getting underway. It's not hard work this kind of story is easy—it's not like Guignol's where everything is transposed. That reminds me, I hope they didn't make too much of a mess of my things—or of my ballet for the Théâtre Royal! I'll put it in *maudits*—around 3 o'clock another walk 25 minutes more in my enclosure—and then back to the cell. There I do a little editing and then I start to read whatever book or newspaper I have on hand. Then around 6 o'clock there's a very hearty dinner. Then after 2 fairly painful hours—they are all over—until bedtime—2 hours when the melancholy of the day accumulates—but I can still escape into my 'secondary' state, if I can call it that, to read and write a little—at 8 the day is over we go to bed after another paraffin-and-linseed tranquilizer— Altogether I must admit the day passes very quickly—I forgot the breath of outside life brought in around 2 P.M. with *Politiken*, whose headlines I translate by dictionary. And there my sweet you now know everything about my life."

And he ends his letter by urging Lucette to continue dancing: "I don't know anything about how you spend your days. I hope you're back at work, it's necessary. If by some miracle we manage to right our miserable little boat we will no doubt be condemned to live by our wits in some godforsaken place. You have a wonderful skill. Don't waste or lose it at any price. You are more than wonderful in your passionate kindness and courageous genius—don't kill yourself with exhaustion, watch out for cars! If you should have an accident! Please don't. We'll soon be waging our last great battle— Yours, Louis."[47]

The text of *Du côté des maudits* [The Way of the Damned] to which he refers in this letter, and which he began in the Vestre Faengsel infirmary in late March, would later bear the title *La Bataille du Styx* [The Battle of the Styx] before being named *Féerie pour une autre fois.* This time he was plunging into his most recent memories, Montmartre at the end of the occupation, before catching up with and describing the present reality of prison in Copenhagen. The ghosts were knocking at his door, the present was shoving aside evocations of the past. Céline no longer had his heart in transposing, recollecting, remembering things past. On the contrary, he transmuted immediate reality into literature, into fiction. As if to distance it from himself and to suffer less—the opposite of his usual approach, which consisted in drawing a past reality closer to himself so as to relive its convulsions.

His letters to Lucette, and the letters she sent to him, had a hard time getting through. With Mikkelsen's return, all that changed. It was officially to his lawyer that the writer now wrote. After two impersonal lines the tone would change, Lucette became the true addressee. In the beginning, Mikkelsen faithfully forwarded this mail (which benefited from the confidentiality enjoyed by all correspondence between lawyer and client). Later he preferred to call Lucette to his office to receive her letters. But he kept them, since, in his eyes, they were "officially" addressed to him.

In the meantime, the legal case continued to develop with excruciating slowness. On April 11, 1946, the head of the Copenhagen police, the faithful Aage Seidenfaden, sent another memo to the Minister of Justice, confirming the thinness or nonexistence of the charges brought against Céline by the French government. The only decision made at a high-ranking interministerial meeting in Copenhagen on May 16 was to appeal to France for a detailed specification of the main counts of the indictment against the accused. The legation was made to understand that the French police were free to interrogate Céline if a request was made to the Danes. But no such request was ever received.

The writer's health continued to deteriorate. He complained of cardiac rheumatism and lumbago. He lost weight continuously. He had to spend much of April in bed. Was his condition known in France? What did it matter? The hour belonged not to objectivity but to passion—and propaganda. On June 27, *Franc-Tireur* described Céline's life in prison as a pleasant vacation with servants in white aprons, sumptuous apartments, elegant meals. Why should anyone be surprised, according to that paper, that the writer had put on fifteen pounds? The slander and lies leave one speechless.

In June, Karen Marie Jensen returned to Denmark.

For Lucette and Louis, many things would change.

Karen's Return and Captivity's End

Karen must have learned in Spain of Louis' incarceration, but she had no reason to hasten her return. What help could she be to him in Copenhagen? And yet there is no doubt that her dismay was real at finding him still imprisoned when she eventually returned home in June 1946. Finding herself face-to-face with Lucette at her apartment at 20 Ved Stranden couldn't have enchanted her much either. After all, it was to Louis alone that she was linked by years and years of a kind of old amorous complicity. Karen was possessive, and touchy too. She liked to rule alone over her lovers, former lovers, paramours, and companions of days gone by. Had she not once contributed to estranging Elizabeth Craig forever? Céline's old dream of cohabiting in perfect harmony with the women he had loved and his present wife, without a hint of suspicion or jealousy, apparently bore witness to singular naiveté. On top of that, Karen found her apartment in a deplorable state. Bébert had done his handiwork, as we have seen. The porcelain was in pieces, the armchairs in tatters. Karen had one priority: to clean everything up, chuck Lucette out, and live by herself. Lucette was promptly shown the door, put out on the street with her cat and her few bags.

"She later told Louis that it was I who wanted to leave, that she couldn't understand why I wouldn't live with her. I remained discreet, I didn't want to insist, to risk bothering Louis with these quarrels. Then a chance for lodgings presented itself thanks to that painter-prison guard at the Vestre Faengsel, Henning Jensen, who was very poor and dreamed of going to the South of France with his wife. So we came to an agreement. My mother put a room at his disposal in Menton with a little money on the side and while he was away he left me his place, a painter's studio, a closet at 8 Kronprincessegade. The least one can say is that there were no amenities. It was terribly cold there the following winter. I'd leave a glass of water out overnight, and the next morning it was iced over. Louis' uncle had sent me a kind of heated coverlet-pillow that Bébert curled up on. One night there was a short-circuit and I found the cat about to go up in flames. I only just saved him."

The studio was very well located in the center of Copenhagen, at the edge of a park, the Kongens Have. But that was no compensation for its meagerness and discomfort. A journalist would later bear witness: "I suddenly found myself within the sloping walls of a student's digs in the Latin Quarter. Dormer, sofa, camp-bed, table (papers and loose leaves), a makeshift (makeshit) stove, goatskin rugs, frameless paintings on the walls and piled in the corners. Next door, a tiny, gray room: dirty dishes, spirit lamp, greasy papers, empty bottles, all speaking of utter destitution. It's classic."[48]

In September, Lucette moved in.

Meanwhile there had been no progress on the legal front. Céline remained in the prison infirmary. The Minister of Justice had taken his vacation in July. Mikkelsen went to England, where he wanted to consult with some jurists and to study English procedure in matters of extradition. On August 7 he sent a memo to the Minister of Justice, pointing out that Céline was in prison for no reason, that the French had never asked to interrogate the writer. In England, Céline would have long since been called before a judge to rule once and for all on his release.

In a personal letter to the minister, Mikkelsen added: "It is now ten months since this writer, highly esteemed and famous throughout the world, has been detained in deplorable conditions and against his doctor's advice; the state of his nerves has been so badly damaged that I doubt he will ever recover from the consequences of his captivity. That is why I ask you to be so kind as to look into this case as soon as possible, not only for humanitarian reasons but to forestall the criticism that it will inevitably entail at some point about our justice and our country's attitude towards proscribed writers."[49]

Thorvald Mikkelsen was not mistaken. There has been no lack of criticism since. The Minister of Justice had no inkling, he was evasive, he thought it clever to tell the lawyer that the final ruling was the province of the Ministry of Foreign Affairs.

For some weeks now, Céline had been at the end of his tether. He had hoped for a prompt release after Mikkelsen's return. He now gave in to despondency. His letters to Lucette are eloquent: "My little darling I asked Mikkelsen this morning since nothing's happening to have me sent back to France— *I can't go on.* It's all very well to spout reason when you're outside—but *inside* it's another thing— I didn't come to Denmark looking for a prison. I can find as many of those as I want in France—For 8 months I've been *doing time* absolutely gratis. . . . They laid a trap for me—they kept me 9 months in security and with full knowledge of the facts and then arrested me and made me even more sick in prison than I had been— If

French justice makes the laws in Denmark why did I exile myself here? I've written so to Mikkelsen, I'm fed up with his bullshit—he gets off on fine words—let me be transferred to Fresnes and have done with it. Enough! I haven't been *interned* here, I've been well and truly *imprisoned*— They don't have the right to do it—I haven't done anything to them— In Switzerland and Spain they *intern* you. What rot that internment doesn't exist in Denmark. What about Vitale? and so many others? Bullshit! The fact is they want to kowtow to France and the Jews! I've been sentenced to prison in the French courts that's charming! I want to go home—I ask that you be spared—you've got nothing to do with all this nobody is after you. Go home to your mother with Bébert and let them do anything they want to me I don't give a damn! I don't care to subject myself to more shenanigans like the first time, answering idiotic questions about crimes that don't exist and that nobody believes in anyway! I've had enough—I've lost 90 pounds—I want to die but not to have to play the clown again into the bargain for all those sanctimonious bullshitters—All my love Louis."[50]

This was only a momentary truth, a declaration of intent on which he did not follow up. It nonetheless bears witness to his anger and despondency.

Lucette Destouches: "No one can imagine Louis' and my despair. It was unbearable. I believe that if you talk about something you belittle it, you make it ordinary. I tried to do away with myself. Louis also wanted to commit suicide. He hesitated because he knew I was there and I was restrained by his presence. We kept telling ourselves: 'It's better to die.' Later, when he got out of prison, he had changed a lot. He wasn't the same man.

"I went to Mikkelsen every day for news about Louis. right from the beginning he was always reassuring, telling me it was just a matter of days, that he only had to meet with various people. I lived with that hope. And then came the disappointments. Louis' letters make you understand all that. Each time, his morale dipped or soared. He was in paroxysms of anxiety, and he was already anxious by nature. He couldn't wait calmly. On top of it he was not doing at all well. When I came to see him, they had to hold him up like a puppet when they brought him in. His vision went blurry. They gave him injections to keep him going, vitamins. Yes, after the prison ordeal, Céline changed entirely. For this guy who loved to talk, whom people listened to for hours, it was over, all over, he didn't want to see anyone."

On August 13 Louis left the prison infirmary to return to K Wing in the Vestre Faengsel. So everything was going from bad to worse. Those close to him were seriously concerned about his health. But what could Mikkelsen do? He was well aware that the authorities only intended to drag their feet. He requested an official health certificate for his client. It was refused. The French legation, having promised a memorandum specifying the charges brought against Céline, was slow in delivering it. It reached the Ministry of Justice only on the 20th and contained hardly any new elements except for the crime imputed to Céline of having denounced Dr. Rouquès in his new preface to *L'Ecole des cadavres* published under the occupation—the same Dr. Rouquès, we will recall, who had brought a suit against Céline and Denoël in 1939 because he felt the writer had slandered him by calling him a Jew, which he wasn't. In conclusion, the French legation was astonished to find that the Danes considered Céline's offenses to be "political misdemeanors," which seemed inadmissible on the part of a country that was not neutral but an ally of France.

The Danish Minister of Justice was hardly persuaded by this memo and continued to hold the charges to be insufficient. Charbonnière was not terribly surprised. On September 21 he wrote to Georges Bidault, his Minister of Foreign Affairs, to express his skepticism concerning Céline's extradition: "The truth is that if the writings of this individual overwhelmingly demonstrate his contemptibility and ignominy, it does not appear that they can be seen to prove in any peremptory manner his collusion with the enemy, i.e., treason. I am even surprised that, in relation to a collaborator as notorious as Céline, it has not been possible for the examining magistrate to collect more persuasive testimony. I am therefore afraid that these new items will not be in and of themselves sufficient to cause the Danish government to change its stance and finally grant the extradition of the accused."[51]

The delays went on.

The Danes had Céline read the charges brought against him by the legation. And on October 19 he was again interrogated by the Danish police, as a defendant. Mikkelsen attended his interrogation and took advantage of the occasion to stress his client's state of health. Céline, who that day as always refuted the accusations, then undertook to write a "statement in defense," "answers to the accusations of treason brought against me by the French justice system and reiterated by the Danish judicial police over the course of my interrogations during my 1945–1946 incarceration in Copenhagen." The text was definitively completed on November 6.

In it Céline took up point by point the accusations aimed at him. For instance, as soon as he had learned that his name figured on the circulars of the Cercle Européen as an honorary member, he had protested by letter and demanded immediate rectification. An anti-Semite? No, he did not recall having written a single anti-Semitic line since 1937, and in any case he had never called for anti-Semitic persecution but merely protested against the actions of certain Semitic clans then pushing France toward war. The private letters signed with his name and published in the occupation press seemed "dubious" or "contrived" to him. He had never set foot in the German embassy. Otto Abetz hated him. "I have always found the political activities of Abetz to be grotesque and disastrous, and the man himself to be a scourge of mediocrity, a spineless person of appalling vanity, a clown for cataclysm. . . ." His literary relationship with Germany was nonexistent. He returned again to the Jewish question, pointing out that he could very well have become High Commissioner to the Jews, and he added these astounding lines: "All things considered in depth, honestly examined, without passion and given the circumstances, *the Jews should erect a statue to me for the harm I didn't do them and which I could have done them.* They persecute me, I have never persecuted them. I did not take advantage of their temporary weakness, I took no revenge for the numberless outrages, lies, and vicious slanders with which they tried to bring me low and destroy me before the war. I have never called for the persecution of anyone. In all this business, the impeccable democrat is me." The denunciations of Rouquès were a joke. Everyone knew Rouquès was a militant communist, a former ambulance doctor for the Reds during the Spanish civil war and the head of a maquis in the South of France; the Gestapo could have learned some tricks from him. Furthermore, recalling the Rouquès case in 1939 and how such rightist papers as *Je suis partout* had abandoned him at the time, it was an indirect lesson Rouquès had given to the occupation press on the occasion.

And he wrapped up his "statement" with these lines: "Certainly, one might have thought, given my books, that I would become a fanatical collaborator with the Germans, but it was exactly the opposite that occurred. But transforming, intimidating, twisting, and misrepresenting a *suspect as guilty* by way of slander, lies, falsehoods, and inventions is the classic sport of every revolution—the pretty game of every form of fanaticism. Exploiting popular fear to behead one's begrudged, envied, and hated adversary is no new trick. It is known as punishment. In this manner were 'punished' in France: Lavoisier, Champfort [*sic*], Chénier and a hundred others—obscure or famous."[52]

Did he sincerely believe all this? Was he convinced that he had not written one anti-Semitic line since 1937? That he had never set foot in the German embassy? Are we catching Céline here *in flagrante delicto* in a lie? Or was he still unconsciously reducing reality, tailoring it to the level of his personal desires and illusions?

Céline had become so weak that the Vestre Faengsel guards soon took the initiative of having his cell washed by a convict. They feared for his life. The Danish authorities had received his "memorandum" rather favorably and seemed inclined to show him more leniency. Rather than send him back to the prison infirmary, they therefore had him admitted to the civilian Sundby Hospital, where Céline was treated more energetically for the constant humming in his ears, his general health, of course, and also for his pellagra, an ancient illness caused by vitamin deficiency that had once been the scourge of prisoners. For the writer, it was almost a foretaste of liberty, the opportunity to enjoy a renewal of strength and a little freedom, in other words to fervently express his most caustic pessimism: "You know I feel like a horse in a Spanish bullfight, whose stomach has been sewn up, who receives general medical care, but always only as much as it takes to send him back into the arena," he wrote to Mikkelsen at the time.[53]

In late October the lawyer briefly went to Paris. He met there with some of Céline's friends and faithful, such as Marie Canavaggia and Dr. Camus. But it seems that he learned very little about the investigation and the circumstances of the proceedings to be brought against his client there. The only trial that really interested public opinion at the time was the one that had just ended on October 1, as if to put an (almost) full stop to the war and its nightmares. In Nuremberg, the International Court had handed down nine death sentences, to Goering, Ribbentrop, Keitel, Kaltenbrunner, Rosenberg, Hans Frank, Wilhelm Frick, Alfred Jodl, and Seyss-Inquart. Céline, who interested few others than the indefatigable authors of the National Committee of Writers and Guy de Girard de Charbonnière, and who was just beginning to be subjected to the most fearsome type of conspiracy—the conspiracy of silence—did not have the strength to take much interest in it. The only trial that preoccupied him was his own. The only victim was him. The only horizon, that of his prison or his hospital room.

For almost three months Karen had been coming to visit him about once a week. Her conversation did not reveal much goodwill toward Lucette. Karen accused her of wasting her money, of buying a luxuriant fur coat, of bankrupting herself left, right, and center on flowers and cologne for one person or another—in short, of dangerously depleting the stock of gold managed by Hella Johansen. Louis had trouble being persuaded of this. But, as he always believed the worst in the long run, he allowed himself to be convinced and wrote Lucette several deeply wounding, if not to say insulting letters, reproaching her for her thoughtless prodigality. If he had written *Les Beaux draps*, it was only to support them. He even went so far as to criticize her state of health, her precarious physical condition. "When they locked me up, they liberated your folly, your romantic fury for spending that will ruin us in the end—you'd walk over corpses for a basketful of strawberries."[54]

We can imagine how cruelly this hurt Lucette. But she knew Louis too well and his way of always magnifying the least of his feelings to excess, in the game of writing, to give in to tragic despair for long. Generous she certainly was. A spendthrift? Perhaps. But she had no access to the gold, it wasn't she who could have depleted Céline's war treasury. She had no trouble convincing him of this. Thus, in November 1946, in his room at the Sundby Hospital, the writer opened a heated confrontation which Lucette remembers to this day. "When Louis was in the hospital, I explained to him that I had never had the gold in my possession, that I couldn't have sold it. Karen had kept it. It wasn't difficult to clear things up. Louis summoned Karen, Mrs. Lindequist, Hella Johansen, and Mikkelsen to the hospital. Karen confessed that she thought at the time that I would leave Denmark, that she'd remain alone with Louis, and that in any case the gold was hers. I couldn't say a word. So the tone heated up. Well might Louis be on his back, sick and all, he summoned up his energy, he raised his voice, it was dramatic. Karen started crying and said, 'Okay, I'll give it back.' Mikkelsen added in English: 'Come to my office tomorrow and bring me the gold.' But the fact is, the gold was no big deal, it was kept in a cookie tin. The way we talked about it you'd think it was a fortune. Karen admitted that she had spent half of it. So Mikkelsen kept the other half. Since he offered us hospitality for four years, that balanced things out. From that day on, he gave us 350 crowns twice a month."

With Lucette acquitted at the Sundby Hospital "court," and Karen found guilty, exiled for life, and characterized by him in his correspondence as an "evil-minded drunken idiot," Louis continued impatiently to await the outcome, if any, of his legal situation in Denmark. But it was better to rot in Copenhagen than to appear before the Seine law courts.

There, on November 16, Le Vigan had been sentenced to ten years' forced labor. The presiding magistrate had encouraged him to compromise Céline, to lay the responsibility on him for his subversive opinions. Le Vigan avoided every trap and every cowardly act. Céline would express his gratitude in *D'un château l'autre*: "Hunted down like quarry as we were . . . no picnic either! . . . and in the Court! . . . my God he was heroic! . . . what a stance! Just think the way he stood up to them! . . . and in handcuffs! . . . how he defended me! . . . there's not many like him! . . . there's no one! . . . and the jackal hordes filling the hall! . . . and they had to listen! . . . forced to! . . . that I was the only patriot! . . . the true patriot! . . . the only one! . . . and that they were nothing but slobbering, ill-tempered, venomous hyenas!"[55]

Le Vigan's sentence might seem light compared to the usual verdicts handed down by the courts at the time (Le Vigan was freed in 1949; he would seek exile in Argentina and die there in 1972). But Rebatet and Pierre-Antoine Cousteau were sentenced to death on November 22 (they were eventually pardoned). Who could ask for better? What did Céline have to complain about? About nothing, everything, life, the only case that mattered to him, his own, about his health, so impaired that he took the trouble, on November 30, 1946, after more than eleven months of detention, to draw up his own medical assessment for the Danish authorities—a catastrophic assessment, naturally. Everything was included: headaches, earaches, insomnia, rheumatism. heart trouble, radial paralysis, intestines, eczema, pellagra, dental problems. He was hardly exaggerating. But mostly he had cause to complain about the indecision of the Danes.

Unexpected support arrived at that moment from the United States by the initiative of Julian Cornell, a New York lawyer who had translated Céline's "statement in defense" and had circulated a petition on his behalf, with the help of a young professor of Jewish birth, Milton Hindus, who taught at Brandeis University in Massachusetts. The writer Henry Miller, the composer Edgar Varèse, and the publisher James Laughlin, among others, signed the petition, which called for the writer's release, pointed out that he was being persecuted purely for differences of opinion, recalled his deeds of arms during the two world wars, and lastly stressed the atmosphere of vengeance and account-settling then pervading France.[56]

In the more clement conditions of Sundby Hospital, Céline reopened his correspondence with his old friends from Paris: Henri Mahé, Marcel Aymé,

André Pulicani, Daragnès, and Dr. Camus. As though he needed to return to his country, his past, and his mother tongue, to write in order to survive, comfort himself, delude himself, protest, howl, curse, complain, be moved, exaggerate—in short, to develop the whole outraged gamut of his feelings, the madness of his writing, his need for a link, a cry as vital as an umbilical cord to fight the suffocation that was threatening him: silence. Few literary correspondences are as fecund as his was during the Danish exile, with its thousands and thousands of letters, a correspondence he had begun in the depths of the despair he shared with Lucette.

Symptomatic of his return to the past is his letter of January 17 to Lucien Descaves, the earliest champion of *Voyage*, who had himself recently published his *Souvenirs d'un ours*, in which he relates, among other things, the misadventures of the 1932 Goncourt. Ah! the Abbé Mugnier whom Céline had enjoyed scandalizing once upon a time at Lucien Descaves' table, and his champions for the Renaudot, like Noël Sabord! . . . "As you know I'm accused of the worst, treason, etc. None of it holds water. Everything I've been told is false: inventions, tissues of gossip, disgraceful and absurd, hatred upon hatred that's all. But it's the suspects who are most often guillotined during revolutions, being a suspect is worse than anything. Exile, then, but exile plus prison, plus illness, it's too much. I have a solid spirit, very resistant, very sturdy, very cheerful—but even so it is beginning to weary— I don't think it will get through spring in this prison, it will then escape, it will go I'm warning you to perch in the phantom of your tree, it will have become a bird again . . . to bid you good day."[57]

On January 24, 1947, Céline left Sundby Hospital to return to his cell in the Vestre Faengsel. An important meeting was held that very day between the Minister of Justice, his counterpart at Foreign Affairs, and several high-ranking bureaucrats. Once again they emphatically decided not to do anything. On the 27th, the exasperated Mikkelsen sent a withering letter to the Minister of Justice: ". . . If, in contempt for the letter and spirit of the extradition treaty in force between France and Denmark, as well as for the most basic human rights and humanitarian principles, we wish to violate the customs to which civilized nations have hitherto adhered, then naturally we mustn't hesitate to extradite this man, whose detention in Danish prisons has turned him into a wreck. But if that is in fact your goal, this man has the right to be informed of the decisions concerning him, so that I can take on his behalf every practical measure to safeguard him, just as it is also his right to demand decent living conditions given that, as already indicated, there is cause only to keep him under observation and close watch, and not to hold him in isolation like a dangerous criminal."[58]

Mikkelsen appended to his letter the appeal made by the leading members of the American literary and intellectual communities. The next day he was received by the minister, who took him to task for the vehemence of his message. But Mikkelsen had scored a minor victory. Consideration had to be given to transferring Céline to a civilian hospital outside the prison.

This was done on February 26. Céline was admitted to the Copenhagen State Hospital, where he remained theoretically under surveillance and where he had to swear on his honor not to leave the premises without authorization from the judiciary police. There he was soon enjoying the benefits of a special diet, was free to move within the confines of the building, to correspond and to receive whomever he liked. He merely had to request special permission from the police if he wished to go into town, for instance to visit his lawyer.

Mikkelsen ceased harassing the Ministry of Justice, as if satisfied with this temporary arrangement. And Helga Pedersen in all seriousness wrote in her work *Did Denmark Save Céline?*: "Meanwhile, the consideration of a permanent liberation was progressing at a lively pace at the Ministries of Justice and Foreign Affairs, and we know that it culminated in a release order on June 19, 1947."[59] As we see, the concept of speed or "lively pace" is rather subjective among Danish jurists.

On March 1, 1947, Céline wrote his first letter to Milton Hindus, who would soon make the journey to Denmark—a Milton Hindus strangely fascinated by the personality of the French writer, attracted by his dark genius, the force of his imagination, the syncopated strength of his style, and the morbid intemperance of his politics. As he wrote in the introduction to the work he would later dedicate to Céline: "I, a Jew living in America, went to see Céline and talk to him last summer in Denmark, because he had reached out for me spiritually in the war and shaken me as Hitler had shaken my whole country, and especially my fellow Jews. I thought of Céline and still think of him as an unparalleled contemporary artistic phenomenon."[60]

Céline, for his part, was moved by the unexpected interest taken in him by the young American intellectual. He would go out of his way to be attentive and congenial toward him, developing in his correspondence a whole philosemitic pattern of wooing, writing him some of his most penetrating letters on his novelistic art, revealing to him his plans to emigrate to the United States, or even to practice medicine in Greenland—that same old escape toward the Great North.

While Céline was recuperating in the Rigshospital, Bébert the cat fell sick. On March 7 he had to undergo surgery for a cancerous tumor. But the Montmartre tom had been around the block. He withstood the trauma and made a speedy recovery, with the slower and wiser serenity of aging cats, faithful, silent, and enigmatic.

In early March, Céline finished *Guignol's band 2* and, on March 20, the new and definitive version of his ballet, *Foudres et Flèches.* But the time was not yet at hand when he could concern himself solely with literature. If the legal pressure was abating in Denmark, it was only just beginning in France. In April 1947 his old friend Antonio Zuloaga, the former press attaché to the Spanish embassy in Paris, asked Albert Naud to consider taking on the writer's defense in Paris. The lawyer, a veteran Resistance member who had been arrested by the Gestapo, imprisoned for two months at the Santé, and had taken part in the fighting to liberate the capital, accepted. Thus began, on April 19, a correspondence between the two men that throws light on the entire legal development of Céline's case in France.[61]

What significant details can be culled from the earliest letters that the writer sent him from the Rigshospital, in which we see him pleading his case as if instructing his own lawyer? He began by describing the personality of Guy de Girard de Charbonnière: "The truth is, he went about it all wrong, the man is a fool—from a legal standpoint the Danes follow the English line, they don't believe in vehemence, any attack they feel to be prejudiced immediately makes them suspicious. Charbonnière went about it all wrong, he tried to get me extradited through 'furia.' "

May 12, 1947: "You've seen my file—it's made up of 95% hatred and 5% collaboration (or so-called). If I say nothing I'm heaped with abuse, if I protest I'm seen as a monster."

On May 25 he returns to the charge: "*Les Beaux draps?* Who read it? No one—there are 100 pages in it that could make up an anthology of patriotism—my so-called letters to the papers? distortions or fakes— Obviously there are 10, 100, 1,000 people in Paris who'd like to see me bayoneted, assassinated, eliminated (like Denoël)! Patriotic? I'm a thousand times more so than my accusers. I only wanted to prevent war from breaking out in such an idiotic manner—and thus revealing *France's weakness.*"

On June 18 he evokes his anti-Semitism in unusual terms, expressing sorrow for what he has soon come to consider the only martyrdom—that of the anti-Semites themselves! "I am the only anti-Semite persecuted for his anti-Semitism who can actually be of use to the Jews at the moment . . . The latter are far from popular, they are hated as much and more as they were before Hitler . . . experience has unfortunately convinced me, however, that anti-Semitism leads to nothing and that, besides, it has lost its *raison d'être*. . . . Anti-Semitism is incited by politicians or the police— Woe unto the sincere man who gets caught up in it! It's a vile farce. I'll never forgive the Germans for having used it as an election platform in the perfect knowledge of the swindle they were committing. . . . No one has ever suggested that I'm calculating or cowardly. I think of my people, MY PEOPLE FIRST, the current sufferings of imprisoned anti-Semites causes me great pain I assure you. . . . I am first and foremost a doctor—may our martyrdom serve some purpose."

Other correspondence begun by Céline at that time includes those with Albert Paraz (totaling 353 letters from Céline) in late May 1946, and with Charles Deshayes (134 letters) in June.

Paraz was born in Constantine, Algeria. In the 1920s he had frequented the anarchist and surrealist circles and the cafés of Montmartre. Two novels published by Denoël before the war—*Bitru* in 1936 and *Les Repues franches* a year later—had gained him little attention in the literary world. He had worked at just about everything: as a fakir, pen salesman, movie extra, and mushroom peddler. What is striking about Paraz—who would be accidentally gassed at the Béni-Ounif research center in the Sahara in 1939 and never fully recover from the damage to his lungs—is his nonconformity, his humor, his freedom of tone and thought, and his vulgar zest. Céline, whom he may have encountered at Denoël's before the war, represented for him the great, inaccessible writer, almost a paragon. Céline's troubles in Denmark, being proscribed, maligned, and awaiting judgment, gave Paraz the opportunity to write and encourage him, challenge convention and conformity of thought, the ideological and persecuting smugness of the day. And Paraz would go to no end of trouble to help the writer, to the extent that his means and connections allowed. For the author of *Voyage*, their correspondence would be like a wonderful lungful of oxygen, a way of breaking his solitude, of breathing a little Parisian air.

Charles Deshayes was a young journalist who wanted to create a climate favorable to Céline in the press. But Naud considered the plan to be ill-conceived and above all inopportune. He dissuaded the journalist. "For the moment," he wrote him, "it would be totally ill-advised to unleash any kind of campaign in Céline's favor. . . . As I write to you, I am almost certain of obtaining from Denmark a refusal to extradite. I must have a formal guarantee and a definitive decision on that point before undertaking anything in France.

Thus, with the summer, the sky was clearing over Copenhagen. In June, Céline signed the contracts for the new American edition of *Mort à crédit*, prefaced by Milton Hindus (whom he would thank in dithyrambic terms, further asking him to pass on his gratitude to Julian Cornell for his petition), and for *Guignol's band* with the publisher James Laughlin. Céline's release and the final decision not to extradite him could only be a matter of days away, despite the campaign waged against him since April by the Danish communist newspaper *Lang og folk* or the petition calling for his expulsion signed by the chief physician and twenty-five doctors at the Rigshospital, hostile to the writer, whom they deemed a collaborator.

On June 24, 1947, at 11 A.M., Céline was finally officially freed. He signed the following declaration (in English): "I the undersigned, Louis Ferdinand Destouches, undertake on my honor not to leave Denmark without the consent of the Danish authorities." He received the rest of his sequestered money—2,025 crowns—and moved in with Lucette into the loft at 8 Kronprincessegade.

Four long years had yet to elapse before he would return to his own country. For the moment, the immediate, physical fear of extradition, the threats against his freedom and his life, faded into the background. The rest was a matter of patience, poverty, boredom, legal proceedings and red tape, anger, impotence, discouragement, and malevolence. He would develop a permanent aversion to Denmark, but the war and its latest tragic consequences were coming to an end for him. The Danes had restored him to freedom. The Danes were not extraditing him. From castle to castle—the end. Céline had just escaped from his last—from prison.

16

Exile

8 Kronprincessegade

Now free, Céline returned to Lucette in the little garret at 8 Kronprincessegade, where he would live for nearly eleven months—a closet too hot during the interminable summer days and freezing through the endless winters. But for them, having grown used to living day-to-day, hand-to-mouth, in suspense since their hasty departure from Paris in 1944, it was an inexpressible relief. With an almost light heart Lucette was able to resume her illicit dance lessons and her training with Birger Bartholin. Before returning home, she was glad to make a detour through the saunas or public baths, which consoled her for the lack of amenities at home. Louis barely left the house, or if so only for a quick walk with Lucette and Bébert (on a leash) through the nearby park. He preferred to stay indoors, to shut out the world with its cries and threats, to isolate himself in his ever more agonizing neuralgia, his resentments, his literary wrath, his failing memory edited by an ever-more-present delirium.

His work-in-progress was still *Féerie pour une autre fois*, which he had begun in prison and no doubt pursued more easily now that he had escaped the cells of the Vestre Faengsel and was enjoying the minimum distance needed to organize and transcribe his experiences as a detainee, as a Parisian intoxicated by the vertigo of nostalgia, as an inconsolable exile from Montmartre, and as a Breton, too, recalling the last happy summers in Saint-Malo.

He had lived through three years of total isolation, during which his only chance of escaping the rigors of the purge had been in his anonymity. He could now begin to show himself again. Thorvald Mikkelsen and Albert Naud, however, did not consider that advisable. They were rightly mistrustful of the whims and provocations of their client, whose best interests were in lying low—or at least in not raising his voice, not granting interviews, not indulging in fits of anger. And Céline, who had received a ration card on leaving the hospital and later had to request vouchers to buy himself a pair of shoes and other basic commodities that were still rationed, took that pretty much for gospel.

His first interview in Denmark, appearing in *France-Dimanche* on June 29, 1947, contained few outbursts. A plaintive, patriotic Céline comes through, a Céline even prepared to enlist in the French expeditionary forces in Indochina(!), who characterizes himself as the most unfortunate and most slandered of all Frenchmen and reduced thereby to living off Danish charity.[1]

On August 1 he wrote a letter to *Combat* which, in its July 11 issue, had reprinted lengthy extracts from an article in *Izvestia* that saw the reissue of *Mort à crédit* in the United States as proof of the decadence of Western bourgeois art. Among other courtesies, the article labeled Céline a literary nonentity and a fascist criminal, and compared him to other decadents: Henry Miller and Jean Genet—not to mention the newly fashionable Marquis de Sade. Céline obviously had no trouble reminding the Soviet journalist that *Voyage au bout de la nuit* had first been launched by Georges Altman in Barbusse's communist *Le Monde*, and that it had been officially translated in Russia; nor in further pointing out, perhaps overdoing it a little, that his novels had been banned in Germany after Hitler's rise. "Such imbecility discourages polemic, one sees why the word is ever more given over to the bomb, the mine, the deluge!"[2]

Céline was equally prolix with Robert Massin—the same Massin who would soon lose his given name to become, under the single name of Massin, one of the most important illustrators in postwar French literature—in an interview for the periodical *La Rue* in November 1947. Still complaining, still talking like a persecuted man. Why had Guitry or Montherlant gotten off so easily and he not? "Some American publishers have made me offers. They give me a pain in the ass. I want to be published in French. Am I working? Fortunately: that's all I have to do." After a pause, Céline added these words: "I'm a stupid jerk [*un con*]," like a regret, a twinge of remorse, perhaps the feeling of having been history's dupe, the down-and-out sucker of the collaboration.[3]

The last conversation of that period was published by the sensationalist weekly *Samedi-Soir*, founded immediately after the liberation and enjoying a circulation of approximately 400,000, in its issue of November 22, 1947. A rather comical interview, and one which, so to speak, never occurred. Mikkelsen must have urged Céline not to see the newspaper's special correspondent. After having arranged a meeting at his, Céline's, house, the author refused to let him in. They negotiated for an hour and a half on either side of the door. Céline seemed to be restraining himself from an angry outburst. The reporter, Jacques Robert, nonetheless managed to have a sort of laconic, farcical, lunatic dialogue with him, without ever succeeding in seeing him.

"Do you ever go out, Céline?"

"No, never."

"You don't go to the restaurant?"

"Are you nuts? On what money?"

"Are you writing?"

"Yes, of course."

"A novel?"

"Yes. *Féerie pour une autre fois.*"

"The subject?"

"Atrocious. A little Apocalypse on behalf of our demented humanity."

"The Jews, Céline?"

"Shut up."

"No, I want to know."

"That's over, it's passé. I'll never talk about the Jews again. Anyway, the disasters that are brewing in the world make these little Aryan matters totally outdated."[4]

More comforting for Céline, of course, were the letters he continued to write to his friends in France, to Descaves, Daragnès, Marie Canavaggia, Albert Paraz. Paraz had gotten in touch with Jean Paulhan, who had accepted in principle to publish a selection by Céline in *Les Cahiers de la Pléiade*, to help break the conspiracy of silence imposed in France on the author of *Voyage*.

Comforting, too, were the friendships established that autumn of 1947 in Copenhagen with Denise Thomassen and the Protestant minister François Löchen. Thomassen was a young compatriot who had married a Dane and had recently opened a French bookstore in the center of town. She wanted to pay a call on Céline. One day an unknown woman knocked on his door. He had every reason to mistrust her. A trap, a journalist's trick, a police provocation? He hesitated. Céline was at the height of his persecution mania—occasionally so unmaniacal. The young woman must have explained herself. He let her in. They got along. They fell into the habit of seeing one another frequently. She brought him books. He could speak to her in French. A godsend! When he left for Korsör, he would write her, order novels, enter into friendly correspondence with her.[5]

François Löchen was the head of the Reformed Church of France in Copenhagen. He had once been a minister in the western suburbs of Paris, at Sartrouville, Houilles, and Bezons, the very place where Céline had been municipal physician.

One day, wrote Löchen, "a Sunday in the autumn of 1947, a man who had attended the service I had led at the Reformed Church of France in Copenhagen, where I was spiritual director, came to introduce himself at the end of the ceremony: 'Doctor Destouches—may I come see you, Father . . . ?' I received not one but several visits from Céline. . . . I'll never forget that Christmas Eve in the old French presbytery in Copenhagen where our two households had come together. We discovered that I had been a minister in the suburb of Paris where Céline himself had practiced medicine. I told him of the death of his nurse, whose funeral I had conducted. In one dramatic and overwhelming moment, he was able to express to us, with his sincerity and vigor, how there was no suffering that did not affect him, and how revolted he was at the idea that there could ever be someone who wished the suffering of 'some one else' under the pretext that it would do him good."[6] Father Löchen is no doubt referring to an incident that had arisen when Mme. Löchen had had the unfortunate idea of remarking that it was only right that the collaborators had been sent to prison.[7] But for the most part the relationship between the two men was unclouded. Father Löchen did everything in his power to help Céline. Unfortunately, his intercessions with the embassy and de Charbonnière met a wall of hostility. Worse still, the French ambassador applied pressures—in vain—to have the minister of the Reformed Church of France in Copenhagen recalled to France for his audacity in trying to help the writer.

The correspondence between Céline and François Löchen is moving. It would be rash to speak of a revival of the religious impulse in the author of *Voyage*. Nonetheless, his first visit to the Protestant church may not have been entirely disingenuous. And he was able to write to his minister: "Though great neither in faith nor in virtue, I do at least possess a certain courtesy and a keen pleasure in listening to you. In the ordeals of the human journey, my soul must have earned its place in heaven a long time ago! All I need now is music . . . I intend no impertinence in these words."[8]

His correspondent was prepared to supply him with material aid. Céline, too proud, declined the offer:

My dear Minister,

I am most touched by your very warm and fraternal gesture, and it pains me to refuse anything so kindly offered, but you know that traditionally stout ships accept help only in the most extreme distress . . . I have not reached that point— not yet . . . But I will let you know, and quickly, I promise, when the waters reach the decks. Alas, that could easily happen."[9]

Two days later he wrote him these impishly melancholy lines: "Preachers have at least two kinds of clients on whom they can count absolutely, whom no one would try to take away from them: lepers and people sentenced to death. I have the good spiritual fortune of belonging to a certain extent to both species . . . It's no surprise, then, that I'm sticking with you."[10]

Another comfort was the November 1947 visit of René Héron de Villefosse and his wife, old prewar friends first met on Henri Mahé's *Enez-Glaz*, moored on the banks of the Seine. Mikkelsen had met them in Paris a few months earlier. Villefosse had believed himself to be invited to Denmark by the lawyer. He embarked at the Gare du Nord, thirty hours by train through German cities still in ruins, children in rags, and a "German miracle" that had yet to make its appearance. In Copenhagen, a room was reserved for them at the Hôtel d'Angleterre, but at their own expense. He made several visits to Céline's garret, which he deemed "rather slovenly" with "socks on the table and shirts hanging from the furniture."[11]

"One day, Mikkelsen took all four of us to Elsinore. A gray November morning. The Danish forest still had its golden leaves, its extraordinary autumn finery, sumptuous and mysterious, certainly the setting that inspired Andersen. Ferdinand had stayed in the car while we visited the historical museums and castles along the way. At Elsinore he got out and accompanied us to the terrace where the old cannons sleep. With the yellow fog over the Swedish coast across the water, sometimes near, sometimes far, and the sea gulls wheeling and crying, the impact is unsettling. You look, you want to see further, you wait for just the right word to rise within you. After staring for a long while, Céline said to us in his hollow voice: 'It's a sea to fish souls from!' "[12]

In France, late 1947 was marked by André Gide's winning the Nobel Prize for literature on October 23, in England by the royal marriage of Elizabeth to her cousin Philip, Duke of Edinburgh, on November 20, and for Céline by the death of Albert Milon on December 1—Milon, the companion of his convalescence in Val-de-Grâce, the old crony with whom he had corresponded for so long but had recently lost sight of, whom he had wanted to lure to the plantations of Africa in 1916, who had followed him to Brittany on behalf of the Rockefeller Foundation, and who was one of the pillars of that youth to which Céline so often referred with affectionate nostalgia.

The writer enjoyed wandering this way among the shadows, reencountering friends of yore. During the winter, the touring ballet company of the Paris Opéra made a stop in Copenhagen. Céline mingled with the crowds several nights in a row, watching the dancers come and go by the dressing rooms and the stage door. Finally, he approached a member of the troupe. Was Serge Perrault among them? What had become of him? He recalled a young dancer friend of Lucette's, whom he had often seen in Montmartre toward the end of the occupation, when the young man was fleeing the STO. He was told that Perrault had left the Opéra eighteen months earlier, that he had joined Roland Petit's company. Céline shook his head, disappointed at not seeing him, then retreated into the solitude of his exile.

Though worn out and prematurely aged since his final release from hospital and prison, he had nonetheless recovered a certain taste for life, no doubt about it. Céline intended to fight, with an energy that was not entirely born of despair. He was well aware of his vigor, his strength as a writer and polemicist, in his struggle against his enemies: against the politicians, for instance, who were relentlessly dogging him. He had warned Albert Naud of his intentions on August 20, 1947: "Nature has endowed me with a rather atomic little pen (compensation for so much weakness!). I can feel it beginning to itch . . . you can imagine I have no lack of opportunities for revenge . . . It's dangerous to push certain characters too far. . . . A patriot I am—100 times more so than the whole cabinet of Ramadier, Bidault, Asshole————and consort! No more or less a traitor than any one of them. And I'll let the whole world know it if they keep giving me shit. No one will read Bidault's books—I can have 500,000 readers in America if I want—Every man according to his place—and as many in Russia and more—again, if I want—These little things should be pointed out. . . . They already have the Brasillach affair on their backs—if they want an even greater Céline affair it's up to them— I know how to make them laugh— Bidault doesn't. And out of the other side of their asses!"[13]

In November, Paraz called his attention to the passage in Sartre's *Réflections sur la question juive*, in which Céline is specifically taken to task, accused of having been in the pay of the Germans. Céline answered Paraz forthwith.

Old Chum,

Many thanks for Temps modernes which I've just received. I'm going after Sartre. Really, the fellow is too asinine, he's depressing. He understands nothing. He is ignoble. It's awful. He's playing at La Bruyère . . . What a mess! What impotence! A jackal he is—a washed-out stoolie. But he's a "jackal that doesn't know how to laugh," who can't laugh. It's shameful. Contemptible as it is, the jackal is intelligent, but not him. Hence his fury. That absurd gesticulating that epileptoid feebleness. . . . He needs a good beating with a heavy stick. I'm going to clean the floor with him but my lawyer advises me to wait . . . not to get the press onto me . . . that my status here is still too precarious."[14]

Precarious or not, Céline nonetheless wrote without delay the few pages of his convulsive, delirious response to Sartre, entitled *"À l'Agité du bocal"* [roughly, To the Restless Fidgeter], in which he would unload scatological garbage trucks on his victim, comparing him to a tapeworm in a turd, a parson's nose, a dung beetle, a little pigeon-shit, a shit-stuffed bastard, a dunce, Cain's Anus, a four-eyed ignoramus, and a phony, puerile brat. Céline the polemicist was in action again, with a breathless, desperate frenzy. But the text moves us because it speaks much more of its author than of Sartre, because it suggests the overtones of misery, pain, and the outraged sense of injustice (no, he had not been paid off by the Germans) that alone could have torn such headlong, excessive, morbid cries from him. "Setting the tone by death-rattles, the sounds of rumbling guts, sobs, clanking . . . 'Help!' "[15]

He sent this text to Jean Paulhan for *Les Cahiers de la Pléiade.*

Meanwhile, the Americans had re-released his early novels. Sought on an arrest warrant in France, however, and threatened with having his property seized, he could have no illusions of receiving any royalties from Paris. Furthermore, he had only one priority: to leave the Denoël publishing house forever after the assassination of his manager and friend. The company's situation, for that matter, was chaotic. Under suspicion of collaboration from the outset of the liberation, it had been placed under the provisional administration of Maximilian Vox. Moreover, Robert Denoël's widow had initiated a lawsuit against Jeanne Loviton—who, as we have seen, had become the company's majority shareholder—to the extent of accusing her of having had her husband murdered by hired assassins. The proceedings, futile and merciless, came to nothing and did not prevent Jeanne Loviton, alias Jean Voilier, the ex-wife of Pierre Frondaie, author of *L'Homme à l'Hispano* and former intimate of Giraudoux and Valéry, from soon taking control of Denoël.

Its literary director, Guy Tosi, who had recently brought the works of Lanza del Vasto, Malaparte, and Miller to the publishing house, nonetheless flew to Copenhagen to meet with Céline. They lunched together at Mikkelsen's. Tosi passed on Malaparte's friendly offer to receive Céline's royalties for him in Italy so as later to restore them to him. Céline declined the offer. Denoël would get the manuscript to *Féerie* only on condition that the royalties be deposited in a Swiss account. This was legally impossible. Tosi explained to him that Vox, the provisional administrator, had no authority for such a move. A few days later, Mikkelsen received from Éditions Denoël an up-to-date statement of Céline's royalties and an inventory of all Céline's works printed to date.[16] On December 8, by registered letter to Jean Voilier, Céline stated his intention of resuming his status as an independent author, pure and simple, based on the fact that not one of his books had been reprinted or reissued since June 12, 1944. Voilier reacted, of course, and signaled her intention, in a further letter on January 8, 1948, of maintaining the status quo for the time being, i.e., neither to reprint nor to break the contract. Céline paid no attention. For him, the divorce was final.

In early January 1948, he met in Copenhagen with the publisher Charles Fasquelle, who was interested in republishing *Voyage*. René Philippon, president of the Publishers Union, may have served as intermediary. But the negotiations came to nothing. In a letter to Pierre Monnier, Céline later claimed that Fasquelle had been scared off by the prospect of a lawsuit by Denoël: "Fasquelle almost took up 'Voyage,' too, you might go see him on my behalf. He backed down before Voilier, the threat of a lawsuit, etc. . . . But he had a hard-on for it. We shouldn't let it drop. I couldn't care less, him or Paulhan!!! He's rich, young Fasquelle, he may run after negresses and be a globe-trotting bum, but he's got some dough in Switzerland. He wanted to advance me a hefty sum."[17]

Paulhan had just received *"À l'Agité du bocal."* He was undoubtedly dismayed by its smutty virulence. Was this the way to go about rehabilitating Céline, to re-establish his presence in French literary life?

"The business of my response to Sartre has fallen through—Paulhan thinks it's too much, that the repercussions would be terrible, etc. There's some truth to that of course. . . . Shit and double shit! I'm sending him a ballet . . . a super-innocuous piece of foolishness," Céline wrote to Paraz on January 10, 1948.[18] But Paulhan was disappointed by the trivial and superficial fairy-tale synopsis of *Foudres et Flèches* and had no use for it in his *Cahiers de la Pléiade*. In March, Céline decided to entrust him with the first unpublished chapter of *Casse-Pipe* (which would appear in *Cahiers* in late summer, "*À l'Agité du bocal*" appearing, along with many of Céline's letters, in Albert Paraz's work *Le Gala des vaches* [The Gala of the Cows], by Les Editions de l'Élan in December 1948).

Two significant events mark the spring of 1948 for Céline. The first was the visit in late March of his old Montmartre friend Jean-Gabriel Daragnès, painter, engraver, and printer, who until his death in 1950 would strive to help the exiled writer and to ease his financial and publishing troubles. It seems that Daragnès had come to Copenhagen to preside over an Exhibition of French Literature. Mikkelsen invited him to dinner. Lucette and Louis were delighted by his arrival. Then, on April 30, they received the news of the Denoël company's acquittal by the Seine law courts. The house of Denoël had been found not guilty of publishing in time of war "brochures and books in favor of the enemy, of collaboration with the enemy, racism or totalitarian doctrines." It was unbelievable. What about its subsidiary, les Nouvelles Éditions Françaises? Its series "The Jews in France"? Its works by Dr. Montandon, Rebatet, and others? What influence, what support had Jean Voilier relied upon? Why prosecute Céline in such circumstances, or blame him for the reprinting of his pamphlets? Voilier had come away with the prize and was now in sole charge of her house. But Céline's prosecution would not be curtailed by the same token. He enjoyed no influence, he remained, in the judges' view, the symbol of anti-Semitism that had to be destroyed—and condemned. Nonetheless, from then on Céline and his lawyers would continually appeal in their defense arguments to the precedent of the judgment rendered on Denoël.

Meanwhile, the painter and former prison guard of the Vestre Faengsel, Henning Jensen, and his wife were thoroughly bored in Menton. The maid's room that the Pirazzolis had given them was tiny. Lucette's mother was not particularly friendly. The Jensens wrote to Lucette that they would soon be returning to Copenhagen and that they intended to resume occupation of their hovel at 8 Kronprincessegade. Lucette could find nowhere in town at a moderate rent. Louis was bent on staying in Copenhagen, but there was no way. Mikkelsen then offered to lodge them on his farm, Klarskovgaard, not far from Korsör, a hundred kilometers or so southwest of Copenhagen, on the Baltic shore.

They moved on May 19.

Baltic Shores, Works and Days

Klarskovgaard ("farm of the clear wood") was an estate of about fifty acres, eight kilometers from Korsör. It was reached by an unpaved road not readily accessible to motor vehicles. Thorvald Mikkelsen had purchased it in the early '20s and often stayed there on weekends and in the summer months. He enjoyed having his friends there, his family, foreign visitors passing through his country. Except through the long winter months, its social life was, as a result, highly animated.

The property was bounded to the south by the sea, the Store Baelt, one of the channels connecting the Baltic to the North Sea, to the east and the west by forests, and opened out to the north on cultivated fields bordered with hedgerows. Klarskovgaard was not strictly speaking an agriculture farm from which Mikkelsen intended to draw an income. He had nonetheless converted it to orchards, the management of which he had entrusted to bailiffs, the Pedersen couple, who lived there year 'round.

Five residences were scattered about the farm. Hovedhuset—"the main house"—where Mikkelsen lived, was naturally the largest, the most comfortable, with its half-timbers and thatched roof, its main body flanked by two wings. It had been built in the early nineteenth century. The lawyer had had an enormous library installed that included many French books. It overlooked a lovely garden. Some twenty meters to the west rose Gaestehuset, "the guest house," more modern, cubic in shape, with its large living room and veranda giving on to four bedrooms. Less than 100 meters to the east, Bestyrer Bolig, "the bailiff house," sprawled with its main building, garages, fruit racks, and farm buildings. Farther away, in a hollow 200 meters to the west of the main house, squatted Skovly, which means "wooded," with its three main rooms at the front of the house, its little kitchen, and its single water tap, unusable more often than not. Beyond the field in front of the house stretched the Baltic, pale and still like a dead sea. Last, some 100 meters at the far southern end, perched on a cliff at the edge of the woods overlooking the sea, was the cottage Fanehuset, "the flag house," with its thatched roof, built in the late eighteenth century. It was incontrovertibly the most rudimentary and uncomfortable on the estate. The kitchen had one little electric hot plate. When Céline moved in, there was no running water and, of course, no toilet. The floor was beaten earth. Like Skovly, it was heated only by a peat stove, which gave scant warmth. In her book *Did Denmark Save Céline?*, Helga Pedersen expresses skepticism about the latter claim. According to her, the orchards provided such an abundance of wood every year that it would have been stupid to warm oneself (poorly) by any other means. Yet Lucette Destouches' testimony is categorical: the stoves were peat-fired, and the winter days as icy as they were damp.

When she, Louis, and Bébert arrived in Klarskovgaard on May 19, in the sudden blossoming of a late spring, in that country without any real transitional seasons, where the endless winter was followed by a miraculous but all too brief summer, they could not have imagined that they would remain there for nearly three years, shuttled across the estate from one residence to another, waiting, growing bored, writing, receiving the rare visit, following from afar the vagaries of the lawsuits brought against the writer, and watching the pitiful efforts of small publishers to reissue his prewar writings. He would suffer from ever more insistent neuralgia. She would fall sick. Old Bébert, now fifteen, would soon be sharing his life and his masters' affections with new companions, a bitch and other cats; above all, after months of being cooped up in a Copenhagen hovel, he would rediscover a certain freedom roaming the forest's edge in the uneasy solitude of nature. A bizarre fate for a Montmartre tom!

In describing Céline's life during this period, we must begin by describing his day-to-day existence, his encounters, his miseries, his discouragements; and then by distinguishing what were at heart his two main preoccupations: the difficulties of republishing his books to break the conspiracy of silence weighing upon him in the postwar atmosphere, and of course the stages of his trials.

Thus, they got off the train at Korsör with their Bohemians' luggage, their shabby valises, their pots and pans, a few books. A taxi brought them to Klarskovgaard. Mikkelsen wasn't there, nor was there anybody to welcome them or help them move in. They lived in the main house for a few days. Louis was able to nose about in the library. Things in general seemed to be looking up. But they had to move out as soon as the lawyer arrived. They withdrew to the guest house, but only for a brief interlude. For Klarskovgaard's social life was starting up, with its "celebrities" whom Mikkelsen took pride in frequenting.

"Louis was not a country man," Lucette explains, "and Korsör was the country. It wasn't the real sea, the kind Louis liked, Le Havre, Saint-Malo, the bustle of ships in port. Stretching out from Korsör was a gray sea, not at all salty, where you caught fish that had no taste. We didn't have the same way of looking at things, he and I. I rather liked the wild feel of that coast. I swam every day, I bathed in the sea. It was ice cold in the winter, that didn't bother me. It came quite naturally to me to live that way. But Louis couldn't adapt, never managed to adapt. He lived tragically through that stay, like a caged lion. And then there were the constant moves from one house to another, like servants you put up any way you could and evicted as soon as you needed to vacate the room they were occupying. You know, even for a prisoner who has almost no possessions, changing cells is a world of confusion. Louis had his bundles of paper on the table, his manuscripts-in-progress, he was surrounded by his cat, his animals, his habits. We had to stuff our belongings into boxes. It was really painful for him. And the hut (Fanehuset) was rudimentary. Not to mention the strange climate. The summer was over from one day to the next. Then it was wind, cold, and night. All you could do was look at the trees. Less than a kilometer from where we were, we could see dunes, and the trees that clung to them looked like dwarves that had been tortured. They clung to the earth because they wanted to live—but under what conditions! Luckily, there were birds everywhere, porcupines, and cats. I enjoyed watching them. . . . Mikkelsen? He loved to entertain. Ambassadors and English personalities especially. He would only just have arrived when he'd invite us for lunch. We weren't particularly keen on it. All those proprieties and that worldliness! Louis didn't want to make a show of himself, to play the fool in front of all those people as Mikkelsen hoped. So he withdrew into himself, scowled. He wouldn't say a word. He pretended not to speak English. And then we'd return to our hut. Later on, we gave up going to those lunches."

For Céline, his first personal visits, shortly after his arrival in Klarskovgaard, were those of the American publisher James Laughlin on May 25 and of the Danish writer and journalist Ole Vinding on June 12. Vinding was then living some fifteen kilometers from Mikkelsen's estate. He immediately felt a keen affection for Céline strengthened by great admiration. From that moment on, they developed the habit of seeing one another frequently. Above all, Vinding was very deft at observing, describing, and understanding him in depth, while at the same time looking for the most apparent symptoms of illness and delirium.

"What was he like? I knew him for almost three years, from June '48 to May '51. He was a very handsome man, although the first impression was somewhat that of a toothless old woman. He suddenly became handsome when his physical pains gave him a moment's respite. His face was truly noble, the features delicate, his eyes unforgettable in their expression, his mouth sensitive but, even when he was relaxed, marked by sarcastic creases in two thin lines at the corners.

"Generally, he was unable to be still. His face was distorted by strange grimaces, and when he spoke he sometimes had foam on his lips or started to drool. He sought his words and always came up with the most unexpected ones, the ones that had the greatest evocative impact or were most sure to be on target.

"I often had the impression that he never actually spoke to an interlocutor, that he was carried away on the tide of his own oratory, as if inspired, that he was actually writing, forgetting the presence of others, forgetting that his words could be heard and that his efforts to find them had become perceptible to others. . . .

"He traded the life that had been offered to him as a youth for the life that his mind ordered him to live. He did not sacrifice intelligence to imagination but subordinated it to the latter. He wasn't concerned with the cost of this to himself. It cost him everything. He died of his juggling."[19]

During that first summer in Klarskovgaard, the most fateful visit—and the most illuminating for our understanding of Céline—was that of Milton Hindus, from July 20 to August 11. The young American academic had finally resolved to make the trip to Europe to meet Céline, the anti-Semitic writer whom he admired and who inspired such troubled fascination in him. In his preface to his personal journal he wrote: "Céline is a splinter in my mind that I've got either to absorb completely or eject completely."[20]*

Before reaching Denmark, Hindus had first stayed in Paris, where he had

* [Here, as in all quotes from *The Crippled Giant*, the translation is Hindus'—trans.]

met with most of Céline's friends: Marcel Aymé, Gen Paul, etc. At Céline's request, he had even gone to see Guy Tosi, the literary director of Denoël, who had entrusted him with a letter for the writer. No sooner had he arrived in Korsör, where Céline had rented him a room above a nightclub, a real dump, the cheapest lodgings he could find, than the young academic (who would very quickly change hotels) was struck by the sadness, the melancholy, the debilitation of this man who seemed so sick and burdened with care. They saw each other almost daily during the American's stay. Sometimes Louis and Lucette would ride their bicycles into Korsör, sometimes Hindus, who had rented a bike, would visit them at Fanehuset. A Frenchwoman, Mme. Dupland, whom Lucette had known in Copenhagen (she had lived one floor below Karen at 20 Ved Stranden), was present at many conversations between Céline and Hindus. She must not have been overly generous toward her old neighbors. "I certainly got the dirt on Céline himself from Mme. D———."[21] She no doubt helped to strengthen the feeling of disenchantment and disappointment that Hindus very soon came to bear toward the author of *Voyage*.

From the outset, Hindus was shocked by Céline's vulgarity. He seemed to bear the former no particular gratitude for all Hindus had done for him. Nor did Céline hesitate to manifest in Hindus' presence his contempt for Mikkelsen. This shocked him. On Sunday, July 25, Hindus went to Klarskovgaard.

"I saw his cat for the first time—gray, large, old, well-fed. Céline talks to him in some subterranean language of purrs. In back of the house, down a long drop of cliff, is the sea. There were paintings on the walls, but when I asked where they had come from, Céline seemed uninterested and said they had been left 'by the bums who had been here before.'

"He is always depressed, and when he talks of his troubles his voice becomes like the whine of a hurt cur, extremely unpleasant in its self-pity."[22]

In his diary, Hindus would readily note all of Céline's little physical characteristics that seemed to disgust him: "He uses a lot of lubrication in talking. His mouth drools saliva at both ends."[23] But that, of course, is not the main thing. Above all, Céline seemed less pleasant, more surly, than in his letters. Hindus never managed to hold a real dialogue with him. His interviewee sometimes appeared to him to be mean, the way a child can be, i.e., gratuitously. Hindus wanted to photograph him. Céline obstinately refused, as if to deprive Hindus of the pleasure. The young academic wanted to broach the question of anti-Semitism. "As to the abuse he heaped upon the Jews ten years ago, he repeats a hundred times: 'I was stupid, stupid, wrong and stupid.' He says that he has been proved wrong 'by experiment.' I did not stop to find out what experiment—I can only guess with horror."[24] Hindus guessed right. Céline was apparently speaking about his own experiment and the consequences of anti-Semitism upon him—in a word, the purge—and not about the genocide of the Jews. As a general rule, Céline moaned continually and saw no real hope in the future. "He can't sleep. My own explanation of that, a mixture of migraine, worry for the future and conscience about the past."[25]

In short, relations between them soon degenerated. So much so that Hindus could note in his diary on July 27: "I see now that this man is across too great an abyss from me to be reached ever."[26] How could he have admired an author who seemed to scorn to such an extent those who helped him, and whose independence was merely a form of ingratitude? Or feel close to an intellectual whose ideas were, at the least, confused and peremptory, who cut short any awkward conversation, who reminded Milton Hindus of his youth (when he was his age he'd understand, Céline told him), who wrapped his racism in more or less dubious generalities and passed from anger to gentleness without the least transition or logic? "Céline and I cannot basically affect each other. We can only witness each other's shame," he noted on August 2.[27] That said it all. Hindus left Korsör on August 11. He would soon start work on the book he planned to devote to Céline, the fruit of his critical reflections and his visit with the writer.

It is hard to imagine what kind of a dialogue they might have entertained. For a start, Céline never held dialogues. He listened, he soliloquized, he shut himself into his illusions or absorbed the world's spectacle for himself alone, nothing more. Above all, he hated toying with general ideas. Milton Hindus was a typical academic, more cerebral than sensitive. He wanted to understand, to theorize. He wanted to hold an abstract conversation with the writer, on politics, the art of the novel, racism, contemporary culture, etc. Céline was thoroughly incapable of that, he loathed general ideas. Moreover, he endlessly repeated after the war: "I am not a man of messages, I am not a man of ideas, I am a man of style." We can clearly ascertain the implicit defensiveness behind such a statement, as if Céline meant to justify his anti-Semitic tirades, to claim a sort of irresponsibility in the face of history. The fact remains that he distorted his ideas, ground them down, mingled them with his hallucinations, wrenched dream into reality, and folded reality in turn to fit his visions, his grimacing, disturbing chimeras. Their correspondence had been misleading. Face-to-face with reality, the masks fell. Céline was alone. Hindus, too naive and too reasonable, hoped to hold a serene dialogue with him. That was impossible. He couldn't see that Céline was in pain, deluding himself, fooling himself with words, ideas, phantasms, tearing himself from reality and rationality. Hindus wanted to take him at his word. Impossible. The fascinating work that the American would write about Céline clearly illustrates the lack of comprehension between them. They didn't speak the same language.

At first, Céline wrote him that he was not interested in reading this work. He was mistrustful. He smelled betrayal. Was he wrong? This was in February 1949, while Milton Hindus was still writing his book. Hindus later found a publisher, and the publisher insisted on sending Céline a copy of the manuscript. After reading it, the author of *Voyage* wrote to its author: "Be happy, dear Hindus! Your book is as vicious as it is possible to be. It will do me the maximum harm. In the extremely critical conditions in which I find myself, your lies, defamatory comments, and abominable inventions are going to lead me to the worst fate, the worst possible reprisals . . . *I have not done you any harm and you are assassinating me!*"[28]

In consequence, Hindus wanted to abandon publication. But the publisher insisted. Céline continued to be so vitriolic, even slanderous, in regard to Milton Hindus, that the latter shed all his qualms. Céline threatened him with a lawsuit, and had his friends write him poison-pen letters. "I needed this final lesson in his almost paternal malevolence toward me to cut whatever ties still bound us together spiritually."[29] Céline even attempted to cost Hindus his teaching job by writing letters denouncing him to the president of the university. He went so far as to deny any meeting between Hindus and himself: "You came to see me here, and I could not receive you, I was too ill to receive anyone, I said nothing to you, and you have extracted from this so-called visit a little ignominy in the form of a libel in which you insult me . . . In addition to everything which is permitted, you attribute designs to me and thoughts which were never mine! You have me befoul a country and men to whom I owe my life. You have *invented* everything with an abominable wickedness. I cannot tolerate such a sadistic fantasy."[30]

It is clear what bothered Céline in Milton Hindus' book: his quoted statements on Mikkelsen, and the Danes, and anti-Semitism. But in denying everything, including the reality of their meetings, was Céline being cynical, was he deliberately lying? I do not believe so. Céline retained his enormous blindness, his way of averting, almost in good faith, any aspect of reality that bothered him. His amnesia remained as selective as his exaggerations. He swept obstacles and disappointments aside. Hindus had manifestly not understood his uniqueness as a creator: too bad for Hindus. Hindus, therefore, had never existed. Céline had barely caught a couple of glimpses of him. He was now convinced of that. Nothing existed beyond Klarskovgaard, Denmark, the narrow realm of his delusions and pain.

And he spent the summer of '48 in the cottage of Fanehuset where, since August 9, he had been corresponding with the Swedish doctor and writer Ernst Bendz, former vice-president of the Göteborg Alliance Française. Bendz never tired of praising him. With Raoul Nordling, the Swedish consul-general in Paris, he would later intercede in support of the writer, attempting to plead his cause before the French courts during the pretrial inquiry.

For that matter, to whom did Céline *not* write? During those endless years in Klarskovgaard, writing remained a way of maintaining his life under pressure, of keeping fit, of breaking out of his isolation. Not a day passed in which he didn't send at least two or three letters to Le Vigan or Paraz, Father Löchen or Daragnès, Jean Paulhan or Albert Naud, Dr. Camus or Marie Canavaggia—a total of nearly 4,000 irascible, violent, contradictory, nostalgic, tender, affectionate, despairing, envious, glowing, dark, lyrical, mischievous, generous letters in which he did not hesitate to criticize his friends, colleagues, family, and rivals, to complain furiously, to envy others, all others, in his concern for himself alone, and then to suddenly give proof of a tender and affectionate compassion for his addressee. He gave Paraz medical care from afar and fretted over manifestations of his tuberculosis. In short, letters that ressembled desultory conversations, free, casual, rambling and intimate, in which Céline lowered his guard, not writing for posterity, to present himself in the best light, but abandoning himself to the contradictory freedom of his passing emotions and rebellions, his pettiness and breadth of spirit.

In the summer of 1948 a new companion took her mute and significant place at his side: the bitch Bessy, whom he spent some time training, whom Bébert at first approached only with the greatest circumspection, and whom Lucette recalls with the most intense emotion. "In the farmhouse where the Petersens lived there was a sort of big, square, metal cage and in it a dog, a very handsome German shepherd, very thin, who looked like a wild, starving wolf. No sooner would you approach than it bared its fangs. A savage dog. So we asked them what the dog was doing there. The Petersens told us that the Germans, in leaving, had left puppies. They had killed them, had kept only one, supposedly to kill rabbits, wild rabbits that proliferated on the estate and devoured the crops. Once a week they freed the dog, which they almost never fed, they let it out like a wild beast, it had to feed itself on rabbits. The bitch would return with bloody paws. They locked her back up until the next time. When we saw the misery of that dog that never had anything to eat, we wanted to adopt her. Louis gave a little money to the farmers. Bessy was really a wild animal. She was afraid of us, of everything. It took us some time to tame her. It took a lot of gentleness, care, patience. At first we tied her up with a rope, we were afraid she'd eat Bébert and another cat that had recently adopted us. Louis worked at his table in the little cottage, with a rope around his waist and Bessy at the other end. I can still see them . . . as soon as she noticed Bébert, wham, she'd go after him. And Bébert wanted to get near Louis and the table. It was awful. I often saw Louis go sprawling with the dog pulling with all her might. She eventually mellowed. She lost her fear of being beaten. She had never known affection. She developed an attachment for everyone. Bébert slept in the hollow of her tummy. He ate from the same bowl, porridge with a little milk that we bought in Korsör. The dog, the cats, us—we all ate the same thing."

In late summer there came to Klarskovgaard a young admirer of Céline's, Pierre Monnier, who worked as a cartoonist for the weekly *Aux écoutes* and had found himself in Denmark by chance that summer, pitchforked into the job of press agent for a folk group from the Auvergne named "La Bourrée," starting off on a three-week tour. It was an opportunity to meet Céline. He didn't hesitate. A taxi ride, and he landed one fine day in front of the cottage of Fanehuset for a first meeting that was to last almost three hours. For Monnier, it was a sort of love at first sight for this immense writer with bright blue-gray eyes, grave voice and, often, companionable fits of laughter. "Back in Paris, I wrote him with a resolve to bring him more than just words of encouragement. . . . I don't quite know what I'm going to do, but my desire to help him is clear and sharp. It must materialize."[31] It would indeed.

On September 3, 1948, according to Mikkelsen's notebooks, we know that the Destouches left Fanehuset for the somewhat more spacious but no more comfortable house of Skovly. This was to become a yearly practice, spending the winter in Skovly and emigrating to Fanehuset in the spring with the arrival of the good weather and the guests in Mikkelsen's other residences.

The first winter in the house was gloomy, cold, damp, scantily heated by the nasty peat stove. Louis was suffering more than ever from dizziness and migraines. He was sick of eating porridge, potatoes, and smoked herring meal after meal. The Petersens sometimes gave them milk and fruit, rather stingily. In late November, Louis reported for a police interrogation in Copenhagen—inconsequentially. Other visits came to ease his boredom—those of Raoul Nordling in January and March 1949, for instance. In February he returned to Copenhagen for two or three days. It was a chance to idle along the streets, do a little shopping, see a movie with Lucette, request a passport at the French consulate, which was of course denied. They stayed in Mikkelsen's little office for the occasion. Mikkelsen, whom Louis and Lucette had spent the whole summer curing of some awkwardly located boils, was preparing to leave for France (perhaps taking with him the remainder of Céline's gold coins, so as to be able to exchange them). Otherwise, it was routine, correspondence to expedite, the manuscript of *Féerie*, which he endlessly, restlessly revised and completed, and which would eventually be divided into the volumes *Féerie pour une autre fois* and *Normance.*

In March 1949 Céline responded to a questionnaire by Paul Guth for *Le Crapouillot*, on the theme "What do our contemporaries dream of?" Soon thereafter, he was visited by a journalist from *France-Dimanche.* Nothing notable in his statements this time. Lucette's mother and stepfather were planning to visit them. On March 3, 1949, Céline wrote them: "The months go by somehow or other. Neither very reinvigorating nor too gloomy. However, our stay here is becoming more and more precarious . . . a certain weariness on the part of our hosts and a *complete lack of water.* We now have to bring the ten-gallon drum by *wheelbarrow* to the pump. Over at the farmers' . . . we also have to go *fourteen kilometers* on foot to mail our letters etc. And all this with an *enormous* smile and *mandatory* chortles of delight. There's nothing to say. My place is in jail. Consequently . . . That's what the Mik and the farmer think too. It's the melody the motif of this whole opera!"[32]

Another letter on March 15 to his father-in-law Ercole Pirazzoli:

My dear Ercole,

"*A surprise! or rather a dirty little trick.* Not very surprising*! We were packed off to the seaside shack on MAY 15. The drilling has brought* water*! it's running!* whence the invitations*! whence we've been expelled! packed off! We'll be staying in this filthy hovel from* May 15 to September 1st*! Of course impossible for you to stay here! Another shack* without water*! and without toilet!* What misery*! But we have to take it or leave it! So you'll have to come in early September when the temperature is still* bearable!*[33]*

In fact, the Pirazzolis had a comfortable stay in Korsör in the spring of that year, in Mikkelsen's own house, but they did not stay long, finding life there to be too gloomy and boring.

Over the summer, Céline was visited by two more reporters, Jean and Marianne Kohler. The former described their meeting in *Carrefour* on September 15, the latter in *Paroles françaises* on December 30, 1949. Each time, Céline was very cautious. Saying nothing against Denmark. Complaining *mezzovoce*. Expressing himself in general concepts. Exuding his nostalgia for France, aspiring to return anywhere, North Africa or New Caledonia, so long as the French flag flew there.

Henri Mahé came to see him in July. It was a happy meeting between the two men, who had nonetheless grown apart, whose closeness related only to the carefree and Bohemian years before the war—a closeness that was unable to renew itself, to take on greater weight in the face of tragedy, the war, reversals of fortune.

Lucien Descaves died on December 7. It was another door closing for Céline, another curtain drawn across his past, an extra mourning, a new ghost to escort him henceforth through a life that resembled one long funeral march.

1948, 1949, 1950 . . .

The days, months, and years dragged on for him, while in France, Justice proved itself patiently and formidably slow. At Mikkelsen's, Céline occasionally ran into Helga Pedersen, who was secretary to the Minister of Justice at the time, and also Ottoström, an old prewar connection, one of Karen's gang, who had become a pharmacist in Korsör. Nor did Céline fail to greet at each of his visits the Copenhagen police chief, Aage Seidenfaden, whose benevolence had been so helpful to him. Beginning in March 1950, he habitually corresponded with Louis Lecoin, the old anarchist and conscientious objector who understood Céline's pacifism very well and undertook his defense out of his own pocket—because of his opinions, Lecoin himself had been continually driven from trial to trial, prison to prison.

My dear Lecoin,

. . . You are a saint in the mold of St. Francis . . . St. Vincent de Paul especially. Quite seriously. Absolutely. I am pretty mystical myself. I understand

you entirely. You construct your life and legend by living off humanitarianism and prison. Your Faith has cost you terribly. I admire you, I love you. Nothing is free, nothing is a cheat.[34]

André Pulicani, an old friend from Montmartre, came to visit Céline in March 1950. "I remember that poor shack outside Korsör where I had the joy of seeing you both again and the sorrow of finding you in terrible destitution."[35]

Two months later, the Destouches had to go to Copenhagen. Lucette had a fibroma. She required an emergency operation.

"When we were arrested in December 1945, I still had my periods. They suddenly stopped, forever. I was suffering hemorrhages every other minute. I was exhausted. A fibroma had formed and was growing on one of my ovaries. And then one day Louis noticed the state I was in. I couldn't get up. We rushed to Copenhagen, where I was operated on that very day. Otherwise, I might have died from one last hemorrhage. Louis stayed in a closet in Mikkelsen's apartment, where the files were stored. No one had asked his opinion about the operation. At first they wouldn't let him come in. He roamed around under the hospital windows. The operation was horrible. I spoke very bad English, I couldn't make myself understood, I was too weak. After the operation, my temperature started to rise and rise. Louis was finally allowed to see me in my room. The wound had become infected. I had a sort of hole in my belly. The doctor had told me at first: 'You have to get up, you have to move around a little!' I didn't have much energy. So they got me up, to avoid any risk of an embolism. I dragged myself to the end of the hall, and the wound abruptly reopened, an evisceration! I collapsed on the floor. They found me there, then brought me back to the operating room and sewed me up again. There was no penicillin at that time. With the infection, it was a dreadful sight. They didn't even knock me out. They sewed me up awake, without anesthesia, nothing. They told me that anesthetic would have no effect since there was too much pus. . . . Afterward, they chucked me under a sheet, on a cart, and I stayed there for hours, without observation, without tranquillizers, under a sheet as if I were dead! Finally, they brought me back to my bed that night. I split open on three separate occasions. How did I survive? 'If she lives, she lives, if she doesn't, she doesn't,' the doctors said very philosophically. They seemed to be thinking that many others had suffered before me, with the war and all. . . .

"I can still see the nurse who took care of me, redoing my bandages while she ate a sandwich over my belly. The wound was open. I had visions of the bread falling into my stomach! It was almost comical. It was less a case of nurses than of chambermaids who did that job. When I returned to Korsör I still had an open wound, not at all sewn up. The doctors hadn't dared close it again. They were afraid it would all start up again. They prescribed me a pomade, cod liver oil, etc. And Louis was the one who healed me. It was months before I could walk again. They must have cut the stomach muscles.

I couldn't do my gymnastics and dancing exercises until much later, at first on my back, trying to rebuild my muscles. I couldn't stand up."

Louis and Lucette did not return to Klarskovgaard from the hospital until July 15, 1950. Jean-Gabriel Daragnès died suddenly on the 25th. Another funeral, another sorrow that Céline could attend only from afar, in his Danish exile. "Certain sorrows may at least help us to stop regretting, I mean, to go quietly along our way, content."[36]

How distant the world seemed to him—politics, current events, involvements of any kind. Certainly, Céline read the newspapers, kept in touch, as they say. He knew all about the cold war between Russia and America, which was growing colder by the day. In June, the Korean War erupted. France was bogging down in Indochina against the Viet Minh. With his *Le Hussard bleu*, Roger Nimier tried to guide French literature toward nonchalance, elegance, swiftness. It was no doubt a literature of the Right, but above all a reaction against the gravity of politics, the spirit of revenge, Sartre's *Les Temps modernes*. . . . This book was important to Céline. Nimier had sent him a copy. Céline wrote back on October 15, 1950: "Ah, *monsieur*, you have pleased me mightily in sending me your hussar. I start laughing at the first page and by the 20th I can't stop! Here's a novel the way I like them—direct yet wise, oh! subtle, clever, wily . . . sensitive—oh! la la, I'm splitting myself. Ah! you know, it's difficult where I am, at the point I've reached!"[37] A keen friendship would develop between the two writers from that moment.

Marcel Aymé in turn, the most loyal of them all, the taciturn friend, made his pilgrimage to Klarskovgaard from March 8 to 11, 1951. The two men probably had little to say to one another. Aymé probably kept silent while Céline lost his breath in monologues. An old habit between them, that is how they understood and valued each other; they were happy to see one another—that was the main thing. Not words and confidences but a mysterious and profound empathy bound the two writers, well versed in silence.

Spring 1951. Céline's stay in Klarskovgaard was coming to an end. He would soon benefit from an amnesty law. With Lucette still slowly recovering, the aging Bébert, Bessy the dog, and the new cats Thomine, Flûte, and Poupine, they take wing for France. No more porridge, potatoes, and smoked herring, the sometimes strained relations with the Petersens, the dubious comforts of Mikkelsen's lodgings where, from November 1949 onward, the amenities at Skovly were at least improved by a new well that brought running water. Céline would be returning to France and his own people.

He had written his daughter, Colette, myriad affectionate letters from Denmark. On June 28, 1950, she had brought a fifth child into the world. These repeated pregnancies dismayed Céline, who held his son-in-law for a perfect idiot. In December, Colette had to undergo surgery for a fibroma. As François Gibault has written, "On that occasion Céline was extremely anxious. He asked Dr. Camus to attend the operation and to send him the surgical report. He phoned Paris frequently for news of his daughter, and suffered for his helplessness and for being unable to be with her. He also solicited help once again from the Marteau family, who stood by Colette and paid the cost of her surgery."[38]

We find other hints of this anxiety in Céline's correspondence, particularly in the letters he wrote at this time to Ernst Bendz. "I have been dazed by some bad news, my daughter (5 children) has had surgery in Paris."[39] We should note, incidentally, that Paul Marteau had been put in touch with Céline in 1948 by Daragnès. The industrialist, owner of the Grimaud playing-card company, was extremely wealthy. He wanted to help Céline any way he could. There was obviously no question of giving him charity. In May 1947 he offered a very inflated price for the manuscript pages, in pencil, of the first version of *Féerie* written in the Vestre Faengsel prison. From then on, Paul Marteau and Céline corresponded continuously. Céline did not hesitate to ask him little favors, for instance to deliver on his behalf a box of candies to his daughter. Sadly, this in no way helped to allay the mistrust, hostility, and bitterness that Colette bore for her father, feelings that her husband probably inflamed.

Nor could anything attenuate the resentment, the thinly masked hostility, which Gen Paul had borne Céline since the liberation. As if he could not forgive Céline for having compromised him, for having dragged him to Berlin in March 1942, for having had him invited to the German embassy, for having closely associated him by asking that he illustrate his works. Gen Paul had scurried off to America at the end of the war. Caution, caution . . . He had complained to anyone who would listen that it was all Céline's fault, that he himself had no opinions, that because of Céline he couldn't sell his paintings, and so on. Céline, who had so much affection for him, did not take umbrage at first, even if he was hurt deep down by being ditched by a man who had been the best friend of his final years in Paris. In November 1950 Gen Paul's new lover, Gaby, visited the Destouches in Klarskovgaard. Why? Gen Paul never wanted to see Céline again, and Céline ended up judging the painter harshly, as this undated letter from Céline to Le Vigan shows: "It seems that he [Gen Paul] is afraid of old age and croaking! The fine life—right down the drain. He only does gouaches now. He doesn't have the stomach for canvas anymore—but it all *sells*—he's rich, not a penny in overhead. 800 francs a year in rent! Rich means *awful*. Léon Bloy's passage is definitive . . . The rich man is a relentless beast who can only be stopped with a scythe or a bellyful of lead."[40]

There is nothing fortuitous about this reference to Bloy. Céline discovered his work in Korsör. Bloy, a vociferous and intolerant Catholic, a loather of the lukewarm, a man persecuted both in reality and in his imagination, a voluntary exile on the Baltic shores who professed for Protestants in general and the Danes in particular a hatred as ferocious as his contempt, reflected a barely distorted image of Céline himself. Both were great stylists, pamphleteers, men of extremes, of passion, of love too often disappointed and violence never contained. To evoke Céline one final time in his desolate stay at Klarskovgaard before his return to France is to see rising behind him the spirit of that other French writer, Bloy, the author of *Le Désespéré*, who was likewise encamped at "the threshold of the Apocalypse."

New Readers, New Publishers?

Céline did not suffer only from being far from his homeland in Denmark. He also ceaselessly deplored the silence that reigned over his work. In the final analysis, that is what he was least able to forgive Jean Voilier and Éditions Denoël: not having reprinted his old books after the liberation, *Voyage au bout de la nuit* and *Mort à crédit* in particular, and having thus contributed to his solitude, his isolation as a writer. He positively did not want to hear anything about the prevailing climate in France after the war, public disaffection with his work, new tastes and new distastes, too, inspired by the latest revelations about Nazi atrocities or the whims of literary fashion. He held politicians, judges, journalists, and his fellow writers solely responsible for the atmosphere that victimized him. It was they and they alone who, through spite and vengefulness, cut him off from his readers, the buyers of his works.

In that regard, his *bête noire* was irrefutably François Mauriac, who nonetheless had been one of the few great French writers of the Resistance to deplore certain excesses of the purge, to appeal for mercy for Robert Brasillach, to have publicly raised the question of amnesty as far back as early '46. From Klarskovgaard, Céline wrote him several jeering, insulting, and gratuitous letters more or less inspired by articles of Mauriac's he had read in *Le Figaro*.

"Oh Scoundrel, that indeed you are! Scoundrel by hypocrisy, black masses, or sheer idiocy, no one knows! Resistance of what? to what, damned imbecile? You brought the Russians to Vienna, would they'd gone as far as Dax! Come may god spew you out for being so dumb, with or without passage of the Evil One."[41]

Or: "Ah Mauriac ever the false spirit! the false judgment! the false taste! (which leads to crime!)."[42]

Or again: "Ah Mauriac / they say you are a novelist, thus a little imaginative all the same / So you may be able to imagine . . . the effect on me of your article *Rossinante*! / The dumb jerk, took him 15 years and what a disaster! . . . ah please stop Mauriac! stop vaticinating, stop mellifluating! . . . You're bringing down thunderbolts! floods!"[43]

That he, Céline, should be forgotten, ignored, he was yet again unable to imagine. Certainly, the intelligentsia pressed on against him. To defend Céline in the press was still an act of the maddest audacity. The least of the conspiracies against him remained that of silence. The fact remains that his readers had grown older, died, or were no longer inclined to follow him; and that the younger generation was slow to recognize him. For every Roger Nimier, who had been writing him since 1949, for every Jean-Louis Bory, one of the first Goncourt winners after the war who, passing through Copenhagen, had tried in vain to meet with him, how many were indifferent, adversaries, or amnesiacs for whom the author of *Voyage* now represented merely a disturbing specimen of a populist pre-war literature that had foundered into racism and barbarity?

But what could be done to help Céline? Reawaken the controversy, stubbornly defend the writer, put an end to the sheepish or guilty silences, recall the circumstances of his exile, the value of his work beyond all political reference? Or, on the contrary, adopt a low profile, avoid controversy, allow the wounds to heal, move ahead cautiously, rushing nothing, unbalancing nothing, provoking nothing through clumsiness, neither the hoped-for sangfroid of Justice nor the hostility of the majority of the press? Albert Paraz was a partisan of the former solution, Jean Paulhan of the latter. Paraz was a born agitator, energetically and muddleheadedly open-handed toward Céline. Paulhan was infinitely mistrustful and clear-sighted. Céline wavered between the two stances. His lawyers, as well as numerous friends, told him to be wary. New admirers like the painter Jean Dubuffet or Pierre Monnier urged him to fight.

The publication of *Gala des vaches* in November 1948, which included Céline's letters and his response to Sartre, "*À l'Agité du bocal*," reawakened every controversy. Those close to Céline, such as Dr. Camus, were indignant. Mikkelsen felt that the book could only harm his client. Céline, himself perplexed, didn't know quite what to think. He wrote to Paraz on December 6:

"Oh you know I think we now have to stop the music of publishing letters. Nothing *should ever be repeated.* The last time it was an accident, innocent on my part it was fine. Now it would be whorishness—a trick—Commerce. . . . I'd be glad to *republish*, earn my living that's all. A worker's requirements *but republish in Belgium or Switzerland.* Forget about France. And I don't see anything concrete on the horizon. . . . A publisher must be first of all a very wealthy *banker.* Authors, a mob. . . .

"Oh fuck the Galas! Let 'em sell them in the grocery stores! I can't give them away *here.* Everything is understood ass-backwards. *Don't send anything*! . . . Now we've got Dr. Camus, Daragnès, Mikkelsen outraged—, and Marie for sure!

"The whole world's riled at us! Nothing left to do. Everything we do is taken the wrong way. On our deathbeds they'll say we rattle wrong.

"But even so I'll be bad so long as they go on stealing my work. It's in the Gospels—by the sweat of one's brow. I've sweated my whole life. Heaven's on my side! They'll see!"[44]

Thus, for him, it all depended on a foreign publisher in expectation of better days to come. It was the only solution to avoid having his property confiscated by the French authorities. He had no new manuscript to offer.

Féerie was far from finished. All he had in his files was a ballet or two—trifles. But he wouldn't let this ideal publisher know that. On the contrary, he'd try to tempt him with his new novel, on the condition that he first reprint his old books. A letter to Daragnès in 1948 neatly sums up that position:

"This can't go on. And on top of it I'll probably soon be sentenced according to custom to having all my *current and future revenue* seized, as the wording goes. So publishing in France becomes an absurdity. But I'm not releasing *Féerie* to any publisher before he's brought out *Voyage, Mort à crédit* and *Guignols.*

"These gentlemen are all as greedy for novelty as whorehouse johns! Let them first screw my old Carmens! who still screw perfectly well. As to Voilier, she can go fuck herself and leave me the hell alone!"[45]

Pierre Monnier, as he had promised, began fighting at that time, knocking on doors, canvassing publishers, initiating a process of republication difficulties of whose he was not initially aware. Could he at least count on the support of some of the press? Monnier worked as a cartoonist on the weekly *Aux écoutes.* He requested an interview with his manager, Paul Lévy, and spoke with him at length about Céline . . .

"Finally, when I was done, he sat in silence for a moment . . . I can still see him, quite small in his enormous chair . . . He leaned back . . . 'Poor, great Céline . . . How can this man be so reviled and what is he accused of? . . . Why can't they understand that Céline is a great poet and that he has the right to say anything? . . .'

"It's true. The first man of any consequence whom I approached who showed true breadth of vision and sincere understanding was Paul Lévy, owner of *Aux écoutes* . . . 'Sure, make waves, write about Céline, his exile and his misfortune . . . and also . . .' He stopped, thought a moment, and almost timidly . . . 'Could you tell him that I am able to send him 100,000 francs on the spot . . . that he should accept . . . it's from the heart . . .'

"Ferdinand did not accept the 100,000 francs. Paul Lévy repeated the offer several times . . . Once, even, through J.-P. Dorian, who had a column on Paris in *Aux écoutes* at the time. But as hardened, as bitter as he was, Ferdinand told me on several occasions how touched he had been by that token of friendship from Paul Lévy, who sided with him right up to the last trial, impervious and indifferent to the insults heaped upon him."[46]

The main battle, however, was to be played out on the field of publishing. At Flammarion, Monnier was politely shown the door by Ukermann, who promised to give it some thought. At Plon, Charles Orengo was even more suspicious. It was a pleasure he preferred to defer to another time. And later, there was decidedly nothing doing, no question of either of them publishing Céline. Monnier then thought of Charles Frémanger, whose small publishing house, Jean Froissart, was preparing to put out Cécil Saint-Laurent's *Caroline Chérie.* In the publisher's offices on the Champs-Élyssés, other than Jacques Laurent (Cécil Saint-Laurent), one might run into André

Fraigneau or Antoine Blondin, who would soon publish *L'Europe Buissonière* there. Frémanger very quickly agreed to reprint *Voyage*. He had no objection to the 18% royalties demanded by Céline, but only after the sale of the first edition of 2,500 copies, from which the author would receive only 8%. The book could be brought out in Belgium, from the fictitious Éditions Froissart address in Brussels.

Céline acceded grudgingly to these conditions. And to Monnier he specified:

"Like any Breton I'm honest to a fault, and I point out the snag to your publisher friend right away.

"The girl . . . , the ultracontested inheritor, an utterly unscrupulous swindler, general director of Éditions Denoël (no one knows how or why!) is a bitch whose only thought is for lawsuits! I'm not getting a penny in royalties from my contract with Denoël. Besides, I have properly and duly informed her of that breach by registered letter. . . .

"If my old novels are published and I receive my royalties, I give the option for *Féerie*; if you like I can give a provisional option today under those conditions, and we're off!

"If all this sounds good to your friend, no doubt the best thing would be for him to come see me in Korsör to work out the details."[47]

Charles Frémanger did indeed visit Céline in early January 1949, while a small publisher, Charles de Jonquières, had just brought out, in late December 1948, the ballet *Foudres et Flèches*, an eighty-eight-page work in a run of 1,000 under the imprint "Actes des Apôtres." Daragnès had served as intermediary between Céline and de Jonquières. This edition would not earn Céline a penny and its publisher barely more.

Despite Frémanger's visit, Monnier remained Céline's preferred spokesman between them. It was to him alone that he wrote tirelessly, smothering him with advice, fretting over a thousand and one details, worrying about the publisher's subterfuges: "I don't understand a thing about Frémanger's dealings. He doesn't write me at all anymore, he doesn't keep me up-to-date on anything. It used to be daily mail, it was night by the time you got through it all . . . I absolutely insist that Marie Canavaggia correct the proofs, she alone, I insist on a definitive correction of the texts. I hate blunderers, and she alone can correct these texts. She also has to get 20,000 francs, that was agreed."[48]

In truth, Frémanger had no bankroll at his disposal and was in no hurry to reprint Céline, much less to pay anyone. It took the writer some time to realize this. He continued to dictate his terms with an impatience and confidence as blind as they were pathetic. He asked for the address of Éditions Froissart in Belgium. He demanded a simple, classic cover without ornament or flashy design. Demanded luxury editions on fine paper to be sent on his behalf to Antonio Zuloaga, Jacques Deval, Georges Geoffroy, and Jean-Gabriel Daragnès. Suggested that Paraz not be kept too well informed:

"Paraz is a tremendous gossip, take every precaution." (He had in mind the controversy raised by *Le Gala des vâches*).

Months went by like this, with no publication in sight. Céline, worn down by despair and dreaming of a change of identity, threatened to cut the whole thing short: "I'd like to be someone else, I'd like to end up like Turner, completely anonymous, in some backstreet neighborhood of a city far from everything. So that no one even knows I exist anymore. But one has to eat and even herring is expensive."[49]

This despair might have been attenuated in April 1949 by Henry Muller's questionnaire, under the pen name *"Le Magot Solitaire"*—The Solitary Grotesque—in *Carrefour*. The literary columnist had requested his readers to name twelve French writers who would be classics in the year 2000. He himself had instantly cited Céline, "the most powerful satirist of our society." For the forgotten, proscribed author in Denmark, the citation was unhoped-for. The results of the questionnaire in May eventually ranked him seventh, between Mauriac and Sartre (a status that could hardly have delighted him). But Céline was unable to appreciate the homage. His letter to the "Magot Solitaire" attests to that:

"Critical judgment is always idiotic, that of the public worse yet. Incompetent, bungling, pontificating, blind, deaf, snobbish or reactionary, never true, never right, always backwards and off the mark.

"One must be able to judge things in themselves, the book, the book's tone, the freshness of spirit, the achievement itself, the rhythm.

"For that one must be an expert. To hell with these millions of muddleheaded, impotent, ignoble blatherers!

"Death alone can clear the stage! The whole public, critical, literary congestion. Then one sees clearly! The housework is done!

"What will they be reading in the year 2000? Not much more than Barbusse, Paul Morand, Ramuz, and myself, it seems to me.

"Vanity? Oh Lord, no! I could care less! I've been worn out enough by all the hatred and controversy while I'm alive! Only I know the product. What the hell! Thus will survive Morand Barbusse, Ramuz and myself! Books can be squeezed like lemons; once all the juice has been sucked out, it's all over! Still enough juice to last 50 years! What a mess."[50]

Céline, ranked seventh in the year 2000? What did he care? There was a much more urgent question to be answered: how to live by his pen, right away. How to afford smoked herring. Frémanger wasn't the man to make him rich. *Voyage au bout de la nuit* finally came out in June 1949, in a printing of 10,000 copies (though only the first 5,000 would be sold, the remaining 5,000 being remaindered to Chaix, it would seem, the following December), with an unpublished preface perfectly suited to the occasion:

"A lot has happened in fourteen years . . .

"I tell you right now, if I wasn't under so much pressure, forced to earn a living, I'd suppress the lot. I wouldn't let one line get through.

"Everything I do is taken the wrong way. I've inspired too much evil-mindedness.

"Looking around at the number of dead, of hatreds around me . . . such treachery . . . the kind of cesspool it all leads to . . . those monsters."

The preface also contains a statement that is mysterious if one cares to read more into it than a simple plea: "Of all my books, the only truly nasty one is 'Voyage' . . . That's right . . . The core of my sensibility."[51]

It was as though Céline were speaking here of a work without hope, its emotions desolate; a work of appalling clear-sightedness in respect to all ideologies, all lies, all vain solutions.

With an essentially nonexistent distribution and a publisher preparing for his summer holidays, it was a swordstroke through water. Not one copy was sent to Céline in Denmark, not one centime paid to anyone, neither to Daragnès, nor to Marie Canavaggia, nor to Monnier, to whom the exasperated author of *Voyage* wrote on August 17, 1949: "Frémanger is more than just a slacker, he's a liar, and that's more serious." Then, on August 20: "Our slacker has turned out to be a ruffian as well. These delays of payment stink of fraud." Or again, on September 7: "I completely agree about Frémanger. That little crackpot is turning into an intolerable shit."[52]

In September, Jean Voilier and Éditions Denoël sued "Jean Froissart" and Céline for copyright infringement. They were unable to accept these "strong-arm" tactics—the release of a pirated edition of *Voyage*, which they deemed an unjustified, unilateral breach of the contract binding them. But their response to the strong-arming was mostly bluff. The house of Denoël was not going to risk a lawsuit they might lose. Voilier eventually withdrew her action and a nonsuit was declared on January 29, 1951.

On September 19, 1949, Céline sent Charles Frémanger a registered letter demanding his royalty statement. "There was an oral agreement between us. You have broken its terms 20 times over . . . *Enough is enough.* I forbid you as of today to print, publish, or sell *Voyage* or any other of my books—in France or abroad." On November 17 he wrote in equally vigorous terms to Charles de Jonquières, who had not paid him a penny in royalties on *Foudres et Flèches.* He was decidedly unhappy with the small publishers to whom he had bound himself. They were not quite swindlers, but rather penniless amateurs who walked a thin line in a publishing market that in any case was not open to the writer.

Monnier then decided to take things directly into his own hands, for lack of better to set himself up as an ad hoc publisher. To him, the important thing was to ensure by any means available Céline's continued presence in the bookstores after five years' absence: "And I get an idea. I'm going to sound out a young publishing house which, unlike almost all the rest, seems to be growing fairly smoothly. It seems that a big bank is backing them. Amiot-Dumont. Céline's name makes them prick up their ears. Why not? But there are risks. Involving a budding business in a legal imbroglio may not be too smart. That's when this idea occurs to me. I create a company . . .

without a penny. I offer to publish Céline under my guarantee, under my name. We'll be 50-50 partners. I bring Céline, Amiot-Dumont brings its credit with the printers. Then we'll be distributed by Chaix, their sole distributor. They'll make their own financial arrangements with Céline."[53]

Thus was born the Frédéric Chambriand publishing house which, in December 1949, launched *Casse-Pipe*, the unfinished manuscript, virtually reduced to its first chapter, that Céline had interrupted before the war to throw himself into the feverish composition of his political tracts. Numerous fragments of this manuscript, left in the apartment on the rue Girardon in Montmartre, had been lost, dispersed, plundered, scattered to the four winds of the liberation.

"It should be told everywhere that if 'Casse-Pipe' is incomplete, it is because the purgers chucked the whole middle section and the end, 600 pages of manuscript, into the garbage cans of the avenue Junot, along with the second and third chapters of 'Guignols' and the manuscript of an entire novel, 'La Volonté du roi Krogold.' That would make a pretty piece of news—and it's true."[54]

Of *Casse-Pipe*, all that remained was the arrival of the hero, a volunteer, at the cuirassier barracks and his plunge into a nocturnal, frightening, fantasmagorical universe, like distant, hallucinated memories of Rambouillet, a dramatic link between the end of *Mort à crédit* and the beginning of *Voyage*.

For Monnier, all this could be only provisional. He had no plans to remain Céline's publisher, for which he had neither the money nor the professional competence. The author was still demanding the reprinting of his novels, 5 million in cash and 18% royalties on each of his titles. That was the goal. Monnier could see only one ideal solution in the long run: to promote Céline's signing with Gallimard (distributed by Hachette), whose literary prestige was incontrovertible.

For the moment there was no budget to devote to the publicity campaigns for republishing Céline's work. He had to do without. He did not take undue exception. "You talk of publicity, of costs? what for? Not one cent on publicity. Denoël never spent a red penny for any of my books; viciousness is what makes publicity, and it is ever watchful."[55]

Nonetheless, Monnier/Chambriand sold *Casse-Pipe* at an almost respectable rate, considering the mediocre distribution, the resolute silence of the press, and the hostility weighing against the writer. Five thousand copies gone in three months, 3,000 returned then sold over the course of the year. Which naturally seemed paltry to Céline, so out of touch with the economic realities of the publishing market. For him, it was much easier to believe that he was being systematically cheated on the numbers. His authorial *amour propre* and his eternal paranoia were well served thereby. Feelings of gratitude or thankfulness were not his strength. Milton Hindus had been shocked by it, but Céline's friends were not offended. Thorvald Mikkelsen had one day confided to Helga Pedersen, concerning Céline: "He was in a dark rage today and lashed out at me unbelievably. . . . That I was a crook and a bastard! (a pause). But he looked so heartened when he left me!" Too much suffering and disappointment, too many fears and troubles, had long contributed to stirring up his anxieties, resentments, and fits of anger.

In December 1949 Pierre Monnier made a return trip to Klarskovgaard for four days of heated professional discussion, but also of rambling gossip, tirades, sarcasms, and memories, a blend of the pathetic and the burlesque. Monnier saw Lucette bathing in the Baltic. He heard Louis speak of the French language to which he felt inextricably bound ("I'd suffer anything for it . . . It's my breath . . . my life's blood"[56]). He watched Bébert the boss policing the dissolute ranks of newly adopted kittens.

After *Casse-Pipe*, the indefatigable Monnier would follow up by reissuing *Mort à crédit* in April and *Scandale aux abysses* (which Denoël had had typeset just before the allied landings but had not had time to issue) in November 1950. A printing of 5,000 copies, with a sober gray cover and a yellow wrapper with the words "The right time" for *Mort à crédit*, and a more fantastic presentation for the ballet, a cover with sketches, illustrations inside—a numbered edition of 3,300 copies. Céline was delighted with it. "My very warm congratulations for 'Scandale,' just received, very good, very witty! (I mean your drawings!) The boat at the end, especially, is wonderful! It's all alive, brilliantly funny! Done like musical comedy, which is exactly what I wanted, perfect!"[57]

In the meanwhile, Paraz's *Valsez, saucisses* [Waltz, Fools] had come out in June 1950, the second volume of his journal containing further letters by Céline, which had been meticulously proofread by the party concerned. No more names or compromising indiscretions, nothing this time that might antagonize his friends or Céline, who had taken care to warn Paraz beforehand: "My dear Fellow— Be careful in your next *Gala* not to yield to the temptation to supply NAMES to land me with any costly mistakes, which I can do without— Stick to *ideeas*! Harmless gewgaws—nonsense—have me mouthing off as much as you like. But about nothing that might harm my case—or earn me new enemies or friends (which comes to the same thing)."[58]

Monnier had advised Paraz to have himself published by Amiot-Dumont. But was the title *Valsez, saucisses* particularly timely? The book's sales were disastrous: it didn't waltz too far.

Nor did Chambriand's edition of *Mort à crédit* sell at all well. The press said not a word, or else just a few insulting paragraphs. Céline fumed. Where was his money, his royalty statements? Poor Monnier, who was exerting himself to the best of his abilities, was sorely beset. His interlocutor complained about everything, about the considerable costs involved in the preparation of *Féerie*, about another Christmas supper (December 1950) again spent eating porridge and smoked herring in a freezing hut, about Lucette's illness, about old age, about the hundreds of thousands of francs that Monnier undoubtedly owed him.

Monnier, at his wits' end, was about ready to chuck the whole thing in. "And then I waited. Predictably, things calmed down very quickly, and I went to Korsör from January 6 to 10, where Lucette welcomed me apologetically. 'You mustn't hold it against Louis. He's so sick . . .' I stopped her short. It all seemed so trivial to me. It was forgotten, erased. It was at that time that I learned one could accord only relative importance to the outrages, imprecations, and insults that Ferdinand had always heaped on his most loyal friends."[59]

On his return to France, Céline would find another whipping boy, i.e., another publisher—Gaston Gallimard. In the meantime, Pierre Monnier had ensured the essential thing, had maintained the contact between the author and his readers—a very weak, flickering, extenuated contact, but one that nonetheless had allowed Céline to keep himself alive, if barely, as if by artificial respiration, by literary reanimation. At the time, that was the most he could hope for.

Investigation, Trial in Absentia, and Amnesty

Appointed on April 19, 1945, examining magistrate Zousman had had a great deal of trouble collecting evidence against Céline. The *Je suis partout* file against Lucien Rebatet, Pierre-Antoine Cousteau, and Claude Jeantet had been much easier for him, since he had only to examine the newspaper's back issues. But the Céline investigation dragged on. The prosecution did not seem to be in any hurry. Zousman had increased the number of rogatory commissions, assembled a few of the writer's texts from the collaboration press, solicited testimony. Dr. Rouquès had zealously taken the initiative to write to him in March 1946 claiming that the reprinting of *L'École des cadavres* in 1942, with the preface in which he was named, had almost cost him his life. The police searches undertaken at rue Girardon, in Céline's apartment, requisitioned by Yvon Morandat after the liberation, had turned up nothing. No more than at Denoël's. There remained the general accusations forwarded to the Danes by the Quai d'Orsay, which, as we have seen, Céline had answered.

The slowness of the investigation, in other words the ever nebulous threats hovering over him, maddened the writer. Month after month, he wrote letter upon letter to Albert Naud in self-justification. Moreover, he requested his help in his fight against the Denoël house. He pleaded, he raged, he was flattering and insufferable by turns, impatient or timid. He promised to settle with Albert Naud at some later date. "My dear counsellor and friend, I remain haunted by the question of your fees. . . . You know that I come from the humblest of pre-1914 families—where we would have hanged ourselves rather than bilk someone of a single penny."[60] And Céline suddenly recalled the apartment he had bought in Saint-Germain-en-Laye before the war. What had happened to it? Did he still own it? He offered to "give" it to Albert Naud—a totally unrealistic offer, since his property was under threat of sequestration at the time. It was his old uncle Louis Guillou, seventy-six years old, who still owned his raincoat store at 24, rue La Fayette and whom Céline believed to be a great miser, who was more or less managing his affairs at the time, and his real estate holdings in particular, distressed at the thought of everything being suddenly confiscated by the Treasury.

In October 1948, on the advice of Paul Marteau, Céline requested the help of a second lawyer, Jean-Louis Tixier-Vignancour. Certainly, with his past as a member of the Resistance, Naud represented useful political security. But hadn't he proven himself too soft, too ineffectual? Tixier would at least be more energetic, but Céline had to be careful not to ruffle the two men's sensitivities. Which of course he did. Stung to the quick, Naud wrote to Céline on October 13: "He [Tixier] has a reputation as a notorious anti-Semite. I wonder whether it would be advisable for his collaboration with me on your case to become known by the prosecution."[61] Céline hastened to reassure him. He explained that he did not want to reject the goodwill that he was offered, but that he, Naud, would of course remain the principal, the defending attorney of record, and that Tixier could in no way take precedence, etc. He made a parallel assurance to Tixier the same day (October 17, 1948) of his trust and friendship, speaking to him in brotherly terms: "Now, as you know, Naud is a little anxious and peevish that I asked you to help me . . . Your friendship and skills grieve him a little—What a fix I'm in."[62]

With varying degrees of subtlety, Céline would play one man off against the other, discreetly flattering them, disparaging the one when he was talking to the other, describing Tixier's "bungling" to Naud, and Naud's culpable indifference to Tixier. After the in absentia verdict of February 1950, it was Tixier who would truly take Céline's defense in hand and win his trust. Naud had never been to see him in Korsör. Did the writer secretly hold this against him, seeing it as a sign of indifference? Tixier was the one who would obtain the revocation of the arrest warrant and, later, the amnesty in 1951. He would visit Céline in Denmark.

Céline's letters to his lawyers do share common ground: the line of defense adopted by the writer. There was no man more patriotic than Louis Destouches, he had never set foot in the German embassy, it was Denoël who had insisted on reprinting *Bagatelles* . . .

"I am a thoroughgoing patriot—too thorough, in short, PERSECUTED. Who are the Frenchmen having lived in France between '39 and '44, what inhabitants of France between those two dates can claim to have been as relentlessly patriotic as me—as little involved in the collaboration? What recent past of any Frenchman could resist the spiteful, relentless, delirious investigation of so many judges, ignoramuses, enemies, the envious? that enormous coalition of fanatical madmen and sadistic vultures? *Let them be counted!*

"You must not forget that I never belonged to any Franco-German medical, literary, or political association, to any party—that I have never written an article in my life. Under the occupation I wrote PRIVATE letters of protest to newspaper directors, who never published them—or else tampered with them—distorted them—throughout the occupation I was harassed by the Beebeecee (for no reason), perpetually threatened—underground newspapers . . . coffins, etc. I can be found neither in *Signal*—nor in the *Cahiers franco-allemands*—nor among the 'visits of Frenchmen of letters to Germany,' nor as an emissary of Pétain's—NOTHING AT ALL— I took no advantage of anything—I took vengeance against nothing, against no one, I LOST EVERYTHING—I didn't bet on Hitler—the Embassy hated me—I am a pacifist patriot—I was against the war— That's all— Nothing nothing NOTHING ELSE."[63]

Céline repeated that he was the victim of an intolerable persecution perpetuated by "sadistic sneaks"—that was the truth! He was Jeanne d'Arc prosecuted by Cauchon, the Duc d'Enghien as Napoleon's victim, the new Dreyfus in a new affair. He bitterly noted France's custom of tearing itself apart in endless civil wars and score-settlings. And yet, upon reflection, the only truly persecuted one was himself. The others had gotten off too easily. He did not hesitate to name them. It no longer involved any danger. "They'd love to see me in Fresnes [prison]—but first let them lock up Paul Morand, twice Pétain's emissary! and Bergery, a good friend of the Embassy—and Chautemps, the prime minister, condemned for treason—all those gentlemen are at large—as pretty as you please! Paul Morand hasn't even been indicted! Montherlant published in the *Cahiers franco-allemands*— Marcel Aymé in *Je suis partout*—*Mercadier*, the publisher of 'La France' in Sigmaringen, is enjoying full freedom in Paris—as are thousands of others! JUSTICE first means EQUITY—ABOVE ALL."[64]

Of course, there had been the execution of Brasillach, but Céline stopped short of reproaching the former editor-in-chief of *Je suis partout* for having had the luck to be arrested, shot, and have done with it. He hadn't liked Brasillach in any case, had never liked him—and it had been mutual. There was nothing in common between the university-educated Boy Scout, who had been a Hitlerite out of passion, a collaborator out of idealism, and a pitiless anti-Semite out of "reason," and the author of *Voyage*, a pamphleteer, a stylist, a desperate, intuitive solitary, an autodidact of literature sprung from the lower-middle class.

Maurice Bardèche's book *Lettre à François Mauriac*, published in *La Pensée libre* in July 1947, had enraged Céline by a passage in which the author, obstinately defending the memory of his brother-in-law, Brasillach (who had remained in Paris during the liberation), claimed that those Frenchmen who had withdrawn to Sigmaringen had basely "abandoned" their country. Céline waxed furious in his letters to Albert Paraz: "There were people at Sigmaringen who were worth a hundred Brasillachs, that zealous little *Propaganda-Staffel* clerk, that scheming, Neronian pansy— he'd have gone just as happily to London if he could have wangled a Ministry of Cinema there—that was *his ambition.*"65 Or further: "Of course I'm against Brasillach's being lined up and Bardèche's being tossed in the can! A cat is a cat— But even if he can't admit to being a cat he is one nevertheless—and Bardèche [is] a jerk and Brasillach ditto."66

Céline's last line of defense was the counterattack, the force that his anger could inspire in him and which he brandished like a threat over his two lawyers, that they might somehow pass on the warning to any lawmen: examining magistrates, judges, the attorney general . . .

"It's easy to rail against some wretch in the dock, to wave red flags in his face, but *I'm the one* with the heavy field guns, the long-range artillery, and I'll use it! *I can make them laugh!* Laugh till they're sick, laugh till they're green, laugh till they croak! Let them remember that I'm not offering a challenge. I am *an accused man defending himself.* Brasillach licked his government commissioner's boots! Brasillach was a fink, he was used to licking. Laval was a fink too. *Not me.* NOT TO BE CONFUSED WITH THEM! NOT AT ALL. With me it'll be lightning! the shit will fly! to the brink! fun and games! *the worst!* I want to be respected and I WILL BE! It's up to you dear counsellor! It's up to your friendship to make these people understand that they won't be accusing some sacrificial lamb! Shit no. That I'm going to drag them into an arena where I'm the master and where they'll be remembered, and for centuries to come, as sadistic, idiotic, stinking clowns."67

In May 1949, the investigation as complete as it could be, Céline's file was turned over to the prosecution and entrusted to deputy public prosecutor Jean Seltensperger. According to François Gibault, he was a remarkable magistrate who was on good terms with Tixier-Vignancour and whose wife was an admirer of Céline's.68 Seltensperger reflected for several months before drafting his indictment. Céline wrote him on numerous occasions to defend himself against various charges.

"I am Déroulède in exile. . . .

"In 1941 in Quimper, I once tried to intervene on behalf of a Breton sailor sentenced to death. I was told that it was none of my business. I undertook this action through official (black zone) channels, through Brinon.

"Had I handed over the Pas-de-Calais, the Eiffel Tower, and Toulon harbor to Hitler, my immediate execution could not have been called for more instantaneously.

"There was also the untimely reprinting of *Bagatelles.* I gave in, I'm not proud of it, to Robert Denoël's pleas."69

Seltensperger, who knew Céline, his high spirits and his excesses, could not have been bored reading his letters. Nor the writer's lawyers. It was hardly customary in the legal world, in which every word of every document was carefully, cautiously weighed, with its technical formulas, its precautionary use of the conditional mood, to find such a talented madman writing and defending himself like a bull in a china shop, a brilliant polemicist in the flimsy, dusty lexical and terminological garden of the legal universe.

Drafted in late October 1949, shortly after the visit Mikkelsen paid to Seltensperger, the prosecutor's indictment was admirably restrained. He cleared Céline of many of the charges against him. The anti-Jewish passages in *Les Beaux draps* were merely extensions of Céline's thinking in 1937. Written immediately after the armistice, this work certainly was not aimed at pleasing the Vichy government (which banned it) or the occupier. Céline had made no changes in *Bagatelles pour un massacre*, as a collaborating writer might have done. The Rouquès affair? His anti-fascist activities were not unknown to the Germans. If Céline had wanted to take revenge against him, he would not have waited until 1943. There was no proof that it had been his intention to denounce Rouquès. Nor was there any proof that Céline had intended to make public his letters to the press. No, he had not visited the Katyn gravesite with Fernand de Brinon. Seltensperger could not even prove Céline's trip to Berlin for a medical congress (where he had well and truly been nonetheless, to entrust Karen with the keys to his bank deposit box).

And the prosecutor concluded:

"In the final analysis, when we examine Céline's activities under the occupation, he can be impugned for:

"—Certain passages in *Les Beaux draps* (1941);

"—his agreement to reprint *Bagatelles pour un massacre* in 1943.

"Taking into account the observations made earlier, these facts reveal neither relations with the enemy nor the intention to serve the enemy's interests and in consequence do not constitute criminal activity as prescribed in art. 75-5 of the Penal Code.

"They are actionable only in Civil Court.

"Consequently, the undersigned remands the accused to Civil Court and calls for revocation of the arrest warrant of April 19, 1945."

It could not have gone more favorably for Céline. He was henceforth safe from prison, liable only to a verdict of "national disgrace [*indignité nationale*]." Unofficially informed by Seltensperger, Tixier-Vignancour immediately informed Mikkelsen of the unhoped-for conclusions of the indictment. The indiscretion may have come from the Danish lawyer. But one thing is certain: on October 26, 1949, the newspaper *L'Aurore* announced the news under the headline L.-F. CÉLINE, THREATENED ONLY WITH CIVIL PROCEEDINGS, SOON TO RETURN TO FRANCE. There was an immediate outcry. Seltensperger was relieved of the case, in disgrace, in favor of René Charrasse. Céline ascribed the maneuver to the Bidault government's new attorney general, René Mayer, whom Céline had soon nicknamed in his letter "Duke Mayer of Vendôme-Montrouge"—Vendôme for the place of the same name, the seat of the Ministry of Justice; Montrouge for the Montrouge fortress where death sentences were carried out. On the other hand, as far as Albert Naud was concerned, the fault lay entirely with Tixier, whom he blamed off the bat for the premature disclosure of Seltensperger's indictment.

On December 9, 1949, Naud wrote to Céline: "It's a disaster. That ranter—you know whom I mean—ruined everything by running around all over the place, to the prosecutors, the court clerks, and the government commissioners, to announce the fine speech he was going to make in your defense. Result: someone who overheard the conversation brought it to the attention of both the attorney general and the press. Another result: the attorney general re-examined your file and referred it to the chancellory. Naturally that was eagerly welcomed in high places: remandment to the Court of Justice and annulment of the remandment to Civil Court.

"That's exactly where we stand. After the effort I've made I am absolutely devastated. . . . Could you please tell me whether I am really your lawyer and if I am the only one so that I might request my distinguished colleagues to leave me the hell alone?"[70]

Céline tried to soothe him and reconcile him with Tixier, which he succeeded to a certain degree in doing. It was a harder task for him to win over René Charrasse. Even so, the new prosecutor's indictment proved to be less savage than was expected. He too had received long letters from Céline and had chosen to find them amusing. A writer who was so immoderate, unreasonable, and vituperative vis-à-vis the whole world could not have been a genuine collaborator. Mayer may not have been equally as amused by the outrageous letter, more bizarre than it was insolent, that Céline wrote him on November 26, 1949, in energetic presentation of his defense.

In any case Charrasse's indictment of Céline charged him with belonging to the Cercle Européen as a member of the honors committee, with having written letters published in *Germinal* and *Au pilori* from 1942 to 1944. In conclusion, he remanded Céline before the Court of Justice. However, he repudiated the applicability of article 75 relative to high treason, retaining only article 83 of the Penal Code, which applied to actions potentially harmful to national defense. The difference was significant. Article 75 could lead to a death sentence. Article 83 carried a prison sentence of only one to five years and a fine of 360,000 to 3,600,000 francs.

The hearing was set for December 15, 1949, before the Seine Court of Justice presided by M. Deloncle. Naud and Tixier-Vignancour represented Céline. Jean-Gabriel Daragnès, Pierre Monnier, Marie Canavaggia, and Dr. Camus attended the proceedings. Mikkelsen had sent a telegram: "Destouches sick impossible to attend request postponement." Naud, speaking for the attending counsel, also requested a postponement of the case, which was granted. The new hearing was set for December 29.

Céline again wrote to Charrasse, pointing out that the acquittal of the Denoël company should by extension clear him too. But he naturally refused to attend the hearing on the 29th. On that day, his lawyers called for another postponement—to no avail. Proceedings for a trial in absentia were thus decided upon and instituted. An order was given to Céline to present himself at the hearing on February 21, 1950. This time, there would be no deferment.

In early 1950, at the instigation of Maurice Lemaître, the newspaper *Le Libertaire* launched an inquiry under the title "What do you think of the Céline trial?" The reporter, obviously partial to the writer, emphasized that it was only Céline's prewar books, his prewar literary successes and controversies, that he was being made to pay for. Lemaître had contacted many writers, artists, and publishers, and opened the columns of *Le Libertaire* to their opinions. Their answers were published in the January 13, 20, and 27 issues.

In Céline's favor, among others, were:

—Marcel Aymé: "Try as his enemies might to muster every resource of their ingenious hatred, Louis-Ferdinand Céline is nonetheless the greatest contemporary French writer and perhaps one of the greatest lyric poets we have ever had."

—René Barjavel.

—Jean-Gabriel Daragnès.

—Jean Dubuffet: "The very painful exile forced upon him for so many years by certain French factions is utterly traumatizing. It must come to an end. We must exonerate him, open our arms to him, honor and celebrate him as one of our greatest artists and one of the proudest and most incorruptible fellows we have. There aren't that many left."

—Jean Galter-Boissière, publisher of *Le Crapouillot*: "That Céline can still be persecuted five years after the liberation proves the hypocrisy of modern justice: it has latched on to a completely disinterested writer, while all the big industrialists, who are guilty of economic collaboration and made billions off the occupier, have for the most part never had to worry."

—Morvan-Lebesque, editor-in-chief of *Carrefour*.

—Paul Lévy, editor of *Aux écoutes*.

—Albert Paraz.

—Louis Pauwels . . .

Hostile to the writer were:

—Charles Plisnier, who spoke of Céline as "one of the greatest corruptors of the free conscience."

—Benjamin Péret, who fretted: "There is a campaign evolving under our very eyes to whitewash fascist and anti-Semitic elements. Yesterday, Georges Claude was back in circulation. Tomorrow, it will be Béraud, Céline, Maurras, Pétain and company. Once all that riffraff has taken the high ground, what will the anarchists, and revolutionaries in general have gained?"

—Albert Béguin, who had only one ax to grind: "After *Voyage*, Céline never wrote a single good line. All the rest is the blathering of a sick mind or a disgraceful explosion of vileness. All anti-Semitism is repugnant, but that of Céline, slimy with rabid slobber, is worthy of a servile dog."

—André Breton, who recalled: "I became nauseated by Céline pretty early on: I didn't need to read further than the first third of *Voyage au bout de la nuit*, where I came to grief against some flattering characterization of a colonial infantry NCO. It seemed to be an outline of some sordid train of thought. As the war approached, I was shown other texts by him that justified my predispositions. I loathe the sensationalist literature that inevitably and quickly descends into slander and calumny, appealing to all that is most base in the world.... To my knowledge *Céline is in no danger* in Denmark. I can therefore see no reason to stir up public opinion in his favor."

Albert Camus sent in the following: "Political justice disgusts me. That is why I believe the trial should be stopped and Céline left in peace. But allow me to add that anti-Semitism, and particularly the anti-Semitism of the '40s, disgusts me every bit as much. That is why I believe that, when Céline gets what he wants, we should stop being bothered with his 'case.' "[71]

In January 1950 Céline's "case" was far from being settled. Drappier, the presiding magistrate, was to rule on it on February 21. All of Céline's friends mobilized themselves on his behalf, as did celebrities and colleagues solicited by them. There were childhood acquaintances, unknowns, a pharmacist writing on the stationery of the Alsatian Society of War Veterans, Arletty, Marie Bell, Jean Paulhan, Marcel Aymé, Marcel Jouhandeau, Thierry Maulnier, medical friends such as Dr. Tuset of Quimper, who recalled Céline's intercession on behalf of a Breton Resistance fighter condemned to death, others who didn't know him, such as Henri Mondor, Ernst Bendz, and Raoul Nordling, who all wrote to the presiding magistrate. Nordling even paid him a visit a few days before the hearing. Maurice Nadeau did not hesitate to communicate to the court a letter he had recently received from Henry Miller:

"In my opinion, it would be a disgrace for France to make Céline a scapegoat.

"For me he will always be not only a great writer but a great man. The world can bring itself to shut its eyes to the 'mistakes' (if mistakes they were) of certain eminent men who have contributed so much to our culture. The truly guilty generally get off easy.

"I know Céline couldn't care less what I think of him. That's OK. Now is the time for us to say what we think. I'm afraid that many will hesitate to speak out until it's too late.

"Let him have his chance."[72]

Along with Marcel Aymé and Albert Paraz, it was Pierre Monnier who made the greatest efforts to come up with testimony on the writer's behalf. He had applied in particular to Montherlant, who rather ingloriously wriggled out of it by reiterating that he felt that Céline's writing was artificial, obsolete, and would be unreadable in fifty years, before specifying that he had no knowledge of Céline's file and that in such circumstances he felt it inadvisable to pass any judgment on a collaboration trial.[73]

Restrained and favorable was the testimony that Monnier extracted from Jean Cocteau: "Céline reproached me savagely for not being an anti-Semite, but these things have nothing to do with a man's freedom. I feel that Céline's significance as a writer outweighs that of which he is accused. And since justice is a matter of balance, I assume, and I hope, that the scales will come down of themselves on the right side."[74] Monnier nonetheless deemed Cocteau's statements unusable in the trial.

The hearing came on February 21. Céline had been excused from attending for reasons of health. Mikkelsen had sent a medical certificate to the presiding magistrate, recalling too that his client had signed a commitment on his honor not to leave Denmark without official approval. In response to the charges brought by deputy public prosecutor René Charrasse, Céline had further written a new "Response to the prosecution's account before the criminal court"[75] on January 24, in which he reiterated the main points of his old line of defense.

The hearing was calm. The great purge trials were no longer box office; the fashion had passed. The public preferred other entertainment in those months of January and February 1950: Louis Armstrong's concerts in Paris, Blaise Cendrars' novels, or the zither melodies of Carol Reed's *The Third Man*. In short, the excitement of the purges had collapsed like a cold soufflé. And what drama could be hoped for in a trial of Céline without Céline, in which his champions, Naud and Tixier-Vignancour, would not even be allowed to speak, in accordance with the rules governing trials in absentia? Nor was there much of the bloodthirsty executioner in prosecutor René Charrasse, even if Céline had deemed his indictment "a nonsensical trial for sorcery."[76] The campaigns waged by the leftist press against Céline in early 1950 had barely succeeded in either influencing justice or dramatizing the developments of the trial.

Extracts of Milton Hindus' preface to the American edition of *Mort à crédit* had appeared in *Combat* on January 19 under the title "A Jew Testifies for L.-F. Céline." This unleashed a lively controversy which the paper echoed in its January 26 issue. There was a certain irony to this, since the preface had been written before the visit to Klarskovgaard, from which Hindus had drawn the disenchanted and rather critical book against which Céline had threatened to take legal action. This work—Hindus had at first called it *The Monstrous Giant Céline* but, deeming the title too biased, had finally settled on *The Crippled Giant*—eventually came out in the United States in February 1950. And *Combat* again published advance proofs from it two days after the trial, on February 23, which could in no way harm the author of *Voyage*. But, in the hostile press campaigns against him that had preceded the trial, neither the statements of the periodical *Regards* describing Céline's luxurious life-style in Copenhagen, statements that were taken up and embroidered by the communist weekly *Action* on January 4, 1950; nor Roger Vailland's article which appeared in *La Tribune des nations* on January 13 under the title "We will no longer spare Louis-Ferdinand Céline" (in which the author, then a member of the Party, regretted not having executed him on the rue Girardon in 1944); nor Pierre Hervé's accusations in *L'Humanité* on January 21, whose title proclaimed in all seriousness that "Céline was a Gestapo agent;" nor, finally, the threats uttered by *Le Droit de vivre*, the newspaper founded by Bernard Lecache, which ended: "Let Céline come back! We're waiting for him at the station. And we promise him a fine welcome!" could succeed in heating up the proceedings.

Judge Drappier read out the letters he had received in Céline's favor. The clerk in turn read Céline's two "defenses." Prosecutor Charrasse took the floor.

Pierre Monnier attended the trial:

"Attorney Charrasse's indictment ended on these words:

" 'I regret that it has not been possible to subject the accused to a psychiatric examination, which seems to me to be justified by the contradictions contained in his sizable correspondence. . . .'"

"There was a great moment when the clerk, instructed to introduce the criminal evidence to the jury, read out extracts of the incriminating works, particularly *Les Beaux draps*. It started off with shocked scowls, which gave way to amused smiles that gradually overtook the audience, until finally an enormous laugh welled up and the whole thing ended in general hilarity."[77]

In conclusion, Charrasse asked for a light prison sentence. And after rapid deliberation, Presiding Magistrate Drappier and the court of justice composed of Mme. Claverie (married name Dumont), MM. Baillon, Pentel, Pages, Bréant and Merle sentenced Céline in absentia to a year in prison, and a fine of 50,000 francs, and declared him to be in a state of "national disgrace" with confiscation of his property present and future not exceeding 50%.[78]

In the context of the period, Céline could hardly have hoped for a more lenient sentence. The proof came the next day, when *L'Humanité* cried scandal. And the writer recognized it too, in this letter to Monnier written two days after the verdict: "They couldn't have done more without disavowing the Resistance! All this goes way beyond my insignificant self"[79] Or again, the same day, to Paraz: "Dear old fellow—here I am disgraced for life, and a year in the hole— But I've already done almost two here. I've had it! But they were as fair as they could be—got to admit. I'd be wrong to bitch. I've paid for reasons of state."[80]

Everything would move very quickly now. Céline had served a far longer prison sentence in Denmark than that to which he was condemned in France. It was theoretically enough for his defenders to prove this in order to have the arrest warrant against him lifted. Without waiting for this formality, immediately after the trial Naud tried to persuade Céline to return to France, to present himself before the court to benefit from a problematic amnesty. No, thanks! Céline did not care to run any risk. He was suspicious. Was he wrong? Perhaps.

It was only on May 13, 1950—nearly four months after the trial—that

Mikkelsen obtained from the Danish Ministry of Justice an affidavit according to which Céline, at the request of the French government, had been arrested in conformity with article 14 of the law on the status of foreigners and placed under surveillance and protective custody in the Vestre Faengsel prison. But it was all as yet too simple. Naud, in no hurry, was unable thereafter to obtain an official acceptance from the French authorities that the prison sentence imposed on Céline had actually been carried out, i.e., a recognition of the principle of the equivalence of sentences, and especially the revocation of the arrest warrant still current against him. Clearly, the chancellery resisted this legitimate request with the greatest illwill. Consequently Céline withdrew his confidence in Naud to place it all in Tixier.

At first Tixier advised Céline to return to France, to accompany him before the Paris military tribunal. "You come forward with me on Tuesday February 20 at 9 A.M. You contest the verdict of the Court of Justice and at 9:05 you leave the military tribunal as free as when you entered it."[81] Céline rejected the plan. He was still mistrustful. No return to France without an amnesty. Tixier changed his tactics. He had gone to see René Camadau, the chief prosecutor of the military tribunal and as staunch an anti-Gaullist as himself (according to François Gibault). And the two men had seen eye to eye. Through M. Thurmel, bailiff of Paris located on the rue de Charonne, Céline contested the adjudication rendered against him by the Seine Court of Justice. The same day, Tixier presented a petition to the presiding magistrate of the military tribunal, emphasizing Céline's precarious health and the dangers involved in any arrest in his condition, recalling the prison sentence the accused had served in Denmark and calling for the revocation of the arrest warrant. This was granted on March 15. Henceforth, Céline was liable to no prison sentence. A first victory—subject at least to the appearance of the accused before the military tribunal before April 15.

Tixier then flew to Copenhagen, went to Korsör, and laid out his strategy for his client. He had him sign a proxy so that he, Tixier, might obtain a passport in his name to return to France. On March 19 he went to the French embassy where he was received by Jacques Thomas, the vice-consul. Tixier presented him with the ruling of M. Liné—a judge of the appeals court and presiding magistrate of the Paris military tribunal, who had signed the ruling revoking the arrest warrant issued against Céline—and requested a passport. Thomas could not make such a decision alone. He referred the matter to the ambassador, who in turn applied to the Minister of Foreign Affairs, Robert Schuman, who on March 29 granted a mere laissez-passer for a single trip to France. But that was not the essential thing. Céline had no intention in any case of returning so fast. The important thing was that Jacques Thomas agreed on March 19 to sign a paper certifying the request on that day by the applicant Destouches for a passport or laissez-passer, a request with which he had been unable to comply.

With this document in hand, Tixier managed, before April 15, to convince the military tribunal that it was not his client's fault that he had been unable to appear. Céline's contestation was thus admissible. The lawyer then prepared his request for amnesty, sanctioned by the law of August 16, 1947, which allowed for the pardon of seriously disabled veterans who had been sentenced to less than three years in prison, whose sentence had been effected before January 1, 1951, and who had been found guilty neither of denunciations nor of actions leading to deportations. Tixier attached to his client's file the testimonial of his *médaille militaire*, his status as a disabled veteran, his service records, and a memorandum from the government commissioner favorable to the amnesty request.

From that point it was all over. Or almost. It remained essential that, at the hearing on April 20, 1951, no one make the connection between the unknown Destouches, Louis-Ferdinand, and the infamous Céline, any mention of whose name Tixier had skillfully avoided; and that there be no leaks that might alert the judges and induce them to refuse the amnesty. Tixier therefore worked in the highest secrecy. Neither the writer's friends, much less the press, had been forewarned. The amnesty was granted.[82] There remained one last threat: that the director of public prosecutions would quash it on appeal. He had five days to do so—five long days, consequently, of waiting, five days of silence, hope, anguish. . . .

Finally, on April 26, the amnesty became irrevocable. Tixier was free to inform the press. The attorney general heard the news and choked. *L'Humanité* was scandalized by the amnesty of a "Gestapo agent and glorifier of the Nazi gas chambers," and the communist daily *Ce Soir* was equally outraged by the freedom granted to the "spokesman of Goebbels and Rosenberg who passionately welcomed the deportation and massacre of patriots."

In Denmark, Céline at first did not dare believe the unhoped-for news. Informed confidentially by telephone of the outcome of the April 20 hearing, he wrote to Tixier on the 23:

> *My dear Counsellor and Friend,*
>
> *We can hardly get over that telephone call, the fantastic excitement! You know that miracles are deemed true miracles only after meticulous investigations, synods, etc. For it does indeed seem a miracle! And you are the astrologer, charmed sorcerer!"*[83]

And when it was all finalized on the 28th:

> *My dear Friend,*
>
> *So now the wonderful news is confirmed, set down in the records! There is nothing left to do but thank Heaven—and especially, if you will, Heaven's Craftsmen—and you the first amongst them! I immediately informed Thomas—he will thus be receiving the photographic copy of the Enactment—*

but *I believe (I have no idea) that he will still have to consult with Paris and his department before giving me a regular passport.*[84]

A good loser (did he have a choice?), Naud had written Céline two days earlier: "You may think that I have long been neglecting you. The truth is that I am a modest man and wanted to leave to Tixier-Vignancour the task of pursuing to its end the initiative he had taken, which could succeed only through personal connections."[85]

There was no longer anything in the way of Céline's receiving a passport. Father Löchen, wonderful in his loyalty, friendship, and devotion, took care of the formalities with the consulate and M. Thomas. It was all settled fairly quickly. A photograph of the smiling Father Löchen handing a visibly delighted Céline his passport at Klarskovgaard immortalized the event. On May 4 Céline again wrote to Tixier: "This is it! I have just received my Passport and my Amnesty enactment—St. Thomas declares himself convinced of the MIRACLE! yours! The terms of the enactment are terrible, one passes under them as if under the blade, only to find oneself magically unscathed on the other side! It's extraordinary!"[86]

After the amnesty, Thorvald Mikkelsen asked the Danish Minister of Justice to release Céline from his promise not to leave Danish territory. This was done only a few days before Céline's departure from Denmark but did not actually pose any problems.

Céline wanted to leave the country as soon as possible. That was hardly surprising. But where to go? To Spain, where his friend Antonio Zuloaga offered him his hospitality? To Corsica, to stay with André Pulicani? To Paul Marteau's home in Neuilly? To Argentina with Le Vigan? The actor had for many months been pressing him to join him. But as early as October 12, 1950, Céline had already answered: "This Argentinian business feels to me like a summary of the whole sordid adventure. . . . No, let it drop, it's not even worth considering! And when I got there, how would I live? on unreliable assistance?"[87] Lucette's health continued to concern him. He at first considered an immediate return to Paris so as to consult with Dr. Tailhefer as soon as possible, staying with Marteau in the meanwhile. But Lucette reassured him: there was no urgent need for such a medical examination. He therefore chose the most practical temporary solution: to live in Menton for a few weeks with his parents-in-law, the Pirazzolis, who had offered to put them up.

Before leaving Korsör, he wrote the following note to the editor of the local paper on June 28. It was published in *Korsör Avis* on July 4:

To the Editor:

As my wife and I prepare to leave the lovely town of Korsör, I ask you to believe that it is not without sadness that we leave the place where we were welcomed in the most friendly, human, and tactful manner.

Through years that were so very critical to us, we were surrounded by genuine sympathy in Korsör, which was a great comfort to us during our very long exile. I would be particularly grateful if you would allow me to pass on through your paper all our feelings of friendship and gratitude to the people of Korsör.

Most sincerely yours,
L.-F. Céline[88]

On Saturday, June 30, Louis and Lucette—followed in baskets by Bessy the dog, Bébert the voyager, and four other cats: Thomine, Poupine, Mouchette, and Flûte—left Klarskovgaard. They reached Copenhagen by train, spent the night at Mikkelsen's, and went to Kastrup airport on Sunday afternoon to catch their plane to Nice. Photographs show us the Destouches at the airport, accompanied by Mikkelsen and two couples, their friends the Ribières and the Sales. Céline wore a light-colored three-piece suit, a bit shapeless. With his cane and his game bag slung across his shoulder, his wrinkled trousers, and his air of a worried vagabond, he looked rather like Charlie Chaplin. Lucette, severely dressed in a black tailored suit, white blouse, and white scarf wrapped in a turban, appears more serene.

Their plane took off at 6:15 P.M. on a direct flight to Nice lasting a little over five hours.

"We had waited so long for the amnesty," Lucette explains. "But we were exhausted from the wait. No, there were no joyous outbursts. We prepared ourselves for our return. We were a little anxious. We ordered special compartmented baskets for the cats. We couldn't put them together. We had to leave Louis' favorite cat in Klarskovgaard, Sarah, so wild, white with brown patches, whose eyes looked like they were underlined with kohl. Sometimes she'd come and wrap herself around his neck, then suddenly go back to being aloof, unapproachable. She's the one who gave birth to the four kittens, Flûte, Poupine, Mouchette, and Thomine, who were able to adapt to civilized life. Before leaving, we left some money with the farm managers to feed the half-wild cats that wandered around there, and Sarah especially, from time to time. We heard later that as soon as we left they organized a beat to kill them all. . . . In short, we prepared to leave, we collected our luggage, our old clothes, blankets, pots and copper boiler, and we chucked it all in trunks—like beggars. Louis had never taken a plane. He really enjoyed it, like a child. He wasn't afraid. There was a terrible storm. The plane bounced around. We could see lightning. A turbulent flight. Louis found all this very amusing."

17

Meudon, or Journey's End

From Menton to Meudon
Céline Forgotten
Success and Controversy
The Old Man and Death

From Menton to Meudon

It was almost 11 P.M. when their plane landed in Nice on July 1. They were met by a heavy heat, thick and humid, which the night had not managed to dissipate. A taxi took them to Menton. Tired and dazed, Louis and Lucette hoped only to be allowed to rest. Alas, the Pirazzolis were waiting for them with great ceremony on the ground floor of the Bellevue, the enormous building where they lived in the hills to the east of town, in the neighborhood of Garavan, overlooking the sea and the gulf as far as the Italian border.

"Big tables had been set up in the entrance hall," Lucette recalls, "with place settings, crystal. Guests and reporters were waiting for us. The champagne had been left to chill. My mother was drunk, my stepfather silent and resplendent, wearing his Italian decorations from before the war. Louis immediately asked, 'Where's my room?' He locked himself in and refused to see anybody. Everyone left, furious. Louis hadn't even had a glass of water. The reception had been my mother's idea. I was devastated. I knew right away that it couldn't last long."

In fact, their stay in Menton, planned to last through the summer (Louis had initially thought to return to Paris in early September, as his correspondence attests), was shortened to under four weeks. Nothing found favor in Céline's eyes: neither his possessive, tactless, and excitable mother-in-law; nor the blazing heat bearing down on the Côte d'Azur that July of 1951; nor the overly formal apartment with its trinkets, in which he felt trapped.

Ercole Pirazzoli had once held an important post in the Italian customs administration. Then he had settled in France. Upon the death of his first wife (a first cousin of Lucette's mother), he had liquidated all his holdings, in particular a factory in Sannois, on the outskirts of Paris, that had belonged to his wife and which he had long managed and had just inherited. With his second wife, he was now running through his capital with no thought for the future. He gambled (in other words, lost) at the casino; not as much as Lucette's mother, however. Pirazzoli was a secretive, taciturn man. He kept aloof. He didn't bother Céline, he just stood at his living-room window in Menton. "He goes out on the balcony to gaze nostalgically at the Italian customs offices," Céline told Pierre Monnier.

515.

"There was such a temperature difference between the North and the South in July," Lucette goes on to explain. "It was awful for Louis, who couldn't stand the heat. His migraines got worse. He wanted to work, he locked himself in his room, he couldn't. Once we took a walk into the center of Menton, which still looked like a big village. One day, on the café terrace, we ordered some ice cream with God-knows-what garbage on it. Louis got terrible food poisoning. He was vomiting. He couldn't digest anything. Sometimes he'd come with me when I went swimming down by the rocks below the building. He never once went swimming. He'd return to his room and to his work, or try to work, not wanting to meet anyone, either my mother or my stepfather. He rejected everything. Open hostility."

There is nothing surprising in his attitude. We might indeed have pictured Céline relaxed, relieved, happy to be back in France, to see a seven-year nightmare finally coming to an end; or at least eager to show a little gratitude to his parents-in-law, who had opened their house to him, his wife, and their animals, which were housed in a hut a stone's throw from the building, on a little patch of ground they owned across the street and down the slope. But no—his years in prison and exile had aged him, exhausted him, made him more solitary still, more sick, more grouchy, more antisocial than ever. He no longer wanted any contact with the world. He did not even visit Albert Paraz, living nearby in Vence, to whom he wrote on July 19: "I'm sick. Lucette is sick—it's not trivial, alas, it's the *real thing*— So there's no question of seeing anyone talking to anyone. The first son of a bitch who speaks to me, I'm down at the cop shop to warn them and *going the hell to the other end of the country.* That's what I'm thinking. Physical and moral repulsion for ALL HUMAN CONTACT except by medical or surgical necessity. Crazy, maybe? Could be. But ain't it my right? I'm not hurting anyone. I feel like a Trappist. Lucette too— As to the book I hope I NEVER have to publish it! ah là là, what a godawful swamp! If I could make a living from medicine, I'd chuck *Féerie* into the deepest shithole I could find!"[1]

No doubt Céline was an egoist as well, vindictive, insufferable, bilious, ungrateful. But that's easy to say, and especially to think, about someone so immoderate, in whom nothing was mediocre, banal, or trivial—neither his bad temper nor his disdain for the world, the strength of his dreams, his dedication to his work, his terror of being dispossessed of his property, his work, the fruits of his imagination. Nothing counted, nothing even existed beyond the objectively narrow and subjectively immense orbit of his life, his view of the world, and above all his visions.

Was Albert Naud no longer useful to him after the amnesty? Not a single letter came from Céline, not a word of thanks, not a token of gratitude, nothing. The lawyer was deeply hurt and let him know it. Too bad. Mikkelsen had helped him, had sheltered him years on end, even if he had peppered his generosity with more or less conscious humiliations inflicted on his guests. Who could deny it? Céline alone could. He got it in his head that Mikkelsen had robbed him, had spent far less on him than the amount of gold he had been entrusted with, of which, by Céline's calculations, there remained 8,000 crowns at the time of his departure. The writer demanded that they be reimbursed. The lawyer turned a deaf ear. He had probably once gotten himself caught in 1949 at the German-Danish border, while attempting to export the gold illicitly in order to exchange it in France—for Céline's benefit. But Mikkelsen, embarrassed, did not boast of it. He didn't even mention it to Céline. The writer took him for a thief. Mikkelsen in return took him for an ingrate—a cruel misunderstanding.

Now, in Menton, Céline became exasperated by the stupid tactlessness of his mother-in-law, who had decided to sell to a lawyer the manuscript of *Féerie* that her son-in-law had offered her in exchange for the indefinite use of the Menton apartment.

"He found that kind of transaction intolerable," wrote Lucette. "He told my mother, 'I don't want anything, I want to clear the hell out.' Her room was at the other end of the hall. She often called for me, she wanted to talk to me, which is understandable, she hadn't seen me in so long. But Louis would say to me, 'No, I forbid you to go to her!' He'd yell until I came back. I shuttled back and forth between them. Five minutes with one, five minutes with the other. You had to know Louis. He couldn't share a friendship. I couldn't be with him and with my mother at the same time. He couldn't imagine it. My mother could have been the most charming woman in the world, it wouldn't have made a difference. On top of it, she never stopped raging. She went around with a revolver, accusing Louis of wanting to take me from her. Quite simply, she wanted to kill him. At least that's what she said."

In Paris, Pierre Monnier continued to go all out for Céline. In early July he received a letter from Jouhandeau, suggesting that he get in touch with Paulhan, who had an important message for him from Gaston Gallimard. Was there finally a contract in the offing? Louis wrote to Monnier on the 13th.

My dear Friend,

> *Gaston is just as much of a pimp and a crook as Frémanger, Dumont, and the rest of 'em. He gets his dough from Hachette, i.e., that thuggish, bluffing Smyrnan Philippaqui [Filipacchi] . . . Okay, don't badger Paulhan or Jouhandeau. Drop 'em. If they don't call you, let 'em go shit! In life, you always have to put your ass on the line. If it doesn't come to anything, too bad, I won't publish, but it will be on my terms or nothing.*
>
> *"You talk about Africa, it's right here! And seedy! Moneygrubbing parents-in-law, jerks, there's little or nothing to eat, and it's boring as hell. It's better than the Baltic because you hear French on the streets, but otherwise it's worse."*[2]

Three days later, Monnier met with Paulhan and was then ushered into the rue Sébastien-Bottin office of Gaston Gallimard.

"Of medium height, dressed in black with a bow tie, he reminded me of a high-ranking chef at Prunier's. After asking me to sit down, he stared at me and smiled. A good 10 seconds passed without anything between us but that smile. And then he spoke. With marvelous cunning and genial false humility. 'I would be glad for the chance to publish Céline. I've had all the great names of literature here, Gide, Claudel, Faulkner, Valéry. All of them! And the only one I missed was Céline. Yes, I missed Céline. It was mistake, a slipup. So you can understand that now I'll do whatever I have to to get him.'

"Down to business. Republication of all the novels, eighteen-percent royalties, 5 million in cash. . . .

"Two days later I'm on the plane (the first time in my life, and at Gallimard's expense) to Nice, with a valid contract in my pocket that meets all of Céline's demands."[3]

Specifically, the contract, dated July 18, 1951, provided for the reprinting of *Voyage au bout de la nuit, Mort à crédit, Guignol's band*, and *Casse-pipe* within six months, with serial, adaptation, and translation rights split two-thirds for the author, one-third for the publisher. Further, Céline promised Gallimard his next book, *Féerie pour une autre fois*, and gave him the right of first refusal for his next five works. The publisher, in turn, would advance him royalties on the first 25,000 copies of these works upon remission of manuscript. Thus, the contract was slanted to Céline's advantage. Monnier, as intermediary, would receive an agent's fee.

The signing of the contract and the first 5 million in hand hastened Céline's return, now that he enjoyed some financial autonomy. The writer asked Monnier to prolong his stay in Menton and to return with him just long enough for him to pack his bags, reserve plane tickets, and forewarn Paul Marteau, who had offered him the hospitality of his mansion in Neuilly. On July 23 they all left Menton together. Not quite all of them: Thomine the cat was on the loose. Lucette had searched for her in vain. She was hiding or living the adventurous and unimaginable life of vagabond cats. (She would reappear at the Pirazzolis' a year later, as if nothing had happened, and would be promptly dispatched by overnight parcel to Lucette, who had been living in Meudon for several months by then and was ecstatically happy to be reunited with her favorite at last.)

The move was again chaotic. The animals in their baskets, the valises, and all their incredible gear were crammed into a taxi for Nice airport. And there, a two-hour wait. Céline was anxious, feverish, pacing the floor, listening to the incomprehensible public-address announcements, ever with his bizarre appearance, his disheveled hair, his cane, his wrinkled clothes, the bus-conductor's satchel in which he kept his money, his plane tickets, and identity papers.

When they finally landed at Le Bourget airport, a shuttle bus took them to Les Invalides. It was 8:15 P.M., and the air less stifling than in Menton. Paul Marteau and his wife, Pascaline, were waiting for them. It was their first meeting, a discovery. Until that moment they had only corresponded; their friendship had been purely epistolary.

A parenthesis—and a symbol: that very day, at the Île d'Yeu, Field Marshal Pétain died in captivity at the age of ninety-five. Vichy would henceforth seem a part of history, like a very, very bad dream. Céline had returned to Paris. The postwar period had finally begun. The ghosts could retire. Or so one hoped.

A taxi took the baggage: three sailor's bags, the manuscript valise, trunks, the cat baskets; Lucette rode in the Marteaus' Packard with Pascaline; Louis, the cats, and Marteau in a Simca. At their mansion at 66 *bis*, boulevard Maurice-Barrès, the Marteaus had set aside a little apartment for the Destouches on the third floor, with a large bedroom, living room, and bathroom.

It was an almost aristocratic life for them in Neuilly: the luxury of devoted friends, a succulent table (Paul Marteau, a gastronome, was president of the Club des Cent), and no immediate material concerns. All the comforts—or all the discomforts for the independent, solitary, ascetic Céline, who hated receiving charity or simply owing anything to anyone. Hence his apparent ingratitude, and his always rather curious relationship to money.

Ingratitude? He preferred to put behind him the moments when he had been forced into an inferior or humiliating position. It was at such times that his terrible lucidity proved useful. It helped him discern the motives that moved his benefactors, whose merits were considerably diminished thereby. Mikkelsen, for example. There had been that stupid misunderstanding over money. But not only had Céline convinced himself that the Danish lawyer had swindled him, he felt that Mikkelsen had wanted to take further advantage of him. In writing his memoirs, Mikkelsen had dreamed of passing into posterity, and Céline had deeply hurt him by his refusal to help him write, to give him the least bit of advice, by telling him off the bat that his pages were worthless. Hence the lawyer's supposed revenge. With Marteau, it was simpler still. The industrialist wanted to play patron of the arts, lover of literature; he took pride in Céline's presence in his house and that of the writer's friends who came to visit him, such as Marcel Aymé and Jacques Deval. Marteau was not exactly a leftist; Céline's polemics had probably delighted him. And again, the writer wondered if his benefactor didn't want to encourage him to write more, to throw himself once again into the front lines of a battle in which he had everything to lose and which, to his eyes, after the war and its revelations, no longer had any *raison d'être*.

Money? With the money he had earned, he was exacting, even rapacious. He fought with his publishers, he demanded more, he was mistrustful, cunning, threatening. It was his money. His own. That which he had earned at terrible cost. Like some old artisan, he'd be damned before he'd be robbed! He was suspicious of the entire planet. And he spent this money only with the greatest parsimony, from the fear of going without, of being in anyone's debt. On the other hand, there was no question of touching other people's money. He hadn't made it himself. He wanted nothing to do with it.

He refused gifts. Nor did he want to know anything about inheritances. It didn't belong to him. He hadn't earned it.

Thus, the Destouches settled in with the Marteaus. The animals took possession of the third floor with a perfectly clear conscience. The cats scampered over the roofs, lounged on the beds, and sharpened their claws on the period furniture. Louis settled into the living room–boudoir with less haste and more exhaustion. His only thought was for writing.

"At the beginning of our stay, Mme. Marteau would come into our apartment at the drop of a hat to see what was going on there. Louis would tell her, 'Madam, you have no business here, so just let me work!' So she'd answer him, 'It's time for lunch (or dinner).' Louis also told her, 'I don't want you to entertain anyone, or else I'm leaving right now.' So the Marteaus, who received all the Paris highbrows at their table every day, had to warn off their friends and stop entertaining them. This lasted a month. Louis didn't want to see any visitors. He came down for meals. He ate in five minutes. It made him nervous. The Marteaus had four servants, the cook (excellent), the chambermaid, the chauffeur, the valet—in a word, the good life. Louis constantly made sarcastic comments in front of the help. The Marteaus were at the end of their rope. I was still feeling very weak. They wanted to give me all sorts of things to pick me up. Louis, who barely touched the stuff, said, 'She should drink some champagne, it'll do her good.' They brought me the best champagne there is, and I started to get tipsy straight off. I was so weak! I wasn't eating much, and champagne on top of it! I stopped drinking it. Louis commended me. He also encouraged me to take up my training again. I had no muscles left after my surgery. He'd take his chronometer and say to me, 'Do ten times three minutes of jump-rope, like boxers, without stopping.'' He'd take my pulse after each series. The rhythm of my heart had to return to normal. This was my only means of training other than my abdominal exercises on the floor. Mme. Marteau's bedroom, with a magnificent crystal chandelier, was below the room where I trained. When I jumped rope like that for half an hour, the chandelier would swing and swing. She'd send up her chambermaid (white cape and little apron), carrying a silver tray with a note: 'Would you be kind enough to stop, because my chandelier is swinging wildly and I'm afraid it may fall, etc.' In other words a very nice letter. And Louis would say, 'Not a chance—keep going!' It was like that every day. We'd receive little notes every five minutes. A kind of war between the two of them. He'd do the opposite of whatever she said or asked."

Over the course of their stay with the Marteaus, Louis saw his daughter, Colette, on several occasions. Their reunions were somber. Louis still refused to meet his son-in-law, Yves Turpin, the irresponsible procreator (in his eyes) of his five grandchildren, whom he was equally as uneager to know. It was as if he were afraid of becoming attached into the bargain, of being bound by ties of affection, of dependence. He wanted to be left alone, and though only fifty-seven, already had the bearing and exhausted shuffle of an old man. The art of being a grandfather meant little to him; he preferred to flee the inevitable mumbling discussions with babies, children, his family. It was far more than egoism, it was the fear of feeling something positive toward the people who would thus invade his life, chasing off his phantasms, driving away his anxieties and hallucinations—and preventing him from writing. He bore within him a sort of exacerbated, burning tenderness that frightened him and that had calcified with the years beneath the lonely violence of his terrors, suspicions, and solitude. He required that wall, that armor, to write, to maintain, there in the isolation of his work, the unique flame of his passions, his memories, his raillery, and his abstract compassion for men and women, children, animals, prisoners. He simply did not want to grow attached to his grandchildren, to get to know them, because he did not want to invest in or project himself into the future, to hope, to be distracted from reflecting on death, or to run the risk of new disillusions. He had come to value only his own way of imagining, withdrawing into the past, and writing.

"Louis often took his dog, Bessy, for walks in the woods. Mme. Marteau sometimes went with him. She had a very Proustian air about her, very *grande dame*. She would give him advice: 'You should have a mistress, and your wife a lover, that sort of thing is done; it would be altogether splendid, would it not?' She and her husband, incidentally, were passionate about esotericism. Louis would shrug his shoulders. During one of these walks, when he was alone, a man came up to him, shook his hand and said, 'I'm Turpin—your son-in-law.' Louis answered, 'Ah, indeed, sir . . . Good day, sir,' and that's all! He went on walking his dog, without adding another word."

Around mid-August the Marteaus left on vacation. They must have been in sore need of one. The Packard and the chauffeur remained in Neuilly at the disposal of the Destouches, who scouted the suburbs and the real-estate agencies that summer looking for a house in which they could settle for good. With the animals, there was no question of an apartment in Paris. Moreover, they needed a place big enough for the dance lessons that Lucette planned to give. They considered Saint-Germain-en-Laye, which they loved; Bougival too. They visited house after house. Their choice eventually fell on a two-story villa with a half-sunken basement, rather run down, at 25, route des Gardes, on the slopes of lower Meudon, overlooking the Seine and the Île Séguin. From the heights, the magnificent view gave and still gives onto Paris and its suburbs. A wild garden rising on a steep slope toward the top of the Bellevue hill, toward Meudon, with a few large trees, cut it off from the two other identical villas built next to it, and from the very rural route des Gardes, on which no residential apartment building had yet been erected. The villa dated from the 1850s, built on an estate that had belonged to the Duke of Bassano and had then been the property of Eugène Labiche and the source, it is said, of lucrative speculations on his part. They signed the deed of trust in early September. The final transfer was enacted on October 1, 1951, by their notary in Bougival. Lucette had inherited two farmhouses in Normandy from her paternal grandmother, some fifteen kilometers north of Mortagne, in the Orne, where her entire family had originated and which she lost no time in putting up for sale. The Meudon villa was thus bought in her name with the proceeds of that sale for the sum of 2.5 million francs. But there was no question of moving in immediately. Essential work had first to be done on the plumbing, heating, carpentry, and walls. Louis and Lucette moved in sometime in late October.

Meanwhile, the Jünger affair erupted in September with Julliard's publication of the French translation of Ernst Jünger's *First Paris Diary, 1941–1943*, his memoirs as a German officer in the occupied capital. In it, Jünger described his encounters with Céline (which we have already noted), Céline's nihilism, racism, and the fanatical glare that had so deeply shocked him. But, anxious not to make trouble for anyone, Jünger had changed the names and designated Céline under the pseudonym Merline. However, in the French translation—initially undertaken by Henri Thomas, then abandoned by him, then vainly urged upon Armand Petitjean before being entrusted to a certain Séchan and proofread by Banine—Céline's real name was reinserted. Was this a mistake or malice on the part of one of the translators or of Julliard? Céline believed it a direct and deliberate attack. Advised by his lawyer Tixier-Vignancour, on October 12 he brought action against the French publisher for libel, defamation of character, and false accusation.

Albert Naud learned of these proceedings, which excluded him definitively as Céline's primary lawyer. He wrote to Monnier, calling upon him as witness of his past devotion to the writer, whom he called a "bastard"; he further requested him to pass the letter on to Céline, who seemed rather bemused as to the source of this irritation.[4] In any case, the bridges between the two men had already been burned.

Having been told of the name switch in the French edition, and without waiting for the lawsuit's deposition, Jünger had written to his friend Marcel Jouhandeau to lament the error. No, it had never been his intention to hurt anyone. He asked him to forward the following note to Céline:

Most esteemed Monsieur Céline,

A painful incident prompts me to write to you. Reading over the translation of my diary that was recently published in Paris, I come across your name— and that in a passage in which the original German edition has the name "Merlin." This alteration, which I most keenly regret and whose hidden motives are unknown to me, was done behind my back. I do not agree with your views, but nothing was further from my mind than wishing to cause you harm. Should you be attacked on the basis of this passage, I beg you to refer it to me. I will deny that you are the person in question.

With my best wishes.
Ernst Jünger[5]

What had actually happened?

Henri Thomas had begun his translation using not the German edition but a photostat of a typed version of the *Diary* in which, according to him, Céline's name was prominently included. But Thomas, having then left to work for the BBC in England, was unreachable, perhaps on the outs with Jünger, and did not respond to any of René Julliard's requests for an explanation.[6] Paulhan, no doubt misinformed, had specified to Céline in a letter on October 25, 1951, that Céline's name did not appear in Thomas's text.[7] He thus believed it to be a case of falsification, as did Mme. Banine. Who had wanted to cause injury to Céline? Séchan? A copy editor? The wildest hypotheses were bandied about. Céline, who did not positively recognize himself in Jünger's portrait, even wondered if it was a case of mistaken identity on the German writer's part between him and a journalist, Philippe Merlen, who had signed himself "Merline" in an ultra-collaborationist rag, *Jeunes Forces de France*, had enlisted in the Waffen SS, and committed suicide in April 1944.

In any case, Céline's lawsuit against Julliard and, at the same time, against two newspapers, *Preuves* and *L'Aurore*, which had reported Jünger's comments annotated with insulting remarks about him (Céline), took an abrupt turn. He very soon abandoned his suit against the newspapers so as not to build up more publicity around the case. On October 12, 1951, as the new French edition of Jünger's *Diary* was coming out with the name Merline re-established, Céline was met by reporters and photographers as he arrived at the law courts to present himself as a plaintiff for damages. He found this extremely unpleasant (perhaps more so than Tixier, who was escorting him).

Apparently the courts did not look very favorably on the writer's suit. The new, corrected edition had come out. And, furthermore, everything was so obscure, responsibilities so indeterminate.

Tixier was very soon convinced that there was little point in hanging on and stirring up more publicity around the case. But Céline at first would not listen to reason. He had suffered too much injustice, insult, and slander, he believed. He wanted his day in court. And to win, for once! The wheels of justice were set slowly turning. On October 26, 1951, and again on July 17, 1952, Céline was called before the examining magistrates handling his case. But on the advice of Tixier and his partner, Dejan de la Batie, he eventually decided to withdraw his suit. His lawyers neglected to inform the examining magistrate of the withdrawal. A ruling of nonsuit on April 16, 1953, closed the books on the case, which had been insignificant when all was said and done but nonetheless instructive on two counts. The first was the way in which it showed Céline's demented conviction that nothing in Jünger's certainly distorted statements had anything at all to do with him. Was this amnesia on his part, mystification, delirium? The second was to show the extent to which he was now prepared to rely on the legal apparatus, of which he himself had recently been a victim, in order to be absolved once and for all, vindicated of all libelous or slanderous accusations.

Between their stay at the Marteaus' and their definitive move into Meudon, Louis and Lucette spent a few days in late October with Lucette's father. Joseph Almansor, still an agent and chartered accountant for several fashion houses such as Patou, had been remarried to a middle-aged woman, an aristocratic Breton of extreme slimness and palor, very proper and guarded, whom Louis nicknamed the Mite, as though he dreamed of crushing her—metaphorically—in his hands. Lucette's recollection of the dates is hazy. In any case, they were not to linger there. One room at the back of their stylish apartment on the rue Dulong in Paris was invaded by the writer, his wife, Bessy the dog, Bébert the old grouch, Flûte the gray tom, and his two sisters, Poupine and Mouchette rounding out the promiscuous feline squad—it was too much for the Mite. They had no sooner moved in than they were out.

They finally disembarked on the route des Gardes in Meudon. It was the last stop. Journey's end.

Céline Forgotten

The house in Meudon was uncomfortable. The central heating didn't work. Remaining was the unique fireplace on the first floor, complemented by a few radiators and a gas stove that nearly asphyxiated the writer one day. It was impossible to fight the damp and cold effectively; the winters there were atrocious.

As they settled in, the ever-thoughtful Mme. Marteau sent them curtains for the windows. But curtains were Louis and Lucette's least concern. Their furnishings were makeshift: an armchair inherited from Marguerite Destouches, some tables, a bench, chairs bought on discount, and a few other pieces, such as a double bed on loan from the Marteaus. In the main, Louis owned nothing, not one decent stick of furniture from his mother's apartment on the rue Marsollier. He had been in Germany when she died. Colette had taken care of the legacy. As to his apartment on the rue Girardon, "requisitioned" after the liberation, and to the furniture in it, he was sick of the whole thing. Strangers had made off with it. For him, the matter was simple: he had been plundered, robbed. He had given up all hope of reconnecting with the past, recovering the trinkets, crockery, and furniture of days gone by. He wanted to draw a line. Start over from scratch.

There was no doubt that he had indeed been plundered in the first days of the liberation of Paris. Most of his manuscripts had been carted off, scattered, lost forever. As for the furniture, things were not so simple. Yvon Morandat, a *Compagnon* of the liberation, had taken over his apartment in September 1944. Gradually replacing Céline's furniture with his own, in 1949 he stored the latter in a warehouse. Upon his return to France, Céline tried to reclaim them from him. Morandat was willing to return them on the condition that Céline pay the storage costs. The writer blustered, refused. It was not for him, the victim, to pay anything! From that moment on, the business became involved. Tixier called on Morandat to settle the bill. On November 30, 1953, a bailiff delivered Morandat's reply: he had paid the storage costs up to December 31, 1951; on that date, had Céline been in France, he could have reclaimed his furniture. This was incontrovertible. It was too bad for him if he had not been there.

The same day, the writer wrote to Tixier:

"I enclose Yvon Morandat's summons, etc. Of course I shall do nothing, write nothing, pay nothing. Let them sell whatever remains of the loot!

"You can imagine that I've resigned myself to all this. Housebreaking, pillage, suffered but *not consented to*! (muddied with lies!).

"That furniture, those manuscripts, were in my place in 1944 (June) as security for the landlord— The apartment itself was 'exchanged' completely illegally by Morandat!

"I lost, was robbed of about 10 million (at today's rate!) at the rue Girardon!

"Those thieves want to 'regularize' things by making me pay Fr 36,739! A pretty clumsy trick."[8]

It all ended with a more or less friendly arrangement. Morandat paid a portion of the costs. Céline's furniture was put up for sale. He wanted nothing more to do with it. He had started a new life in a new setting.

In the basement of the Meudon villa, lit by barred windows opening onto the front of the building, Louis and Lucette had set up a little kitchen, near the cellar and the nonfunctional central-heating boiler. When Lucette, from the garden, saw Louis in the kitchen, she had the painful feeling, as she would later say, of seeing him back in prison.

Céline set up his office on the first floor, in the main room, near the fireplace. A table covered with a cloth of plain, coarse fabric, a whatnot, his mother's armchair, another armchair, a sofa and, soon, anatomical prints pinned to the wall and birdcages in a corner, made up the decor that would be described by reporters come to interview him. Next to the office (which would later serve as a medical consultation room as well) was a bedroom that Lucette would soon make over for Louis' sole use.

The second floor was taken up by a small bathroom and a dance room where Lucette started giving her lessons, next to a room that she soon took over. The third floor remained neglected. Louis would not hear of any work being done on it. He dreaded the bustle of workmen, the noise, anything that might disturb his concentration or aggravate his headaches.

But Lucette had her own ideas. "When we moved in, we found a sort of attic broken up into five small rooms. I came to an arrangement with an old fellow, half gardener, half mason, for him to take down the partitions gradually, quietly, gently, so Louis wouldn't hear. And that's how I made the dance studio on the third story. Next, the floor needed redoing. Louis agreed to it. You can't dance without a good floor. I had mirrors and barres installed. In the beginning I financed the work on the third floor with the money from the lessons on the second. Later on, I used the two rooms simultaneously. On the second floor, stretching exercises, work on the large beam, balancing exercises; above, dance proper. I sometimes gave two classes at a time, too. The grown-ups on the second, the children on the third. I had students starting at age four."

The Destouches' arrival in Meudon touched off a good deal of gossip and scandal in the neighborhood. "Céline the Nazi" had moved in, folks whispered. Certain shopkeepers were loathe to serve them. Lucette remembers little handbills nailed to the telephone poles and trees of lower Meudon, calling on them to leave. Upper Meudon, richer, more bourgeois, remained indifferent. But it all seems to have calmed down soon enough. The Destouches didn't go out much. The butcher delivered meat for the animals. Louis went down for some shopping twice a week. Lucette took the train for Paris, where she preferred the shopkeepers. In brief, their neighbors saw very little of them. They were barely able to make out the sign Lucette had hung to the left of the gate, a few days after they had moved in, which proclaimed: LUCETTE ALMANSOR, CLASSICAL AND ETHNIC DANCING.

Naturally, she couldn't hope this to be enough to bring the pupils pouring in. She had to build up her clientele little by little, with the help of old professional connections at first, or of friends who sent their families. There was no dance school in Meudon at the time. Word-of-mouth very soon worked in her favor. Thus, Claude Maupome and Judith Magré, Marcel Aymé's granddaughters; Roger Nimier's wife, Louise de Vilmorin's sister-in-law; and Simone Gallimard became regular students of Lucette's, working at movements that resembled breathing and stretching exercises, an entire gymnastic discipline that she had perfected, somewhere between yoga and dance. Many students soon befriended Lucette and Louis, such as Mme. Pinson, a native of Meudon who had watched them move in, or, somewhat later, Dr. Robert Brami and his fiancée, Christine.

Very often, Céline would "intercept" the young doctor, who was finishing his internship, and would spend hours discussing matters of medicine, hygiene, current events, anything, with him. Consequently, Brami would miss his lesson. It didn't matter. A cardiologist, he would provide detailed answers to everything the insatiably curious Céline had to ask. They discussed articles in the *Presse medicale*. In Céline, Brami observed a man partially paralyzed in the right arm, of shuffling gait, who clearly suffered from problems of balance consequent to lesions of the labyrinth of the inner ear. Most probably, this was an aftereffect of a fracture of the petrous bone, which explained his buzzings and constant headaches. And yet, Dr. Brami never examined Céline. The writer—too modest, too surly to surrender himself to a colleague—was not anxious to seek help. Only once did Dr. Brami take his blood pressure, which confirmed what Céline already knew very well: arterial hypertension, which was chronic in him and would kill him after a burst aneurism. Today, Dr. Brami and his wife, Christine, remember a man often laughing, cheerful, and infinitely humane. Céline was very reluctant to talk to him about the war or the Holocaust, in which a part of his interlocutor's family had perished. Or, if he did, it was implicitly as of an enormous blunder he had committed before the war, believing at the time that he was helping the weak, the future victims of a conflict he feared and wanted to prevent by protesting. Whereas he had ended up inadvertently on the side of the strong, the butchers.

It was Louis' habit to rise very early. How could he sleep with his endless, pounding headaches, the trains speeding through his head, as he was so fond of saying? He was up at six and set to work immediately. These were his best hours, the most productive and least pain-ridden. Around nine, Lucette would make him some weak tea; he would eat a croissant or two. And the morning wore on: he reworked or wrote letters, edited his correspondence, read the papers—*Le Figaro*, *Le Monde*—or medical journals. He followed the news, the musical chairs of the Fourth Republic governments, colonial wars, the election of Eisenhower in November 1952 and that of René Coty in December 1953, the battle of Dien Bien Phu and Nasser's rise to power in Egypt in 1954. He especially followed the so-called "society" articles, the new fashions. He was fascinated and amused by the ads, which he felt revealed the mores, tastes, and desires of the age. In the afternoon he attended to various tasks: housework, shopping. Occasionally his neuralgia became so unbearable that he had to lie down, wait, remain still.

"His only relaxation," Lucette says, "consisted of sitting on the armchair that was by the front door, near the stairs. He'd look at the garden, at the dogs coming and going. The students had to pass by there on their way up. He loved the children, the youngest ones, he'd talk to them a little. Some of them were afraid of this gaunt, weirdly dressed gentleman, others weren't. Yes, Louis adored children. I often saw him treat them. It was extraordinary. This man, who was usually so impatient, gave them injections, bandaged them with infinite gentleness and patience. He wanted to avoid making them suffer, hurting them, at all costs. He always caught the clinic nurses when they'd rip off plasters or bandages, and pow! He managed to do it himself without hurting them, with endless care, calm and sweet."

In accordance with their agreement, Gaston Gallimard began reselling *Casse-Pipe*, *Guignol's band*, and *Mort à crédit* in November 1951, with Céline barely settled in Meudon. For a while the publisher was happy just to glue new Gallimard covers on the unsold stock of Denoël and Chambriand copies he had bought. The publishers Amiot-Dumont protested, having come in time to see that they preferred to keep Céline, whom they had distributed (and financed) through the agreement reached with Pierre Monnier/Chambriand. It was purely formal. No contract bound Céline to them.

Purely formal, too, was the supreme court of appeal's censure, on December 6, 1951, of the amnesty granted to the writer. It did nothing to alter his situation. But the authorities, feeling that they had been hoodwinked by the way in which Tixier-Vignancour had pulled off the amnesty by cloaking

Céline behind his real name, Destouches, wanted to have the last word. "In the interests of the law," went the official pronouncement.

Gallimard republished *Voyage au bout de la nuit* for real in March 1952, and *Casse-Pipe, L'Église, Guignol's band 1*, and *Semmelweiss* in May. Céline had recently remitted the manuscript of *Féerie pour une autre fois 1*, and the contract for this book was signed on April 3.

At that time, relations between the author and the publisher were sunny. They had met for the first time in October 1951, at Paul Marteau's. The industrialist had been reluctant at first to give this dinner. He had a grudge against Gaston Gallimard for having once "stolen" his mistress, the actress Valentine Tessier.[9] Basically, Céline was responsible for their reconciliation.

Immediately after this soirée, Gaston Gallimard wrote his new author a rather toadying letter that ended with these words: "I also hope that we shall soon be able to meet again. I can truly say that I owe our first meeting to Paul Marteau—I listened to you too assiduously not to be eager to hear you once again. You must believe me when I say that I am proud, proud and happy to be your publisher, and that I already consider myself your humble servant Gaston Gallimard."[10] And Céline answered him with a "Dear Sir, publisher and, I hope, friend."[11]

Naturally, things could not stay like this. The writer had to rebel, protest, scent conspiracies. His works were not coming out fast enough, he claimed. Gallimard was blocking their distribution, "while I see so much tripe emerging from your synods."

This letter, dated October 2, 1956, is highly revealing of Céline's foul temper:

". . . you do no publicity for my books, either editorial or graphic, nor in your disastrous NRF, and it would thus be quite surprising if anyone were aware that I have published with you . . .

"What a surprise! . . .

"Everybody I talk to, hundreds of them, it's like they're emerging from a dream when I tell them that I've published with you—and big books—since my return from Denmark.

"You've been pimping off my dreams, don't say a word against them! you'd be nothing without my dreams! you and all your tribe of dimwitted cretins!

"Stop dreaming!

"That's not your job! You don't know the first thing about it! Your job is to turn dreams to account, you catastrophic philistine!"[12]

Obviously, Céline saw the publisher as the boss, the exploiter of his labor, and thus the ideal target. He couldn't very well deny himself the pleasure of attacking him. In his later novels, and *D'un château l'autre* in particular, he would swipe at him, caricaturize him under the name of Achille Brottin, call him a double-crosser, hypocrite, pimp, insensitive clod, a libidinous old voyeur, an old busybody caught in the act, a fanatical botcher, a sluttish philatelist, and other flavorsome niceties. Clearly, his works' lack of success and the critical silence with which they were met reinforced his bitterness and anger against Gallimard and his adviser, Jean Paulhan, alias Norbert Loukoum.

But there was a certain amount of fun in Céline's vociferating. Gaston Gallimard must have known that his author needed to rant in order to pacify himself. Henri Godard correctly perceived it: "An insulting letter is followed by the following amendment: 'We laugh about it, and that's all. If it's no longer permitted to have fun . . . You're in danger of becoming 'objective' [February 16, 1955]. Another letter, extremely ferocious, ends with the phrase 'In fun and friendship.' Punctuated with declarations of this sort, the insults are defused. Even in their most strained moments, the relationship always retains something of a game. Céline provokes and insults, but never makes it possible to decide whether he is in earnest or jesting."[13]

In June 1952, then, was published *Féerie pour une autre fois 1*, Céline's first novel since *Guignol's band* in 1944, with an initial print run of 33,000 copies retailing at 620 francs, bearing a publicity wrapper with the simple endorsement "Unpublished Céline." A blurb had been drafted that included the following lines: "In his exile, Céline meditated and wrote. With *Féerie pour une autre fois*, he now offers us ten years of emotion and experience. With virulence, but not without melancholy, he reckons with the hatreds directed against him, retraces the misfortunes of his life, evokes the men who admired and then betrayed him."[14] But Céline, fearing legal repercussions, had the blurb withdrawn. He even asked the publisher to abandon all publicity for three months following the book's release. He was still afraid of the law and potential libel suits.

It may not be quite correct to call *Féerie* a novel. It should rather be seen as the first of his great "chronicles." Bardamu no longer exists. It is Céline speaking now, writing, taking the stage, drunk on the recounting of his own adventures. There is no longer the time to transpose the howl he emits into novelistic terms. Characters torn from his daily existence spring to life around him: his cat Bébert, Lili-Arlette (Lucette), Marc Empième (Marcel Aymé), and Jules, in whom we recognize Gen Paul. Céline further evokes Nartre (Sartre), Montandon, and many others. He describes Montmartre, the avenue Junot (avenue Gaveneau here), and his apartment on the rue Girardon. In short, he gives the impression that he is sticking to the truth. This is hardly surprising. In the end, his past had almost caught up with him. Life in Paris toward the end of the occupation, his captivity in Danish prisons—all of this, evoked in *Féerie*, is almost coeval with the moment in which he is telling the story, as we have already pointed out. These are living images and agonies, pulsating wounds that he exhumes and describes. The functions of imagination and authorial prudence are erased: the chronicler describes what he has experienced, what he has seen, that to which he bears witness. Such is Céline's infinite ambition: "I have so many things to tell that I'd have to live 120 years and never stop writing just to give you the premise."

As a chronicle, *Féerie* anticipates the final trilogy, of which it constitutes the opening or, more accurately, the monumental display case. Jumping from the years 1942–1944 in Paris to 1945–1948 in Copenhagen, Céline creates a sort of void, a zone of silence that would be filled by the adventures described in *D'un château l'autre*, *Nord* and *Rigodon*.

But what is also striking about the book is the way in which he also evades a scrupulous respect for the events of the story. Its title is eloquent: *Féerie pour une autre fois*—a sort of pantomime based on magic or fairy tales. And Céline proclaims in his epigraph: "I loathe realities. . . . Down with any form of reality!" A profession of faith. His book remains nonetheless like a series of escape ports through which the author flees his times and his suffering: prison, exile, and the rest. His memories form a string of fairy tales; he displaces his exaltations and his rages.

Irritated by a reporter who asked him overly personal questions about his life, Vladimir Nabokov said that a writer's true biography is not the account of his adventures but the history of his style. Céline's life is the history of his style, and it could be told starting with the still sluggish rhythms of *Voyage* and ending on the pure music of *Rigodon*. Motivated by a strange and contradictory evolution, the author progressively abandons the deceptive illusions of fiction for a chronicler's testament, he drops his (relative) lexical and syntactical moderation for an "emotive speech" in which reality is disjointed, in which the thing observed is less important than the observing gaze, in which Céline's dementia, the hallucinatory solitude of the individual/victim in a moribund world relentlessly destroyed and destroying itself, blazing up in the final glow of its decadence, is re-created in language—no longer the support, the solid foundation of a society or a world secure in their values, but a worm-eaten illusion, equally indescribable. Céline, the modern writer par excellence, perhaps the greatest of the modernists, explodes the pleasant and feigned coherences of that world, throwing us back on the music of his emotions, on the phenomenal harmony of dying worlds and individuals who feel persecuted, who cry out in their self-imposed solitude—though for whom, for what? Perhaps like Céline, not to lacerate but to heal themselves, to soothe their pain by that form of cleansing or catharsis that literature has always permitted. That perhaps is where we find Céline: in the history of his style, the story of increasing suffering, a "loathing for reality" combined with the ambition to create a chronicle—of which *Féerie* constitutes a decisive stage.

Written in Denmark from 1945 to 1951—years that were so trying for him—the book soon assumed immense proportions. Céline had to divide it into two volumes, and he envisaged a third that he later abandoned. The first, published in June 1952 under the title *Féerie pour une autre fois 1*, actually represented the section written last. Céline had started with the book that would come out in June 1954 under the title *Normance* and which relates in the form of a nightmare the allied air raids over Paris at the end of the occupation, as the narrator was able to observe them from his apartment.

Who was capable at that time of understanding the novelty of *Féerie* and *Normance?* Céline's more diplomatic friends confessed their consternation in whispers. They saw it only as incomplete, repetitious, its shrill cries lost in a fog of unreality. For the others, the unsilent majority of critics and writers, Céline was still proscribed, accursed, the archetypical anti-Semite on whom the reproach of silence must weigh as the most merciful of his punishments. Céline had ceased to exist, had lost his talent, was nothing. There was, however, one very encouraging comment by Maurice Nadeau in his book *Littérature présente*, in which he re-examines harshly but without spite Céline's work up to *Guignol's band.* "What Joyce did for the English language, which remains a phenomenal laboratory experiment, what the surrealists attempted to do for the French language, Céline achieved effortlessly and on a vast scale,"[15] he wrote.

In *Carrefour* on August 6, 1952, Nimier published an article devoted to *Casse-Pipe* and *Féerie.* "It is very natural to dislike Céline. He can be seen as too affected or too oratorical. But it is equally acceptable to like him. In any case, he is very poorly known. He is unjustly accused of having invented foul language for the pleasure of it, when all he was doing was hurling invective, in the Greek sense of the word: exhortation to fight against life's evil forces."

About the hero of *Féerie*, he goes on to state: "He is accused of every collaboration crime. He feels as though he were the scapegoat for hordes of people. But the goat is not an accommodating animal. So he kicks out. The time has passed for Bardamu's brand of humility. It is time to rise to circumstances. He must glorify himself, first in order to be able to tolerate an almost unbearable existence; next to avenge himself and even the score. They locked Céline up. They destroyed his manuscripts and rescinded his military medal. Well, he brims over with an exultant rage, and will drown them all in its flood. Those he resents are clearly not the victims of the Germans, but all who constituted themselves lawgivers either out of a need to see blood flow or to put their consciences to sleep. The species is not a rare one. It must be acknowledged that we have seen very few martyrs amongst the purgers."[16]

It would have been easy to point out to Nimier that the martyrs of the Germans had died before the liberation. But that is beside the point. His article in *Carrefour* went unnoticed. Nimier further believed that "an important sector of modern youth finds nourishment or, lacking that, a voice it can relate to" in this "underappreciated writer." He seemed to be anticipating the course of time with his own hopes. The nonexistent critical reception was echoed by dismal sales; Céline remained the forgotten man of Meudon. Youth (that dubious abstraction beloved of demagogues) had not rediscovered him. His old readers were laying down their arms, licking their wounds as defeated Pétainists, as more or less purged *collabos*, as anti-Semites no longer very proud of being or having been so. In a word, Céline was alone. Which suited him fine. Without a readership. Which suited him less. He had become so conscious of this that, in November 1952, he asked Gallimard to have a book commissioned about his work.

The end of 1952 was plunged into mourning for him by Bébert's death. The cat had already had a tumor excised a few years earlier in Denmark. This time the cancer had metastasized, and nothing could be done. He faded away at the far end of his life—at the far end of old age, having lived one of the most remarkable cat's lives there ever was. Bébert the solitary, Bébert the boon companion, grumpy and cautious, bold and enigmatic, Bébert the "merry sprite" who had seen—understood?—everything, who had returned from the war, from Sigmaringen, from the Baltic exile to his Parisian home—Bébert had vanished into silence.

"... he died here after many an adventure, jail, bivouac, ashes, all of Europe ... he died agile and graceful, impeccably, he had jumped out the window that very morning ... We, who are born old, look ridiculous in comparison!"[17]

Lucette and Louis buried Bébert at the top of the garden. For a while, his grave was marked by a stick painted red and white. No pet was ever really able to replace Bébert. There were many other cats and dogs, surrounding the writer, consoling him for lack of human intercourse. But Bébert of Montmartre remained the First, the Only, the sole companion of the Apocalypse, Bébert the soft-furred hero.

Nonetheless, a newcomer arrived in Meudon in 1952: Toto the parrot. Lucette often saw Louis alone in his office when she had to go up to the second floor to work with her students. "I'd like a bird," he had told her. She chose a West African parrot, gray-blue and red, still very young, which she brought back from La Samaritaine. No sooner had Céline seen it than he angrily demanded that she return it to the store. She turned a deaf ear. Two days later he and Toto had become inseparable. The parrot could gloat. Soon he would be whistling himself hoarse to the tune of "In the Steppes of Central Asia," which his master had taught him.

"The parrot had no cage. Louis let it fly free. It made messes everywhere, on the table, the armchair, the floor. Louis couldn't have cared less. Toto broke his pencils, played outrageous tricks on him. Louis would yell at him. Toto yelled back. They got along fantastically, they were hardly ever apart. When Louis went down to the kitchen to make some tea or cook supper in the evening, Toto was on his shoulder. Poor Louis could hardly stand, he sometimes fell down the stairs. Toto fell with him. From upstairs I'd hear the parrot screaming furiously. I went down to pick them up. Toto got back on his shoulder and they were off. I never saw two creatures like them—what a triumph! And Toto had one advantage, he got rid of people who came to see him. He gave them ten minutes, no more. After ten minutes, Toto would start biting Louis' visitors on the shoes or the tips of their feet, and they had no choice but to beat a retreat. Things worked out fairly well with the dogs and cats. Of course, there were a lot of fights, but they were of no consequence. Sometimes you'd think the house was going to burst, it was torn apart by squawking, furious barking, a whirlwind. Two minutes later the quiet returned, just as miraculously."

And then, in 1954 or 1955, came the death of Bessy, the dog rescued from Denmark—yet another dreamlike and poignant death, perfect and silent, which overwhelmed Lucette and Louis. Bessy suffered for fifteen days, without complaint. And then one morning she went off by herself. Here is what Céline said about her in *D'un château l'autre*:

"... she wanted to be somewhere else ... on the coldest side of the house and on the pebbles ... she lay down gracefully ... she started to rattle ... it was the end ... I had been told, I didn't believe it ... but it was true, she was lying in the direction of a memory, of where she had come from, the North, Denmark, her muzzle northwards, pointing north ... the dog was very faithful in a way, faithful to the woods where she had run, Korsör, up there ... faithful, too, to the awful life ... the woods of Meudon did nothing for her ... she died with two ... three little rattles ... very discreet ... never once complaining ... so to speak ... and in a really beautiful position, as if in full leap, running ... but on her side, beaten down, finished ... her nose toward her hunting forests, up there where she came from, where she had suffered ... God knows!

"Oh, I've seen plenty of deathbeds ... here ... there ... all over ... but none even close to being so beautiful, discreet ... faithful ... what disrupts men's death is all the fuss ... it seems that man is always on stage."[18]

Bessy was buried in her turn in the garden, behind the house. Lucette planted a hawthorne bush on her grave, as she would for all the animals that were to die in turn: the cats, the dogs that would soon join the Destouches colony: Agar, Balou the endearing black colossus, Frieda, Yasmine, Bonzo the Great Dane, Delphine, Totem and the others, rescued from the neighborhood, abandoned or collected in a shelter in Chaville.

In January 1953 Marcel Aymé accompanied André Parinaud, who came to interview Céline for *La Parisienne*. It was the first of the pilgrimages to Meudon, the first time that a reporter would describe the dilapidated villa, the furious barking of watchdogs, the bizarre figure of Céline walking to the gate like a ragged beggar, dressed in animal skins, layers of sweaters, old corduroy pants, and snow boots with their fur protruding, note the appalling disorder of the writer's office, and listen to the Célinian monologue on such subjects as medicine, Denmark, and the paucity of true stylists. Soon Céline would be talking about the yellow peril and the Chinese in Cognac, the ravages of alcoholism and circus games; paid vacations and the Passage Choiseul. ... To Parinaud, he proclaimed: "Here's a book ... Hours, hour after hour spent torturing paper ... Why? Who reads me today? Who am I writing for? Of course you don't give a damn, but I can't wait a hundred years. I've got to eat every day, I've got to pay the gas bill. So I write . . . what the hell. I write like crazy. The more I bug myself the more I bug them. I've got my back to the wall."[19]

If, in September 1953, Céline decided to register with the Seine-et-Oise medical roll, to open a practice at his home, and to hang out a sign on the gate—DR. L.-F. DESTOUCHES OF THE PARIS MEDICAL FACULTY, 2 P.M. TO 4 P.M. EXCEPT FRIDAYS—it was not solely by way of a pastime or to rejoin the profession that he loved, that he needed, that put him in touch with people, their anguish and their deepest secrets. It was also, incontestably, by way of improving or the hope of improving his income. The failure of *Féerie* and of *Normance* soon thereafter, in June 1954, and the debit account accruing at *Gallimard* all compelled him to find other work—which, on the material level, ended in fiasco: "The first patients came, but when they saw how Louis was set up! Decor counts a lot in patients' eyes. There was no waiting room. Louis saw them in his office. I came down to receive them—I was supposedly the nurse. Women told me about their diseases. Some came out of curiosity, too. There were a few people in the winter, maids, janitors, poor folk. Louis made a lot of house calls. He didn't mind going out of his way. There weren't many who would go out like that, on foot, in the winter, with the rain and the bad weather. But he never had much of a clientele. Just as he was never able to collect his fees."

Céline thus brought out *Normance*—with the subtitle *"Féerie pour une autre fois II"*—in June 1954. His fingers burned, Gallimard reduced the first run to 11,000 copies, which still showed optimism in the face of enduring public disaffection and the dismayed or resolute silence of the press. Robert Poulet, in *Rivarol*, did not beat about the bush: "The monster has lost his amazing agility; all that remains to him is to bite endlessly in the same place, with the dreadful, disenchanted mastication of a sick lion. The truth is, he wearies, he bores."[20]

Normance was an impossible book—one of Céline's borderline works, dedicated to Pliny the Elder, the chronicler of Vesuvius who tried to save the inhabitants of Stabiae, threatened by the volcano, and died of asphyxiation. The allusion was transparent. The author of *Voyage* and *Bagatelles pour un massacre* was trying to tell us yet again that he had never been an actor in history but a witness, that he had never influenced events but had confined himself to relating them, and finally, that if there was anything to reproach him for, it was his excessive courage, if not foolhardiness. Like Pliny, Céline had wanted to raise the alarm and save his compatriots from the massacre he dreaded. Later, he had wanted to observe the cataclysms of World War II and had become their victim, skirting death on several occasions, exiled and imprisoned in Denmark. Misfortune indeed—what, then, had he always been doing, if not bearing witness? Certainly, Céline at his window, describing the air raids on Paris over nearly 400 pages, that unique and crazy eruption, had a right to compare himself to Pliny the Elder. He had captured a style more volcanic than ever, a torrent of lava, words at the melting point, explosions, blasts. It was a spectacle of fire that offered itself to his distorted vision. "The Butte is erupting," he noted before going on to describe "displays of magical volcanic fury" and the emergence of "ten little volcanoes born in the crevasses here on the Butte, between the Avenue and Sacré-Coeur." This was more exaggeration than illusion. And just as Céline turned the unfortunate one-legged Gen Paul into a lecherous and demonic legless cripple (with that same old "respect for the grandiose"), so did he see Montmartre collapsing like a huge gruyère with too many holes, or the Eiffel Tower flattened under the bombs. This is what can be called, in the clinical sense of the word, an hallucination: the distortion of reality under the effect of a diseased consciousness—or of convulsive writing.

This time public disaffection and the indifference of reporters deeply disturbed the writer. What did he care that *Voyage au bout de la nuit* had been optioned by the Club du Meilleur Livre? Or that *Guignol's band* had been translated in England? His new book was going nowhere. Paulhan had not even mentioned it in the NRF. Céline, furious and sarcastic, wrote to him: "We do not hear the same public voices! For pity's sake! mine howl out their astonishment to me at having found nothing in your (deficient) journal on *Normance*— . . . not one review! (not Israelo-assholish and mental-defective as usual!) but a good old-fashioned invitation, the way it ought to be, to buy at the house of our poor Gaston, who has such trouble making ends meet and with whom you commiserate with such lyrical tenderness that it brings tears to my eyes . . . Don't worry JP you'll get your medal as a true servant of the last remaining feudal lords. You'll get your place in Nanterre!* so well deserved! O inadequate one!"[21]

But the fact that there were no reviews, no serious interviews, no compliments, and above all no opportunity to describe his "poetic art" did not prove to be an obstacle. He'd do his own criticism, write his own interview! In 1954, having finished *Normance*, he got to work on *Entretiens avec le professeur Y* [Conversations with Professor Y], which would appear in five nonconsecutive installments in *La Nouvelle Revue Française* starting in June 1954, and in one slim, limited-edition volume of 7,120 numbered copies in March 1955.

It is a curious text—farcical, sarcastic, delirious, solemn—in which Céline reveals for the first time a few of his literary secrets. Of course, he starts with complaints. The decline in book sales has been catastrophic, and a lyrical writer like himself bears its full brunt. His laments very quickly give way to anger: against cynical, swindling publishers, novelists who write in "technicolor," Americans who are good only at publicity. His clownish dialogue with "Professor Y"—a senile, prostatic, and bilious colonel—gives him above all the opportunity to talk about himself. Not as a man of ideas, messages, thoughts, but as a stylist. What style? His answer is based on two points:

---

* Nanterre is the site of a well-known home for the aged poor.

To written language, frozen in its stale conventions and stereotypes, Céline returned an affective dimension. "Emotion in written language! . . . written language was dried out, I was the one who returned emotion to it! . . . it's just as I'm telling you! . . . I swear to you, it's no mean feat . . . the trick, the magic, that any jerk nowadays can move you 'in writing'!"

And that affective dimension was made possible by capturing spoken language in writing. ". . . the novel of 'emotive rendering' is unbelievably exhausting . . . emotion can be captured and transcribed only through spoken language . . . the memory of spoken language! and only after infinite patience! after tiny little retranscriptions!"

For Céline, this is merely a humble invention on the order of the three-gear bicycle. But it is also a crucial invention. His literary goal: to lure readers into his famous "emotive subway" with the accelerations of his writing, his beveled rails. He would endlessly propound it to the visitors and journalists who came to see him: emotion is everything in life.

Was Céline alone through the years 1951 to 1956? He was in any case a man whom Paulhan, fed up with his mockery and incessant cackling, could no longer abide. Their break was made effective in early 1955, Paulhan sadly noting in the postscript to his last letter to Céline: "This is all painful and when all is said and done I am fond of you. Why the devil be so ill-natured?"[22]

But Céline's real, old friends, those who were familiar with his "ill nature," his passing whims, had soon learned and committed to memory the road to Meudon: Marcel Aymé, who came to see him on Sunday mornings, René Héron de Villefosse, André Pulicani and Henri Mahé, Dr. Camus and Pierre Duverger, Arletty and Lucien Rebatet, Jacques Deval and Pierre Monnier. Lucette occasionally received her father and stepmother on Saturday afternoons. Louis also welcomed new admirers and friends, such as Roger Nimier, sometimes accompanied by Antoine Blondin, Kléber Haedens or Stephen Hecquet. He was very fond of Nimier, his enthusiastic youthfulness, his unpedantic culture, his sincerity, his seriousness hidden beneath wild flights of imagination. To Céline, who hated cars and weekends, Nimier showed off his new toys, such as his Aston Martin, and Céline humored his friend.

But more often, in the rediscovered solitude of Meudon, where Céline, who never asked anyone to lunch or supper—he nibbled at his lunch, and supper was boiled vegetables, which he cooked after a fashion while Lucette gave her last lesson, and which he hastily swallowed before going to bed at an early hour—stopped playing, he dreamed, he chewed over old grievances or new novelistic projects.

But Céline was not entirely forgotten. A few rumblings indicated that the quarantine of silence and proscription would not long hold out against his forceful literary presence, the muted violence of his writings. *Voyage au bout de la nuit* came out as a Livre de Poche paperback in early 1956.[23] Robert Poulet came to visit him in the same period to prepare his future *Entretiens familiers avec L.-F. Céline*, to be published by Plon in the "Tribune libre" series in January 1958. Poulet found the writer "muffled in a filthy greatcoat from which emerged the hollow face of an exhausted recluse, in which the pain-ridden mouth contrasts with the half-closed eyes sometimes flashing with a hard flame," expressing himself "in the voice of an awakened sleepwalker who falls back to sleep from time to time or else wavers between cursing and laughing and resolves the dilemma by cursing."[24]

A young admirer of Céline, Paul Chambrillon, recommended by Paraz, had the idea of making a record of extracts of *Voyage* and *Mort à crédit*, read by Michel Simon and Arletty. A first recording in March 1955 proved unusable because of a technical error. At the end of the next session, in April 1956, Céline, thinking that the microphones had been cut, sang the two songs he had composed in the old days, "À noeud coulant" and "Règlement." An accordion was later dubbed in. This Célinian impromptu rounded out the record, which came out the same year, marketed first under the Uranus label and reference number URLP003.

That was not all. In its April 6, 1956, issue, *France-Dimanche* devoted a feature to him. Gérard Jarlot noted a statement that would soon become one of Céline's leitmotifs. "The French? They don't want to work anymore. They eat, they drink, they drink, they eat. Me, I eat black bread, noodles, I drink water and I work. What do I want? To write my books and to be left the f——— alone. What am I looking for in my books? A little French music, some Couperin or Rameau."

On August 8 Céline answered a questionnaire on the subject of vacations in the weekly magazine *Arts*, a pretext for him to evoke the nightmare of the automobile and, once again, France gone to seed, flabby and indolent. "No, I'm not against vacations. We've become a land of vacations, Capua. No virtue can hold out for long here. Cognac, the Paris Casino . . . On top of it, everyone has some family in the provinces where they can go eat some country cooking. . . . France is one big tourist hotel. The danger is that others might want a room here, since you don't live too well in the deserts of Mongolia."

Again in *Arts*, on November 14, 1956, to the question "Do writers have a conscience?" he answered that this was a luxury he had never had the leisure to entertain. "I have a thirty-five-year-old daughter, my son-in-law hates me; I have five grandchildren I've never seen. But everything's fine. Regrets, yes, some regrets. As for the rest, matters of conscience, it's just masturbation. Gide perfected all that."

In his Louis-Philippe villa in lower Meudon, Céline the disliked, even hated witness to barbarism, the contemporary of that absolute evil which, with Hitler, had so recently outraged the conscience of the world, blinded by a human ignominy of which, since *Voyage*, he had been an insufferable chronicler; Céline, unable to find any other response to the great pre-war fear than a cry that sounded to most like gratuitous hectoring; Céline, the delirious with his splendid imprudence, the ideal scapegoat for the mediocre, the specialists in trivial cowardice, ready denunciation, and lightning tergiversation; Céline, the inadvertently amnestied, was beginning to make his voice heard, the voice of a prophet booming against decadence. He was about to undertake *D'un château l'autre*.

In the long run, his purgatory had been brief.

Success and Controversy

One man had yet to visit Céline: Albert Paraz. He had been corresponding with Céline for years, going out of his way to help him, contacting newspaper editors, waging war with a sometimes muddleheaded recklessness but with a brave and fraternal friendship. Céline answered him scrupulously, confided in him, offered him medical advice on how best to treat the chronic tuberculosis from which Paraz had suffered since 1939, when he had been accidentally gassed in the Sahara. But they had never met. Céline did not seem overly anxious to do so. His circle of old friends had always been a little suspicious of the newcomer Paraz, with his often annoying high spirits and his crude outspokenness. The author of *Voyage* did not particularly admire Paraz's literary work. One need only read Céline's letters to note all the pirouettes, evasions, and superficial compliments that avoided his having to come down harshly. Paraz was too naive, too extroverted, too popular and slangish for Céline, an adept of mystery who, despite his effusions, was introverted to the point of timidity and was an intemperate yet painstaking writer. Their friendship was based, one might say, on mistaken identities, a sort of misunderstanding. Certainly, Céline could not deny Paraz's devotion, but he simply did not care to meet the man. From Menton, he could have visited him in Vence, where Paraz had settled after a sanatorium stay, but he did not do so. It was Paraz who finally got his doctors' permission to go up to Paris in June 1956. He hastened to Meudon. Monnier and Céline were waiting for him.

"From the house, where we had gathered, we saw Paraz appear at the garden gate. He was walking with little steps, leaning on a friend's arm. His face was beaming. He was still very handsome despite his illness, and with a smile of happiness on a face that tuberculosis had not managed to ruin. Céline, too, seemed happy. They spent the whole afternoon together, there are photographs of that meeting.

"I think Paraz experienced one of the greatest joys of his life that day."[25]

The two writers met again, in May 1957, during a lawsuit brought by *L'Express* against Paraz and *Rivarol*, and again in August that same year. Paraz then returned to Vence, where he died on September 2 at the age of fifty-seven.

It is unlikely that Céline spoke to Paraz, on his first visit, of the new novel on which he was working. He did not like to discuss his works-in-progress at length, their multiple versions, the groping by which he eventually managed to establish their central theme and prune their superfluous scenes. He treasured the secrecy of his creation, like a craftsman jealous of his techniques.

The failure of his previous books had perhaps discouraged him. But Gallimard, at least, still believed in his talent, though not to the extent of jumping for joy at Céline's repeated requests to be included in the Bibliothèque de la Pléiade. And yet, on February 8, 1955, the writer had dotted his *i*'s: "Ever desirous to play the game, I wonder whether my trash might not be accepted by the Bibliothèque de la Pléaiade, between Bergson and Cervantes, for instance. Might I ask your eminent opinion?"[26]

Gaston Gallimard's eminent opinion was somewhat negative. The decision would not be taken until 1959. This temporary rebuff may consequently have made Céline more receptive, between 1955 and 1957, to the wooing of other publishers who were suddenly interested in enticing the writer away. Around that time, Jean-Claude Fasquelle paid several calls on Céline, to whom he had been recommended by François Michel. The advances paid him by Gallimard were too low, Michel explained. Éditions Fasquelle could be far more generous. Michel had met Céline through Roger Nimier. He was in charge of the "Libelle" series at Fasquelle. The idea of requesting a work from Céline for the collection was tempting. But everything about Céline was already libelous, imprecatory. In François Michel's presence the writer gave vent to long, scabrous monologues against Gaston Gallimard; he would later heap ridicule on Roger Vailland for him, or poke fun at Louise de Vilmorin's affectations.

"More rubbish! . . . the director of Éditions Bérengères is making 'attacks' on me! yes! . . . 'attacks,' as in cavalry! . . . he's looking for me, I'd say . . . he's hunting for me so I can come over to them, so I can go lock, stock, and manuscripts to his 'Bérengères'! can you picture it? . . . me, my manuscripts! obviously, he hates Achille! . . . and not since yesterday! . . . since always! a rancid hatred! he'd give anything to see him foreclose, go bankrupt, sell out! . . . him and his whole fleabag of tricks! and have all his files and dirty dealings looked into . . . this one cleaned up . . . that one . . . the whole thing plucked from under him!"[27]

Does the Bérengères publishing house described by Céline at the beginning of *D'un château l'autre* bear any resemblance to Éditions Fasquelle? And its director, Gertrut Morny, an aging, monocle-wearing dandy, vaguely anti-Semitic, to Jean-Claude Fasquelle, his father, or François Michel? The answer must be negative. In many ways Gertrut is reminiscent of Paul Marteau. Nevertheless, Céline's literary comedy was somewhat inspired by Jean-Claude Fasquelle's interest in his work, which he would have liked to publish at that time. But in his counterattack, Gallimard must have stumbled on some convincing arguments to secure his author's fidelity.

In the early morning light, Céline feverishly wrote page after page of his new book; he called upon his memory, his emotions, ghosts. What else is there to say about his life? The crux was played out there on the first floor of the Meudon villa, when he was not in too much pain—in other words, when he was able to transpose his suffering into words. The rest was just trifles, anecdotes, petty storytelling, the dregs of the day. In Meudon, Céline lived from 6 A.M. to 9 A.M., in the silence of his office, under the parrot's astonished or attentive gaze. Full stop, new paragraph . . .

Occasionally, in the evenings, he'd call on Lucette to bear witness. He asked her to remember. He'd give her the clues: *Sigmaringen—crossing Nuremberg—Bessy's death.* . . . Yes, she remembered. The words came naturally to her, words and emotions. She would begin spontaneously to re-experience the story she told—the recent past, so alive for her, that recaptured the music of long-lost feelings, the movement, the rhythm, the dance perhaps. With Lucette, intuition won out. She spoke of Bessy's death and she cried. That is what must have captivated Louis in her words: not facts or sentences, but the emotion, the essence, the very substance, all that he would later have to organize and transpose in the endless labor of style.

And this time Céline sharpened his style on his memories of Sigmaringen, intermingled with the chronicle of the Meudon years during the writing of the book, from summer '54 to spring '57, while one colonial war followed another, from Algeria to Indochina, and the Russian tanks in Budapest crushed the Hungarian uprising of October 1956. These current events hovered thus at the periphery of the manuscript-in-progress. And with Sigmaringen, as Céline sensed and hoped, he had a good subject this time. If it was scandalous, so much the better. Thus far no one had approached history from the elevated, twilit vantage point of the collaboration, the tremendous tragicomedy played out on the deathbed of the Third Reich. What did Céline care if he compromised himself in recalling his presence on the banks of the Danube among the shipwrecked militiamen, Vichy fugitives, and former ministers of Field Marshal Pétain? He had nothing to lose. When he described the air raids over Paris, in *Normance*, he hadn't made an impression. Now, his "scandalous" presence in Sigmaringen might attract readers.

"I am going to ask you a perhaps rather naive question: What are your reasons for bringing out this new work, *D'un château l'autre*?

"Well, obviously, it's mostly for reasons—I might as well confess it yet again—for economic reasons, to put it nicely. I have been subject to a kind of interdict for a number of years now, and in bringing out a work that despite everything is rather public, since it speaks of facts that are well known and are of some interest, after all, to the French—since it's a little part—a very little part—but even so, a little part of French history: I talk about Pétain, I talk about Laval, I talk about Sigmaringen, it's a moment in French history, like it or not; it may be regrettable, people may not like it, but just the same it's a moment in French history, it happened, and they'll be teaching it in schools one day."[28]

In late 1956 Gallimard hired Roger Nimier as literary consultant. Since his break with Paulhan, Céline had no one to talk to on the rue Sébastien-Bottin, except of course for Gaston Gallimard, and he was unapproachable most of the time. Nimier henceforth became his preferred interlocutor. It was Nimier who would oversee the publication and marketing of his books. The two men respected and liked each other. Nimier knew all the literary high society in Paris and the intrigues of the seraglio. Moreover, as a novelist himself, he was able to encourage Céline, understand his problems, further his ambitions. Nimier sensed it: *D'un château l'autre*—whose marvelous title, with its omission of the "à"* that abruptly accelerates the image, seems to have been hit upon after the book was written—could be the vehicle for Céline's triumphant return to the forefront of contemporary literature.

"I'm up to the 1,300th page, the 50th rehash . . . without being stupidly optimistic, I think that I'll be reaching the end soon (about a month)," Céline wrote him on February 25, 1957. He would keep his word. On March 25 Céline signed his contract with Gallimard upon remission of the manuscript. For once, it had not been Marie Canavaggia who had supervised his typing. Céline may have been fed up with her sometimes possessive affection. Marie hated going all the way to Meudon to pick up the manuscript pages, taking them to the typist, overseeing her work, and then bringing them back to Meudon. And Céline did not care to go to Paris. So, for *D'un château l'autre*, one of Lucette's dance students took on the twofold task of typing and proofreading. It was simpler that way. But Louis, urged on by Lucette, was appreciative of Maria's admirable and long-standing loyalty, and requested her assistance once again for *Nord*.

D'un château l'autre came out on June 4, in a first run of 11,000 copies, selling at 850 francs retail. But even before it reached the bookstore shelves officially on June 20, the book had become the object of curiosity, controversy, and scandal.

An interview in *L'Express* on June 14, given to Madeleine Chapsal on Roger Nimier's initiative and accompanied in the same issue by page proofs from the book, set the tone from the start. For the leftist weekly, Céline stank of infamy. The interview was capped with the warning headline JOURNEY TO THE END OF HATRED and an introductory paragraph clearly delineating the paper's position: "[Céline's] answers, or rather his monologue, shed a harsh light on the mental processes of those who, like him, have chosen to hold mankind in contempt. The confession of his remarkable failure, and the pity that might be inspired by this portrait—grown almost impersonal by dint of being stripped to the bone by existence—must not and cannot lead us to forget that others still dream of that triumph over the spirit known as fascism."

Concerning his pre-1939 pacifism, his vision of the white race overrun by the Chinese, there was nothing particularly new, other than the intemperate virulence reported by Chapsal, who suppressed none of the writer's remarks. Céline described his infinite pains concerning style, only to qualify

---

* In correct grammar, the title would be *D'un château à l'autre*.—Trans.

his statements immediately afterward: "As to that stuff, even my stylistic and rhetorical fanaticism doesn't have such a hold on me that I wouldn't give it up. If your paper offered me a lifetime annuity of 100,000 francs a month, I'd throw it all in, sure, I'd ban my works, gladly, joyfully!"

Céline may have regretted *Bagatelles pour un massacre.* Faced with Chapsal, there was no question of remorse: "That was perhaps the only book I have written for the French in which I abandon my personal reserve. . . . Yes, I believed we had to create one Europe! And that's exactly what they're trying to do now! Too late! . . . History doesn't offer second helpings. We can't make one Europe now! When there was a German army we could have made it. With the German army, the last German army. We chucked it all away!"

A little further he added: "I have suffered like no one and I'm still suffering . . . I'll die in shame, ignominy, and poverty, and all that out of stupidity . . . My only regret is having been a dope!"

He defined the atmosphere in Sigmaringen: "The story of *D'un château l'autre* is unique because it's kind of funny to see 1,142 Frenchmen condemned to death in one little town . . . It's not an everyday sight! It's very rare to write the memoirs of 1,142 people condemned to death! . . . A tiny little hostile German town with the whole world against you . . . Because everybody was waiting for the good folks in Buchenwald with open arms, to greet them with kisses, whereas the world hunted down those in Sigmaringen to rip their guts out . . . It's a pretty strange situation, and it doesn't happen very often! It's kind of funny, 1,142 guys with death closing in, and each of them trying to point the finger at the one who would pay for the rest! And me, I was among them because I was an anti-Semite."

Was this an unrecognizable Céline in *L'Express*? Ready to be bought off to keep quiet? A Céline who would gladly make a spectacle of himself, more vicious than he actually was, as if to justify the weekly's a priori judgment against him? The writer let it be known at once.

To Paraz, on June 18, he wrote: "You should know that Nimier did not attend this conversation, *L'Express* being afraid that in his presence I would restrain my usual excesses and vulgarity . . . that's what they wanted! . . . They didn't censor or cross out a thing, it seems to me . . . you know, when you've had the whole world breathing down your neck for so long, in the slammer and out, you get the knack for finding exactly the right word . . . How could those baboons hope to catch me out? It would take me years to teach them! They're so dull that they'll never understand anything but their own heavy-handed muck!"[29]

And to André Parinaud, who also came to interview him, he declared sarcastically: "All those turds rediscovering me when they find out I've just published *D'un château l'autre.* They come to visit the wreck . . . to see if it's holding together. If I don't stink too bad. But I give them their money's worth. I know the ropes, I always respond to a request. Gentle as lamb is Céline, drooling or spitting. And what may I do for you today? The *Express* came by Meudon. I decked out the station with all my vileness just to welcome him. He must have been delighted! They'll be able to edify their readers and with a clean conscience. I rolled about in my sty like a fat pig . . . And then *Match* . . . I've become the fashionable item. It excites them. How may I help you?"[30]

At heart, Céline was rejoicing at having suddenly become the object of scandal, the recognized writer, the prophet of a new decadence, that of Europe, the white race, Judeo-Christian civilization. I do not believe that he was parodying himself in his interviews: he was exaggerating, not lying.

He had no trouble offending the readers of *L'Express*, who wrote to their weekly in droves. To the extreme Right, he shocked people like Pierre-Antoine Cousteau, the former ultra-collaborationist, a member of the *Je suis partout* team sentenced to death at the liberation. "M. Céline has rallied to the gilded dungheap of the System," he exclaimed in the June 20 issue of *Rivarol*. To his eyes, granting an interview to *L'Express* smacked of disgraceful compromise. Worse still, in minimizing his anti-Semitism, in insisting that he had been above all pro-Aryan, pro-French, and a pacifist, Céline suddenly seemed to him to be a traitor, an irresponsible coward who—having sent to the front lines myriads of young Frenchmen who had read *Bagatelles* or *L'École des cadavres* and enlisted in the LVF—was now washing his hands of them. Cousteau's fierce attack also appeared in *Lectures françaises*.

The diatribes and jockeying for position began to multiply. Rebatet rightly pointed out in *France-Dimanche* that he had trouble seeing how a writer who had never belonged to any party or newspaper could be accused of repudiating anything. In the columns of *Rivarol*, Paraz too protested against the accusations of betrayal. Céline wrote to him on June 20: "Cousteau would love to see me hanged, along with all the 'intellectuals' from Siegmaringen . . . as vile as I am for being free of charge . . . a 'liberated woman' and not a whore . . . I never took anything and I'd never take anything from anyone . . . I never had any business with the *Staffel* or the *German censor*, while they, the *JSP*, *slithered around* in those places, *dependents* and *under orders* as they were . . . Those are old reasons for hatred warmed over, obviously horror at seeing me resurrected . . . when I was dead and 'buried' . . . what a relief! Disgusting zombie!"[31]

The controversy dragged on this way throughout the summer, a godsend in those months of rather gloomy news that saw Nasser nationalize the Suez Canal and the Italian ocean liner *Andrea Doria* slowly sink beneath the waves off Nantucket.

Maurice Clavel, in *Jeune Europe*, observed with cold contempt the attacks on Céline by old *collabos* "warming over their bitterness and stewing in it." The *Express* interview inspired the following commentary from him: "Being so 'sectarian,' I may be attacked for harboring a soft spot for a genius. I can't help it, that's how it is. Collaboration is moral turpitude—it's cowardice, it's delegating law and order and personal vengeance to the enemy.

Céline has paid amply. He has not finished paying. *L'Express*, proud of itself, interviewed him so they could make a fairground attraction out of him. They succeeded. They entitled it *Journey to the End of Hatred*. That is not quite accurate: the journey is still to the end of night."[32]

Other critics preferred to speak exclusively of the book. From *Le Figaro* to *Paris-Presse*, from *Carrefour* to *L'Aurore*, from *France-Soir* to *Le Canard enchainé*, there was hardly a single periodical not to devote long columns— mostly favorable—to the new work. And the interviews continued. For Swiss-French radio with Louis-Albert Zbinden. For *Artaban* with Jean Callandreau. Most importantly, on July 17, Céline was Pierre Dumayet's guest on his famous television show, "Lectures pour tous" [Reading for All]. *L'Humanité* headlined forthwith SCANDAL ON TELEVISION. It was nothing of the sort. Céline had rehashed most of his old obsessions for the cameras, described his childhood in the Passage Choiseul, talked about Sigmaringen (which he continued to spell "Siegmaringen" in his books, playing ironically on the German word *Sieg*, meaning "victory"), denied he was a violent person, and finished by lamenting human stupidity. "I mostly see people drinking, eating, sleeping, doing all the . . . concerned with all the human functions, which are all rather vulgar, and I would say they are dull. And their minds are dull, that's what I sense above all. And they have always been so."[33]

In a letter to Céline, Gaston Gallimard referred to the book's "staggering takeoff." Everything is relative. The first run of 11,000 copies sold out quickly. Gallimard ordered a reprinting of 11,000 in July and 5,500 in September. And then the pace slackened. A year later, the sales of *D'un château l'autre* had yet to reach 30,000. During the same period, Roger Vailland's *La Loi* [The Law], published, ironically, by the same house at the same time, won the Goncourt on December 2. Two hundred and fifty thousand copies were printed, while Camus' *L'Exil et le Royaume* [Exile and the Kingdom] had passed the 80,000 mark. In a word, Céline was still no best-selling author. He could hardly hope to be. The critical success of his book had been based largely on its subject matter: Sigmaringen, Pétain, Laval. For the writer, this was a partial misunderstanding. Far more important to him was narrative technique, the quality of the writing, the "pure lace" of the style. "From that point of view, *Château* is a whopping success. I've freed myself from a lot of clichés. Painters have gradually abandoned subject matter. I've pursued the same adventure, but I'm the only one concerned."[34]

It was the success of *La Loi* that drew Céline's attention to Vailland. The article by the communist novelist that had appeared in *La Tribune des nations* in January 1950 could not have been known to him, exiled in Denmark at the time. Nimier confirmed, after *La Loi* won the Goncourt, that it had been Vailland who once boasted of wanting to assassinate Céline during the closing days of the occupation. Céline wrote his derisive response in *Le Petit Crapouillot* in February 1958.[35]

It was not only reporters and columnists who rediscovered Céline after

D'un château l'autre. Writers and artists got in touch with him. Chaval wrote to him. The tragic absurdity and suicidal hilarity of the marvelous cartoonist was in harmony with the writer's morbid extravagances. Paul Morand also wrote to him. If Céline's latest books had perplexed him, if he had deemed *Entretiens avec le professeur Y* staggering but opaque, the "chronicle" of Sigmaringen, on the other hand, had enthused him. "Your triumph is tremendous. Young people worship you. Your message is awaited, received, understood. The coming generation is like the others: it hates its fathers but loves its grandfathers, whom we are. That will help us get along."[36] But Morand, back in France—Morand, whom Céline loved because he had managed to jazz up the French language—did not have the opportunity to meet the author of *Voyage* again; the imprecating hermit of Meudon suddenly burst into the news with *D'un château l'autre.*

The news gradually died down, of course, as the months passed, and as Céline withdrew once more into Meudon and began his new work, *Nord,* calling forth other memories of Germany, other emotions, other ghosts, between Baden-Baden and Berlin, Dr. Hauboldt's bunker and the Scherz estate near Neuruppin. For such was the subject matter of *Nord*: the lives of the narrator, Lucette, Bébert, and Le Vigan before they reached Sigmaringen, the story of the summer of '44 in the Shakespearian luxuriance of dying dynasties. But the trend had been set, the road to Meudon mapped out, Céline's "liveliness" made familiar to interviewers. and his literary genius pretty well established.

On October 22, 1957, Céline recorded a half-hour of rambling talk for the "Leurs oeuvres et leur voix" series on the Festival label. On the flip-side Arletty and Pierre Brasseur read extracts from his first two novels. In January 1958 Plon published his *Entretiens familiers* [Casual Conversations] with Robert Poulet. On the 12th of that month, Céline answered Jacques Chancel's questions on "Télémagazine." He had become a "personality," someone who has to be urgently questioned on everything and nothing, and preferably on subjects that have nothing to do with his speciality or area of expertise.

What did he think of television?

"It's a phenomenal propaganda tool. Unfortunately, it also makes people stupid in the sense that they have to rely on what they're shown. They stop imagining. They watch. They lose the concept of judgment and happily surrender to laziness.

"TV is dangerous.

"Alcohol, gossip, and politics have already made morons out of them. Was it necessary to add something new?"

A year later, in January 1959, the journal *Arts* asked his opinion on the conquest of the moon. *Paris-Presse l'Intransigeant* wanted to know, in February, if he'd like to be told the truth if he developed cancer. Céline's answer: as a doctor he would know it, obviously. *Arts* again solicited his opinion of *Don Quixote.* It was endless.

At the time of *Normance*, Céline had asked Gaston Gallimard to commission a book on him. In March 1959 he received two visits from a young Belgian academic, Marc Hanrez, who recorded one of their conversations. He was in fact preparing a work devoted to the author of *Voyage* for Gallimard's series "La Bibliothèque idéale" managed by Robert Mallet. Hanrez expressed his astonishment to Céline at the almost total absence of sentimental love in his books. His interviewee answered: "The association of two beings is a very respectable thing, and quite normal as an aid in resisting life's blows, which are innumerable. It's nice, it's pleasant, but I don't think it merits a literature. I also find it vulgar and dull, this whole 'I lo-ove you!' business . . . It's an awful word which I myself have never used, because it can't be expressed, only felt, and that's all there is to it. A little self-restraint isn't a bad thing. These things exist, but should be spoken only once a century, a year . . . not all day, like in the songs."[37]

During that same month of March 1959, Céline received a French television crew with Louis Pauwels and André Brissaud, to interview him for the series "En français dans le texte." He talked about his childhood, his mother's lace-making, the Passage Choiseul, his sufferings, his disease, and the difficulties in achieving a style. The greatest joy in his life? "Well, by God, I have to tell you—I haven't had many! I'm not a creature of joy, I'm not one for fleeting passions. I don't mind saying that I'll be glad to die, that's the truth. Only that I'd like to die as painlessly as possible, especially since I'm not fond of pain."[38]

Was Céline's trial on appeal on the way to being won in the court of public opinion? No. The conversation with Pierre Dumayet had already caused loud howls of outrage. The announcement that Pauwels and Brissaud's show would be aired on June 19 inspired a call to arms. The MRAP and the Association of Resistance Veterans protested, leading the Ministry of Information to ban it.

Céline's interpretation of the affair in *Nord*: "Now I've attained the honor, no matter how you look at it, of getting myself excommunicated, an undesirable eccentric . . . why just two days ago the television! . . . they came, they wanted to, they took one look at me, they ran away in a panic . . . busted up all their equipment, fogged all their film stock! . . . they didn't even apologize . . . nothing! . . . I ask you! . . . where we've gotten to! 'It'll all end in rabble' . . . Nietzsche predicted it, all right . . . and here we are! Ministers, satraps, Dien-Pen-Hu everywhere! tail-turning and pink underwear!"[39]

That was not the end of it. The announcer Jacqueline Caurat was threatened with a serious reprimand merely for mentioning Céline's name on the air.[40] At the writer's death, the network canceled the report it had planned for the news. In a word, Louis Destouches still stank of infamy. His mere presence on the screen, the mention of his name continued to be a subject of scandal—like an incitement to anti-Semitism. Ignoring Céline was a way of shutting one's eyes, of forgetting the past, the defeat, the occupation.

Céline no longer expected or hoped for anything. On March 31, 1959, he gave up his medical practice, had himself stricken from the Seine-et-Oise medical roll, and claimed his pension. He was going on sixty-five. He was wasting no time. In May, Gallimard published his *Ballets sans musique, sans personne, sans rien* [Ballets Without Music, Without Characters, Without Anything] in an edition of 5,500 copies at 700 francs, illustrated by Éliane Bonabel, the niece of his old friend from Clichy, from years past, from the days of *Voyage*. It was less a joy for him than a little consolation for all the synopses written over the course of the years which had never been produced onstage, brought to life, illuminated by dance music, lifted from the earth. The signing on June 2, 1959, of the contract for the long hoped-for and awaited reprinting of *Voyage* and *Mort à crédit* in the Bibliothèque de la Pléiade must have brought him a certain comfort. But his account with the publisher remained nonetheless desperately in the red, to the tune of nearly 6 million old francs.*

This was all the more incentive to grapple with his new book, to exhaust himself with work, to try to reach the North with the utmost despatch. He worked on it from the spring of '57 to late '59. As with *D'un château l'autre*, the years in which he wrote were the "backdrop" for the book in progress, through brief references and short contemporaneous scenes set parallel with the main action, that of the past, the summer of 1944. The Russians had just launched their first Sputniks. They appeared to be on their way to winning the space race under Kruschchev. France was bogged down in Algeria in a colonial war to which no end seemed in sight. On May 13, 1958, it changed Republics. De Gaulle was returning to power. "I understand you," he would proclaim on June 4 to the Algerians, who didn't understand what there was to be understood.

In Meudon, Céline watched current events with a weary detachment. He could have said of himself what Jules Renard had said in his *Journal*: "It is not my way of thinking that matters to me, it is my way of feeling." And as always, to Céline, feeling meant capturing emotion, expanding his vision to the plane of an immense imaginative fresco, fitting his prose style into the framework of his most tragic, most subtle music.

Despite the visits from his friends, he remained a man alone. A man who could grant himself a few minutes' distraction, nostalgia, happiness in meeting once more with Max Revol, the Montmartre cabaret singer; André Neufinck, his old buddy from the 12th Cuirassier Regiment in Rambouillet, who had saved his *Carnet du cuirassier Destouches*; Marie Le Bannier, who had been the mistress of his father-in-law Follet, and then his landlady in Saint-Malo, with her daughter Sergine; Dr. Bécart, another collaboration figure and the soul of the Cercle Européen; Mme. Mitre, the former secretary and lover of Fernand de Brinon; Dr. Jacquot, his Sigmaringen colleague;[41] the sculptor Arno Brecker, whom Hitler had praised to the skies for his robust realism, who had been living in Montmartre since 1950 and was

---

* The franc was devalued in 1960. One new franc is worth 100 old francs.—Trans.

considering doing Céline's bust; Hermann Bickler and Karl Epting in early 1961. ... But a man who immediately afterward plunged back into his manuscripts, his memories, his obsessions, his exhaustion, his headaches, his solitude.

The dancer Serge Perrault, in turn, had found Lucette and Louis again, lost in the upheavals at the war's end. He spent long hours with them in Meudon. He introduced them to Dr. Willemin, who also became one of the couple's regular visitors. Louis, as we have said, rarely went to Paris. He constantly promised Lucette that he would take her to the Musée de la Marine. He never went. Only once did he take her to the Louvre. Marcel Aymé, in 1952, somehow managed to convince them to attend a performance of his play *La Tête des autres*. Céline dragged himself to one other show, a few years later, in the company of Lucette and André Willemin, to see the ballets of the Marquis de Cuevas at the Théâtre du Champs-Élysées. That was it. Not one film, one review, ballet, or play.

Occasionally, on Thursdays, Serge Perrault took Louis into Paris in his rickety Citroën 2CV to see his dentist, whose office was located near the Opéra. Perrault would later meet the writer on the terrasse of a Grands Boulevards café near the Madeleine. As soon as he had finished teaching his classes at the Opéra dance school, he would drive Louis back to Meudon. He once witnessed an incident that he saw, deeply moved, from afar. At the terrace of his usual café, dressed as raggedly as ever, Louis had just sat down, worn out from his session with the dentist. There was a small bloodstain on his shirt. A new waiter at the establishment, noticing this apparent tramp, approached him, took him gently by the arm, and helped him to his feet. "This isn't any place for you—come along, my friend!" and he escorted him to the sidewalk. Docile and resigned, Céline put up no fuss. The overzealous waiter had no idea that he had bounced one of the greatest French writers of the century.

As we have said, Céline reserved all his strength for writing, for summoning his memories. When, in 1958, his first mother-in-law, Mme. Athanase Follet, died, he wrote a letter to Édith—a letter that deeply moved the woman who had shared his life from 1919 to 1924, and which helped to reforge the bonds of an old and affectionate complicity between them.

My dear Édith,

I embrace you—all one can do in such circumstances—and share your sorrow. I would be with you if I hadn't behaved so foolishly.

Marie Follet is joining G. Sand, she was altogether of another era. She was always good to me, I have a great recollection of her most generous gifts (Degas) and her hospitality—how brutal I was to her as well! On top of my stupidity, I perhaps have the excuse of my horrible ear problem, a very feeble excuse! I hope I shall see you, whenever you choose, between the two of us, my God, getting away from life, there is nothing but perfectly innocent memories! but I value those memories and your forgiveness.

> *All my love,*
> *Louis* [42]

But Édith no longer had anything to forgive. Time, that balm to bitterness and disappointment, had passed. Long ago she had asked for a divorce; he too had suffered. There was nothing but tenderness between them now. "I'm a fool for memories," he told her. "I want to remember only the best times I spent with Louis, only the amazement and enrichment he brought me," Édith Follet-Lebon confided to me.

At each of Édith's visits to Meudon, Louis insisted on reimbursing her taxi fare. One day, while the two of them were strolling near the promenade of the lower Meudon station, Louis told her:

"You know, when I was a kid, my mother came here by train and sold her lace by the station exit."

She looked at him, astonished.

"Really, Louis, who do you think you're talking to?"

He started. He had forgotten that Édith had known his parents very well, witnessed their petty-bourgeois dignity. Mme. Destouches had never personally sold her lace on the street or in front of stations. She might on occasion have gone to important markets or to visit clients to repair antique lace, but nothing else.

"A writer has to invent his biography," he finally said, smiling, in excuse.

Memories ... It was perhaps because the important things between Colette and himself had been forgotten that he hardly saw his daughter in the last years of his life. Their relationship had become difficult. As we have seen, he did not want to meet his grandchildren, place any bets on the future. He valued only his past. Édith and Lucette nonetheless conceived the idea of introducing him to the eldest, Jean-Marie Turpin, who was about fifteen years old. Céline had not been forewarned. They feared being rebuffed. So Jean-Marie presented himself to him. Rankled at being caught off-guard, his grandfather greeted him coolly.

"Have you graduated from high school?" he asked.

No, he hadn't graduated yet.

"Well then, sir, come back to see me after you graduate."

That was all. He walked his grandson to the door. He never saw him again. Then, with Lucette, he gave full vent to his anger.

"But his rages didn't mean anything," she explains. "Had Louis' grandson been a little smarter, had he done what I told him to do and not come pipe in mouth, with a floppy bow tie and affectations straight out of Lamartine, telling him that he wanted to write too, if he had come a little more simply and asked his advice, I'm sure Louis would have taken to him on the spot."

With Mikkelsen, in any case, there were no memories or sentimentalities that counted for anything. The gold in Denmark, that distressing misunderstanding, stood between them. One day the Danish lawyer showed up unexpectedly at the gate of the Meudon villa with bottles of a sleeping potion that Louis had used in Copenhagen and which had done him a lot of good. Louis parleyed with him from the balcony and refused to let him in.

"There was nothing I could do," says Lucette. "I tried to intervene. A thousand times I tried to intercede with Louis. We had bad arguments. People said that we fought all the time. But that wasn't it at all! I simply tried to persuade him to be more diplomatic, I told him to be more tactful with Mikkelsen or the Marteaus. In vain. When someone said, 'I'll be glad to help you but you have to do this or that in return,' he couldn't stand it."

Nonetheless, Céline finally listened to reason and received Mikkelsen on later occasions, when the lawyer paid his brief visits to Paris. He also got into the habit of corresponding with him. The weight of the past was ever present, of which he unburdened himself primarily through writing.

On January 27, 1959, he specified to Nimier: "My next saga is coming along . . . it's finished (2,600 pages) . . . I just have to polish it up for a few more months."[43]

On December 23 all was ready and the manuscript sent to Gaston Gallimard. From then on, Céline was impatient to see it in print. In January 1960 Nimier received another letter: "I'm afraid of the future, Roger . . . the printing, quick!"[44]

Death was prowling around the writer, more insistent, more persuasive than ever. Céline sensed it. He was afraid. He hadn't yet finished his work.

The Old Man and Death

Two young men, Jacques Darribehaude and Jean Guénot, set out on the road to Meudon in early 1960. To see the Master, record his words, and perhaps to dream of a film that they would devote to him. Céline began by showing them to the door. "I do not converse!" And then he fixed appointments for February 6 and 20. Later on, Guénot would meticulously retranscribe the writer's statements—statements that are beyond any doubt among the most complete and concise he ever gave. His interviewers particularly wanted to know his opinion of the great writers that might have influenced him. Céline spoke to them of La Fontaine and Villon, Racine and Shakespeare, Proust and Saint-Simon, Stendhal and Mme. de Staël.[45] In his panting, somewhat nasal voice, he also described for his two interviewers his childhood, his years of apprenticeship, once again giving life to the Passage Choiseul, never tiring of summoning forth his recollections.

In May 1960 the producer Claude Autant-Lara wrote to him. He was considering adapting *Voyage* for the cinema. Another return to the past, an old dream that would not be fulfilled. It was impossible to put *Voyage* on the screen. Autant-Lara abandoned it a few months later.

And on May 20 Gallimard brought out *Nord* in a first edition of 8,000 copies, at the retail price of 17.50 francs ("francs" now meant new francs). Nimier had drafted the publisher's blurb. Céline found it marvelous.

"Céline in the middle of a Germany in flames: such is the theme of *Nord*. A participant, narrating and observing at the same time, the author finds himself in Baden-Baden in the months preceding the Reich's downfall. A strange luxury hotel where caviar, bouillabaisse, and champagne count for more than the air raids. The astonishing Baroness von Seckt, a survivor from another world, judges Hitler: 'You know, Monsieur Céline, the Devil owes his triumph above all to the fact that those who knew him well are no longer among us.'

"Then on to Berlin, with its disemboweled houses, a petty, oppressive bureaucracy operating among the ruins. Céline and his companions in misfortune—his wife Lili, the actor Le Vigan, Bébert the cat—are sent 100 kilometers from the capital to Zornhof, an immense estate managed by a madman. To the East, the plain stretches all the way to the Urals. And around the four Frenchmen (for Bébert definitely counts as a Frenchman) lives a Shakespearian family in a village inhabited by Poles, prostitutes from Berlin, and conscientious objectors, all plump and hearty, forced by the Reich to build coffins.

"Céline calls himself a chronicler, but he describes Germany in defeat like Dante visiting the circles of his Inferno.

"On one side are the powerful of this world, ever determined to milk life for all they can. On the other are the unfortunate, to whom they toss 'ideals' like so many bones to gnaw on. And, ever present, 'the world of the Greeks, the tragic world, miseries every day and every night.' "

Immediately after drafting the blurb, Nimier published, in the June 1 issue of *Arts*, one of the most beautiful of the book's reviews. Without too many moral scruples, as both judge and plaintiff, publisher and journalist, he wielded every conceivable weapon in defense of an author whom he loved.

"What Circle of Hell, what Inferno, what Germany are the themes of *Nord*, his most beautiful book since *Voyage au bout de la nuit*? First, the empire of gluttony in Baden-Baden; that of ruins in Berlin; that of madness at Zornhof in Prussia. The gluttonous, the violent, and the mad parade through this chronicle in which mankind, lost, reels in drunken circles."

And he ends his article with this closing remark: "The terrible chronicle of our times, with the melody of a song far off in the distance, far off in the depths of evil."

The publication of *Nord* was marked by few polemics or controversies. Céline granted almost no interviews that summer. Only his conversation with Claude Sarraute for *Le Monde* on June 1 deserves special attention. This time it was no longer a case of laying traps for the writer, of setting him up for the readers' admiration or opprobrium, or of recalling what was now known to all (or should have been): Céline's anti-Semitism and prewar ravings, Sigmaringen, and all that followed. The book was out: *Nord*, an incontestable masterpiece. To Claude Sarraute, Céline explained why he had become a "tragic chronicler" at the end of the war, which for him presaged the end of Europe. He emphasized his style, his famous "little music," the prodigious effort of transposition he had to make to catch his readers unaware, to move them.

"When people talk about me, they say: 'He has natural eloquence . . . he writes the way he talks . . . you can tell.' Only, the thing is, it's 'transposed.' It's not quite the word expected, the situation expected. It's transposed into the realm of dream, between what's true and not true, and in this way the word used becomes both more intimate and more precise than the way it is normally used. You make your own style. You have to. The craft is easy, it can be learned. Good hands have no use for ready-made tools. Style is the same way. It only serves to draw from oneself what one cares to reveal."[46]

Nord received exceptional critical acclaim. In *L'Express* on May 26, Jean-Louis Bory waxed lyrical in the intense admiration he had long held for this "picaro of the Paris suburbs, this verbal dynamiter, this churlish Pierrot, guzzler of clouds sailing between memory and prophecy, from repetitiveness to vaticination, this detestable, inspired, doddering geezer, this awesome òld clown in a circus magnified to the scale of our planet, where he simultaneously spouts the patter and struts in the parade, performs the somersaults and the painted face, the trapeze and the lion-taming— sneering with distress at the thought of the final shore." Elsewhere, Bory rightly stresses the evolution of Céline's style. "Writing in trances, a hurricane of hues, *Nord*, it seems, is a further progression on the road to stylistic liberation, to the expressive immediacy of the emotive rendering, the precise reverberation of vertigo. One cannot conceive of a tighter harmony between the abrupt, disconcerting style, whose ultimate refinement leads to the use of a syntax in the 'savage state,' and the savage Apocalypse of our recent history, the fall of that House of Usher that was Nazi Germany."

It is impossible to list all the book's reviews: the warmth of Kléber Haedens in *Paris-Presse* on June 4, the more subtle admiration of Maurice Nadeau in *France-Observateur* on June 9, the predictable praise of Robert Poulet in *Rivarol*, which called *Nord* superior to *D'un château l'autre*, and even, surprisingly, the laudatory article of André Rousseaux in *Le Figaro littéraire*—the same Rousseaux who, ever since *Voyage*, had stubbornly cut Céline down for each of his works and who, suddenly, was struck by his gracefulness and concluded his article on these words: "Certain pages of this book give contemporary literature its most stirring vibrancy."

Nord is Céline's last masterpiece, perhaps his greatest book, sumptuously wild and sumptuously structured, with that cryptic, magnetic fascination that draws its heroes all the way to the desolate Brandenburg plains, endless plains, lines of glaciary umber, with the vague, harrowing threat of Barbarism's advance—meaning the arrival of the Russians but even more, of Doomsday—a deluge that has only to wash across the plain to signal the end of civilization, to drown Céline, Bébert, Lucette, Le Vigan forever; the German medical service, the prisoners, the little Polish women, the Prussian aristocrats, the Gypsies, the Berlin prostitutes; in short, that sampling of humanity huddled in the Noah's ark of the Kränzlin estate. After Baden-Baden and its anachronistic hotel, after Berlin in ruins and the air raids, the action is concentrated in the heart of the farm, which is directly controlled from the Scherz home, in a mythological tragicomedy orchestrated somewhere between vaudeville and horror, the epic and the grotesque. No longer isolated episodes set end-to-end, as in *D'un château l'autre*, but a chain of bizarre, demented occurrences and visions.

With tremendous breadth, Céline seems to recapitulate every possible emotion, every feeling that can animate characters: love, venality, fear, hatred, desire for vengeance, envy, lust, or the survival instinct . . . and he shuffles them with desperate humor. He has nothing left to lose, since he has already lost almost everything, since his days are numbered. He thus goes to the heart of the matter—and that by the most marvelous detours anywhere in fiction. *Nord* sometimes makes one want to laugh: the greatest works of world literature always contain a comic element. But our laughter chokes on itself. And that too is the sign of a masterpiece, with its hallmark of lucidity.

Céline could have—should have—rested after writing *Nord*. But he plunged into his new novel, a sequel of the last, twofold crossing of Germany from north to south to reach Sigmaringen, then from south to north as far as Flensburg, to reach Denmark a few months later. Another epic, another journey beneath the bombs and through chaos, from train to train, "a digression across a landscape," as Céline would so neatly define the book that he would end up naming *Rigodon* [Rigadoon], after having long planned on the title *Colin-Maillard* [Blindman's Buff].

The title, *Rigodon*, is typical of Céline's genius, managing in one word or one short phrase to sum up an obsession, suggest a hue, a theme, make a novel sing by shedding inevitable yet unexpected light upon it. "*Rigodon*" has two meanings, according to the French dictionary. The first: a lively and merry dance that was fashionable in the seventeenth and eighteenth centuries. The second: in target practice, a drumbeat, bell, or flag signal to indicate that a bullet has hit the center of the target; by extension, a bull's-eye.

And, that said it all: gracefulness and strength, nimbleness and violence, elegance and fatality. *Rigodon* would resemble all his other books in the comic tone underlying the darkest passages: an Apocalypse in lace. Thus, when Bébert unearths in the ruins of Hamburg the remains of a grocery store buried beneath the rubble or when, a little earlier in Ulm, Le Vigan stops Field Marshal Von Runstedt's car, we are incontrovertibly in full comedy. Céline writes alertly, elegantly, he smiles through revolutions, he is a man of the eighteenth century who writes the way one dances, who has a sense of measure, grace, spontaneity. But let there be no mistake. The smile is but a façade, the lively, merry rigadoon a fragile illusion. These characters swaying to the dance beat are in reality being shaken by the jolts of death; they are dancing an endless round in the arms of death, but they have the supreme courtesy to lie, to smile. The trains roaring through hell and speeding off toward nowhere—these are the rigadoons, the Célinian bull's-eyes, the sense of urgency, the prose rushing headlong toward intense emotion, toward the shadowy certainties rising from blood-drenched landscapes.

A few months earlier Céline had suffered a minor stroke. Only a few intimate friends had been told. He had risen abruptly from his desk one day and scattered his papers on the floor. Lucette had found him later, prostrate on his bed, spittle at the corners of his mouth, barely able to recognize her. "It lasted a few weeks," she recalls. "And then one day he got up and asked me, 'What did you do with my papers?' He didn't remember a thing. His life returned to normal."

Other than writing *Rigodon*, Céline spent a part of the summer of 1960 preparing, with Jean A. Ducourneau, the Pléiade edition of *Voyage au bout de la nuit* and *Mort à crédit*, to be prefaced by Professor Henri Mondor. Recall the blank spaces left in the first edition of *Mort*, the passages deemed scandalous that Céline had refused to rewrite more respectably—he began to write passages to fill these blanks.[47] Over the course of that summer, he met for the first time with Claude Bonnefoy, who, in their conversations, would urge Céline to talk about his childhood, his years in the Rambouillet barracks and, later, his missions for the Rockefeller Foundation.

Gallimard was paying him 1,000 francs a month as advances on his royalties. It wasn't much. It may have been too much, though, for the publisher, who watched as Céline's balance dipped ever further into the red and could only urge him on to ever greater productivity. Despite its staggering critical success, *Nord*'s sales had been disappointing. The first commercial edition of 8,800 copies was followed in June by a second of 5,500. And this last edition was far from being sold out.

Lucette sensed that Louis was at the end of his tether, more short of breath, sickly, and exhausted than ever. His headaches came on stronger. He rejected any form of distraction. A few years earlier, she had thought that a stay at the seaside would do him some good. He had inherited two little houses from his parents in Dieppe. Lucette had made several trips by herself to fix one of them up, after a fashion. When she finally managed one Sunday to drag him to Dieppe, it was only to note his disappointment at what he deemed a miserable, meager dwelling on a street corner. He refused to spend a single night there. They both took the next train back to Paris. He had not allowed himself one day's vacation since.

"A few days before his death, I said to him, 'We're selling everything, we sell the house, we go to the seaside, you can drop your work, you're not finishing your book, we're leaving.' But he wanted to finish his book, so that I'd have something after his death. He explained it all very clearly to me. He took barely two years to write *Rigodon*, he overworked himself, and everything was done, in draft, on the eve of his death, he had just written the last page. I think he realized it, he knew that he had overdone it, that he had made an effort from which he wouldn't be able to recover, his head wouldn't bear up under it. You can't imagine how he worked. He sometimes spent hours on a single word or sentence, he'd start over, cross out, come back to the same passage."

The Pléiade edition was delayed. Céline became despondent, having rejoiced at being included in the imprint during his lifetime, as if into some sort of Pantheon, after Malraux and Montherlant.

"If I understand you, your plans for me have been deferred by at least six months! But six months for me means total decrepitude and the desire to vanish from the scene for good and all!"[48]

On June 30, 1961, he completed the second draft of *Rigodon*. It has been claimed that he considered the book to be finished. But he told a reporter in May that he did not think he would be done for another two years. He had written in the pages of *Rigodon* itself: "I'll be seventy when this work is published." In other words, he did not anticipate publication until 1964. The text bears traces of this relative incompleteness. Several passages are repeated at various places in the novel. The narrative suffers from inconsistencies and surprising ellipses in the thread of the discourse. On the way to Augsburg, for instance, Céline is told that he will have to change trains to get to Ulm. The train stops soon thereafter . . . in Ulm. The plot chronology, too, is whimsical. We go from the month of November to the month of May, then June, then September, with astonishing alacrity. But all of this is of little importance. More serious is the erratic style of the writing. Céline the stylist clearly did not have time to reread this version, to comb through his text. And the writing sometimes drags imperceptibly, betrays a forced tone, a self-conscious effort to sound natural. *Rigodon* is evidence by default of Céline's genius—the perfection that may be lacking here but in no way prevents many passages from being among his very best work.

In any case, he knew that it was all over, that he would go no further, that the journey was drawing to an end. *Rigodon* would not have the breadth of his earlier novels. *Tant pis.* He would not relate therein his life on the Baltic shores, which, as several pages of the book attest, had been his intention: "Korsör . . . everything in its place, I'll show you around."[49] Death was present, watching, losing patience. He didn't want to keep it waiting. What was the use? So he abridged his novel. And we can sense death's unwavering presence between the lines and pages he was writing at the time. "I'm digressing, I'm going to lose you, but I have the feeling that I may never finish this book . . . very beautiful, a chronicle of events and gestures that were important twenty . . . thirty years ago . . . but what about today's events? . . . all the people in my class have vanished except a few failures whose minds are gone, who quibble, scratch, sit on the can from one spluttering newspaper to the next. . . . We've only got one life it's not much, especially in my case, feeling the Fates pulling on my string, and just for the fun of it . . . yes! plaything!"[50]

On June 30 he wrote two more letters. One to Gaston Gallimard:

> *My dear Publisher and Friend,*
>
> *I think it is nearly time to bind ourselves by another contract for my next novel* Rigodon *. . . on the same terms as the last except! for the sum of 1,500 NF [new francs] instead of 1,000—otherwise I too am going to rent a tractor, knock down the NRF and sabotage every school kid's exams!*
>
> > *Keep that in mind!*
> > *Yours ever,*
> > *Destouches*[51]

The other to Roger Nimier:

> *Dear Roger,*
>
> *I briefly met with that novelist lady, I don't have a minute to lose, I want to pass my 70th in full steam, in a whirlwind, to hell with the public!*
> *"What great advice! So I sit down and write to Gaston and hurrah for the 1,500 NF! I've got 'em! Everything I do has got to sell well, since the others cling to Bourget, Maizeroy . . . It's not my fault, those stubborn old new waves keep me permanently fresh!*
>
> > *Affectionately,*
> > *Louis*
>
> *Not* Colin-Maillard, *the next one,* Rigodon.
> *You know, I ponder very slowly but years ahead—the publicity wrapper already:*
> Over here! quick! Over there![52]

The next day, Saturday, July 1, the heat was crushing. When Lucette got up, she found Louis in the cellar, trying to find a little respite. She took him up to his room. The light hurt him. She closed the shutters. "That day, his head hurt him more than usual. I gave him compresses. He lay down, naked, he was that hot. And his right arm was freezing, which was amazing on such a scorcher. The blood had stopped circulating in it. I think the hemorrhage in the left side of the brain had already started. I realized immediately that the attack was worse than usual. I wanted to call the doctor but his regular doctor wasn't there. I thought of Willemin. Louis told me, 'I forbid you to call, I don't want it, I want to be left to die quietly, I don't want injections or doctors, I don't want anything.' I know that if I had called a doctor he would have refused to see him. He knew he was dying. He said to me again: 'I don't want to see anyone, stay here, I don't want to see anyone!' I gave my classes that day as usual. Serge Perrault came with a young girl who was my student and wanted to get into the Opéra, and she wanted a letter of reference from Céline. I told her, 'He's too sick, not today, it's not possible.' I think he saw her for two minutes and then sent her away. He also told Serge to leave. Serge came up to join me. And Louis lingered on like that all day, on his back. My students finally left. I went down to Louis. He hiccuped, hiccuped, and it was over. I hadn't wanted to bother him. It wouldn't have helped to bring in a doctor. A ruptured aneurism. He knew perfectly well what he had."

It was 6 P.M. "The truth of this world is death," Céline had written in *Voyage au bout de la nuit*. The journey was over. He had finally found his truth. In the silence of eternity, far from the dullness of men, from their lies and illusions.

Dr. Willemin, called by Lucette, certified the death by a hemorrhage in the left side of the brain. Lucette asked Serge Perrault to go find a priest. The parish priest of lower Meudon may have refused to put himself out, or the only nun on duty at the Saint-Joseph Institute may have been unable to leave her post and suggested that Serge Perrault talk to a nurse instead. Lucette today is convinced of the truth of the first hypothesis; Perrault leans toward the second.

Soon notified, the intimate friends—Marie Canavaggia, Roger Nimier, Arletty, the Bramis, Robert Poulet, Max Révol, Pierre Duverger, Lucien Rebatet, Marcel Aymé, Gaston Gallimard—filed past Céline's deathbed.[53] Dr. Willemin wanted an expert to take a cast of the writer's right hand and face.

"The press was not informed. Céline hadn't wanted them to be. I didn't say anything. I kept vigil for three days. But it was very hard. Perched in the trees, they watched the comings and goings, spied on the house with its shutters closed. A priest whom Gallimard had brought came to bless the corpse."

All the same, on Monday, July 3, Lucette allowed the following statement to be broadcast: "Suffering for several months from a heart condition, Louis-Ferdinand Céline's state of health took an abrupt turn for the worse."

A warm, heavy drizzle fell on the morning of July 4 when Céline was buried in a temporary vault in the Meudon cemetery. There were no more than fifty persons in attendance. The old friends. The faithful. "A splendid burial, just what Céline deserved," Lucien Rebatet would say of it.

In November 1961, on the permanent vault ordered by Lucette, was the double inscription

Louis-Ferdinand
Céline
Doctor L.-F. Destouches
1894–1961

Lucie Destouches
Née Almansor
1912–

Beneath this, his wife had engraved a cross and the image of a three-master. The last dream-ship for the writer of imaginary journeys, the Breton who dreamed of the open sea and remained bound to the earth, the sailor of phantom crossings, finally lost on the other side of life, of death, in the solitudes from which no man returns.

Notes

1. Birth . . . and Before

1. *Cahiers Céline*, no. 6, Gallimard, 1980, 37, 41, 47.
2. Letter to Albert Paraz dated October 4, 1947, ibid., 35.
3. Final passage of *Voyage au bout de la nuit.*
4. The first to do so, Jacques Boudillet, published the Destouches family tree in *Album Céline* in Gallimard's Pléiade series, 1977.
5. Cf. *Cahiers Céline*, no. 4, 1978.
6. Ibid., 144.
7. Ibid., 157.
8. Cf. Jean-Pierre Dauphin's explanatory note in *Cahiers Céline*, no. 4, 140.
9. In François Gibault, *Céline, 1894–1932, le temps des espérances*, Mercure de France, 1977.
10. Cf. *Album Céline*, 15.
11. *Cahiers Céline*, no. 4, 139–140.
12. Denoël, 1944, 10.
13. Cf. Photographic documentation in the F. Gibault collection, first published in *Album Céline.*
14. *Cahiers Céline*, no. 2, 63.
15. Ibid., 121.
16. Ibid., 165.
17. *Mort à crédit*, in "Céline, Romans I," La Pléiade, Gallimard, 1981, 560–561.
18. Ibid., 593.
19. Gibault, op. cit., 34.
20. Cf. Jean-Denis Bredin, *L'Affaire*, Julliard, 1983, 153.
21. Ibid., 14–15.
22. Léon Poliakov, *Histoire de l'antisémitisme*, vol. 2, le Livre de Poche "Pluriel," 1981, 297.
23. Cf. Bredin, op. cit., 133ff.
24. The author of this work was Georges Vitoux, my grandfather. Before his death in 1933, his pseudoscientific theories, strangely enough, found approval with Drumont and Barrès. He would later take up the cause of the Dreyfusards.
25. Poliakov., op. cit., 303.

2. Passage Choiseul, Passage Toward Adolescence

1. Letter quoted in Gibault, *Céline 1894–1932*, 39.
2. Letter to Albert Paraz dated October 4, 1947, *Cahiers Céline*, no. 6, 35.
3. La Pléiade, 1981, 544.
4. Gallimard, 1952, 84.
5. La Pléiade, 1974, 7.
6. Ibid., 551.
7. *Mort à crédit*, 551.
8. Ibid., 549.
9. Ibid., 552.
10. Gallimard, 1954, 194.
11. *Mort à crédit*, 552.
12. Cf., in particular, F. Vitoux, *Céline, misère et parole*, Gallimard, 1973.
13. *Mort à crédit*, 553.
14. Ibid.
15. Ibid., 554.
16. Ibid., 568.
17. Ibid., 239–240.
18. Ibid., 70.
19. Ibid., 576.
20. Ibid., 560.
21. Ibid., 65.
22. In Gibault, op. cit., 49–50.
23. Quoted, ibid., 58.
24. *Les Beaux draps*, Nouvelles Editions françaises, 1941, 171 and 178.
25. *Mort à crédit*, 632.
26. Ibid.
27. Ibid., 598.
28. In *Cahiers Céline*, no. 1, op. cit., 35.
29. *Mort à crédit*, 632.

3. The Schools of Life

1. Interview with Louis Pauwels and André Brissaud, *Cahiers Céline*, no. 2, 123.
2. *Mort à crédit*, 634.
3. *D'un château l'autre*, 196.
4. Ibid., 276.

5. *Mort à crédit*, 557.
6. Ibid., 558.
7. Quoted in Gibault, op. cit., 78.
8. *Voyage au bout de la nuit*, 10.
9. Letter quoted in Gibault, op. cit., 91.
10. Ibid., 93.
11. *Mort à crédit*, 721.
12. Ibid., 725.
13. *Rigodon*, 857.
14. *Mort à crédit*, 722.
15. Ibid., 652.
16. Quoted in Gibault, op. cit., 94.
17. Ibid., 102.
18. Cf. *Cahiers Céline*, no. 2, 164.
19. Cf. Robert Poulet, *Entretiens familiers avec L.-F. Céline*, Plon, 1958, 76ff.
20. *Cahiers Céline*, no. 6, 322.
21. *Voyage au bout de la nuit*, 102ff.
22. Letter to Albert Paraz dated April 5, 1951, *Cahiers Céline*, no. 6, 320.
23. *Cahiers Céline*, no. 4, 147–148.
24. Quoted in Gibault, op. cit., 117.
25. *Voyage au bout de la nuit*, 10.

4. The Good Old Days and the War

1. *Casse-Pipe* suivi du *Carnet du cuirassier Destouches*, Gallimard, 1970, 7–8.
2. Interview with Pauwels and Brissaud, op. cit., 124.
3. Interview with Jean Guénot and Jacques Darribehaude, *Cahiers Céline*, no. 2, 164.
4. Interview with Claude Bonnefoy, *Cahiers Céline*, no. 2, 212.
5. Cf., in particular, *Rigodon*, 825 and 882.
6. Letter to Roger Nimier dated November 14, 1950, *Bulletin célinien*, no. 24, Brussels, n.d.
7. *Carnet du cuirassier Destouches*, 112.
8. Ibid., 111.
9. Cf. Gibault, op. cit., 131.
10. *Carnet du cuirassier Destouches*, 114.
11. *Voyage au bout de la nuit*, 236.
12. *Féerie pour une autre fois*, 200–202.
13. Records of the 12th Cuirassier Regiment, quoted in Gibault, op. cit., 137.
14. Quoted, ibid., 137.
15. Cf. interview with Pierre Ordioni, *Commandos et Cinquième Colonne en*

mai 40, Nouvelles Éditions latines, 1970, reprinted in *Cahiers Céline*, no. 1, 130.

16. *Voyage au bout de la nuit*, 140.
17. Quoted in Gibault, op. cit., 139.
18. *Maudits Soupirs pour une autre fois*, Gallimard, 1985, 210f.
19. Cf. Bredin, op. cit., 365.
20. *Maudits Soupirs*, 211.
21. Letter from Louis Destouches to his parents, quoted in Gibault, op. cit., 140.
22. Interview with Ordioni, op. cit., 125–127.
23. *Guignol's band 2—Le Pont de Londres*, Gallimard, 1964, 33.
24. Unpublished chapter of *Casse-pipe*, in Poulet, op. cit., 104.
25. *Guignol's band 2*, 34.
26. Gibault (op. cit., 144ff) took precise note of the enlistment dates of the 12th Cuirassiers as they appear in the regiment's *Records*.
27. *Nord*, 482.
28. Éditions Gallimard, 1954, 11–12.
29. Unpublished letter, archives Lucette Destouches.
30. This letter, quoted *in extenso* for the first time in Gibault, op. cit., 147–149, ended with the following lines: "I reproduce WORD FOR WORD the letter I have just received from Captain Schneider, Commander of Company 2 of the 12th Cuirassier Regiment."

                                          On campaign near Ypres, Belgium

Sir:

    Your son was recently wounded. He fell valiantly, braving the bullets with the spirit and courage he has continually shown since the beginning of the campaign.
    I wanted to tell you about his injury myself so as to describe the exemplary way in which your son has always conducted himself.

                                          Signed Captain Schneider
                                          12th Cuirassier Regiment.

    "I will treasure this letter in my archives. Most cordially yours. Destouches."
    We should note Fernand Destouches' rather touching claim of reproducing the letter received from Captain Schneider word for word.

31. Reproduced in facsimile in *Cahiers Céline*, La Pléiade, 40.
32. *Guignol's band*, Denoël, 1944, 288–89.
33. *Nord*, 458.
34. Interview with Merry Bromberger in *L'Intransigeant* on December 8, 1932, reprinted in *Cahiers Céline*, no. 1, 30.
35. *Rigodon*, 826.

36. From unpublished conversations with the author. Unless otherwise specified, all of Lucettes Destouches' statements to follow in this work are culled from the same source.
37. *Voyage au bout de la nuit*, 94.
38. Ibid., 96.
39. Quoted in Gibault, op. cit., 154.
40. *Voyage au bout de la nuit*, 49.
41. Ibid., 90.
42. Cf. *La Revue célinienne*, nos. 3–4, Brussels, 1981.
43. *Maudits Soupirs*, 37.
44. Ibid., 40.
45. Ibid., 49.
46. *Cahiers de l'Herne*, no. 3, 11.
47. Cf. Sam Waagenar, *Mata-Hari*, Appleton-Century, 1965.
48. Cf. Gibault, op. cit., 170ff.
49. *Guignol's band*, 51.
50. *Le Pont de Londres*, 309.
51. Ibid., 319.
52. *Guignol's band*, 40.
53. Ibid.

5. Impressions of Africa

1. This boilerplate was published *in extenso* in *Cahiers Céline*, no. 4— *Lettres et premiers écrits d'Afrique, 1916–1917*, Gallimard, 1978, 15–18.
2. Cf. in particular Jean-Pierre Dauphin's long explanatory note in *Cahiers Céline*, no. 4, 38–39.
3. *Cahiers Céline*, no. 4, 21.
4. Ibid., 26.
5. Cf. Letters to his parents dated May 6 and 9 and August 20, 1916.
6. *Cahiers Céline*, no. 4, 31.
7. Ibid., 34.
8. To Simone Saintu, June 28, 1916, *Cahiers Céline*, no. 4, 43.
9. Ibid., 43–44.
10. Ibid., 43.
11. Ibid., 52.
12. *Féerie pour une autre fois*, 183–185.
13. *Cahiers Céline*, no. 4, 79–82.
14. Ibid., 64.
15. To Simone Saintu, October 22, ibid., 131.
16. Ibid., 75.

17. Ibid., 92.
18. To Simone Saintu, December 11, 1916, ibid., 156.
19. To Simone Saintu, October 12, 1916, ibid., 117.
20. Facsimile of the diploma in *Cahiers Céline*, no. 4, 184.
21. Ibid., 187–188.

6. *Eureka, Medicine!*

1. Cf. Pascal Fouché's research in *La Sirène*, Bibliothèque de littérature française contemporaine de l'université Paris-VII (BLFC), 1984, 203–204.
2. In Pierre Monnier, *Ferdinand furieux*, L'Age d'Homme, 1979, 52.
3. In Fouché, op. cit., 220.
4. *Nord*, 519–520.
5. Letter to Milton Hindus dated July 7, 1947. This letter appears in *L.-F. Céline tel que je l'ai vu* (L'Herne, 1969, 152), the French translation of Milton Hindus, *The Crippled Giant*, Boar's Head Books, 1950, but not in the original.
6. See Chapter 10.
7. *Mort à crédit*, 83.
8. François Gibault noted that Courtial des Péreires' given name, Roger-Marin, was inspired by Céline's father-in-law, Athanase-Marin Follet. But I believe it would be difficult to extrapolate or discern any shared characteristics between the fantastical inventor of *Mort à crédit* and the respectable doctor of Rennes.
9. Cf. Henri Mahé, *La Brinqueubale avec Céline*, La Table Ronde, 1969, 143.
10. In Poulet, op. cit., 77.
11. In *Cahiers Céline*, no. 1, 87.
12. Interview and statement taken by the author.
13. In *Cahiers Céline*, no. 1, 87.
14. Concerning Louis Destouches' early years in Rennes and his medical experiences, the doctoral theses in medicine of Jacques François (*Contribution à l'étude des années rennaises du docteur Destouches*, faculté mixte de médecine et de pharmacie de Rennes, 1967) and especially of François Balta (*La Vie médicale de Louis Destouches, 1894–1961, état actuel de nos connaissances*, académie de Paris, université René-Descartes, 1971), which occasionally draws on Jacques Boudillet's (unpublished) research, provide the main matter of available documentation.
15. *Cahiers Céline*, no. 2, 214.

16. Mahé, op. cit., 215.
17. Jacques François (cf. note 14) proposes in particular the possibility of a fortuitous encounter between Carrel and Louis Destouches in Saint-Brieuc, at a bookstore which both men were known to have frequented regularly. But where did he obtain this information, which he himself deems dubious? He also refers to the presence of Lindbergh, a close collaborator with Carrel. Is he really certain of this? Lindbergh (the famous aviator) did in fact work with Carrel, but he was only sixteen-years old at the time. Could this be a different Lindbergh? In a statement published in *Cahiers de l'Herne*, no. 3, 15, Marcel Brochard mentions the correspondence between the two men, who would have met through the Rockefeller Mission, which seems much more probable.
18. Personal statement to the author.
19. Cf. François, op. cit.
20. *Cahiers Céline*, no. 2, 214.
21. Poulet, op. cit., 78.
22. Undated letter to Albert Milon, quoted in Gibault, op. cit., 226.
23. *Cahiers de l'Herne*, no. 3, 16.
24. Statement noted by Éric Mazet, *Bulletin célinien*, no. 29, January 1985.
25. Ibid.
26. Statement made by Édith Follet to the author.
27. In his medical thesis (op. cit.), Jacques François details these exams and their evaluations. Thus: 1st exam: Anatomy (not including topographical anatomy), practical dissection test—GOOD; Anatomy (not including topographical anatomy), oral examination—FAIR; 2nd exam: Histology, physiology, including physical and chemical biology—GOOD; 3rd exam: surgery and topographical anatomy (practical test)—GOOD, surgery and topographical anatomy, external pathology and obstetrics (oral examination)—GOOD, practical test in pathological anatomy—GOOD, general pathology, parasites, animal and vegetable kingdoms, microbes, internal pathology (oral examination)—GOOD.
28. François, ibid., 35.
29. Balta, op. cit., 69.
30. Quoted, ibid., 70–71.
31. Cf. ibid., 12.
32. Ibid., 13.
33. Cf. the letters to Albert Milon quoted in Gibault, op. cit., 241.
34. *Voyage au bout de la nuit*, 280.
35. In *Le Figaro littéraire*, April 7–13, 1969.
36. In *Cahiers Céline*, Gallimard, no. 3, 1977, 28.
37. Ibid., 52.
38. Ibid., 19–20.
39. Ibid., 18.

7. *Final Preparations Before The "Journey"*

1. Statements quoted by Céline in his interview with Jean Guénot and Jacques Darribehaude, *Cahiers Céline*, no. 2, 148.
2. Quoted in Gibault, op. cit., 249.
3. Ibid., 247–248.
4. *Bagatelles pour un massacre*, Denoël, 1937, 101–102, 111.
5. For further detail, cf. in particular Balta, op. cit., 18, in the League of Nations–WHO–UNO Archives, section 12B, Geneva. The correspondence later exchanged between Louis Destouches and Dr. Abbatucci is pure comedy. The former, well schooled by Ludwig Rajchman, does not hesitate to correct the writings of the latter with learned and unconsciously comical self-importance.
6. *Voyage au bout de la nuit*, 184.
7. Ibid., 192.
8. Ibid., 194.
9. Letter to Erika Irrgang dated July 19, 1934, *Cahiers Céline*, no. 5, 56.
10. *Voyage au bout de la nuit*, 201.
11. Letter dated February 26, 1925, WHO Archives, Geneva, quoted in Gibault, op. cit., 257–258.
12. *Bagatelles pour un massacre*, 99.
13. The daily schedule of the delegation led by Louis Destouches, as we can imagine, bears witness to erudite scruples more precise than actually educational. It has been referred to, among others, by Balta in his medical thesis and in notes to Gibault, op. cit.
14. This is a typewritten text signed by Louis Destouches, sent en route to the Health Section of the League of Nations, and reproduced in its entirety, as well as an earlier report on Louisiana and a note on the health service of the Westinghouse Company in Pittsburgh, published in *Cahiers Céline*, no. 3, 113ff.
15. Cf. correspondence with E. Bendz, *Cahiers de l'Herne*, no. 3, 127.
16. *Cahiers Céline*, no. 3, 123.
17. *Voyage au bout de la nuit*, 226.
18. *Cahiers de l'Herne*, no. 3, 86.
19. Quoted in Balta, op. cit., 24.
20. Letter by Louis Destouches dated August 3, 1925, mailed from the Excelsior Hotel in Rome (WHO Archives), quoted by Gibault and Balta, which again provides a detailed daily itinerary of the South American doctors' journey through Italy.
21. Statements quoted by Mazet, *Bulletin célinien*, no. 29, January 1985.
22. A photocopy of the judgment rendered by the county court, including

all documents and thus Louis Destouches' letter, is held by the bibliothèque Céline de l'université Paris-VII.

23. Again, for the expedition's daily agenda, cf. Balta, op. cit., 26ff.
24. Cf. *Cahiers Céline*, no. 1, 77.
25. Cf. *Cahiers Céline*, no. 2, 163.
26. *Bagatelles pour un massacre*, 102–103.
27. In Helga Pedersen, *Le Danemark a-t-il sauvé Céline?*, Plon, 1975, 86.
28. In Mahé, op. cit., 27.
29. Cf. Gibault, op. cit., 294–295.
30. In *Cahiers de l'Herne*, no. 3, 18.
31. *Bagatelles pour un massacre*, 100–101.
32. Gibault, op. cit., 282.
33. In *Cahiers de l'Herne*, no. 3, 19.
34. *Voyage au bout de la nuit*, 237.
35. Ibid., 238 and 240–241.
36. Dr. Rosenthal introduced Louis Destouches in the following terms:

"With his military as well as civilian distinctions, Dr. Destouches' candidacy is certainly to be welcomed.

"Decorated on October 28, 1914, sergeant-at-arms in the cuirassiers, he was then honorably discharged for disability.

"As a member of the Rockefeller Commission's antituberculosis campaign, he helped to set up clinics in Brittany.

"After he became a doctor (a graduate of the *faculté*), he worked for four years for the Health Section of the League of Nations. This took him around the world and led to his founding an epidemiological office in Western Africa (1926).

"He is currently hoping to study work organization among patients and workers.

"Dr. Destouches' orientation is unique. His background is our guarantee that he will be a man of bold initiatives and progress in social health. He has a place waiting for him in our Society." (cf. *Cahiers Céline*, no. 3, 138).
37. Cf. ibid., 159.
38. In *Cahiers Céline*, no. 3, 161–162.
39. Ibid., 162.
40. In *Cahiers de l'Herne*, no. 3, 20–21.
41. Interview with Claude Bonnefoy, *Cahiers Céline*, no. 2, 207.
42. In *Cahiers de l'Herne*, no. 3, 21.
43. Ibid., 21–22.
44. Ibid.

8. *Finally, on October 15, 1932: Celine . . .*

1. Mahé, op. cit., 24.
2. Ibid., 27–28.

3. Letter to Milton Hindus dated February 28, 1948, in Hindus, *L.-F. Céline tel que je l'ai vu*, op. cit., 182.
4. In *Bulletin célinien*, no. 29.
5. Testimony quoted in Pierre Lainé, *De la débâcle à l'insurrection contre le monde moderne: itinéraire de L.-F. Céline*, Bibliothèque universitaire de la Sorbonne, Chap. 6, 141.
6. Mahé, op. cit., 43–44.
7. Cf. *Voyage au bout de la nuit*, 400–405.
8. Mahé, op. cit., 33.
9. In *Céline, textes et documents I*, BLFC, 1979, 5.
10. Statements noted by the author.
11. Cf. *Cahiers Céline*, no. 6, 330. For Grégoire Ichok's life, cf. in particular Balta, op. cit., 35ff., and Gibault, op. cit., 283–288.
12. Mahé, op. cit., 15.
13. Statement by André-Louis Lejay, in *Cahiers de l'Herne*, no. 5, 281.
14. Mahé, op. cit., 42.
15. For a detailed description of and the publicity brochure for this medicine, cf. *Cahiers Céline*, no. 3, 248–250.
16. In *Cahiers Céline*, no. 3, 238–239.
17. Ibid., 240.
18. Ibid.
19. Letter quoted in Balta, op. cit., 50, and in Gibault, op. cit., 294.
20. In Poulet, op. cit., 39.
21. Response to an inquiry in *Nouvelles littéraires*, no. 774, August 14, 1937, in *Cahiers Céline*, no. 1, 119.
22. In Poulet, op. cit., 40.
23. Cf. *Cahiers Céline*, no. 1, 46–47.
24. In *Cahiers Céline*, no. 2, 23.
25. Ibid., 148.
26. Ibid., 214.
27. Cf. in particular Henri Godard's historical analysis in the Pléiade edition of *Voyage*, 1227–1232.
28. Statements quoted by Eric Mazet in *Bulletin célinien* no. 25, September 1984.
29. Pierre Lainé, in his *De la débâcle à l'insurrection contre le monde moderne: l'itinéraire de L.-F. Céline* (1982, Bibliothèque universitaire de la Sorbonne), not only revealed the existence of these two men, Marcel Lafaye and Joseph Garcin, but also published many previously unpublished letters to them from Céline. We owe our current knowledge to his research. The quotation is from his chap. 5, 121.
30. Lainé, op. cit., 149.
31. Ibid.
32. Ibid., 149.
33. Ibid., 146.
34. Letter quoted in its entirety in *Bulletin célinien*, no. 6, February 1983.

35. Lainé, op. cit., 146–147.
36. Ibid., 148.
37. Ibid., 150.
38. Cf. The Oran (Algeria) *Écho-Soir*, July 16, 1961: "Céline almost burned *Voyage au bout de la nuit* 30 years ago."
39. Mahé, op. cit., 47.
40. Cf. statement quoted earlier, *Bulletin célinien*, no. 29.
41. Statement noted by the author.
42. Ibid.
43. In *Cahiers de l'Herne*, no. 3, 22.
44. Patrick Modiano, *Emmanuel Berl: Interrogatoire*, Gallimard, 1976, 127.
45. Cf. in particular Gibault, op. cit., 311–312, and Henri Godard's notes in the Pléiade *Voyage*, 1251ff.
46. In Hindus, *L.-F. Céline tel que je l'ai vu*, op. cit., 156–157.
47. Statement by Max Dorian, in *Cahiers de l'Herne*, no. 3, 26.
48. That, at least, is the theory offered by Henri Godard in the Pléiade *Voyage*, 257.
49. *Cahiers de l'Herne*, no. 23, 26.
50. Cf. Robert Denoël's interview with André Roubaud in *Marianne*, May 10, 1939, 7.
51. Dorian, op. cit., 27.
52. In Poulet, op. cit., 23–24.
53. In *Marianne*, May 10, 1939, 7.
54. A photocopy of the complete contract can be found in Jean-Pierre Dauphin and Pascal Fouché, *La Bibliographie des écrits de L.-F. Céline*, op. cit.
55. Statement by Jeanne Carayon in *Cahiers de l'Herne*, no. 3, 22.
56. In *Le Magazine littéraire*, no. 116, 19.
57. In *Cahiers de l'Herne*, no. 5, 36–37.
58. Cf. *Cahiers Céline*, no. 5, "Lettres à des amies," Gallimard, 1979, 31, 40.
59. Ibid., 154.
60. Ibid., 37–38.
61. Ibid., 146.
62. Ibid., 73–74.
63. Ibid., 75.

9. Story of a Book

1. Facsimile of the publisher's blurb, in Dauphin and Fouché, op. cit.
2. In *Magazine littéraire*, no. 116, 19.
3. Cf. Godard, op. cit., 1256–1257.

4. Letter quoted in the catalogue of the Libraire Morssen, Paris, Spring 1975, and reprinted in Godard, op. cit., and Gibault, op. cit.
5. Letter to Jean Proal, quoted in Dauphin and Fouché, op. cit.
6. In Poulet, op. cit., 25–26.
7. *Cahiers de l'Herne*, no. 3, 43.
8. Ibid., 44.
9. For a more detailed overview of the reaction of the press and writers to the publication of *Voyage*, cf. Godard, op. cit., 1262ff.
10. Lucien Descaves, *Souvenirs d'un ours*, Éditions de Paris, 1946, 268.
11. *Cahiers Céline*, no. 5, 41 and 43.
12. Ibid., 81–82.
13. Ibid., 85.
14. Quoted by Max Descaves (Lucien Descaves' son) in *Vu*, December 14, 1932.
15. Interview in *Lectures du soir*, December 10, 1932.
16. Statement by Jeanne Carayon, strangely speaking of herself in the third person, in *Cahiers de l'Herne*, no. 3, 24.
17. Letter to Erika Irrgang dated December 8 (?) 1932, *Cahiers Céline*, no. 5, 44.
18. Letter to Cillie Pam dated the week of December 10, 1932, ibid., 86.
19. Letter to Pam dated the week of December 18, 1932, ibid., 88.
20. Letter by Rosny the Elder in *L'Intransigeant*, December 9, 1932.
21. *Cahiers Céline*, no. 5, 21.
22. François Gibault, a lawyer by profession, devotes some excellent pages to the legal misadventures of the Goncourt scandal in *Céline 1932–1944: Délires et persécutions*, Mercure de France, 1985, 29ff.
23. In *Cahiers Céline*, no. 3, 241.
24. Ibid., 241.
25. Ibid., 178, 212.
26. Ibid., 188.
27. Ibid., 210.
28. Quoted in the Pléiade *Voyage*, 1108.
29. Letter dated January 16, 1933, in *Cahiers Céline*, no. 5, 22.
30. Ibid., 116.
31. Ibid., 88.
32. Ibid., 65–66.
33. Quoted in the Pléiade *Voyage*, 1108 and elsewhere.
34. In *Cahiers Céline*, no. 3, 217.
35. Ibid., 218.
36. *Le Magazine littéraire*, no. 116, 19.
37. Quoted in Jean Lacouture, *François Mauriac*, Seuil, 1980, 432.
38. *Journal de l'abbé Mugnier*, Mercure de France, 1985, 531–532.
39. In *Cahiers Céline*, no. 1, 49–50.
40. Ibid., 51.

41. Cf. the letters (mostly undated) published in *Cahiers de l'Herne*, no. 5. In this case, 48.
42. Ibid., 52.
43. Ibid., 55.
44. In Clément Rosset, *Le Réel—traité de l'idiotie*, Éditions de Minuit, 1977, 37.
45. *Cahiers de l'Herne*, no. 5, 57.
46. Ibid., 58.
47. Ibid., 61.
48. Statement by Élisabeth Porquerol published in *La Nouvelle Revue française* on September 1, 1961, and reprinted in *Cahiers Céline*, no. 1, 44.
49. Ibid., 45.
50. Ibid., 48.
51. In *La Revue célinienne*, no. 3/4, statement by Évelyne Pollet, 15.
52. Letter of early March 1933, in *Cahiers Céline*, no. 5, 166.
53. Letter of February 1933, ibid., 165–166.
54. Letter of late March 1933, ibid., 167.
55. In *Bulletin célinien*, no. 14, October 1983, 4.
56. Letter quoted in Gibault, *Céline 1932–1944*, 79.
57. In *La Revue célinienne*, no. 3/4, 15.
58. Évelyne Pollet, *L'Escalier*, La Renaissance du Livre, Brussels, 1956, 40.
59. Letter published in *L'Oeuvre*, June 10, 1933, and reprinted in *Cahiers Céline*, no. 1, 73.
60. *Cahiers Céline*, no. 5, 104.
61. Letter from Céline quoted in Mahé, op. cit., 77.
62. *Cahiers Céline*, no. 5, 108.
63. Ibid., 51.
64. Ibid., 100.
65. Ibid., 173.
66. In *Le Magazine littéraire*, no. 116, 20.

10. Chronicle of a "Death" Foretold

1. In *Cahiers Céline*, no. 5, 179.
2. Émile Henriot's text and the principal critical reviews of *L'Église* were anthologized and published by Jean-Pierre Dauphin in *Les Critiques de notre temps et Céline*, Garnier, 1976.
3. In *Cahiers de l'Herne*, no. 3, 88.
4. Statements published in *Marianne*, November 25, 1933.
5. In *Le Canard enchainé*, October 25, 1933, and reprinted in *Cahiers Céline*, no. 1, 91.

6. An allusion to the French novelist Marc Chadourne, whose past as a colonial administrator made him particularly suspect to Louis Aragon.

7. Letter to Cillie Pam, late November / early December 1933, in *Cahiers Céline*, no. 5, 113.

8. Céline recalled Stavisky's stance vis-à-vis *Voyage* for the journalist Sterling North, come to interview him for the *Chicago Daily News*, July 18, 1934.

9. In *Cahiers Céline*, no. 5, 54.

10. Letter dated April 28, 1934, ibid., 118.

11. This is the theory developed by Henri Godard in the Pléiade *Voyage* and *Mort à crédit*, 1339ff.

12. Unpublished letter, a typewritten copy of which is preserved in the Bibliothèque Céline de l' université Paris-VII.

13. In *Cahiers Céline*, no. 1, 103.

14. Letter to Robert Denoël, June 1934, in *le Magazine littéraire* no. 116, 21.

15. Ibid., July 12, 1934, from Los Angeles.

16. In Mahé, op. cit., 101–102.

17. Letter dated August 28, 1934, in *Cahiers Céline*, no. 5, 120.

18. In Hindus, *L.-F. Céline tel que je l'ai vu*, 169.

19. Ibid., 167.

20. In Mahé, op. cit., 103.

21. We owe the last information we possess on Elizabeth Craig's life to the testimony of her friend Estelle Reed, reported by Gibault in *Céline 1894– 1932*, p. 300. In August 1973 Elizabeth was still corresponding with one of their mutual friends, Mrs. Helen Sheldon Berquam. Her husband, Ben Tankle, was seriously ill at the time, she explained. Elizabeth has since ceased corresponding.

22. Cf. note 15.

23. In Hindus, *L.-F. Céline tel que je l'ai vu*, 154–155.

24. Letter to Henri Mahé, in *La Brinquebale avec Céline*, 104.

25. Letter dated July 23, 1934, in *Le Magazine littéraire*, no. 116, 21.

26. In *Cahiers Céline*, no. 5, 157.

27. Letter of September or October 1934, in *Textes et Documents*, no. 1, Paris BLFC, 1979.

28. Letter to Karen Marie Jensen dated February 7, 1935, in *Cahiers Céline*, no. 5, 226.

29. Letter dated September 6, 1934, ibid., 183.

30. Letter of late January 1935, ibid., 124.

31. Undated letter (spring 1935), ibid., 126.

32. Same letter as in note 28, ibid., 227–228.

33. Pol Vandromme, *Robert Le Vigan*, in *La Revue célinienne*, 1980, 65.

34. Letter from Le Vigan to André Bernard dated January 6, 1972, in Vandromme, op. cit., 197.

35. Letter dated May 19, 1972, to Bernard, ibid., 199.

36. Personal statement noted by the author.

37. Cf. the personal account of Lucienne Delforge which he reports, along with Céline's letters, in *Cahiers Céline*, no. 5, 257ff.
38. Ibid., 265. Another encomium, written by Céline a year later, would appear under the artist's photo for her recital on March 18, 1936: "Lucienne Delforge was born in music. Her lyricism is real and natural. Such grace arises but once or twice in a generation, and almost never in a woman." The misogyny of his note needs no commentary.
39. Letter to Karen Marie Jensen dated June 17, 1935, ibid., 231.
40. Letter to Lucienne Delforge, 262.
41. Ibid., 262.
42. Ibid., 263.
43. In *Cahiers Céline*, no. 5, 233.
44. Ibid., 138.
45. In Mahé, op. cit., 117.
46. Cf. in particular Jean-Noël Schifano's preface to Gian Dauli, *Magie blanche*, translated by Marie Canavaggia, Desjonquières, Paris, 1985.
47. Personal account of Marie Canavaggia in *Cahiers de l'Herne*, no. 3, 31.
48. In Poulet, op. cit., 53.
49. René-Marie Auguste Tardivaux, pseudonym René Boylesve: author (1867–1926) of social histories of the provinces known as *romans tourangeaux.*
50. In *Cahiers Céline*, no. 1, 107.

11. Cries and Solitude

1. In their monumental *Bibliographie des écrits de Louis-Ferdinand Céline*, op. cit., Dauphin and Fouché reproduced in their entirety the texts of the advertisements that appeared almost daily in *Paris-Soir* from May 14 to 31 and from June 18 to 25, 1936.
2. In *Cahiers Céline*, no. 5, 58–59.
3. Ibid., 59. The letter is dated April, but we repeat that *Mort à crédit* would not be published until May 12.
4. In *Cahiers de l'Herne*, no. 5, 40.
5. We refer to the pages devoted by Henri Godard to the critical reception of *Mort à crédit*, in its Pléiade edition, pp. 1401–1415, and to Dauphin's selection in *Les Critiques de notre temps et Céline*, op. cit.
6. Letter published in *Céline, textes et documents*, op. cit., no. 1, 71.
7. In Mahé, op. cit., 147.
8. Document of the Bibliothèque Céline de l'université Paris-VII, cited in part in the Pléiade *Mort à crédit*, 1405.
9. Undated letter (probably late May 1936), quoted in the Pléiade edition, 1121.

10. *Bagatelles pour un massacre*, 46.

11. In *Cahiers Céline*, no. 5, 139. The letter is dated late July 1936. Late August 1936 is more likely. The other dates, personal testimony and cross-checking suggest that Céline's stay in Leningrad lasted about a month, from mid-August to September 21.

12. *Bagatelles pour un massacre*, 46.

13. Ibid., 332.

14. Ibid., 362–363. In *Céline 1932–1944*, 140. Gibault reports the account of a certain M. de Fonscolombe, who made the return trip on the *Meknès* with Céline and had previously accompanied him to the Aleksandrovski palace. The female guide had emphasized the poor taste of the tsar's study and neighboring rooms, decorated in an overwrought art-nouveau style. Céline had cut her short. "You lousy bastards, you've already wiped them out, so you can cut the crap now." The stories may be two parts of one anecdote.

15. Ibid., 342.

16. Ibid., 347–348.

17. Letter of October 1936, in *Cahiers Céline*, no. 5, 140.

18. Ibid., 238.

19. Cf. *Cahiers Céline*, no. 1, 112.

20. Ibid., 114.

21. The French public would have to wait for François Joxe's faithful and sensitive direction at the théâtre de la Plaine, in Paris 1973, to be able finally to attend a series of productions of the play.

22. In *Cahiers de l'Herne*, no. 3, 36.

23. In the edition of Céline's *Oeuvres* by the Club de l'honnête homme, Paris, 1982, vol. 4, 102.

24. Statement noted by Daniel Rondeau in *Libération*, June 26, 1985.

25. Letter dated March 2, 1937, in *Cahiers Céline*, no. 5, 242.

26. In *Cahiers de l'Herne*, no. 3, 16.

27. In *Cahiers Céline*, no. 5, 243–244.

28. Ibid., 246.

29. Letter published in *Paris-Midi*, May 13, 1937, relating the incident in an article by Roger Giron (a barely legible facsimile of which appears in *Album Céline*, Pléiade, 149).

12. *Phony Peace, Phony War*

1. Robert Brasillach, *Notre Avant-guerre*, Le Livre de Poche, no. 3702, 1973, 244.

2. Quoted in Léon Poliakov, *Histoire de l'antisémitisme 2*, Le Livre de Poche "Pluriel," no. 8371, 1981, 450.

3. Ibid., 467.
4. Ibid.
5. *Bagatelles pour un massacre*, 94.
6. Ibid., 89.
7. Ibid., 317–318.
8. Ibid., 125.
9. Ibid., 178.
10. Ibid., 219.
11. In *Cahiers de l'Herne*, no. 3, 44.
12. In Dauphin, *Les Critiques*, 68–70.
13. Article reproduced in *Cahiers de l'Herne*, no. 5, 335–337.
14. Quoted in Dauphin, *Les Critiques*, 70–80.
15. Ibid., 82.
16. Ibid., 88.
17. Letter to Évelyne Pollet of early January 1938, in *Cahiers Céline*, no. 5, 195.
18. Letter dated January 31, 1938, ibid., 196.
19. In *Bulletin célinien*, no. 21, May 1984, 5.
20. *D'un château l'autre*, 246.
21. In Mahé, op. cit., 176.
22. In *Cahiers de l'Herne*, no. 3, 33.
23. "Quand Céline séjournait au Canada, [Céline's visit to Canada]" an article appearing in 1963 in *Aspects de la France* and reprinted in *La Revue célinienne*, no. 3/4, 8–9.
24. In *Cahiers Céline*, no. 5, 198.
25. *Féerie pour une autre fois*, 108.
26. Ibid., 110–111.
27. Concerning Olier Mordrel, the Breton autonomous movements and their connections to the German authorities, cf. Gibault, *Céline 1932–1944*, 309–310.
28. *L'École des cadavres*, 22.
29. Ibid., 223.
30. Ibid., 282.
31. Ibid., 287.
32. In *Cahiers de l'Herne*, no. 3, 45.
33. Article reproduced *in extenso* in Dauphin, *Les Critiques*, 89–95.
34. Personal testimony of Robert Durand published in *La France enchaînée*, December 15–31, 1938, and reprinted in *Bulletin célinien*, no. 28, introduced by Paul Chambrillon.
35. In *Cahiers Céline*, no. 5, 144.
36. Cf. *Céline, textes et documents III*, op. cit., 100–101.
37. In *Cahiers Céline*, no. 1, 121.
38. Ordioni, op. cit., reprinted in *Cahiers Céline*, no. 1, 132.
39. In *Cahiers de l'Herne*, no. 3, 114.

40. Letter from Céline to Jean Bonvilliers, quoted in Gibault, *Céline 1932–1944*, 202.
41. Lucien Rebatet, *Les Décombres*, Denoël, 1942, 425.
42. *Les Beaux draps*, 11–12.
43. Letter from Dr. Detrieux dated June 20, 1940, quoted in Gibault, *Céline 1932–1944*.
44. Yvelines departmental archives; letter quoted by Balta, op. cit.

13. The Occupation

1. *Les Beaux draps*, 44.
2. Ibid., 115.
3. Ibid., 78.
4. Ibid., 81.
5. Ibid., 128–129.
6. Ibid., 162–163.
7. Ibid., 171.
8. According to Henri Mahé, op. cit., 202.
9. According to Lucien Rebatet in *Cahiers de l'Herne*, no. 3, 45.
10. In *Cahiers de l'Herne*, no. 3. Rebatet places this encounter at Céline's home on the rue Girardon in October 1940. However, the writer did not move there until February 1941. He has no doubt either mistaken the date or placed the conversation in the wrong setting. But the mistake does not alter the conclusions we can draw from their conversation.
11. Céline wrote, for instance, to Frédéric Empeytraz, who replaced the ousted mayor of Bezons: "Events [i.e., the hostilities on the Russian front] are moving apace! as it happens, for the best, on the whole." Letter dated July 17, 1941, quoted in Gibault, *Céline 1932–1944*, 226.
12. In *Cahiers Céline*, no. 6, 311.
13. In *Catalogue de la vente de manuscrits autographes de Céline*, Paris, Nouveau Drouot, Friday, June 28, 1985.
14. Summary calculated by Henri Godard in his preface to the Pléiade "Romans 1." The entirety of Céline's statements in the occupation press can be found elsewhere, in issue no. 7 of *Cahiers Céline*, entitled *Céline et l'actualité, 1933–1961*, Gallimard, 1987.
15. Facsimile of the original manuscript published in Dauphin and Fouché, *Bibliographie*, s.v. 1941.
16. In *Je suis partout*, March 7, 1941, and reproduced in its entirety in *Bulletin célinien*, no. 28, December 1984.
17. In *Le Pays libre*, April 5, 1941.
18. Interview with Maurice-Yvan Sicard in *L'Émancipation nationale*, No-

vember 21, 1941. Published in Marseille, this newspaper was the central organ of Jacques Doriot's Parti populaire français. Doriot led the first LVF contingent to leave from the Gare de l'Est on September 4 for the Russian front (he would return to Paris in late December). It was this same Sicard, one of the earliest pro-Céline journalists, who was found guilty of slander in 1933 in connection with the Goncourt affair. A close collaborator with Doriot, he would re-encounter Céline in Sigmaringen. After the war he would publish many books under the pseudonym Saint-Paulien, including a voluminous *Histoire de la collaboration* (L'esprit nouveau, 1964).

19. Unpublished letter dated September 14, 1941, quoted in Gibault, *Céline 1932–1944*, 288.
20. Again, from the *Au Pilori* letter dated January 8, 1942.
21. Letter dated July 7, 1946, to an unknown addressee, quoted in Gibault, *Céline 1932–1944*, 291.
22. In Saint Paulien, op. cit., cf. note 9.
23. Cf. Dauphin and Fouché, *Bibliographie*, 1942.
24. In *Cahiers Céline*, no. 7, 317–318.
25. Letter reproduced in facsimile in Dauphin and Fouché, *Bibliographie*, 1942.
26. Ibid., 1943.
27. In *Album Céline*, 184.
28. *Je suis partout*, February 11, 1944.
29. In *Germinal*, April 28, 1944.
30. Theory developed particularly by Maurice Bardèche in *Louis-Ferdinand Céline*, La Table Ronde, 1986.
31. Sentence quoted by Robert Aron in *l'Histoire de l'Épuration*, vol. 1, Fayard, 1967, 285.
32. Concerning Céline's life in Bezons, cf. in particular the three personal accounts of Raymond Simeon, Joannin Vanni and Mme. D., noted by Marie Alchamolac-Emery in *Bulletin célinien*, no. 26, October 1984.
33. Letter quoted in part in Mahé, op. cit., 224, recto reproduced in facsimile in *Bulletin célinien*, no. 26.
34. Personal testimony of Raymond Simeon, in *Bulletin célinien*, no. 26.
35. *Bezons à travers les ages*, in *Cahiers de l'Herne*, no. 3, 181–182.
36. Personal testimony of D., *Bulletin célinien*, no. 26.
37. In *Cahiers de l'Herne*, no. 3, 45–46.
38. Letter to Thorvald Mikkelsen (November 1946), quoted in Gibault, *Céline 1932–1944*, 234–235.
39. Letter quoted, ibid., 249–250.
40. Letters appearing *in toto* in *Bulletin célinien*, nos. 16, 22, and 26. Other extracts of letters to Henri-Albert Mahé were published by his son in *Le Brinquebale avec Céline*, op. cit., 210–211.
41. Cf. F. Vitoux, *Bébert le chat de L.-F. Céline*, Grasset, 1976.
42. In Arletty, *La Défense*, La Table Ronde, 1971, 140–141.

43. Quoted in Poliakov, op. cit., vol. 2, 502.

44. In *Cahiers de l'Herne*, no. 3, 48–49.

45. Anecdote described by a witness, Paul-Yves Rio, in a letter to F. Gibault dated April 15, 1979.

46. Letter to Alphonse de Châteaubriant, quoted in Gibault, *Céline 1932–1944*, 239.

47. Ernst Jünger, *Premier Journal parisien*, in the edition prefaced by Nicole Chardaire, Le Livre de Poche "Biblio," 1984, 69. In the first French edition of this work soon after the war, the name "Merline," which Jünger had taken the precaution of substituting for "Céline," was replaced by the writer's real name. A lawsuit ensued.

48. Ibid., 69–70.

49. Ernst Jünger, *Second Journal parisien*, Le Livre de Poche "Biblio," 1984, 49.

50. Ibid., 203.

51. Summary account of this conference in *Le Concours medical*, February 15, 1942, and reproduced *in toto* in its June 16, 1979, issue.

52. Personal account of Professor Rudler (1977), quoted in Gibault, *Céline 1932–1944*, 246.

53. "Response to the exposé of the criminal court prosecutor," a document written from his Danish exile in answer to the accusations brought against him.

54. Report of January 28, 1942, held in the archives of the international military tribunal of Nuremburg, quoted earlier in G. Loiseaux, *La littérature de la défaite de la collaboration*, Publications de la Sorbonne, 1984, and in Gibault, *Céline 1932–1944*.

55. *Premier Journal parisien*, op. cit., 132.

56. In Poliakov, op. cit., vol. 1, 504.

57. In Dominique Veillon, *La Collaboration, textes et débats*, Le Livre de Poche, 1984, 37.

58. Quoted in Aron, op. cit., vol. I, 357.

59. Extracts of unpublished diary of Théophile Briant, quoted in Gibault, *Céline 1932–1944*, 307–308.

60. *Maudits Soupirs pour une autre fois*, 135. Marcel Aymé appears under the patronymic Marc Empième.

61. Personal account of Jacques-Bénoist Méchin noted by the author.

62. Letter quoted in Gibault, *Céline 1932–1944*, 327.

63. Account by Pierre Duverger in "Mon ami Céline," published in *Le Magazine littéraire*, March 1967, and reprinted in *Bulletin célinien*, no. 25.

64. Account by Simone Mitre, in *Cahiers de l'Herne*, no. 5, 283.

65. Karl Epting, "Il ne nous aimait pas," in *Cahiers de l'Herne*, no. 3, 57–58.

66. Letter published in *Le Petit Crapouillot*, June 1958. Under the explicit title "Céline ne nous a pas trahis [Céline Did Not Betray Us]," Champfleury set down for *Cahiers de l'Herne*, no. 3, the substance of his recollections of the Vailland affair.

67. *Maudits Soupirs pour une autre fois*, 32–33.
68. Article quoted almost in its entirety in Dauphin, *Les Critiques*, 108–113.
69. *Maudits Soupirs pour une autre fois*, 61.
70. *Nord*, 334–335.
71. Cf. François Gibault, *Céline, cavalier de l'Apocalypse, 1944–1961*, Mercure de France, 1981, 20.

14. One Summer, '44

1. *Nord*, 304.
2. Ibid., 305.
3. Ibid., 307.
4. In her memoirs *Le Ballet des crabes* (Fillipachi, 1975), Maud de Belleroche recounts her stay in Baden-Baden and her friendly encounters with Céline.
5. *Nord*, 323.
6. In Corinne Luchaire, *Ma Drôle de Vie*, Sun, 1949, 177–199.
7. Account by Pierre Petrovitch published in *La Revue célinienne*, no. 3/4, 13.
8. *Nord*, 333.
9. Ibid., 339.
10. Ibid., 382.
11. The Scherzes' home is today in Germany. At least one photo of it is known to us, published in *Paris-Presse–l'intransigeant*, June 3–4, 1962, in connection with the lawsuit brought by the Scherz family against Céline following the publication of *Nord*.
12. In L.-F. Céline, *Lettres à Tixier*, La Flûte de Pan, 1985, 31–32.

15. Castle and Prison

1. In *Cahiers de l'Herne*, no. 3, 51.
2. *D'un château l'autre*, 102–103.
3. Henry Rousso, *Pétain et la fin de la collaboration*, Éditions Complexe, 1984, 51.
4. Luchaire, op. cit., 205.
5. Quoted in Rousso, op. cit., 47.
6. In *Cahiers de l'Herne*, no. 3, 51.
7. Ibid., 52.
8. Cf. Luchaire, op. cit., 204–220.

9. In *Cahiers de l'Herne*, no. 3, 52.
10. Ibid., 53.
11. In *Lettres à Tixier*, op. cit., 29–30.
12. Anecdote quoted by André Brissaud and set down in Rousso, op. cit., 140.
13. In G. T. Schillemans, *Philippe Pétain, le prisonnier de Sigmaringen*, Éditions M.P., 1965, extracts reproduced in *Cahiers Céline*, no. 7, 343–347.
14. Ibid.
15. Article by Dr. Schillemans, "L'engrenage," in *Tribune médicale*, no. 169, February 8, 1986.
16. Cf. Rousso, op. cit., 148.
17. Letter quoted in Gibault, *Céline 1944–1961*, 162.
18. Account by Lucien Rebatet, *Cahiers de l'Herne*, no. 3, 53.
19. That, at least, was the theory developed by Doriot's secretary, Maurice-Yvan Sicard, who was then staying with him in Constance, and which he would develop in his *Histoire de la collaboration*, op. cit., 496ff.
20. In *Cahiers de l'Herne*, no. 3, 54.
21. *Écrits de Paris*, October 1961, 104.
22. Germinal Chamoin preserved a map of Germany on which he had carefully noted all stations passed through. François Gibault, having consulted this document (*Céline 1944–1961*, 68), was thus able to reconstruct Céline and his companions' itinerary.
23. Cf. note 20.
24. Undated letter written by Céline in Denmark to Dr. Jacquot, and quoted in Gibault, *Céline 1944–1961*, 71. Chamoin would visit Céline after the war at his home in Meudon. The latter expressed his undying gratitude to him. Chamoin died in 1977.
25. *Rigodon*, 903.
26. Undated letter in *Céline, textes et documents 1*, op. cit., 87.
27. Article by Vercors in *Carrefour*, February 16, 1945.
28. Conversation with Frédéric Grover on March 9, 1973, published in *Six Entretiens avec André Malraux sur des écrivains de son temps*, Idées/Gallimard, 1978, 96.
29. Document cited *in extenso* in Pedersen, op. cit., 44–46. As a general rule, this is the work to consult for a complete investigation of Céline's legal dossier in Denmark, with the pertinent official documentary evidence.
30. According to Gibault, *Céline 1944–1961*, 87.
31. Quoted in Herbert Lottman, *L'Épuration 1943–1953*, Fayard, 1986, 305.
32. Ibid., 306.
33. Two letters of December 1945, in *Céline, textes et documents 1*, op. cit., 89–91.
34. In Pedersen, op. cit., 26–27.
35. Ibid., 34–35.

36. Letter quoted *in extenso*, ibid., 47–50.
37. Quoted in Gibault, *Céline 1944–1961*, 101.
38. Pedersen, op. cit., 54–55.
39. Unpublished letter, coll. Lucette Destouches.
40. Unpublished, undated letter, coll. Lucette Destouches.
41. Ibid.
42. Ibid.
43. Letter dated March 20, 1946, same source.
44. *Féerie pour une autre fois*, 60, 63.
45. Ibid., 159–160.
46. Unpublished letter, coll. Lucette Destouches.
47. Unpublished, undated letter, coll. Lucette Destouches.
48. Robert Massin, "Rencontre avec Céline," *La Rue*, no. 12, November 1947, reprinted in *Cahiers Céline*, no. 7, 262.
49. Pedersen, op. cit., 67.
50. Unpublished, undated letter, coll. Lucette Destouches.
51. Document reproduced in Gibault, *Céline 1944–1961*, 100–101.
52. This memorandum has often been reproduced at length, as in Pedersen, op. cit., or *Cahiers Céline*, no. 7, 245–258.
53. Undated letter quoted in Gibault, *Céline 1944–1961*, 116.
54. Ibid., 118.
55. *D'un château l'autre*, 73. Cf also Pol Vandromme's invaluable book *Le Vigan*, Ed. La Revue Célinienne, Brussels, 1980, 30–31.
56. The entire text of this petition, in English with a French translation, appears in Pedersen, op. cit., 97–100.
57. In *Textes et documents 2*, op. cit., 99–100.
58. In Pedersen, op. cit., 96–97.
59. Ibid., 129.
60. Hindus, *The Crippled Giant*, 11.
61. L.-F. Céline, *Lettres à son avocat—118 lettres inédites à Me. Albert Naud*, La Flûte de Pan, 1984. All quotations of Céline's letters to Albert Naud are from this work.

16. Exile

1. Cf. *Cahiers Céline*, no. 7, 259–262.
2. Cf. *Cahiers Céline*, no. 1, 145–146.
3. Cf. *Cahiers Céline*, no. 7, 262–267.
4. Ibid., 268–272.
5. Cf. *Cahiers de l'Herne*, no. 5, 113–115.
6. In *Cahiers de l'Herne*, no. 3, 131.
7. Anecdote set down in Gibault, *Céline 1944–1961*, 147.

8. Undated letter in *Cahiers de l'Herne*, no. 3, 131.
9. Letter dated December 26, 1947, ibid., 132.
10. Letter dated December 28, 1947, ibid.
11. Account by René Heron de Villefosse in *Cahiers de l'Herne*, no. 3, 34.
12. Ibid.
13. In *Lettres à son avocat*, 39–40.
14. Letter dated November 13, 1947, in *Cahiers Céline*, no. 6, 40–41.
15. "À l'Agité du bocal" has often been reproduced: in *Cahiers de l'Herne*, in the deluxe edition of Céline's works by the Club de l'honnête homme, etc. This text can also be found in *Cahiers Céline*, no. 7, 382–387.
16. To give a sense of the print runs of Céline's works at the time, we note that the commercial edition of *Voyage au bout de la nuit* reached 148,353 copies; *Mort à crédit*—70,537 copies; *Bagatelles pour un massacre*—86,142 copies; *L'École des cadavres*—37,669 copies (for all these titles, a cumulative total of the prewar editions and those illustrated by Gen Paul under the occupation); and *Guignol's band*—36,692 copies. A photocopy of the inventory of these print runs appears in Dauphin and Fouché, *Bibliographie*.
17. Letter dated September 4, 1949, in Monnier, op. cit., 65. The publisher Fasquelle to whom Céline refers here is the father of Jean-Claude Fasquelle, head of Éditions Grasset-Fasquelle and hence the publisher of this biography.
18. In *Cahiers Céline*, no. 7, 51.
19. Article of October 7, 1968, reproduced in Pedersen, op. cit., 143.
20. Hindus, *The Crippled Giant*, 21.
21. Ibid., 96.
22. Ibid., 40.
23. Ibid., 42.
24. Ibid., 49.
25. Ibid., 50.
26. Ibid., 60.
27. Ibid., 80.
28. Ibid., 151.
29. Ibid., 152.
30. Ibid., 153.
31. Letter dated August 9, 1948, in *Cahiers de l'Herne*, no. 3, 117.
32. In Monnier, op. cit., 16.
33. In *Textes et documents 2*, op. cit., 117.
34. Undated letter of 1950, in *Textes et documents 1*, op. cit., 119.
35. In *Cahiers de l'Herne*, no. 3, 39.
36. Letter to Raoul Nordling dated March 24, 1951, concerning Daragnès' death, in *Cahiers de l'Herne*, no. 3, 140.
37. In *Textes et documents 1*, op. cit., 120.
38. In Gibault, *Céline 1944–1961*, 187.
39. In *Cahiers de l'Herne*, no. 3, 29.

40. In Gibault, 181.
41. Letter dated December 30, 1948, in *Textes et documents 2*, op. cit., 113.
42. Letter of 1949, ibid., 114.
43. Letter dated August 15, 1949, ibid., 123.
44. In *Cahiers Céline*, no. 6, 107–108.
45. In *Le Lérot rêveur*, no. 39, December 1984, Éditions du Lérot, 24–25.
46. In Monnier, op. cit., 20.
47. Letter to Pierre Monnier dated October 27, 1948, ibid., 24–25.
48. Letter dated February 12, 1949, ibid., 46.
49. Letter dated May 25, 1949, ibid., 57.
50. In *Cahiers Céline*, 389–390.
51. This preface was later used in every edition for nearly thirty years. As of 1952, however, Céline felt that it had lost all meaning.
52. In Monnier, op. cit., 62, 63, 66.
53. Ibid., 74.
54. Letter dated February 15, 1950, ibid., 115.
55. Letter dated November 17, 1949, ibid., 81.
56. Ibid., 93.
57. Letter dated November 29, 1950, ibid., 158.
58. Letter dated September 14, 1949, in *Cahiers Céline*, no. 6, 180.
59. In Monnier, op. cit., 169.
60. Letter dated April 18, 1948, in *Lettres à son avocat*, 65.
61. Ibid., 74.
62. *Lettres à Tixier*, 20.
63. Letter to Albert Naud dated January 9, 1950, op. cit., 106–107.
64. Letter to Tixier dated September 17, 1949, op. cit., 41–42.
65. Letter to Paraz dated March 17, 1949, *Cahiers Céline*, no. 6, 140.
66. Letter to Paraz dated March 27, 1949, ibid., 142.
67. Letter to Naud dated October 17, 1948, op. cit., 77–78.
68. Cf. Gibault, *Céline 1944–1961*, 202.
69. Ibid., p. 203.
70. In *Lettres à son avocat*, op. cit., 90–91.
71. For the principal responses to this inquiry, cf. *Cahiers Céline*, no. 7, 350–359.
72. Quoted in Gibault, *Céline 1944–1961*, 228.
73. Montherlant's letter to Pierre Monnier, dated February 16, 1950, can be found in Monnier, op. cit., 116.
74. Ibid.
75. The complete text of this "response" was published in *Cahiers Céline*, no. 7, 313–324.
76. Letter to Albert Naud dated January 24, 1950, in *Lettre à son avocat*, 116.
77. In Monnier, op. cit., 118.
78. The complete text of the enactment rendered on February 21, 1950, by the Seine court was published in Pedersen, op. cit., 204–211.
79. Letter dated February 23, 1950, in Monnier, op. cit., 119.

80. Letter to Albert Paraz, same date, in *Cahiers Céline*, no. 6, 240.
81. Letter from Tixier to Céline dated January 23, 1950, in *Lettres à Tixier*, 55.
82. The complete text of the amnesty judgment rendered by the military tribunal of Paris, composed of Presiding Judge Reynaud, judges Sentis and Maillet of the first Seine magistrate's court, and officers Corsini, Alazet, Jan, Colombies, Arnoult and Chambert, appears in *Cahiers Céline*, no. 7, 366–370.
83. In *Lettres à Tixier*, 81.
84. Ibid., 82–83.
85. In *Lettres à son avocat*, 181.
86. In *Lettres à Tixier*, 85.
87. Letter published in part in the autograph catalogue of the Librairie de l'Échiquier, Frédéric Castaing, 1987.
88. In Pedersen, op. cit., 116–117.

17. Meudon, or Journey's End

1. In *Cahiers Céline*, no. 6, 349.
2. In Monnier, op. cit., 188.
3. Ibid., 189–190.
4. Ibid., 204.
5. Official translation by Louis Muller, sworn expert translator to the Seine civil court, quoted in *Lettres à Tixier*, 111.
6. Cf. the letter from Henri Thomas to F. Moresi dated May 30, 1980, in *Le Lérot rêveur*, no. 29, December 1980. Jacques Brenner, who corresponded with Thomas in connection with the Jünger-Céline affair, confirms this version in his *Mon histoire de la littérature française contemporaine*, Grasset, 1987, 109.
7. Cf. the facsimile of Paulhan's letter in *Lettres à Tixier*, 136–137.
8. In *Lettres*, 122–123.
9. Strangely enough never noted hitherto, an allusion to the rivalry between the two men for the same actress can be found in *D'un château l'autre*, 42: "Gertrut and Achille were hot for the same person, one of those gold-digging babes! Whew! a real rival for the Bank of France! ... those who remember those days, 'Happy France,' will remember Suzanne ... what a silver-screen artist she was! and her steamy nightgowns on a 'soft blue light' or a 'moonlight' background! ... what a sublime artist, well and truly silent, not a 'talkie.' "
    Here, Achille Brottin represents Gaston Gallimard. The character of Gertrut may have been inspired by the industrialist Paul Marteau and, for other circumstances of his life, by the publisher Fasquelle, as we

shall see. In his critical Pléiade edition, Henri Godard does not suspect the allusion or seek to identify the character of Gertrut. He simply wonders whether "Suzanne" might not be the actress Suzanne Bianquetti, merely based on the thin coincidence of their given names.

10. Quoted in Gibault, *Céline 1944–1961*, 266.
11. Quoted in Henri Godard's preface to "Céline, Romans II," op. cit., 1007.
12. Ibid., 1007 and 1009.
13. Ibid., 1010.
14. Quoted in Dauphin and Fouché, op. cit.
15. Cf. Dauphin, *Les Critiques*, 122.
16. Ibid., 123 and 125.
17. *Nord*, 670.
18. *D'un château l'autre*, 116.
19. In *La Parisienne*, no. 1, January 1953.
20. *Rivarol*, July 22, 1954.
21. Quoted in Henri Godard's preface to "Céline, Romans II," 1008.
22. Ibid., 1015.
23. On March 7, 1958, Céline wrote to Henri Fillipachi, creator of the Livre de Poche series and general secretary of Librairie Hachette: "My enemies and enviers managed to completely empty the bookstores of all my books, I believe, and I am pleased to be read finally in your 'livres de poche'!" (In *Bulletin célinien*, no. 12, 8).
24. In Poulet, op. cit., 1, 3.
25. In Monnier, op. cit., 207.
26. Preface to the Pléiade "Romans II," 1013.
27. *D'un château l'autre*, 34–35.
28. Conversation between Céline and Louis-Albert Zbinden for Radio-Suisse romande, July 25, 1957, reprinted in *Cahiers Céline*, no. 2, 67–68.
29. In *Cahiers Céline*, no. 6, 417–418.
30. *Arts*, June 19–25, 1967, reprinted in *Cahiers Céline*, no. 2, 36–37.
31. In *Cahiers Céline*, no. 6, 421.
32. In *Jeune Europe*, July 15, 1957, article quoted in part in the Pléaide "Romans II," 1018.
33. Retranscription of this conversation in *Cahiers Céline*, no. 2, 66–67.
34. Conversation with André Parinaud in *Arts*, June 19–25, 1967, reprinted in *Cahiers Céline*, no. 2, 40.
35. Cf. above, 390.
36. Letter from Paul Morand to Céline dated July 29, 1957, quoted in Gibault, *Céline 1944–1961*, 317.
37. Statement retranscribed in *Cahiers Céline*, no. 2, 115. Marc Hanrez's book would come out in November 1961, five months after the writer's death.
38. This conversation was first set down in Louis Pauwels, Jacques Mousseau, and Jean Feller, *En Français dans le texte*, Éditions France-Empire, 1962, and reprinted in *Cahiers Céline*, no. 2, 119–129.

39. *Nord*, 543. We note that in 1969, eight years after the writer's death, the conversation would be partially broadcast in a two-part program, "D'un Céline l'autre."
40. Jean-Pierre Dauphin took note of this broadcast in his *Bibliographie*.
41. François Gibault, in *Céline 1944–1961*, reports that on two visits to Meudon, Dr. Jacquot brought Germinal Chamoin, who had accompanied Céline and Lucette from train to train to the Danish border in 1945. For her part, Lucette does not recall these visits.
42. Letter to Édith Follet dated August 10, 1958, and preserved by its addressee. François Gibault was the first to publish it, in *Céline 1944–1961*, 304.
43. In the Pléiade, "Céline, Romans II," 1145.
44. Ibid.
45. Céline's conversation with Jean Guénot and Jacques Darribehaude first appeared in *Cahiers de l'Herne*, no. 3. Jean Guénot reused it in his self-published *L.-F. Céline damné par l'écriture* (1973). Lastly, it appears in *Cahiers Céline*, no. 2, 171.
46. *Le Monde*, June 1, 1960, reprinted in *Cahiers Céline*, no. 2, 171.
47. Céline would not have the satisfaction of seeing this volume in print or of being included in the Pléiade series in his lifetime, as he hoped. The work came out in February 1962, eight months after his death.
48. Undated letter quoted in *Album Céline*, op. cit., 257.
49. *Rigodon*, 904.
50. Ibid., 906.
51. Quoted in the Pléiade "Romans II," 1183.
52. Ibid. We do not know to which female novelist Céline is referring here. Lucette would find this letter and the one addressed to Gaston Gallimard on Céline's desk after his death. She passed them on to their respective addressees. The manuscript of *Rigodon* was also found on his desk. It would be published for the first time in February 1969 by Gallimard, after having been deciphered by André Damien and François Gibault.
53. According to Lucette Destouches, Céline did not want his family to be informed about his death. She nonetheless telephoned Colette Turpin, who hurried to her father's deathbed, where his friends were holding vigil. Later, the inventory of Céline's holdings would come up short and his account with Gallimard remain in the red, not to mention the lawsuit with which Gallimard, Céline, or his inheritors had been threatened since September 11, 1961, when Mme. Asta Scherz, recognizing herself in the portrait that Céline had made of her and her family at Kränzlin in *Nord*, had at first demanded and obtained the work's immediate withdrawal from sale before suing for slander (as had Dr. Hauboldt, for that matter). At the time the book came out, Céline was convinced that the war's end and the arrival of the Soviet troops had destroyed the estate forever and dispersed the family, henceforth shorn of liberty under the

trusteeship of East Germany. Mme. Scherz, however, was living in West Berlin with her two children. In short, on March 17, 1962, Colette Turpin's lawyer announced that his client, Céline's only daughter, and her children relinquished claim to the writer's estate. Lucette thus became the sole beneficiary.

THE WORKS OF CÉLINE

(first editions)

La Vie et l'Oeuvre de Philippe Ignace Semmelweis, Rennes, Simon, 1924.
Voyage au bout de la nuit, Paris, Denoël et Steele, 1932.
L'Église, Paris, Denoël et Steele, 1933.
Mort à crédit, Paris, Denoël et Steele, 1936.
Mea culpa, Paris, Denoël et Steele, 1936.
Bagatelles pour un massacre, Paris, Denoël, 1937.
L'École des cadavres, Paris, Denoël, 1938.
Les Beaux draps, Paris, Nouvelles Éditions françaises, 1941.
Guignol's band, Paris, Denoël, 1944.
Casse-Pipe, Chambriand, 1949.
Féerie pour une autre fois I, Paris, Gallimard, 1952.
Féerie pour une autre fois II Normance, Paris, Gallimard, 1954.
Entretiens avec le professeur Y, Paris, Gallimard, 1955.
D'un château l'autre, Paris, Gallimard, 1957.
Ballets sans musique, sans personne, sans rien, Paris, Gallimard, 1959. This book contains the ballets: *La Naissance d'une fée, Voyou Paul. Brave Virginie et Van Bagaden*, which appeared earlier in *Bagatelles pour un massacre*, as well as the ballets *Foudres et Flèches* and *Scandale aux abysses* published in booklet form in 1948 and 1950.
Nord, Paris, Gallimard, 1960.
Guignol's band II, Le Pont de Londres, Paris, Gallimard, 1964.
Carnet du cuirassier Destouches, dans *Casse-Pipe*, Paris, Gallimard, 1970.
Rigodon, Paris, Gallimard, 1969.
Progrès, Paris, Mercure de France, 1978.
Arletty, jeune fille dauphinoise (scénario), Paris, La Flûte de Pan, 1983.
Maudits soupirs pour une autre fois, Paris, Gallimard, 1985. This is an early unfinished version of *Féerie pour une autre fois*.

OTHER WRITINGS BY CÉLINE

Les Cahiers de l'Herne n° 3, Paris, 1963.
Les Cahiers de l'Herne n° 5, Paris, 1965.
This book contains, among other things, Céline's minor writings: *A l'Agité*

du bocal, Vive l'amnistie, Monsieur! Rabelais, il a raté son coup . . . , his introductions to *Bezons à travers les âges by Albert Sérouille* and *to 31, cité d'Antin by* Henri Mahé, as well as various correspondences.

Cahiers Céline I et Cahiers Céline 2: Céline et l'Actualité littéraire, Paris, Gallimard, 1976.

An anthology of all his non-political essays: statements and interviews between 1932 and 1961.

Cahiers Céline 3: Semmelweis et autres écrits médicaux, Paris, Gallimard, 1977.

Cahiers Céline 4: Lettres et premiers écrits d'Afrique 1916–1917, Paris, Gallimard, 1978.

Cahiers Céline 5: Lettres à des amies, Paris, Gallimard, 1979.

This is Céline's correspondence with Erika Irrgang, Cillie Pam (here referred to as N., though her identity was later revealed), Élisabeth Porquerol, Évelyne Pollet, Karen Marie Jensen et Lucienne Delforge, between 1932 and 1939.

Cahiers Céline 6: Lettres à Albert Paraz 1947–1957, Paris, Gallimard, 1980.

Cahiers Céline 7: Céline et l'actualité 1933–1961, Paris, Gallimard, 1987.

Lettres à son avocat—118 unpublished letters to Albert Naud, Paris, La Flûte de Pan, 1984.

Lettres à Tixier—44 unpublished letters to Tixier-Vignancour, Paris, La Flûte de Pan, 1985.

These two volumes of letters, from 1947 to 1951, edited and annotated by Frédéric Monnier, shed light on the legal fiasco of Céline's trial during his exile in Denmark.

Letters, writings, and documents by Céline that were never published elsewhere appear in the three following volumes:

Textes et documents 1, Paris, BLFC, 1979.

Textes et documents 2, Paris, BLFC, 1982.

Textes et documents 3, Paris, BLFC, 1984.

CÉLINE WORKS AVAILABLE IN ENGLISH

Castle to Castle. 1987, Carroll & Graf.

Conversations with Professor Y. Bilingual edition. Luce, Stanford, tr. from Fr. 1986. University Press of New England.

Death on the Installment Plan. Manheim, Ralph, tr. 1971. New Directions.

Guignol's Band. Frechtman & Nile, trs. 1969. New Directions.

Journey to the End of the Night. Manheim, Ralph, tr. 1983. New Directions.

Mea Culpa & the Life & Work of Semmelweis. Parker, Robert A., tr. from Fr. 1979. Reprint of 1937 ed., Fertig.

North. 1972, Delacorte.

Index